Pregnancy loss and the death of a baby:
Guidelines for professionals

4th edition

**Updated and edited by Amanda Hunter
Based on original text by Judith Schott,
Alix Henley and Nancy Kohner**

Sands
Stillbirth & neonatal death charity

Published by Tantamount
Coventry University Technology Park,
Puma Way, Coventry CV1 2TT

First published in Great Britain in 2016
by **Tantamount** on behalf of
Sands, the stillbirth & neonatal death charity
Victoria Charity Centre, London, SW1V 1RB

Charity registration number 299679. Company limited by Guarantee Number 2212082.
Scottish Charity Registration Number SC042789.

Office: 020 7436 7940
Email: info@uk-sands.org
Web: www.uk-sands.org

ISBN: 978-1-909929-16-6

Pregnancy loss and the death of a baby: guidelines for professionals
Copyright © 2016 Sands

Cover and layout design by Tantamount
Email: publishing@tantamount.com
Web: www.tantamount.com

The Sands guidelines are a compilation of research findings and the guidance and feedback given to the Authors by health professionals, other relevant experts and bereaved parents. The Guidelines are not intended to be prescriptive directions defining a specific course of management or care, but are offered as an aid to good practice. They should not be relied on in isolation. Staff must make their own judgements and apply them when appropriate, taking into account professional guidance, trust and other protocols and all the circumstances and facts of the particular case. Neither Sands nor the Authors shall be responsible or liable for any loss, damage, liability or claims (whether direct or indirect) that arise out of or in connection with the Guidelines.

Contents

Introduction

The fourth edition of *Pregnancy Loss and the Death of a Baby: Guidelines for Professionals* builds on the information presented in the third edition of this guidance by incorporating new research findings and practice recommendations that have become available since 2007. The incorporation of new evidence-based information about providing care and support for parents and other family members following a pregnancy loss or the death of a baby strengthens this updated version of Sands' guidance for professionals. However, gaps in the available research base mean that it continues to be necessary to include "anecdotal" evidence that is based on parents' experiences of bereavement care to make practice recommendations in some areas of this guidance.

Many of the recommendations are aimed at healthcare professionals and services. However, the guidelines also provide information and guidance that is relevant to other practitioners and supporters including peer supporters, cemetery and crematorium staff, registrars, doulas, administrators, receptionists, auxiliary staff and family and friends who may be supporting parents.

In these guidelines, Chapters 1 to 5 focus on principles of care that all practitioners should be aware of when working with bereaved parents and which relate to all of the guidance presented in this document. Chapters 6 to 13 emphasise the care that should be offered to parents experiencing different types of perinatal losses. Chapters 14 to 23 provide information about the care and support that should be offered to parents after a pregnancy loss or the death of their baby. Chapters 24 and 25 provide guidance for staff, managers, Trusts and Health Boards regarding the support and training that should be available to staff and the policies and service provisions that should be in place to ensure that parents receive the best care possible.

It is important to note that these guidelines are intended to provide best practice suggestions and recommendations for services, organisations and staff who are providing care and support for parents following a pregnancy loss or the death of a baby. Sands recognises that the resources and practices that are highlighted throughout this guidance are not currently available in many areas of the UK. Sands also commends the many professionals who are doing the best that they can to provide high quality care and support to parents, even when the resources available to them are limited.

However, this guidance is also meant to help staff and services evaluate and improve their current practices, policies and services that they provide to ensure that bereaved parents and families receive the best bereavement care possible following a perinatal loss. The importance of providing high quality bereavement care to improve the well-being of parents and families both immediately following a loss and on a longer-term basis is highlighted throughout these guidelines.

The main requirements for providing good bereavement care following a pregnancy loss or the death of a baby require few resources except that staff have time, training and support to provide this care. The main elements of providing high quality bereavement care to parents that are highlighted throughout these guidelines include:

- **Good communication.** Good communication is one of the most important elements of bereavement care as it is needed for providing all of the other aspects of care for parents during and following a perinatal loss. This includes listening to bereaved parents and ensuring that they receive sensitive, accessible information about what is happening as soon as possible when their baby has died or a problem is suspected.

  The importance of good communication between healthcare staff, teams and services is also highlighted throughout this guidance to ensure that parents receive high-quality, sensitive and consistent care and information from all staff during and after a perinatal loss. This includes good communication between public and private healthcare services where necessary.

- **Informed choice.** Providing parents with opportunities to make informed choices about their care and that of their baby before, during and after a perinatal loss is crucial. Good communication with parents is important to ensure that they have complete, impartial information about all of their available options and the benefits and limitations of each available option. Different parents will want different amounts of information. However, it is important that parents have sufficient information so that they are able to make the right decisions for them, their baby and their family.

- **Individualised care.** Parents have different needs and preferences that are unique to them as individuals. Therefore, care and support should be tailored to the individual needs and preferences of all bereaved parents without making assumptions about their wishes or decisions. To provide individualised care, it is important that parents are offered opportunities to make informed choices about the care and support that is right for them and their families. Good communication with parents is also a crucial element of providing individualised care as this tailored care requires listening to parents and providing clear information.

Good communication is also an important element of care that may help to reduce and prevent more stillbirths and neonatal deaths. As many of these deaths may be preventable, good communication and support are needed to ensure that women are aware of some of the things they can do to have a safer pregnancy. These can include stopping smoking, avoiding alcohol and drugs, monitoring their weight, eating healthily and reducing their risk of infection (Sands 2016a). Additionally, women need good information about the importance of monitoring their baby's health during pregnancy by attending regular antenatal appointments, being aware of their baby's movements and immediately reporting any bleeding or abdominal pain to their midwife or doctor (Sands 2016b). Listening is another area of communication that may help reduce the number of babies' deaths as some women have not felt that their concerns during pregnancy (particularly around the baby's movements) were listened to by healthcare staff (Redshaw *et al.* 2014; Knight *et al.* 2015).

A dedicated chapter looking at prevention efforts to reduce the number of stillbirths and neonatal deaths in the UK has not been included in this bereavement care guidance as this information is better placed in clinical guidance. In addition, recommendations for preventing and reducing the numbers of babies who die are quickly changing as a result of research efforts in this area. Stillbirths and neonatal deaths are not inevitable and it is important for healthcare professionals to engage with local and national prevention strategies and reviews of babies' deaths (see Chapter 15). Staff should also be aware of the need for better intrapartum care, signs of poor growth and the increased risks of stillbirth for women who:

- have twin or multiple pregnancies;
- are older than 35 years of age;
- are teenage mothers;
- have been diagnosed with certain medical conditions such as diabetes, hypertension and thrombophilia;
- have a history of past obstetric complications;
- smoke;
- have a body mass index over 30;
- live in socially deprived areas; and/or
- are from some ethnic minority groups (Sands 2016c).

Healthcare professionals working in maternity care should also be familiar with research into preventing babies' deaths including, for example, the Lancet Stillbirths Series (2016), the AFFIRM Study to promote awareness of fetal movements (AFFIRM 2014), the Pregnancy Outcome Prediction (POP) study (Sovio *et al.* 2015) and the Midland and North of England Stillbirth Study (MiNESS) (Platts *et al.* 2014).

Hopefully, research aimed at preventing babies' deaths and improving bereavement care will continue to be undertaken. This research is crucial to both reduce the number of babies who die and provide recommendations so that parents who experience the death of their baby receive the best care possible.

Terminology

These guidelines are intended for all healthcare professionals and staff who see bereaved parents and parents whose baby may die during pregnancy, be stillborn or die shortly after birth. The terms "healthcare professionals" and "staff" are used throughout to denote all of those practitioners that a bereaved parent may come into contact with.

We have used the phrases "childbearing loss" and "perinatal loss" to cover all losses at any gestation and losses in the first few weeks after birth.

For consistency, the term "parents" is used to refer to expectant and bereaved mothers, fathers and partners. This is applied in a wide range of situations, including when referring to individuals who experience early miscarriage, late miscarriage, termination for fetal anomaly, stillbirth and neonatal death. Many people will consider themselves parents from the time they discover they are, or were, pregnant while others will not. Therefore, it should be acknowledged that not all people who have experienced a childbearing loss would consider themselves to be, or have been, a parent. It is also important for those who do identify themselves as parents to have this recognised. As is set out in these guidelines, healthcare professionals should use the terminology preferred by those experiencing the loss when communicating with them.

Similarly, the term "baby" is used throughout to describe the child from the early stages of pregnancy through to the neonatal period. Many people will conceptualise their baby and develop strong attachments to them from the moment they discover that they are, or were, pregnant. However, others will be more comfortable with medical terminology such as "fetus" and may not find the term "baby" to be appropriate in their situation. Again, while we have used the term baby, it is important to recognise that the wishes and viewpoints of those experiencing the loss should always be the most important factor when communicating with them. Healthcare professionals will need to adapt the terminology they use accordingly.

We have used the phrase "Trusts and Health Boards" because the rapid changes in the way that health services are structured and managed in England, Wales, Scotland and Northern Ireland make it impossible to use a phrase that covers all the bodies involved. However, the Guidelines are also applicable to independent health care establishments and to all other bodies that may be set up in the future to organise and provide care for women and families experiencing a childbearing loss.

Acknowledgements

We are most grateful to all the parents who have shared their stories and given us permission to use their words in the text.

We are also very grateful to the many people and organisations who have helped us by sharing their expertise, and by reading and commenting on drafts of these Guidelines:

Cheryll Adams, Director, Institute of Health Visiting

Elizabeth Allan, Chief Registrar, City of Edinburgh Council

Gemma Andrew, Medical Advisor, Coroners Service Northern Ireland

Susan Ayers, Lead, Centre for Maternal and Child Health Research, City University London

Carmel Bagness, Professional Lead Midwifery and Women's Health, Royal College of Nursing (RCN)

Ruth Bender-Atik, National Director, The Miscarriage Association

Jane Brewin, Chief Executive, Tommy's

Yvonne Bronsky, Local Supervising Authority Midwifery Officer (LSAMO), NHS Scotland

Caroline Browne, Head of Regulation, Human Tissue Authority (HTA)

Sally Buller, Specialist Midwife, Project Lead for Maternity Notes, Perinatal Institute

Andrew Buttress, Senior Additional Superintendent Registrar, Birmingham Register Office

Ann Chalmers, Chief Executive, Child Bereavement UK

Zoe Chivers, Head of Services, Bliss

Catherine Coppinger, SCT Programme Manager, NHS Screening Programmes

Rosalind Crawley, Reader in Cognitive Psychology, University of Sunderland

Sharon Darke, Tamba Bereavement Group Coordinator, Twins and Multiple Births Association (Tamba)

Jane Denton, Director, Multiple Births Foundation (MBF)

Amy Dickson, Paralegal, Foot Anstey LLP

Elizabeth Duff, Senior Policy Adviser, NCT

Kath Evans, Experience of Care Lead – Maternity, Newborn, Children and Young People, Nursing Directorate, NHS England

Alan Fenton, President, British Association of Perinatal Medicine (BAPM)

Jane Fisher, Director, Antenatal Results and Choices (ARC)

General Register Office for Northern Ireland

Rachel Hayden, Trainer and Founder, Gifts of Remembrance

Arlene Honeyman, Head of Care Strategic Development, Rainbow Trust Children's Charity

David Howe, Consultant and Honorary Senior Lecturer in FetoMaternal Medicine, Princess Anne Hospital, Southampton, on behalf of the British Maternal and Fetal Medicine Society (BMFMS) and the Royal College of Obstetricians and Gynaecologists (RCOG)

Gail Johnson, Professional Advisor Education, The Royal College of Midwives (RCM)

Emma E. Jones, PhD Research Student in Psychology, University of Sunderland

Sarah Jones, Family Services Manager, Bliss

Sue Jose, Local Supervising Authority Midwifery Officer (LSAMO), Health Inspectorate Wales

Lydia Judge-Kronis, Senior Mortuary Manager, Great Ormond Street Hospital for Children

Debbie Kerslake, Chief Executive, Cruse Bereavement Care

Jenny Kurinczuk, Professor of Perinatal Epidemiology, Director, National Perinatal Epidemiology Unit

Alex Mancini, Pan London Lead Nurse for Neonatal Palliative Care, Chelsea and Westminster Foundation Trust and the True Colours Trust

Annette McHugh, Programme Manager, Fetal Anomaly Screening Programme, Public Health England

Mandy Myers, Director of Operations and Nursing, British Pregnancy Advisory Service (BPAS)

Heather Neil, NCT Policy and Communications Tutor, NCT

Mohamed Omer, Board Member – External Affairs, Gardens of Peace Muslim Cemetery

Munira Oza, Director, Ectopic Pregnancy Trust

Alison Paxford, Deputy Superintendent Registrar, Cardiff Register Office

Helen Pearce, Local Supervising Authority Midwifery Officer (LSAMO), Regional Directorate of Nursing (South), NHS England

Julia Petty, Senior Lecturer in Children's Nursing, University of Hertfordshire, on behalf of the Neonatal Nurses Association (NNA)

Peter Pinto de Sa, Office of the Chair and Chief Executive, Nursing and Midwifery Council (NMC)

Maggie Redshaw, Associate Professor, Social Scientist, National Perinatal Epidemiology Unit

Julie Richards, Local Supervising Authority Midwifery Officer (LSAMO), Health Inspectorate Wales

Devender Roberts, Consultant in Obstetrics and Fetal Medicine, Liverpool Women's NHS Foundation Trust, on behalf of the British Maternal and Fetal Medicine Society (BMFMS) and the Royal College of Obstetricians and Gynaecologists (RCOG)

Mary Ross-Davie, Education Projects Manager, Maternal and Child Health, NHS Education for Scotland (NES)

Rehanah Sadiq, Muslim Chaplain, Birmingham Women's NHS Foundation Trust

Neil J Sebire, GOSHCC Professor of Paediatric and Developmental Pathology, NIHR Senior Investigator, NIHR GOSH BRC Theme Lead Diagnostics and Imaging, Great Ormond Street Hospital and ICH (UCL), on behalf of The Royal College of Pathologists (RCPATH)

Judy Shakespeare, Clinical Champion for Perinatal Mental Health, on behalf of The Royal College of General Practitioners (RCGP)

Claire Stoneman, Partner, Foot Anstey LLP

Caroline Strickland, Policy Officer, Standards and Ethics Team, General Medical Council (GMC)

Şebnem Susam-Saraeva, Senior Lecturer in Translation Studies, University of Edinburgh

Helen Tourle, Training Manager, Cruse Bereavement Care

Helen Turier, Support Services Manager, Twins and Multiple Births Association (Tamba)

Sara Twaddle, Director of Evidence, Healthcare Improvement Scotland

Anne Wadey, Bereavement Information and Consulting, on behalf of the Bereavement Advice Centre

Jenny Ward, Director of Services, The Lullaby Trust

Jason Warriner, UK Director of Quality and Clinical Services, Marie Stopes United Kingdom

Valerie Watts, Chief Executive, Health and Social Care Board (HSCNI)

Gillian Weaver, Imperial College Healthcare NHS Trust and UK Association for Milk Banking

All of the listings above reflect the role of advisers at the time when assistance was given.

Sands is very grateful to the Northern Ireland Sands Network and the Scottish Government for their generous contributions to the costs of producing the Guidelines.

Additionally, the help and support that has been received from Sands for this project has been invaluable. In particular, I would like to acknowledge Cheryl Titherly (Improving Bereavement Care Manager) for her contribution to these guidelines in terms of both her support and crucial editorial guidance. I would also like to thank Judith Schott and Alix Henley, former Sands Advisors and the authors of the third edition, for their support and thorough handover, as well as Janet Scott (Research and Prevention Lead) and Charlotte Bevan (Senior Research and Prevention Officer) for their comments and guidance.

Sands principles of bereavement care

Parents' perspectives and collaborative working with healthcare professionals have informed these principles of bereavement care.

1. Care should be individualised so that it is parent led and caters for their personal, cultural or religious needs. Parents should always be treated with respect and dignity. Sensitive, empathetic care is crucial and may involve spending time with parents. This should be recognised by managers and staff.

2. Clear communication with parents is key and it should be sensitive, honest and tailored to meet the individual needs of parents. Childbearing losses can involve periods of uncertainty and staff should avoid giving assurances that may turn out to be false. Trained interpreters and signers should be available for parents who need them.

3. In any situation where there is a choice to be made, parents should be listened to and given the information and support they need to make their own decisions about what happens to them and their baby.

4. No assumptions should be made about the intensity and duration of grief that a parent will experience. It is important that staff accept and acknowledge the feelings that individual parents may experience.

5. Women and their partners should always be looked after by staff who are specifically trained in bereavement care and in an environment that the parent feels is appropriate to their circumstances. In addition to good emotional support, women should receive excellent physical care during and after a loss.

6. A partner's grief can be as profound as that of the mother; their need for support should be recognised and met.

7. All staff who care for bereaved parents before, during or after the death of a baby should have opportunities to develop and update their knowledge and skills. In addition, they should have access to good support for themselves.

8. All parents whose babies die should be offered opportunities to create memories. Their individual wishes and needs should be respected.

9. The bodies of babies and fetal remains should be treated with respect at all times. Options around sensitive disposal should be discussed and respectful funerals should be offered.

10. Good communication between staff and healthcare teams is crucial in ensuring that staff are aware of parents' preferences and decisions; therefore, parents do not need to repeatedly explain their situation. This includes the handover of care from hospital to primary care staff, which should ensure that support and care for parents is seamless. Ongoing support is an essential part of care and should be available to all those who want it and should continue to be made available to all women and their partners during a subsequent pregnancy and after the birth of another baby.

CHAPTER 1

Providing holistic care

Other relevant chapters

2: Providing inclusive care   5: Communication across language and other barriers

3: Loss and grief   24: Staff support and training

4: Communication

After the death of their baby, it is very important that holistic care is provided for parents that is sensitive to their individual needs, as this may affect parents' experiences of care (Redshaw *et al.* 2014). How parents experience bereavement care after the death of their baby is important because it can have longer term implications for their emotional well-being (Downe *et al.* 2013).

In order to provide holistic care, a person-centred and integrated approach to care should be used. Staff should focus on the individual needs and wishes of parents for emotional care and support in addition to providing any physical and practical care. Providing holistic care will also require staff to consider parents' personal, cultural, spiritual and religious needs.

Providing person-centred and integrated care for parents

To provide holistic care, it can be helpful to take a person-centred approach to care. The Health Foundation states that:

> *In person-centred care, health and social care professionals work collaboratively with people who use services. Person-centred care supports people to develop the knowledge, skills and confidence they need to more effectively manage and make informed decisions about their own health and health care. It is coordinated and tailored to the*

needs of the individual. And, crucially, it ensures that people are always treated with dignity, compassion and respect. (2014: 3)

The Health Foundation (2014) also identifies some main barriers to providing such holistic person-centred care, including:

- Organisational processes and systems, including the culture of care found in different parts of the healthcare system.

- The personality and beliefs of individual patients that may affect their willingness and ability to engage in their care.

- The belief of some healthcare professionals that they are providing person-centred care when the evidence suggests that this is not the case.

The Sands guidelines address some of these potential barriers to providing holistic, person-centred care to bereaved parents. With regard to the organisational factors that may affect care, Chapter 25 provides an overview of guidance for Trusts, Health Boards, managers and healthcare services. Information that is relevant for the organisation of healthcare services is also highlighted in appropriate areas throughout the text.

This guidance also focuses on how staff can support and encourage bereaved parents to become more actively involved in the healthcare provided for themselves and their baby or babies. This information is provided throughout the text. However, potential barriers to parents' involvement in this care, which are related to the inclusiveness of care, barriers to accessing care, communication and communicating across language barriers, are addressed in Chapters 2, 4 and 5. A review of how staff can communicate sensitively and effectively with parents, facilitate informed choice and consider the specific needs and challenges for individual parents is also highlighted in these sections and throughout the guidelines.

The role of integrated care is also important when providing holistic care. Integrated care means ensuring that there is good coordination, cooperation and communication between and within services provided by the healthcare system, social care systems and local and national support organisations (National Collaboration for Integrated Care and Support 2013). Information about communication between staff and services and referring parents to local and national support organisations is included throughout these guidelines.

Unfortunately, there may be some systematic barriers to providing person-centred, integrated healthcare services to parents (National Collaboration for Integrated Care and Support 2013; The Health Foundation 2014). However, staff should aim to do as much as they can to ensure that the individual needs of bereaved parents are being met and to promote good communication within and across teams, departments and services. Hopefully, the relevant sections of the Sands Guidelines will help staff to identify areas where they can work as individuals and teams to ensure that parents receive the most holistic care possible. While these efforts are important, Trusts, Health Boards and managers also have a responsibility to ensure that all parents are able to receive good care, regardless of their location (National Collaboration for Integrated Care and Support 2013).

Providing emotional and physical care

Individual parents will have different needs for emotional and physical care. All parents should be offered full information about their available options for care and be supported to make decisions about their care and care for their baby wherever possible (see *Giving information and facilitating informed choice* in Chapter 4).

Some of the potential specific support and care needs of parents experiencing losses under different circumstances are highlighted in Chapters 6, 7, 8, 9, 10 and 11. This includes using care pathways and checklists as tools for facilitating informed choice rather than seeing them as lists of tasks or rote procedures that must be completed (see *Parental choice and checklists* in Chapter 14).

Considering parents' personal, cultural, religious and spiritual needs

Provisions should be in place to meet the cultural, religious and spiritual needs of bereaved parents and all staff have a responsibility to provide care on this basis (NHS Education for Scotland 2009). Meeting these needs in an inclusive manner that is accepting of difference is an important element of providing holistic care (NHS Education for Scotland 2009).

Staff should be aware of how parents' personal, cultural, religious and spiritual needs may affect their decisions regarding care for themselves and their baby who has died or is expected to die. For example, parents' opinions and beliefs may affect the decisions that they make regarding antenatal screening and diagnostic testing, miscarriage, termination of pregnancy, continuing a pregnancy after a fetal anomaly is diagnosed, post mortem examinations and/or funeral practices. These factors may also influence how parents experience and express emotions and grief or view themselves as parents.

While staff should be aware of how personal, cultural, religious and spiritual beliefs may affect parents' wishes and decisions, assumptions should never be made based on these factors. Staff should always ask parents about their personal, cultural, religious or spiritual needs and preferences. This is important as it is impossible to guess what any parent will feel or want when their baby dies on the basis of their culture, socioeconomic status, religion, personal circumstances or the community in which they live or were raised.

While a person's decisions and behaviour may be strongly influenced by their culture or religion, they will not necessarily be determined or dictated by these factors. Within any culture, religion or spiritual group, there is a very wide range of attitudes and opinions. Some of these differences may be influenced by social class, age, gender, education and/or life experiences. Some parents may also be surprised by the decisions they make when they are faced with a childbearing loss, particularly if the choices they have made are not usually seen as being acceptable based on their personal, cultural, religious or spiritual beliefs. Parents who make choices that are against the norms and values of their communities may fear that they will experience conflict with or be stigmatised by their families, friends or wider networks as a result of their decisions. It is important that these parents are offered extra, non-judgemental support and they are reassured that confidentiality will be maintained.

Providing spiritual care for parents

When thinking about spiritual care, it is important to recognise that spirituality is not the same as religion, even if some people express their spirituality through their religion (NHS Education for Scotland 2009). Additionally, spiritual needs are highly individual and no assumptions should be made about the spiritual support that parents may want (see *Considering parents' personal, cultural, religious and spiritual needs* above).

When a baby dies, parents' beliefs, values and sense of self may be profoundly challenged. Parents may ask questions such as "Why did this happen to me?", "What did I do wrong?", "Am I being punished in some way?", "How will other people see and react to me now?" and "How can I possibly cope with this?" Many parents may also feel isolated as they try to make sense of their baby's death or grieve for their loss.

On the other hand, having a strong spiritual or religious faith may be a great source of comfort and strength for some parents. Spiritual and religious beliefs may become particularly important to some parents at this time, including parents who do not normally consider themselves to be religious or spiritual. Some parents may feel that their faith and acceptance of the power of God's will helps them to continue with their lives and cope with their grief. Other parents may experience doubt or lose their faith as a result of their baby's death. Some parents may be angry that such a thing could happen to them despite their faith.

All staff can provide spiritual care to parents even if their beliefs are not the same as those of parents (NHS Education for Scotland 2009). However, some parents may prefer to speak with someone with the same spiritual or religious beliefs as themselves or a hospital chaplain. Staff should offer to arrange this if necessary (see *The role of hospital chaplaincies in providing holistic care* below). The hospital chaplaincy can also often provide contact details for various religious and spiritual organisations.

Offering to listen to parents as they discuss how they are feeling can be an important component of spiritual care (NHS Education for Scotland 2009). Staff can offer parents opportunities to discuss their feelings about their baby's death as well as any spiritual or religious questions or thoughts that this experience raises for parents (see also *Support and listening* in Chapter 15). In addition to not making assumptions, it is important that staff are able and willing to listen without judgement or making reference to their own beliefs when parents discuss their beliefs and preferences. Staff should also aim to normalise parents' feelings, experiences and decisions without comparing them to other parents or their own experiences. However, it may also be helpful for staff to acknowledge that parents' feelings are often experienced by other bereaved parents to help parents understand that what they are feeling is not unusual.

Offering this kind of care can be exhausting and may sometimes challenge the beliefs and assumptions of the care provider. It takes generosity, insight and discipline to fully listen to bereaved parents and resist the temptation to reassure, find solutions, compare or talk about one's own experience and beliefs. It is important that staff are aware of their own beliefs and that they know their own limits when providing support. It is also important that support is available for staff supporting bereaved parents (see Chapter 24 for more information about support and training for staff).

A multi-faith room should also be provided in hospitals for the use of parents and families of all faiths and those with no spiritual affiliations or beliefs. Some parents may want to pray or spend quiet time in these areas alone, with family members or with other members of their community.

Some parents may also want to bring religious or spiritual items to the hospital. Religious items that have been placed in the room where parents are receiving care or with the baby should not be moved without first consulting the parents.

Some parents may perform rituals around the time when their baby dies. Religious or spiritual rituals can have an important spiritual, social and/or emotional significance and may be comforting to some parents. Most religious rituals that parents might want to perform when a baby dies can be easily accommodated and many may go unnoticed by staff. However, lamps, incense or candles often clash with institutional safety regulations. Parents' requests to use such items should be met with understanding and sympathy, and, wherever possible, accommodated safely. Any health and safety concerns about any religious items or rituals should be sensitively and respectfully explained to parents.

The role of hospital chaplaincies in providing holistic care

Hospital chaplaincies aim to ensure that all people within the hospital have access to pastoral, spiritual or religious support regardless of their faith and whether they have no religious or spiritual beliefs (NHS England 2015a). In larger areas, chaplaincies also often have a multi-faith team depending on the main religious and spiritual groups living in the local area (NHS England 2015a). Additionally, chaplaincies can help parents to make contact with other religious and spiritual support organisations should parents wish to access help or support from a spiritual adviser from their own faith.

Chaplains who work in health care settings should receive specialist training in communicating and supporting individuals and families during very distressing times (NHS England 2015a). They also often have an insight into the very difficult personal, religious and ethical dilemmas that can arise in relation to childbearing loss. Some parents, other family members and/or staff members may find it helpful to talk to a chaplain as they are not directly involved in clinical decisions and they can bring a different perspective to discussions. Parents may also feel that a chaplain has more time to sit with them and listen as they discuss their feelings (McHaffie 2000). Also, some parents may have no experience of traditions and rituals associated with pregnancy loss or the death of a baby for their faith. These parents may want advice on the rituals or observation that they are expected to engage in when their baby dies.

Chaplaincies are also responsible for checking and maintaining multi-faith rooms to ensure that meet the needs of people from different spiritual backgrounds (NHS England 2015a).

Some of the information in this chapter is adapted from Schott and Henley (1996) and Henley and Schott (1999).

CHAPTER 2

Providing inclusive care

Other relevant chapters

1: Providing holistic care

3: Loss and grief

4: Communication

5: Communication across language and other barriers

24: Staff support and training

It is important that healthcare and social care services are inclusive and can be accessed by all parents and families who experience the death of a baby. This includes meeting the care needs of parents who have different personal, cultural, religious and spiritual needs (see Chapter 1). However, it also means that high quality care must be provided for.

> ...everyone, including those who [sic] are vulnerable, who live in poverty and who are isolated. By seeking to deliver high quality care for all, we are striving to reduce inequalities in access to health services and in the outcomes from care. (NHS England [n.d.])

Why providing inclusive care for bereaved parents is important

Childbearing loss affects people from all social groups and there are risk factors that may result in a baby's death that are not related to ethnicity, poverty or the mother's age (Manktelow et al. 2015). However, parents who live in the most socially deprived areas of the UK are more than 50 per cent more likely to experience a stillbirth or neonatal death than parents in more affluent areas (Manktelow et al. 2015). Manktelow et al. (2015) found that parents had a higher risk of their baby being stillborn or dying neonatally if they are:

- from ethnic minority communities (particularly Black, Black British, Asian or Asian British parents who have over a 50 per cent higher risk);

- teenage mothers or mothers over 40 years of age (39 per cent higher risk); and

- living in poverty (57 per cent higher risk).

The risk of experiencing a miscarriage, stillbirth or neonatal death is also higher for parents in Gypsy and Travelling communities and for refugees and asylum seekers (Parry *et al.* 2007; Maternity Action and Refugee Council 2013; The Traveller Movement 2014). The higher risk rates for women in these groups highlight that bereavement care must be available that meets the needs of parents from diverse backgrounds. This data also suggests that it is crucial to provide more inclusive maternity care to women from more socially disadvantaged backgrounds as this may help to prevent more babies' deaths (Manktelow *et al.* 2015).

However, it is important to recognise that there may be barriers to accessing healthcare services for some women who may be more "vulnerable" or socially disadvantaged.

For some parents, these barriers may result from discrimination that they experience when accessing or attempting to access healthcare services. Legal protection is offered against discrimination based on age, disability, gender reassignment, marriage and civil partnership, pregnancy and maternity, race, religion or belief, sex and sexual orientation under the Equality Act 2010 (Section 4). However, healthcare inequalities and barriers to accessing care continue to exist for women from different backgrounds despite this protection (Maternity Action, Women's Health and Equality Consortium 2014; Lindquist *et al.* 2015; Manktelow *et al.* 2015).

Providing healthcare services that are inclusive

It is important to ensure that healthcare service provisions are tailored to meet the needs of parents from a range of backgrounds, including those who:

- are experiencing poverty or homelessness;

- are teenage parents;

- are from specific ethnic minority backgrounds;

- are lesbian, gay, bisexual, trans and queer;

- speak little or no English;

- are refugees and asylum seekers;

- have substance abuse problems;

- have mental health problems or a history of mental health problems;

- have a physical, learning or sensory disability;

- are experiencing or have experienced domestic violence or other forms of violence and abuse;

- have been referred to child protection services;
- have experienced female genital cutting;
- have been involved in sex work or trafficking; and/or
- are in prison.

The needs of these parents, and some of the barriers and difficulties that they face with regard to accessing care, will be different, and possibly compounded, if they have experienced more than one of these factors that may make them vulnerable.

The most important thing is that all parents are provided with care that is sensitive, non-judgemental, holistic and person-centred (NICE 2008a; Downe *et al.* 2009) (see also Chapter 1). This involves treating all parents with dignity and respect while working in partnership with them to help them make fully-informed decisions about their care (NICE 2008a). Good communication is a crucial part of providing this type of high-quality, inclusive care to parents (NICE 2008a) (see Chapter 4).

While many healthcare professionals attempt to provide inclusive care that is sensitive to the needs of patients from different backgrounds, many staff may feel uncertain about their understanding of patients' backgrounds (Kai *et al.* 2007). However, it is important that staff do not feel that they need to have expert knowledge about parents' backgrounds to provide inclusive care (Kai *et al.* 2007). Instead, Kai *et al.* emphasise that:

> *Fundamentally, health care professionals need to be supported to respond to patients as individuals, whose cultural diversity embraces not only ethnicity, but other influences such as gender, social background, and education.* (2007: 7)

By focusing on parents as individuals, this will help staff to better understand parents' needs, regardless of their background. That said, it can be important for healthcare services to consult parents and ensure that basic care provisions are sensitive to the needs of as many parents as possible. For example, healthcare services can be more sensitive to parents' needs by ensuring that the language used in forms and written information is inclusive of single parents and those in lesbian and gay relationships (Peel 2010). It is also important that all partners are offered support and included in discussions (with the woman's consent when discussing antenatal care) (Peel 2010).

It is also important to recognise that some women from socially disadvantaged backgrounds may seek less antenatal and postnatal care and that they often have poorer experiences of care when they do engage with maternity services (Lindquist *et al.* 2015). Special consideration is needed for providing care that is more accessible and better meets the needs of these women and their families. For example, maternity care should be provided in a variety of settings that are accessible to women (including homeless women) (Downe *et al.* 2009; Lindquist *et al.* 2015). Flexible opening hours are also important as some women may not be able to take time off work to attend appointments during regular opening hours (Downe *et al.* 2009; Maternity Action, Women's Health and Equality Consortium 2014). Parents on low incomes may also need help with travel costs for specialist care for themselves or their baby if they are staying on a specialist neonatal unit. Staff should offer all parents information about benefits that may be available for them (see *Discussing entitlement to time off work and benefits* in Chapter 15).

Additionally, information needs to be in a variety of formats that parents can understand and that are tailored to meet the needs of parents with learning, physical or sensory disabilities (NICE 2008a; Lindquist *et al*. 2015). This includes providing information in other languages and interpreters when necessary (NICE 2008a) (see also Chapter 5).

Downe *et al*. (2009) also highlight how some of the following measures might also help to improve parents' access to care:

- Advertising information about healthcare services in areas where women from different backgrounds and other service providers may encounter this information.

- Providing one-to-one, continuous care for parents.

- Building up trust and building relationships with communities and other service providers.

- Promoting referral and good communication across different healthcare services, social care services and local and national support organisations.

Trusts, Health Boards and managers have a responsibility to ensure that services are accessible to parents from different backgrounds and that systems and standard practices do not intentionally or unintentionally discriminate against parents. Trusts, Health Boards and managers should also be aware of the costs that parents may incur if they or their baby need specialist care and funding should be available to assist parents on low incomes.

Training and support for staff

Training should be provided for staff to support them and build their confidence in providing inclusive care for all parents (Kai *et al*. 2007). As well as providing information to staff, this training should offer staff opportunities to:

- Identify their own culture-based values and assumptions and those of the organisation in which they work.

- Consider how these values and assumptions may affect their responses to parents who have different backgrounds, views and opinions.

- Think about how they could find out about and respond to the needs and wishes of parents and families of different cultures.

In addition to ensuring that training on providing inclusive care is available for all staff, Trusts, Health Boards and managers should identify and train specialist midwives and nurses. These specialist staff should develop knowledge and skills for supporting vulnerable parents with specific needs. For example, some midwives and nurses specialise in bereavement, mental health, child protection, screening, teenage pregnancy or substance misuse. These midwives and nurses should not be expected to support all parents who are experiencing such difficulties or who may be vulnerable. However, these staff can be a valuable resource and source of support for other staff members who are caring for parents with extra support needs and they can ensure that services are in place to meet the needs of these parents (see also *Bereavement midwives and nurses* in Chapter 25).

Staff working in specialist roles should also receive support from their managers and colleagues so that they can adapt care to meet the specific needs of parents wherever possible.

CHAPTER 3

Loss and grief

Other relevant chapters

1: Providing holistic care

2: Providing inclusive care

4: Communication

5: Communication across language and other barriers

24: Staff support and training

A loss during pregnancy or around the time of birth is complex and unique (Hutti 2005). For parents, a childbearing loss may be the loss of hopes, dreams and expectations for the future, including the loss of a person who would have been. This may also be the first experience of loss and bereavement for parents and the potential emotional chaos, grief and devastation that these experiences can entail.

Putting theories of grief into practice with bereaved parents

Grief is both universal and highly individual in that people may have a wide range of feelings and physical reactions (Wortman and Silver 1989; Scrutton 1995).

Grief has historically been described as a series of "tasks", "stages" or "phases" through which people move. This can be a useful model for starting to think about grief. For example, Kübler-Ross and Kessler (2005) describe five stages where people typically experience denial, anger, grief, depression and acceptance in relation to their loss. However, Kübler-Ross and Kessler (2005) also highlight that people do not necessarily experience all of these stages or the emotions associated with these stages and they may not experience them in a particular order. That is, the experience of grief is different and unpredictable for each person.

Therefore, it is unhelpful to impose a framework of "normal grieving" on bereaved parents or to expect them to progress through a series of prescribed stages (Murray

Parkes 1985; Wortman and Silver 1989; Littlewood 1992; Davies 2004). If staff do expect parents to experience grief as a linear progression, parents may feel judged or that there is something wrong with them if their feelings and reactions do not fit into a formula (Leon 1992).

Stroebe and Schut's (1999) dual-process model of grief suggests that bereaved people often move backwards and forwards between confrontation and avoidance rather than experiencing grief as a series of stages or phases. They argue that people sometimes confront their loss and emotions or engage in mourning rituals or other tasks related to their grief. However, they also highlight that people on occasion also deal with other tasks that are required for living or seek distractions (Stroebe and Schut 1999). Worden (2003) argues that people can attend to their feelings of grief at the same time as they engage in these other tasks.

> *My grief does not seem to leave me alone for very long and when it does leave me it only seems to do so because of the demands of my work ... It seems incredible that I should be able, or even willing, to carry on as normal. Sometimes I catch myself laughing and joking with work colleagues and feel as though I have let my little boy down.* Father

It is important to normalise the experiences and emotions of parents. Some parents may also find it helpful to know that other parents commonly have similar experiences.

Resolution or continuing bonds?

People often develop attachments or strong affectionate bonds to other people in their lives and usually experience strong emotional reactions when these bonds are broken (Worden 2003). It is important for others to recognise that many bereaved parents will already have developed a bond with their baby.

Older models of grief generally assume that, after a period of time, the bereaved person should reach "resolution" and be able to "let go" of their emotional relationship with the person who has died. However, it is increasingly acknowledged that many bereaved people continue to feel a bond with the person who has died and that the person continues to be part of their lives (Worden 2003) and that this is a conscious and healthy part of grieving (Hall 2014). Studies have also confirmed that many bereaved parents do not want to forget their dead babies: they may continue to feel a bond with them and find solace in doing so (Klass 1996; Walter 1999; Wilson 2001; Davies 2004).

> *Dear Charlie and Joshua, it is five years since you were born. You should both be starting school now. It seems longer ago now, but at other times not as long as five years. You have a younger sister, Jessica, who is four and talks about you regularly, and a two-year-old brother, Samuel, who doesn't really understand yet, but knows you are Mummy's babies.* Mother

At first, we were terrified if at the end of the day we realised that we had not thought about her, in case that meant we were forgetting her; but as time went by we realised that not consciously thinking of her was fine, she would creep into our thoughts on her own. Mother

Parents' experiences and expressions of grief

Grief is what the person experiencing it says it is. (Mander 2006: 111)

Each parent will grieve and express their grief in their own way (Worden 2003). It is also impossible to predict the significance of a pregnancy loss or the death of a baby for any parent. The depth and length of each parent's grief varies and depends to some extent on many factors, including their personality, circumstances, life experiences, previous experiences of loss, attachment to this baby or pregnancy, the significance of the loss to them and the support network available to them (Worden 2003).

A shorter gestation or the nature of the loss does not necessarily determine parents' experiences of, feelings about or reactions to the loss (Zeanah *et al*. 1993; Bagchi and Friedman 1999; Mander 2006). Some parents may be devastated while others may see it as the end of a pregnancy rather than the loss of a life and find it easier to move on (Leon 1992). In some situations, parents may distance themselves and withdraw both emotionally and physically (Enkin *et al*. 2000). For example, parents may distance themselves from their feelings or the situation when there is a very poor prognosis antenatally or the baby is in a neonatal intensive care unit (Enkin *et al*. 2000). Some parents may also experience anticipatory grief in these situations, where they grieve before their baby dies, as they anticipate their death but also experience this grief again after the death (Kübler-Ross and Kessler 2005).

For many parents, losing a baby affects their self-esteem and self-confidence and some parents may feel that they have failed. Some parents might also feel that they have lost control over their lives (Worden 2003). The loss of their baby may also be a traumatic experience for some parents (Worden 2003). However, it is important to recognise that bereavement is not always experienced as being traumatic (Worden 2003) (see *Post-traumatic stress and post-traumatic stress disorder* in Chapter 18).

Parents may also experience a number of physical and emotional reactions. These feelings and reactions may last for hours or days and may recur over the following weeks. However, it is important to remember that each parent's reactions will be different.

Initially, most parents feel shocked and numb even when the loss or death of their baby has been expected. Some parents may not be able to absorb the reality of what has happened or understand what is being said.

Parents may also experience physical reactions as a result of their grief. These could include pain, palpitations, diarrhoea, nausea, tightness in their throat or stomach and/ or exhaustion (Sands 2014h). They may also feel shaky, cold, weak or breathless and their appetite or sleep may be affected (Sands 2014h). Some parents may also feel that their arms ache to hold their baby or that they can hear their baby crying (Sands 2014h). Some women may feel that their baby is still kicking inside of them or feel distressed by their own physical reminders of their baby after the birth (for example, lactation, vaginal bleeding, after pains or stitches) (Sands 2014h).

 The pain of grief was so physical. My chest hurt, I could not move about and certainly could not think straight. Every now and then a wave of grief came crashing over me and all I could do was crouch down and scream until I was exhausted. Then there was calm until the next wave came. Mother

 I had thought that terms like "your arms aching to hold him" belonged in trashy romance novels. But they are true. Your arms do ache. Your chest does feel as if a huge stone has settled on it. Your heart does break into a million pieces. It's the loneliest feeling in the world. Mother

 I just feel so cheated, like part of me has died, and that my insides have been ripped out. I'm just so angry and all these feelings I have been told are natural. Mother

Parents also commonly feel sad and tearful. Some parents may also experience recurring waves of despair, sadness and crying spells or find it hard to function. They may also feel guilty and resentful. Some parents may be angry at the staff who were involved, their partner, relatives, friends, the baby who has died or parents with healthy babies. Sometimes, the anger is turned inwards and some bereaved parents feel guilt or shame and sometimes blame themselves (Barr 2004; Cacciatore 2010; Brierley-Jones *et al*. 2014) For example, some parents may have thoughts such as "If only I had…" (Cacciatore 2010). Other parents may also feel envious or jealous of parents with healthy babies (Barr and Cacciatore 2007). Additionally, some parents may question their faith or be angry that their baby has died despite their faith.

 I blamed myself for the death of our baby, for drinking coffee, the occasional glass of wine, the prawn sandwich I had eaten. Mother

 Babies don't die for no reason. It was my responsibility, as Kieran's mother, to nurture my son through the first nine months of his life and to see him safely into this world. And even if you don't smoke, didn't drink, took all the multivitamins advised, avoided soft cheese and even hair dyes and nail varnish for fear of harmful chemicals – that guilt is still there. It was my responsibility and I failed. Mother

Outward expressions of grief do not necessarily indicate what an individual parent is experiencing or what they need. Some individuals, families and cultures value stoicism, others feel more comfortable or encourage private but not public expressions of grief and some value and encourage loud and open grieving (Schott and Henley 1999). It is important to avoid assumptions about how a person feels based on the way they behave in grief.

There may also be some cultural, religious or spiritual factors and norms that determine how people experience, express and make sense of or explain their grief. There may also be some cultural, religious or spiritual expectations that affect how bereaved parents behave in public, how they organise funerals, the restrictions that they observe and/ or the clothes they are expected to wear. In some cultures and faiths, there may be no formal grieving rituals following a childbearing loss. In some faiths, parents may be expected to hide or suppress their grief as loss is seen as something that should be accepted without questioning the will of God or another deity (Schott and Henley 1999).

However, it is always important to remember that individuals from the same background will have different experiences of grief. They will also have ways of expressing and dealing with grief that are unique to them (Cowles 1996). Despite the presence or absence of expectations, traditions or rituals for parents from different backgrounds, parents will have their own personal preferences and needs and they may not adhere to all of the expectations and norms.

Although intense grief usually eases with time, many people find that grief continues to return over months and years. Some parents may find that grief is like a wound that can be re-opened time and again and memories of childbearing losses may continue to surface many years later (Cowles 1996; Dyson and While 1998; Sands 2014e).

 Now six months later, to most of the world I am just like any other mother of two healthy, lively young children. Inside I often fight to control my emotions and tears which seem triggered off by so many things. Mother

Some significant dates such as the baby's due date, the date when the baby died, the baby's birth date, Mothers' day, Fathers' day, festivals, celebrations and important life events may trigger parents' feelings of grief. Parents may also experience grief as a result of certain sights, sounds and smells.

 I miss what might have been. I will never be able to pick them up and comfort them when they fall over. I will never get to see their paintings from the toddlers group or their first day at school and I will never get to see them playing with my daughter. Mother

The important thing to remember is that each parent (regardless of their background) will have feelings and experiences of grief that are unique to them. People who are supporting parents should be supportive of each parent's way of grieving and their choices regarding rituals such as funerals. It is important to listen to bereaved parents, respond to their needs and normalise their experiences and emotions, regardless of the time that has passed since their baby's death.

To ensure that appropriate support is offered to bereaved parents, it is also important to be aware of the potential experiences of grief that fathers and other partners might have, as well as the grief experiences that some parents may have as a couple.

Fathers and same-sex partners

 My closest male friend John ... gave me what I can only describe as the kind of hug only fathers can give their sons. I will be forever indebted to him. For that moment he could not change the pain but he carried some of it for just long enough when I could not. Father

The effects of childbearing losses on fathers and same-sex partners are not always recognised. Additionally, most of the available research in this area has focused on bereaved fathers. The term "father" has been used here when men are being specifically discussed and "partner" has been used in other areas. However, some of the information here about "fathers" may also apply to women and some of the research cited may have focused on men even when the term "partner" is used.

It is often assumed that fathers do not bond as deeply with an unborn child and so are not as severely affected by loss as mothers, especially in cases of early loss (Duncan 1995). However, many fathers respond to the loss of their baby with deep and intense grief (Di Clemente 2004; Don 2005). They may, however, experience more feelings of distress several weeks later rather than immediately following the loss (Puddifoot and Johnson 1999). This may be particularly the case for fathers who had seen the baby on ultrasound (Puddifoot and Johnson 1999).

Gender expectations of men may also affect their ability to acknowledge their own needs and their willingness to seek support from other people. Consequently, men may be more isolated both socially and psychologically (Clare 2000). Additionally, they may not have a network of people to whom they can express their feelings. Many men rely on their partners for support, although they may not feel they can do so following a childbearing loss. Additionally, family, friends and staff often focus on the mother's needs and may not consider, or know how to deal with, the father's needs. These factors may cause some fathers to feel excluded or suppress or ignore their own feelings and needs (Murphy 1998).

 I was unable to give a name to my feelings let alone feel in a position to articulate them to anyone whatever their capacity. A supportive GP prescribed anti-depressants which I didn't think helped. I wasn't depressed. I was a bereaved Englishman. Father

Grieving was hard because we did not seem to be able to communicate much and so did not really talk to each other about how we were feeling or how we were coping. I later discovered that my partner had started to drink and by the time I realised it, he had a serious drink problem. Mother

 It took a long time for someone to ask me how I was. Father

Many partners often feel helpless, frightened and angry at the pain and distress that the mother is experiencing (Bennett *et al*. 2005). Partners may also feel the strength of the woman's emotions very strongly and/or feel guilty and responsible for her unhappiness and physical distress. It may be very hard for partners to see a woman's distress and be unable to help (Sands 2014c). They may also feel the need to "switch off", "close down" or "get away" for a while (Sands 2014c).

 I felt suffocated with grief. I could not bear my pain, but more, the pain my wife was suffering. I could not fix it. Father

Partners may also feel that they need to put their grief on hold in order to be strong to support the mother who was pregnant and focus on other practical tasks (Stroebe *et al*. 2013; Sands 2014c).

This feeling may be reinforced by other people's expectations or their need to return to work (Sands 2014c). If a partner must or feels that they want to return to work quite soon after their baby's death, they may want to contact their employer and colleagues beforehand (Sands 2014c). This may help to ensure that some support is in place for them in their workplace. They may find it helpful to use Sands' support booklets on *Returning to work after the death of your baby* and *Information for employers: helping a bereaved parent return to work* (for ordering information, see the details for the Sands website in Appendix 2).

 I was shocked at how little I could do, I felt constantly distracted, lacking energy, and looking back now, I really didn't function effectively for six months. Father

For most partners, it is important that they are recognised and acknowledged – by their partners, by other family members and by staff – as parents who are grieving the loss of their baby and not simply as supporters and comforters (Samuelsson *et al*. 2001; Cacciatore *et al*. 2013). They should also feel able to grieve in their own way and in their own time, without having to comply with other people's expectations of them (Koopmans *et al*. 2013).

Couples

 The first few months were very hard. We seemed very separate and at times I wondered if we would ever get through this. But looking back on it now, I think it has made us stronger as a couple. Mother

Grieving is very individual. Each parent is likely to have different perceptions of their loss and different ways of managing and expressing their feelings, as well as having their own unique relationship with the baby who has died.

Grieving couples often find that their needs and feelings do not coincide and may find it hard to talk and give each other support. Each may try to protect the other by keeping their more painful thoughts and feelings to themselves (Bennett *et al.* 2005; Stroebe *et al.* 2013). As a result, each parent may feel increasingly lonely and isolated and their relationship may become strained and difficult (Schaap *et al.* 1997; Mander 2006). Additionally, parents' grief may be experienced more intensely if they do not feel supported by their partner (Hutti *et al.* 2015).

Some parents may also experience difficulties in their relationship if one parent's grief persists for longer than that of their partner, they are unable to accept each other's different ways of grieving, they do not feel that their partner feels the loss as intensely or they do not feel supported by their partner (Wallerstedt and Higgins 1996; Avelin *et al.* 2013; Koopmans *et al.* 2013; Hutti *et al.* 2015). When parents' grief experiences are not similar, this may also increase their likelihood of separation (Koopmans *et al.* 2013). The effect of experiencing a perinatal loss on a couple's relationship may also be related to the quality of the relationship prior to the loss (Avelin *et al.* 2013).

 I think, if truth be told, we've probably moved a bit further apart. I don't think we communicated our experiences or how we were feeling particularly well. Maybe it's our inability to share how we feel, or maybe me just thinking I've shut that chapter door. I want to get on with life. Father

When parents share their experiences of grief with each other and feel that they have support from their partner, this may strengthen their relationship and improve their emotional well-being (Statham *et al.* 2001; Swanson 2003; Avelin *et al.* 2013; Koopmans *et al.* 2013). Parents' relationships may also be strengthened if they are able to respect and accept each other's individual experiences of grieving (Cacciatore *et al.* 2008; Avelin *et al.* 2013). Additionally, couples who talk to each other about their feelings and experiences may also perceive their relationship as being closer.

Some parents may also experience sexual difficulties after a childbearing loss that may affect their relationship (Swanson 2003; Cacciatore *et al.* 2008). Parents' desires for sex may be affected by their grief and parents may have different needs and desires for sex (Sands 2014a). A parent's desire or lack of desire for sex is also not necessarily dependent on whether they are a man or a woman.

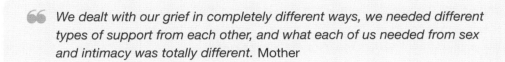
We dealt with our grief in completely different ways, we needed different types of support from each other, and what each of us needed from sex and intimacy was totally different. Mother

I wanted to want sex but felt nothing. Mother

Our physical needs were quite different. I just needed to be held tightly, to feel comforted, wanted, desired, reassured, but I didn't want sex. My husband needed sex to give him that comfort and reassurance. Mother

Some parents may also find it difficult to discuss sex with each other, especially if they did not talk about sex before their baby died (Sands 2014a).

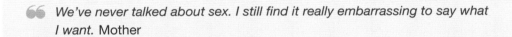
We've never talked about sex. I still find it really embarrassing to say what I want. Mother

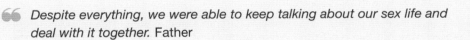
Despite everything, we were able to keep talking about our sex life and deal with it together. Father

Some parents may fear getting pregnant again or disagree about whether or when to try for another baby (Sands 2014a) (see also *Parents considering subsequent pregnancies* in Chapter 23). Parents may also feel guilty about enjoying sex after their baby has died or find that sex releases other emotions (Sands 2014a). They may also fear hurting their partner, particularly if she is still recovering from the birth (Sands 2014a). Some women's relationship with their body may also be affected and they may no longer feel attractive or may experience flashbacks during sex if they experienced a traumatic birth (Sands 2014a). Parents may also find it difficult to start having sex again if some time has elapsed since they had physical contact with each other (Sands 2014a).

It may help couples to know that:

- It can be very difficult for either parent to support the other when they are both grieving.

- It is common for people to react differently at different times, but that this does not mean that their partner does not care about how they feel or that one parent cares more about the loss.

- Although it can be difficult, taking time to listen to each other is helpful and important. Parents who are anxious that talking may make things worse or make their partner cry more, may find it reassuring to know that talking does not *cause* the pain, rather it allows the pain to be expressed.

- Parents may have different needs and desires for sexual contact. Parents may find it helpful to read the Sands booklet on *Sexual relationships after the death of a baby* (see Appendix 2).

Grief experiences of other family members and friends

In addition to parents, other family members and friends may also be affected by a pregnancy loss or the death of a baby. It is important for staff to recognise that grandparents and other family members may need help and support in their own right and that they are not merely additional supporters for the parents. However, grandparents, other family members and friends may also be able to offer important support to parents and other children on a long-term basis and they may benefit from being offered information about how they might be able to support parents.

If the parents wish, involving the baby's grandparents, other family members and friends at the time of the loss may also be a way of helping the parents in the future. This is because other people can share memories with the parents if they have seen the baby and/or were present at important events.

Some people may not live near their close family and friends and this may affect the support these people can offer to parents. For example, they may not be able to be with the parents around the time of a childbearing loss or the funeral. If family or friends need to travel, this may also cause delays to funerals. It is important for staff to recognise the effect that this may have on parents as they may need extra support as a result.

Being aware of some of the potential support needs of other children, grandparents and other family members and friends may be beneficial for staff who may also need to offer support to these individuals. This information may also be useful for parents who need to support other children or who need support from other family members and friends.

Other children

Existing children are usually profoundly affected when their parents are grieving. Children may also experience their own grief if they have been expecting to have a new baby brother or sister (Sands 2014i). Children born after a pregnancy loss or death of a baby may also be affected if grief and loss affect how their parents view another pregnancy and relate to these children.

Many people feel that children should be protected from the reality of death. The decision to tell a child about a loss is very personal and will depend on several factors. However, children who know that a new baby was expected should be told about the loss. Some parents may decide not to tell a child who does not yet know that their mother was pregnant. However, parents need to know that children often sense when something is wrong or overhear adult conversations and their behaviour may change as a result. If parents feel unable to talk to the children themselves, they may wish to ask a close family member or friend for support in talking to children (Sands 2014i).

There is not a right way to talk with a child about death (Sands 2014i). However, explanations should usually be short and clear and children should be able to ask questions (Sands 2014i). It is also important to choose words or advise parents to choose words that cannot be misinterpreted when talking to a young child and to be as open and honest as possible (Sands 2014i). For example, telling a young child that the dead baby is "sleeping", "unwell", "an angel" or has been "lost" could cause the child to feel great anxiety about going to sleep, being ill or having a family member or friend who is ill, being called an angel or getting lost (Sands 2014i). It is better to use the terms "died" or "death" and answer the child's questions, if there are any, about what this means. Some children may have questions immediately or they may ask questions at other times and parents should try to respond to these questions as truthfully as possible (Sands 2014i).

Parents may find it useful to read leaflets on talking to children about a pregnancy loss produced by Sands, Child Bereavement UK (CBUK), Cruse Bereavement Care, Antenatal Results and Choices (ARC), the Miscarriage Association and other support organisations (see Appendix 2). For example, parents may benefit from reading the Sands booklet on *Supporting children when a baby has died* (see Appendix 2). Some of these organisations publish books to help young children understand the concept of death and the feelings it can generate. These organisations also offer support to parents and children at this time. If parents are still worried about how to support their other children, or are having difficulties, staff should offer to put them in touch with a counsellor or other professional who is experienced in the area of child bereavement.

It is also important to recognise that young children may be ambivalent about the impending arrival of a sibling and, as a consequence, some may feel that the death is somehow their fault (Worden 1996). Children should be reassured that they are not to blame for the death of their baby brother or sister.

There is also some debate about whether young children grieve in the same way as older children or adults (Worden 1996). How children respond to a loss is determined by a number of factors, including their level of development. Support from adults is important as children also learn how to grieve from the adults around them and they need the support of these adults (CBUK 2011).

Daisy had a massive impact on our family. Rosie, our one-year-old, was too young to understand what she'd lost. Matthew, her big brother, felt it very keenly and was very, very sad. Cathy and I were devastated – and could have been destroyed – by our grief. But with two tots depending on us, we couldn't let that happen. We sought out anything that could help us cope. Father

Small children may find it difficult to understand the meaning or permanence of death. Children may also have a limited capacity to express their grief and feelings verbally and may be more likely to express their feelings about the loss or the changes in the adults around them by "acting out" (CBUK 2011). For example, children may regress to earlier behaviours, cry, become clingy or become angry or difficult. These behaviours may increase the pressure on their parents and make it harder for them to cope. Children may also hide their feelings if they fear adding to their parents' distress or if the adults around them are controlling their feelings very strictly (Sands 2014i). Children should be encouraged and supported to express how they are feeling. Parents can also explain to children that it's okay to be sad and that they have not done anything wrong to upset adults if they become emotional while talking to children (Sands 2014i). Parents should also be encouraged to inform the child's nursery or school so that any changes in behaviour are seen in the context of the family's loss. Parents may need to explain to other family members and friends that children can be deeply affected by a loss and that this may affect their behaviour for some time.

How much children are involved in rituals after a childbearing loss depends to some extent on personal preferences and cultural norms. Some parents actively include children while others try to shield children from death. It is important for parents to be aware that it is unlikely to be possible to shield children completely from death and grief and that involvement may benefit children by helping them to feel involved or because their involvement can be discussed with them in the future even if they are too young to remember (Sands 2014i).

Some parents encourage children to make their own choices about matters such as seeing the body, helping to plan the funeral, attending the funeral, visiting the grave and participating in other memorial activities. It is also important to be aware that children may change their mind about taking part in these activities or anniversaries over time (Sands 2014i).

A small study by Wilson (2001) identified three main categories of support that parents belonging to a Sands group in Edinburgh gave to their children after the death of a baby:

- *Recognising and acknowledging the child's grief*. For example, telling children what is happening, understanding mood and behaviour changes as reactions to loss, listening and answering questions honestly and trying not to burden children with their own grief.

- *Including the child in family rituals to do with the baby who has died*. For example, offering the child an opportunity to see and hold the baby, photographing them with the baby, including them in funeral or memorial services if they want to attend.

- *Keeping the baby's memory alive in the family.* For example, visiting the grave or crematorium garden and/or lighting candles in memory of the baby on anniversaries and at important festivals and celebrations.

Parents may also be preoccupied with their own grief and their existing children may feel excluded (Sands 2014i). It is important that parents let children know that they are there for them even when it is difficult for parents (Sands 2014i). Children in these situations can also be helped by long-term consistent support from another adult who they are close to and who is able to listen and respond to them.

Parents and children may also need long-term support from other family, friends, healthcare staff and supporters. If parents feel unable to care for their other children after 6 months, they should be referred to their GP or health visitor (Sands 2014i). Some parents may also become over-protective of existing and future children and may need support to gradually give children more independence in a way that gives parents time to adjust and manage any anxieties (Sands 2014i).

Grandparents

 Never underestimate what a grandparent goes through when a baby dies. For their suffering is doubled: they mourn for the child they will never get to see grow and they watch their own child suffer the cruellest of agonies. They feel heartbroken, yet try to be strong. They see their own child's heartbreak and feel helpless. Father

 As I was wheeled out of the delivery room, I saw my father pick up my baby boy, his grandson, and cradle him, sobbing quietly. Mother

Many grandparents are deeply affected and distressed by a childbearing loss. For some grandparents, the loss also evokes painful memories of their own childbearing losses and they may not have received support for this loss previously. Grandparents may also experience grief for both their anticipated grandchild and their own child who is also grieving (Sands 2014i). It can be very distressing for grandparents to be unable to lessen the pain and grief of their child who is grieving for their baby (Sands 2014i). They may also feel guilty if the baby was diagnosed with a genetic anomaly.

 I have felt so helpless. I have been unable to "kiss it better" and make my daughter's pain go away, nothing can. I have simply held her hand and listened. Grandmother

Provided the parents want them to be involved, grandparents may want to see and hold the baby and participate in funerals and memorials.

Grandparents may also benefit from support from organisations such as Sands or from the Sands booklets on *Information and support for grandparents: When a grandchild dies before, during or shortly after birth* and *Long ago bereaved* (see Appendix 2).

Other family members and friends

Ideas about what constitutes a family vary from person to person. Some people may see "the family" as the parents (or parent) and their child or children and other relatives may form the "extended family". For some families or cultures, there may be no division between the immediate and extended family. Grandparents, aunts, uncles, siblings and cousins may all be regarded as close family and a new baby may be considered an addition to the whole family. The definition of family for some people may also include close friends. This means that a larger number of people may experience grief over a childbearing loss or want to be directly involved.

 I can't believe how much the loss of my niece has affected me. Seeing my sister-in-law and my brother in such distress has been heart-breaking. I never realised how much you could miss someone that you have never known. Aunt

 I had seen my friend the day before - everything was fine and it didn't occur to me that anything could go wrong. When I heard that her baby had died shortly after birth I was very upset and sad. But my overriding feeling was fear. I never knew this could happen. Nothing that horrendous had happened to anyone we know. I realised it would have a massive effect on everyone. Friend

In some cultures, any activities associated with pregnancy and childbirth may be the sole responsibility of women and some women may not expect or want their husbands to be involved. In these instances, female relatives or friends may sometimes be more important sources of support for a bereaved mother.

However, in any circumstances, it is important not to make assumptions about who parents may want to involve in creating memories or making arrangements after a baby dies. With the parents' consent, staff should involve other family members and friends in activities following a childbearing loss and offer support.

Other family members and friends may also benefit from support from organisations such as Sands or from the Sands booklet entitled *For family and friends* (see Appendix 2).

Offering emotional support to bereaved parents

The importance of offering emotional support to bereaved parents

The support that is given to bereaved parents is important and can have long-term implications for their well-being (Schott and Henley 2009; Crawley *et al*. 2013; Downe *et al*. 2013; Redshaw *et al*. 2014). This includes the support they receive around the time of their baby's death as well as longer-term support (Harper *et al*. 2011; Redshaw *et al*. 2014). It is also important that this support is offered to partners and not only to the woman (see *Fathers and same-sex partners* above).

Around the time when a baby dies, parents' experiences and perceptions of the support and care that they receive can affect how parents experience grief later on and may have implications for their mental health (Crawley *et al*. 2013; Downe *et al*. 2013; Redshaw *et al*. 2014) (see Chapter 18). An important part of this care is related to sensitive communication by staff and the quality of the information and support that they provide for parents as they make decisions about care (Redshaw *et al*. 2014) (see Chapter 4). However, the quality of the emotional support that staff are able to offer to parents is also important and many parents appreciate the warmth and caring demonstrated by staff (McHaffie 2001; Säflund *et al*. 2004; Mander 2006). Conversely, parents may have negative experiences of care if they feel that staff are uncaring, unsupportive or are emotionally distancing themselves from the situation (Downe *et al*. 2013). Downe *et al*. highlight that:

> *No parent whose baby is stillborn should experience inadequate, unsupportive or even uncaring behaviours from staff ... By ensuring that parents receive care that is clinically skilled, emotionally intelligent, consistent and authentically caring, there is the best chance that, even in the midst of a difficult situation, they will have the healthiest experience possible, as well as the best chance of achieving optimum well-being in the longer term. Staff in all relevant health settings need to be supported and encouraged to recognise and respond to their one chance to get it right, for the sake of all future parents who experience such a loss.* (2013: 9)

A member of staff may also be the only person who met their baby or was with the parents at very important moments. For example, staff may have been with parents during a scan when the baby's death was confirmed, when the baby was born or when the baby died. Some parents may find it helpful to discuss what happened with members of staff who were present and share their recollections of the experience and their baby. Sharing these memories of their baby with other people (in addition to creating memories with their baby) may also be beneficial for parents' long-term emotional and mental health (Crawley *et al*. 2013) (see *Creating memories* in Chapter 14).

Even though social support may be important for some parents when they are grieving, they may find that this support is not present (Cacciatore 2010). Some family members and friends may be shocked, experiencing their own grief and/or unsure of what to say or how to offer support (Brierley-Jones *et al.* 2014). They may also feel anxious about upsetting parents, feel uncomfortable when the loss is discussed and/or avoid parents. Some family members and friends may also not understand the impact or significance of the loss for parents and may inadvertently say things that are hurtful to parents (Sands 2014h). For example, they may attempt to provide comfort by saying things that can be hurtful to parents such as "It was probably for the best" or "At least you can have other children" (Sands 2014h).

Parents in relationships may feel isolated if they feel unable to share their grief or experiences with their partner or are experiencing difficulties in their relationship (see *Couples* above). Single parents may feel even more isolated in their experience.

Some parents may also experience or fear stigma as a result of a perinatal loss (Murphy 2012; Brierley-Jones *et al.* 2014). For example, some people may blame the parents for their loss or fear that their misfortune is catching. If the loss resulted from a termination for fetal anomaly or maternal medical condition, some family members or friends may strongly disapprove. In some communities, women who have lost a baby may be excluded from family events and celebrations for some time.

All of these factors may contribute to the amount of support that parents receive from family and friends and any feelings of isolation that some parents may experience. Therefore, parents may also benefit from the emotional support that staff can offer if family members and friends are unable to offer appropriate or adequate support. Parents may also need longer-term support from healthcare staff and other support organisations at times when their grief resurfaces (see *Resolution or continuing bonds?* and *Parents' experiences and expressions of grief* above).

The importance of long-term support is highlighted by the finding that parents whose baby has died are two to four times more likely to die than other parents (Harper *et al.* 2011). The reasons for this increased mortality rate are uncertain but it may relate to the higher number of health problems experienced by these parents or an increased risk of alcohol misuse or suicide (Harper *et al.* 2011) (see also *The importance of care and support for parents in the community* in Chapter 17).

How staff can offer emotional support to parents

There are many ways in which staff can offer emotional support to bereaved parents. The skill in providing this support involves being sensitive to what individual parents need at a particular time. Sometimes parents need someone to listen and at other times they appreciate the offer of information or suggestions (see *Support and listening* in Chapter 15). It is important that private rooms are available for any discussions with parents (see more information about place of care in Chapters 6 to 14).

When offering and providing emotional support to parents, it is important to remember that parents will express grief in different ways (see *Parents' experiences and expressions of grief* above). Some parents may express their feelings openly while others may not show any outward signs of emotion. A parent who grieves silently and inwardly may appreciate the offer of an opportunity to talk about how they feel as much as a parent who expresses their feelings openly. Assumptions should not be made about whether or not parents need emotional support based on their outward expressions of grief. Many parents are particularly grateful when staff offer emotional support without being asked (Statham *et al*. 2001).

It is also important not to pathologise "normal" grief or to expect parents to fit into a prescribed pattern of grieving (see *Putting theories of grief into practice with bereaved parents* above). When providing emotional support to parents, they may find it helpful to know that different parents experience a wide range of physical and emotional reactions when they are grieving (see *Parents' experiences and expressions of grief* above). Staff should reassure parents that there is no "right" or "healthy" way to express or deal with grief, that grief can persist for much longer than most people expect and that grief usually eases over time but it may be triggered by certain dates, events or experiences (Leon 1992; Dyson and While 1998; Mander 2006) (see *Parents' experiences and expressions of grief* above).

However, staff may also need to be aware that some parents may experience prolonged and intense grief and may benefit from an offer of specialist support and a referral to mental health services (see Chapter 18). Some parents may also experience mental health problems and staff should be aware of the signs and symptoms of these conditions and offer a referral for specialist help when necessary.

When offering emotional support to bereaved parents, it is always important for staff to:

- Listen to parents and be prepared to listen again and again.
- Treat parents as individuals and offer them support based on their particular needs.
- Accept what parents say without judgement or comparison.
- Acknowledge parents' feelings and respond with empathy.
- Avoid assumptions, platitudes, comparisons and empty reassurances.
- Remain calm when parents express strong feelings. This may be particularly difficult if parents are angry with staff or blame staff for their baby's death (see *Responding to parents' feedback about their care* in Chapter 22).
- Express sympathy and sorrow when appropriate, but only if these are genuinely felt (Leon 1992).
- Be genuine with parents, willing to help and show kindness.
- Support parents to have as much control over their care as possible and support them to make informed choices (see *Giving information and facilitating informed choice* in Chapter 4).
- Resist the temptation to give advice unless specifically asked.
- Offer parents ongoing support from community staff and arrange this support if the parents wish to accept this offer.
- Offer parents information about other sources of ongoing support such as counselling and other relevant support services and organisations.

- Provide written information for parents about the support available and their choices for care.

This is not an exhaustive list of the ways that staff can provide emotional support to bereaved parents and families but is it a list of the essential support that should be offered.

Counselling

Some parents or other family members may want, at some stage, to see a professional counsellor. Staff should ensure that parents are aware of the counselling services available and offer parents this information if they do not ask for it themselves.

A counsellor has specific skills that may help parents to express and gain some understanding of how they feel. A counsellor may also be able to help parents find ways to manage any practical concerns. Parents may see a counsellor for one session or for a number of sessions over a period of time. Sometimes, parents may want to see a counsellor on their own while others may find it helpful to see a counsellor with their partner if they have one.

Some hospitals have a counsellor who specialises in perinatal losses. However, some parents may prefer to access counselling in another location if they find it too painful to return to the hospital where their baby died. Parents may also be able to access a referral to their counsellor through primary healthcare staff or a local bereavement service. All counsellors who support bereaved parents should have specific knowledge about the unique nature of perinatal losses.

Multiple pregnancies

Rates and risks of childbearing loss are higher for parents expecting multiple pregnancies (Bazian 2012). Parents who experience a loss during a multiple pregnancy may have different experiences and support needs from parents who experience a loss in a single pregnancy. For example, Bryan (2002) highlights that parents may experience the loss of one multiple baby as profoundly as if the loss was of a single child although their experience of grief may be more complex.

Parents who lose all the babies in a multiple pregnancy may grieve more intensely and for longer than parents who lose a single baby (Swanson *et al.* 2002, 2009). Parents may grieve for each baby individually rather than as a "collective baby" and it is important that staff acknowledge each baby (Pector and Smith-Levitin 2002). Parents may also experience grief more intensely if the grief for their multiple babies is not acknowledged. Additionally, parents may also experience grief over the decreased likelihood that they will have another multiple pregnancy.

However, the grief of parents who have lost all their babies may be better understood by other people than that of parents who have one or more surviving babies from a multiple pregnancy (MBF 1997a). Therefore, the rest of this section primarily focuses on parents who have lost one or more babies during a multiple pregnancy as the complexities of experiencing this type of loss may not be very well understood by others. This is not to suggest that the loss of parents who experience the death of all babies in a multiple pregnancy is not as intense. These parents may experience intense multiple losses as they grieve for each baby.

Parents with a multiple pregnancy who lose one or more of their babies at any stage in the pregnancy may have to deal with the complexity and difficulty of grieving for the child who has died while also welcoming and caring for any surviving baby or babies (Richards *et al*. 2015) (see *When one or more babies die during a multiple pregnancy* in Chapter 11 and *Multiple births* in Chapter 14). Parents' feelings may be more complex if they have decided to have a selective termination of pregnancy when one or more multiple babies have been diagnosed with a fetal anomaly or if they have decided to have a multifetal pregnancy reduction (see Chapter 8). If the pregnancy was conceived using an assisted reproductive technology, parents' feelings may also be very complex (see *When parents use assisted reproductive technology* below). Parents may also face additional challenges if any surviving baby or babies are also unwell and vulnerable (see *Parents with more than one baby* in Chapter 13).

Parents who are trying to care for a surviving baby while grieving for the baby or babies who have died (and perhaps organising a funeral and completing other practical tasks) may feel that they cannot enjoy or focus on the living baby as much as they would like. In some cases, grieving is delayed or supressed while parents focus on the surviving baby or babies (Richards *et al.* 2015) only to emerge or re-emerge later, often unexpectedly. Some parents may also feel guilty about their grief and may worry about possible long-term effects on the relationship with the surviving baby or babies.

 It was a difficult time, sharing the feelings of the joy of a new baby and mourning the loss of his beautiful twin sister. The first year was definitely the hardest, our friends and family could not possibly understand what we were going through. Mother

Parents who have one or more surviving babies rarely receive the same degree of sympathy from other people for the baby or babies who have died, especially if the losses occurred before the birth (Pector and Smith-Levitin 2002; Richards *et al*. 2015). Well-meaning friends and relatives may focus on the surviving baby or babies and encourage and expect the parents to do the same (Richards *et al*. 2015). They may try to comfort parents by pointing out that looking after several babies would have been difficult and stressful. They may also discourage parents from grieving for or talking about the baby or babies who have died (MBF 2000).

However, the presence of a living baby in no way lessens parents' grief for those who have died and can emphasise their absence in many ways. It is very important that staff acknowledge all of the babies – both those who have died and those who survive (Wilson *et al*. 1982; MBF 1997a; Fraser 2010). Parents who were expecting twins or more babies also lose the excitement and special status generally given to parents expecting more than one baby. The birth of the surviving baby may be an anticlimax. It is important that parents are supported to express their feelings of loss openly. It may also be helpful if staff acknowledge the difficulties that parents are likely to be experiencing (Wilson *et al*. 1982; MBF 1997a).

The conflicting emotions that parents are likely to experience may persist for a very long time. Every event in the life of the surviving baby or babies may also be a reminder of the babies who have died and may trigger renewed grief. For example, birthdays, learning to walk and talk, festivals such as Christmas and milestones such as weaning, starting nursery and starting school may all be events that remind parents of the baby or babies who have died who would have been experiencing these milestones at the same time. At these times, some parents may keep their feelings, memories and thoughts about their dead baby or babies to themselves, particularly if they feel that these feelings will not be understood. Parents should be told that many parents experience grief at these times and they should be supported to discuss their feelings. They should have access to support and counselling at any time following their baby's death.

At some point in the future, parents who lose one or more babies and also have one or more who survive will also have to decide whether, when, how and what to tell their surviving child or children about the circumstances of their birth.

> *Everyone was in so much shock as we had expected all three babies to be fine … Feeling excited for two babies and sad for one baby was very hard and confusing. Our little man will always be loved and never be forgotten. Eliot and Jake are thriving now, and as they grow older we will ensure that they know they were triplets and that their brother Ben will always be with them.* Mother

Some multiples may also develop a relationship in the womb that would normally continue after birth. Any surviving children may have a sense that something is missing even if they are not aware of the baby or babies who died (Bryan 2002; Leonard 2002). It is generally recommended that surviving children are told early about their dead siblings. It may also be easier for parents to discuss the dead baby or babies with surviving children if they have been named or if they have copies of ultrasound scans, photographs or other keepsakes of the dead baby or babies to share with any surviving children (MBF 2000) (see also *Creating memories* in Chapter 14).

It may also be important for some parents to know whether their same sex babies were identical (monozygotic). In some cases, this may already be known. If not, a member of staff should sensitively discuss zygosity testing with the parents as they may not think of it at the time. If the parents do not know whether or not the babies were identical, they may have unanswered questions and/or experience regret later. Knowing about the zygosity may be an important part of creating memories of the dead twin and distinguishing between the two babies. As the surviving baby grows up, they may also want to know whether they had an identical twin. For most surviving twins this is very important to their sense of self and how they think of their twin who died (MBF 2006, personal communication). Knowing the zygosity may also be essential for later genetic counselling and parents of dizygotic twins may want to know that they have an increased chance of having twins again in a future pregnancy. Parents can contact the

Multiple Births Foundation (MBF) if they want more information about zygosity testing (see Appendix 2).

All parents should be told where they can access support at any time, including in the future. They should be given the contact details for relevant support organisations such as TAMBA, the Multiple Births Foundation, Sands, ARC and Bliss (see Appendix 2). It may also be important to acknowledge that parents of multiple babies who have died may find support from specialist support organisation such as TAMBA and the Multiple Births Foundation most helpful. TAMBA has a bereavement support group specifically for parents of multiples. Parents who have one or more surviving babies may also benefit from being told about the potential benefits of accessing support as soon as they are ready as these parents may be more likely to delay accessing support.

Support for same-sex couples

Cacciatore and Ratho (2011) found that lesbian mothers often felt more marginalised after their baby died because of their sexuality. It is important that staff are aware of the many possible family types and structures and that sensitive support is offered to meet the needs of all bereaved parents.

It is also important that forms and documents are sensitive to the needs of different parents and family types. It may be distressing for some parents when the only available categories on official forms and documents are "mother" and "father".

 There was no place to put [my partner's] information on the death certificate ... and, well, that's just not right. Mother (Cacciatore and Ratho 2011: 174)

Staff should also be aware that some parents in same-sex couples may not feel comfortable in some support groups or settings and be aware of local or national support organisations that offer support for gay and lesbian parents (Cacciatore and Ratho 2011).

 There is always that risk of are you going to get that sideways look because you are a gay couple walking into what is all straight people. Mother (Cacciatore and Ratho 2011: 172)

 Well you know, the thing that was different about that is they were all like these couples that were there. And I felt sort of out of place there, because there I was by myself, and I couldn't share with them that part of my life ... about being a lesbian because the last thing I needed was to be ostracised because of that. Mother (Cacciatore and Ratho 2011: 172–3)

Trusts, Health Boards and managers should ensure that all staff have training in supporting parents in same-sex relationship and ensure that sensitive documentation is available to support the needs of all parents (Cacciatore and Ratho 2011).

Support for parents who have used assisted reproductive technology

Some parents use assisted reproductive technology if they have experienced difficulties conceiving as a result of fertility problems. They may also use this technology to conceive a baby if they are in same-sex partnerships or are single parents.

It is important to recognise that bereaved parents may also include parents who have used assisted reproductive technologies such as in vitro fertilisation (IVF), artificial insemination and surrogacy to conceive a baby. Parents who use IVF to conceive a baby may also have a higher risk of experiencing a loss (Wisborg *et al.* 2010).

It is important that staff are aware that parents who have used assisted reproductive technology may not be able or not want to conceive another baby for a number of reasons including the emotional stress of using assisted reproductive technologies or financial constraints. Staff should be aware of the additional distress that this may cause.

> *I can't just get pregnant like everyone else.* Mother
> (Cacciatore and Ratho 2011: 174)

Trusts, Health Boards and managers should ensure that all staff have training and awareness of all family types and are aware of the potential needs and experiences of bereaved parents who have used assisted reproductive technology to conceive their baby (Cacciatore and Ratho 2011).

Organisations such as the Human Fertilisation and Embryology Authority (HFEA) may be able to offer parents helpful information about their available options (see Appendix 2).

Support and training for staff

While staff should strive to offer high-quality supportive care to bereaved parents, providing this care can be challenging and emotionally draining (see *The importance of support and training for staff* in Chapter 24). Trusts, Health Boards and managers should recognise the importance of ensuring that staff have adequate support and training to support bereaved parents (see Chapter 24).

CHAPTER 4

Communication

Other relevant chapters	
1: Providing holistic care	5: Communication across language and other barriers
2: Providing inclusive care	22: Receiving and responding to feedback: parent experiences
3: Loss and grief	24: Staff support and training

After their baby dies, parents need care from staff who have good communication skills and who are able to support parents to make informed choices that are right for them as individuals (Redshaw *et al.* 2014; Siassakos *et al.* 2015, unpublished results). It is also important to recognise that other elements of communication, such as staff behaviour and the timing and way in which information is provided, are important factors that affect parents' experiences of care (Redshaw *et al.* 2014). It is therefore crucial that all staff who work with bereaved parents receive training in the relevant communication skills (Redshaw *et al.* 2014; Siassakos *et al.* 2015, unpublished results) (see *Staff training* in Chapter 24).

 Everyone we came in contact with that night, the nurse, the registrar, the consultants, they were so fantastic. They took time to talk to me. And they really showed how upset they were as well. Mother

Communication is probably the single most important component of effective care and excellent clinical care can be overshadowed by poor communication. Failures of communication are a significant cause of dissatisfaction and poor communication is one of the top three reasons for complaints made to the NHS - three out of ten complaints relate to the quality or accuracy of information provided (Parliamentary and Health Service Ombudsmen 2014). Another two out of ten complaints are about staff attitudes, which include staff behaviours and communication styles (Parliamentary and Health Service Ombudsmen 2014). Downe *et al.* highlight that:

From the moment of diagnosis through to postnatal care, parents were extremely sensitive to the messages that professionals sent out through both verbal and non-verbal communication, and through caring, indifferent, or, at the extreme, hostile behaviours. When these messages were poorly communicated or inconsistent or led parents to question clinical judgement or skill, their sense of loss was augmented. (2013: 6)

Quotes from parents further emphasise how parents experience poor communication from staff:

 The midwives were all amazing. They dealt with our grief and confusion in a very comforting way. The doctor who told us that our son's heart had stopped was the only person who was very short and abrupt ... his initial words still ring in my ears. Parent (Redshaw *et al.* 2014: 15)

 I felt the midwives were caring and respectful towards my husband and I, however, we were aware they were discussing things without involving us. It was clear there was something going wrong which they didn't want to mention, and we were in no state to discuss circumstances having contractions every 2 to 3 minutes. Parent (Redshaw *et al.* 2014: 19)

Conversely, good communication helps parents trust in staff and feel cared for during their experience of loss (Coulter *et al.* 1999; Downe *et al.* 2013; Redshaw *et al.* 2014). There may also be positive effects on the emotional well-being of parents when they have confidence in staff and feel that they are being guided and supported through the decision-making process after their baby dies (McCourt and Pearce 2000; Downe *et al.* 2013; Redshaw *et al.* 2014).

 The midwives read our birth plan and ensured all we had hoped for could happen; details such as [my husband] announcing she was a girl. We felt as much in charge as possible, whilst being reassured that they were monitoring everything well. We had a calm and peaceful labour as we had hoped for, only possible with the midwives' support. Parent (Redshaw *et al.* 2014: 29)

 Amazing, I knew my baby wouldn't survive. The staff informed me of [the] decisions we would have to make beforehand so we weren't so rushed or shocked when we had to make them. Parent (Redshaw *et al.* 2014: 31)

The care from the professionals on the neonatal unit was wonderful. They made sure we understood everything - they would always check we were ok even though they were extremely busy. We were included in most consultations about our baby. They were all considerate, kind, caring and professional whilst working very hard. Parent (Redshaw *et al*. 2014: 32)

Good communication with parents

Good communication involves good verbal and non-verbal communication and the communication needs of different parents will be highly individual.

The main aims of communication when supporting bereaved parents are to:

- Sensitively inform parents about what is happening or what is expected to happen (see *Breaking bad news* below).

- Discuss the current situation with the parents and ensure that they are fully informed about what is happening and all of their options for their care and the care of their baby (see *Giving information and facilitating informed choice* below).

- Ensure that parents have time to absorb information and ask questions.

- Listen to the views and wishes of parents and support them to make decisions that are right for them.

- Offer support and listen to parents as they talk about their feelings, concerns and wishes (see *Listening and support* below).

Good communication with bereaved parents also includes:

- Ensuring that an appropriate place to talk with parents is available (GMC 2008). Discussions should, whenever possible, take place in a private room that contains tissues and no images of babies or children (see more information about place of care in Chapters 6 to 14). Discussions should not take place in public spaces or when women are partially clothed or when lying on an examination couch.

- Allocating sufficient time for discussions and being able to extend discussions with parents if needed. It is essential that staff set aside time so that they will be uninterrupted by other staff and mobile phones. Parents should be assured that the discussion can go on for as long as they need or that other times for discussion can be arranged. If parents wish to arrange further discussions because they are tired or because staff are unable to stay with them for a longer period of time, staff should offer to make these arrangements before the end of the discussion.

- Introducing oneself by telling parents one's name and role.

- Including partners or other supporters in discussions (with the woman's or parents' consent).

- Providing parents with clear, comprehensive, honest and succinct information (GMC 2008).

- Providing parents with as much information as they want or need to make an informed decision (GMC 2008). Parents may need time to absorb information and it may be helpful to offer them more than one discussion.

- Ensuring that parents feel able to ask questions or raise topics that they would like to discuss.

- Responding flexibly and sensitively to parents' specific needs.

- Using accessible and appropriate language (GMC 2008) and avoiding euphemisms.

- Being aware of the messages that are conveyed by body language.

- Listening to parents by giving them full attention and responding appropriately.

- Showing genuine empathy and sensitivity when speaking with parents.

- Remaining calm and supportive when parents express strong emotions.

- Offering parents written information or information in other formats that reiterates what has been discussed.

- Ensuring that parents have a named contact and the details of how to contact them should they have any questions, concerns or topics they would like to discuss between formal discussions.

- Reassuring parents that confidentiality will be maintained at all times and that they are aware of how information might be shared with other staff and that they can object to this information sharing (GMC 2009; NMC 2015) (see *Communication between staff and confidentiality* below).

Verbal communication and choosing words

Many parents appreciate when staff verbally communicate with them in a sensitive but clear and honest way (Siassakos *et al.* 2015, unpublished results). It is also important that staff pay attention to details in their language when speaking with parents (Downe *et al.* 2013).

> *Our baby was born at 24 weeks and died a few hours later. We each spent some time with her and eventually, exhausted, drifted into sleep in the early hours. At 3am we were woken by a midwife who said, "Have you finished with your baby? If so I'll put her back in the fridge". I was shocked at what had been said so I quickly had to put it to the back of my mind as I did not want to contemplate our baby "in a fridge", it was too heart-breaking to dwell on. I did wonder if it would have been better to just take care of her and tell me when I woke that I could ask to see her again at any time.* Mother

Staff should follow parents' lead with regard to the terminology they use when referring to the loss and recognise that the meaning of a loss will be different for each parent (see *Parents' experiences and expressions of grief* in Chapter 3). For example, some parents may prefer to refer to their "baby" or use the baby's name while other parents may feel more comfortable using the word "fetus". While many parents may be grateful when staff acknowledge the loss of a wanted baby (regardless of the gestation or type of loss), other parents may prefer to think of it as the end of a pregnancy. Some parents may also find the use of clinical terms distressing. For example, some parents may be distressed if their loss is referred to as "the products of conception", "the embryo" or "the fetus" even if they are clinically correct. It is important that staff use the same language as parents when referring to their loss.

Staff should also avoid referring to miscarriage, incomplete miscarriage and delayed or silent miscarriage as "spontaneous abortion", "incomplete abortion", "missed abortion", "missed miscarriage" and "anembryonic pregnancy". Terms such as "pregnancy failure", "abnormal pregnancy", "blighted ovum" and "incompetent cervix" should also normally be avoided and "miscarriage with infection" should be used instead of "septic abortion".

Language should also be tailored so that it is accessible for individual parents. The use of medical terminology should be avoided and medical terms should be clearly explained when they are used.

Staff also need to think about the possible impact on parents of the words and phrases they use when talking to each other. A sentence that seems inoffensive and practical when speaking to a colleague may be very distressing for bereaved parents to hear.

Non-verbal communication

Non-verbal communication is an important component of communication and can affect how people understand what is being said to them (Lewis 2012). Non-verbal cues such as posture, gestures, facial expression and tone of voice all send powerful messages when communicating with other people. For example, people may discount a speaker's words if his or her body language "says" something different to what they are saying verbally (Guirdham 1990).

Research has also shown that bereaved parents are sensitive to non-verbal communication from staff and often sense that something is wrong or that something has happened before staff tell them (Downe *et al.* 2013; Siassakos *et al.* 2015, unpublished results).

Staff need to be aware of the non-verbal messages they may be sending and also respond to parents' non-verbal cues. For example, it can be important for staff to have confident body posture and relaxed shoulders, make good eye contact (but not constant eye contact), have a relaxed facial expression and be facing parents during discussions (Coogler 2012). When parents are speaking, staff should also ensure that they appear supportive and encouraging by nodding and responding appropriately with facial expressions and sounds (Coogler 2012).

It is also important to recognise that some individuals may interpret non-verbal signals differently and that there may be differences in the meanings of some gestures, facial expressions and eye contact across cultures. As gestures and facial expressions can be misunderstood, especially when people are anxious and distressed, it is important that staff do not make assumptions about what people mean or understand by reading body language alone. Staff should always gently check that parents understand what they have been told and confirm parents' decisions if they have given a non-verbal indication of their wishes (for example, by nodding).

Touch is another form of non-verbal communication. Some parents may welcome a supportive gesture such as a hand being placed on their shoulder. However, other parents and staff may be uncomfortable with this contact. It is important for staff to be aware of their own preferences and assumptions in relation to touch and they should ask parents if it is okay before using touch as a way offering comfort.

It is also important for staff to be aware that touch may be viewed differently by people from different cultures. For example, touch may be seen as friendly and positive in some cultures or it may be seen as intrusive and impolite in other cultures. There may also be some cultural restrictions regarding physical contact. However, it is important to recognise that individual preferences vary within cultures and assumptions should not be made about whether touch is acceptable to parents on a cultural basis.

At the end of each discussion

Before leaving parents, staff should ensure that parents know what decisions they need to make next and they should be offered another appointment or meeting time. They should also be offered referrals for any additional tests or procedures that they have consented to. Referrals should be made as soon as possible, depending on the parents' wishes. If parents are distressed by any delays to further appointments, staff should acknowledge that this can be difficult and stressful. When making a referral, staff should also inform staff in other teams, departments and units of the reason for parents' visit so that staff are expecting them and parents do not need to explain why they are there (Statham *et al*. 2001) (see *Good communication between staff* below).

At the end of each discussion with parents, staff should clearly document what topics have been discussed with parents and what parents have been told during all discussions. This will ensure that parents have a record of this information and that other staff can read these notes to avoid giving parents conflicting information (see *Good communication between staff* below). Parents should also be given written information containing contact details for a named contact who they can speak with between formal discussions. They should also be given written information or information in another format containing the information they have discussed with staff and about their available options (see *Written information and information provided in other formats* below).

Listening and support

Listening is a crucial part of communication and offering support to bereaved parents. The *Listening to parents* report highlights:

*The need for a responsive care system and pathway which ensures that health professionals listen to parents at every stage: during pregnancy and if parents have concerns about their baby, during periods of difficult decision-making once the death has been confirmed, and in the postnatal period, both immediately afterwards and in the longer term. (*Redshaw et al. 2014: 49)

In addition to listening to parents' concerns, needs and wishes regarding their and their baby's care, many parents also appreciate opportunities to speak with staff about their feelings and experiences (see also *Support and listening* in Chapter 15). When a staff member is able to listen supportively to parents as they discuss their feelings and experiences, this can be beneficial for parents' well-being in both the short and long term (Leoni 1997; Moulder 1998; Swanson 1999; Kenworthy and Kirkham 2011; Crawley et al. 2013).

> 66 *I felt I wasn't listened to about my headaches and other problems, and could never get hold of my midwife even when I was told she would contact me.* Parent (Redshaw et al. 2014: 13)

> 66 *I saw at least four different midwives during the later stages of my pregnancy and at several different venues. It was impossible to build relationships or feel confident enough to "chat" through "silly concerns".* Parent (Redshaw et al. 2014: 13)

> 66 *You need somebody to just sit with you and talk you through all these different feelings that you've got. One midwife was very good: she'd come in and sit with us and talk for a little while and then she'd go off again.* Mother

In addition to their physical and emotional needs, parents may have urgent practical concerns that they want to discuss. For example, parents may want to talk about any challenges they may be facing around arranging care for other children, taking time off work for appointments and/or arranging or paying for travel related to their care. Staff should listen to these concerns and offer to arrange appointments at times and in locations that minimise inconvenience wherever possible and be aware of any financial support that may be available to parents (Statham *et al*. 2001) (see *Discussing entitlement to time off work and benefits* in Chapter 15).

Staff should ensure that they actively and supportively listen to parents by:

- Being attentive and using encouraging body language (see *Non-verbal communication* above).

- Not interrupting parents.

- Not moving on to discuss new topics until parents are ready.

- Taking parents' concerns seriously.

- Asking clarifying questions if necessary while being careful not to sound like they are challenging parents.

- If appropriate, reflecting back to parents a summary of what has been said to ensure that staff are clear about parents' decisions and that parents fully understand the provided information.

Breaking bad news

Breaking bad news can be extremely difficult and stressful for staff and it is important that all staff have training so that they have the skills to sensitively inform parents when something is wrong (Siassakos *et al.* 2015, unpublished results). Breaking bad news in a sensitive way cannot reduce the pain that parents feel but it can affect how they experience care from staff (Statham *et al.* 2001). However, it can add to parents' immediate and long-term distress when they are not given this news sensitively (Redshaw *et al.* 2014; Siassakos *et al.* 2015, unpublished results).

 First the student midwife checked the heartbeat, then midwife, then the resident doctor and he said to me, "There is no movement". I was shocked. At that time I was on my own, my husband was on [his] way [to] hospital, and they just told to me. I think they should have waited for my husband to come and then informed me. Parent (Redshaw *et al.* 2014: 15)

 Doctor said there doesn't seem to be a heartbeat and asked if I know what that means?! Why did she have to make me go through the hardship of telling her that my baby is dead, is this an exam/test? I think she should have gently explained it herself. Parent (Redshaw *et al.* 2014: 15)

Parents should be told as soon it is suspected that something is wrong, even if it is not yet confirmed or certain. Parents often sense from the reactions of staff that something might be wrong and this may cause them additional distress and anxiety and reduce their trust in staff if they are not told what is happening (Downe *et al.* 2013; Siassakos *et al.* 2015, unpublished results).

Sands' Bereavement Care Training highlights the following best practice points that staff should follow when breaking bad news to parents:

- Before breaking bad news to parents, staff should prepare what they are going to say and ensure that they have accurate information. Many parents appreciate an indication that the member of staff understands the impact of what they are saying. Phrases such as "I am afraid it is bad news…"; "I am sorry to say that the results are not what we expected…" or "I am afraid this is not the news you wanted…" may be helpful.

- Find the most appropriate private place available to break the news (see more information about place of care in Chapters 6 to 14).

- If a woman is on her own, check whether she would like to contact a partner or another supporter who might be able to join her.

- Check whether an interpreter or other support for communication is needed.

- Use warm, open body language by sitting near parents, facing them, making eye contact and using touch if appropriate (see *Non-verbal communication* above).

- Use clear, straightforward communication and do not use euphemisms. For example, when a baby's death is confirmed during a scan, use words such as "your baby has died" and not euphemisms such as "I'm afraid your baby has gone". It is important that the message is clear and that parents are not left with false hope (Siassakos *et al.* 2015, unpublished results).

- Be honest with parents while continuing to be as sensitive as possible.

- Express genuine concern and empathy by using phrases such as "I'm very sorry" or "What a terrible shock for you – I'm so sorry". Staff should avoid being "cold and calculating" when giving information as this can add to parents' distress (Siassakos *et al.* 2015, unpublished results).

- Ensure that parents have sufficient time to absorb what they have been told, check their understanding of the information they have been given and ensure they have time to express their concerns and ask any questions.

- Be honest when a baby's diagnosis or prognosis is uncertain and acknowledge that this is likely to be very difficult for parents.

If the member of staff who is with parents at the time cannot give them accurate or sufficient information, they should be honest about this and offer to arrange for parents to speak with someone more knowledgeable as soon as possible. Parents should not be given information that they may later discover is incorrect (Statham *et al.* 2001).

Parents will likely be shocked and distressed after receiving bad news and they may find it hard to absorb and remember what they are being told. Parents may only hear the first one or two things that are said and then be unable to focus on additional information. Staff may need to repeat themselves and should check that parents have understood what they are being told. It may sometimes be helpful for staff to phrase information in different ways. While staff should provide parents with as much information as they want, they should also ask parents how they are feeling and offer to arrange further discussions to discuss additional details. Repeated discussions may be necessary, particularly if there is a lot of information to convey.

 I remember the silence. I asked "the baby?" and the Registrar said "I'm so sorry, she died". That was all I could take in and I was very grateful that the details were given later. Parent (Redshaw *et al.* 2014: 21)

If there is a lot to discuss, staff should start by dealing with any topics that parents want to discuss and the immediate decisions that parents may need to make (see *Giving information and facilitating informed choice* below). Staff should be prepared to leave discussing less pressing information until later, depending on the parents' wishes. It is important to watch for signs of distress and exhaustion and to ask parents if they would like to take a break and continue the discussion later.

If a woman is going home alone after receiving bad news, staff should suggest that she might like to call somebody to accompany her. This can be very important if she is driving herself home.

Dealing with parents' reactions

For staff, one of the hardest aspects of breaking bad news to parents is not knowing how parents will react. Parents may respond to bad news in many ways. Some parents may, for example, be silent, tearful, angry, disbelieving, distressed, feel guilty or blame themselves or other people (including staff). Staff should be aware of the different responses that parents may have to the news and remain calm and supportive (see *Parents' experiences and expressions of grief* and *Offering emotional support to bereaved parents* in Chapter 3). This may be very distressing for staff and support should also be available for them (see Chapter 24).

Giving information and facilitating informed choice

Full information about all test results, diagnoses and any available procedures or care options should be offered to parents (GMC 2008). This information should be conveyed honestly and sensitively. Any uncertainties that staff have should be acknowledged (RCOG 2015c) and a more knowledgeable member of staff should be asked to provide parents with further information if needed. Time and encouragement should be given for parents to absorb any information provided, discuss their thoughts, concerns and/ or feelings and ask any questions. Staff should take parents' thoughts, wishes and concerns seriously and answer any questions directly and honestly.

However, it is also important to recognise that all parents are different and that the type and amount of information that parents want will vary. Parents may also have different levels of medical knowledge and some parents may need more explanation to help them understand the information they are given. Some parents may also need information to be presented in different ways or using the support of interpreters (see Chapter 5). All communication should be tailored to the needs and wishes of individual parents.

It is also important that all staff discussing information with parents are aware of what parents have already been told. It can be very distressing for parents to receive inconsistent or contradictory information. If parents are receiving care from different staff, it is crucial that there is excellent communication between staff (see *Good communication between staff* below).

Parents experiencing a perinatal loss may have to make a number of difficult decisions that they did not expect or want to make. Whenever there is a decision to be made, the informed consent of women (before the birth) and parents (after the birth) must be sought before any procedures, tests or examinations are performed. Parents need to be given sufficient information to make informed decisions (GMC 2008) but it is also important not to overload them with information. While the woman has the legal right to make any decisions about care before the birth, she may wish to involve her partner if she has one. However, where a woman's partner is involved in decision-making before the birth, staff should ensure that they speak to the woman alone to be certain that she is not being coerced in anyway. After the baby is born, both parents have a responsibility to make decisions about the baby's care.

> *I was given plenty of time to let me think about all the decisions and help in making them. Lots of opportunity to ask questions, but I didn't know what I needed to know as I was in deep shock.* Parent
> (Redshaw *et al.* 2014: 16)

> *To be honest it all seemed a bit of a blur after we were told. It felt as though I was being bombarded with so much information and making decisions all at once within a few minutes.* Parent
> (Redshaw *et al.* 2014: 17)

With regard to the information provided and making informed decisions about care, the Care Quality Commission (CQC) states that:

> *We want everyone who uses care services to shape their care around their own needs. But people can't make informed choices about their care without the right kind of information.* (CQC 2014)

Information must be:

- accurate and complete;
- in a format each person can understand; and
- readily available when a person wants to make decisions.

Different parents will have different approaches to making decisions. Staff should also be aware that some parents may feel unable to ask questions or request additional information about their options if they fear being seen as difficult or as questioning the authority of staff (Ahmed *et al.* 2005). Staff should ensure that all parents are encouraged and supported to ask for more information.

Some parents may not have the mental capacity under the Mental Capacity Act (MCA) to make a decision about care (NHS Choices 2015a). However, under the MCA, these parents should still be involved in the decision-making process and be supported to express their preferences and make decisions (NHS Choices 2015a). They should also be provided with an independent advocate to support them through this process (NHS Choices 2015a).

When parents need to make decisions about care, staff should:

- Ensure that parents are provided with information about the situation and all of their available options while acknowledging any uncertainties (GMC 2008; RCOG 2015c).

- Provide information that is accurate and objective, including the potential benefits and risks related to any options or procedures (GMC 2008; RCOG 2015c). Staff should be aware of their own values, beliefs and choices so that they can be certain that they give parents impartial information. Staff should also be aware that it may be difficult for parents to state their preferences or decline care when the information given is perceived as instructions or recommendations from staff (Lundqvist *et al*. 2002; Siassakos *et al*. 2015, unpublished results).

- Be sensitive and gentle when providing information (GMC 2008).

- Use clear, unambiguous language (GMC 2008). Receiving good quality, clear information can be reassuring for parents (Siassakos *et al*. 2015, unpublished results).

- Check whether parents need additional support to help them make a decision (GMC 2008).

- Whenever possible, offer information about potential decisions before parents need to make them (Siassakos *et al*. 2015, unpublished results). Except in emergencies, parents should not be expected to make decisions in a hurry or, for example, when they are recovering from general anaesthetic.

- Be careful not to overload parents with information. Staff may also need to repeat information and parents may find this helpful (Siassakos *et al*. 2015, unpublished results).

- Support parents to make one decision at a time. If parents have to make several decisions, staff should explain the information related to each decision clearly and support parents to make each decision separately.

- Empathetically acknowledge that the situation may be very difficult for parents.

- Wherever possible, give parents as much time as possible to think about their decisions (GMC 2008). If a decision is time-limited, they should know when a decision needs to be made and who they need to contact and how to contact them (GMC 2008).

- Support parents to make decisions that are right for them (GMC 2008) based on their individual needs, preferences, beliefs and values.

Some parents may want decision-making to be shared with staff or they may request guidance or advice. Other parents may prefer to make decisions completely independently once they have the necessary information. For some decisions, such as making decisions to withdraw or continue with life-sustaining treatment for a baby, staff and parents should make decisions jointly (see *Making decisions about critical care* in Chapter 13). Some parents may also want to ask advice from other family members or religious advisers or involve them in decision-making. With parents' consent, staff should involve these people in any discussions.

If parents ask staff for advice and guidance, staff should ensure that they give impartial guidance based on the best available information and evidence. However, parents should still be supported and encouraged to make the best decisions for them as this may help to prevent them from experiencing regret and guilt in the future.

Unless a decision is needed urgently, parents should be given time to absorb the information and consider their decisions without pressure (Statham *et al.* 2001). Some parents may want some alone to talk privately, although they should be told how they can reach staff when they are ready. Other parents may want to go home to think about their decisions and they should be offered another appointment and the contact details for a named contact. Some parents may change their minds several times before they settle on a decision.

Once a woman or parents have made a decision, this should be documented in the woman's or baby's medical notes. Where consent forms are required, they should be available in different formats and all the main languages spoken in the area. Staff should offer to help all parents complete any forms. If necessary, an interpreter should be provided to help parents with the forms if they are not available in their primary language. Parents should be given a copy of any decisions that have been made and any consent forms that they have signed in case they wish to refer to this information at any point in the future.

Written information and information provided in other formats

Verbal explanations and information are essential for providing effective care. However, people's ability to listen and remember what they are told is limited, especially if they are in shock or distressed. Written information and information in other formats can be an extremely useful resource that staff can offer to look at with parents or give to parents to look at in their own time and refer to when they need it. Despite the potential benefits of providing parents with this type of information, it should not be used instead of face-to-face discussions. Staff should also not assume that parents have looked at, used or remembered all of the information from these materials when discussing any information or options with parents.

If parents have difficulty reading or understanding written material, it may be helpful to offer to go through it with them. Information should also be available in other formats for parents with sensory or learning disabilities, such as large print, Braille, DVDs, CDs and visual images. These materials should also be available in the main local languages.

Producing written information and information in other formats

Many Trusts, Health Boards, hospitals and clinics produce their own leaflets and other materials. This information should provide parents with specific information about the type of loss they are experiencing, local services, their options for care and information about the support available (including from local and national support organisations that are not part of the healthcare service). Some hospitals and clinics may also use material produced by support groups or organisations (for example, the Sands support booklets for bereaved parents and families). All material should be checked on a regular basis to ensure that the information is consistent, up-to-date, relevant and easy to read.

Successful leaflets and materials require considerable thought and planning. Materials should be developed in consultation with relevant support organisations and bereaved parents, including parents from different communities who have used specific services. Parents should be asked what information would be or would have been useful for them before a draft is produced, rather than only being given a draft to review.

The content of any materials should be sensitively worded, impartial, factual and evidence-based. Common concerns and misconceptions should be addressed and relevant risks, benefits and uncertainties should be acknowledged and clearly described. Any evidence used should be cited in case parents want more information about these sources. Sources of further information should also be given for parents who want to know more (Coulter *et al.* 1999).

The language used should be clear and sentences should be short. When producing translated leaflets and other materials, the content should be developed with members of the relevant communities and trained translators. Translation software and programmes such as Google Translate should not be used as these translations may be incorrect or insensitive to parents' needs. It may also be important to provide additional information that is of cultural relevance.

The tone should be sensitive and encourage parents to make their own decisions. Materials should also avoid telling parents how they will or should feel. For example, it may be helpful to use phrases such as "Some parents feel X and others feel Y".

The layout should be clear and uncluttered. The title of the resource and each section should accurately reflect the contents. Each topic should begin with a clear heading. Important information should be highlighted or boxed. Question and answer formats are also effective and should include common questions that parents may have.

Illustrations can be used if they will increase understanding but it is important to check with parent representatives that these are acceptable and helpful. People's tastes vary enormously and what might seem comforting and appealing to some parents might be off-putting for others. Pink and blue should be avoided. Careful thought should be given to any design features and logos, other than the standard logo of the Trust, Health Board or hospital. In order to be inclusive, religious symbols should also be avoided.

All materials should be piloted with and evaluated by parents and/or their representatives. This will help to ensure that the content is sensitive and adequate and that the language is clear. It is crucial that this process is completed before the materials become a standard part of care.

All leaflets and other materials should be dated and include the date on which they will be reviewed and updated wherever possible. These materials should include the name and contact details of the issuing Trust, Health Board, hospital or clinic. All materials should be produced to a high standard and look professional.

Good communication between staff

Good communication between staff is important as poor communication can cause parents to be exposed to inadvertently insensitive queries or comments that may add to their distress (Siassakos *et al.* 2015, unpublished results). For example, if staff cannot respond appropriately if they do not know about a parent's situation. Therefore, it is essential that all the staff who parents encounter are well informed about what is happening, particularly as staff generally approach expectant and new parents assuming that all is well.

 The anaesthetist who came to put in my epidural knew my baby had died. But he didn't say anything about it at all. Just joked and chatted as though nothing bad had happened. Mother

Providing supportive care requires that all of the staff involved in caring for parents work together in a co-ordinated way and communicate well with each other. This includes staff taking the time to hand over information to other staff within their team who are providing care to parents at the same time or who will be caring for parents after a shift change.

Keeping records

Ensuring medical records are completed accurately and fully is essential for providing supportive care to parents. The information recorded should include notes detailing discussions with parents and any decisions that have been made. This will help to ensure that parents do not receive conflicting information. It will also help to ensure that parents are not asked about their decisions again once a decision is made. If parents are repeatedly asked about a decision they have already made, they may feel that staff are questioning their decision and may lose confidence. All staff should check a woman's or baby's medical notes regularly to ensure that they know what parents have been told and what decisions have been made.

Communication between staff and confidentiality

Although most people accept that information about them will be shared between different healthcare staff, parents should be informed of how their information might be shared between staff (GMC 2009; NMC 2015). Seeking parents' consent before sharing information with other staff will help to ensure that they are able to exercise their legal right to object to this information being shared (GMC 2009; NMC 2015). Even if information does not appear to be sensitive, it may be very sensitive to an individual parent in their particular circumstances (DoH 2003). Staff have a responsibility to ensure the confidentiality of all parents, including young parents under the age of 16 (BMA 2014). If parents object to their information being shared by staff, this must be respected unless there is a legal reason why this information must be disclosed in the interest of the public or a child (GMC 2009).

A formal discussion or written consent to pass on information is not usually necessary. For example, it is enough for a member of staff to tell parents that they will phone ahead to the relevant department or healthcare team so that they are expected. They should also mention that it is customary to inform the woman's GP, community midwives and health visitors so that they can offer appropriate care and support. This gives each woman an opportunity to say if she does not want this to happen.

Communication between units and healthcare teams

Bereaved parents may find it difficult and painful to have to explain their situation to a series of members of staff or at a reception desk in front of a queue of expectant parents. If parents are referred to another department, the staff there (including receptionists and cleaning staff) should be informed so that they are expecting them and can greet them when they arrive.

When a woman or baby is transferred from one unit or healthcare team to another, it is also essential that all medical records, any specific decisions or requests that parents have made and details of any investigations, test results and treatment are passed on immediately.

This also includes providing primary care staff with information about women in their care before and after a woman leaves the hospital. It is important that primary care staff know about what has happened (unless a woman objects) as they are able to offer ongoing follow-up care and support (see Chapter 17). It also helps to avoid women receiving invitations to antenatal or postnatal clinics or appointments and helps to ensure that midwifery staff or health visiting staff who are scheduled to contact parents or visit parents at home are aware of what has happened. There should also be a system for informing antenatal education staff so that they do not send parents an invitation to classes. This will help to avoid causing additional distress to parents.

Good communication between staff will also help to ensure that all staff have access to sufficient information to offer effective support and care to bereaved parents. For example, some primary care and midwifery staff may not have an in-depth understanding of the healthcare needs of some parents or babies. This may particularly be the case if a fetal anomaly has been diagnosed. Community staff should know whom they can contact at the hospital in order to obtain information (with a woman's consent).

All units and healthcare services should have policies and procedures in place to ensure that the transfer of information is prompt and efficient. A designated member of staff should be responsible for ensuring that this happens in each case by following up with staff who are receiving the referral. A checklist of people to inform should be available for staff and a completed copy should be attached to medical notes. The list should include the mother's GP, community midwife and health visitor. When a referral is being made or parents are being discharged from hospital, all relevant staff should be informed:

- By telephone (immediately).

- In writing (as soon as possible). Written information should include a full history of a woman or baby's care. Post mortem examination/test results (if applicable) should be sent later.

Information should not be faxed or emailed unless confidentiality can be guaranteed. Parents should also be told which unit or healthcare team to contact if problems arise and should be given written information containing the contact details of a named contact.

Trusts, Health Boards and managers should ensure policies are in place that have been agreed to by primary and secondary care staff to ensure that efficient processes are in place to keep all staff informed about a pregnancy loss, a diagnosis of a fetal anomaly or the death of a baby and any treatment or care that has been received or decided upon.

CHAPTER 5

Communication across language and other barriers

Other relevant chapters

1: Providing holistic care

2: Providing inclusive care

3: Loss and grief

4: Communication

No agency can provide a fair or effective service to people with whom it cannot communicate. (Shackman 1984: 4)

Some of the communication challenges faced by parents whose primary language is not English and parents who have a sensory impairment when accessing healthcare services may be very similar. The inclusion of these topics in the same chapter is not intended to imply that parents experiencing language barriers are disabled or that there are not considerations that are specific to communicating across different types of communication barriers. Rather, the aim of this chapter is to help staff understand some of the ways in which they can work to facilitate communication with parents when there are barriers to communication present.

The Equality Act 2010 underlines the legal requirement that parents are not discriminated against because of their ethnicity or disability. This legislation helps to ensure that "reasonable adjustments" are made to healthcare services to ensure that:

- the physical building where services are provided can be accessed by users with specific needs resulting from a disability;

- policies and practices are updated and changed to meet the needs of service users; and

- specific equipment, auxiliary aids and services are in place to meet the communication needs of service users (for example, providing information in accessible formats, special equipment such as induction loops or support staff such as interpreters) (Government Equalities Office 2010).

Trusts, Health Boards, managers and service commissioners should ensure that adjustments are made to all services to ensure that the needs of bereaved parents with disabilities such as sensory impairments or bereaved parents who need language support can access and receive good quality care that is tailored to their individual needs (Government Equalities Office 2010).

The challenges of supporting parents when communication barriers are present

Communication barriers can be significant obstacles to parents receiving good-quality healthcare (Davies and Bath 2001; Roberts *et al.* 2005; Sheldon 2005; Pitkin Derose *et al.* 2007; Lindholm *et al.* 2012). Some parents may experience communication barriers as a result of language barriers or because of a sensory impairments (for example, if parents are deaf or have a hearing impairment).

Parents who have difficulty communicating with healthcare staff may be provided with less information, be offered fewer choices and/or feel disempowered or vulnerable (feelings that parents may already be experiencing during a childbearing loss). Without interpreters, these parents may not understand what is happening or what care is being offered (Pitkin Derose *et al.* 2007). Parents may also not be able to ask questions, raise concerns or make informed decisions. This may cause parents to be less satisfied with their care and it may also affect their safety, particularly in instances where parents are unable to explain their symptoms or they are sent home with information that they do not understand about medications, instructions or potential complications (Pitkin Derose *et al.* 2007; Lindholm *et al.* 2012; NHS England 2015b). When staff work with interpreters who are inadequately trained or by using family members or friends to interpret, the potential errors introduced may create a greater risk to parents and staff than having no interpreter at all (NHS England 2015b).

Staff may also become frustrated or feel stressed if they cannot understand what a parent is trying to tell them and are not sure that the information that they have provided has been understood. It is important that staff are aware of these frustrations and try to avoid expressing them as some parents may perceive staff frustration as discrimination. Staff may also feel that they cannot give the good-quality care that they want to give and may instead focus primarily on essential practical tasks without explanation or discussion (Bulman and McCourt 2002). This may be exacerbated if there are time pressures on staff as trying to communicate across a language barrier or another communication barrier can take more time and effort.

Staff should also never assume that they can anticipate the needs of any individual with a sensory impairment or who is experiencing a language barrier. Staff should ask all parents if they need additional support and about their preferences. Staff should also record this information in a prominent place in parents' medical notes (with their consent). This may help to reduce the frequency with which parents have to explain their needs to different members of staff. This can be important as the need to provide repeated explanations may affect how parents experience care at what is likely to be a very distressing time.

Providing interpreters for parents

Staff should have easy access to trained and experienced interpreters when supporting parents whose primary language is not English or those who have a sensory impairment that may affect communication. An interpreter can translate for parents and staff to facilitate discussions and help to ensure that bad news is broken to parents sensitively, that parents receive full information about what is happening and that parents are able to make informed choices about their and their baby's care.

Offering interpretation services and providing interpreters for parents who speak little or no English or who have difficulty with communication as a result of a sensory impairment is an essential part of providing parents with safe and effective care (Pitkin Derose et al. 2007; Lindholm et al. 2012; NHS England 2015b). Even when one parent's primary language is English or they speak English fluently, they should still be offered an interpreter so that one parent is not expected to translate for the other (particularly if they are shocked and distressed). Shock, distress and trying to understand what is happening in a new context such as the UK healthcare system may also drastically affect a parent's ability to understand what they are being told and their capacity to express themselves (see Chapters 3 and 4). Providing an interpreter may help to ensure that both parents understand the information provided and are able to ask questions and express their concerns. However, it is also important to be aware that some parents may prefer not to use an interpreter.

Despite the importance of having trained professional interpreters to interpret between parents and staff, the provisions for good quality interpreting services within the healthcare service are still inadequate (NHS Commissioning 2015). This may particularly be the case in areas with smaller minority communities and for languages that are less common.

Although it may not always be possible to have interpreters for all of the languages spoken by parents, Trusts, Health Boards and managers should provide the best and most comprehensive service possible to reduce communication barriers for parents so that they receive the same quality of care as other parents (NHS England 2015b). Therefore, all Trusts, Health Boards, managers, service commissioners and staff should ensure that:

- A local policy regarding best practice when using interpretation services has been agreed with input from local service users and that this has been made available to all staff.

- Trained, registered interpreters are employed to interpret for people with sensory impairments and to provide language interpretation for the main languages spoken in their area (NHS England 2015b). When face-to-face interpretation is not possible within the healthcare service, access to interpreters should be arranged through outside agencies or using telephone interpreting services and/or visual (or video) relay interpreting (NHS England 2015b).

- All interpreters have training in bereavement care.

- All interpreters maintain the confidentiality of all parents (NHS England 2015b).

- Equal weight is given to considerations of cost and quality when commissioning interpreting services (NHS England 2015b).

- Interpreters should be available for the use of all staff, including primary care staff who work in clinics and visit families at home (NHS England 2015b).

- Appropriate interpreting services should be available when booking appointments so that parents can book appointments appropriately to meet their needs (NHS England 2015b).

- Extra time is allocated for appointments where interpreting services are required (NHS England 2015b).

- Parents should not experience delays in accessing appointments because of the need to provide interpreting services (NHS England 2015b).

- Parents are able to express preferences for a female or male interpreter and that these preferences are accommodated wherever possible, particularly if they are to be present during an examination, labour or birth.

- Policies and practices are in place to ensure that parents are asked about their communication needs, and that these needs (including their language preferences) are highlighted in parents' medical notes and that this information is passed to staff when parents are referred to other healthcare teams or units (NHS England 2015b).

- All staff should be trained in working with interpreters and be aware of the types of interpreting services that are available (NHS England 2015b) (see *Working well with an interpreter* below).

- All staff should know how to contact interpreters when parents need extra support with communication and be aware of their responsibility to ensure that this service is booked (NHS England 2015b). They should know how to book an interpreter in advance for a planned appointment and how to contact one in an emergency. They should be encouraged to use interpreters whenever necessary.

- Whenever possible, and with parents' consent, the same interpreter is contacted to provide interpretation for parents so that they have continuity of carer (NHS England 2015b) (see also *After any discussion* below).

- When an interpreter has been booked, clinic staff and receptionists should try to ensure that parents are seen as soon as possible when staff are running late to ensure that the interpreter is available (NHS England 2015b).

- Many hospitals have a list of bilingual staff members who can be called upon to translate when there is no interpreter. However, these staff should only be used to explain delays or appointment issues, greet parents or to facilitate information exchange in emergency situations (Health Scotland 2008). It is important that it is recognised that interpreting is a specialist skill and that it is unethical to have staff interpreting in clinical situations, regardless of their fluency in a language, unless they are trained and it is part of their job role (Health Scotland 2008; NHS

England 2015b). It is also important to check that bilingual staff are willing to act as interpreters (Health Scotland 2008) and that their role will not be adversely affected if they are frequently asked to take time out to interpret.

- Staff document information about any interpretation services, informal interpretation services used or any other barriers to communication in parents' medical notes (Health Scotland 2008).

- Patients should never be expected to pay for interpreting services (NHS England 2015b).

- There is an annual audit of local interpreting services.

- Support and training should be available for interpreters who work with bereaved parents and this need should be recognised by their managers (Sheldon 2005). This should be the same as the support and training that should be available for other staff who work closely with parents who experience a childbearing loss (see Chapter 24). This may be particularly important as many interpreters work in isolation, on a sessional basis, work under a great deal of pressure with little or no time between consultations and/or without breaks.

 During the delivery you see dead babies delivered and then ten minutes later you are bleeped and you have to go to another call. There is no support at all and you have to keep your emotions inside of you until the end of the day. Interpreter (Sheldon 2005)

The role of interpreters

NHS England state that:

> *The interpreter is present only to facilitate communication during the appointment. They should not be asked to undertake additional/ancillary duties during the appointment time (e.g. those which may be delivered by a carer or advocate).* (2015b: 7)

Part of facilitating communication with bereaved parents, however, involves communicating with parents in a sensitive and honest way to ensure that parents have the best possible experience of care under difficult circumstances (Siassakos *et al.* 2015, unpublished results). That is, communicating with bereaved parents is not only an activity involving the facilitation of communication but it also involves knowing how to break bad news to parents as sensitively as possible, express condolences and be empathetic, using sensitive language and non-verbal communication (see *Good communication with parents* in Chapter 4). Interpreters must be aware of these issues as the behaviour of healthcare staff and the way in which information is provided can affect the parents' experiences of care (Redshaw *et al.* 2014). Therefore, in addition to having the appropriate language and/or signing skills, it is important that interpreters are:

- able to introduce themselves, explain their role to parents and provide interpretation for all individuals involved in care including parents, any other supporters or advocates and healthcare staff (NHS England 2015b);

- able to respond empathetically to parents' distress or emotional responses;

- aware that parents may need time to absorb information;

- aware that different parents may need information to be presented in different ways so that they are able to fully understand what they are being told;

- able to avoid using any medical terminology;

- able to understand grief and grieving and the different emotional responses that parents may have (see Chapter 3);

- able to work with other staff as part of a team while interpreting to give the best possible care to parents; and

- able to encourage parents to ask questions or raise concerns.

More comprehensive information about the communication skills that interpreters and other staff need to sensitively communicate with bereaved parents are available in Chapter 4.

Working well with an interpreter

Working well with an interpreter involves ensuring that:

- Staff retain overall responsibility for the discussion.

- Parents are able to make fully informed decisions and express their preferences and concerns (see *Giving information and facilitating informed choice* in Chapter 4).

- The interpreter understands all of the information that has been provided and the purpose of each discussion. Staff should check that the interpreter understands this information before speaking with parents.

In addition, it is important that staff continue to follow the basic principles of good communication set out in Chapter 4.

Before any discussion

Before working with an interpreter (especially for the first time), staff should:

- Check that parents have given consent for an interpreter to be involved (Health Scotland 2008).

- Ensure that the identification documentation of the interpreter has been checked (Health Scotland 2008).

- Explain the purpose of the discussion or appointment.

- Ensure that the interpreter is well-briefed about the circumstances and is emotionally prepared (Health Scotland 2008).

- Acknowledge the importance of the interpreter's role in the discussion and encourage them to explain any cultural concerns that arise and/or intervene if people talk too fast. However, it is important to note that interpreters should not be expected to be cultural experts, provide support or counsel parents (Health Scotland 2008).

- Ensure that sufficient time has been allocated for interpretation as these discussions may take more than twice as long as other discussions.

- Check whether there are any constraints on the interpreter's time and the timing of their next appointment.

- Check with them how to pronounce and use the parents' names correctly.

- Discuss how the interpreter and the other staff present should respond if the parents become upset.

At the beginning of a discussion

At the start of any discussion (especially during an initial discussion with parents), it may be necessary for staff to:

- Ensure that everyone is seated so they can see each other in face-to-face discussions (Health Scotland 2008).

- Ensure that the interpreter has been introduced.

- Check that the interpreter fully understands and speaks the parents' language and (if appropriate) dialect.

- Explain to the parents the roles of the member of staff and the interpreter. That is, they should make it clear that the interpreter should translate everything that is said and that they will not give advice other than that given by the member of staff (Permalloo 2006).

- Explain the code of confidentiality to the parents and ensure that parents feel comfortable. Some parents may have concerns about speaking about sensitive topics in front of the interpreter, particularly if they are making decisions that may not be generally acceptable within their cultural or religious communities. For example, termination for fetal anomaly or post mortem examinations may be particularly sensitive topics for some parents.

During the discussion

Staff continue to be responsible for parents' care and well-being during all discussions. Therefore, it is important for staff to ensure that:

- They behave as normally as possible and try not to become physically or emotionally distanced from the parents because the discussion is through an interpreter. For example, staff should greet the parents, face them during the discussion and speak directly to them rather than to the interpreter.

- They use all their usual communication skills such as listening, observing, responding, explaining and checking. They should also avoid using medical terminology and speak in a way that is easier for the interpreter to translate by pausing so that information is given in translatable chunks. See Chapter 4 for full details about good communication.

- Information is not being explained to parents when staff are not present (Health Scotland 2008).

- They are aware that parents may understand some or most of what is being said. In some cases, parents may want to speak in English but ask the interpreter to listen and help if there are any misunderstandings.

- Avoid using closed questions where a "yes" or "no" answer is required and use open questions instead to check parents' understanding (Health Scotland 2008).

- Parents are given time to absorb information, ask questions, discuss their concerns and feelings and think about and make decisions about any available options.

After any discussion

Parents, staff and interpreters should be aware of how to provide feedback about interpretation and parents should be able to access feedback systems directly in their own language or in a format that is accessible to them (NHS England 2015b) (see also Chapter 22).

Staff should also document the details of the interpreter used in parents' medical notes and make time to have a debriefing discussion with the interpreter wherever possible (Health Scotland 2008). It may also be helpful to write down the key points of what was discussed in clear and simple language and give a copy to parents. Staff should offer to have this information translated by a translator for parents wherever possible.

Support for interpreters

Providing interpretation services for bereaved parents is likely to be very distressing for interpreters. Interpreters may also be expected to go directly from working with bereaved parents to provide interpretation services in another healthcare setting. Therefore, it is important that interpreters have support systems in place. If formal support is not available, it is important that these staff are able to access informal support such as peer support groups (see Chapter 24 for more information about support for staff).

Telephone interpreting services or interpretation using a video conference

Telephone or video conferencing interpreting services can be useful for emergency and out-of-hours interpreting, consultations in languages for which there is no professional interpreter available locally, when an appointment would have taken place over the phone anyway, when the information to be discussed is simple and straightforward and consultations for which it has not been possible to book a professional interpreter in advance (Pointon 1996; Health Scotland 2008). This may also be important if privacy and confidentiality are important to parents and local interpreters are part of their community (Health Scotland 2008). However, telephone interpreting services may be less suitable for what are often sensitive and complex discussions with bereaved parents who are likely to be shocked and distressed. In these situations, a face-to-face interpreter is essential.

To help ensure that telephone and video conferencing interpretation services meet parents' needs, staff should:

- Be aware of how to use the equipment and some of the issues such as background noise that may be present if using speaker phones (Health Scotland 2008).

- Introduce themselves and parents to the interpreter.

- Explain the situation, their role and the purpose of the call to parents and the interpreter.

- Allow the interpreter time to say who they are and explain their role.

- Avoid or explain technical terms and abbreviations.

- Speak clearly and break up questions or information into short points.

- Check or rephrase information where necessary for parents' or the interpreter's understanding.

- Pause frequently and long enough for the interpreter to translate.

Communicating if there is no interpreter

All staff should have training in how to communicate better across a language barrier when there is no interpreter present. In some instances, parents may decline the offer of an interpreter, prefer to use family or friends for interpretation or an interpreter may not be available immediately in the case of an emergency. Staff should also allow more time for these discussions and avoid making parents feel that time is pressured.

Using family and friends to interpret is strongly discouraged as errors in interpretation may negatively affect the care provided to parents and babies and this can carry more risks to parents, babies and staff than if no interpreter is used (NHS England 2015b). However, some parents may prefer to have family or friends interpret for them. If family members or friends are to act as informal interpreters, staff should seek consent from the pregnant woman before the baby is born or both parents after a baby is born (NHS England 2015b). This consent should be sought in the parents' own language and independently of the informal interpreters (NHS England 2015b). In these instances, this should be documented in parents' medical notes (Health Scotland 2008).

Staff should also be aware that parents may not want the informal interpreter to know everything about them and may not feel able to discuss things fully or truthfully. For example, they might fear that the family member or friend who is acting as an interpreter will disapprove or tell other people. Staff should also try to determine the nature of the relationship between the informal interpreter and parents and whether there are things that the person interpreting feels unable to interpret because they are too embarrassed to discuss some things, they find the information distressing or they object to the information being provided. An informal interpreter who is a family member or friend may themselves be deeply affected by the situation and they may need support. Their ability to interpret may also be affected if they become distressed.

It is never acceptable to use a child or a teenager under the age of 16 years to interpret for parents who are experiencing a perinatal loss unless immediate emergency care is required and no other options are available (NHS England 2015b). The situation may be very distressing for any young person and they may find it difficult to convey intimate details about their mother's or female relative's condition. Some parents may be accustomed to their children interpreting for them. They may also have a cultural expectation that their children will interpret for them and feel proud that their child is taking responsibility in the family. However, staff should inform parents that it is the hospital or clinic's policy to not allow children to interpret in order to avoid possible misunderstandings.

Staff should also try to ensure that all parents have continuity of carers, but be aware that this may be particularly beneficial in these situations. Familiarity with one or two members of staff may help parents and staff to work out ways of understanding each other better over time.

When managing communication through an informal interpreter or with parents without any interpreter, it is important that staff should [adapted from Henley and Schott (1999) and Schott and Henley (1996)]:

- *Use all of the verbal and non-verbal communication skills highlighted in Chapter 4.*

- *Try to simplify the language they use* to make it easier to understand and/or translate. It may be advisable to convey only essential details and leave more complex information until a trained interpreter is available (if parents have consented to using one). Try not to condense what has to be said as denser language is more difficult to understand. It is helpful to break up what needs to be said into smaller chunks and use a short sentence for each piece of information that needs to be conveyed.

- *Avoid using expressions, euphemisms and colloquial language.*

- *Avoid speaking louder than usual.* It can be helpful, however, to speak clearly and perhaps more slowly, depending on the language ability of the parent or informal interpreter.

- *Draw diagrams or point things out on a picture* rather than only relying on spoken words. Staff should check whether this is acceptable to parents first.

- *When explaining something complicated, stop and plan what to say and in what order*, dealing with one subject at a time, choosing words carefully, and pausing to check that the parents have understood before moving on to a new subject. When giving instructions, it is helpful to give them in the order in which things need to be done.

- *Listen carefully to the person's command of English* and decide how much they understand. Most people understand more of a language than they can speak.

- *Listen for the words that parents and informal interpreters use and understand and try to use the same words*. It is particularly important to avoid medical language and jargon.

- *Encourage parents to ask questions, tell staff when they have not understood what they have said and be willing to explain things more than once and in different ways if necessary*.

- *Check understanding of information and consent.* When checking understanding, it is helpful to try to avoid asking questions that can be answered with "Yes" or "No". When parents or informal interpreters say "Yes", or its equivalent, they may not necessarily understand or agree with what they have been told or offered. If possible, open questions should be used to check understanding. For example, instead of "Do you understand?" it may be better to ask parents to say *what* they have understood. Some parents may also feel that saying "No" directly is rude and they may use other indirect but polite ways of refusing a request or answering a question negatively. These may include not responding to the request, changing the subject, asking for time to think, making a non-committal reply, or using a polite phrase that insiders understand as meaning "No" but is less offensive.

- *Watch for signs of weariness*. Everyone may have to concentrate more when communicating across a language or communication barrier and they may get tired quickly. Staff should ask if parents and informal interpreters would like a break or if they would like to continue discussions later.

- *Keep accurate written records* of what has been discussed and decisions that have been made so that different members of staff do not have to keep asking the same questions. Also, keep a record of whether or not an informal interpreter was used and how this may have affected the discussions.

When working with informal interpreters, staff should also:

- *Encourage any informal interpreters to relay the questions and information to and from parents rather than answer for parents.* Many informal interpreters may find it very hard to relay questions and information without joining in the discussion. They may start answering for the other person if they think they know the answer.

- *Help the informal interpreter as much as possible and offer them support*. It may help to explain the content and purpose of the discussion beforehand and to find out if the interpreter feels able to manage the situation. If there are things the interpreter does not understand or is not sure how to translate, they should be encouraged to tell staff.

- *Thank the person for interpreting.*

> *A single mother with fairly good English was told that her baby girl was being transferred from the regional neonatal intensive care unit back to the special care unit at her local hospital. The staff thought the mother understood that the baby was being transferred because she was dying. But the mother thought it meant she was getting better. When the baby's condition deteriorated the mother was devastated and wanted her to go*

back to intensive care. The staff realised she had no idea that her baby was going to die. (Bliss 2006, personal communication)

Written information, reference materials and translations for parents

Correspondence with bereaved parents and any supplementary information such as leaflets and materials in other formats should be available in the main local languages and in written, braille, audio and visual formats (including large print and sign language videos) (NHS England 2015b) (see *Written information and information provided in other formats* in Chapter 4). Trained, professional translators should be employed to translate these materials and this should not be done by practice staff unless they are appropriately trained (NHS England 2015b). Automated translation services such as Google Translate should never be used to translate documents (NHS England 2015b).

Information should be sent to parents in their preferred language or format where it is known by staff (NHS England 2015b). Parents should not be expected to follow-up if they do not receive information in an accessible format.

Additionally, parents should be able to access their medical records in their preferred language or format without incurring charges in addition to those that may be in place for obtaining access to these records (NHS England 2015b).

When providing written information, staff should also be aware that parents may not be literate and they should ensure that all information has been verbally discussed with parents.

Specific communication considerations when caring for parents with a sensory impairment

Staff should be aware that there are many different degrees of sight and hearing impairment and that each person has their own preferred ways of managing their sensory impairment. Staff should ask parents how they would like to be alerted when they are called in for an appointment or discussion.

Trusts, Health Boards and managers should ensure that all staff have adequate training in supporting parents with sensory impairments and other disabilities (Government Equalities Office 2010).

Communicating with parents who are deaf or who have a hearing impairment

People who are deaf or who have a hearing impairment may use a hearing aid, lip reading, sign language, an induction loop or a combination of these communication techniques. In addition to offering to arrange for a sign language interpreter, staff who are communicating with parents who a deaf or have a hearing impairment should ensure that:

- A quiet place is available for discussions.
- They avoid wearing a mask or covering their mouth.
- They avoid shouting, speaking slowly or exaggerating speech or facial expressions.
- They use clear, simple language.

It is also important to recognise that some parents who sign may not use British Sign Language (BSL), which is the standard type of sign language used in the UK. There may also be regional variations in the signs used by parents who use BSL.

Communicating with parents who are blind or who have a visual impairment

Staff should introduce parents who are blind or visually impaired to everyone involved in any discussion and told where everyone is located.

Staff should also ensure that they offer parents who are blind or visually impaired opportunities to create memories and take photographs of their baby as they may wish to share these with other people (see also *Creating memories* in Chapter 14).

CHAPTER 6

Antenatal screening and diagnostic tests

Other relevant chapters

1: Providing holistic care

2: Providing inclusive care

3: Loss and grief

4: Communication

5: Communication across language and other barriers

7: Continuing the pregnancy

8: Termination of pregnancy for fetal anomaly or maternal medical conditions

12: Labour and birth when a baby has died

Screening and diagnostic tests are a widely accepted and increasing part of care during pregnancy. Different types of screening and tests are available antenatally for various fetal anomalies to assess fetal growth and check for anything that may affect the health of the woman and/ or baby, including haematological conditions, infections and clinical conditions (such as gestational diabetes, pre-eclampsia or placenta praevia) (NICE 2008a). Some tests and screening may also be offered as part of pre-conception care or for newborns. For example, screening may be offered if parents or a newborn may be genetic carriers of a particular condition such as a major haemoglobin disorder (NHS Sickle Cell and Thalassaemia Screening Programme 2012).

Some tests offered may involve blood tests, ultrasound examinations or more invasive procedures such as amniocentesis or chorionic villus sampling (CVS) depending on what anomalies or medical conditions are being tested for. Up-to-date information about various screening programmes and tests is available through the UK government website (see Appendix 2). More detailed information about screening tests and when they should be offered is also available from NICE's (2008a) *Antenatal care* guidelines, the NHS Antenatal and newborn screening timeline and ARC (see Appendix 2).

Informed choice and consent around screening and diagnostic testing

Care during pregnancy should enable a woman to make informed decisions, based on her needs, having discussed matters fully with the healthcare professionals involved. (NICE 2008a: 6)

Some screening and diagnostic tests may be offered routinely to all women and others may only be offered if a particular risk is identified for a woman and/or her partner. Good communication between staff and parents around the available options for screening and diagnostic tests is important for women to make fully informed choices about the tests offered (see also *Giving information and facilitating informed choice* in Chapter 4). Staff should be aware of how they present this information and it should be made clear to parents that all screening and diagnostic tests are optional (NICE 2008a; Skirton and Barr 2010; Tsouroufli 2011).

Some partners may also want to be involved in decision-making around antenatal testing. With the woman's consent, her partner (where applicable) should be included in discussions with healthcare staff and an effort should be made by staff to involve partners in these discussions (Skirton and Barr 2010). This may be particularly important when tests are being offered where the father should also be offered testing (for example, during screening for sickle cell disease or beta thalassaemia). Despite a partner's involvement, the woman has the legal right to make the final decision about any antenatal testing offered for herself and/or her baby.

 For many men pregnancy is not just something that happens to their wife or partner. It happens to the two of them. Father

It is important that women are offered information about and have access to screening and diagnostic testing as soon as possible so that they have time to consider their options (Skirton and Barr 2010). To allow women time to consider and discuss their choices about screening offered in the first trimester, procedures should be in place to ensure that women receive screening information as early as possible in pregnancy (Tsouroufli 2011; Ahmed *et al.* 2013). The offer of early screening may also be important as women may need time, depending on the results, to make other decisions around further testing, termination of pregnancy, continuing the pregnancy and/or palliative care planning (NHS Sickle Cell and Thalassaemia Screening Programme 2012) (see also Chapters 7 and 8).

Flexible appointment times should be available when discussing antenatal screening and diagnostic testing with parents so that healthcare staff have time to give women sufficient information and women have time to ask questions (Tsouroufli 2011; Ahmed *et al.* 2013). Trusts and Health Boards should have a policy in place to ensure that adequate time is available for these appointments (Tsouroufli 2011; Ahmed *et al.* 2013).

In addition to verbal information, women should be given written information which should also be available in other formats and the main local languages.

When being offered screening or diagnostic testing, women and their partners (where relevant) should be given full, impartial, consistent, clear and up-to-date information about:

- The purpose of all tests offered (including for combined tests offered in the first trimester of pregnancy).

- The optimal timing for particular types of testing.

- Procedures performed during diagnostic testing and screening and any associated risks.

- Whether it is a screening test that provides information about a potential risk to the baby or a diagnostic test that tells parents whether or not their baby has a particular condition.

- The accuracy of the test offered that is relevant to the time when it will be performed.

- The potential implications of test results and the potential need for further testing.

- Any other information that the test may provide.

- Any benefits that the tests may offer such as early treatment for particular conditions.

- When and how the woman can expect to receive test results (Marteau and Dormandy 2001; NICE 2008a; Skirton and Barr 2010; Tsouroufli 2011).

Women should also be told about their options for terminating the pregnancy if a fetal anomaly is diagnosed at this stage as this may affect some women's decisions about accepting or declining testing (Lyus *et al.* 2014). However, care should be taken to ensure that women do not feel that testing is only available or appropriate if they will agree to terminate the pregnancy.

Women's choices regarding screening and diagnostic tests may be affected by a number of factors. Some women may want reassurance that all is well with their pregnancy or see consenting to testing as a way of caring for their baby (Tsouroufli 2011). Others may want as much information as possible to enable them to make decisions about their pregnancy (UK NSC 2014). Some women may make decisions based on the potential risks of testing for their baby.

The choices of some women may also be affected by their partner's and/or family's wishes (Skirton and Barr 2010). Women and/or their families may have personal, religious or cultural values and beliefs about prenatal diagnosis or termination of pregnancy that may affect their decisions regarding screening (NHS Sickle Cell and Thalassaemia Screening Programme 2012). In some communities, there may also be a stigma attached to being a sickle cell disease or beta thalassaemia carrier or having certain infectious diseases and parents may need reassurance regarding confidentiality (Ahmed *et al.* 2002; Dyson 2005).

When women make choices about screening and diagnostic tests, their choices should be respected and documented regardless of whether they consent to or decline offers of testing. Staff should also give women information about when results will be available and ask the woman how any testing results should be given if a problem is detected. If this cannot be done in person and the results are to be given by phone, staff should discuss with the woman when this should be done. It may be possible to set a time to call when she will be at home or in another private space. She may also wish to receive results when her partner or another supporter will be with her. This information should be documented and referred to when the results are available.

Giving results of screening and diagnostic tests

Women should be given the results of all screening and diagnostic tests as soon as possible. During the consent process for any testing, staff should have documented when and how the results should be given to the woman if a potential problem is detected. The woman should also be told how results are normally given if the test results are normal. If a potential anomaly is detected during testing, staff should check a woman's medical notes before results are given to determine the woman's preference for receiving this information.

If possible, an appointment should be made with the woman to discuss results in person when staff have bad news.

Alternatively, women and staff may have arranged for results to be given by telephone. In these instances, staff should always check whether the woman is able to talk when she answers the phone and before giving results. If the woman is told bad news, she may respond with a long silence. This may be very hard for staff and they may be tempted to say something. However, it may be better to wait until the woman feels able to speak. Before the end of the call, it is important to give the woman a named contact and phone number so that she or her partner can call back later if they have any additional questions or need information to be repeated (ARC 2006, personal communication). The woman should also be offered a face-to-face appointment as soon as possible to further discuss the results and their implications.

Parents may be unprepared for bad news when results are available following screening or diagnostic tests (Lalor *et al*. 2007, 2009), and they may experience a variety of emotions. These feelings may include grief for the baby they had hoped for, grief for the baby they are carrying, relief that they have time to make decisions about the pregnancy or the baby's care or a mixture of emotions (Bijma *et al*. 2008; ARC 2012). Parents' reactions to the news and/ or their grief are also unlikely to be affected by the information given to them before the screening or diagnostics tests were performed (ARC 2015, personal communication). Staff should acknowledge that the situation is likely to be very distressing for parents and offer support. Parents may simply need staff to supportively listen at this time (see also *Support and listening* in Chapter 15).

Women and their partners (where they have one) should also be offered appropriate counselling including genetic counselling where needed (NICE 2008a; NHS Sickle

Cell and Thalassaemia Screening Programme 2012). Parents should also be given information and contact details for support organisations such as ARC that offer support for parents around testing and results (see Appendix 2). If a woman is planning to travel home alone after being told bad news, staff should suggest that she may want to phone someone and ask them to accompany her.

The woman should be offered another appointment as soon as possible to discuss the results and their implications further and discuss any available options for care and further testing. See *Further tests and appointments* below for arrangements that should also be made to offer parents additional testing, care and support after they receive potentially distressing or unexpected news.

Informing parents of screening results and discussing the potential implications

All women having an antenatal or newborn screening test must be informed of the result, even if it is negative or if the level of risk identified is very low (NDSSPE 2004).

The information that women and their partners need in order to make informed decisions about results from screening tests can be complicated and difficult to explain. Workloads should be organised so that staff have enough time to fully discuss the results and implications with parents and answer any questions. Staff who give parents screening results should also be well informed about the significance and implications of the results before discussions with parents. If necessary, the member of staff who will be speaking to parents should ask a colleague to explain the results to them. This may not be possible during an ultrasound scan and staff should offer parents the opportunity to speak with someone who is able to provide them with more information after breaking the news. If staff are unable to adequately answer parents' questions during a discussion, they should explain this and arrange for the woman and her partner (if applicable) to speak with someone who has a better understanding of the results as soon as possible.

A screening test often provides information about a baby's level of risk for being affected by a particular fetal anomaly or medical condition, rather than a clear diagnosis. Discussing risk should be a two-way process involving an exchange of information between parents and healthcare staff. The aim of this information exchange should be to enable parents to make informed and individual decisions about further testing and options for the pregnancy where necessary. It may sometimes be helpful to provide and discuss information over several consultations, although this may not always be possible if options for further testing or terminating the pregnancy are time limited (Edwards *et al*. 2002).

A parent's perception of the meaning of a certain level of risk is highly individual and may depend on the parent's life experiences, the severity and implications of the identified anomaly and how the statistical risk is explained (Edwards 2004a).

Two women with exactly the same results, explained in exactly the same way, will not necessarily perceive their risk in the same way. (UK NSC 2005: 5)

A parent's understanding of risk may also be affected by their ability to assimilate complex information. Staff should tailor their explanations and examples to suit individual parents.

The language used when presenting screening results should also be chosen with care. Staff need to be aware of how parents may understand words and their connotations and choose language that accurately conveys the situation and the level of risk (Abramsky and Fletcher 2002). The examples below illustrate how parents' perceptions or understanding of risk may be affected by the language used:

- Parents may be more likely to assume that something "rare" is more serious than something "uncommon" and that something "abnormal" is more serious than something "unusual" (Abramsky and Fletcher 2002).

- The words "syndrome", "disorder" and "anomaly" may also worry parents even if the test results show a variation from a norm that is unlikely to cause problems for the baby (Abramsky and Fletcher 2002).

- The word "risk" has negative connotations for many people and using "chance" may be more neutral.

- In the context of screening results, the implications of "positive" and "negative" are often reversed where a positive result is likely to be bad news and a negative result is probably good news. The words "negative" and "positive" should be avoided when giving results or the meaning of these terms should be fully explained.

- Some parents may find hearing the chance of a desired outcome more reassuring than the chance of an undesired outcome (Abramsky and Fletcher 2002). Reframing information from a different perspective may be helpful for some parents but it is important to offer them information about the likelihood of both desired and undesired outcomes.

- Technical words such as "trisomy" may worry some parents more than equivalent phrases such as "extra chromosome" (Abramsky and Fletcher 2002). All technical terms should be fully explained to parents.

- Some people may understand "high risk" as meaning that the baby has a fetal anomaly or medical condition and "low risk" as meaning that the baby is healthy (Ryder 1999). These terms should be clarified for parents so that they understand that a "high risk" does not confirm a diagnosis and that a "low risk" is not a definite indicator that the baby is healthy.

- Words such as "likely", "unlikely", "high", "low" and "probable" mean very different things to different people and must be further discussed and clarified (Edwards *et al.* 2002).

- The technical screening terms "false positive" and "false negative" are unfamiliar to most parents and should be explained.

It may also be important to give information about the screening results to parents in different ways. For example:

- Some people prefer verbal or descriptive information about risk while others find numbers easier to understand (Edwards 2004a). The best approach may be to provide both types of information by using, for example, a verbal probability phrase such as "very unlikely" as well as the corresponding numerical probability (Marteau *et al.* 2000).

- Some people find numbers easier to understand if they are presented visually in a diagram such as bar or pie chart (Lalor *et al*. 2007). ARC (2005) suggests that a result of 1 in 100 could be represented by 100 circles on a page, one of which is a different colour from the rest. For larger numbers, it may be helpful to have a visual aid such as an illustration of a jar of marbles or beans containing one of a different colour to demonstrate the level of risk.

- Some people find ratios easier to understand. For example, saying there is a "1 in X" chance. Other people prefer information about risk or chance to be given as a percentage. For example, saying there is an "X per cent" chance. Abramsky and Fletcher (2002) found that many people perceived "1 in X" as larger than the equivalent percentage. Some parents may also focus on the "1" and assume that that "1" must be their baby (ARC 2006, personal communication). Information about risk should be presented using both ratios and percentages. It is also important to be consistent by not giving the chance of one outcome as a percentage and the chance of another as a ratio (Abramsky and Fletcher 2002).

- To people who are unfamiliar with the language of probability, "1 in 300" may sound like a higher risk than "1 in 100". Calman and Royston (1997) suggest comparing a specific risk to numbers of people. For example, a risk of 1 in 100 (or 1 per cent) could be compared to one person in a street with 100 people; 1 in 1,000 (or 0.1 per cent) to one person in a village with 1,000 people; 1 in 10,000 (or 0.01 per cent) to one person in a small town with 10,000 people and so on. Analogies based on the maximum capacity of well-known local venues such as a local football stadium could also be used.

Many people find it hard to remember specific information about risk. Each woman should be given a written record of the discussion to take away with her and the contact details for a named contact who she can speak with if she has additional questions or is unclear about the information that she has been given. She should also be given information about any further tests that are offered that may provide more information and/or a diagnosis. If the woman wants further testing, these appointments should be scheduled as soon as possible (see *Further tests and appointments* below).

Informing parents of diagnostic test results and discussing their implications

An appointment to discuss a diagnosis of a fetal anomaly can be very stressful for parents and may be very demanding for staff. All staff who give parents the results of diagnostic tests must be fully informed about the condition(s) they are discussing, including information about how the condition may affect the baby's life (Skirton and

Barr 2010). The information provided to parents about a fetal anomaly and the woman's options must be as complete as possible, accurate, up-to-date and impartial. The possible severity and impact of a fetal anomaly should be neither exaggerated nor understated.

Parents may feel shocked and may find it difficult to understand the information given or think clearly. Staff should speak clearly and use simple language, Staff may also need to repeat information more than once and parents should be encouraged to ask questions (see also *Breaking bad news* in Chapter 4).

Staff should offer parents the following information regarding the diagnosis:

- A clear explanation of the fetal anomaly or medical condition.

- The reliability of the diagnosis, what further confirmation might be recommended and how this might be obtained. If the findings are uncertain or cannot yet be confirmed, the potentially stressful nature of such uncertainty should be acknowledged.

- How the pregnancy may be affected by the fetal anomaly or medical condition.

- Whether special care or treatment will be needed before the birth.

- The possible long-term prognosis for the baby and what treatment or support might be available.

- How the anomaly or condition might affect the baby's quality of life.

- Options for continuing or ending the pregnancy where applicable.
  (ARC 2005)

Parents often want as much information as possible about the fetal anomaly or medical condition after a diagnosis (Lalor *et al.* 2007; ARC 2012). Parents may also have questions or concerns about the causes of a fetal anomaly and may wonder if it could have been avoided if they or healthcare staff had done something differently (ARC 2012).

Staff should offer to refer parents to specialists such as geneticists, fetal medicine specialists, neonatologists, paediatricians or disability organisations where parents can get additional information about the baby's condition. This is important as parents may need to have access to a multi-disciplinary team in order to gather as much information as possible about the possible prognosis. Whenever possible, parents should also be given supplementary written information that has been developed specifically for parents about the condition affecting their baby. This information should include the details of other sources of information and support such as ARC (see Appendix 2). The information should also be available in other languages and formats.

Staff should offer parents another appointment as soon as possible for further testing (see *Further tests and appointments* below) or to discuss their options regarding the pregnancy and future care (see *Choice and decision making after a fetal anomaly is diagnosed or suspected* below). Parents should also be encouraged to write down any questions that occur to them after any discussions so they can ask these questions at the next appointment.

Ultrasound examinations

All of the information given in this chapter regarding discussions with parents about choices regarding screening and diagnostic testing, results and further testing also applies to ultrasound examinations. However, this section discusses some of the additional considerations that staff may need to be aware of when discussing ultrasound examinations and their results with parents.

Before an ultrasound

For most women, seeing their baby on a scan is an exciting and much anticipated event that is often shared with their partner, a family member or another supporter. Many women are aware that ultrasound is used to check their due date, the size of the baby and the position of the placenta. However, they may not realise that the scan also checks for possible structural anomalies and/or markers for chromosomal anomalies, particularly the 18 to 20-week anomaly scan that many women do not realise is for screening (Skirton and Barr 2010).

NICE states that:

The purpose of the scan is to identify fetal anomalies and allow:

- Reproductive choice (termination of pregnancy).

- Parents to prepare (for any treatment/disability/palliative care/termination of pregnancy).

- Managed birth in a specialist centre.

- Intrauterine therapy (2008a: 25).

It is important that women are well informed before a scan about the purpose of each ultrasound examination, the scan procedure, the possibility of detecting a fetal anomaly during the scan and how they will be given the results (Garcia *et al*. 2002; Mitchell 2004; NICE 2008a; Skirton and Barr 2010). Women should also be told about the limitations of routine scans when checking for fetal anomalies and how their body mass index and/ or the baby's position may affect detection (NICE 2008a). Any potential risks associated with ultrasound scans including the recent recommendations against having "keepsake" ultrasounds that are not medically indicated should also be explained to women (RCOG 2015a).

If a transvaginal scan is recommended, women should be given this information in advance along with the reasons for recommending this type of scan, a description of the procedure and an acknowledgement that women may find this uncomfortable. Some women may find transvaginal scanning or the idea of this type of scan distressing (Clement *et al*. 2003) and should be aware that they can decide to decline this offer. Women should also be able to request that any scans are performed by women and that no men are present during examinations if this is their preference.

Women must be given complete and impartial information during the consent process so that they are able to make an informed choice about whether or not to have ultrasound scans (NICE 2008a). Verbal and written information should be provided. Women should also be made aware that they can choose to decline the offer of an ultrasound examination. A woman's decision regarding any scan that is offered should be respected and documented.

During the scan

A woman should be able to have her partner or another support person with her throughout all examinations. Any request to have a scan carried out by a female sonographer should also be accommodated wherever possible. It is also important that privacy is offered to all women during scans and this may involve closing the door, keeping the woman covered as much as possible during the examination or limiting the number of staff present.

Before beginning the scan, the sonographer should check that the woman understands the purpose of the examination. They should also ask if the woman or her partner (if present) would like to look at their baby. Ideally, a second screen should be positioned so parents can see the baby. If it is not possible to have a second screen, the sonographer should explain that parents will see their baby briefly at the beginning of the examination, that they will then turn the screen away to perform the necessary checks and that they will then invite parents to see their baby for a longer period at the end and they will explain what parents are seeing.

Communication during an ultrasound examination

Whenever possible, sonographers should explain what they are doing during an ultrasound examination as long silences may be very hard for parents. If the sonographer needs some time to concentrate, it may be helpful to use phrases such as, "I am going to be quiet for a moment so that I can concentrate on the screen". Staff should be aware that parents are often highly sensitive to non-verbal messages and body language. Parents may become alarmed if the screen is turned away from them without prior warning or if the sonographer's facial expression and demeanour change (Mitchell 2004).

> *I can remember every detail of the room and the moment the chatty sonographer stopped talking and turned the screen away from me. She then asked her assistant to get a doctor. That is the moment I knew deep inside me that my baby daughter Heather had died and my heart broke.*
> Mother

If an anomaly or another reason for concern is found during a scan, the sonographer should tell the woman as soon as possible that there is something on the scan that needs to be looked at more closely. This may be very difficult and distressing for the sonographer who may need a moment to compose their feelings although parents must not be kept waiting for any length of time. It is also important not to pretend that all is well or offer false reassurance.

Parents should then be informed if an anomaly is detected or suspected during the scan to enable them to make an informed choice about their pregnancy options (NICE 2008a). In these instances, sonographers should be able to inform parents of ultrasound scan results during the examination and to discuss the potential implications (RCOG 2010b). Clear, honest information about the results should sensitively be given to parents (Mitchell 2004; Lalor *et al.* 2007) (see also *Breaking bad news* in Chapter 4). Additionally, staff should acknowledge any uncertainties about the findings. Parents should also be asked if they would like the sonographer to show them what they have seen on the screen (Mitchell 2004).

If the sonographer is uncertain about the ultrasound results, they should say that there may be a problem and explain why a second opinion is needed. The sonographer might find the following phrases helpful: "I'm very sorry but I think I might have found a problem", "I will have to get a doctor to have another look" (ARC 2006, personal communication). The second opinion should be organised as soon as possible and the sonographer should acknowledge that the wait may be very difficult for parents (Lalor *et al*. 2007).

If another ultrasound examination is recommended and parents' consent to another scan, this should be organised as soon as possible as delays may add to parents' distress (Lalor *et al.* 2007). The reasons for any delay in arranging this scan should be explained to parents and staff should acknowledge that waiting may be very difficult and stressful for parents.

When necessary, sonographers should be able to access support from staff such as bereavement midwives and obstetricians who can offer additional support to parents (Lalor *et al.* 2007). These staff should be able to offer parents more information about the results, their implications and the options available to parents (see also *Giving results of screening and diagnostic tests* above). Parents are often not expecting to hear bad news during an ultrasound examination (Bijma *et al.* 2008) and should be given time to begin to absorb the results of the examination before staff offer to discuss the next steps and available options with them (see also *Further tests and appointments* below). If an anomaly is detected during a private scan, staff should offer to contact the woman's midwife or obstetrician to discuss the results and arrange further appointments with healthcare staff.

Parents should also be offered a scan photograph. Some parents will appreciate a scan photograph while others will not. If the parents do not want a photograph, the sonographer could offer to take one and keep it in the woman's medical records so that they can ask for it later if they want (see also *Photographs* in Chapter 14). Parents should not feel pressured to accept the offer of a photograph.

Ultrasound examination when a problem is suspected

Sometimes a woman requests or is referred for a scan because a problem is suspected or to confirm a diagnosis. These ultrasound examinations should be carried out by a member of staff who specialises in fetal medicine and who can interpret and explain the information obtained during the appointment. If this is not possible, the woman must be informed beforehand and told what arrangements will be made to explain the findings fully to them as soon as possible. Women should also be advised to bring their partner (if they have one) or another person for support and not to bring other children.

 When they returned with the scanning machine I could not look at it. I watched my husband's face. When I saw the incredible sadness that spread across his face I knew that we had lost our baby. Mother

The person performing the scan should speak to parents before the scan to make sure that they understand the reasons for the scan and are well prepared. They should acknowledge that having a scan in these circumstances may be very upsetting and stressful for parents. It may help to say something like, "I'm sorry. This must be very hard for you …".

Ultrasound policy and procedures

Every unit should have an agreed procedure for talking to women about ultrasound examination findings. This procedure should be developed and agreed by a multi-professional group that includes parents or their representatives, sonographers, nurses, midwives, radiologists, obstetricians and genetic counsellors. The policy should ensure that the time between the detection of an anomaly, explaining it to parents and discussing the next steps is as short as possible. This will be easier if several members of staff from different disciplines are all trained in ultrasound examination and in the necessary communication skills (see Chapter 4).

In order to facilitate best practice, sonographers should receive information from the relevant department (e.g. histology laboratory or fetal medicine unit) about the outcomes of pregnancies in which they have identified anomalies. Wherever possible, they should also be involved in case and audit meetings. Good informal and formal support should also be available to sonographers.

Further tests and appointments

If further tests are recommended to obtain or confirm a diagnosis after the results of a screening or diagnostic test are received, these should be discussed with parents as soon as possible. Staff should ensure that parents are given sufficient information about the purpose and implications of further testing and support parents as they make an informed choice about whether to proceed with further testing (see *Informed choice and consent around screening and diagnostic testing* above). The woman's choice regarding further testing should be respected regardless of whether she accepts or declines this testing and her decision should be documented.

With a woman's consent, referrals for appointments with specialists to discuss recommendations for care and parents' options should be made as soon as possible. An appointment should be arranged with an obstetrician within three working days and a specialist unit if needed within five working days (NHS Screening Programmes 2015). The woman should be given clear verbal and written information about the date, time and place where the tests or appointments will take place, directions if it is in another unit or department and details of whom she will see (their name and role). She should also be invited to bring her partner (if she has one) or another supporter with her to the appointment. Women should also be given the details for a named contact who can answer questions and offer support before or between appointments. Additionally, staff should be aware of the costs that women may incur if they have to travel longer distances to access specialist care during pregnancy and that this may affect some parents' ability to access this care. If possible, funding should be available to help parents on low incomes.

When making referrals, good communication within and across healthcare teams, departments and units is important and policies and procedures should be in place to facilitate this process between the different specialties involved in screening and diagnostic testing (NHS Screening Programmes 2015). Good coordination and regular communication between specialties are essential to make sure that policies and procedures are coherent and offer the best possible care for parents. This will also help to ensure that the information given to parents by staff in different departments is consistent.

The member of staff who arranges further appointments should phone ahead to make sure that the woman is expected for the appointment or arrange to accompany the woman if she is going to another department immediately. The woman should not have to explain to staff why she has, especially in front of other parents (Chitty *et al.* 1996). Staff who are expecting the woman for further testing or specialist appointments should be waiting to welcome her and her partner or supporter (where applicable). Wherever possible, parents should not have to wait in an area with other pregnant women who are having scheduled scans or tests.

 We booked in at reception and were asked if we had attended before. Nobody seemed to know or care that we had been referred from another hospital. We were told to wait in a large square bare room with six or seven other women, some with partners and young children. Then we were led to a darkened room with a very large ultrasound machine by a doctor with a soft friendly voice. He asked, "So what can I do for you today?" I couldn't believe that he had to ask. Surely everybody in the world knew that ours had come crashing down around us? Mother

Choice and decision making after a fetal anomaly is diagnosed or suspected

There are no right or wrong decisions, just decisions that parents can live with. (ARC 2005: 3)

When a fetal anomaly is suspected or detected in pregnancy, parents are suddenly forced to make decisions that they never wanted to make. Parents may need time to absorb this information, grieve for themselves and their baby and consider their options for the pregnancy and their care (Lalor *et al.* 2009). The "severity" of the fetal anomaly or the degree of risk may also not be an indicator of parents' response to the results or their subsequent decisions (Lalor *et al.* 2007, 2009). The Royal College of Obstetricians and Gynaecologists state that:

> It should not be assumed that, even in the presence of an obviously fatal fetal condition such as anencephaly, a woman will choose to have a termination. A decision to decline the offer of termination must be fully supported. (RCOG 2010b: ix)

Decision-making support for parents following the diagnosis of a fetal anomaly

Some parents will want a lot of information to help them make decisions about their pregnancy and care while others will immediately know what they want to do. A few women may have decided in advance what they will decide if their unborn baby has a fetal anomaly, although some may change their mind following a diagnosis. Some parents may also want to know about the implications of the diagnosis or suspected fetal anomaly for future pregnancies as this may influence their current decision.

Although staff "cannot take the pain of the situation away, sensitive supportive care at this time plays an important part in helping parents come to decisions that are right for them" (ARC 2005: 10). Many women value continuity of carer with a known member of staff during discussions about their options for the pregnancy (Lalor *et al.* 2009). Parents should also be given the contact details for their designated care provider or another named contact who they can contact between appointments if they have any questions.

It is important never to make assumptions about what parents will decide and all parents should be offered opportunities to discuss all available options (See also *Giving information and facilitating informed choice* in Chapter 4). Staff should give as much impartial, factual information as the parents want about the diagnosed or suspected fetal anomaly, acknowledge any uncertainties and offer information about the potential implications, risks and benefits of each available option. The information that is given to parents should be tailored to reflect their baby's diagnosed or suspected fetal anomaly and parents should be encouraged to ask as many questions as they want during these discussions.

Parents should also be offered non-directive counselling support to help them consider and make their decision and they should be referred as soon as possible if they wish to accept this offer (Breeze and Lees 2013). Wherever possible, parents should be given written information about their available options, their baby's fetal anomaly and further support that is available from organisations that offer parents support during this decision-making process (for example, Antenatal Results and Choices – see Appendix 2) or that support families with children with specific conditions. This information should be available in different languages and formats.

Discussing potential options
for the pregnancy and care with parents

In the case of a non-lethal anomaly, staff should suggest that parents may want to contact relevant support organisations. This might help parents to learn how the condition might affect their child's quality of life and about the potential impact of caring for the child on them and/or their existing or future children.

Some fetal anomalies may be treatable or there may be a chance that treatment and intervention before or after the birth might save the baby's life. In these instances, staff should explain the available options to parents and any potential risks, benefits and outcomes. Staff should also offer parents an opportunity to discuss recommendations for the baby's birth and how the baby would be monitored during the labour and birth.

If the baby might be born alive but is not expected or is unable to survive, staff should offer parents information about how long the baby may be expected to live after the birth, even if uncertainty makes this difficult to predict (Chiswick 2008; Breeze and Lees 2013). Parents should also be told if it will not be possible to determine whether the baby is likely to survive or whether the baby may live but with significant morbidity until after the baby is born (Breeze and Lees 2013). Any uncertainty should be explained to parents along with parallel planning options for treating the baby and providing palliative care (Breeze and Lees 2013) (see also Chapters 7 and 13).

Parents should also be offered information about their options for termination of the pregnancy. This can be a very difficult topic to bring up with parents. Staff may start by saying something such as, "There are a number of choices open to you/for you to think about" (Statham *et al.* 2001: 40). Women should be offered information about the available methods of termination that are available locally and in other areas for her gestation of pregnancy (see also Chapter 8). If the pregnancy is approaching 24 weeks' gestation, the woman also needs to know how long she has to make her decision.

Support for parents who are deciding
whether to continue or terminate a pregnancy

Parents may be in shock following the diagnosis of a fetal anomaly and/or experience a mixture of feelings at this time including grief, anger, isolation, failure, detachment, confusion and guilt (ARC [n.d.]). Some parents may also blame themselves, their partners or the healthcare professionals providing their antenatal care (ARC [n.d.]). Parents may need reassurance that it is very unlikely that anyone has done something to cause their baby's condition (ARC [n.d.]).

Parents may also be facing a very difficult decision if they are considering whether to continue or terminate the pregnancy. Unless they are approaching 24 weeks' gestation, parents should be given as much time as they need to make a decision and discuss their feelings without feeling pressured (ARC 2005; Fisher and Lafarge 2015). If parents are approaching 24 weeks' gestation, the restrictions on termination after this time should be explained to them so that they understand why a decision must be made more quickly and whether they want access to a second opinion (ARC 2005).

Decisions may be particularly difficult if parents are making decisions based on the *probability* that their baby has a fetal anomaly, rather than on a definite diagnosis. Staff should acknowledge that this may be difficult for parents. When there is uncertainty, parents should also be offered a referral to a fetal medicine unit for an expert opinion about the baby's condition (Lalor *et al*. 2009; Lyus *et al*. 2014). Although there may be little new information to be gained, it may confirm the results that parents have been given and/or provide them with more information. Many parents have found this helpful afterwards when they look back at the decisions they made (ARC 2006, personal communication).

Parents' decisions may also be affected by a number of other factors including their personal, religious and/or cultural values and beliefs, their feelings about the pregnancy, their ability to cope with uncertainty, their obstetric history or their knowledge of other parents whose babies were diagnosed with fetal anomalies. Sometimes, parents may need time to consider their own needs, beliefs and values before they reach a decision.

When parents do not agree with each other about the decision, they may appreciate it if a trained member of staff offers to support them while exploring their options so they can attempt to reach a joint decision. A woman who decides on a course of action that is against her partner's wishes will likely need additional support. In these circumstances, women may need to cope with "going it alone" while continuing the pregnancy or undergoing a termination, in addition to coping with her feelings about the decision (ARC 2005).

Some women and/or their partners (where applicable) may want to discuss their options with other family members. One advantage of such collective decision making is that parents may be more likely to feel that they will receive support from their family (Ahmed *et al*. 2006). However, some parents may fear or know that their family will disapprove of their decision. It is particularly important in such cases to reassure parents that strict confidentiality will be maintained.

Many parents may find that they change their minds frequently while trying to come to a decision. This may be very distressing, especially for people who are used to being decisive. It can be helpful to reassure parents that such vacillation is very common and to acknowledge how difficult it may be to make a decision.

Parents may also ask staff about what they would do in this situation. Staff should not discuss their personal views regarding the condition or what they would decide in this situation (Abramsky *et al*. 2001). However, they might ask parents questions to help them figure out why they are asking staff about their choices (ARC 2005). Some parents may be seeking acknowledgement of the enormity and responsibility attached to making a decision, while others may be trying to determine if their choice is acceptable to others at the same time as trying to come to terms with their decision themselves (ARC 2005). It may be helpful to acknowledge that making the decision may be overwhelming for parents and that there are no right or wrong choices but that parents need to make the choice that is right for them (ARC 2005).

Once a decision has been made about continuing or terminating a pregnancy

Once the woman has made her decision about continuing or terminating a pregnancy, this should be documented and staff should offer to discuss the next steps and make the appropriate referrals as soon as possible. Parents' decisions about the pregnancy or their care should be respected.

If a woman decides to terminate the pregnancy, she may want the termination to be carried out as soon as possible. However, some women may want to wait for a while. As much as possible, the woman should determine the timing and the pace of events although she should also be told about any medical or legal considerations (such as the gestation of the pregnancy) that may affect her options (see also Chapter 8). It is important that staff discuss timing with women to find out what is appropriate for each woman as some women may experience additional distress if there are delays for referral and others may be more upset if they feel rushed (Fisher and Lafarge 2015).

If a woman decides to continue the pregnancy, the member of staff who is caring for her should offer to arrange for her to discuss care options for her and her baby with her midwife, obstetrician and/or any relevant specialists (see also Chapter 8). If the baby is expected to die in utero, the woman should be offered scans to check the condition of the baby and an induction after the death. Parents should be offered support and the difficulty of waiting for the baby to die should be acknowledged by staff.

 She had Down's syndrome which caused her heart to be hopelessly underdeveloped. There was no intervention that could have saved her and we were told she could die in days or in weeks. We watched powerlessly on ultrasound as her heart beat slowed and faded. She died soon after and, perversely, her death was something of a relief. Her struggle was over; she died in the only place she had ever known. We were spared days or perhaps weeks of waiting and frequent visits to the hospital for repeat scans. Father

Communication between secondary and primary care staff regarding test results and parents' decisions

After a fetal anomaly is diagnosed or suspected, good communication between primary and secondary care staff is very important. Trusts, Health Boards and hospitals should have a policy that ensures prompt and accurate communication between secondary and primary care staff when a fetal anomaly is diagnosed or suspected.

Information sharing between healthcare teams is important as parents may want and expect to discuss test results, their options for the pregnancy or their decisions with their GP, community midwife or health visitor. Ongoing support from their GP may also be needed as they are responsible for providing parents with long-term care. Some primary care staff may be uncertain about what they can or should offer to women with a suspected or diagnosed fetal anomaly (Statham *et al.* 2003). Good communication between secondary and primary care staff will also help to ensure that primary care staff understand women's test results and know what support and information they should offer parents.

Training and support for staff who support parents to make informed choices about antenatal testing and results

Screening and diagnostic tests are often discussed with women and/or their partners by midwives but they may also be offered testing by other healthcare staff including an obstetrician or their GP. Results of tests may also be given by midwives, obstetricians, GPs, sonographers or other members of staff. It is important that all relevant staff receive training regarding sensitive communication, facilitating informed choice and breaking bad news (Lalor *et al.* 2007; RCOG 2010b; Lyus *et al.* 2014) (see also Chapter 4).

The available tests and information about these tests changes regularly and staff should ensure that their information is up-to-date when discussing screening and diagnostic tests with prospective, expectant or new parents. Staff who are discussing screening options and results with parents should also be provided with training regarding the testing involved and parents' choices for testing (Skirton and Barr 2010; Tsouroufli 2011). This is important as some staff may overestimate the amount of information that could be gained from screening and diagnostic tests or misunderstand the purpose or potential implications of testing (Skirton and Barr 2010). Antenatal Results and Choices is one organisation that offers training for healthcare professionals in communication with parents around testing and results.

Support should be available for staff who discuss results and pregnancy options with parents after a risk or diagnosis has been identified. ARC also offers support to healthcare professionals regarding decision-making around antenatal screening and diagnostic tests and the results of these tests.

CHAPTER 7

Continuing the pregnancy

Other relevant chapters

1: Providing holistic care

2: Providing inclusive care

3: Loss and grief

4: Communication

5: Communication across language and other barriers

6: Antenatal screening and diagnostic tests

11: Late miscarriage between 14 and 24 weeks' gestation and stillbirth

13: Care in neonatal units and neonatal death

Some parents whose baby is diagnosed with a fetal anomaly decide to continue their pregnancy even if their baby is unable or unexpected to survive. There may be a number of reasons why parents make a decision to continue the pregnancy under these circumstances (Wool 2013). Some parents may decide to continue the pregnancy as their baby's prognosis is uncertain. Some parents may feel that the diagnosis was made too late in the pregnancy for them to accept a termination. Other parents may want time to prepare for their baby's birth and death and possibly spend time with their baby after the birth. Some parents may find termination unacceptable for personal, religious, cultural or ethical reasons. Some parents may not believe the diagnosis or may find it too hard to accept.

 I do not regret for a moment continuing the pregnancy. It meant that we had six precious hours with our beautiful daughter and those hours mean so much to me. And although it was awful knowing so early in the pregnancy that she could not live, it meant we were able to prepare ourselves and other people, and to plan exactly how we wanted her birth and her short life to be. The doctors and midwives were surprised at our decision but they accepted it and supported us. Mother

Antenatal care when a baby is expected to die

Parents who decide to continue their pregnancy following the diagnosis of a life-limiting or potentially life-limiting fetal anomaly need sensitive, respectful and well-coordinated care and support (Statham *et al*. 2001). Women and their partners (if they have one) should be offered extra support during the remainder of their pregnancy and additional appointments to discuss care for them and their baby. It is important that support is extended to partners as this is also likely to be a very distressing situation for them (see *Fathers and same-sex partners* in Chapter 3).

> *The staff were great, really supported us and cared for us. There were only one or two people who seemed to think we had made a weird decision.*
> Mother

Any care provided should be individualised to meet the needs of parents and their specific situation. Wherever possible, parents' requests for their care should be accommodated. Some women may want to be treated as normally as possible during the remainder of their pregnancy (Wool 2013). These women may fully understand the situation but want to "enjoy a normal pregnancy" before their baby dies. Other women may find it hard to believe or accept a diagnosis of a life-limiting fetal anomaly. These women are likely to need time and support to help them absorb and process the diagnosis and they should not feel pressured to make non-urgent decisions about their or their baby's care.

If it is known that the baby will not live, the woman still needs routine antenatal care for her own health (BAPM 2010a). In these circumstances, some women will not want any more tests or ultrasound examinations unless these are essential for their own well-being. For other women, scans may offer a valuable opportunity to see their baby alive (Wool 2013) and/or may be helpful in confirming and explaining the diagnosis. Some partners may also find it important to see a scan, particularly if they were not present when an anomaly was identified during a previous ultrasound examination. A photograph of the ultrasound scan should also be offered to parents as some may appreciate having this keepsake of their baby (see also *Creating memories* in Chapter 14).

If there is a chance that treatment or other interventions may save the baby's life, women may be offered a constant stream of scans, tests or procedures. If the woman accepts this care, good co-ordination of her care is extremely important to ensure that her appointments run smoothly (see *Continuity of carers and staff communication after a fetal anomaly is diagnosed* below). Staff should acknowledge that it may be very stressful and distressing for parents to deal with prolonged uncertainty as they undergo further tests and procedures and wait for results. Parents may also find it distressing if they must travel to access this care (see also *Place of care during pregnancy* below). In addition to the care offered for the baby, staff should ensure that the woman is offered appropriate physical and emotional care for herself. During antenatal appointments, staff should make sure that a woman whose baby has a life-threatening condition does not feel like "a container for the baby" but is recognised as an expectant mother (Statham *et al*. 2001: 266; Wool 2013).

Continuity of carers and staff communication after a fetal anomaly is diagnosed

After a fetal anomaly is diagnosed, women should be offered continuity from the same carers for the remainder of their pregnancy (Lalor *et al*. 2007). Each woman should be assigned a named midwife and consultant obstetrician. She should also be given contact details for these staff members in case she has any questions or concerns between appointments (Lalor *et al*. 2007; BAPM 2010a).

You are going to have some questions when you go home, so you can ring me [consultant] or the midwife tomorrow and he circled the number and said that is no problem. Mother (Lalor *et al*. 2007: 85)

In addition to providing support and care for parents, the woman's named midwife should be responsible for co-ordinating the woman's care by:

- Guiding parents through the maternity care system and explaining the reasons for particular appointments, who they will see at each appointment and how to get there when necessary.

- Co-ordinating all staff who are providing care for the woman and ensuring that they are informed about the baby's diagnosis, the care plan and any changes to this information.

- Liaising with different departments, hospitals, the woman's GP, community midwife and/or health visitor to ensure smooth transitions between the care parents receive in different departments, hospitals and clinics.

- Ensuring that parents have verbal and written information about what to do if there is an emergency during the day and out of hours.

- Offering practical and emotional support to all staff who are caring for parents.

It is important, however, that the named midwife and consultant obstetrician are not the only staff that the woman sees during the remainder of her pregnancy. She should be introduced to a small team of staff who she can get to know and trust. These staff will be able to offer the woman care when her named midwife or obstetrician is unavailable, although it is important that the woman does not see a different member of staff at every antenatal visit (Chitty *et al*. 1996).

I have never seen the same two people … I am very wary of going up there now. Mother (Lalor *et al*. 2007: 85)

Good communication between staff, departments and/or hospitals is crucial to ensure that parents receive seamless care and consistent, up-to-date information. All staff (including receptionists) should be expecting parents for appointments (BAPM 2010a). This will help to ensure that parents do not have to explain themselves and will help to avoid inappropriate comments from staff (BAPM 2010a). Any staff who are caring for parents should also ensure that they have read the woman's medical notes before any appointment and be aware of any updates.

Place of care during pregnancy

Wherever possible, parents whose baby has been diagnosed with a fetal anomaly should be able to access antenatal care in their place of preference (Wool 2013). For some parents, it may be distressing to receive antenatal care or go for tests and procedures in the same place as other parents who are expecting healthy babies. To avoid unnecessary distress, women should be offered appointments to see their doctor or midwife in another clinic, out of hours or at home (Lalor *et al*. 2007; Wool 2013). However, it is important for staff to ensure that parents do not feel stigmatised or isolated and parents should be made aware that they can attend the standard antenatal clinic if they wish to do so.

If parents do not want to attend antenatal clinics with other parents and it is not possible to make other arrangements, staff should acknowledge that this may be distressing for parents. Parents should also be offered a private room to wait for appointments (BAPM 2010a).

Staff should also be aware that it may be difficult for parents to travel to appointments, particularly if they require care at a specialist fetal medicine unit that is some distance away from where they live. This potential difficulty for parents should be acknowledged. Wherever possible, funds should be available to help parents on low incomes with any travel costs associated with their care.

If the woman is admitted to the hospital for antenatal care, she should be offered a single room wherever possible. Staff should give the woman privacy during her stay but also take care to ensure that she does not become isolated. Staff may also need to be prepared for the anxieties that other women on the ward may experience if the woman chooses to tell them about her baby's prognosis.

Emotional support for parents

Parents may experience shock, grief and/or a mixture of other emotions after their baby is diagnosed with a life-limiting fetal anomaly (ARC [n.d.]). For some parents, these feelings may include grief for their expectation of a healthy baby and/or anticipatory grief for their baby who is expected to die (ARC [n.d.]; Bennett *et al*. 2011). Parents' feelings about the pregnancy may also be very conflicting. Some parents may feel that there is very little they can do except wait for their baby to die. Parents who are expecting their baby to die may find it difficult to consider their pregnancy further (ARC [n.d.])

and/or cope by expecting the worst outcome (Wool 2013). Other parents may find that normalising their pregnancy is an important coping strategy (Wool 2013).

Staff who are caring for parents during a pregnancy after a fetal anomaly is diagnosed should acknowledge parents' loss and the specific difficulties of their situation (Chitty *et al*. 1996; Lalor *et al*. 2007; Wool 2013). It is also important that staff offer parents ongoing emotional support throughout their pregnancy after their baby is diagnosed with a fetal anomaly (Bennett *et al*. 2011).

 I felt they cared – I was not just another interesting science experiment. They said we know this is very disappointing for us – focusing in on the emotional. Mother (Lalor *et al*. 2007: p.85)

Support from staff may be very important for parents who may feel isolated during this time (Wool 2013). Some parents may feel that their family members and friends find it difficult to listen as they talk about their distress and negative feelings. Parents may also be reluctant to talk about their feelings and situation for fear of having to deal with hurtful remarks, false reassurance and/or other people's distress as well as their own. Some parents may also find it helpful to talk to staff about what to say to relatives, friends and acquaintances and how to respond to any insensitive or unhelpful remarks.

Staff should offer parents time to talk about their feelings during appointments as parents may benefit from talking to someone who is able to supportively listen without judgement (see *Support and listening* in Chapter 15). Parents should also be offered an opportunity to see a counsellor and/or a genetic counsellor (if appropriate).

During any discussion with parents, it is important for staff to be sensitive to parents' needs while remaining realistic and focused on the current situation. Parents should not be offered false reassurances about the outcome of the pregnancy. Staff should also avoid talking about "when all this is over" or a future pregnancy (Statham *et al*. 2001: 175). Well-meaning attempts to provide unrealistic comfort or to distract parents from the situation may increase parents' distress and isolation by making them feel that they are unable to talk honestly with anyone.

Parents should also be given written information with the contact details of support organisations, such as Sands, Bliss, ARC, Child Bereavement UK and Together for Short Lives, who offer parents support when a fetal anomaly has been diagnosed and their baby is expected to die before, during or shortly after birth (see Appendix 2). Offering parents the details of these organisation may be particularly useful for some parents as they may find it easier to discuss their feelings with someone who is not involved in their care.

Parents with a multiple pregnancy should also be offered information about organisations that specifically offer support for parents having multiple births such as TAMBA or the MBF (see Appendix 2). See also *When one or more babies die during a multiple pregnancy* in Chapter 11 and *Parents with more than one baby* in Chapter 13.

Care planning for the woman and baby

When parents have decided to continue a pregnancy where their baby is expected to die, they should be offered an assessment of their baby's diagnosis and prognosis by a specialist fetal medicine network. These assessments are often critical for understanding the choices available to parents when planning for the pregnancy and birth. Assessments should take place at a specialist fetal medicine unit and parents may need to travel some distance from their home and/or referring hospital for these appointments. If possible, support should be available to facilitate parents' travel if needed (see *Place of care during pregnancy* above).

It is essential that any information gained from these specialist fetal medicine assessments is communicated to the woman's midwifery and obstetric team as soon as possible (see *Continuity of carers and staff communication after a fetal anomaly is diagnosed* above). Women should then be offered an appointment for a multidisciplinary meeting with the key staff who will be involved in their care. This meeting will often take place at the woman's local hospital and should always include her named consultant obstetrician and midwife who will oversee her care during the remainder of her pregnancy and her labour and birth. Other people should be involved in this meeting as appropriate. For example, it may be appropriate to invite a genetic counsellor, a consultant neonatologist, a neonatal nurse and/or the labour ward manager or their deputy. The woman should be invited to bring her partner and/or another supporter to this meeting.

The purpose of this multidisciplinary meeting is to develop an individualised care plan that is based on the specialist fetal medicine network assessment and the woman's wishes (Wool 2013). This meeting should also aim to determine the support needs of the whole family (Breeze *et al*. 2007). During this meeting staff should:

- *Confirm and discuss the baby's diagnosis and prognosis with parents and answer any questions that parents have*. Staff should ensure that parents understand the diagnosis and prognosis and that they have as much information as they want about the baby's condition and the pregnancy. Any information that is discussed with parents should be sensitively conveyed, tailored for their situation, unbiased, clear and up-to date (Wool 2013). Some parents will want a lot of information while other parents may want very little information. Some parents may also want to know the baby's sex to help them bond with the baby and staff should tell them this information if it is known.

- *Based on the most likely outcome for the baby and any other possible outcomes, staff should offer to fully explain the available care options for the woman and baby*. Staff should then support the woman to make informed decisions about her care and feel as in control of what is happening as possible (see *Giving information and facilitating informed choice* in Chapter 4). With the woman's consent, staff should also ensure that the woman's partner (when relevant) is included in decision making if they want to be involved (Lalor *et al*. 2007).

- *Discuss and agree a care plan for the woman during the rest of the pregnancy and during the labour and birth*. Parents may also wish to make a birth plan and prepare for their baby's birth (BAPM 2010a; Breeze and Lees 2013).

  - The details of the place where the woman will labour and give birth should be discussed – for example, at a specialist unit, the local hospital or at home (BAPM 2010a). When planning for the place of care during labour and birth, it is important to consider the woman's wishes, the likelihood of the baby's survival and any interventions that might be needed for the woman and/or baby. If the woman is to be transferred to a specialist unit to give birth, she should be offered the opportunity to visit the hospital beforehand to meet and talk with the staff who will be caring for her and her baby. Funding should be available to help parents on low incomes with travel costs (see *Place of care during pregnancy* above).

  - Parents should also be told if it is likely that pre-term labour will occur or the baby will die before or during labour (Breeze and Lees 2013).

  - If the baby is not expected to survive, it is important to make sure that no inappropriate intervention is made during the labour and birth (BAPM 2010a). For example, a caesarean section should normally only be offered if it is necessary for the woman's well-being or she requests this procedure (BAPM 2010a; Kilby *et al*. 2011; Breeze and Lees 2013).

  - If there is a chance that the baby might live, the various options for the labour and birth (including monitoring of the baby) should be discussed with the woman (BAPM 2010a; Breeze and Lees 2013). Staff should offer to discuss how choosing to monitor the baby during labour may mean that a woman planning for a vaginal birth will need to consider a caesarean or instrumental birth if the baby is in distress (BAPM 2010a; Breeze and Lees 2013).

- *Discuss and agree a care plan for the baby if they are born alive*. This may involve planning palliative care or active treatment if there is a chance that the baby could live. If the baby's prognosis is unclear, this may also involve anticipatory parallel care planning for both active and palliative care (see *Antenatal palliative and parallel care planning* below). In the case of a multiple pregnancy, a separate care plan should be drawn up for each baby (BAPM 2010a) (see also *Parents with more than one baby* in Chapter 13).

- *Determine which staff will be present during the labour and birth and put systems in place to ensure that there will be clear and consistent communication between everyone involved, throughout the pregnancy, birth and postnatal period* (Kilby *et al*. 2011) (see *Continuity of carers and staff communication after a fetal anomaly is diagnosed* above).

- *Offer parents any additional specialist appointments that are relevant for the care of the baby or woman*. For example, parents should be offered an appointment with a neonatologist to discuss the baby's care and an opportunity to visit the neonatal intensive care unit (Wool 2013) (see also Chapter 13).

Meetings with parents should not be rushed and staff should allow time to discuss the plan with parents in detail and explain anything that parents do not understand (Lalor *et al*. 2007). The care plan that is agreed by the woman and healthcare staff should be clearly documented in the woman's hospital notes and she should be given a copy of the care plan for her hand-held notes (BAPM 2010a). Staff should advise the woman to carry her hand-held notes containing the care plan in case she goes into labour unexpectedly and the baby is born elsewhere (Breeze *et al.* 2007). Copies should also be sent as appropriate to the specialist fetal medicine unit, the referring hospital, the woman's GP, her community midwifery team, the consultant neonatologist and/or consultant paediatrician.

The planning meeting may be very stressful for parents and it may be difficult for them to absorb everything that was discussed and decided. Therefore, the woman's named midwife should offer to arrange a follow-up appointment with parents to go through the care plan again. This appointment will help to ensure that parents understand and agree with everything that was discussed and decided at the multidisciplinary meeting.

As the pregnancy progresses, the plan should be continuously reviewed with parents to reflect any changes in the woman's wishes, her or the baby's condition or place of care (BAPM 2010a; Kilby *et al.* 2011). If any changes are made to the care plan, these updates should be documented and copies of the updated plan should be given to the woman and all relevant healthcare staff as soon as possible (BAPM 2010a).

Antenatal palliative and parallel care planning

Staff should offer all parents information about the available palliative care options when their baby has been diagnosed with a potentially life-limiting fetal anomaly (BAPM 2010a; Wool 2013; Wilkinson *et al.* 2014). Staff should also gently explain that palliative care involves supportive care to promote the well-being of the whole family and not only end of life care (BAPM 2010a; Kilby *et al.* 2011).

If parents accept this offer, they can be referred for palliative care discussions antenatally, even if their baby's prognosis is uncertain (BAPM 2010a; Wilkinson *et al.* 2014). Staff should also be aware of any local children's hospices that accept antenatal referrals for palliative care and offer parents information and a referral for these services.

Antenatal palliative care discussions should involve parents and a multidisciplinary team of healthcare professionals (BAPM 2010a). This team of healthcare staff should include the woman's named midwife and consultant obstetrician as well as staff from the neonatal unit, the community team, a hospice and/or any other relevant specialists that are involved in the baby's or woman's care (BAPM 2010a).

During these discussions, the benefits of palliative care, such as ensuring that the baby is comfortable and pain-free, should be explained to parents, particularly if they are uncertain about or unaware of the need for this care (Bliss 2010; Larcher *et al.* 2015). It is important that parents know their options for their baby's care and that their baby will receive the best possible care if they are born alive (see also *Continuing care when life-sustaining treatment is withdrawn or withheld* in Chapter 13).

If the baby is expected to die, staff should offer to discuss options for resuscitating the baby with parents. Any decisions that parents make about resuscitation should be clearly documented in the woman's notes and communicated to all staff. However, parents should be made aware that this decision may need to be reconsidered after the baby is born if resuscitation appears to be in the baby's best interest (Chiswick 2008; Wilkinson *et al*. 2014).

If the baby may live for some time after the birth, it is important that parents are gently prepared for this possibility and that staff offer to discuss parents' options for this care and its location (Wilkinson *et al*. 2014) (see *Care and discussions with parents when a baby may live for a while following the move to palliative care* in Chapter 13).

If there is uncertainty about the baby's prognosis, it is important that this is clearly discussed with parents (Breeze and Lees 2013) and that staff acknowledge any additional distress that this uncertainty may cause (ARC [n.d.]). In these instances, staff should gently suggest parallel planning of palliative and active care for the baby to parents. Having a parallel care plan in place will help to ensure that the baby receives care that is in their best interest after the birth (Wilkinson *et al*. 2014) (See also *Making decisions about critical care* in Chapter 13).

Staff should also offer to discuss parents' options for spending time or holding their baby when they are born and/or die (see *Discussing redirection of care with parents* in Chapter 13), creating memories with their baby (see *Creating memories* in Chapter 14) and any emotional support that parents or other siblings may benefit from accessing (BAPM 2010a).

Parents should be given time to consider all of their options and make the decisions that are right for them and their family. Any decisions made during palliative care discussions with parents should be documented and included in the care plans devised for the woman's antenatal care, the labour and birth and the baby's care (BAPM 2010a) (see *Care planning for the woman and baby* above).

Antenatal classes for parents after a fetal anomaly is diagnosed

Many parents, especially if this is their first baby, will want information about labour, giving birth and their options for pain relief and positions for labour. Despite wanting this information, parents whose baby has been diagnosed with a fetal anomaly may not feel able to attend a standard antenatal class (Kobler *et al*. 2012).

Parents whose baby has been diagnosed with a fetal anomaly should be offered individual preparation sessions with a childbirth educator who is aware of the potential challenges that these parents may be facing. The childbirth educator should be able to tailor information about parent's options for labour, birth, the baby's care and creating memories with the baby based on the parents' individual needs and situation (Kobler *et al*. 2012).

It may be a helpful starting point during these sessions for the childbirth educator to ask parents about their particular questions, concerns and wishes regarding the labour and birth (Kobler *et al*. 2012). In addition to discussing parents' options for the labour and birth and their baby's care, a childbirth educator may also be able to offer parents emotional support before and after the birth by giving parents opportunities to discuss their feelings and experiences (Kobler *et al*. 2012).

Support for parents during labour and birth

Continuous support and care should be available to parents during the labour, birth and postnatal period (see also Chapter 12). Additionally, the woman should be cared for in labour by members of the team that provided her care during the pregnancy. This continuity of carers will help to ensure that parents receive care from staff who are fully aware of their situation and wishes.

For women who know that the birth will cause their baby's death, staff should be aware that the process of pushing the baby out can be extremely distressing.

> *I knew my baby was alive and safe inside me but I also knew that when he was born he would die. It made pushing the last thing I wanted to do. It was a truly horrendous situation to be in.* Mother

If the baby is born alive and the parents have decided against resuscitation, staff should not attempt to resuscitate the baby after the birth. However, this decision may need to be reconsidered if the parents change their mind or the baby's prognosis changes after birth (see *Making decisions about withdrawing or withholding life-sustaining treatment* in Chapter 13). If a baby is not receiving active care, palliative care should be provided to keep the baby as comfortable as possible (see *If a baby may be born alive but is expected to die during or shortly after birth* in Chapter 12).

Parents also should be offered opportunities to see and hold their baby before, during and after the baby's death if the baby is expected to die shortly after the birth. Staff should be aware that some parents will want to be with their baby while others may prefer for the baby to be cared for by staff in the neonatal unit (see also *Being with the baby and caring for the family when the baby dies* in Chapter 13).

I was referred for a specialist heart scan when I was 20 weeks as there is a family history of heart defects. I was very nervous and my worst fears came true – my baby had a serious heart defect. They asked me to decide if I wanted to continue with the pregnancy – for me this was an easy decision as I believe that every life is sacred. When he was born, we were shocked to find that he also had a hole in his skull. He was taken to special care, but then they said that there was nothing more they could do to save him. So they took the tubes out and I held my baby until he died. I do not regret my decision to continue with the pregnancy as I got to spend three precious days with my baby boy. Thankfully I now have three healthy children. Mother

If the baby dies, parents should be offered:

- Opportunities to spend time and create memories with their baby (see Chapter 14).

- Information about postnatal care (see Chapter 15).

- The relevant information about registering their baby's stillbirth, birth and/or death (see Chapter 19).

- Opportunities to discuss having a post mortem examination of their baby to confirm the diagnosis of the fetal anomaly (Breeze and Lees 2013) (see Chapter 16).

- Opportunities to discuss their options for burying, cremating or having a funeral for their baby (see Chapter 20).

CHAPTER 8

Termination of pregnancy for fetal anomaly or maternal medical conditions

Other relevant chapters

1: Providing holistic care

2: Providing inclusive care

3: Loss and grief

4: Communication

5: Communication across language and other barriers

6: Antenatal screening and diagnostic tests

12: Labour and birth when a baby has died

14: After a loss

Some of the information in this chapter applies primarily to care provided in England, Wales and Scotland. It is important to be aware that different legislation is in place in Northern Ireland where fetal anomaly alone is not recognised as a ground for termination of pregnancy (RCOG, 2011a; DHSSPSNI 2013) (see *Northern Ireland* under *Legal requirements for performing a termination of pregnancy for fetal anomaly or a maternal medical condition* below).

Parents' experiences of termination of pregnancy for fetal anomaly or a maternal medical condition

 The pain of loss, and the pain of being the one to make the decision to create that loss, are the hardest things I will ever have to bear. Mother

Parents who decide to have a termination of pregnancy for fetal anomaly or a maternal medical condition at any gestation may feel a range of emotions including grief, anger, guilt and/or relief that they found out in time to make a decision about the pregnancy

(ARC 2012). Parents may also experience other feelings such as doubt, anxiety, failure, shame, self-blame, vulnerability and loneliness. Parents may be expecting some of these feelings but may be surprised by other feelings that they experience (ARC 2012). Staff should reassure parents that their feelings are not unusual and that everyone grieves in their own way (ARC 2012).

 She couldn't have lived, and she was only 18 weeks when she died, but I loved her as much as I love my two boys. Mother

The intensity of grief that may be experienced by parents who decide to terminate a pregnancy for fetal anomaly can be as profound as that of any other parent who experiences the death of their baby (Zeanah *et al*. 1993; Statham *et al*. 2001) (see also *Parents' experiences and expressions of grief* in Chapter 3). For many parents, the additional burden of having decided to end the pregnancy may make it more difficult for them to come to terms with their loss. This may be the case even if their decision was well thought through. That said, it is important to remember that every experience is individual and the feelings and responses of parents who decide to terminate a pregnancy for fetal anomaly or a maternal medical condition may be influenced by many factors.

Providing care for parents undergoing termination for fetal anomaly or a maternal medical condition

Many women who have had a termination of pregnancy for fetal anomaly have expressed some level of dissatisfaction with their care (Fisher and Lafarge 2015) This finding is significant as a parent's satisfaction with their care may affect their emotional well-being following the termination (Fisher and Lafarge 2015).

Women should be offered continuity of carer when they have decided to terminate a pregnancy for fetal anomaly or a maternal medical condition (RCOG 2010b; Fisher and Lafarge 2015). Having this continuity, particularly from a named and experienced midwife, may help to ensure that women are able to make informed decisions about their care and are not exposed to inappropriate or hurtful comments from care providers (Fisher and Lafarge 2015).

It is also important that there is good communication between all staff and that staff read a woman's notes before meeting with her to ensure that they are aware of her situation and provide appropriate care (Fisher and Lafarge 2015).

[Unhelpful] Being handed a leaflet about dealing with a miscarriage almost immediately afterwards when I was clearly dealing with an awful decision which was NOT a miscarriage. Parent (Fisher and Lafarge 2015: 11–12)

Parents may experience additional distress if they perceive staff to be unsupportive or disapproving of their decision to terminate the pregnancy (Statham 2002; RCOG 2010b). It is important that parents receive supportive, empathetic, non-judgemental care and information from staff so that parents can make decisions about terminating their pregnancy that are right for them (Fisher and Lafarge 2015). Empathetic care may also be crucial for parents who fear being judged for their decision (Fisher and Lafarge 2015).

Except in the case of an emergency, any staff member who has a conscientious objection to termination should refer the woman's termination care to another member of staff as soon as possible (RCOG 2011a; GMC 2013b; BMA 2014; NMC 2015). Wherever possible, managers should also support staff with a conscientious objection to opt out of providing care before and after the termination procedure to ensure that parents receive the best care possible (RCN 2013) (see also *Conscientious objection* in Chapter 9*).*

Discussion and planning

Once parents have decided to have a termination for fetal anomaly or a maternal medical condition, staff should offer to discuss the woman's options for her care including the termination procedures that are offered locally and in other areas (where necessary) (see *Discussing termination of pregnancy procedures* below). However, it is important that parents are given adequate information so that they know what to expect and can make informed choices about their care (Fisher and Lafarge 2015). It has been highlighted that parents do not always receive sufficient information about their options or are unable to process the information given in this situation (Fisher and Lafarge 2015). It is important that staff offer to repeat information to parents and that parents have a named contact who is available to discuss any questions and concerns that they may have (Fisher and Lafarge 2015).

Staff should acknowledge the difficulty of these unique circumstances for parents who are planning a termination for a wanted baby (Fisher and Lafarge 2015). They should also ensure that they use the language that parents use when referring to their baby. For example, some parents may use the word "baby" or refer to the baby by name, others may be more comfortable with "fetus" and some may be distressed by the use of terms such as "products of conception" (Fisher and Lafarge 2015).

 I was made to feel like my baby wasn't a baby. Parent (Fisher and Lafarge 2015: 12)

> *The midwife was a natural birth midwife and kept referring to the fetus as a baby which I found upsetting.* Parent (Fisher and Lafarge 2015: 12)

Staff should sensitively offer to tell parents how the baby is likely to look and how this may be affected by the type of termination procedure used.

> *I was really scared about how my baby would look. Nobody mentioned it and I didn't dare ask.* Mother

Some parents who have had a termination for a fetal anomaly have also welcomed suggestions and valued opportunities for seeing and creating memories with their baby (Moulder 1998; Statham *et al.* 2001). Staff should sensitively offer to discuss parents' options for seeing, touching, holding and/or creating memories with their baby and normalise these choices when speaking to parents (see Chapter 14 for more information). Some parents may also want to have a blessing or other type of ceremony for the baby before or after the termination procedure (see Chapters 20 and 21).

Some parents may want to discuss other concerns with staff. For example, parents may want to discuss what they would like say to other people about their loss, whether they want visitors if they will be in hospital after the termination and/or whether they will want cards or flowers to be delivered. If parents have decided not to tell family members and friends about the termination, it is extremely important that staff are aware of this decision and reassure parents that complete confidentiality will be maintained (ARC 2005).

Written information that has been specifically compiled for parents who decide to terminate a pregnancy for fetal anomaly or a maternal medical condition should be given to parents. This should include information about the available local termination procedures, where the procedures are performed, after care and the details of support organisations such as ARC (see Appendix 2). This information should be available in other languages and formats.

Discussing termination of pregnancy procedures

As most women whose baby is diagnosed with a severe fetal anomaly decide to terminate the pregnancy, midwives and other staff working with pregnant women should be aware of all the available termination options (Lyus *et al*. 2014; Fisher *et al*. 2015). This will help to ensure that parents receive the best and most supportive care possible when making decisions about termination (Lyus *et al*. 2014).

Regardless of gestation, terminations can be performed medically (using medicines to induce the expulsion of the pregnancy) or surgically (the physical removal of the pregnancy from the uterus using surgical tools such as vacuum aspiration or forceps). However, a medical termination is usually performed after 24 weeks' gestation.

It is important to be aware, however, that local policies may differ regarding what procedures are offered at different gestations. Most women who are considering a termination after 14 weeks' gestation are offered a medical termination in a hospital setting and may be unaware or surprised that they are expected to labour and give birth to their dead baby (RCOG 2010b; Fisher *et al*. 2015). This information should be sensitively explained to women when they are being given information about medical procedures (RCOG 2010b). Women who opt for a medical termination should also be offered information about their choices for the labour, birth and pain relief. They may also want to plan for this experience (see Chapter 12).

Some women may feel daunted by the prospect of labouring and giving birth to their dead baby and provisions should be made for a woman to access a surgical termination if she would prefer this procedure as this can be accommodated by independent sector providers who are contracted by the NHS. Women who decide to have a surgical termination of pregnancy should be gently prepared for waking up after the surgery and no longer being pregnant and the potential effects of the general anaesthetic (ARC 2012).

In any situation, it is important that women seeking terminations receive accurate, realistic and accessible information about the termination methods available to them, what each procedure involves, what to expect before and after procedures and the potential risks and complications of each procedure (Fisher and Lafarge 2015; Fisher *et al*. 2015). This information should include the relevant information about the expected length of each procedure, how long a woman will need to stay in a hospital or clinic and any arrangements that she needs to make to travel home afterwards. This information may be particularly important for women who need to arrange childcare or make other arrangements for their absence from home or work (ARC 2012).

Women should also be told where procedures will be performed (for example, in a gynaecological ward, day clinic or on labour ward) and whether other women will be having different procedures in the same place (including terminations for other reasons) (RCOG 2010b; Fisher and Lafarge 2015). The location of the procedure may be important for some women and they may be distressed if they are admitted to the "wrong ward" (Fisher and Lafarge 2015). For example, some parents may find it difficult if they are on labour ward and are able to hear crying babies or are leaving the unit without their baby (Fisher and Lafarge 2015). Other parents may feel that their wanted pregnancy is unacknowledged if they are admitted to a gynaecological ward or independent clinic, particularly if other women are having terminations in the same place for non-medical reasons (Fisher and Lafarge 2015).

Parents should also be gently offered information about post mortem examinations and how the termination procedure used may affect their post mortem examination options for their baby (Fisher *et al*. 2015) (see *Discussing a post mortem examination with the parents* in Chapter 16).

Women should be supported to access the termination procedure of their choice (Fisher and Lafarge 2015; Fisher *et al*. 2015). This is important as women's ability to access their procedure of choice may have implications for how they experience the termination (Lyus *et al*. 2014; Fisher and Lafarge 2015). If women are not able to access their procedure of choice through the healthcare service, they should be given information about independent sector services that provide these procedures (Fisher and Lafarge 2015). Some women may be willing to travel and/or pay for a private procedure in areas where there is no contract between an independent clinic and the healthcare service (Fisher and Lafarge 2015). If possible, support and funding should be available for women on a low income who need to travel to access the procedure of their choice.

Termination of pregnancy before 21 weeks + 6 days' gestation

It is uncommon for a baby to be born alive following a medical termination before 21 weeks + 6 days' gestation (RCOG 2010b). However, women who undergo a medical termination before 21 weeks + 6 days' gestation should be prepared for this possibility (RCOG 2010b). These women should be gently and sensitively told that the baby may make movements at birth but that this does not mean that the baby could survive even with intensive care.

In circumstances where the baby is born alive, parents should be offered palliative comfort care for the baby (including pain relief, warmth and fluids when appropriate) and staff should have training to provide this care (RCOG 2010b). Parents should also be told that they can see, touch and hold the baby if they wish, regardless of whether the baby is born alive or dead (see *Moving to and providing palliative care for babies and their families* in Chapter 13).

Termination of pregnancy at or after 21 weeks + 6 days' gestation

The RCOG (2010b) recommends that feticide (where an injection is administered using an ultrasound scan to bring about fetal asystole) is used for terminations that take place after 21 weeks + 6 days' gestation. The RCOG also states that:

> The only exception to this rule is when the fetal abnormality itself is so severe as to make early neonatal death inevitable irrespective of the gestation at delivery. (RCOG 2010b: 29)

Despite this recommendation, it is not a legal requirement for women to have feticide for a termination of pregnancy that is performed at or after 21 weeks + 6 days' gestation and women should not be pressured to have this procedure.

When feticide is discussed, it is very important that the woman is told what the procedure involves, where it will be performed and what she may feel during and after the procedure. The woman also needs to know when and where her labour will be induced after the feticide procedure (see *Induction* in Chapter 12).

Some women may decide to have feticide as they feel that their baby will not suffer during the labour and birth. Other parents may decide not to have feticide before the termination and this decision should be respected (Nuffield 2006: 4.16). Staff should gently tell the parents that if the baby is born alive with a non-lethal anomaly, the baby may survive and care will need to be administered that is in the baby's best interests (RCOG 2010b) (see *Making decisions about critical care* in Chapter 13). Parents should also be assured that palliative comfort care will be available if the baby is born alive but is expected to die (see *Moving to and providing palliative care for babies and their families* in Chapter 13). The healthcare team should involve the parents in any care planning if the baby is born alive.

If the termination is to be performed after 24 weeks' gestation, the parents must also be told that the stillbirth will need to be registered if the baby is born dead or that the birth and death of the baby will need to be registered if the baby is born alive and then dies (see *Certification following a termination after 24 weeks' gestation* in Chapter 19).

Travelling to a fetal medicine unit

In many cases, women need to travel a considerable distance to and from another unit to have feticide performed by a fetal medicine specialist (RCOG 2010b). If the local obstetric unit is unable to offer the procedure, staff should be aware that this travel may increase parents' distress and ensure that support is in place for parents (RCOG 2010b).

A woman travelling to a different unit should be given a map and clear information about how to get there. The staff in the unit should be expecting her so that they can welcome her without her having to explain why she has come (RCOG 2010b). If she is planning to travel alone, staff should discuss with her whether she might like to travel with her partner or another supporter so that she does have to make the journey alone. Women who plan to travel by car should be told that they should not drive themselves. If possible, funding should also be available to help with travel costs for parents on low incomes.

 Travelling to the fetal medicine unit for the feticide was the hardest journey I have ever made. I knew Ella couldn't live but she was my baby and I loved her just as much as I love her brothers. I always will. Mother

Selective termination and feticide

Women having a multiple pregnancy may be offered selective termination or feticide if one or more of their babies is diagnosed with a fetal anomaly. Since 1990, selective feticide has been covered under the Abortion Act even though the woman will remain pregnant following the termination (RCOG 2010b).

Parents who are considering selective termination or feticide should be offered full information about the procedures offered for the gestation, chorionicity and amnionicity of the pregnancy. It is important that the risks to other babies are explained for each procedure including the risk that the procedure may also cause the death of other babies (RCOG 2010b). Parents may need time to consider the available options and should be offered support and counselling if they want to discuss their concerns or the particular issues surrounding selective termination or feticide.

The woman should also be told about any physical changes that she might notice after the baby has died and any potential side effects of drugs that may be offered to prevent premature labour. Some parents may find the idea of the dead baby remaining in the womb beside the living baby or babies disturbing while other parents may find the thought comforting (MBF 1997b). The woman should also be told about what to expect during the remainder of the pregnancy, labour and birth (see also *When one or more babies die during a multiple pregnancy* in Chapter 11).

Some parents may also want to discuss what to tell family, friends and/or other siblings (including the surviving babies as they grow up) (see *Multiple pregnancies* in Chapter 3). Parents may also welcome suggestions and discussions about naming the baby, creating memories and/or arranging a funeral after the babies are born (see Chapters 14 and 20).

If feticide is to be carried out after 24 weeks' gestation, parents must also be told that they are required to register the stillbirth of the baby who has died (see *Certification following a termination after 24 weeks' gestation* in Chapter 19).

Once the feticide has been carried out, staff should inform their colleagues who will be providing the woman's ongoing maternity care. This will help staff to avoid making inappropriate comments and ensure that the woman does not need to explain what has happened. For example, the woman should not have to explain the situation to a sonographer if the dead baby is seen during a subsequent ultrasound examination. Informing the relevant staff requires a careful communication plan, especially if the feticide has taken place at a specialist centre that is not linked to the obstetric or midwifery teams who are providing the woman's maternity care.

Staff should also be aware that parents may experience very mixed feelings when the babies are born even if they are certain about their decision to have a selective termination. Parents may feel intense grief for the baby who died while also experiencing joy for the birth of the surviving baby or babies (see *Multiple births* in Chapter 14). Staff should acknowledge the baby who has died and offer parents opportunities to talk about the baby. Parents may also find it helpful to talk to other parents who have had similar experiences and they should be given the contact details of the relevant support organisations including ARC, Sands, TAMBA and the MBF (see Appendix 2).

Multifetal pregnancy reduction

If a woman has a multiple pregnancy, she may be offered fetal reduction to reduce the risks for the mother, the risks of losing the pregnancy or the possibility of going into very premature labour. These risks must be considered in relation to the risks of the termination procedure, including the potential loss of the pregnancy. Parents should be offered clear, unbiased information about all options and any associated risks so that they can make a fully informed choice (see *Giving information and facilitating informed choice* in Chapter 4). Staff should also offer parents information about fetal reduction procedures (using a transvaginal or transabdominal ultrasound-guided needle to aspirate or inject the fetus) (Dodd and Crowther 2012). Parents should be made aware that the fetuses that have died will remain in the uterus but will not harm the surviving baby or babies and that there are unlikely to be any visible remains after the birth of the surviving baby or babies if the procedure is carried out in early pregnancy.

Parents must then be given as much time as they need to consider their options and make a decision about reducing the pregnancy that is right for them (Fraser 2010). For many parents, this may be a very difficult decision and they should not feel pressured to make a decision (Fraser 2010). While making their decision, parents should also be offered support from staff, a referral for counselling and information about support organisations such as TAMBA and the MBF (see Appendix 2).

Parents may or may not decide to reduce the pregnancy for a variety of reasons (Dodd and Crowther 2012). When parents make a decision, this should be documented in the woman's notes and the decision should be respected and supported (Maifeld *et al*. 2003).

Parents who decide to have fetal reduction should be offered sensitive care and emotional support from staff before, during and after the procedure (Bergh *et al*. 1999). Support from staff may very important for parents who may feel very isolated around the time of making the decision, undergoing the procedure and/or after the birth of the surviving baby or babies. Some parents may not feel able to talk about their feelings with family members and friends who may not understand the complexity of the decision or the distress that parents may be feeling (Bergh *et al*. 1999).

While most parents feel that they made the right decision after a successful fetal reduction, they may also experience mixed emotions after deciding to reduce their pregnancy which may include grief, guilt and/or a fear of criticism (Bryan 2002; Fraser 2010). Some parents may also find the random selection of the fetus or fetuses for reduction to be distressing and may struggle with the idea of how it was decided which fetus would die (Fraser 2010; Denton and Bryan 2002). For parents who have had fertility treatment, it may also feel particularly bizarre and frightening to decide to terminate one or more fetuses after their struggle to become pregnant. Parents may appreciate an offer from staff to discuss how they are feeling before, during or after the procedure. Staff should also offer to refer parents for counselling.

Parents may also want to discuss what to say to the surviving children and what they might tell them in years to come (Fraser 2010). If the parents are planning not to tell other children, they should be aware that their children may inadvertently find out if parents discussed the reduction with family members or friends (Fraser 2010; MBF 1997b). Parents should be told about available counselling and support that they will be able to access in the future if they want support before or after telling their other children about the reduction.

Continuous support should be available for parents throughout the procedure as they are likely to find the reduction procedure stressful and distressing. It is also important that the staff carrying out the procedure are sensitive to the parents' needs and feelings. For example, staff should ensure that any discussion about which fetus to select is discreet and cannot be overheard by the parents.

After the surviving babies are born, staff should be aware that parents may also experience immediate and/or long-term grief. With the woman's consent, staff should inform the woman's midwife, GP and/or health visitor of the fetal reduction so that they can offer ongoing support and care for parents (see also Chapters 14 and 17).

Legal requirements for performing a termination of pregnancy for fetal anomaly or a maternal medical condition

England, Wales and Scotland

Once a woman gives consent for a termination procedure, two doctors will need to verify that the conditions for termination have been met (except in an emergency) (RCOG 2010b). For terminations before 24 weeks' gestation, these can be performed under section 1(1)(a) of the Abortion Act 1967 and Section 37 of the Human Fertilisation and Embryology Act 1990 (see also *Termination of pregnancy and the law* in Chapter 9).

For terminations after 24 weeks' gestation, the practitioner must verify as per Section 1(1) of the Abortion Act 1967 that:

> *(b)* the termination is necessary to prevent grave permanent injury to the physical or mental health of the pregnant woman; or

> *(c)* the continuance of the pregnancy would involve risk to the life of the pregnant woman, greater than if the pregnancy were terminated; or

> *(d)* there is a substantial risk that, if the child were born, it would suffer from such physical or mental abnormalities as to be seriously handicapped (Ground E on the abortion notification form).

It is important to note that no legal definition exists for "substantial risk" or "seriously handicapped" and that each baby would need to be assessed on a case-by-case basis (RCOG 2010b). The RCOG (2010b) recommends that doctors consult maternal-fetal medicine specialists and/or colleagues with experience in treating the condition in question if a given situation is not straightforward. The legislation also does not impose a gestational limit for terminations that satisfy the necessary criteria after 24 weeks' gestation (Fisher & Lafarge 2015).

While many staff may find the feticide procedure distressing, the primary concern for most fetal medicine specialists is ensuring that it is lawfully performed (RCOG 2010b). If a practitioner does not feel that a termination is required for fetal anomaly before 24 weeks' gestation, the woman should be able to have the procedure performed under another clause in the Abortion Act (RCOG 2010b). If the practitioner still does not feel that the grounds for a termination are met or the pregnancy has exceeded 24 weeks' gestation, they should refer the woman to another doctor for a second opinion without delay (RCOG 2010b). If a woman is not offered a termination under these circumstances, she should be offered emotional support and counselling with a referral being made as soon as possible if she accepts this offer (RCOG 2010b).

Northern Ireland

The Abortion Act does not extend to Northern Ireland where operations carried out to terminate pregnancies are unlawful unless there is a threat to the life of the mother or a risk of real and serious adverse harm to her long-term or permanent health (Sections 58 and 59 of the Offences Against the Person Act 1861 and Section 25(1) of the Criminal Justice Act (Northern Ireland) 1945, as interpreted by case law). In Northern Ireland, fetal anomaly alone is not recognised as a ground for termination (RCOG 2011a; DHSSPSNI 2013). However, women from Northern Ireland may qualify for a termination if there is a risk to her life or a long-term or permanent risk to her physical or mental health. Women are also able to travel to other parts of the UK to undergo a termination, although this may be difficult and distressing for women.

During the termination procedure

When a woman arrives for a termination procedure, all staff should be aware of the reason for her appointment so that she does not need to explain her situation and to avoid inappropriate comments from staff (RCOG 2010b). Good co-ordination and communication is needed between staff making the referral and the unit or clinic (including independent sector services) where the procedure is being performed to ensure that women receive the best care possible (Fisher and Lafarge 2015). It is important that parents do not need to wait in waiting areas with other pregnant women or women who are having a termination for reasons other than a fetal anomaly or a maternal medical condition (Fisher and Lafarge 2015).

 I fully support women's choice to have terminations, but at the time, it was hard to be in the same room as many young girls, when I did not want to be there at all. I did not have a choice as the diagnosis meant my baby would die anyway. Parent (Fisher and Lafarge 2015: 11)

Privacy is important for many parents and each woman should be offered a private room where she will be cared for during and after the termination regardless of the type of procedure that is being performed or the location (RCOG 2010b; Fisher and Lafarge 2015). Women should also be able to have their partner or another supporter with them at all times.

Careful thought should be given to which staff should be present during the procedure (Statham *et al.* 2001). Parents must be asked for consent if medical students want to be present during the termination. Parents should be told that they can refuse to have medical students in the room and should not feel pressured to give their consent.

Staff should be available to stay with parents during the procedure and the labour and birth if relevant. Some parents may ask for privacy at times but they should not feel abandoned and should know how to call for staff if needed (see also Chapter 12). Women should also have access to sufficient pain relief (Fisher and Lafarge 2015) (see *Pain management* in Chapter 12).

> *It was a very busy maternity ward and the midwives did not spend much time with me. I ultimately gave birth to my baby on the toilet into a bedpan in the absence of any midwives with my husband with me, which was a horrific experience for both of us.* Mother (Fisher and Lafarge 2015: 9)

During a feticide procedure, the ultrasound screen should be placed so that parents or any other supporters are unable to see it unless they wish to look. A woman should also be offered sedation if she feels unable to cope with the feticide procedure. Fetal asystole will be checked shortly after the procedure and should be reconfirmed using ultrasound approximately 30 to 60 minutes following the procedure (RCOG 2010b). Some parents may want to see the screen afterwards if they want confirmation that the baby is dead.

Care after the termination procedure

It is important that women are offered appropriate care following the termination procedure and that staff (including those in the private sector) are aware of their potential needs (RCOG 2010b; Fisher and Lafarge 2015). For example, some women may find it distressing if they are offered contraception following a termination procedure for fetal anomaly or a maternal medical condition (Fisher and Lafarge 2015). Parents should also be offered opportunities to see, hold or create memories with their baby (see Chapter 14), postnatal care (see Chapter 15), discussions about and a post mortem examination (see Chapter 16), registering their baby's death if necessary (see Chapter 19) and a funeral for their baby (see Chapter 20).

Well-organised follow-up care to check on parents' emotional and physical well-being is also essential following a termination for fetal anomaly or a maternal medical condition (RCOG 2010b; Lyus *et al.* 2014; Fisher and Lafarge 2015) (see also Chapter 17). With the woman's consent, it is important that primary care staff and the woman's community midwifery team (where appropriate) are informed following the termination so that they are able to offer appropriate postnatal care and other types of ongoing care and support (Lyus *et al.* 2014). This care and support should also be extended to partners (where applicable) (see *Fathers and same-sex partners* in Chapter 3). Ongoing follow-up support may also be important as some parents may also experience mental health difficulties following the termination, such as post-traumatic stress disorder, and they may benefit from being offered referral to specialist services (Zeanah *et al.* 1993; Kersting *et al.* 2005; Korenromp *et al.* 2005) (see also Chapter 18). Signposting parents to support organisations such as ARC and Sands may also be beneficial for some parents (see Appendix 2).

Support for staff

Providing care for women undergoing termination and/or feticide for fetal anomaly or a maternal medical condition can be very distressing for staff (RCOG 2010b; Fisher and Lafarge 2015). It is important that appropriate formal support is in place for staff (Fisher and Lafarge 2015) (see also Chapter 24). Staff should also be aware that they are able to access support from the ARC helpline (see Appendix 2).

CHAPTER 9

Termination of pregnancy for reasons other than fetal anomaly or maternal medical conditions

Other relevant chapters

1: Providing holistic care

2: Providing inclusive care

3: Loss and grief

4: Communication

5: Communication across language and other barriers

8: Termination of pregnancy for fetal anomaly and maternal medical conditions

In Great Britain, at least one-third of women will have undergone a termination for reasons other than fetal anomaly by the time they are 45 years of age (Birth Control Trust 1997, cited in RCOG 2011a). In 2014, 184,571 terminations were performed in England and Wales and 11,475 terminations were performed in Scotland (Department of Health 2015; NHS National Services Scotland 2015). Performing terminations of pregnancy for reasons other than fetal anomaly is "a significant proportion of the workload of many gynaecologists" and the procedure is generally safe for all gestations in a sterile, legal setting (RCOG 2011a: 1). Termination of pregnancy for reasons other than fetal anomaly is often referred to as abortion. Termination of pregnancy is legal under certain circumstances in England, Scotland and Wales but this legislation does not apply in Northern Ireland (see *Termination of pregnancy and the law* below regarding access to terminations).

Standards of care

There are many reasons why women may decide to terminate a pregnancy and women's decisions may be related to a combination of factors. "Over 98% of induced abortions in

Britain are undertaken because of risk to the mental or physical health of the woman or her children" (RCOG 2011a: 1).

It is important to ensure that women who are undergoing a termination of pregnancy are treated with respect and care, regardless of the reason for the termination. Women should be cared for by staff who are appropriately trained, non-judgemental and have no objection to termination. All care should be individualised based on the needs and wishes of each woman (RCN 2013).

Care may take place in a hospital, NHS clinic or private clinic. Ideally, women having a termination should not be cared for at the same place and time as women who are having antenatal care or care for miscarriage (RCOG 2011a). Women's privacy and dignity should be maintained in all settings and by all staff, including sonographers, receptionists and other support staff (RCOG 2011a). Whenever possible, female staff should be available to care for women who prefer a female care provider for personal, cultural or religious reasons (RCN 2013).

All women (including women under 16 years of age) are legally entitled to confidentiality except under exceptional circumstances (for example, where concerns exist regarding a woman's ability to consent or child protection) (BMA 2014). Some women may choose not tell their partner about the termination and this decision should be respected (BMA 2014). Additionally, young women may choose not to tell their parents or legal guardians even if they are encouraged to do so by healthcare staff in order to access parental support during this process (BMA 2014).

If women speak little or no English or prefer to speak in their own language, professional interpreters should be used (with a woman's consent) who have no objection to termination, are non-judgemental and respect the importance of confidentiality. It is not appropriate to use friends or family members as interpreters, particularly during any discussions about pregnancy options or during the consent process (RCOG 2011a; RCN 2013).

Some women and girls who access termination services may be particularly vulnerable (RCN 2013). For example, women and girls may have experienced or be at risk of substance problems, sexual abuse or violence, domestic abuse or other types of violence against women (RCN 2013). Service providers should have robust safeguarding policies and procedures in place to effectively identify and offer support for women and girls under these circumstances (RCOG 2011a; RCN 2013; BMA 2014). Services should also have information available about local specialist support services and how they can be accessed.

Access to services

Women should be given information about local termination services and what can and cannot be offered by each service (RCOG 2011a). Some women may also need information about care that is available in clinics and hospitals in other areas. This may include information about private clinics where women may need to pay for care depending on their local NHS service arrangements (NHS Choices [n.d.(a)]).

It is important that women seeking termination of pregnancy for any reason can access a procedure of their choice as conveniently as possible without delay (RCOG 2011a). Local services should be available wherever possible and referral to termination services should be available through health professionals and self-referral (RCOG 2011a; RCN 2013). Service commissioners should ensure that prompt access to termination services is available for women seeking care at all gestations to the legal limit or that a robust mechanism for referral to the appropriate service is in place (RCOG 2011a).

The RCOG recommends that services should minimise delay and ensure that:

- Referral to an abortion provider should be made within two working days.
- Abortion services must offer assessment within five working days of referral or self-referral.
- Services should offer women the abortion procedure within five working days of the decision to proceed.
- The total time from seeing the abortion provider to the procedure should not exceed ten working days.
- Women requiring abortion for urgent medical reasons should be seen as soon as possible (RCOG 2011a: 8).

Service commissioners should also ensure that there is provision within the NHS for women with complex health problems seeking termination. These women cannot usually be cared for by independent service providers because they require specialist medical care as well as a termination. This may be particularly difficult for women seeking later terminations that are more often provided by the independent sector. When NHS providers are not available to preform later terminations, it is important that NHS and independent sector services collaborate effectively to ensure the availability of services to women in these circumstances.

When local termination services are not available, some women may have to travel considerable distances and incur the costs of travel, overnight stays and possibly childcare. Although the termination procedure itself will likely be funded by the NHS, the associated costs of accessing it may make termination unaffordable for some women. One Scottish study found that some women felt that the expense, distress and stigma of travelling to England were barriers to accessing later terminations (Purcell *et al*. 2014). If possible, funding should be available to assist women who are on low incomes that need to travel to access a termination.

The utility of a centralised booking system to cover all service providers that carry out terminations after 20 weeks' gestation should also be considered. This would facilitate faster referrals for women who are nearing the legal limit.

If a pregnant woman presents at or beyond the legal limit for termination, staff should recommend that she accesses antenatal care as soon as possible. With her consent, clinic staff should arrange for her to be referred to maternity care. She should also be given information about how to access antenatal and any other support or safeguarding services that are available. Staff should also offer to discuss her options for when the baby is born including adoption or becoming a parent. Additionally, staff should offer the woman a referral for counselling.

Conscientious objection and access to care

Doctors and other health service staff who have a conscientious objection to termination because of their personal values or beliefs should arrange for women who are seeking a termination to be referred immediately to another colleague who is willing to provide this care (RCOG 2011a; GMC 2013b; BMA 2014; NMC 2015). This is not applicable in an emergency situation where the woman's life is at risk.

Staff should be non-judgemental when explaining the reason for this referral and the woman's dignity and opinion must be respected (GMC 2013b). Staff should also not obstruct women from accessing a termination procedure (GMC 2013b). See also *Conscientious objection* below.

Care before, during and after termination of pregnancy

Staff should offer to discuss all available options with women regarding the pregnancy including becoming a parent, giving the child for fostering or adoption or termination of the pregnancy (RCN 2013). They should also offer to discuss all available termination options that their facility offers for the woman's gestation of pregnancy (RCN 2013) (see *Discussing termination of pregnancy procedures* in Chapter 8). It is important to ensure that women have the relevant information required to make an informed decision.

Women should be reassured of the safety of termination procedures undertaken in Britain and that major complications and mortality are rare at all gestations (RCOG 2011a). To help ensure that women access available services, reassurance regarding confidentiality should also be highlighted in all discussions and written information (RCOG 2011a). Women must give consent before any information is shared with their GP and a woman's wishes must be respected if she does not want information to be shared (BMA 2014).

Staff should follow women's lead regarding the language they use to discuss the pregnancy. Some women may be ambivalent about having a termination and other women may be certain about their decision. Women should be given time to discuss their feelings and consider their decisions regarding the termination and method of termination (if applicable). All women should be offered a further opportunity to discuss their available options and counselling but should not be pressured to use these services if they decline (RCOG 2011a). Where women want access to these services, rapid referral should be available (RCN 2013). If there are any concerns that a woman is being coerced to have a termination, every effort should be made to ensure that staff have an opportunity to speak with her alone (RCOG 2011a; RCN 2013).

If the woman has been referred for the reduction of a multiple pregnancy, the potential risks and benefits of the procedure to the mother and babies should be discussed with the woman to help her make an informed choice (RCN 2013; BMA 2014) (see also *Multifetal pregnancy reduction* in Chapter 8).

Women must also be given information about physical assessments that are required to determine whether a termination procedure is medically suitable and, when appropriate, be referred for these procedures promptly (RCN 2013). As part of these assessments, a scan may be performed to determine the estimated gestation of the pregnancy and women should be told that they do not need to see the screen. Staff involved in scanning should take care to adhere to the woman's wishes regarding seeing the screen.

The termination options that are available to women should be fully discussed with women. Facilities that offer termination of pregnancy should also have clear written information available that is given to women upon referral describing which methods they offer and the gestation limit for each method (see *Discussing termination of pregnancy procedures* in Chapter 8). This written information should be up-to-date, comprehensive, non-judgemental, evidence-based, include the contact details of the termination service provider and be available in different languages and formats (RCOG 2011a).

Medical or surgical termination procedures can be performed at any gestation but local policies may affect what is offered to women at different gestations. Women should be supported to choose the termination procedure that is right for them wherever possible and flexibility in local policies may be important. When a woman gives consent for a procedure, she should be given relevant information regarding the expected length of the procedure, her expected length of stay in a hospital or clinic and the arrangements she should make for travelling home following the procedure.

An increasing number of women are choosing early medical termination [also referred to as an early medical abortion (EMA)] when their gestation allows. The RCOG (2011a) recommends that women who choose EMA are able to leave the healthcare facility after they receive the second of the abortifacient medications (misoprostol) to complete their termination at a place of their choosing. Evidence shows that this is both safe and acceptable to women choosing EMA (Ngo *et al.* 2011). If women choose to leave the healthcare facility to complete the termination, it is very important that they have all of the necessary information to manage their termination at home. This information should include how to manage pain and bleeding, what possible immediate complications to look out for, what action to take in the event of an emergency such as haemorrhage and how to dispose of the pregnancy remains.

When a woman gives consent for a termination, it will be ensured that two doctors determine in good faith that the woman meets the terms of the Abortion Act, the procedure is medically appropriate for the woman and that she has the relevant information needed to give informed consent. During the consent process, any enquiries regarding a woman's certainty about and reasons for her decision should be carefully and sensitively worded in a way that does not question her decision (RCOG 2011a). She should also be told that she can change her mind at any time before the procedure (RCOG 2011a) and be given contact details that she can use if she has any additional questions or wishes to cancel the termination. Following the termination, the doctor who performed the termination fills out an abortion notification form, which is sent in confidence to the Chief Medical Officer for England, Wales or Scotland as appropriate.

All women should be provided with verbal and written information about what to expect in the days and weeks following the termination that is relevant to their procedure type (RCOG 2011a). This should include information about expected and abnormal bleeding and pain, symptoms of infection, other possible complications and what action to take should they experience any of these symptoms (RCOG 2011a). A 24-hour helpline should be available for women to call for advice after termination and they should be provided with a letter containing the details of the treatment and care she has received to enable another practitioner to offer care for any complications (RCOG 2011a).

Women undergoing termination should be offered advice on contraception and testing for sexually transmitted infections. Most contraceptive methods can be initiated at the time of the termination (FSRH 2009). Women should be able to access a contraceptive method of their choice at the time of their termination procedure (RCOG 2011a). The wishes of women who decline contraceptive advice or a method of contraception should be respected. Women should be offered contact information for local primary care or contraception services should they wish to access contraception advice in the future.

Women should also be given verbal and written information about the range of emotions they may experience following termination of pregnancy and what sources of support or counselling are available and how to access them if they wish. Staff should ensure that women are referred to support services that are offered by the NHS or other organisations such as Marie Stopes UK or the British Pregnancy Advice Service (BPAS) (see Appendix 2). It is important that staff refer women to support services that have been carefully assessed to ensure that they offer impartial and non-judgemental support following a termination.

Some women feel relief following a termination and may not need to discuss how they feel. Others may experience mixed feelings, grief or other emotions. The RCOG (2011a) reviewed the available evidence and recommends that women are told that they are not at a higher risk of having mental health problems after a termination of pregnancy. This is supported by a recent US study which found that the majority of women (95 per cent) surveyed over three years felt that they had made the right decision to have a termination and felt able to manage their emotions (Rocca et al. 2015). The women surveyed who had intentional pregnancies or experienced difficulty making a decision about the termination were more likely to experience emotional difficulties (Rocca et al. 2015). Women with a past history of mental health problems who have an unintended pregnancy may also be at a higher risk of experiencing further difficulties whether they decide to have a termination or continue with the pregnancy (RCOG 2011a). For a few women, they may not feel they need support initially but may require support later, sometimes years after the termination. Appropriate, non-judgemental support and mental health services should be available to all women should they feel they would benefit by accessing this care immediately after the termination or at some point in the future.

Disposal of pregnancy remains

All women should be offered the opportunity to discuss their options for disposing of their pregnancy remains following a termination (HTA 2015). Staff should be aware of the available local options for burial, cremation and sensitive incineration through the hospital or by making private arrangements and discuss these options with women if they wish (HTA 2015). Sensitive incineration is not available in Scotland. Staff should also respect a woman's choice to decline being involved in any discussions or decision-making regarding disposal (RCN 2015). However, it should not be assumed that women will not wish to discuss their options for disposal.

If women wish to take the pregnancy remains from the healthcare facility and make their own arrangements for disposal, staff should support this decision (HTA 2015). There is no legal requirement for the woman to be given documentation when she takes pregnancy remains from the healthcare facility. However, staff should give women a form to confirm that this has been done in case any difficulties arise (see a sample form in Appendix 1 and more information in *Taking the baby's body home* in Chapter 15). There are also no legal requirements for the disposal of pregnancy or fetal remains before 24 weeks' gestation.

A record should always be kept of a woman's decision regarding discussing disposal and/or her choice regarding disposal where relevant (RCN 2015). A record should also be kept of when and how the pregnancy remains where disposed even if a woman does not wish to be involved in these decisions as she may want this information later (RCN 2015).

If a woman chooses to have an EMA at home or outside a healthcare facility, it is important that they are given information about what they can expect to see after the termination based on the gestation of the pregnancy. They should also be given information about their options for disposing of the pregnancy remains (Myers *et al*. 2015)

See Chapter 20 for more information about the disposal of pregnancy remains and HTA guidance.

Termination of pregnancy and the law

Termination has been legal in certain circumstances in England, Scotland and Wales since 1967. Under the Section 1(1)(a) of the Abortion Act 1967 and Section 37 of the Human Fertilisation and Embryology Act 1990, termination of pregnancy is permitted before 24 weeks' gestation if:

- The continuance of the pregnancy would involve risk to the life of the pregnant woman, or of injury to the physical or mental health of the pregnant woman or any existing children of her family, greater than if the pregnancy were terminated.

The Abortion Act does not apply in Northern Ireland. For more information about when termination is permitted after 24 weeks' gestation and in Northern Ireland, see *Legal requirements for performing a termination of pregnancy for fetal anomaly or a maternal medical condition* in Chapter 8.

Except in an emergency, a termination must be agreed by two doctors, performed by a doctor and carried out in a government-approved hospital or clinic (Section 1(1), (3) and (4) Abortion Act 1967).

Additionally, the European Convention on Human Rights does not confer the right for a woman to have a termination of pregnancy unless there are risks to her health or safety (Article 8) but she does have the right to not experience degrading treatment (Article 3).

The use of emergency contraception or the insertion of an intrauterine device (IUD) to prevent the implantation of a pregnancy is not considered to be termination as the pregnancy is not established (BMA 2014). This interpretation was clarified in 1983 by parliament in relation to the Offences Against the Person Act 1861 and it was later tested and confirmed in 1991 in the case of *R v HS Dhingra* and a 2002 judicial review (BMA 2014).

Young women and termination

Young women are able to seek medical advice and give consent to termination of pregnancy and other treatments regardless of their age if the healthcare professional caring for them is of the opinion that they understand the procedure and its possible outcomes. This is often referred to as Gillick or Fraser Competency. This ability for young people to independently seek treatment was granted by the House of Lords' ruling in *Gillick* (BMA 2014). The ruling in *Axon* later confirmed that the *Gillick* principles applied to young people's decisions regarding their treatment and care for sexually transmitted infections, contraception and termination of pregnancy (BMA 2014). A competent young person's consent for termination cannot legally be overridden by their parents' refusal for the procedure (BMA 2014).

Women under 16 years of age are entitled to the same confidentiality as women aged 16 and over (see *Standards of Care* above). While young women may be encouraged to confide in their parents or legal guardians, this is not mandatory (BMA 2014). Some young women under 18 years of age in England and Wales and under 16 years of age in Scotland may also be at risk of harm and staff should be aware of local child protection procedures and make referrals as needed (RCN 2013).

Conscientious objection

Section 4(1) of the Abortion Act (1967) includes a clause on conscientious objection that allows health care staff to refuse to "participate in any treatment authorised by the Act" to which they have a conscientious objection. The law does not define "participation". However, under Section 4(2) of the Act, staff are obliged to provide treatment in an emergency when a woman's life is at risk. In Northern Ireland, staff can also object to participating in performing a termination unless the woman's life is in immediate danger (DHSSPSNI 2013).

Under the European Convention on Human Rights, healthcare staff cannot refuse to perform a termination under their right to freedom of expression (Article 10) or discriminate on any basis and refuse an abortion (unless conscientious objection applies in which case they are required to refer the patient on to a practitioner who will provide the care) (Article 14).

Therefore, staff who have a conscientious objection to termination are able to refuse to participate in the termination procedure (RCN 2013; NMC 2015). However, they are not able to refuse to provide care for women before or after the termination (RCN 2013). If staff have a conscientious objection to termination, they are advised to inform their employer as soon as possible (RCN 2013; NMC 2015). Wherever possible, managers should try to ensure that nurses or midwives with a conscientious objection are not involved in termination care if they are not comfortable to ensure that women's care is not affected (RCN 2013).

Staff should be aware of their relevant professional regulatory body's code of conduct and guidance regarding conscientious objection and referral to another healthcare practitioner.

CHAPTER 10

Early miscarriage before 14 weeks' gestation

Other relevant chapters

1: Providing holistic care

2: Providing inclusive care

3: Loss and grief

4: Communication

5: Communication across language and other barriers

12: Labour and birth when a baby has died

14: After a loss

17: Follow-up appointments and ongoing care

20: Funerals and sensitive disposal

21: Memorials

Miscarriages that occur before 14 weeks' gestation have been included separately from later miscarriages and stillbirths as the type of care that may be offered to parents and the place of care may be different. In addition to the gestation of the miscarriage, the type of early miscarriage that a woman experiences may also affect the care that she is offered.

Support and care for parents experiencing early miscarriage

Women may not remember all the information they are given in hospital, but they do remember the kind of care they had. It's clear that kindness, compassion, sensitive language and clear explanations can make all the difference in helping people through the toughest of times. (Miscarriage Association 2015, personal communication)

The physical and emotional care that staff can offer to parents experiencing a miscarriage is important as it may affect parents' long-term emotional well-being (Leoni 1997; Evans 2012; NHS Improving Quality 2014). Staff often recognise that parents experiencing a miscarriage may be very distressed and that this is not a routine and minor medical event for many parents (Murphy and Merrell 2009). However, some parents have felt that their physical and emotional needs were not recognised by healthcare staff (Rowlands and Lee 2010).

It is important for staff to ensure that parents experiencing miscarriage receive adequate emotional and physical care. However, it is also important to be aware that there is variation in the amount and type of practical care and support that is appropriate for individual parents (NHS Improving Quality 2014). For example, some women may not want much contact with healthcare staff at this time while others may want a great deal of contact (Murphy and Merrell 2009).

Communication with parents is an important part of this care and staff should be trained in sensitively communicating with parents when breaking bad news and offering information about their available choices for care (see Chapter 4 and *Confirmation of a miscarriage* below). Staff should also be aware that parents may be in shock or distressed and that communication about the situation and their options for care needs to be clear, honest and presented in a way that parents can absorb and understand (see *Giving information and facilitating informed choice* in Chapter 4).

Emotional care for parents experiencing early miscarriage

Parents may experience a range of feelings during or following a miscarriage, which may include grief, distress, shock, confusion, regret, anger, relief, guilt, blame (of themselves or others), stress and/or mixed emotions (Callander *et al.* 2007; Murphy and Merrell 2009; Miscarriage Association 2015a). Some parents may experience these feelings very intensely or feel overwhelmed by their emotions (Miscarriage Association 2015a). Other parents may not have these feelings or may not experience them with the same intensity (Miscarriage Association 2015a). Some parents may feel relieved if the pregnancy was unwanted.

 I spent a week lying on the sofa pretending that I wasn't bleeding and that my heart wasn't breaking. Mother

No assumptions should be made about parents' feelings about the miscarriage as these are intensely personal and not necessarily determined by the gestation of the miscarriage (Murphy and Merrell 2009). In discussions with parents, staff should use the language that parents use to describe their baby. Some parents may refer to their "baby" or use the baby's name if one has been given. Other parents may be more comfortable using words such as "fetus" or "pregnancy".

 I lost our baby before I knew I was pregnant. I couldn't believe how hard this was, losing a baby I didn't even know I had. Mother

Staff should also offer emotional support to all parents experiencing miscarriage (including partners where applicable) (see *Fathers and same-sex partners* and *Offering emotional support to bereaved parents* in Chapter 3 and *Support and listening* in Chapter 15). The compassion offered by staff at this time may have a lasting effect on how parents experience their care (NHS Improving Quality 2014). Additional support and help should be offered to parents who may be particularly anxious because they have experienced one or more miscarriages (Callander *et al*. 2007), are older or have undergone fertility treatment. This may include, for example, offering opportunities for parents to discuss how they are feeling or a referral for counselling.

However, staff caring for parents during miscarriage do not always feel that they have time to offer adequate emotional support (Murphy and Merrell 2009; NHS Improving Quality 2014).

Therefore, it is important for managers, Trusts and Health Boards to ensure that policies are in place in units to ensure that time is allocated for staff to talk with parents and listen to their feelings and concerns during miscarriage.

Staff who only have brief encounters with parents when they are being referred for care should also offer parents emotional support. These staff can be supportive of parents by, for example, showing kindness, being willing to help and offering a few words of sympathy such as "I am sorry that this is happening to you". While some healthcare staff may be concerned that an expression of sympathy will "open the floodgates", many parents may appreciate an acknowledgement of their loss and these supportive actions may also help some parents to feel cared for and supported.

Continuity of carer and communication between staff

Wherever possible, a woman should have a named member of staff who is responsible for her care during and following a miscarriage to help provide her with the best care possible. This named member of staff should also be responsible for ensuring the woman has as much information as she wants about her options for care and that her care is smoothly transferred between departments where necessary (Moulder 1998).

Even where a woman has a named carer, any member of staff who is referring her to another team or unit should contact the ward or healthcare team where the woman is being transferred to ensure that they are expecting her and that she does not have to explain why she is there.

While many women receive care for early miscarriage in primary care settings (NHS Improving Quality 2014), staff caring for a woman in another healthcare setting should provide written information to her GP (with the woman's consent). See also *Communication between units and healthcare teams* in Chapter 4.

Place of care

There is currently a great deal of variation in terms of where care is provided for women experiencing early miscarriages (NICE 2012; NHS Improving Quality 2014). However, the place where a woman receives care during a miscarriage is important as it can affect how she experiences this care (Murphy and Merrell 2009).

All Trusts and Health Boards should provide an early pregnancy assessment unit (EPAU), which can be accessed directly by primary care physicians and accident and emergency (A&E) units (RCOG 2010c). All staff working in EPAUs should be trained to offer sensitive, empathetic care for parents who are, or may be, experiencing a miscarriage (see *Support and care for parents experiencing early miscarriage* above and Chapter 24). EPAUs should be available on a daily basis and women should be able to access care within 24 hours of referral (RCOG 2010c). All EPAUs should have access to transvaginal ultrasound and staff who are trained to use this equipment (RCOG 2010c).Where it is not possible for an EPAU to be open every day because of resource constraints, it should be open five days a week as a minimum (RCOG 2010c). In these cases, women should be able to access an emergency gynaecological unit at any time although it is important to note that these units do not always provide specialist support for women who are experiencing a miscarriage (NHS Improving Quality 2014). It is important that the staff working in any unit where a woman is referred when she cannot access an EPAU have training in offering sensitive care to parents who are experiencing a perinatal loss.

NICE (2012) has called for an audit of EPAUs to determine the benefits and cost effectiveness of providing these services. However, EPAUs can be beneficial as these multidisciplinary units have specially trained staff who can streamline women's care to provide them with rapid assessment of their symptoms (such as pain or bleeding in early pregnancy) and diagnosis confirmation in some instances (Murphy and Merrell 2009).

After a miscarriage diagnosis is confirmed and depending on the circumstances, women should be offered information about their care options (see *Physical care for early miscarriages* below). In relation to each type of management offered, women should be given information about their options for going home (either to wait for the miscarriage to occur or while awaiting a procedure) or being allocated a room or bed on a gynaecological or surgical ward where appropriately trained staff are available to support them. A woman should only be referred to a surgical ward if there is no gynaecological ward. Except in an emergency, a woman should not be expected to miscarry in an A&E department. Women who are admitted through A&E should be transferred to a ward or be offered support to go home as quickly as possible. Women should also never be left on a trolley in a public place. When being transferred or moved, women should be offered a covering so that bleeding is not visible to people who are passing by.

Ideally, a single room or dedicated bereavement room should be available to parents on a gynaecological or surgical ward and parents are likely to appreciate the privacy (Murphy and Merrell 2009) (see also *Place of care* in Chapter 14). However, it is important that parents do not feel isolated or unsupported if they are moved to a single room on a busy ward where staff are expected to prioritise patients whose physical needs are more urgent (Murphy and Merrell 2009). Staff should be aware of this potential difficulty and ensure that a designated member of staff is responsible for periodically checking on parents (at least once every hour unless parents request otherwise) and ensuring that they know whom to contact if they need support or assistance.

If a woman is not allocated a private room, she should not normally be placed in a room with other women who are terminating pregnancies for reasons other than fetal anomaly or a maternal medical condition. The place where care is provided on wards should also have a comfortable chair for any partners or supporters who are with the woman and easily accessible toilet facilities for men and women (see *Space for partners* in Chapter 14).

If a woman is undergoing medical or expectant management while miscarrying and is already at home or has decided to go home, she should be offered verbal and written information about what to expect, pain relief, whom to contact if they have any questions, what to do in an emergency and potential options for what will happen with any pregnancy remains (see also *Physical care for early miscarriages* below and *Offering choices to parents* in Chapter 20) (NICE 2012; Miscarriage Association 2015b). Women should not be made to feel that they are being sent home or that they do not have support at home.

Physical care for early miscarriages

The first signs of a possible miscarriage can cause intense anxiety for parents (Murphy and Merrell 2009) and many parents will want to know if anything can be done to prevent the miscarriage. Even if they are unable to prevent the miscarriage (which is often the case), staff can offer parents physical and emotional care. This care is important as some parents may become angry or distressed if they feel that staff are not taking their concerns seriously (even if the miscarriage is not diagnosed until later) (Jansson and Adolfsson 2010).

The care recommendations or considerations for a woman's care may depend on the type of miscarriage that she is experiencing or is thought to be experiencing. In any circumstances, it is important that parents are given clear information about what is happening, any medical procedures that are being recommended (including their benefits and risks) (Rowlands and Lee 2010) and the reasons for being asked to wait for further care (where appropriate). A clear, individualised care plan should then be developed in consultation with each woman based on her particular circumstances and wishes. This plan should include details of the place and type of care that a woman has decided upon, what she should do if she has any concerns during or after the miscarriage and arrangements for follow-up care. With the woman's consent, her partner (when she has one) should also be involved in developing this plan although the woman has the legal right to make any final decisions about her care. Providing information to parents and involving them in developing a care plan may help to increase their sense of control in a situation where they may feel that they have little control (Smith *et al*. 2006).

Before a care plan is devised, it may also need to be confirmed that a woman is experiencing a miscarriage. Once a miscarriage has been confirmed, staff should offer to discuss care options with women (see the sections below for more details).

Parents should also be offered information about what they might expect their baby or pregnancy remains to look like depending on the gestation and the type of management used. Some parents may wish to see their baby or any remains and others parents may not (Ogden and Maker 2004; Smith *et al.* 2006) (see also *Seeing and holding the baby* in Chapter 14). After a surgical procedure, staff should offer to gently describe what parents will see beforehand if they wish to see their baby or any pregnancy remains (see also *Seeing and holding the baby* in Chapter 14). This may include sensitively telling parents whether any remains will be recognisable and/or complete.

Parents should also be offered information about their options for what to do with their pregnancy remains and funerals (HTA 2015; RCN 2015) (see *Offering choices to parents* in Chapter 20). Depending on the circumstances, some parents may want to make special arrangements and other parents may decide to flush any pregnancy remains down the toilet (Miscarriage Association 2015b). Parents should be assured that it is their decision and whatever they decide is all right (Miscarriage Association 2015b). Some parents may flush the pregnancy remains by mistake and may be distressed that they were unable to see the remains or make other arrangements for them. It may help parents to know that this can and does happen to other parents and that there may be other ways of marking their loss.

A woman's consent should be obtained before any samples are sent for examination (see *Histological examinations after miscarriage* below).

Confirmation of a miscarriage

As many staff will encounter parents around the time when a miscarriage is confirmed, it is crucial that these staff feel confident and have training in sensitively breaking bad news to parents (see *Breaking bad news* in Chapter 4). Good communication with parents is important at this time and staff should be aware of the range of reactions that parents may have when receiving this news and offer emotional support (see *Dealing with parents' reactions* in Chapter 4).

Confirming a miscarriage, incomplete miscarriage or ectopic pregnancy

For some women, a miscarriage may involve all of the pregnancy tissue being spontaneously expelled from the uterus (Miscarriage Association 2015b). Other women may experience what is often referred to as an incomplete miscarriage where some of the pregnancy tissue remains in the uterus after some tissue is expelled (Miscarriage Association 2015b). Some women may continue to bleed and experience pain following an incomplete miscarriage (Miscarriage Association 2015b). Some women who have ectopic pregnancies may also experience pain or bleeding (see *Care and aftercare for ectopic pregnancy* below).

When a woman visits or calls any medical service (including their GP or midwife) because of pain or bleeding in early pregnancy, she should be offered a referral for an assessment to confirm whether she is miscarrying as soon as possible. However, some women may need to wait until their pregnancy reaches six weeks' gestation before an assessment will provide useful information and the reasons for this should be explained to women. Ideally, this referral should be made to an EPAU. Women should also be able to self-refer to an EPAU if they have previously experienced recurrent miscarriages, ectopic pregnancy or molar pregnancy (NICE 2012).

Rather than be referred for an assessment, some women may prefer to access support and information from staff over the telephone. To ensure that these women feel that they have enough information, staff should speak with them for as much time as they need and give them the details of a named person who they can contact if they have any further questions or concerns.

Whenever possible, all women should be able to telephone or see the same person if they need further advice and support after accessing information over the phone or being referred for assessment (see also *Continuity of carer and communication between staff* above).

Despite the potential limitations of ultrasound scans for determining the viability of a pregnancy before 49 days' gestation, women who have a previous history or symptoms of an ectopic pregnancy should be offered a scan to determine the location of the pregnancy without delay (Bottomley *et al*. 2009) (see also *Care and aftercare for ectopic pregnancy* below). If a woman is waiting for an ultrasound scan, she should be given information about what to expect at this time (NICE 2012). Parents may appreciate the offer of an appointment even if it is considered too early to confirm the miscarriage using an ultrasound scan (Jansson and Adolfsson 2010) as long as it is explained to them that a scan may not provide useful information at an early stage.

Confirming a missed or delayed miscarriage

Women who experience delayed or missed miscarriage may not experience any signs or symptoms of miscarriage although some women may have a feeling that something is wrong with their pregnancy (Jansson and Adolfsson 2010). A missed miscarriage (also called a delayed or silent miscarriage) is when a baby has died or not developed but remains in the uterus (Miscarriage Association 2015b). A delayed or missed miscarriage may also refer to early embryonic or fetal demise where the amniotic sac has developed but the baby has not developed (this may also be called a "blighted ovum", "anembryonic pregnancy" or "early embryo loss") (Miscarriage Association 2015b) (see *Verbal communication and choosing words* in Chapter 4).

Missed or delayed miscarriages are often diagnosed at a woman's first routine ultrasound examination. It is important that this information is sensitively communicated to parents during the examination by appropriately trained staff (NICE 2012) (see also *Breaking the news to parents* in Chapter 11). Some parents may be shocked by this diagnosis or unable to process this information (Jansson and Adolfsson 2010). Some women may still be feeling pregnant and/or have a positive pregnancy test (their hormone levels may still be continuing to rise). Other women may not have felt pregnant or felt that something was wrong prior to the ultrasound scan (Jansson and Adolfsson 2010). Other women may feel guilty or ashamed that they had not realised that anything was wrong. Staff should clearly and sensitively tell women that, in many cases, something has gone wrong at a very early stage and the embryo could not continue to develop. When appropriate, women should also be made aware that this is unlikely to recur in future pregnancies.

Some women may bleed and experience pain following a missed miscarriage (Miscarriage Association 2015b) and staff should tell them about this possibility.

Care options and aftercare for miscarriage (including incomplete, missed or delayed miscarriage)

Current NICE (2012) guidance recommends that women who have had a diagnosed early miscarriage use expectant management of the miscarriage for seven to 14 days before considering other management options (see also *Expectant and medical management* below). Some exceptions to this recommendation include where a woman has experienced a previous childbearing loss or is at risk of haemorrhage or infection (NICE 2012). According to this guidance, women should be offered medical management if expectant management is not acceptable for them (NICE 2012).

Despite these recommendations, expectant or medical management may not be suitable care options for some women. Additionally, women may have a wide range of views and preferences regarding how early miscarriage is managed (Ogden and Maker 2004; Smith *et al*. 2006). For example, some women may wish to wait for the miscarriage to occur naturally while others may want the miscarriage to be over as soon as possible (Ogden and Maker 2004; Smith *et al*. 2006). Some women may also feel safer in hospital while others prefer to be at home (Ogden and Maker 2004; Smith *et al*. 2006).

Where medically appropriate, women should be able to decide on their place of care and whether their miscarriage care will be expectant, medical or surgical (see the relevant sections below). Therefore, staff should offer all women the opportunity to fully discuss their available miscarriage care options (Miscarriage Association 2015b) (see *Giving information and facilitating informed choice* in Chapter 4). The information discussed with women for each care option should include details of:

- How long each type of management may take and what it involves.

- Any associated risks and benefits (including for the woman's future fertility).

- What they might see following each type of management.

- How long a woman may expect to bleed or experience pain after the miscarriage (NICE 2012; Miscarriage Association 2015b).

Staff should also offer parents information about histological examinations that may be available or recommended to examine tissue from the pregnancy (see *Histological examinations after miscarriage* below).

Women should be given written information to supplement what they have been told about each care option (NICE 2012). This information should also be available in other languages and formats. The Miscarriage Association's leaflet for parents *Management of miscarriage: your options* may also be helpful for some parents (see Appendix 2).

Parents may also have other questions and concerns that they wish to discuss with staff. For example, some parents may want information about what their baby might look like. Staff should offer to sensitively and honestly describe to parents how their baby might look (even when a fetus may not be distinguishable from other pregnancy remains) and their options for seeing the fetus or any pregnancy remains after the miscarriage (see specific considerations under *Expectant and medical management* and *Surgical management* below).

Staff should ensure that sufficient time is available to discuss all relevant information with parents and offer to schedule another appointment if necessary (NICE 2012). Except in an emergency, parents should be given time to consider all of these options. Some parents may wish to go home while making a decision and others may make a decision quite quickly. Once a decision has been made, staff should document the woman's decision and then offer to arrange any necessary appointments for further care and/or follow-up appointments (see *Follow-up appointments and ongoing support* below). At this time, parents may also want more detailed information about what to expect from the type of care they have chosen (Smith *et al.* 2006).

Expectant and medical management

All women who are offered either expectant or medical management should be given a clear explanation of what these care options involve and what to expect during the miscarriage. Some parents may also want to make a plan of what they would like to happen during the miscarriage (including, for example, their preferences regarding pain management and/or seeing any pregnancy remains) and may appreciate staff support while doing so (see also Chapter 12).

Providing information about the range of experiences that women may have is important as some women have felt unprepared for the amount of bleeding and pain that they experienced and the length of time that the process took (Smith *et al.* 2006). For example, many parents are surprised to find that an early miscarriage may be similar to labour and staff should explain that there is variation in how much pain different women experience (Ogden and Maker 2004; Smith *et al.* 2006). Staff should also offer to discuss women's options for pain relief and pain relief should be provided to women if they want it. It is important that adequate pain relief is available to women in all circumstances and that staff recognise that over-the-counter pain medication may not be enough.

Most expectant or medically managed miscarriages occur at home. When women are returning home during or after an expectant or medical miscarriage, it is important that they are given verbal and written information about their chosen care option that includes:

- The details of a named contact who they can reach if they have any further questions or concerns.

- The details of whom to contact in an emergency (NICE 2012) and encouragement to contact this number if they are worried.

- Information about how long they might expect to bleed during the entire process and when to seek medical advice and/or further treatment if bleeding or pain persist

(NICE 2012). There is a great deal of variation in the amount of bleeding that women experience and this should be explained clearly to women (Ogden and Maker 2004; Smith *et al*. 2006). Women should also be advised to have a supply of extra-absorbent sanitary pads available (Miscarriage Association 2015b).

- Advice about when to take a urine pregnancy test after the bleeding has stopped (NICE 2012).

- Information about signs of infection and what to do if an infection is suspected (Miscarriage Association 2015b).

- The details of any further treatment that may be needed and any follow-up appointments that are offered (NICE 2012).

- Information about options for what to do with their pregnancy remains (see *Physical care for early miscarriages above* and *Offering choices to parents* in Chapter 20).

Some parents may be anxious about miscarrying at home or seeing their baby (Miscarriage Association 2015b). It is important that parents who wish to access physical care or emotional support from staff are able to do so.

Additional considerations for expectant management

Expectant management may also be referred to as natural or conservative management (Miscarriage Association 2015b). Some parents who decide to have expectant management for their miscarriage may feel that it is important for them to allow this process to happen naturally (Smith *et al*. 2006). However, parents who have expectant management of their miscarriage may not know whether the baby or pregnancy remains have been passed for a long period of time. This uncertainty can be very distressing for some parents and they should be offered emotional support from staff and an appointment for further assessment. Parents should also be told that they can change their mind later and decide to have medical or surgical management (Miscarriage Association 2015b).

Additional considerations for medical management

Women who have medical management for their miscarriage will be given medication (misoprostol) that they can choose to insert into their vagina or take orally (NICE 2012). Women who choose to have misoprostol vaginally should be given the option of inserting the medication themselves or with the assistance of a healthcare professional. Women should also be told about possible side effects of the medication (NICE 2012) and suggestions for alleviating any symptoms they experience. Additionally, women should be given the contact details of whom to contact for further medical advice if they do not start bleeding within 24 hours of taking the medication (NICE 2012). While medical management is largely successful, women should be told that they may need surgical management if this procedure is not effective (Miscarriage Association 2015b).

Surgical management

Surgical management of miscarriage is sometimes also referred to as SMM or dilatation and curettage (D&C) (Miscarriage Association 2015b). Evacuation of retained products of conception (ERPC or ERPoC) should no longer be used as this language can be upsetting for some parents and is no longer considered to be sensitive to their needs (Miscarriage Association 2012) (see also *Verbal communication and choosing words* in Chapter 4). Also, D&C is not an accurate description of the surgical procedure for miscarriage (Miscarriage Association 2015b). Staff should, therefore, refer to surgical management of miscarriage when speaking with parents.

Some women may prefer surgical management for their miscarriage as it is more predictable and the miscarriage is over more quickly (Smith *et al.* 2006; Ogden & Maker 2004). Other women wish to avoid this type of care and may be frightened by the idea of being hospitalised, having a general anaesthetic and/ or undergoing an operation (Ogden and Maker 2004; Smith *et al.* 2006). Some parents may have concerns about surgical management if they think that the baby could still be alive (Miscarriage Association 2015b). These parents should be offered an ultrasound examination if they are considering surgical management for their miscarriage (Miscarriage Association 2015b).

A surgical procedure may also be medically recommended for some women experiencing miscarriage. The reasons for this recommendation should be clearly explained to parents and staff should offer to discuss any concerns that parents may have about the procedure.

Women who decide to have surgical management for their miscarriage should be offered the choice of manual vacuum aspiration (MVA) under local anaesthetic or a surgical procedure under general anaesthetic, depending on their medical history and the available facilities (NICE 2012). Women should be told about what to expect during and after each procedure and the benefits and risks associated with each procedure and anaesthetic type (NICE 2012). Women should also be given information about pain, cramping and/or bleeding that they may experience (again the potential variation in the length and amount of bleeding should be explained) (Miscarriage Association 2015b). They should also be told that the procedure may need to be repeated if it is not successful the first time but that this only happens very occasionally (Miscarriage Association 2015b). Any arrangements that women may need to make to travel home afterwards should also be discussed. Written information about the procedures should be given to women (NICE 2012) and be available in a variety of languages and formats.

Once women have decided on a procedure, staff should offer to refer them for an appointment as soon as possible. Some women may want to have the procedure without delay while others may wish to wait a while. Wherever possible, women's preferences should be accommodated.

If there is a long delay when women are waiting for a procedure to take place, the potential difficulty of the situation should be acknowledged and women should also be offered emotional support including opportunities to discuss how they are feeling.

Before going home, women should also be given information about signs of infection, what to do if bleeding persists or becomes heavier (Miscarriage Association 2015b) and any follow-up appointments that are offered. They should also be provided with written emergency contact information as well as the details of a named contact who they can reach if they have any additional questions or concerns.

Care and aftercare for ectopic pregnancy

Ectopic pregnancy affects approximately 1.7 in every 100 pregnancies in the UK (HESonline 2012). An ectopic pregnancy is a pregnancy that develops outside the uterus, usually in the fallopian tubes (Miscarriage Association 2014).

Women who have a positive pregnancy test and are experiencing symptoms, such as abnormal bleeding, abdominal pain or shoulder-tip pain, should be referred without delay to a hospital or an EPAU for assessment as an ectopic pregnancy may be suspected (Tay *et al.* 2000; Walker 2002; Bottomley *et al.* 2009) (see also *Physical care for early miscarriage* above). Staff should also consider offering a pregnancy test to women who are of reproductive age and experiencing symptoms that may indicate an ectopic pregnancy even if their symptoms overlap with other conditions (NICE 2012).

A diagnosis of an ectopic pregnancy is usually confirmed using a transvaginal ultrasound (RCOG 2010c; NICE 2012; Miscarriage Association 2015b). Women may also be offered a blood test to determine their hCG levels, which is usually repeated after 48 hours as part of the diagnosis (RCOG 2010c; NICE 2012; Miscarriage Association 2015b). The results of any examination should be communicated sensitively and clearly to parents (see *Breaking bad news* in Chapter 4). In any discussions with parents, staff should also choose their language carefully and avoid using clinical terms. For example, parents may find references to "an ectopic" or "removal of a tube" distressing. Staff should use the language that parents use when discussing their baby or fetus (see *Emotional care for parents experiencing early miscarriage* above).

Parents may be very frightened or distressed if they are waiting for confirmation of a suspected ectopic pregnancy or receiving treatment for an ectopic pregnancy. Some parents may not have known they were pregnant and may also be trying to absorb this information. Staff should offer parents emotional support during this time and parents should be given the contact details for a named contact who they can speak with if they have any questions or concerns. Parents who have an ectopic pregnancy should also be offered condolences by staff. This is important as some parents have felt that staff have not recognised their loss following an ectopic pregnancy in the same way as parents who experience other types of early miscarriage (Jessica Farren, Speciality Trainee, Imperial College Healthcare Trust, personal communication) (see also *Emotional care for parents experiencing early miscarriage* above).

In terms of physical care, women who have an ectopic pregnancy will be offered different care options from those offered to women experiencing other types of early miscarriages. NICE (2012) recommends that women are offered medical or surgical management for an ectopic pregnancy depending on their circumstances. When a woman's choices for care during an ectopic pregnancy are limited for medical reasons, these reasons should be clearly explained to her. In instances where a woman's options are not medically limited, she should be offered the choice of medical, surgical and, in some cases, expectant management (see the relevant sections below).

Except in an emergency, all parents should be offered clear information about any procedures being suggested for care during an ectopic pregnancy. This information should include the advantages and disadvantages of each procedure (including potential risks to the woman's future fertility), what to expect in terms of pain and bleeding, their expected recovery time and when they will be offered follow-up appointments for further assessment. Wherever possible, parents should be given time to absorb and process what they have been told before they make a decision. Parents should also be given written information about any procedures discussed and this should be available in other languages and formats. Parents may also find the Miscarriage Association's *Ectopic pregnancy* leaflet helpful and they should be offered information about support organisations such as the Ectopic Pregnancy Trust (see Appendix 2).

Before women go home (either before or after any type of management), they should be provided with written information about whom to contact in an emergency, when to seek further help and the details of a named contact who they can speak with if they have any additional questions or concerns. They should also be offered information about their options for seeing and/or making arrangements for any pregnancy remains and any follow-up appointments that are offered (see also *Seeing and holding the baby* in Chapter 14, Chapter 20 and *Follow-up appointments and ongoing support* below).

Medical management for ectopic pregnancy

Women who are offered medication (methotrexate) to stop the growth of an ectopic pregnancy should be offered information about any side effects and the potential need for further treatment (RCOG 2010c). It may be recommended that women are admitted to the hospital for observation during medical management for ectopic pregnancy as it can be difficult for women to distinguish between the pain related to the procedure and the pain of tubal rupture (RCOG 2010c). Women will also need follow-up for up to six weeks after the medication is administered to check that their hormone levels have returned to normal (Miscarriage Association 2014).

Women who have had medical management of an ectopic pregnancy should also be advised to avoid sexual intercourse and alcohol during treatment in case of tubal rupture (RCOG 2010c). They should also be advised to use barrier contraception for three months following treatment as methotrexate is potentially teratogenic (RCOG 2010c; Miscarriage Association 2014). Some parents may be distressed by the delay in conceiving again and staff should acknowledge this potential difficulty for parents.

Surgical management for ectopic pregnancy

Different care options are available for the surgical management of an ectopic pregnancy. It is recommended that laparoscopy (keyhole surgery) is used wherever possible and Trusts, Health Boards and managers should ensure that appropriately trained staff and equipment are available to perform this surgery (NICE 2012). When this procedure is not available, open abdominal surgery may be required. In either instance, women should be offered information about what the procedure involves, her expected length of stay in hospital, her recovery time and any support that she may need after being discharged from hospital.

When discussing surgery for an ectopic pregnancy, staff should also offer to discuss the options of completely removing the fallopian tube (salpingectomy) and removing the pregnancy but leaving the tube behind (salpingotomy) (NICE 2012; Miscarriage Association 2014). This information should be explained clearly and staff should avoid using technical terms. The complete removal of the fallopian tube is often recommended unless women have other fertility problems such as the removal of a tube during a previous pregnancy or damaged tubes (NICE 2012; Miscarriage Association 2014). The potential need for further treatment or assessment and the possibility of a future ectopic pregnancy following salpingotomy should also be explained to women (NICE 2012; Miscarriage Association 2014). Wherever possible, parents should be given time to absorb this information and make the best decision for them.

Some parents may be very distressed if one or both fallopian tubes are removed (Miscarriage Association 2014). Staff should offer emotional support to parents as they may be very distressed or grieving for this loss of fertility as well as the loss of their baby (Miscarriage Association 2014). These parents may only be able to conceive future pregnancies using IVF (Miscarriage Association 2014). However, staff should be aware that IVF may not be an option for some parents for a number of reasons (for example, financial and emotional reasons). Parents should be offered information about organisations such as the Human Fertilisation and Embryology Authority (HFEA) (see Appendix 2).

If a woman is admitted for surgical management of an ectopic pregnancy in an emergency, she and/or her partner may be very distressed and anxious about her safety. Even when there is very little time before surgery to explain what is happening, it is still important that parents are given as much information as possible. Any partner or supporter of the woman may be alone and have an anxious wait while the woman is undergoing surgery. A named member of staff should be responsible for offering support to any partner or supporter and for updating them as soon as possible regarding the woman's condition. Once the woman is fully recovered from the anaesthetic, she and her partner (if she has one) should be given clear information about the reasons for the surgery, what was done, any implications for the future and their options for seeing and/ or deciding what will happen to any pregnancy remains.

Before a woman leaves hospital, she should be given advice about taking care of herself during the recovery period, what to expect in terms of bleeding and pain and details of whom to contact if she has any concerns. She should also be offered a follow-up appointment to check her physical and emotional well-being within six weeks of surgery (EPT 2016). For example, staff should check that the incision is healing properly.

Expectant management for ectopic pregnancy

Some women may also be offered expectant management of an ectopic pregnancy if there are minimal risks to the woman and she has easy access to a hospital and follow-up care (RCOG 2010c) (see *Expectant and medical management* above). More frequent assessment is required for these women and they should have an emergency contact information readily available (Miscarriage Association 2014).

Women who decide to have expectant management for a tubal ectopic pregnancy should be told that there is a chance that their fallopian tube could rupture (Miscarriage Association 2014). They should also be advised to avoid sexual intercourse as it may cause the tube to rupture as well as drinking alcohol as this may cause other problems if there is a complication (Miscarriage Association 2014).

Care and aftercare for molar pregnancy

Few people are aware of the existence of molar pregnancies and many clinicians are unlikely to encounter molar pregnancies on a regular basis (RCOG 2010d; Miscarriage Association 2013).

A molar pregnancy or hydatidiform mole is a type of gestational trophoblastic tumour (tumour that grows from pregnancy tissues in the uterus) and it occurs in approximately one out of every 600 pregnancies (Miscarriage Association 2013). These moles may be complete or partial, which is determined using genetic and histopathological information (RCOG 2010d):

- Complete moles usually occur when one or two sperm fertilise an ovum that does not contain any genetic material (RCOG 2010d; Miscarriage Association 2013). There is no evidence of fetal tissue present in these pregnancies, which become implanted in the uterus in rare circumstances (RCOG 2010d; Miscarriage Association 2013).

- A partial mole usually occurs when two sperm fertilise the same ovum (RCOG 2010d; Miscarriage Association 2013). The placenta may develop more quickly than the fetus, which would be unable to survive even if some fetal tissue is present (Miscarriage Association 2013). Very few live babies have been born following a pregnancy when a partial mole has been thought to be present which could have resulted from a multiple pregnancy (Miscarriage Association 2013).

In very rare cases (approximately 1 per cent of partial moles and 14 per cent of complete moles), the cells may grow very rapidly and sometimes these tumours may become deeply embedded in the uterus and have the potential to become malignant (cancerous) (Miscarriage Association 2013). These are known as invasive moles and may develop into choriocarcinoma if they are untreated.

Some women do not discover that they have had a molar pregnancy until after a histological examination has taken place following their miscarriage as many of the symptoms are the same as those of pregnancy or miscarriage (Miscarriage Association 2013) (see also *Histological examinations after miscarriage* below). In some instances, a woman's healthcare practitioner may suspect that she has a molar pregnancy if she has hyperemesis (severe or prolonged vomiting), irregular vaginal bleeding, her uterus is larger than expected for the gestation of the pregnancy and/or she has other more rare symptoms (RCOG 2010d; Miscarriage Association 2013). Healthcare staff who care for pregnant women should be aware of the symptoms of molar pregnancy and refer women for a urine pregnancy test if one is suspected (RCOG 2010d).

If the woman is still pregnant and a molar pregnancy is suspected, she should be offered a blood test to confirm her hCG levels (these may be higher than usual), an ultrasound examination and/or a referral to a gynaecologist or EPAU for assessment (RCOG 2010d; Miscarriage Association 2013). Her options for surgical or medical management of the miscarriage should then be explained to her and she should be told that this is not the same as termination of pregnancy (Miscarriage Association 2013). While surgical management is strongly recommended as a care option for molar pregnancies (particularly for complete moles), medical management may still be an option (RCOG 2010d).

Before speaking to a woman who may have or has had a molar pregnancy, staff should ensure that they are fully informed about what a molar pregnancy is and the potential implications. Staff should carefully, sensitively and clearly explain any relevant information and implications of test results or symptoms that lead them to suspect a woman may have a molar pregnancy. Women should also be offered information and referrals for any recommended treatment and/or follow-up care. Written information about molar pregnancy (including information in other languages and formats) should be available and given to women who have had or are believed to have a molar pregnancy. It is crucial to provide women with an explanation of molar pregnancy and answer their questions as early as possible as some women may search for information online and immediately find information about cancer that may cause unnecessary distress. The Miscarriage Association's *Molar Pregnancy* leaflet may be a useful resource for parents (see Appendix 2).

After either procedure, parents should be offered follow-up appointments and a histological assessment of the pregnancy tissue to confirm whether it was a molar pregnancy and whether any additional treatment may be required (RCOG 2010d; Miscarriage Association 2013) (see *Histological examinations after miscarriage* below). Follow-up appointments will include monitoring the woman's hCG levels using blood tests until these levels return to normal and/ or offering additional treatment such as chemotherapy if the levels do not return to normal (Miscarriage Association 2013). Any blood samples must be sent to a specialist centre for testing.

Parents should be advised to use barrier contraception or a contraceptive pill to prevent another pregnancy while the woman is still receiving follow-up treatment and before any test results are received (RCOG 2010d; Miscarriage Association 2013). Staff should acknowledge that this delay to becoming pregnant again may be difficult for parents.

It is important that staff offer emotional support to all parents who have a molar pregnancy (see *Emotional care for parents experiencing early miscarriage* above). Some parents may be frightened by the potential implications of a molar pregnancy. Some parents may also be grieving for their expected baby and/ or feel uncertain about their grief if they are wondering if they were ever pregnant (Miscarriage Association 2013). It is important to reassure parents that whatever they are feeling is normal (Miscarriage Association 2013).

 It was painful to realise that for all these weeks there wasn't a baby growing inside me. It felt like we had been tricked. Parent (Miscarriage Association 2013: 7)

I thought nothing could be more devastating than losing a baby, until a month later when they told me it was a partial molar pregnancy. Parent (Miscarriage Association 2013: 7)

Histological examinations after miscarriage

The RCOG (2010d) recommends that all pregnancy remains following a miscarriage should be sent for histological examination to exclude potential malignancies and to address the difficulties of diagnosis of molar pregnancies. For example, ultrasound examination does not prove a definitive diagnosis of molar pregnancy and partial moles are not always identified during these examinations (RCOG 2010d). There should be a clear local policy on histological examinations of pregnancy remains and all relevant healthcare staff should be familiar with this policy.

The value and purpose of histological examinations should be explained to all parents and they should be asked for their consent before any histological examinations take place. Consent should be sought as a matter of best practice even if it is not legally required to examine tissue from pregnancy remains before 24 weeks' gestation as this is considered to be tissue from a living person (the mother) (HTA Code 1 2014). Parents should also be told that histological examinations cannot be used to diagnose the cause of the miscarriage or determine the baby's sex. As part of the consent process, parents should be told when to expect the results and be given written contact information if they want to follow-up on the test results. Current systems of informing parents about histological examination results vary. However, informing parents of test results would be recommended as reflects best practice.

Given the RCOG (2012d) recommendation for tissue from all miscarriages to be sent for histological examination, it is important to address how women having expectantly or medically managed miscarriages at home provide tissue for these investigations. It is important that these women are offered information about histological examination when this treatment option is available. Some women may be distressed by the idea of taking a tissue sample to their GP or hospital. However, some women may want the tests even if the idea is distressing. Women who wish to provide a tissue sample should be given clear instructions and information about how and when to take the tissue sample and about the times when the sample can be taken to their GP or local hospital.

When the results are available, these should be sent to the woman's GP and local hospital who should offer her an appointment to discuss the results if a problem is detected (Miscarriage Association 2013). In instances where a woman has an invasive mole or has developed a choriocarcinoma, staff should break the news sensitively (see *Breaking bad news* in Chapter 4). Staff should then offer to clearly and simply explain the potential implications and treatment options available when the woman is ready for this information.

Follow-up appointments and ongoing support

Even though miscarriage is so common, it's still something of a taboo subject – people just don't talk about it. This can leave women feeling very alone. What's more, most women never find out why they have miscarried, so they often assume that it must have been something they did or didn't do. (Miscarriage Association 2015, personal communication)

Even when specialist follow-up is not usually required after an early miscarriage, women should be offered follow-up appointments in case they need ongoing support or have any questions or concerns (NICE 2012) (see also Chapter 17). Despite this recommendation, a Miscarriage Association survey found that 79 per cent of women did not receive any aftercare after early miscarriage (NHS Improving Quality 2014). Trusts, Health Boards and managers should ensure that care pathways for women who experience miscarriage include the offer of a follow-up appointment with either their GP or with a member of their consultant team if appropriate. Some parents may want to have a follow-up appointment in person while others may only wish to receive a telephone call (Jansson and Adolfsson 2010).

Some women may also require ongoing physical care. Other women may need follow-up appointments to discuss results and/ or access treatment following histological examinations of pregnancy remains (see *Histological examinations after miscarriage* above). Parents who have experienced miscarriage may also want an opportunity to ask for more information, discuss why the miscarriage occurred and find out whether it is likely to happen again. Parents who have experienced recurrent miscarriage (defined as three or more miscarriages) should also be offered additional screening and diagnostic tests to determine whether they would benefit from specialist treatment (RCOG 2011b).

The emotional support that staff can offer to parents at follow-up appointments may also be important. For example, some women have received beneficial support from family and friends following miscarriage (Rowlands and Lee 2010). However, other women have found that they were unable to talk to family and friends about their experiences of grief and loss (Rowlands and Lee 2010). This feeling of not being able to talk sometimes resulted from other people being insensitive to parents' needs, trivialising their experience of grief or being unable to cope with parents' emotions (Mander 2006; Rowlands and Lee 2010). For example, some parents may encounter insensitive and unintentionally hurtful remarks such as, "It was nature's way of telling you there was something wrong with your baby"; "You're young, you can always have another one"; or "At least you can be grateful you've already got two children". Staff could offer to discuss with parents some of the ways that they might deal with these types of comments or tell other people about what they would find helpful.

Everyone said it was for the best, that the baby wasn't growing properly, that it would never have survived. They say at least it happened before it had a chance and that you just have to move on. I know all those things. I know it was only a tiny thing that didn't look much like a baby, but it was my baby, it was Jason, it was part of me, and it took a part of me when it died. Mother

Additionally, friends, family members and colleagues may be unaware of the miscarriage if parents have chosen not to announce their pregnancy until the end of the first trimester. Support from staff may be particularly important for these parents. Staff may also be able to help parents consider family members or friends who may be helpful and supportive if they decide to tell them about the miscarriage.

All parents should be offered information about local and national support organisations that may be able to offer them additional support such as the Miscarriage Association, Sands, TAMBA and the Multiple Births Foundation (see Appendix 2).

Some parents may also want or benefit from the offer of information about counselling or other specialist mental health support services that are available (see Chapter 18).

CHAPTER 11

Late miscarriage between 14 and 24 weeks' gestation and stillbirth

Other relevant chapters

1: Providing holistic care

2: Providing inclusive care

3: Loss and grief

5: Communication across language and other barriers

12: Labour and birth when a baby has died

14: After a loss

15: Postnatal care

16: Transfer to the mortuary and post mortem investigations

17: Follow-up appointments and ongoing care

19: Certificates and registration

20: Funerals and sensitive disposal

21: Memorials

Many of the care considerations for parents experiencing stillbirth (when a baby is born dead after 24 weeks' gestation) will be similar for late miscarriage (when a baby is born dead between 14 and 24 weeks' gestation). However, local policies may affect the type of care offered or the place of care available to parents depending on the gestation when their baby died. Some of the information in Chapter 10 may be more relevant for some parents depending on their local care provisions for miscarriage and the gestation of their pregnancy.

Support and care for parents who experience a late miscarriage or stillbirth

> " *I had perfectly wonderful, excellent care. There is not one concern or regret in my heart or mind that things could have been done better or different.* Parent (Redshaw *et al.* 2014: 13)

> " *Although the medical care was excellent, we really felt that there was a lack in emotional support. No one to talk to. I so desperately wanted and needed to talk to somebody, a professional, about what we were going through, and the decisions we had to make.* Parent (Redshaw *et al.* 2014: 17)

The *Listening to Parents* report found that many parents were provided with good quality care around the time when their baby was stillborn (Redshaw *et al.* 2014). However, there is still room for improvement in the care received by some parents who experience stillbirth or late miscarriage (Sands 2010; Redshaw *et al.* 2014). For example, better emotional support, access to ultrasound assessments, improved facilities and the provision of written information have been highlighted as areas for improvement (Sands 2010; Redshaw *et al.* 2014).

The care that parents receive from healthcare staff around the time when their baby dies is crucial as it may affect parents' long-term well-being (Downe *et al.* 2013; NHS Improving Quality 2014; Redshaw *et al.* 2014;). In addition to the physical care provided to parents during late miscarriage or stillbirth, staff should offer parents emotional support and information about what is happening. Parents may be experiencing a range of emotions at this time and may appreciate opportunities to talk with staff who can offer condolences and listen while parents talk about their feelings and experiences (see *Offering condolences and listening* in Chapter 14 and *Support and listening* in Chapter 15). It is important that staff offer support to partners or other supporters in addition to the woman where relevant (see also *Fathers and same-sex partners* in Chapter 3). Staff should also refer to the baby using the words that parents use. For example, some parents may refer to their "baby" while others may prefer to say "fetus" or refer to the baby by name.

Where relevant, staff should offer parents full information about their choices for giving birth to their baby, making a birth plan (see Chapter 12), creating memories and spending time with their baby (see Chapter 14). Parents should also be offered information about postnatal and ongoing care (see Chapters 15 and 17), post mortem examinations (see Chapter 16), registering their baby's birth, death and/or stillbirth (see Chapter 19) and arranging a funeral for their baby (Chapter 20). However, when this information is provided may vary depending on individual parents' needs.

Trusts, Health Boards and managers should ensure that policies, practices and procedures are in place to make sure that the emotional and practical care needs of parents are met around the time when their baby has died (Redshaw *et al.* 2014).

Care Pathways

In some areas, care pathways have been developed detailing the stillbirth or late miscarriage care that parents should receive. These care pathways can be helpful reminders for staff of the care options that should be offered to parents. However, care pathways should not be used as checklists that must be completed (see *Parental choice and checklists* in Chapter 14).

It is important that all parents receive sensitive, empathetic, individualised care based on their particular needs and wishes (Redshaw *et al.* 2014). Staff should offer parents detailed information about their available care options and support parents to make informed choices about their care (see *Giving information and facilitating informed choice* in Chapter 4). Some of the care offered to parents may also depend on when their baby's death occurs (see the sections on *Intrauterine death, Spontaneous late miscarriage, Premature labour* and *Intrapartum death and stillbirth* below).

Communication with parents

Good communication with parents is important both before and after a baby's death has been confirmed (see Chapter 4).

Listening to parents' concerns

During pregnancy, labour and birth, it is important that staff listen to parents' concerns (Rance *et al.* 2014; Redshaw *et al.* 2014; Siassakos *et al.* 2015, unpublished results). The *Listening to Parents* report found that around two-thirds of parents whose babies died before labour and almost half of parents whose babies died during labour felt that something was wrong (Redshaw *et al.* 2014). However, only 57 per cent of the women whose babies died before labour and 41 per cent of women whose babies died during labour felt that staff took their concerns seriously (Redshaw *et al.* 2014).

The InSight study also found that there was a range of responses when parents told staff about their concerns (Siassakos *et al.* 2015, unpublished results). For example, some parents were told that it was nothing when they contacted staff with their concerns while other were told to come to the hospital for a check (Siassakos *et al.* 2015, unpublished results). It is important that parents receive consistent offers of care when they have concerns about their baby's well-being and that appropriate care is provided (Siassakos *et al.* 2015, unpublished results).

Breaking the news to parents

When a baby dies before or during labour or birth, or shortly afterwards, the parents should be told straight away. Most parents remember what is said and done at this critical and potentially traumatic time (Downe *et al.* 2013; Redshaw *et al.* 2014). Although it is not possible for staff to make the situation better or to reduce the parents' distress, they should try to use clear, unambiguous language and to choose words that convey genuine sorrow, warmth and respect (see *Breaking bad news* in Chapter 4 and *Staff training* in Chapter 24 for more information).

Sometimes parents expect or anticipate the death but they still need clear and sensitive confirmation that their baby is dead (Siassakos *et al.* 2015, unpublished results). Parents who were expecting to welcome a healthy baby may be completely stunned and may find it impossible to believe that their baby has died. Staff need to be gentle and sensitive. They should allow time for parents to understand the reality of what has happened (Siassakos *et al.* 2015, unpublished results). While many parents value privacy at this time, it is important that they know that staff are available and nearby and that they do not feel abandoned if staff leave the room (Redshaw *et al.* 2014; Siassakos *et al.* 2015, unpublished results).

Continuity of carer and communication between staff

Continuity of care provided by known carers is often valued by parents who are experiencing a late miscarriage or stillbirth (RCOG 2010a; Kenworthy and Kirkham 2011; Siassakos *et al.* 2015, unpublished results). Parents can benefit from the support offered by a continuous team of carers who are trained in providing bereavement care and understand their potential needs (Siassakos *et al.* 2015, unpublished results) (see *Continuity of carers, bereavement midwives and communication between staff* in Chapter 12). In some areas, it is also possible for parents to be supported in hospital by a midwife who cared for them in the community (Kenworthy and Kirkham 2011).

Despite the potential benefits for parents of having continuity of carer, *Listening to Parents* found that 81 per cent of women had not met the midwives who provided their care during labour after their baby died (Redshaw *et al.* 2014). Additionally, most of these women received care from three or more midwives during their labour (Redshaw *et al.* 2014). Trusts, Health Boards and managers should ensure that systems are in place to offer parents care from a known carer and/or the same team of staff during late miscarriage and stillbirth.

Good communication between any staff providing care for parents is also essential to ensure that inappropriate comments are not made to parents and that their care is transferred smoothly between departments and healthcare teams if necessary (Draper *et al.* 2015) (see *Informing other carers* in Chapter 14). This will also help to ensure that parents do not need to repeatedly explain their situation.

Place of care

It is important that privacy is available when parents are being told that their baby has died and for discussions with staff around this time (Siassakos *et al.* 2015, unpublished results). If it is suspected that a baby has died, parents should not have to wait in an area with other expectant parents (Siassakos *et al.* 2015, unpublished results). In these instances, staff should offer to show parents to a separate room if they must wait before an examination.

During examinations where parents may learn that their baby has died, it is ideal to have a room with a door that can be closed (Siassakos *et al.* 2015, unpublished results). An interview room should also be available where staff and parents can have private discussions about options for care after their baby has died and where parents can have some time to absorb this information (Siassakos *et al.* 2015, unpublished results). It is important that these rooms are comfortably furnished and that there are not images of healthy babies in the room (Siassakos *et al.* 2015, unpublished results).

During and after labour, it is important that parents are offered a private room away from the sounds of other women in labour and crying babies (Redshaw *et al.* 2014). Trusts, Health Boards and managers should ensure that policies are in place and facilities are available to provide such rooms and make sure that any partners and supporters are able to stay with the woman overnight (Redshaw *et al.* 2014). See *Place of care* in Chapter 14 for more details of how these facilities should be arranged and maintained.

While women who are experiencing late miscarriage and stillbirth should be offered a special bereavement room on the labour ward, these facilities are not always available. Staff should acknowledge the potential difficulties of this situation for parents and offer parents support. Some parents may also wish for their baby to be born at home (see Chapter 12).

Local policies regarding place of care vary greatly and it may also be the case that parents who are experiencing late miscarriages may not be offered a room on the labour ward (Sands 2010; NHS Improving Quality 2014). Most commonly, the cut-off point for access to the labour ward is 20 weeks' gestation although a small number of units do not allow women onto the labour ward before 24 weeks' gestation (Sands 2010; NHS Improving Quality 2014).

These restrictions on place of care are important as many parents feel that their baby is not acknowledged as a baby if they are not admitted to the labour ward (Sands 2010). The labour ward may also be more likely to have more suitable facilities and staff who are trained to provide parents with good quality bereavement care (Sands 2010). However, it is important to remember that some women experiencing late miscarriage may also prefer to give birth on the gynaecological ward or at home (see *Place of care* in Chapter 10). Ideally, parents should be given options for their place of care regardless of gestation.

 We lost twins at 14 and 16 weeks. This was hard to deal with, as a miscarriage is considered an "invisible death" with no funeral or place of rest to visit. Mother

I was put in a gynae ward because I was only 20 weeks. I wanted my baby to be acknowledged and recognised as a baby, but I wasn't allowed into the labour ward. Everyone around me was having Ds and Cs and hysterectomies. Mother (Sands 2010: 7)

Specific considerations for care during late miscarriage and stillbirth

The circumstances around a baby's death may affect the types of care and support that should be offered to parents. The following sections detail some of the specific care needs of parents whose baby dies in utero, during labour and birth or as a result of a spontaneous late miscarriage or premature birth.

Intrauterine death

A baby's death may be confirmed while the woman is still pregnant and parents should be told immediately. It is important that parents are told gently but clearly that their baby has died (see also *Breaking the news to parents* above).

 We had to wait what seemed like a long time to be visited by a doctor who could operate the ultrasound and confirm the death. Parent (Redshaw *et al.* 2014: 17)

For some parents, the baby's death may a complete surprise if it is confirmed during an ultrasound scan (Miscarriage Association 2011) (see also *Confirmation of a miscarriage* in Chapter 10). Other women may already suspect that something is wrong (Redshaw *et al.* 2014). For example, some women may notice reduced fetal movements and they should be offered an appointment and assessment of the baby's heart rate using a hand-held Doppler device or cardiotocography (CTG) as soon as possible (RCOG 2010a, 2011c). Even when a baby's heart rate assessment appears to be normal, women should then be offered an ultrasound examination as soon as possible (RCOG 2010a, 2011c). The RCOG (2010a) recommends that a real-time ultrasound assessment should ideally be available to women for these assessments at all times.

When a baby's death is confirmed, parents may need some time to absorb this information. When parents are ready, staff should sensitively offer to discuss parents' options for the labour and birth of their baby (see Chapter 12) and seeing and holding the baby after the birth (see Chapter 14).

> *To be honest it all seemed a bit of a blur after we were told. It felt as though I was being bombarded with so much information and making decisions all at once within a few minutes.* Parent
> (Redshaw et al. 2014: 17)

Parents should also be told that the baby may make passive movements in the womb before the birth (RCOG 2010a). This is important as some parents may mistake these movements as a sign that the baby is alive which may cause additional distress.

When one or more babies die during a multiple pregnancy

When one or more babies in a multiple pregnancy die and this is confirmed during an ultrasound examination, parents may experience a range or mix of emotions (see also *Multiple pregnancies* in Chapter 3). Some parents may feel torn if they are looking forward to the birth of their healthy baby or babies while they are simultaneously grieving for the baby or babies who have died. Some parents may feel intense grief that may affect their ability to enjoy and/or develop a relationship with their surviving baby or babies. Other parents, however, may feel relief if one or more of their babies survive or are expected to survive (Fraser 2010).

Additionally, some parents may feel that they are unable to start grieving for their baby or babies who have died until after the birth (Fraser 2010). For some parents, this delayed experience of grief may be because they are unable to say goodbye to their baby or have a funeral until after the babies are born (Fraser 2010). Some parents may also have concerns that their fear and grief may affect the surviving baby or babies (Fraser 2010).

In some instances, parents may be advised to continue the pregnancy for the benefit of any surviving babies (Fraser 2010). Waiting to give birth may be difficult for parents who feel fearful for their surviving baby or babies although some parents may feel reassured by the extra checks that are often recommended (Fraser 2010). Some parents may also be distressed about the idea of the dead baby remaining with any surviving baby or babies (MBF 1997a; Fraser 2010). However, other parents may find this thought comforting (MBF 1997a; Fraser 2010).

Staff should acknowledge the potential difficulties for parents who have a multiple pregnancy where one or more babies have died and offer parents emotional support and reassurance that whatever they are feeling is normal. Support from staff may be particularly important if some family members and friends discount the reality of the loss and focus only on the surviving baby or babies (MBF 1997a; Fraser 2010).

Spontaneous late miscarriage

> *My baby was born following several hours of very painful contractions. The release of pain when my waters broke came as a relief, but also a nightmare at the same time.* Parent (Miscarriage Association 2011: 3)

Some women may experience a late miscarriage that starts in a way that is similar to going into labour (Miscarriage Association 2011). For example, women may experience their waters breaking (or not) and/or have strong contractions (Miscarriage Association 2011).

For some women, the labour may progress quickly and they may give birth at home or in another place (Miscarriage Association 2011). Women should be offered a physical assessment for themselves and their baby even if no healthcare professionals were present when the baby was born.

Other women's labours may take longer and they may come to the hospital (Miscarriage Association 2011). In these situations, women should be offered a physical assessment and information about what is happening, options for their care and pain relief (see Chapter 12). If there is a fetal heartbeat, parents should also be offered information about any care that would be offered for the baby if they are born alive (see *Premature labour* below). In these instances, some parents may see late miscarriage and premature labour as being very similar even if some staff may view these as very different situations.

Experiencing a spontaneous late miscarriage may be a very distressing and frightening experience for many women. Staff should offer parents continuous care and emotional support during the labour and birth (see Chapter 12). If parents are offered care on a gynaecological ward, it is important that they are offered a private room and that appropriately trained staff are available to provide sensitive, empathetic care (see *Place of care* above). After the birth, staff should offer parents emotional support and an opportunity to discuss their experience in addition to offering physical care and information about recommended follow-up care, post mortem examinations and funeral options.

Premature labour

Experiencing a premature labour can be very frightening and distressing for parents who may also be in shock (Sawyer *et al*. 2013). In one study, parents whose babies were born prematurely valued when staff appeared to be empathetic, calm, confident and in control of the situation (Sawyer *et al*. 2013). However, these parents felt it was most important that staff provided them with information and explanations about what was happening, even in emergency situations (Sawyer *et al*. 2013). While 80 per cent of the parents involved in this study were extremely satisfied with their care, parents who viewed their care negatively often felt that staff did not listen to them or that their partners were not included (Sawyer *et al*. 2013).

Wherever possible, staff should offer to explain parents' options for care during a premature labour and birth and give them time to think about the options that are right for them (Wilkinson *et al*. 2009). A Cochrane Review found that there is no reliable evidence to suggest that a planned caesarean birth or a planned vaginal birth would be recommended for a pre-term birth (Alfirevic *et al*. 2013). However, staff and parents may need to consider whether:

- A caesarean birth might be protective for the baby (Alfirevic *et al*. 2013).

- A caesarean birth may cause the baby to be born pre-term even though many women who are thought to be in pre-term labour give birth weeks later (sometimes at term) (Alfirevic *et al.* 2013).

- An emergency caesarean birth may be needed if complications arise during a planned vaginal birth (Alfirevic *et al.* 2013).

- A planned caesarean may not be possible if a woman's labour progresses too quickly and she gives birth vaginally (Alfirevic *et al.* 2013).

- A caesarean or vaginal birth is indicated for the mother's health and well-being (Wilkinson *et al.* 2009).

- There are implications of having a caesarean birth for future pregnancies (Wilkinson *et al.* 2009).

Parents who are experiencing pre-term labour should also be offered continuous support and care throughout the labour, during the birth and afterwards (see Chapter 12).

Discussing care for very premature babies with parents

Before or after a premature birth, parents should be offered opportunities to be involved in all decisions made about their baby's care (Bliss 2010).

When parents are unable or do not want to make decisions

Offering parents opportunities to be involved in all decision-making may not always be possible. For example, detailed discussions with a woman may not be possible before the birth if a labour progresses quickly, she is in strong labour or has had analgesia that affects her ability to concentrate. If another parent is present in these situations, staff should offer to discuss the available options with them and involve them in the decision-making process. Even when staff are able to offer parents opportunities to be involved in decision-making, some parents may not want to make decisions.

If parents are unable or do not want to participate in making decisions about their baby's care, staff should use their clinical judgement to make a decision about the care that is in the baby's best interests (NMC 2007). If there is time before the birth, parents should be told what has been planned for their baby's care and be given an opportunity to discuss these plans. If parents were not able to participate in decision-making before the baby's birth, they should have an opportunity afterwards to discuss the decisions that were made and what happened. Ideally, the doctors providing care for the woman and baby will be available for these discussions.

Involving parents in decision-making

Whenever possible, any decisions about the potential care a baby will receive should be made during discussions between parents and a multidisciplinary team of healthcare professionals (BAPM 2010a; Larcher *et al.* 2015) (see *Making decisions about critical care* in Chapter 13). During decision-making, parents should be offered clear information about the care that may be offered for their baby if they are born alive, including information about resuscitation and palliative care (Kaempf *et al.* 2009; BAPM 2010a;

Wool 2013; Wilkinson *et al*. 2014) (see *Care planning for the woman and baby* in Chapter 7 for more information). As the baby's prognosis will often affect care recommendations, parents should be offered an opportunity to discuss their baby's prognosis and care options with a neonatal paediatrician.

Wherever possible, parents should be given as much time as possible to consider their available options and be able to ask questions. More than one discussion with parents may be required to help parents understand their available options or discuss their feelings about these decisions (Aladangady and de Rooy 2012). Further discussions may also be required if there are disagreements between parents and staff about the care that should be provided for the baby (see *Conflicts when parents and staff disagree* in Chapter 13). More information about antenatal discussions with parents and other considerations is available in Chapter 7.

Discussing the baby's prognosis

When discussing the baby's prognosis, it is important that staff sensitively but realistically explain the likelihood of the baby surviving or having a severe disability using information on local and national data for the gestation of the pregnancy and any other relevant obstetric information (for example, the baby's estimated birth weight, gender or any diagnosed or suspected fetal anomalies) (Nuffield 2006; Wilkinson *et al*. 2009; EPICure 2012a; Manktelow *et al*. 2013).

As the gestation of a pregnancy increases, the baby's chances of survival are more likely to increase (Wilkinson *et al*. 2009; EPICure 2012b). For example, an increasing number of babies are surviving at 24 and 25 weeks' gestation and even more babies survive after 25 and 26 weeks' gestation (EPICure 2012b).

In line with these findings, EPICure's 2006 study found that a baby's chance of survival is not likely to be very high before 24 weeks' gestation (EPICure 2012b). There has been much debate among both professionals and the public about the responsibilities and duties of healthcare staff in relation to the care of these very premature babies who are born alive at the threshold of viability (between 22 and 24 weeks' gestation). However, it is often not possible to make a clear prognosis based on gestational age alone (Brunkhorst *et al*. 2014). Therefore, decisions about care should be based on the best interests of each baby if they are born alive and the baby's best interests should determine staff's duty of care to the baby (Nuffield 2006; Brunkhorst *et al*. 2014). That is, there is no legal requirement to provide life-sustaining treatment if parents and staff agree that this care is not in a very premature baby's best interests (Nuffield 2006). However, it may not be clear what care will be in the baby's best interests based on their prognosis. Additionally, all decisions should be made in partnership between parents (if the parents wish to be involved) and the healthcare teams involved in the woman's and baby's care (Mancini *et al*. 2014; Larcher *et al*. 2015) (see *Antenatal palliative and parallel care planning* in Chapter 7 and *Making decisions about critical care* in Chapter 13). Parents should also be informed that these decisions may need to be discussed again based on the baby's prognosis after birth (Chiswick 2008; Wilkinson *et al*. 2014).

Discussing parallel care planning and palliative care options with parents

Where a baby's prognosis is uncertain, this should be honestly explained to parents. Staff should suggest to parents that a parallel care plan for providing both active and palliative care be devised in these situations (Wilkinson *et al*. 2014) (see *Antenatal palliative and parallel care planning* in Chapter 7 and *Making decisions about critical care* in Chapter 13).

Parallel care planning may be beneficial for parents who fear that they are "giving up" on their baby by considering palliative care. It may also help if staff explain that palliative care is a type of supportive care for the whole family and not only end of life care. Additionally, staff should explain the benefits of palliative care for the baby to parents (for example, keeping the baby comfortable and pain-free) (Bliss 2010; Larcher *et al.* 2015) (see *Continuing care when life-sustaining treatment is withdrawn or withheld* in Chapter 13). These discussions may help to reassure parents that their baby will receive excellent care and be kept as comfortable as possible under any circumstances.

Discussing resuscitation and intensive care with parents

Parents should also be offered information about resuscitation and be involved in decision-making about whether or not to resuscitate the baby if they are born alive (see *Discussing the baby's prognosis* above). When a baby will be born before 22 weeks' gestation, staff will often inform parents that resuscitation is unlikely to be in their baby's best interests (Wilkinson *et al*. 2009). However, parents should have opportunities to discuss this recommendation with staff and express their thoughts, feelings and concerns (Wilkinson *et al*. 2009). See *Making decisions about withdrawing or withholding life-sustaining treatment* in Chapter 13 for more information.

Many parents are understandably anxious that everything possible should be done for their baby. Some parents may also be influenced by press reports of the "miraculous" survival of an extremely premature baby and have unrealistic expectations about what can be done for their baby. It is therefore important that parents of very premature babies are given clear, realistic information about their baby's prognosis, the available care options (Kaempf *et al*. 2009) and the potential implications of starting intensive care (Wilkinson *et al*. 2009).

> *The practicalities of starting, withholding and withdrawing intensive care and the positive role of palliative care where appropriate should be described to the parents. This will help to prepare them for the different possible outcomes after delivery.* (Wilkinson et al. 2009: F2)

If babies are to be offered intensive care, the parents should be offered an opportunity to visit the unit beforehand if there is time (Wilkinson *et al*. 2009). The intensive care plan should also be discussed with the parents and they should be told what to expect when their baby is born. For example, what members of staff will be in the room, information about the paediatrician who will assess and initiate treatment for the baby and how and when the baby will be transferred to the neonatal intensive care unit. For more information about intensive neonatal care see Chapter 13.

Preparing parents when a baby will receive palliative care after they are born

When a decision has been made not to resuscitate a baby after they are born, staff should gently prepare parents for what to expect in terms of how palliative care will be provided and their baby's potential reactions. Staff should offer to discuss the ways parents can spend time with and comfort their baby during this time (see *Providing care for parents around the time of their baby's death* in Chapter 13). Parents should also be gently and sensitively informed that some very premature babies may make movements at birth. They should also be told that this movement may continue for some time but that it does not mean that the baby will survive if they are born too early.

If the baby is unlikely or unexpected to live, staff should also offer to discuss parents' options for spending time with their baby and creating memories (see *Being with the baby and caring for the family when the baby dies* in Chapter 13 and *Creating memories* in Chapter 14).

When a decision is made about the baby's care

Any discussions with parents and any decisions made about care plans for the baby should be documented and a copy should be given to parents (Wilkinson *et al.* 2009). Parents should also be made aware that decisions about resuscitation, active and palliative care may need to be reviewed when the baby is born to determine the care that is in their best interest (Chiswick 2008; Wilkinson *et al.* 2014).

If there is uncertainty about the baby's prognosis, an experienced paediatrician should be present at the birth to assess the baby, resuscitate the baby if necessary and make further recommendations for care (Wilkinson *et al.* 2009; Nuffield 2006). See Chapter 13 for more information about care in the neonatal unit, discussing the baby's condition with parents after the birth and making decisions about the baby's care after the birth.

Intrapartum death and stillbirth

The unexpected death of a baby during labour or at birth is very distressing for parents and the quality of care that parents receive at this time is very important (Redshaw *et al.* 2014). Receiving supportive and empathetic care from staff in addition to high-quality clinical care is important to parents and can affect parents' long-term emotional well-being after a stillbirth (Downe *et al.* 2012).

The *Listening to Parents* report highlighted that women whose babies died during labour and birth were more critical of their care and felt less involved in decision-making than women whose babies died before labour began (Redshaw *et al.* 2014). The study also found that of these women whose babies died during labour and birth:

- 24% felt that staff communication was poor.

- 14% rarely or never felt trust or confidence in the staff providing their care.

- 43% did not feel that staff listened to them.

- 41% did not feel that their concerns were taken seriously (Redshaw *et al.* 2014).

With regard to these findings, it may be important that 84 per cent of these women had not previously met any of the midwives caring for them and that 69 per cent had three or more midwives providing their care during labour (Redshaw *et al*. 2014).

Additionally, the realisation that something is wrong during labour and birth often triggers a flurry of activity. This can be very frightening for parents, particularly if there is not much time for explanations. In these situations, parents are often aware that staff are very busy and preoccupied (Redshaw *et al*. 2014). However, a member of staff should be designated to explain what is happening to parents.

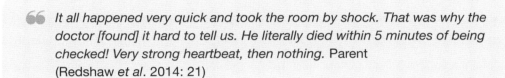

> *It all happened very quick and took the room by shock. That was why the doctor [found] it hard to tell us. He literally died within 5 minutes of being checked! Very strong heartbeat, then nothing.* Parent
> (Redshaw *et al*. 2014: 21)

> *Consultants, midwives missed things, and did not explain what was happening. During caesarean I was so scared, shouting out asking if baby was ok and no one talked to me!* Parent (Redshaw *et al*. 2014: 21)

Staff should also be aware of the support needs of partners and any other supporters during this time. This situation can be particularly hard for partners who may be left on the sidelines with no understanding of what is happening while staff focus on the mother and the baby. A designated member of staff should also explain to partners what is happening when a woman is receiving emergency care.

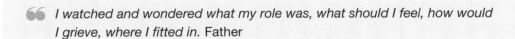

> *I watched and wondered what my role was, what should I feel, how would I grieve, where I fitted in.* Father

Telling parents that their baby has died during labour and birth

Listening to Parents also found that most women felt they were treated with kindness, sensitivity and respect at the time when they were told that their baby had died (Redshaw *et al*. 2014). However, some parents felt that they had been left alone during the labour and birth or immediately following the birth without any information (Redshaw *et al*. 2014).

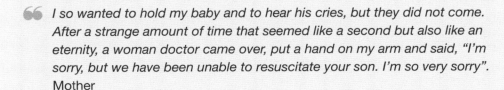

> *I so wanted to hold my baby and to hear his cries, but they did not come. After a strange amount of time that seemed like a second but also like an eternity, a woman doctor came over, put a hand on my arm and said, "I'm sorry, but we have been unable to resuscitate your son. I'm so very sorry".* Mother

The midwives were supportive but the Consultant... wouldn't explain what was happening... I had to raise my voice to get her to tell me that my baby had died no-one used the words died – "No fetal heartbeat" are the words that were used. Parent (Redshaw *et al.* 2014: 21)

 It was awful. We were left on our own for 1 hour before the Consultant actually told us he had died. I was lying in a pool of my own blood from the episiotomy and a third degree tear I sustained... None of the staff would stay in the room with us. It was chaotic, nobody knew what was going on and nobody took charge. Parent (Redshaw *et al.* 2014: 21)

Good communication with parents after their baby's death is very important. Parents should be sensitively but clearly told that their baby has died as soon as possible (see *Breaking the news to parents* above).

Parents may need time to absorb the reality of what has happened and staff should offer parents support. However, staff should also give parents as much time as they need before offering parents information about creating memories and/or asking parents to make any other decisions.

 I remember the silence. I asked "the baby?" and the Registrar said "I'm so sorry, she died". That was all I could take in and I was very grateful that the details were given later. Parent (Redshaw *et al.* 2014: 21)

 The silence is the thing that will stay with me forever, and seeing my beautiful son with his eyes closed. He was so still. Mother

When a baby who is full-term dies following incidents during labour and birth, staff should register the stillbirth with national review bodies such as MBRRACE-UK and the RCOG's Each Baby Counts project (see Appendix 2) (see *Recording, reporting and reviewing the baby's cause of death* in Chapter 16). By contributing to these reviews, staff will be providing information that can be analysed to improve the care received by women and babies in the future with an aim of reducing the number of babies who die during labour and birth (RCOG 2015b). In addition to contributing to these national reviews, staff should also review deaths on a local level in order to better understand why these deaths occurred and learn from these deaths to improve care for future patients (GMC and NMC 2015) (see *Being open and honest with colleagues* in Chapter 22).

When a baby is expected to die around the time of birth

Parents who have decided to continue a pregnancy after their baby has been diagnosed with a potentially life-limiting fetal anomaly need special care and support during labour and birth (see *Support for parents during labour and birth* in Chapter 7). These parents should also be offered referral to a local hospice if this service is available (see *Antenatal palliative and parallel care planning* in Chapter 7). This referral can be beneficial as parents can spend time with their baby in the hospice and receive support from staff before and/or after their baby dies.

CHAPTER 12

Labour and birth when a baby has died

Other relevant chapters

1: Providing holistic care

2: Providing inclusive care

3: Loss and grief

4: Communication

5: Communication across language and other barriers

7: Continuing the pregnancy

8: Termination of pregnancy for fetal anomaly or maternal medical conditions

10: Early miscarriage before 14 weeks' gestation

11: Late miscarriage between 14 and 24 weeks' gestation and stillbirth

14: After a loss

Many of the considerations for care during labour and birth after a baby has died apply to women who are experiencing a miscarriage, stillbirth, termination for fetal anomaly or maternal medical condition or whose baby is expected to die during labour and birth. Specific considerations for providing care and support for parents experiencing losses at different gestations and under varying circumstances are discussed in Chapters 7, 8, 10 and 11.

Discussing options for labour and birth with parents

It is important that women are able to make fully informed choices about their care during labour and birth after their baby has died. Being involved in the decision-making process may help parents to feel a sense of control at a time when they feel that they have little or no control. This sense of control may be important for some parents as it may have longer-term implications for their mental health (Moulder 1998; Harris and Ayers 2012) (see also Chapter 18).

To make an informed choice, a woman needs to know about all of her available options for labour and birth, including the benefits and risks of each option and recommendations based on her medical condition (see *Giving information and facilitating informed choice* in Chapter 4). This includes providing parents with information about the benefits and risks of their options for having a vaginal birth (either through expectant management or induction), a caesarean birth and pain management (see the relevant sections below). Recommendations may also be made based on whether a woman has a multiple pregnancy and whether or not her baby is expected to be born alive but die shortly after birth.

While the woman has the right to make the final decision regarding where and how she gives birth, some women may also want their partner (if they have one) to be involved in these discussions and the decision-making process. With the woman's consent, staff should include partners in discussions regarding care during labour and birth.

The information that staff provide to parents should be tailored so that individual parents can understand what they are being told (see *Giving information and facilitating informed choice* in Chapter 4). Parents who are in shock after learning that their baby has died may also find it difficult to process and retain information (see *Breaking bad news* in Chapter 4). Staff may need to repeat information on several occasions and check that parents have understood what they have been told.

The amount of information that individual parents will want may also vary. Some parents may only want the basic information needed to make an informed choice about their care while other parents may want more detailed explanations about their options and any potential risks and benefits. Staff should allow enough time during these discussions for parents to absorb the information and ask questions. Staff should also be aware that it may be difficult for parents to make decisions under these circumstances, particularly if the woman is in pain or has had analgesia.

> *To be honest it all seemed a bit of a blur after we were told. It felt as though I was being bombarded with so much information and making decisions all at once within a few minutes.* Parent
> (Redshaw *et al*. 2014: 17)

A woman whose baby has died in utero or who is having a termination for fetal anomaly may not expect to labour and to give birth. Women may also have fears or concerns about the labour and birth (ARC 2012). Additionally, women may not know much about labour and birth and may need a lot of information especially if this is their first pregnancy. Staff should offer parents an explanation of the labour and birth process and an opportunity to discuss any feelings and concerns.

It is important that parents are given support and as much time as possible while considering their options for labour and the birth of their baby (RCOG 2012; van der Kooy 2015). However, they may need to make decisions more quickly if the woman is already in labour or there are certain risks that may affect her health (Sands 2013c).

During the decision-making process, some parents may change their minds a number of times (van der Kooy 2015). Other parents may make a decision more quickly. Unless a woman is already in labour, she should be offered the option of going home to consider her options. If parents decide to go home to make a decision, they should be given a 24-hour contact number for a named contact or contacts who can offer help and support (RCOG 2010a). Some parents may value having this time to make a decision and absorb the reality of what has happened. Other parents may decline this offer to go home as they want to give birth to their baby as soon as possible after finding out that the baby has died (Sands 2013c).

 They offered me a chance to go home first. I suppose they were giving me the chance to get my head round it, but I just couldn't face going home, knowing what I did. I just wanted to get on with the birth. Mother

 The midwife and doctor team that we saw at the hospital at this time were very good. We were told about what would happen next (medically) and given information and leaflets ... which we read before returning to the hospital for the birth. Parent (Redshaw et al. 2014: 17)

Any discussions with parents should be documented in the woman's medical notes and they should be given a copy of the notes for their reference. Parents should also be given written information with details about their options for labour and birth and any relevant local or national support organisations such as Sands, ARC, the Miscarriage Association, Child Bereavement UK, TAMBA and the Multiple Births Foundation as appropriate (see Appendix 2).

 I was also told a Doctor would visit me to explain my options but instead my midwife came with a tablet, told me to take it and come back in 2 days. I was sent home with no information or leaflets ... I had no idea what I had been given or any effects. Parent (Redshaw et al. 2014: 17)

Parents should also be offered information about their options for seeing, holding or creating other memories with their baby, post mortem examinations and a funeral for their baby (see Chapters 14, 16 and 20, respectively). Some parents may find it helpful to consider these options or have questions that they raise with staff before their baby is born. For example, some parents may want information about what their baby might look like. Staff should sensitively but honestly explain how the baby might look based on their gestation and any other relevant information (see *Seeing and holding the baby* in Chapter 14). Other parents may prefer to discuss this information after the birth. In either situation, it is important that parents are not overloaded with information as these choices can also be offered and explained after the baby is born.

Care options for labour and birth

Most of the care options listed here are most relevant for late miscarriage and stillbirth. The section on induction is also relevant to women who are having a medical termination or feticide for a fetal anomaly after 21 weeks + 6 days' gestation. See specific chapters for more information about care options for parents experiencing a termination for fetal anomaly or maternal condition (Chapter 8), an early miscarriage (Chapter 10), premature labour (Chapter 11) or whose baby is expected to die around the time of birth (see *Support for parents during labour and birth* in Chapter 7).

The information about pain management in this section applies to all parents.

Vaginal birth is generally the recommended type of birth for women whose baby dies before labour begins unless there are medical reasons for recommending a caesarean birth (RCOG 2010a, 2012). This is because of the risks to the mother and potential implications for future pregnancies that are linked with caesarean births (RCOG 2010a). However, all potential options for the baby's birth should be discussed with parents. Parents should also be reassured that staff will be available to provide continuous support regardless of the type of care parents choose.

 I remember the feeling of absolute disbelief that anyone was really expecting me to go through labour and childbirth. I just kept saying "I can't" over and over again. At that moment if someone had told me I could have a general anaesthetic and a caesarean section I would have said yes without question. I wish there had been someone there to tell me that giving birth to my beautiful little girl would be something I would never regret, and a memory that I would always cherish. Mother

Women will also usually be offered tests to check their health and examine the cause of the baby's death (RCOG 2010a, 2012; Sands 2013c). However, it should be explained to parents that it may not be possible to determine the reasons at this stage (RCOG 2010a, 2012; Sands 2013c).

If there is time, staff should also suggest that parents may want to plan for the labour, birth and/or what they would like to happen after their baby is born. Some parents may want help and support in deciding what they would like to include in a birth plan. Any members of staff caring for parents should read this plan and be aware of parents' wishes (see *Providing care during labour and birth* below).

If they are going home before returning to a hospital or a freestanding-midwifery unit, parents may also wish to consider things that they might like to bring to the hospital. For example, they may want to bring snacks, comfortable clothing, toiletries, a camera, a special toy, blanket or other item for their baby and any clothes that they may wish to dress their baby in (Sands 2013c). Parents may appreciate suggestions from staff about items that they could bring.

Induction

Some women may want to have their labour induced (started using medication) after their baby dies, including after a termination for fetal anomaly (see *Termination of pregnancy at or after 21 weeks + 6 days' gestation* in Chapter 8). Induction of labour is generally recommended if there are signs of sepsis, pre-eclampsia, placental abruption or the woman's waters have broken as these carry potential risks to the woman's health (RCOG 2010a).

Parents should be offered information about:

- The types of medication that are available to induce labour. These options include vaginal pessaries or gels containing prostaglandin, tablets that can be taken orally or vaginally (i.e. Misoprotol) or an intravenous syntocinon drip (RCOG 2010a, 2012).

- The process, and the potential benefits and risks associated with each medicine used for induction (RCOG 2010a, 2012).

- The time each type of induction may take (Fisher and Lafarge 2015).

 I was not told that it could take so long and had not expected to be in hospital for nearly 6 days. I learnt that at 34 weeks' gestation my body had to be coaxed into delivering. Mother

If a woman has previously had a caesarean birth, a consultant obstetrician should offer to discuss the safety and risks of induction based on the number of caesarean sections she has had, the location of her scar and the recommended medications (RCOG 2010a). These women may wish to further consider their options for expectant management or a caesarean birth.

When parents decide to have their labour induced, they should be offered time between the confirmation of the baby's death and induction. This time may help some parents to absorb the news about their baby and the idea of labouring and giving birth to their dead baby, make any necessary practical arrangements at home and think about how they want to say goodbye to their baby (Geerinck-Vercammen 1999; RCOG 2012; Sands 2013c). If a woman goes home before the induction, she should be given a 24-hour contact number for named contacts should she want any support or information (RCOG 2010a). Other women may want the induction to take place as soon as possible and may find it very distressing to carry a dead baby. For some parents, a long delay between the confirmation of their baby's death and the birth may cause distress (Rådestad 2001). It is important that women are supported to make a decision that is right for them.

 It was absolutely important to get back into our own home, to get away from the maternity ward, to inform family and prepare for the next morning. I believe having this space gave us the mental strength to prepare in our own way for what was to come. Mother

When I did manage to get to sleep over the next few days, waking up was unbearable. You were still in my belly and I'd hold you thinking I'd had a bad dream. When reality sank in, the devastation would wash over me again and again. Mother

Expectant management

After a baby's death has been confirmed, some women may want to go home and wait for labour and birth to start naturally. Most women (more than 85 per cent) will go into labour within three weeks of their baby's death (RCOG 2010a, 2012). Parents should be reassured that waiting for labour to start is generally safe if they are medically well. However, if there are signs of sepsis, pre-eclampsia, placental abruption or that their waters have broken, women are generally advised to have their labour induced (RCOG 2010a) (see *Induction* above).

If women decide to go home to wait for labour and birth to start, it is usually recommended that they return to the hospital twice a week for testing (RCOG 2010a, 2012). This testing is for disseminated intravascular coagulation (DIC), which is the formation of blood clots in the body's small blood vessels (RCOG 2010a). These visits may also help staff to assess parents' emotional and mental well-being and offer support. Staff should be aware when parents are coming for these assessments so that parents do not need to explain the reason for their visit (see *Continuity of carers, bereavement midwives and communication between staff* below). Parents should also be given a 24-hour contact number where they can reach named contacts for further information and support (RCOG 2010a, 2012).

Parents who are waiting for longer periods of time for labour to start should be supported in their decision. However, they should also be made aware that they can change their mind at any time if they decide they want their labour to be induced (RCOG 2012). They should also be advised that their baby's appearance will start to change and that the results of any post mortem examinations may be less informative (RCOG 2010a).

Caesarean birth

Some women may prefer to have a caesarean birth after their baby has died or this may be recommended for medical reasons. Women should be made aware of the benefits and risks of caesarean birth, including the increased physical recovery time after the surgery (RCOG 2010a, 2012; Sands 2013c). Staff should also ensure that the woman is aware of how a caesarean birth may affect future pregnancies (RCOG 2010a; Sands 2013c).

Some women may not feel able to cope with giving birth to their baby vaginally or have had previous experiences that make the thought of vaginal birth very distressing (RCOG 2010a; Sands 2013c). Women expecting healthy babies have the option of having a caesarean birth following a documented discussion with staff about the risks associated with a caesarean section and their options for a vaginal birth (NICE 2013). Women whose babies have died should also be able to request a caesarean birth under these circumstances and should be supported in this decision.

When women have decided to have a caesarean section, staff should also offer to discuss the options for local or general anaesthetic with parents. A local anaesthetic may be safer, make it possible for the woman to be awake when the baby is born and allow her partner or another supporter to be with her in theatre (Sands 2013c). However, a general anaesthetic may be advisable for some women and the reasons should be explained to parents (Sands 2013c).

Pain management

Women have different experiences of pain during labour and birth (Jones *et al*. 2012). However, a woman who is frightened, shocked, distressed or feels unsupported may feel pain more intensely (Haines *et al*. 2012; Jones *et al*. 2012). Induction of labour may also increase the pain that a woman experiences and this should be explained to women when discussing induction and pain management (NICE 2008b). In addition to this, many women may not expect the pain and duration of their labour after their baby dies (Moulder 1998).

Women whose babies have died need full information about pain relief and should be reassured that all pain relief options will be available to ensure that they are comfortable (unless they have a history of allergies or adverse reactions to certain drugs). All women who are experiencing a perinatal loss should be offered information about all available pain relief options, including advantages, disadvantages, side effects and evidence for the efficacy of each type of pain relief.

Women should also be aware that the place where they are receiving care may affect their options for pain relief. For example, women who are receiving care on a midwifery-led unit or at home would not have access to an epidural or some other pain relief options. This may also be the case for women who are being cared for on a gynaecological ward as epidurals are often only available to women on labour wards (Sands 2013c).

It is important that all women, including those being cared for on gynaecological wards, have access to adequate pain relief if they need it. Trusts, Health Boards and managers should ensure that it is possible for women to access adequate pain relief regardless of where they are receiving care. If it is not possible for women to access an epidural on a gynaecological ward, they should be offered a room on the labour ward and policies should be in place to facilitate this process (see *Place of care* below).

If women want pharmacological pain relief (such as diamorphine or epidural anaesthesia), they should be offered an opportunity to discuss these options with an anaesthetist (NICE 2014b). However, women who have sepsis or problems with blood clotting may not be able to use epidural anaesthesia as this may cause complications for the woman (RCOG 2010a, 2012). Some methods of pain relief, for example opioids, may make women feel drowsy, nauseated or cause them to vomit (NICE 2014b). Drowsiness caused by opioids may diminish a woman's ability to understand and participate in what is happening. She may feel confused later on about events that she wants to remember and understand and this may add to her distress. For example, a woman may want to have a clear memory of seeing and holding her baby at the time of birth.

Women may also be interested in considering the use of entonox (gas and air), breathing, water (a birth pool, bathtub or shower), visualisations, massage, aromatherapy, acupressure or music (NICE 2014b). Women should be supported to use these pain relief methods and techniques during their labour and birth.

Ideally, information about pain relief options should be offered to women before and during labour as necessary. Staff should ask women about what approaches to pain management they would prefer and which they would like to avoid (NICE 2014b). However, they should be aware that some women may feel uncertain about how they will experience labour and birth if the discussion is taking place beforehand (Lally *et al*. 2014). Therefore, staff should also support women to make and reconsider decisions during labour as needed (Lally *et al*. 2014).

It is important to find the appropriate type and level of pain relief for each woman and address the situation immediately if a women's pain relief is found to be inadequate (NICE 2014b). Without a healthy baby to look forward to following the birth, some women may find it particularly difficult to cope with labour pains. Staff should offer these women additional support and pain relief as needed (see also *Providing care during labour and birth* below).

Special considerations for intrapartum care

Multiples

When one or more babies have died during a multiple pregnancy and one or more babies have also survived, parents may experience mixed feelings during labour and after the birth (see *Multiple births* in Chapter 14). Some parents may feel torn between experiencing joy for the impending birth of any surviving babies and intense grief for the baby or babies who have died. Some parents may not feel able to grieve until after their babies are born when they are able to say goodbye to the baby or babies who have died (Fraser 2010). They may also have been concerned that their grief would affect any surviving babies before the birth (Fraser 2010). Staff should acknowledge the baby who has died and avoid only focusing on the baby or babies who have survived during and after the labour and birth. Staff should also offer parents opportunities before, during and after the labour and birth to discuss how they are feeling.

Sometimes parents are advised to continue a pregnancy if one or more babies have died to give any surviving babies more time to develop (Fraser 2010) (see *When one or more babies die during a multiple pregnancy* in Chapter 11). This may be the case if a baby dies unexpectedly in utero. In other instances, one or more babies may have been diagnosed with a fetal anomaly and some parents may have had a selective termination or feticide (see also *Selective termination and feticide* in Chapter 8). Other parents may have decided to continue the pregnancy after a fetal anomaly was diagnosed and one or more babies may be expected to die around the time of birth. Staff should be aware of any care plans that have been made for each baby in these circumstances (see also *If a baby may be born alive but is expected to die during or shortly after birth* below and *Care planning for the woman and baby* in Chapter 7). Some parents may also be experiencing complex emotions if they had a reduction of a multiple pregnancy (see also *Multifetal pregnancy reduction* in Chapter 8).

If there is likely to be a body, recognisable remains of the baby or babies who have died or a fetus papyraceous, staff should offer to gently describe to parents how the baby or babies may look. Many parents do not regret seeing their baby or babies even if their appearance has deteriorated or they have a visible fetal anomaly (Fraser 2010). Staff should also offer parents opportunities to discuss their options for seeing and holding their baby and creating memories after the birth (see also *When the baby has an anomaly or is macerated* and *Creating memories* in Chapter 14). For example, staff may want to suggest that parents take photos with all of the babies together. Even if a surviving baby or babies may need care in a neonatal unit, staff can offer parents information about spending time with all of their babies after the birth (see *Parents with more than one baby* in Chapter 13).

If a baby may be born alive but is expected to die during or shortly after birth

Parents who know that their baby will die as a result of the process of labour and birth may be very distressed and need extra support during this time (see also *Support for parents during labour and birth* in Chapter 7). Parents may also find labour and birth very difficult if their baby will be very premature and unable to survive (see *Premature labour* in Chapter 11).

When it has been decided that a baby will not be resuscitated or offered active treatment, they can be provided with palliative comfort care in the same place where the mother is receiving care (de Rooey *et al.* 2012). That is, palliative care can be offered to babies who are born alive on the labour ward or at home. Trusts, Health Boards and managers should ensure that policies and provisions are in place to provide palliative care in any setting where the mother is giving birth. This may include releasing a member of staff from the neonatal unit to offer support and care to parents and babies who are on the labour ward or at home.

Examples of the comfort care that may be provided for these babies can include pain relief, warmth, fluids, skin-to-skin contact with parents, being put to the breast and/or being held by parents or other family members. Palliative care also includes supportive care for parents when their baby is expected to die (see *Providing care for parents around the time of their baby's death* in Chapter 13).

Parents should also be offered opportunities to spend time with and care for their baby and may benefit from the emotional and practical support that staff can offer at this time (de Rooey *et al.* 2012). Some parents may wish to participate in their baby's care. However, other parents may decline opportunities to be involved in their baby's care at this time and this should be respected. Staff should reassure parents that their baby will receive excellent care and be kept as comfortable as possible. If parents were not present when the baby died, staff should offer parents opportunities to discuss the care that their baby received at that time (see *If the parents were not there at the death* in Chapter 13).

Place of care

The place where a woman receives care during labour and birth after her baby dies may affect how parents experience this care (Redshaw *et al.* 2014; Fisher and Lafarge 2015). Women and their partners (if they have one) should be provided with full information about the places where they can choose to give birth and be supported to make a decision about their place of care. Some parents may decide to give birth in the place where they had originally planned or they may change their mind (van der Kooy 2015). With regard to determining place of care during labour and birth, the RCM state that:

> *Midwives should take action to ensure that … women have a full discussion of the evidence to help them make the best choices for themselves.* (RCM 2014: 12)

As most research around place of birth has studied women who were expected to give birth to live babies, the evidence base is limited for parents whose baby has died before labour begins. Therefore, staff should support women to make a decision about where they give birth to their baby who has died by giving them information about their available options, the benefits and risks of each option for the woman and recommendations based on the mother's medical condition and history (see *Care options for labour and birth* above). A woman's preferences for the labour and birth will also affect where she gives birth. For example, a woman will need to give birth in a hospital if she decides to have a caesarean birth, induction of labour, surgical termination of pregnancy or surgical management of miscarriage. The types of pain relief that a woman may want may also affect her decisions about place of care (see *Pain management* above).

It should be possible for women to decide whether to give birth to their baby who has died in a hospital (on a labour ward, gynaecological ward or midwifery-led unit), in a freestanding midwifery-led unit or at home. The available choices will be dependent on the woman's medical condition and birth preferences.

However, the availability of choices may also be affected by policies that determine where care is offered based on the gestation when the baby died (Sands 2010; NHS Improving Quality 2014). For some parents who experience a late miscarriage or termination for fetal anomaly, it may be particularly distressing if they are unable to access care in the place of their choice (Sands 2010; Fisher and Lafarge 2015). Some of these parents may find it upsetting to receive care on a gynaecological ward as they may not feel that the loss of their wanted baby has been acknowledged (Sands 2010; Fisher and Lafarge 2015). Other parents may prefer to receive care on a gynaecological ward (Fisher and Lafarge 2015). Women should be able to access care in the place of their choosing under these circumstances and no assumptions should be made about the place where they will want to receive care (Fisher and Lafarge 2015) (see also *Discussing termination of pregnancy procedures* in Chapter 8 and *Place of care* in Chapter 11).

It has also been highlighted that gynaecological wards may not be able to provide parents with care that is as good as that available on labour ward (Sands 2010). For example, gynaecological nurses may not have adequate training in supporting bereaved parents or offering them choices about seeing, holding and creating memories with their baby (Sands 2010). However, this problem is not isolated to gynaecological wards as gaps in staff training have also been identified on some labour wards (Redshaw *et al.* 2014; Siassakos *et al.* 2015, unpublished results).

It is important that Trusts, Health Boards and managers ensure that policies and practices are in place to provide all parents with care from appropriately trained staff in their place of choice wherever possible.

Care in a hospital or freestanding midwifery-led unit

Some of the recommendations here will be more relevant for care on labour wards. However, these best practice points also highlight some of the considerations regarding the place where care is provided in gynaecological wards and midwifery-led units.

Many parents find it distressing to give birth in a place where live babies are being born or they can hear the sounds of crying babies (Redshaw *et al.* 2014; Fisher and Lafarge 2015). It is recommended that labour wards have dedicated, soundproofed bereavement rooms or suites where parents can have complete privacy and comfort (Redshaw *et al.* 2014). These rooms should be a short distance from the main labour ward rooms so that staff are quickly and easily able to provide care for parents. There should also be space for partners and other birth supporters in these rooms, including a comfortable place to sleep. Where these facilities are unavailable, staff should acknowledge that this may potentially be difficult for parents and prepare parents for potentially distressing sights or sounds on the way to the room where they will receive care (Hunter 2015). For more information, see *Place of care* in Chapter 14.

It is also very important that parents are never shown into these rooms before they know that their baby has died or is likely to die as this may cause parents additional distress.

 We were shown into a very nice, comfortable room and only realised that something might be seriously wrong when we saw a label on the kettle saying "dedicated to the memory of…". We were devastated. Mother

After the birth, parents should also be cared for in rooms that have been specially designed for bereaved parents (see *Place of care* in Chapter 14).

Trusts and Health Boards should ensure that each labour ward has one or more specially equipped bereavement rooms or suites. The number of rooms should be dependent on the size of the unit and the number of births per year.

Home

While it is less common, some women may decide to give birth at home after their baby has died or is expected to die around the time of birth. Some women may already have been planning a homebirth before their baby died (van der Kooy 2015). Other women may decide to give birth at home after they learn that their baby has died.

If a woman plans to give birth at home, it should be clearly documented in the woman's hand-held maternity notes that the baby has died or is expected to die around the time of birth. If there is a chance that the baby might be born alive, any care plan detailing comfort care for the baby should also be included in the mother's notes.

The woman's midwife should arrange for gas and air and any other equipment to be delivered to the woman's home as soon as possible. Any equipment that may be needed to provide care for the woman or comfort care for the baby should be included in this delivery. The midwife should ensure that a delivery pack for the baby is not sent to the home unless the baby may be born alive. Staff should also double-check that these items have been delivered.

Providing care during labour and birth

Labour ward staff should be expecting parents who arrive at a hospital for an induction after their baby has died. Staff should be available to welcome parents and ensure that they do not have to explain why they are there (Draper *et al*. 2015) (see *Continuity of carers, bereavement midwives and communication between staff* below). This also applies if labour has started following expectant management and parents have called ahead to inform staff that they are coming in to the labour ward or midwifery-led unit. These parents should not be expected to wait at home until contractions are closer together unless they wish to do so.

Parents should be shown to a private room as soon as possible after arrival. One benefit of having a dedicated bereavement room or suite is that the room is more likely to be available so parents would not need to wait until a room is free (see *Place of care* above). Additionally, parents should not be expected to wait for a scheduled induction or caesarean section under these circumstances unless it is absolutely necessary.

Before caring for parents, all staff should ensure that they have read the woman's medical notes and birth plan if one has been prepared.

Women whose babies have died should be offered the same quality and content of care as other women (Draper *et al*. 2015).

Continuity of carers, bereavement midwives and communication between staff

All women should be offered continuous support and care from the same carers throughout the labour and birth as this may affect their well-being and their experience of care (RCOG 2010a; Kenworthy and Kirkham 2011; Redshaw *et al.* 2014; Siassakos *et al.* 2015, unpublished results). This continuity will help to ensure that parents do not need to repeatedly build new relationships with staff at such a difficult time and it may also affect the quality of care that staff can provide. For example, it may be easier for staff to provide support for parents if they have had an opportunity to get to know them (Kenworthy and Kirkham 2011). Building a relationship with parents may also help staff to avoid distancing themselves from parents as a potential way of coping with this very difficult situation (Kenworthy and Kirkham 2011). Wherever possible, staff should be able to arrange for parents to be supported in hospital by a known midwife who cared for them in the community (Kenworthy and Kirkham 2011).

 There was a sensitive awareness of our needs and excellent continuity of care in the labour ward. I was cared for by three key midwives throughout my stay who showed great understanding of my needs and who obviously communicated well with each other. Mother

It is also important that staff support parents as a team so that no member of staff feels that they have been left on their own to care for parents (Kenworthy and Kirkham 2011). The same members of staff (including bereavement midwives) should not be expected to care for all bereaved parents on the unit as providing this care can be very distressing for staff (Kenworthy and Kirkham 2011; Sands 2015i). It can also be exhausting for staff to be constantly monitoring their words to avoid saying something that may cause additional distress for parents (Kenworthy and Kirkham 2011). Having a continuous team of carers will help to relieve some of this pressure on staff and ensure that they receive support from colleagues.

In the event that a member of staff absolutely must be called away to another emergency, they should tell parents that they will be back as soon as possible. They should also ensure that another member of staff is able to stay with parents and offer care and support in their absence. Parents whose babies have died should be a priority for staff, even when they are busy.

 The delivery was just awful from beginning to end. They almost treated me like "The Woman With The Dead Baby" [mother's emphasis]. There was no sympathy. When I asked to see a doctor, this particular doctor came in and said "we're very busy". And his exact words, I'll never forget them "Well, with all due respect, your baby's dead already". Which was just the most awful thing you could say. Mother (Downe *et al.* 2012: 7)

The other staff on the unit should be told about the baby's death or expected death. This will help to prevent inappropriate comments being made by well-meaning staff. It may also help to ensure that the staff caring for parents whose baby has died are offered support from their colleagues. After parents arrive at the labour ward or midwifery unit, the patient board should be marked with a special symbol to notify all staff that a woman is in labour whose baby has died. All staff should be familiar with this symbol – including administrative, cleaning and support staff. This symbol will give staff information about what room parents are in and make them aware that they will have different support needs from other parents on the unit.

Support for staff

It is important that staff receive support from managers and other colleagues when providing care for parents whose baby has died (Kenworthy and Kirkham 2011) (see also Chapter 24). Trusts, Health Boards and managers should ensure that policies and practices are in place so that arrangements can be made for staff to stay with parents throughout the labour and birth (see *Continuity of carers, bereavement midwives and communication between staff* below).

In addition to the emotional effect that constantly providing this care may have on staff, relying on one or even a handful of staff to care for all bereaved parents may cause other staff to become de-skilled or feel that they are not able to support parents (Kenworthy and Kirkham 2011; Sands 2015i). Dedicated bereavement staff may also not always be available. Therefore, it is important that all staff have training in empathetic communication and are aware of the potential needs of bereaved parents so that they are able to provide good quality care for parents when their baby dies (Downe *et al.* 2013; NHS Improving Quality 2014; Sands 2015h, 2015i; Siassakos *et al.* 2015, unpublished results). Training may also benefit staff who do not feel confident providing care to bereaved parents (Kenworthy and Kirkham 2011).

Having bereavement midwives available on every unit may also help to ensure that parents receive the best care possible as these specially trained midwives are able to:

- Offer support and information to all staff who are providing care for bereaved parents.

- Ensure that all relevant staff have bereavement care training.

- Promote good communication between staff (Sands 2015i).

See *Bereavement midwives and nurses* in Chapter 25 for more information about the role of bereavement midwives.

Emotional support and care for parents during labour and birth

It is important that women and their partners (if they have one) feel completely supported throughout the labour and birth and are not left alone unless they request privacy.

Throughout the labour and birth, women should be offered information about their care options as needed and staff should obtain informed consent before any procedure is performed (see *Giving information and facilitating informed choice* in Chapter 4). Even in an emergency, a designated member of staff should explain what is happening to parents.

The emotional support that staff can offer to parents during the labour and birth is also crucial. Many women have concerns or fears about labour and birth and how they will cope. However, these feelings may be intensified when the baby has died and there is no reward of meeting a healthy baby at the end (Woods 1997). Women whose babies have died or are expected to die around the time of birth are likely to need extra encouragement and support to keep going during the labour and birth (Woods 1997).

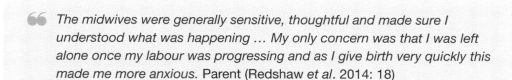

The midwives were generally sensitive, thoughtful and made sure I understood what was happening … My only concern was that I was left alone once my labour was progressing and as I give birth very quickly this made me more anxious. Parent (Redshaw *et al.* 2014: 18)

I felt like strangers around me became more like family. Their grief was obvious and a comfort to me. I felt like a person not their job … They watched my reactions carefully and behaved accordingly. Parent (Redshaw *et al.* 2014: 18)

Offering this support may be challenging for staff as the usual words of encouragement that focus on the positive experience of the baby being born cannot be used with parents whose baby has died (Kenworthy and Kirkham 2011). It may be tempting for staff to focus on the future in these situations. However, it is important that staff stay focused on the present situation as focusing on the idea of a future baby may cause additional distress for parents or cause them to feel isolated.

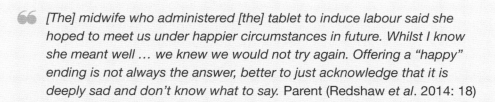

[The] midwife who administered [the] tablet to induce labour said she hoped to meet us under happier circumstances in future. Whilst I know she meant well … we knew we would not try again. Offering a "happy" ending is not always the answer, better to just acknowledge that it is deeply sad and don't know what to say. Parent (Redshaw *et al.* 2014: 18)

During the birth, parents may need extra emotional support when pushing the baby out. This may particularly be the case for parents whose baby is expected to die as a result of the process of giving birth (see *If a baby may be born alive but is expected to die during or shortly after birth* above).

From the moment I started pushing, our delivery room was very quiet. My husband was very supportive and our midwife talked to us throughout everything and helped carry us both through it all. We desperately wanted to see our baby, but at the same time we knew that once she was born it would be real and we would have to accept that she was really gone.
Mother

After the birth, parents may not be expecting the silence that follows and some parents may be in shock or be very distressed (Trulsson and Rådestad 2004; Sands 2013c). Staff should be present to support parents following the birth. Staff are also able to offer parents opportunities to meet their baby at this time and parents may value guidance from staff around seeing, holding and creating memories with their baby (Trulsson and Rådestad 2004) (see also *Seeing and holding* in Chapter 14).

 I remember saying to one of the midwives that I'd so looked forward to saying hello to my son. Her response was that I still could. Mother

Care for partners and supporters

A woman should be able to have her partner and/or another supporter with her at all times. A woman who wants supporters to be with her should be able to have them present regardless of the gestation when her baby dies. Some women may want to have more than one person with them and this should be accommodated.

 It was so good to have my partner with me the whole time. I don't think I could have got through labour without him. Mother

Even if a woman has someone else with her, it is important that staff offer support and make it clear that they are available whenever needed. Some women do not wish to be left alone at any time and should not be left on their own. Other women may prefer to be alone, provided that they know that they can get help immediately if it is needed.

Any partners or supporters who are present should be kept fully informed and involved whenever possible (with the woman's consent). This is important as it may add to their distress if they do not feel informed about what is happening.

 It was terrifying. Staff were rushing around and nobody had time to talk to me or tell me what they were doing. They rushed her out and I was left alone for what seemed like ages. I then realised that not only was our baby dead, but I might lose my wife as well. Father

Partners and supporters may also feel protective towards the woman and may become very anxious that staff should be doing more to help her and, where appropriate, the baby. In some cases, this may lead to aggression towards staff. Acknowledging the partner's or supporter's concerns and giving clear explanations may help to reassure them that everything possible is being done.

Staff should also offer emotional support to any supporters as they are likely to be experiencing their own grief for the baby as well as fear for the woman. Additionally, they may feel powerless and worried if they see that the woman is distressed and in pain.

 It's bad enough watching the woman you love suffer the pain and sickness of labour when it's for a living baby. But knowing that it was for a dead baby was brutal. I have never longed so hard and so long that I could have shared some of the burden. But I couldn't. Having said that – despite the difficulty of being there – I think if I had been somewhere else, I would be regretting it for the rest of my life. Father

It may be helpful for staff to acknowledge that partners may feel that there is very little that they can actively *do*. However, they can emphasise the support they are offering by *being there*. It is also important to acknowledge that most people find it very difficult to "just" be there.

Care after the birth

Chapter 14 focuses on the care that should be offered to parents after the birth of their baby who has died. In addition to this immediate care after the birth, staff should also be aware that parents should be offered relevant information about postnatal care (see Chapter 15), a post mortem examination (see Chapter 16), registering their baby's birth, death and/or stillbirth (see Chapter 19) and a funeral for their baby (see Chapter 20).

CHAPTER 13

Care in neonatal units and neonatal death

Other relevant chapters

1: Providing holistic care

2: Providing inclusive care

3: Loss and grief

4: Communication

5: Communication across language and other barriers

7: Continuing the pregnancy

11: Late miscarriage between 14 and 24 weeks' gestation and stillbirth

14: After a loss

15: Postnatal care

16: Transfer to the mortuary and post mortem investigations

17: Follow-up appointments and ongoing care

19: Certificates and registration

20: Funerals and sensitive disposal

21: Memorials

Care and support for parents in the neonatal unit

Many parents find being in a neonatal intensive care unit frightening and threatening at a time when they are already extremely anxious and distressed. Parents may experience a wide range of emotions. They might feel scared, disempowered, angry, loving, vulnerable, detached, guilty, like they want to run away, that they cannot control their emotions, unable to bond with their baby and/or inadequate for not knowing how to help their baby (Lundqvist *et al.* 2002; Charchuk and Simpson 2005; Meyer *et al.* 2006; Bliss 2010; Woodroffe 2013). They may have little opportunity to feel that they are parents to their baby (or babies) or they may feel that their baby belongs to healthcare staff (Aagaard and Hall 2008). When a baby is not expected to live for long, parents may also not be able to believe that their baby is going to die or need time to accept that this is going to happen (Woodroffe 2013; Smith 2014).

Personal, cultural and religious variations may influence the way that parents experience and deal with having a baby in the neonatal unit and the decisions they wish to make for their baby's care (Butt 2012; Das 2012; Scott-Joynt 2012; Weitzman 2012). Staff should be aware of this diversity so as not to question parents' views or see some parents' responses and behaviour as "abnormal" or uncaring (Fowlie and McHaffie 2004; Woodroffe 2013). For parents who are not familiar with UK hospitals or medical practice, the experience may be particularly alien and terrifying, especially if they are experiencing language barriers (see also *Providing interpreters for parents* in Chapter 5).

Parents are likely to be exhausted after the birth and may find that their sleep is disturbed by their fears and concerns. Some parents may also experience depression, anxiety or traumatic stress symptoms (Woodroffe 2013; Redshaw *et al.* 2014). These factors may make it harder for parents to deal with the often rapid changes in the baby's condition, understand what is happening and make difficult critical care decisions (Woodroffe 2013). The emotional and possible financial stresses linked with having a sick baby may also affect parents, their relationship and/or other family members (Fowlie and McHaffie 2004; Bliss 2014). Staff should be aware of signs of exhaustion and strain in parents and offer sensitive help and support if necessary.

> *It was a six-month roller coaster ride. There were periods of great excitement and also fear as Emma's condition took a step forward or back. I also had the added responsibility of supporting Julie and my only son Timothy.* Father

Providing emotional and practical support for parents and families is an essential part of caring for very ill babies. Having continuity of carer may help parents to feel more confident in themselves and their baby's care (Aagaard and Hall 2008). Parents should be offered opportunities to become involved in their baby's care and staff should encourage and support parents who wish to help with caring for their baby. Staff should also support parents to help them feel that they have some control over the care planning for their baby. It is important to:

- Explain how the neonatal unit functions, parents' role in the daily routine and what they need to know (Bliss 2011).

- Listen to parents and try to understand their values, priorities and concerns.

- Give parents as much information as they want (see *Discussions with parents about their baby's condition* below).

- Acknowledge parents' feelings about the situation and the difficulties caused by the nature and pressures of the neonatal unit.

- Invite parents to be present during doctors' rounds, routine medical procedures and when their baby is examined.

- Take parents' observations about their baby's condition seriously (Wocial 2000; Aagaard and Hall 2008).

- Talk about the baby as an individual rather than just focusing on their medical condition and use the baby's name if they have one.

- Ask if parents would like to care for and create memories with their baby (see also *Spending time with the baby* below).

- Ensure that the mother is receiving appropriate postnatal care (see also Chapter 15).

- Acknowledge siblings who visit the baby on the neonatal unit and also consider siblings who are unable to visit the neonatal unit.

- Discuss options with parents about referral to local children's hospices for emotional and practical supportive care where parents may be able to arrange respite care, spend time with their baby outside of a medical environment while having support readily available and use a "cool room" to spend time with their baby after the baby's death (see *Parents' time with and access to their baby* in Chapter 14 and *Taking the baby's body home* in Chapter 15).

- Give parents advice about financial support that is available (see *Special considerations for parents with babies in neonatal units* below).

- Inform parents if their baby's cot has been moved before they visit the unit to avoid unnecessary distress.

- Ensure that care for the baby and their family is integrated and multidisciplinary and that there is good communication within and across teams.

The Bliss Baby Charter (2011) provides more detailed information about the family-centred care that should be provided for babies and their families on neonatal units (see Appendix 2).

 I was by the incubator and was asked if I minded medical students having a look at such a premature baby. I said it would be OK as they have to learn. They asked the consultant questions about Lily-anne but referred to her as "it". Lily-anne was a very small but nonetheless human being, and deserved the same respect as any other patient. I didn't complain or say anything at the time because my brain was all over the place. "It" is not an appropriate way to talk about a child, especially in the presence of a parent. I have been really distraught by this: it has stuck with me for five years. Mother

In addition to support offered by clinical staff, parents may value the support of a counsellor, a member of the hospital chaplaincy or their own religious adviser. It is important to ensure that fathers and female partners are also offered emotional support (see also *Fathers and same-sex partners* in Chapter 3). Partners are often seen as the mother's supporter, which may make it difficult for them to express their own feelings (Hugill *et al.* 2013). Parents may also benefit from the support of organisations such as Bliss, Rainbow Trust, Child Bereavement UK, Lullaby Trust, Sibs, Together for Short Lives, Sands or local children's hospices (see Appendix 2 for more information about these services). It is important to remember that older siblings and other family members, such as grandparents, may also need support (see also *Other children* and *Grandparents* in Chapter 3).

Place of care

The layout of neonatal units has been found to have an effect on the health of babies, parents and staff (Shahheidari and Homer 2012).

Open plan units may promote interactions between parents and staff and allow staff to monitor several babies at the same time (Shahheidari and Homer 2012). Staff should also be aware of the possible interactions between the different families in the unit. Relationships between parents can be supportive but can sometimes also add to parents' tension or be counter-productive. Parents tend to compare and contrast their baby's progress with that of other babies in the unit. Hearing other people's stories and witnessing the ups and downs of other babies can be stressful. It may also lead to a highly charged atmosphere that staff may need to defuse.

The use of single family rooms on neonatal units may improve patient care and satisfaction by reducing noise, sleep deprivation and risk of infection while providing privacy and promoting increased parental involvement in care and satisfaction with parenting (POPPY Steering Group 2009; Shahheidari and Homer 2012; Örtenstrand 2014). However, a single room does not ensure that parents will receive family-centred care and may limit parents' interactions and communication with staff, which continues to be important (Örtenstrand 2014).

Spending time with the baby

Listening to Parents found that most women and their partners were able to see and touch their baby before they died (Redshaw *et al.* 2014). Parents should be encouraged to spend as much time as they want with their baby. Visiting should only be restricted when absolutely necessary (for example, if there is risk of infection). Nevertheless, it may sometimes be helpful to suggest that parents take a break and get some rest. Ideally, the unit should have a quiet room where parents can relax and make themselves tea and coffee. There should also be a private area or way to create privacy (for example, by drawing a curtain) as some parents may feel privacy is important or missing when they spend time with their baby (Aagaard and Hall 2008).

> *We know we are luckier than some, at least we had three bitter-sweet days with our baby. But losing her just broke my heart.* Mother

Almost half of the mothers who responded to the *Listening to Parents* survey changed their baby's nappy and more than a third cuddled and cleaned their baby (Redshaw *et al.* 2014). Some babies were too sick for these interactions to be possible (Redshaw *et al.* 2014).

Staff should ask parents if they would like to do normal parental activities wherever possible and support them in doing so by providing gentle guidance when needed

(Wocial 2000; Bliss 2011). Providing care for their baby may help parents feel like they are parents (Aagaard and Hall 2008; Arockiasamy et al. 2008).

Many parents will welcome suggestions and ideas from experienced staff such as touching and talking to their baby, having skin-to-skin contact, changing their baby's nappy or feeding their baby (Bliss 2011). Mothers may wish to put the baby to the breast for comfort rather than only for feeding. Skin-to-skin contact could also be discussed with parents as this may have benefits for preterm and sick babies by promoting bonding or providing pain relief during painful procedures (Campbell-Yeo et al. 2013; Conde-Agudelo and Díaz-Rossello 2014).

Parents should be supported but not pressured (see also *Giving information and facilitating informed choice* in Chapter 4). Over time, some parents who are initially overwhelmed by the situation and the neonatal unit may feel that they want to play a more active role and should be encouraged to do so (Charchuk and Simpson 2005).

Staff could also suggest that the parents might want to create keepsakes or take photographs or videos of their baby in the unit. Some neonatal units provide journey boxes or parents may wish to make one where they can store keepsakes from their baby's time spent on the neonatal unit (Bliss 2010) (see also *Creating memories* in Chapter 14).

Some parents may want to put a toy, family photograph, drawings or "get well" letters from siblings in the incubator. Others may want to bring in religious items. For example, some parents may wish to tie a religious object around the baby's wrist or body to help protect the baby from harm. However, it is important to note that holy water, which some parents may wish to use to bless the baby, is a potential source of infection (Kirschner et al. 2012). If necessary, parents should be asked to check with staff before they bring anything in so as to reduce the risk of infection. Religious and other valued items should not be disturbed or removed without prior discussion with the parents.

Parents should also be offered information about transferring their baby's care to a local children's hospice when this option is available. The environment in a children's hospice is less clinical and parents will be supported to spend as much time as they would like with their baby and their family with no time restrictions. Family rooms may also be available in the hospice where parents can comfortably stay while spending time with their baby.

Visitors

When a baby is unlikely to live for long, there should be no or few visiting restrictions for siblings, grandparents and other family members, provided that the parents have agreed to these visits. Parents may also want friends or religious advisers to see their baby and this should be allowed if possible. Other people may be able to be more supportive to the parents later if they too have memories of the baby to share (Canadian Paediatric Society 2001; Crawley et al. 2013). However, restricted space in the unit may mean that the number of visitors present at any one time has to be limited. It may also be appropriate to ask visitors (other than the parents) to leave during doctors' rounds or when procedures are carried out. It can be helpful if staff acknowledge and introduce themselves to other family members (especially siblings) when they visit the ward.

Special considerations for parents with babies in neonatal units

Some parents may need to make special arrangements to enable them to stay at the hospital for any length of time. For example, they may need to arrange care for other children, transportation to the neonatal unit or accommodation if they live farther away from the unit where there baby is staying. Parents who observe religious dietary restrictions may also need to bring in their own food and drink or have food and drink brought in for them.

Parents may find it particularly hard to spend time with their baby when the baby requires specialist care and is transferred to a neonatal unit that is many miles away from their home. A map has been developed by the Neonatal Data Analysis Unit and North West London CLAHRC with information about all of the different levels of neonatal units, children's hospitals and hospices in the UK (see Appendix 2).

A Bliss report has also found that the costs of having a baby on a neonatal unit can be "crippling" for families who need to spend money on transport, accommodation, meals, childcare and/or take unpaid leave at this time (Bliss 2014). This report also found that this financial stress caused many parents' mental health to worsen (Bliss 2014). It is important that parents are made aware of the financial support available to them through benefits, the health service or local charities (see *Discussing entitlement to time off work and benefits* in Chapter 15 and Bliss' *Financial Advice for Families* in Appendix 2).

> *The Neonatal staff were amazing. Very informative and supportive …*
> *They provided details for a nearby charity offering accommodation and*
> *facilitated this.* (Redshaw *et al*. 2014: 32)

Some parents cannot spend a lot of time with their baby because they have other commitments and pressures. Others may find it too distressing or frightening. Gentle encouragement and support may help some parents to feel more confident. When caring for parents who may be apprehensive about spending time with their baby, staff could gently suggest that they will stay with parents or be present just outside the door if parents would prefer. Parents should be told that there is no rush and they should be supported to decide what feels right for them with no pressure.

Some women may also be reluctant to travel on public transport by themselves. Additionally, some women who speak little or no English may be afraid to visit without their partner or another family member. Interpreters should be arranged to support families where necessary (see also Chapter 5). Women who follow the tradition of resting at home for several weeks after giving birth may also be unable to come.

It is important to reassure all parents who find it difficult to spend time in the unit that their baby is receiving the best possible care and attention from staff.

If the mother is ill

If the mother is in the same hospital but is unable to walk to the neonatal unit, and her physical condition allows, she should be brought to the unit in a wheelchair or hospital bed. This will allow her to spend as much time as possible with her baby. If the baby is transferred to a regional unit where specialist care can be provided and it is not possible to move the mother with the baby, midwifery staff at the referring hospital should be asked to phone the regional unit regularly to check the baby's progress and pass this information on. The information should be not only about the baby's condition and prognosis but also anything the staff can tell her about the baby's personality and reactions. This may help the mother to picture her baby as an individual.

Some units take digital pictures of babies and relay them to the mother's bedside. Taking a video or using a video calling service such as FaceTime or Skype to contact the mother may also be beneficial. Some units have a password-enabled site for each baby, where the mother can view computer readings from her baby and comments and observations entered by nurses. While the use of technology may be beneficial, bad news should always be given face-to-face with both parents (if applicable) or another family member or friend present to offer support (if possible).

Parents with more than one baby

In the case of a multiple birth, parents may feel torn between their babies and feel even more pressure if they have other children (TAMBA 2014). Parents should be encouraged to spend time with healthy babies and babies that are sick or unlikely to live (TAMBA 2014).

Many hospitals will also try to keep babies together (TAMBA 2014). If parents have two or more babies in the unit, they should be placed near to each other if possible. The babies' incubators should be visually distinguishable from each other and individual care plans should be devised for the babies (BAPM 2010a).

 I just wished my twins could have had cots next to each other. It would have made such a difference. (Redshaw et al. 2014: 33)

For many parents it is very important to see, hold and/or photograph all their babies together and with the family. This may be their only chance to do so if one of the babies is critically ill and this opportunity should be offered to parents (Kollantai and Fleischer [n.d.]).

> *The nurses and doctors who cared for Charlie and Joshua were wonderful. We cannot thank them enough for all that they did for our twins. The neonatal unit helped to provide us with our wonderful memories and allowed us to get to know Charlie and Joshua as individual characters.* Mother

If one or more babies have already died, it is important that the staff caring for the surviving baby or babies in the neonatal unit recognise the importance of all the babies to the parents and listen when the parents want to talk about the baby or babies who have died (Richards *et al.* 2015) (see also *Multiple pregnancies* in Chapter 3). Support from staff may be crucial for parents' well-being (Richards *et al.* 2015). Many parents appreciate it if staff bring up the subject of the baby who has died, as this gives them an opportunity to express their feelings. Parents should be offered specialist bereavement support if one baby has died and another baby is still being cared for on the neonatal ward (Mancini *et al.* 2014). However, some parents may find that they are not ready to access this support, particularly if they are putting their feelings on hold while focusing on the surviving baby or babies (Richards *et al.* 2015) (see also *Multiple pregnancies* in Chapter 3). Some parents may also want to place a photo of the baby or babies who have died with or near the surviving baby or babies (Richards et al. 2015).

Staff should be aware of the position of the cot or incubator of the surviving baby or babies. It may be distressing for some parents if surviving babies are located near other multiples on the unit.

Some parents may feel pressured to make funeral arrangements in haste for the baby or babies who have died, particularly if they feel that they need to focus on the surviving baby or babies (Richards *et al.* 2015). Staff should offer parents informed choices about their options for a funeral (see Chapter 20). Parents may also choose to delay the funeral for the baby who has died while any other siblings remain in the hospital.

Discussions with parents about their baby's condition

> *Care from the Nurses was very variable. Some were great – very competent and good at explaining what they were doing to anxious parents. But others were rushed, seemed stressed and made us feel as if we were not welcome, and this upset us as we really didn't want to make things any worse but we also really wanted to spend time with our little baby daughter.* (Redshaw *et al.* 2014: 33)

Within 24 hours of admission, all parents should have a documented consultation with a senior member of the neonatal team (NNAP 2014). They should also have opportunities to talk with a senior member of staff if their baby is seriously ill or dying.

Additionally, parents should be kept informed and be involved in discussions about changes in their baby's condition, prognosis and care as soon as possible (Bliss 2011). For many parents this is an important part of taking parental responsibility and their identity as a parent, especially when they feel that they have no control over the situation (Wocial 2000; Arockiasamy *et al.* 2008).

A private, comfortable room should be available for discussions with parents on the neonatal unit (Bliss 2011; Mancini *et al.* 2014). It is very important that information is given sensitively to parents by staff who are trained in breaking bad news and the baby's name should be used if they have been named (Bliss 2011) (see also Chapters 4 and 24). Interpreters should also be arranged when needed (see also Chapter 5).

Parents need to be given clear, understandable, consistent and honest information about all tests, developments and interventions. Staff should normally avoid using technical terms or these should be explained using everyday language. Parents should be encouraged to ask questions (more than once) and to say if they find anything difficult to understand. It may be necessary for staff to repeat what they have told parents on several occasions as stress and anxiety can strongly affect people's ability to take in and remember information (see *Giving information and facilitating informed choice* in Chapter 4). Parents may wish to write this information down. Some parents may also want to invite another person such as a family member or friend to be present for these discussions. Whenever possible, parents should be offered an opportunity to privately discuss important matters together in a quiet place or room.

At the end of formal discussions, parents should also be given a time when they can meet with staff again. Parents should be encouraged to write down any questions as they occur to them so that they can ask them when the opportunity arises. However, parents should also have easy access to members of staff who can answer their questions between formal discussions (Wocial 2000). Some parents may have questions and concerns at times when the consultant team is not there. Others may find it easier to talk to less senior members of staff. In both cases, parents should be encouraged to raise issues with any member of staff with whom they feel comfortable. If their questions cannot be resolved immediately, the member of staff concerned can approach the consultant team on their behalf. It is important that all staff are trained in supporting families on the neonatal unit (BAPM 2010b).

All discussions with parents should be documented to ensure parents receive consistent information (Bliss 2011). In order for parents to receive consistent information, it is essential that staff work in a well-functioning multidisciplinary team where information is shared with all staff (including junior staff) and across disciplines and teams (Mancini *et al.* 2014). To ensure consistency, it is good practice to have a differently coloured parent communication sheet in the front of the notes where staff can record what parents have been told.

Parents should have designated members of staff (including a named nurse) who take the main responsibility for checking that the parents feel informed and listened to and who raise and discuss sensitive and difficult issues and decisions with them.

If a baby dies suddenly on the neonatal unit

Parents should be sensitively informed as soon as possible after their baby dies if they were not present. This information should be shared with parents in a private place and in person wherever possible. The baby's death should be confirmed to parents using clear, simple, unambiguous language. Parents may need time to process this information and some parents may not be able to believe that their baby has died when the baby's death is sudden or unexpected (Woodroffe 2013) (see also *Breaking bad news* in Chapter 4).

Parents should be offered a private space such as a family room or a room in a local children's hospice where they can spend time with their baby (see *Place of care when moving to palliative care* below and *Place of care* in Chapter 14). Parents should be able to spend as much time as they want with their baby and have opportunities to create memories. See also Chapter 14 for more information about supporting parents at this time.

Making decisions about critical care

The *Listening to Parents* study found that most women felt that staff always discussed their baby's problems and treatments with them (76 per cent) while less than 10 per cent felt that this was never discussed or explained (Redshaw *et al*. 2014). *Listening to Parents* also found that only 67 per cent of mothers felt that they were always involved in decisions about their baby's care (Redshaw *et al*. 2014).

Parents should be offered the opportunity to participate in all important decisions about the care of their baby, including critical care decisions when their baby is in very critical condition (Bliss 2010). Whenever possible, staff should avoid implementing a major change in the baby's care without first explaining it to the parents. If decisions have to be taken in an emergency and the parents cannot be reached, staff should document the reasons for their decision. Parents should then be informed as soon as possible by telephone or when they arrive at the unit about the treatment their baby has received and the reasoning for staff's decisions (Charchuk and Simpson 2005).

If the baby's prognosis is poor and their viability is considered to be borderline, it may be difficult for healthcare staff to discuss care options with parents when they are unable to predict a likely outcome (Chiswick 2008). Open and honest communication with parents about their baby's condition from the time of diagnosis is important (Smith 2014). This will allow staff to support parents who remain hopeful about their baby's prognosis to simultaneously start considering potentially necessary palliative care options for their baby (Smith 2014). It is important for staff to recognise that hope may be an important coping mechanism for some parents (Smith 2014).

Parallel or anticipatory planning may be beneficial in such instances as care plans can be discussed by staff and parents for active treatment of the baby while also planning for palliative or end-of-life care should it become necessary. This parallel planning may also help parents to avoid feeling like they are "giving up" on their baby.

Critical care decisions are guided by the baby's best interests, which staff have a duty to act upon in partnership with the parents (Mancini *et al.* 2014; Larcher *et al.* 2015). Consideration of the parents' interests are also important as these are linked to the baby's best interests (Chiswick 2008). During discussions about critical care, parents should be treated as full partners in the discussion and with respect and dignity at all times (Bliss 2010).

Making decisions about withdrawing or withholding life-sustaining treatment

> *Professional duties and responsibilities do not cease when a child dies. The quality of care at the end of life and after the child's death can have a major impact on the family's grieving.* (Royal College of Paediatrics and Child Health (RCPCH) in Larcher *et al.* 2015: s20)

Decisions about withdrawing or withholding life-sustaining treatment from a baby who has a life-limiting or life-threatening condition are inevitably difficult. The RCPCH (Larcher *et al.* 2015) considers that it is ethical to limit life-sustaining treatment in three instances where treatment is not thought to be in a child's best interests:

- When the child's life is limited in quantity, such as when brain-stem death has occurred, where death is imminent and the child's condition is deteriorating and not responding to treatment or when the death is certain and there are not benefits to life-sustaining treatment.

- When the child's life is limited in quality including when life could be significantly prolonged but the pain or burden of treatment may outweigh the benefits, when the sufficient pain and distress that may be caused by the child's condition may outweigh the benefits of treatment or where continuing the child's life is unlikely to be of benefit because of their condition.

- When the child is able to provide informed competent refusal of treatment.

Even in these instances, many parents and staff find it especially distressing to withdraw treatment once it has been initiated (Larcher *et al.* 2015). This makes it even more important that, wherever possible, the decision to initiate intensive care is based on a realistic assessment of the baby's prospects (Wilkinson *et al.* 2009). However, it may also be difficult to determine the best interests of the baby when a neonatal prognosis is unclear (Chiswick 2008).

Guidelines such as those published by the RCPCH (Larcher *et al.* 2015) are available to help medical staff determine when life-sustaining treatment should be withheld or withdrawn. However, making this decision may be more difficult than simply following clinical guidance (Smith 2005).

Discussions amongst healthcare staff about the decision-making process

Neonatal staff have their needs too, and it is easier to be caring and compassionate when we are at ease with our own thoughts and feelings surrounding end of life decisions. This is more likely in neonatal units where there is leadership, teamwork, and a forum for discussing ethical issues. In their absence, end of life decisions challenge staff each time as though it was a new experience, and conflicting and unclear advice may be given to parents, reflecting uncertainties and conflicts between staff members. (Chiswick 2001)

It is important that inter-disciplinary communication takes place involving all staff involved in decision-making about a baby's care (Bloomer *et al.* 2015). The focus of this communication should be on the baby and their life, which may have a positive influence on the decision-making process (Bloomer *et al.* 2015).

 Thank you for remembering throughout everything that Louisa was a person, not just a body with a complex of medical problems. Parents

Different members of a health care team inevitably have different experiences, responsibilities and perspectives. All members of the team should be asked for their views on the baby's care and each opinion will be given weight according to the individual's knowledge, experience and understanding (Larcher *et al.* 2015). If there is disagreement within the multidisciplinary team about continuing or withdrawing further treatment, it is important that each team member is able to state and explain their views openly and honestly in an atmosphere of mutual respect. It also important that each team member hears, understands and respects the views of others. Some people may feel afraid to voice their opinion and encouragement is important. If all members of the team have shared in the decision-making process, each person is more likely to be committed to whatever has been agreed and the responsibility is shared amongst the team (McHaffie and Fowlie 1996; Larcher *et al.* 2015).

The timing of the discussions with the parents about withdrawing or withholding treatment can also be a source of tension within a team. Sometimes it is the staff who have most contact with the baby (often nurses) who may feel that continuing life-sustaining treatment is not in the baby's best interests and that it is time to discuss this option with the parents (Mendel 2014). All members of the team should feel able to raise the issue of withdrawing or withholding further life-sustaining treatment with their colleagues and should be taken seriously in these situations (Mendel 2014). Staff may feel distressed or that they are lacking respect or support in their working environment when they are not supported to make these decisions about discussions with parents (Mendel 2014). The situation may be further complicated when there is disagreement between staff about the viability of very pre-term babies and whether or not they should be resuscitated or have life-sustaining treatment withdrawn (Rijken *et al.* 2007). The baby's condition should be discussed within the team and then, when agreement is reached, with the parents. It is important that staff reach an agreement as most complaints around neonatal care result from staff not having an agreed protocol in place or because of disagreements with parents (Chiswick 2008).

All units should have a protocol in place for moving to palliative and end of life care (Neonatal Expert Advisory Group 2013). All staff (including neonatologists) should also have training in end of life care as this may also help influence staff perspectives by helping them to see the value of palliative care as a holistic and supportive type of care rather than care that is only provided at the end of life (Twamley *et al*. 2014). The influence of training on staff perspectives may also increase the number of babies who are referred to specialist palliative care services (Pradhan 2011; Cortezzo *et al*. 2013; Twamley *et al*. 2014).

Raising the issue of withholding or withdrawing life-sustaining treatment with parents

It can be difficult to raise the issue of withdrawing or withholding life-sustaining treatment with parents. Occasionally, parents raise the subject themselves, particularly if they are concerned that their baby is suffering and that further intervention will not be helpful. Other parents may not want to initiate this discussion about their baby's treatment but may be relieved if staff do so.

Some parents may not be able or ready to consider withholding or withdrawing life-sustaining treatment for their baby. Some parents may not be able to believe that their baby will not survive. Other parents may feel that it is wrong to consider the situation hopeless or they may have strong personal or religious objections to withdrawing or withholding treatment (da Costa *et al*. 2002; Garros *et al*. 2003; Roy *et al*. 2004).

Wherever possible, anticipatory planning discussions with parents may be beneficial as these may give parents time to consider withdrawing or withholding life-sustaining treatment before it is necessary. It may also help parents to fully realise that withdrawing or withholding life-sustaining treatment may become an option and that their baby is extremely ill but that their baby will still receive other types of care if this happens.

Parents' involvement in decision-making around withdrawing or withholding life-sustaining treatment

> 66 *She was struggling and in great distress and the outlook was dire. My instinct was that keeping her alive was not right. I was desperate for her not to suffer any more or be left trapped inside a body she could not control with an appalling quality of life. I would have gone round pulling out the tubes myself if I hadn't been given the option to let her die.* Mother

Parents' views and wishes differ a great deal and no assumptions should be made about how much they will want to be involved in making decisions regarding withdrawing or withholding life-sustaining treatment for their baby. All parents should be given the opportunity to be included in the decision about whether to withdraw or withhold life-sustaining treatment. Receiving information about their baby's prognosis and care may be important for some parents as it may reduce their stress in comparison to when they do not feel informed about the situation (Arockiasamy *et al.* 2008). Parents also have a legal responsibility to be involved in critical care decision making for their child alongside medical staff (Larcher *et al.* 2015).

Some parents feel strongly that they themselves should take on the responsibility of deciding what is best for their baby and that this is part of the rights and duties of being a parent. However, even when parents want to make the decision themselves, they should not be left feeling that they are carrying the burden alone and should receive support from healthcare staff during decision-making (Chiswick 2001; Larcher *et al.* 2015).

Some parents want to be fully informed about the issues but feel that they should not make the decision themselves. Parents may feel that they lack the requisite medical knowledge and professional experience to make a decision or they may be more familiar with a more traditional paternalistic relationship with doctors.

Both parents and staff are likely to have views and opinions about what should and should not be done when considering withdrawing or withholding life-sustaining treatment. It is important that there is excellent communication and co-operation during these discussions and that everyone has opportunities to voice their views and feelings, listen to each other and, if possible, reach a consensus (Mancini *et al.* 2014; Larcher *et al.* 2015). Co-operation is important as staff offer their medical expertise, experience and reasoning while parents contribute their values, preferences, family circumstances and understanding of the situation (McHaffie 2001).

> Decisions regarding the end-of-life care of neonates, especially those at the limits of viability, cannot be made on the basis of clinical facts alone. They should take into account the values and beliefs of all concerned. (Larcher 2013:105)

Staff should offer to fully explain the baby's condition and options for care, including parents' options for symptom control and taking the baby home or to a hospice for extubation (ACT 2009; McNamara 2013; Mancini *et al.* 2014). This information may be important as some parents may have lingering doubts about their decision to withdraw or withhold life-sustaining treatment if they were not convinced that there was sufficient evidence to confirm their baby's poor prognosis (McHaffie 2001). Additionally, McHaffie (2001) found no evidence that parents felt guilty about having taken the decision to withdraw or withhold life-sustaining treatment from their baby if they were certain that this had been in the baby's best interests.

Some parents may also want to involve family members, friends or a spiritual adviser in discussions with medical staff (Brinchmann *et al.* 2002; da Costa *et al.* 2002; Soffritti *et al.* 2014). Hospital chaplains, other religious figures or support organisations such as Bliss, Rainbow Trust or Child Bereavement UK may also be able to assist some parents while making decisions regardless of their faith or beliefs (Woodroffe 2013) (see Appendix 2). Support from these sources may help parents gain a sense of control, help them to reflect on their baby's best interests and encourage confidence in the healthcare team. Some parents may also feel that a chaplain or other supporter has more time to sit and talk about their concerns (McHaffie 2000) and they may be able to offer ongoing comfort and support. Staff should offer parents information about local resources and the Bliss helpline that is available to support parents. Parents may also find the *Making Critical Care Decisions* booklet helpful – this resource can be ordered from Bliss by healthcare professionals (see Appendix 2 for more information about Bliss).

Following the initial meeting about withdrawing or withholding life-sustaining treatment for a baby, parents should be given time to think about the decision (Mancini *et al.* 2014; Larcher *et al.* 2015). Another appointment should be arranged for them to discuss their baby's care further with a senior member of their care team (Mancini *et al.* 2014). It is important that making a decision is a process rather than a singular event as parents and others involved in decision-making may better understand the available options over a period of time (Aladangady and de Rooy 2012).

Parents' decisions about withdrawing or withholding life-sustaining treatment should not be rushed and they should be given enough time to consider and evaluate all options (Goggin 2012). Parents may also disagree with each other about the decision being made about their baby's care (Larcher *et al.* 2015). These parents may need additional time and appreciate an offer of support from staff to help them reach an agreement about their baby's care.

Waiting can be distressing for staff (particularly if they believe they are causing the baby to suffer) and support should also be available for staff while parents make these decisions (Mendel 2014; Bloomer *et al.* 2015). Staff may also deliberately delay death while parents and families make a decision or prepare for their baby's death (Bloomer *et al.* 2015). Whenever possible, staff should not have to carry out clinical procedures that they strongly believe are not in the baby's best interests as these situations may damage individual and team morale (Chiswick 2001).

Despite staff concerns, it is important to respect the parents' decision-making process and timescale. Only the parents can fully understand what the decision means and they will have to live with the consequences for the rest of their lives (Walsh 2000). However, some parents may find it too difficult to make a decision and staff may need to gently encourage them to do so in the baby's best interests. For personal, religious, cultural or other reasons, some parents may choose to partly, or entirely, delegate the decision to the medical team that is caring for their baby (Wocial 2000). However, it is always important that parents know that their feelings and views have been heard and taken seriously (Wocial 2000).

Even though the final decision regarding the baby's care rests with senior medical staff, healthcare teams making a decision in partnership with the parents will hopefully help everyone feel they can live with the decision (Mancini *et al.* 2014; Larcher *et al.* 2015).

Explaining severe hypoxic ischemic encephalopathy

BAPM (2010a) suggests considering withdrawing or withholding life-sustaining treatment for babies who are expected to have a very limited quality of life and whose condition is not compatible with long-term survival. Babies with severe hypoxic ischemic encephalopathy fall into this category (Mancini *et al.* 2014).

Decisions to withdraw or withhold life-sustaining treatment for these babies may not be acceptable for some parents and may be even more difficult for some parents with strongly held religious beliefs. For example, some Muslims and some orthodox Jews define death as the absence of a heartbeat and breathing. Because both of these are present when a baby is receiving life-sustaining treatment, some families may see the withdrawal of life support as murder (Goh *et al.* 1999; Inwald *et al.* 2000; da Costa *et al.* 2002). These parents may need more time and explanation to help them understand the reality of their baby's condition. Some may wish to talk to their spiritual adviser or family members or have them present at the discussions.

Discussing organ donation

Newborn organ donation is not currently common practice in the UK although it is feasible and there have been positive outcomes reported from transplants from neonatal donors (Wright and Barlow 2015). Some parents also take comfort from knowing that their baby's organs will be used to help another child (Bliss 2010).

When a baby has anencephaly or has been confirmed as having severe hypoxic ischemic encephalopathy, it may be appropriate to discuss the option of organ donation with parents or they may ask about this possibility. Organ donation should not be discussed with parents or confirmed as a possibility until staff have determined this option is possible following multidisciplinary discussions that include transplant teams (Mancini *et al.* 2014). If parents have asked about donation and it is not possible, the reasons for this should be explained to parents (Mancini *et al.* 2014).

Parents should be reassured that their baby's care will not be affected if they decide to consider donating their baby's organs. To allow parents to make a fully informed choice, they should also be told how donating their baby's organs will affect their options regarding end of life care, post mortem examinations or spending time and creating memories with their baby after their baby dies. Parents' decisions regarding organ donation must always be respected.

All staff who are discussing neonatal organ donation with parents should receive training around how to communicate sensitively with parents (Wright and Barlow 2015).

> *Discussing the possibility of organ donation with the parents of a child who is approaching death requires skill, sensitivity and tact ... The independence of organ donation from clinical care should be established at the outset of any discussion.* (Larcher *et al.* 2015: s17)

Conflicts when parents and staff disagree

If the parents are unhappy with the recommendation of the medical team, several meetings may be necessary at which the different viewpoints of parents and staff can be sensitively explored. In these discussions, staff should try to understand parent's views and should not be judgemental if parents wish to continue with life-sustaining treatment (Mancini *et al.* 2014).

If it is difficult for the parents to believe that their baby's condition is very poor or deteriorating, it may help to show them concrete evidence of a poor prognosis (McHaffie 2001). Some parents find it helpful to see x-rays or scans of their own baby and of healthy babies for comparison (Wocial 2000). Staff should explain to parents that life-sustaining treatment is not curative and that it will not change the baby's underlying condition (Mancini *et al.* 2014). It may also be helpful to reassure parents that care will not be withdrawn for their baby when life-sustaining treatment is withdrawn or withheld but that the care will change in its focus (Mancini *et al.* 2014).

It may also be helpful to offer parents a second opinion. The consultant caring for the parents should arrange for this second opinion unless parents wish to make arrangements independently or with the support of the hospital's patient advice and liaison services (PALS) (Larcher *et al.* 2015). Parents may also wish to consult advice or advisory services or a local mediation service (Bliss 2010).

If an agreement still cannot be reached between parents and medical staff after repeated discussions, a Clinical Ethics Committee should be consulted (Mancini *et al.* 2014; Larcher *et al.* 2015). While awaiting the outcome of the committee's decision, staff should reassure parents that their baby's care will remain unchanged (Mancini *et al.* 2014).

On the very rare occasion that staff and parents are still unable to reach an agreement after a Clinical Ethics Committee has made a decision, it may be necessary to resort to legal proceedings. Litigation should be avoided wherever possible as it may be distressing and costly for everyone involved.

When there is disagreement it is important that staff are well supported if they are expected to continue or to instigate treatment that they do not consider to be in the baby's best interests. All staff should be given time and opportunities to express their views and feelings away from the parents.

When a decision is reached

Once a decision has been reached between medical staff and parents to withdraw life-sustaining treatment or not to resuscitate the baby, it is very important that this information is documented and passed on to all staff as soon as possible and that the decision is recorded prominently in the baby's notes (McHaffie *et al.* 2001c; Bliss 2011; Larcher *et al.* 2015). Some neonatal units will have specific documentation for the continuation of the baby's treatment at this stage.

At this stage, parents should know that the final decision is supported by all staff and should be assured that staff will continue to provide the best possible care for their baby.

Continuing care when life-sustaining treatment is withdrawn or withheld

The way in which the withdrawal of intensive treatment is handled is very important. The development of a palliative care pathway or plan on each neonatal unit may improve the experiences of parents and staff when discussing and implementing palliative care, without increasing the frequency of withdrawals of life-sustaining treatment (Soni *et al.* 2011; Younge *et al.* 2015). The implementation of a written care pathway, improved documentation of end-of-life care provided to babies and increased awareness and training for staff can also improve the comfort care received by dying babies (Samsel and Lechner 2015; Younge *et al.* 2015). However, it is important that care pathways or plans should not be used as checklists where all items or interventions must be completed (Samsel and Lechner 2015). Instead, these guides should be used as prompts for ensuring the best care possible is provided to babies and their families during this time.

The guidance document *"Practical guidance for the management of palliative care on neonatal units"* (Mancini *et al.* 2014) offers additional practical guidance on preparing families and providing palliative care for babies.

Discussing redirection of care with parents

It is essential to prepare parents by offering them information about what palliative care for babies normally entails and the opportunity to be involved in their baby's care at this stage (Chiswick 2008). Before life-sustaining treatment is withdrawn, staff should offer to have a private, face-to-face discussion with parents to discuss the options for their baby's care and give parents adequate time to ask questions and talk about their views and feelings (Mancini *et al.* 2014). Parents may appreciate someone being able to listen to their concerns, particularly as many parents will not have seen anyone die before and may feel frightened by the prospect.

The process of moving to palliative care should be thoroughly explained to parents and they should be reassured that this does not mean that care is being withdrawn from their baby (Larcher *et al.* 2015). This explanation should include a discussion of the benefits of palliative care (including keeping the baby pain-free and comfortable) and its ability to reduce harm to the baby, particularly if parents are sceptical or uncertain about the need for this care (Bliss 2010; Larcher *et al.* 2015). The following information and options should also be discussed with parents before their baby starts to receive palliative care (Mancini *et al.* 2014):

- *The time and place for the withdrawal of life-sustaining treatment.* It is important that staff are aware of the available options for the location of palliative care and offer these options to parents (Craig and Mancini 2013). Parents should be offered information about the available options for taking the baby home or to a hospice to receive palliative care (even if the baby is not expected to live for long) (Neonatal Expert Advisory Group 2013). If the baby has been transferred to a unit that provides specialist neonatal care, consideration should also be given to transferring them to a neonatal unit or hospital that is closer to parents. If the mother is ill and still in hospital, the possibility of the baby receiving palliative care on the postnatal ward could also be discussed (Mancini *et al.* 2014).

- *Whether or not parents want to be present when life-sustaining treatment is withdrawn or their baby dies.* Parents should also be told that they can change their mind.

- *Whether or not parents wish to have a dedicated member of staff available to be with them or nearby when life-sustaining treatment is removed.*

- *The possibility of parents inviting family members or close friends for support.*

- *The baby's possible physical reactions to the change in care.* It should be explained to parents that the baby may gasp or change colour when the ventilator is removed. The role of opiates in diminishing pain and distress during extubation should also be discussed with parents while acknowledging that the use of opiates may also hasten the baby's death.

- *Any spiritual or religious needs or requirements that they parents may have.*

It is important that staff are trained in providing neonatal palliative care so that they can provide parents with full information about the available options for their baby's care (Mendel 2014; Tosello *et al.* 2015).

Parents should also be offered opportunities to care for their baby, choose specific clothing and dress their baby (if appropriate) and hold their baby during or after their baby's death (BAPM 2010a; Mancini *et al.* 2014). Additionally, parents should be offered information about their options for creating memories with their baby before and after the baby's death (Mancini *et al.* 2014) (see also *Creating memories* in Chapter 14). Staff should support parents in these activities but also try to give parents space to engage in these activities themselves (Eden and Clark Callister 2010). It may be helpful for staff to ask parents about the best way to offer support at this time.

Parents should have a designated member of staff who is available to offer information and support before, during and after their baby's death (Larcher *et al.* 2015). This may be particularly important if the baby is expected to live for a while (Larcher *et al.* 2015). The name and contact details of this staff member should be recorded on the care plan that is given to parents (BAPM 2010a).

Care and discussions with parents when a baby may live for a while following the move to palliative care

The length of time that some babies are expected to live may be uncertain. Some babies live for hours or even days after of life-sustaining treatment is withdrawn and parents should be warned about this during the discussions before moving to palliative care. Parallel planning is important in these instances and clear care plans should be discussed and agreed with parents should the baby live or die (Mancini 2015, personal communication). Support can then be put in place with local community palliative and primary care teams or a children's hospice if the parents choose to have their baby cared for at home or in a hospice (Breeze *et al.* 2007). Parents should also be told what to expect in terms of the baby's physical response and practical care needs (Mancini *et al.* 2014).

Some parents may welcome more time with their baby. However, it may be very distressing for parents who have assumed that the baby's condition and prognosis will mean that the death will be swift. They may begin to question whether they were right to withdraw life-sustaining treatment or whether their baby could have survived if this treatment had been continued. It can also be exhausting for parents to keep saying their goodbyes again and again (McHaffie *et al.* 2001c). Parents whose baby takes a long time to die may need comfort and support during this time and reassurance that the decision to withdraw life-sustaining treatment was correct (Goggin 2012).

Place of care when moving to palliative care

This will depend on the available local options and where parents decide to have their baby receive palliative care. This could be on the neonatal unit, postnatal ward, at home or in a hospice. It is important that the options discussed with parents are realistic and that they are clearly told what may or may not happen (Mayer 2014).

Providing privacy for families is essential. Whenever possible, parents who want to stay with their baby should be offered a separate family room on the neonatal unit (or a private room on the postnatal ward if the mother is still receiving care). Staff should remove as much equipment as possible from this room. The unit or hospice should also have a comfortable sitting room where parents can spend time with their baby that is large enough and has enough chairs to accommodate several people if necessary. This room should have a cot or Moses basket available, a settee and soft, non-fluorescent, side lighting.

Parents may also want to take their baby out of the neonatal unit, particularly if the baby is expected to live for a while. Some parents may want to take their baby home, into the hospital grounds or to a local park. This may help them feel that their baby has experienced more than the hospital environment and has been a part of the wider world. It may also be helpful for parents to spend time with their baby away from the public space of the hospital in a private and/or familiar place. Some parents will feel able to do this alone while others will need some reassurance and support. This may also be helpful for other family members (especially older siblings) or people who will be important sources of support for parents in the subsequent months and years.

If the baby is to be moved home or to a hospice to receive end of life care, it is important that the move and plans to withdraw life-sustaining treatment are well-planned (Mayer 2014). It is crucial that the transport team, the neonatal unit team and any community-based care providers (for example, a GP, nurse or hospice staff) work well together and have good communication (Mayer 2014). If parents want to take their baby home or to a hospice to die, neonatal staff should give them a letter explaining the situation and containing the contact details of the unit. The community care team, including the parent's GP should also be informed. It is also important that parents are given details about other types of community support and outreach programmes that are available to offer them support while caring for their baby at home or in a hospice.

Staff should ensure that the parents know that they can telephone or bring their baby back to the unit at any time of the day or night. They should also be told what they will need to do if the baby dies at home and be given information about how to obtain a medical cause of death certificate.

Moving to and providing palliative care for babies and their families

> *Maintaining warmth, dignity, human contact, and pain relief are the basic elements of palliative care.* (Walther 2005: 970)

Staff should ensure that the parents have been prepared (if they are present) and that the ventilator's alarms have been turned off before removing the baby's ventilation support (Mancini *et al.* 2014).

Babies receiving palliative care should be provided with comfort care that includes pain relief, symptom and secretion control, physiological monitoring, fluids and oral nutrition (unless it causes the baby discomfort) (Mancini *et al.* 2014). More detailed clinical palliative guidance is described by Mancini *et al.* (2014).

If parents choose to be present when their baby is receiving palliative care, the benefits of holding the baby and allowing them to suckle for comfort should also be discussed with parents (Mancini *et al.* 2014). Parents should be offered opportunities and be supported to care for their baby (but not feel forced). Nurses can help parents to hold and cuddle their baby or put them to the breast, which may help them to bond with their baby as well as provide comfort (Bliss 2010). Parents may also wish to dress their baby. Some parents may want to do this while the baby is still on the ventilator. Other parents may want to be alone when they dress their baby or do it when all of the tubes have been removed. The unit should have suitable clothes available to parents who do not have their own baby clothes. Babies who have been ill since birth may never have been dressed in normal baby clothes and this may be the first time that the parents have seen their baby dressed.

Being with the baby and caring for the family when the baby dies

 They stopped the ventilator and we sat in a side room and held her. We thought she would die quite quickly, but she didn't. It took forever. Just when we thought she had finally stopped breathing, she took another breath. She was struggling and it was too much to bear. So the doctor gave her an injection of morphine to ease her distress and she died shortly after that. Mother

Most parents will want to be with their baby until he or she dies. Some parents may find this time very precious even if it is also very distressing. Parents may also feel very anxious about watching their baby die. Parents should be offered the support of a nurse who will stay with them for the whole time or for as long as they want. The nurse could also offer to be outside of the room if the parents need them.

Parents may have personal or religious reasons for not wanting to be present when their baby dies. They should be sensitively asked how they would like to be informed that the baby has died and support should still be offered to these parents at this time.

Providing care for parents around the time of their baby's death

Parents may want time alone with their baby in privacy before, during or after the death. Others may wish to have a member of staff present to support them, answer any questions and confirm the death when the time comes. If parents want privacy, they should be aware that a member of staff is available just outside of the room.

Some parents may want to hold their baby before the death and while they are dying. The designated member of staff supporting parents could also make gentle suggestions about parents' options to comfort their baby by holding them or putting them to the breast. They could also gently remind parents about their options for creating memories. It is important that staff make suggestions tentatively and gently as it may be particularly difficult for distressed parents to refuse if they perceive these suggestions to be instructions from staff (Lundqvist *et al.* 2002).

Some parents may also have family members and friends with them for support and/ or to care for older children. Parents might want to offer these people the opportunity to see, possibly hold and/or say goodbye to the baby. Staff might offer to take photographs of family members (particularly siblings) spending time with or holding the baby.

> *I have a precious photo of my whole family, taken when Sharon came out of the ventilator before she died. All my three children together for the first and last time.* Mother

Some parents may appreciate seeing other staff members who have been most involved in caring for their baby. The staff concerned may also find this helpful.

Some parents may want to pray alone or with a chaplain or spiritual adviser. They may also want to hold a religious ceremony. Parents should be asked what they would like and staff should offer to contact whoever is needed and to help with arrangements. The parents should be offered privacy to hold any ceremony that they choose to perform. Some parents may be grateful if staff take part.

After their baby's death, parents should be able to be alone with their baby in quiet and privacy for as long as they want. They may also want to spend this time taking more photographs, making hand or footprints, washing or dressing their baby. Staff could also offer parents keepsakes from their baby's time in the neonatal unit or hospice to take away with them (for example, clothing or blankets used by their baby, wristbands, cot cards or other items used in their baby's care) (Bliss 2010). See also *Creating memories* in Chapter 14 for more information.

> *After he had been disconnected from all his equipment he was placed in my arms for the first time, and as we cuddled him he died peacefully... I never thought that the first time I bathed my baby would also be the last ... I wanted to do everything for Charlie; it just didn't seem fair that he wasn't alive ... We felt torn between spending time with Charlie and putting our will into Joshua, his twin, to survive.* Mother

If the parents were not there at the death

If the parents were not able or chose not to be present when their baby died, they may be very worried that their baby may have died alone and unsupported. It is important to reassure them that someone was there to comfort the baby and that the baby died peacefully and without distress. If possible, the person who was with the baby at the time of death should talk to the parents and gently and sensitively describe what happened.

Informing primary care and other staff of the baby's death

One member of staff in the neonatal unit should be responsible for informing the appropriate staff and updating the local safeguarding team and Child Death Overview Panel within 24 hours of the baby's death. They should also ensure that the baby's hospital record is updated electronically.

With parents' consent, other staff in the hospital and the community who have cared for them and their baby should also be informed as soon as possible. This will help staff to avoid making inappropriate comments and allow them the opportunity to offer their condolences and support. The mother's GP or primary health care team should also be informed about the baby's death within 24 hours.

It is very important to inform the community midwifery and health visitor teams that the baby has died as they will see the mother for her postnatal check-up and follow-up care. This will also help to ensure that the parents are not invited to bring their baby to baby clinics or for immunisation (see also *Before the parents leave the hospital* in Chapter 15).

Before parents leave the neonatal unit

 It was hard leaving the hospital but they told us we could come back any time of the day or night to see our baby and they would find us somewhere quiet to be with him. Mother

Before parents leave the unit, they should be given opportunities to ask questions and talk at length with staff about anything that concerns or worries them. Parents should also be given information about a named person who they can contact if they have any questions. They should be given an email address or telephone number where they can reach this person.

Additionally, parents should be offered information about postnatal care (see Chapter 15), including their options for any breast milk being stored on the neonatal unit (including milk donation) (see *Milk donation* in Chapter 15), post mortem examinations (see Chapter 16), medical certificates and registering the baby's birth and death (see *Certification and forms following a neonatal death* in Chapter 19), funeral options (see Chapter 20), benefits (see *Discussing entitlement to time off work and benefits* in Chapter 15) and support that is available to them in the community from the health service and other organisations (see Chapter 17).

Staff should also ensure that parents have copies of care plans and any other forms that they have signed giving consent for their baby's care. This may be important as parents may want to reassure themselves about what they have signed if they are worried and unable to recall what they did afterwards.

All parents should be offered at least one follow-up appointment to see the doctor and nurse who were primarily responsible for the care of their baby in the neonatal unit (see also Chapter 17).

Keeping in touch and ongoing support for parents

 The staff were devastated when Poppy died, they cried - we really felt that they cared. When we left the unit they said phone at any time. They also sent lovely cards which was so nice, you develop such intense relationships with the staff when your baby is in the unit. Mother

Ongoing care for parents from neonatal unit staff and in the community is important after a baby dies (Walther 2005). Some parents will have built relationships with neonatal unit staff and may miss these people after they leave the unit. Having a named contact on the neonatal unit who can continue to answer any questions that parents might have and having staff who cared for families attend any follow-up appointments may be beneficial in these situations. It is also important to ensure that parents are referred to primary care staff for care and support. Seeing primary care staff may also help parents re-establish themselves in the community.

 I was in hospital for several weeks during my next pregnancy and four of the neonatal staff came down to the ward to visit me. They were so pleased when my baby was born strong and healthy. Mother

For some parents it is important to remain in touch with the staff in the neonatal unit where their baby died and where so many momentous and life-changing events occurred. Parents should be assured that they can return to the unit during the coming weeks and months. Many parents are also extremely appreciative if one or more members of staff attend the baby's funeral. Some staff may also appreciate the opportunity to attend the baby's funeral while others may not feel comfortable attending or feel that this violates their professional boundaries (Kain 2013).

Many neonatal units have a book of remembrance in which parents can make an entry (see also Chapter 21). They may not want to do this until some weeks or months after their baby's death. If and when parents come to make the entry, they should be welcomed onto the unit and time should be made for them to sit down and talk with those members of staff who cared for their baby if they would like to do so. Parents may also want some quiet time alone in the place where their baby lived and died.

Many units telephone or send letters or cards to parents on the anniversary of their baby's death. Neonatal units should have a system to ensure that this is done. Anniversaries are times when many parents may gain comfort from knowing that their loss has been remembered and acknowledged by others. Cards should have no religious content or symbols unless they are specially chosen for a family whose religious faith is known to staff.

An annual remembrance service for all the babies who have died on the unit may also give parents the chance to meet with others who have had similar experiences and can give staff the opportunity to share in parents' grief (see also *Memorial services* in Chapter 21). It is important that a service of this kind is acceptable to people from a wide range of religious backgrounds and outlooks (see also Chapter 2). It is useful to ask the parents to let the unit know whether they will be coming so that some of the members of staff who looked after their baby can possibly arrange to attend. Ideally, these staff should have time to talk to the parents after the service and answer any questions or set up a further meeting to do so.

Support for neonatal unit staff

Caring for parents and babies in a neonatal unit can deeply affect staff who routinely deal with feelings of grief and loss while continuing to support families (Kain 2013; Bloomer *et al.* 2015). Providing palliative care for babies and families may help some staff to deal with their distress (Mendel 2014). However, providing palliative care may also cause moral distress for some nurses (Cavinder 2014).

It is extremely important that the stresses and demands of the job are acknowledged and that senior staff and management make it clear that it is legitimate for all staff to ask for and get help and support when they need it (Kain 2013). Both formal and informal support must be readily available and staff should be encouraged to make use of it. This support should include training for staff (Pradhan 2011; Mendel 2014). Offering and encouraging different types of support such as peer support amongst staff is also important (Kain 2013). It is also important to recognise that support sessions may not be held when staff are most in need of support (particularly if these are postponed) and staff should be able to receive support from other staff on an ad hoc basis when it is needed (Kain 2013). Stigma and concerns about not appearing to be coping with their job may cause some staff to avoid coordinated professional counselling (Kain 2013) and this should be offered as a confidential service through the central hospital human resources team.

Senior staff may wish to set up support systems with other members of staff at their own level as they often have to take very difficult decisions and to deal with the most complicated and difficult situations. See Chapter 24 for more information about staff support.

CHAPTER 14

After a loss

Other relevant chapters

1: Providing holistic care

2: Providing inclusive care

3: Loss and grief

4: Communication

5: Communication across language and other barriers

15: Postnatal care

16: Transfer to the mortuary and post mortem investigations

17: Follow-up appointments and ongoing care

18: Mental health

19: Certificates and registration

20: Funerals and sensitive disposal

21: Memorials

This chapter discusses some aspects of the care that parents may need immediately after a miscarriage, a termination of pregnancy for fetal anomaly, a stillbirth or a death. However, some of the suggestions in the chapter for seeing and holding the baby or creating memories may also be relevant after parents have left the hospital. More information about postnatal care is found in Chapter 15.

The quality of the care that parents receive during the time when their baby dies is crucial as this support may have long-term effects on parents' emotional and mental health (Schott and Henley 2009; Crawley *et al.* 2013; Downe *et al.* 2013; Redshaw *et al.* 2014; Ryninks *et al.* 2014). All individuals who provide support and care for bereaved parents should see every interaction as their "one chance to get it right" as what they say and do may affect bereaved parents for the rest of their lives (Downe *et al.* 2013).

 It is the detail of events that matters so much. Mother

Communication

Communication with parents

Informed Choice

Unless parents have lost a baby before, or been close to someone who has, they may not know their options for labour or think of asking to see and hold their baby or create memories. It is therefore important that options are explained and parents are given time to make a decision.

Harm may be caused by staff who rely on rote procedures (Robinson 2002). For example, when the options relating to seeing and holding a baby who has died or "creating memories" appear in a detailed checklist with tick boxes, inexperienced staff may feel under pressure to ensure that each item is ticked. As a result, parents may feel that their experience has been so routine and rushed that they have lost control over what happens to them and to their baby, the exact opposite of the aims of good care (Leon 1992) (see also *Parental choice and checklists* below). Simply following rote procedures may result in staff prioritising the completion of these tasks when interacting with bereaved parents rather than responding and listening empathetically to parents (Leon 1992).

Timing is also important. Parents often need time to think about what they want or do not want, especially if the idea is new to them. Women should not be expected to make decisions when they are in shock, immediately following what may have been a stressful and traumatic labour or when they are still affected by opiates or a general anaesthetic. They should be offered time and be supported to make informed decisions at their own pace (see *Giving information and facilitating informed choice* in Chapter 4).

Offering condolences and listening

Medical and other staff who were involved in the mother's care should make a point of seeing the parents after the loss to offer their condolences. Junior staff (including doctors) with little or no experience of speaking with bereaved parents may find it helpful to be accompanied by another doctor or midwife.

Parents may also need someone to supportively listen at this time. See *Support and listening* in Chapter 15 for more information.

Afterwards, managers or colleagues should ensure that all the staff affected are offered support and time to talk before they go home. Staff may also be shocked and upset and may value the help and support of an experienced colleague in caring for the parents. Sands recommends that bereavement midwives are available on every unit who are able to offer guidance and support to all staff who work with bereaved parents (see Chapter 25 for more information about the role of bereavement midwives and Chapter 24 for information about staff support and training).

The sex of the baby

Many parents know the sex of their baby from previous scans. However, when parents do not know the sex (particularly in the case of earlier losses), they are often anxious to know whether their baby is a boy or a girl as soon as possible. However, it may be very difficult or impossible to confirm the baby's sex after pre-term losses (up to 20 weeks' gestation) or if the baby is badly damaged or has an anomaly. In babies born at early gestations, female genitals can look very similar to male genitals. When a baby is born at or under 20 weeks' gestation, the sex should be identified by two members of staff before the parents are told.

If there is any uncertainty, staff should explain to the parents that it is difficult to determine the baby's sex and that they may have to wait to learn the baby's sex until after examination by a pathologist or paediatrician. Although this delay can be difficult, it is better for parents to have to wait than to be given information that they later find out was wrong. Staff should only confirm the baby's sex if they are very sure about their identification.

Waiting to confirm the baby's sex may be important as parents may view and relate to their baby differently based on the sex of the baby.

 My twins were born at 18 weeks, five years ago and lived for an hour. They were named, blessed, registered and cremated as boys. We scattered their ashes as boys. Six weeks later, after the post mortem, we were told they were girls. Up till then we'd been grieving for our boys. All our love, memories, sympathy cards, photos, wrist bands were for "the boys". We talked about the boys and missed them as boys. Suddenly we had to start thinking about them as girls. We had to give them girls' names, mourn them as girls. When people ask me if I have children I don't know what to say any more. This happened five years ago and I still feel that I have lost four babies and not two – it's a nightmare. Mother

If the parents do not want a post mortem examination it may still be possible for the pathologist or paediatrician to examine the baby externally and (in most cases) confirm whether the baby is a boy or a girl.

Telling the family or friends

At some point, the mother or parents will likely need to tell their family or friends what has happened. Breaking bad news is never easy and it may be doubly difficult for parents who are themselves shocked and grief stricken. If appropriate, professionals could direct parents to the *Telling family and friends* section of the Sands *Saying goodbye to your baby* booklet, which has practical suggestions for communicating this bad news.

Then we had to tell our family. How on earth can you tell your loved ones such awful news … I shall never forget the look on Mom and Dad's faces as I told them the baby was dead. There was disbelief, tears and so many unanswerable questions. Their grief and pain was doubled, love for the unborn grandchild and the inability to do anything to ease the pain of their son and daughter. Mother

Informing other carers

 I was on the ward still and someone came in and said, "Where's your baby?". Mother

Midwives, nurses, doctors and health care assistants who will be directly involved in the mother's immediate postnatal care should be informed promptly about the death or loss. This helps to protect parents from well-meant but inappropriate comments and staff from the distress of having caused unnecessary pain. Consideration should also be given to informing ancillary staff who are likely to be in contact with the parents. The hospital chaplain or their own religious adviser should also be contacted if the parents would like this.

If the mother agrees, the front of her medical notes should be marked with a sticker that all staff recognise and understand. It may also be possible to include an alert or flag on a woman's electronic medical notes. This will help to ensure that all staff are aware that she has had a childbearing loss and that she is cared for with tact and sensitivity.

Teardrop Stickers

The Sands teardrop sticker can be used to identify the hard copy of a mother whose baby has died immediately following the baby's death and in any subsequent pregnancies. It can be used on hospital and GP records, antenatal notes and appointment cards to ensure that everyone who comes into contact with a bereaved mother is aware of her loss and does not inadvertently say things that will add to her distress. These stickers can also be used in subsequent pregnancies and for other family members who are affected by the death of a baby.

These teardrop stickers can be ordered online from the Sands Shop. See also *Medical notes used during postnatal care* in Chapter 15. Sands is looking to develop an electronic version of this teardrop for electronic medical notes.

Written information

Written information should also be available on every unit to support parents and professionals. This should include information about parents' choices and support literature, such as Sands support booklets which can be ordered from the online Sands Shop.

Staff should keep an up-to-date list of the resources available to parents on the unit. This should include the names and contact details of local organisations that offer support, details about registering the baby's death and certificates, information about post mortem examinations and local mortuary practices and information about local funeral arrangements (Hunter 2015). One member of staff should be designated as being responsible for keeping this listed updated at least every six months.

Place of care

Forget-Me-Not bereavement suite, Royal Surrey County Hospital

The *Listening to Parents* report highlighted the importance of place of care by emphasising how being able to see or hear other parents and their babies may compound parents' anguish and distress (Redshaw *et al.* 2014). Parents may remember this experience for the rest of their lives.

Ideally, bereaved parents will be cared for in a dedicated bereavement care room or suite following the death of their baby. These rooms should only be used to care for bereaved parents and families and should offer complete privacy, comfort, and adequate soundproofing so that parents do not have to hear crying babies or other parents (Redshaw *et al.* 2014). The location of these rooms should also be carefully considered so that parents and other family members do not have to pass expectant and new parents or babies on their way in or out of the room. If the baby has died before birth, the room should also be positioned so that it is near enough to the labour ward to ensure that the mother receives continuous care and support during labour and birth.

The door of a bereavement room or suite should be discreetly labelled so that other parents are not necessarily aware of the room's purpose. Some hospitals use a symbol or have a special name for the room. Ideally, the room should be equipped with a double bed, en-suite bathroom and small kitchen area that will allow parents to spend time with their baby and any visitors if they wish. A cot or suitable-sized basket should be available to put the baby in. Some units also have a cooling facility in the bereavement suite so that babies do not need to go to the mortuary during a parent's stay in hospital.

The upkeep of this room is important as this may affect parents' perceptions of their care.

> *Occasionally the issue of Sands/bereavement suites comes up during a call (or we may receive a call directly about it). Parents often express extreme gratitude for such a private space in such a time of need. Most parents feel terrified and out of control of what is happening to them and such a room is truly valued and appreciated. All callers, without fail, are keen to emphasise this point, but at the same time, some of them felt let down by what they felt to be the neglect of the room. It seemed to counteract the support they felt they received in some way. Due to the hyper-sensitivity in grief and the often vivid recall of the unfolding events, details such as staff attitudes and care, the sounds, the venue and the visual appearance of equipment and spaces becomes very heightened. The issues of concern around private Sands/bereavement suites are usually basic wear and tear, but also the finer details too such as dust, untidiness, grubby appearance, a lack of literature, no clean cups or water, empty tissue boxes or none at all, unemptied bins etc. ... They don't want to see that it may be neglected or an afterthought. The small details, as well as the larger ones, really do count.* Sands Helpline Staff Member

The decoration of the rooms in which parents are cared for at the time of and after the loss is also important. The room should be both homely and comfortable. Additionally, posters of women with babies are entirely inappropriate and reproductions of well-known paintings should be avoided. Many parents find that their surroundings during this time are etched on their memories and that, long afterwards, a particular picture or image can trigger very painful memories.

 I was wheeled into the delivery suite to deliver my stillborn daughter and was faced with a large photo of a smiling and emotional mother who had just delivered a live baby. I had had an epidural and couldn't turn away. All I could think was, "This is not how it's going to be for me". I asked the midwife and she quickly removed it. Mother

Sometimes a bereavement room or suite is not available as a result of limited resources, space or availability of the room. It is important to manage parents' expectations and acknowledge any disappointment that arises when a special bereavement room is not available. In such instances, staff should prepare parents for potentially distressing sights or sounds (such as seeing expectant parents or hearing crying babies) that they may encounter on their way to the available room (Hunter 2015).

Space for partners

Consideration should be given to the practical needs of partners or birth partners who may be spending many hours with the woman. Many maternity units have double rooms where couples can stay after a stillbirth, but partners also need to be catered for beforehand. It may be possible to arrange for a parking permit for any supporters for the woman. Also, they should not have to go home simply because there is nowhere for them to be. In any ward or room (including on an EPAU) where women who are experiencing a childbearing loss are cared for, there should be:

- A comfortable chair in the same room.
- Toilet facilities nearby for men as well as for women.
- Facilities that are available 24 hours a day so that partners can eat and drink at any time.
- Ideally, a room nearby with comfortable, reclining chairs and tea and coffee making facilities where partners can take short breaks or sleep.

It is also important to acknowledge that it may be difficult for partners to walk through a labour ward and pass other parents, babies and partners who are bringing balloons or flowers.

More information about supporting partners is included in *Fathers and same-sex partners* in Chapter 3.

Much of the detail in this section has been updated using the Improving Bereavement Care sections of Sands' Groups Handbook.

Multiple births

Special consideration is needed for the parents of twins or multiple babies, especially if one or more babies have survived.

 The emotions that swamped us over the next few days were completely overwhelming. How does one integrate the feeling of grief for one baby with the feeling of joy for the other? After all we had only wanted one healthy baby and we still had that. So why did we feel so terrible? Mother

It is important that staff acknowledge the importance of the baby (or babies) who have died, and avoid focusing only on the baby or babies that are alive (Bryan 2002) (see also *Multiple pregnancies* in Chapter 3). If parents want to see the baby or babies who have died, it may be helpful to see and perhaps hold the living and the dead babies together if this is possible. Without this opportunity it may be difficult for parents to grasp the reality of what has happened. Later on, the parents may value the memory of being with all their babies together.

Seeing and holding the baby

As recommended by the updated NICE Guidance on Antenatal and Postnatal Mental Health, parents should be given the choice of seeing and holding their baby following stillbirth or neonatal death by an experienced practitioner (NICE 2014a). This recommendation is in line with the clarification statement that NICE issued in 2010 for their 2007 guidance following a campaign by Sands (Sands 2015g).

The 2007 NICE guidance that discouraged parents from seeing and holding their baby after stillbirth was based on the small study by Turton *et al.* (2001) of women whose babies were born dead after 20 weeks' gestation (Sands 2015g). This study found that a higher percentage of women who saw their dead baby experienced post-traumatic stress disorder (PTSD) after stillbirth, although Turton *et al.* acknowledged that these results were statistically insignificant. Additionally, a subsequent study by Turton *et al.* (2006) found that there was no significant association between fathers' having depression, anxiety or PTSD and seeing their dead baby. NICE's 2007 recommendation did not account for the statistical insignificance of these associations, criticisms of the research of Turton *et al.* (Lovett 2001; Robinson 2002) or the existence of other studies that found seeing and holding to be beneficial to parents following stillbirth or neonatal death (Geerinck-Vercammen 1999; Rådestad 2001).

NICE's 2014 recommendation is also based on the findings of Ryninks *et al.* (2014) that parents should be given an informed choice about seeing their stillborn baby where all of the possible risks and benefits are discussed with parents. It is also important to note that parents' decisions to see or hold their baby may be influenced by staff attitudes (Rådestad et al. 2009). Additionally, professional support and follow up when parents see their baby are seen to be important prevention measures against the development of maternal mental health problems (Turton *et al.* 2009b; Ryninks *et al.* 2014).

Many mothers felt that they made the right decision to see their baby even when they experienced intense distress upon seeing their baby (Ryninks *et al.* 2014). As with any other contentious issue, it is essential to guard against the tendency for practice to swing from one extreme to the other. The current focus in healthcare, particularly in maternity care, is informed choice. Removing choice from bereaved parents and deciding what will be best for them is paternalistic and can be damaging. Most people would rather live with the consequences of their own decisions, good or bad, than with the consequences of decisions that are imposed on them by others, however well meaning.

Some people also find it important to see the body when someone they love dies even when the circumstances of their loved one's death has been traumatic or sudden (Chapple and Ziebland 2010). This may help to make the death real and can help people to accept that it has happened. If there is no body, it may be harder to believe and to come to terms with the person's death. However, seeing the body may be particularly important or forbidden for some people or in some cultures (Schott and Henley 1996).

Seeing and holding their baby may be important to parents regardless of the size, condition or gestation of their baby. It may sometimes be hard for staff to treat a tiny baby of an early gestation in the same way that they might treat a larger, more developed baby. However, for parents, gestation is not necessarily an indicator of feeling for or attachment to their baby and it is important that all babies are handled respectfully and with care.

 The midwife behaved as if he was a normal live baby, she didn't treat me as if this was awful, she was just like, isn't he beautiful, look how much he weighs. Mother

It is important for healthcare professionals to offer **all** parents the option of seeing and holding their baby while recognising that some parents will decline this offer. For example, staff could say: "Many parents have said that it helped to see and hold their baby. Others have decided not to. What would you like to do?".

When suggesting to parents that they might want to see and to hold their baby, it is important to remember that:

- Current evidence and recommendations suggest telling parents about the risks and benefits associated with seeing and holding their stillborn baby and allowing parents to make an informed choice.

- It is impossible to predict who will regret not seeing their baby and who might suffer more intense distress after seeing their baby.

- Being expected to behave in certain ways can exacerbate the loss of control and autonomy that parents may already be experiencing.

Facilitating genuine choice about seeing and holding a baby who has died is complicated. Parents may have many reasons for being uncertain or refusing. These may include:

- Shock at the suggestion as this possibility has never occurred to them.

- Fear of seeing a dead body, especially if they have never seen one before.

- Fear of what their baby will look like (Brierley-Jones *et al*. 2014), especially if he or she is known to have died some time before birth or to have a serious visible anomaly.

- An established personal coping style of dealing with stressful issues by not confronting them directly.

- Fear of how they will be affected by seeing the baby (Brierley-Jones *et al*. 2014).

- A cultural or religious prohibition against seeing a dead body. For example, some orthodox Jews may decline as seeing or handling a dead body unless absolutely necessary is considered to be wrong. Also, some men of certain orthodox Jewish families are forbidden to be near a dead body and may leave abruptly after a baby has died. Despite cultural restrictions, assumptions should not be made about parents' choices and they should be offered the opportunity to see their baby.

- Feeling that seeing and holding the baby is simply not right for them.

 Shona was tiny but perfect when she was born. They handed her to me in a tiny blanket and she was so beautiful. Jade was born a bit later and we chose not to see her because of her abnormalities. I wanted to think of her as perfect too, just like her sister. I didn't want to have horrible memories of her. Mother

When the baby has an anomaly or is macerated

If there is a visible anomaly or maceration, the parents should be gently told what to expect and be offered a description of their baby's appearance before deciding whether to see the baby. Parents may need extra support from healthcare professionals (Ryninks *et al*. 2014). If parents accept the offer of a description, it is important that the explanation is factual and without judgement or any implication that the baby looks unpleasant. Parents often see the beauty of their baby regardless of the baby's actual appearance. Sometimes, it may help if the baby is wrapped in a blanket or dressed and the parents look first at the baby's other features. Some parents may want to see the anomaly. They may find this important for understanding why their baby died. If the pregnancy was terminated for medical reasons, seeing the anomaly may help parents to understand the decision they made to end the pregnancy. Other parents may want to keep the anomaly covered if this is possible. It is important to respect the parent's choice and follow their lead while also providing them with opportunities to discuss how they feel (Ryninks *et al*. 2014).

When parents are undecided about seeing or holding their baby

Some parents will want to see and hold their baby straight away while others may want time to decide. Some parents may choose to see but not to touch or hold their baby. Some parents will decide that they do not want to see or hold their baby, and their decision should be accepted and respected. They should be told where the baby's body will be kept and that they can ask to see their baby if they change their minds. Parents should not feel pressured. However, if there are time limits, this should be explained. For example, time may be a consideration if the baby is to have a post mortem examination.

In most cases it is reasonable to make the offer once more at a later time. If possible, this should be done by the same member of staff who asked the parents in the first instance. This will help to avoid repeated offers that may leave parents feeling harassed and unsure. In addition, careful notes must be kept about what has been offered to parents and what has or has not been done. This should ensure that all staff know the situation *before* they speak to the parents.

If the parents are unsure about seeing their baby, it may be helpful for an experienced member of staff, preferably someone whom they already know, to talk to them and ask whether they would like:

- The baby to be washed and carefully wrapped or dressed first. *Staff should always ask first if they may wash or dress the baby*. Some parents may wish to do this themselves, others may want or have a religious need for their baby's body to be washed before they touch it and some may not want anyone who is not of their faith to touch the baby but may want the baby washed by members of their religious community. See below for more information about *Washing and dressing the baby*.

- The baby to be placed in a cold cot or a suitably sized Moses basket beside the parents so that they can see their baby and then decide, without pressure, whether to hold him or her.

- A member of staff to hold the baby first and stay with the parents for a while.

- A member of staff to take a photograph of the baby for the parents to see before they decide.

- The baby to be kept in a nearby room for a while. It can be easier for parents to ask for their baby to be brought to them if they know that he or she is not far away.

These suggestions must be sensitively made as it is important that parents do not feel under pressure from staff to do anything that is against their better judgement. See the Creating Memories form in the *Creating memories* section of this chapter for more details.

I could have been better prepared for how my baby would look after he was born. I was so scared … I didn't know if I could hold him … I needed to be given time … I felt that someone was going to swoop in at any moment and take him away to the morgue. I would have loved more time.
Parent (Redshaw *et al*. 2014: 22)

Naming the baby

Parents often decide to name their baby. This may help to make the baby feel more real to parents and may help parents and their family to talk about the baby in the future. A name may also be important for existing and future siblings, especially in a multiple birth where one or more babies survive. Staff should always use the baby's name when they have been given one by the parents. However, staff should bear in mind that some parents will not want to name their baby.

It is easier to choose a name if the baby's sex is known. If there is any doubt about the sex, the parents may want to wait for definite confirmation (see above) before they choose a name. Some parents may still want to give their baby a name, even if it is not possible to identify the baby's sex. They may want to choose a name that could be used for either sex or a name with a special meaning to them.

Creating memories

Why create memories?

Normally when a person dies, those who were closest to them have a store of memories to help them remember and remain connected to the dead person. Physical keepsakes (for example, photographs, clothes, possessions, letters connected with the dead person) can trigger memories and may bring comfort to the bereaved (Davies 2004). These memories and keepsakes may enable the bereaved to hold on, in some sense, to part of the person they have loved (Davies 2004).

Perinatal loss involves losing someone who may be very important and who may have already changed their parents' lives in many fundamental ways. However, there are generally few or no tangible memories of the baby or babies and often there are no memories that can be shared with other people. In most cases, the parents have never seen their baby alive and there may be no body in early pregnancy loss.

Parents may find making memories following the death of their baby valuable and sharing these memories may be beneficial to the grieving process (Crawley *et al*. 2013; Brierley-Jones *et al*. 2014). Parents may wish to have these activities photographed (see *Photographs* below). Talking about the baby who has died and sharing memories of them may help to confirm the parent's identity in the absence of their baby who continues to be important despite their lack of physical presence (Crawley *et al*. 2013;

Brierley-Jones *et al*. 2014). Also, being able to share these memories with other people has been found to have a positive effect on maternal mental health following stillbirth (Crawley et al. 2013).

Many parents also feel a strong desire to cherish and remember their baby and to preserve his or her continuing importance in their lives. Physical items connected with their baby may help to confirm the reality of his or her short existence and provide comfort as well as a focus for their grief (Davies 2004).

Staff may be able to help by offering those parents who want opportunities to create positive memories and physical keepsakes.

Parental choice and checklists

It is now commonplace for staff to offer parents various ways of creating memories and tangible keepsakes of their baby. Protocols, procedures and checklists have been created to ensure that these are offered. However, these checklists and procedures should not be adhered to as directives, rules or tasks that must be completed but should be used to offer suggestions and choices to parents (Leon 1992) (see *Informed choice* above and *Giving information and facilitating informed choice* in Chapter 4). Checklists inevitably emphasise *what* should be done at the expense of *how* it is done. They cannot reflect the diversity of parents' individual needs or the sensitive issue of *when* to discuss things with parents.

Checklists for creating memories are different from lists containing information about samples collected, completed paperwork and information that has been passed on to colleagues. In such checklists, a tick or a Yes/No response in a column may be sufficient. However, checklists aimed at creating memories should be clearly marked in a way that makes it immediately obvious that these forms are different from the clinical checklist. For example, these lists could be copied on coloured paper (not pink or blue). It may also be helpful if these checklists are included in bound bereavement care notes so that they are not overlooked by staff with little experience of providing bereavement care.

Space should be provided on these checklists to record what has been discussed with parents. The way the items are set out should also make it clear that parents who decline an option should not be asked repeatedly if they have changed their minds. Sands suggests that parents who decline to create memories should only be asked about each option twice (if appropriate) to ensure that they have an opportunity to change their minds but to prevent parents feeling pressured. Using the form below should ensure that this happens.

When suggesting to parents that they might want to create memories of their baby, staff should remember that *parental choice is paramount. It is essential to offer genuine choice and not to steer parents towards a particular course of action in the belief that it will help them*. However, it is important to let parents know that they can change their minds later if they decline to create memories and to "normalise" the options for creating memories that are available to parents by mentioning that some parents find this helpful. Parents should be reassured that whatever choice they make is acceptable.

Some parents may find the idea of creating memories strange and unnecessary. For example, this may be the case for parents who have grown up in parts of the world with high infant mortality rates. However, no assumptions should ever be made on the basis of people's background or origins. It is important to listen to individual parents and find out what they would like to do in their own time. Sands' *Saying goodbye to your baby* booklet has a section on creating memories that may be helpful for some parents. Some parents may have already started to create memories if their baby died neonatally in hospital, at home or in a hospice.

Storing keepsakes

Parents may agree to having photographs taken of their baby or other keepsakes created even if they do not wish to take these keepsakes home with them. This choice should be recorded and keepsakes should be stored in the mother's medical notes where possible (Sands 2015j).

With the move to digital medical records, hospitals and clinics may no longer be able to store such keepsakes. In such cases, keepsakes can be placed in a sealed envelope to give to parents or a person designated by the parents for safekeeping (Sands 2015j).

When hard copy keepsakes are part of the medical notes and can no longer be stored by a hospital, the parents should be contacted and given the choice of whether to have these items sent to them (Sands 2015j). Any correspondence to parents should acknowledge that this may be distressing for them and they should be given clear information about the different methods available for contacting the hospital about these keepsakes (telephone, email or postal address) (Sands 2015j). The items should be sent in a sealed envelope inside of the envelope used to post the item(s) by recorded or special delivery to ensure that the items are not lost (Sands 2015j). Information should also be provided to parents stating that the keepsakes will be stored by the hospital for the foreseeable future if the parents do not make contact (Sands 2015j).

Creating memories – offering choices

This form provides a record for staff and should be kept prominently in the notes. It helps to ensure that:

- Parents are offered genuine choices.
- They are given time to reflect and decide what they want.
- Parents who have declined previous offers are not asked repeatedly if they have changed their minds.

It is very important to use the form sensitively and flexibly and to take into account:

- Any views the parents may have expressed earlier.

- The condition of the baby.

If the parents make it very clear that they definitely do not want to see the baby, the offer should not be repeated. However, parents should be told that they can change their minds.

Creating memories – offering choices

	Offer made	Accepted	Declined	Postponed	Second offer (if appropriate)	Accepted	Declined
Seeing the baby (or fetal remains)							
Holding the baby							
Photographs							
Lock of hair (if baby has hair)							
Foot and handprints (if feasible)							
Naming the baby							
Taking the baby home							

This form can be copied, modified and used by healthcare professionals, clinics, Trusts and Health Boards. A copy of the form can be downloaded from the Sands website. **More rows can be added to this form if needed.**

Washing and dressing the baby

Parents may want to wash their baby or assist or watch a member of the staff washing the baby. It may be beneficial if staff wait until after they have asked the parents twice if they would like to wash the baby themselves before staff wash the baby. Some parents may feel that washing and dressing their baby provides them with an opportunity to "parent" or care for their baby as well as look more closely at their baby.

If there is maceration, skin slippage should be explained first to prevent further distress to the parents. Using lukewarm or slightly cool water with no soap when bathing the baby may help to prevent skin slippage. It is also important not to wrap a very premature baby in a paper towel because the paper may stick to the baby's delicate and friable skin and is very difficult to remove. For very tiny babies and some that are macerated, washing may not be appropriate and this may need to be discussed with parents.

Some parents may want to dress their baby in clothes they have chosen. They may need help to dress their baby or may want to ask someone to do it for them. Some hospitals provide clothes (including very tiny ones) but it is still important that parents are able to choose what their baby wears. Some parents prefer to wrap their baby in a shawl. For very tiny babies who can be difficult to dress, a small knitted poncho is often a good alternative. It is possible to order very small clothes and shawls from several online retailers.

> *We carefully wrapped her in the shawl that Mom had knitted and together placed her in the cot with her toy. I remember kissing her gently on her cold cheek and leaving her forever. It was the hardest thing we have ever had to do.* Mother

> *I brushed his hair and put him in the new cardigan I had bought him. I got to do all the things I'd looked forward to doing, it was my chance to show him all the love I had.* Mother

Photographs

> *The community midwife suggested that I pack a camera to take pictures of our baby – I can remember thinking how terrible to take pictures of a dead baby. The pictures we now have of him are truly precious: vivid and beautiful memories of our treasured son. I'm so grateful she mentioned something so simple, important and caring.* Father

Many parents cherish for the rest of their lives the photographs that have been taken of their baby and the time they spent with their baby. Photographs often also help other family members and friends to understand and empathise with parents.

Staff should not assume that parents will not want photographs because their baby is very tiny, macerated or has been diagnosed with a fetal anomaly. With the exception of facial disfiguration, most visible anomalies can be covered by wrapping the baby in a shawl, blanket or hat or positioning the baby so that the anomaly is not visible. Some parents will want photographs of their baby showing the anomaly. It may be helpful for parents if a range of photographs are taken with and without covering any anomalies.

Photographs should never be taken without the parents' knowledge and permission. Additionally, parents' wishes must be respected if they say clearly that they do not want any photographs taken. Some parents may simply find the idea unacceptable or may not feel it is necessary. Some parents including some conservative Muslims may regard it as forbidden to make an image of a person and may not want photographs or hand and footprints taken. However, staff should never assume for any reason that any parents will not want photographs of their baby. Photographs should always be offered.

If parents are not sure whether they want photographs, it may be helpful to say gently that many people have greatly valued photographs of their baby, especially in the months and years after the loss (Blood and Cacciatore 2014). Other parents have expressed regret that they did not have photos of their baby or that they did not take more photos, better quality photos or different photos (Blood and Cacciatore 2014). Staff could also offer to take photographs and keep them safely with the medical records until the parents have decided whether they want to have them. If this offer is accepted, the parents should know that they can ask for the photographs at any time in the future and whom to contact (see also *Storing Keepsakes* above).

 I decided that it would be better to have a photo I might never look at than to want to have a photo that I do not have. Father

Staff may offer to take photos for parents. Some parents may want staff to take some or all of the photographs for them, as it can be difficult to concentrate in such a distressing situation. Alternatively, they may want to take photos themselves or ask a family member or friend. Some hospitals have a digital camera available on the labour ward to take photographs although many parents now use cameras on their phones to take photographs. Despite this, Sands suggests that a camera is made available on every unit and that staff are familiar with using these cameras.

The use of digital images allows parents to reprint and edit photos as they wish. It is extremely important to suggest that parents download or print these images in case these devices or memory cards are lost or damaged.

Staff can receive training on taking photographs from organisations such as Gifts of Remembrance. Volunteer photographers may also be available in some areas such as those listed on the Now I Lay Me Down to Sleep or Remember My Baby websites. See Appendix 2 for more details about these organisations. It may also be possible for a hospital to develop contacts with one or more local professional photographers who would be prepared to give their time to take high-quality photographs for bereaved parents. Staff should be aware of their available local resources.

Quality

The quality of photographs is important. For example, blurred photographs or photographs taken with a flash that are very stark can be very hard for parents to look at or show to other people later. Despite this concern, all photos should be sent to parents regardless of quality so they can decide which photos they might want to keep or edit. Although it is not easy to take good-quality photographs in this situation, staff should try to make sure that parents have high-quality pictures and to meet any special requests from parents.

Deciding what to take

Some parents in this situation know what kinds of photographs they want while other parents may be grateful for sensitive advice and suggestions. Unless they have sophisticated photographic equipment, it may be helpful to advise them to take the photos in natural light if possible with a simple backdrop. Parents may also appreciate documentary-style photos taken by themselves or by staff of the activities and interactions that they or family members engage in with their baby.

Parents may need time to think about the pictures they want and to arrange different shots. They may want to take a lot of photos so that they can select the best. They should be offered privacy so that they can take the photographs they want without worrying about what other people might think. Parents should not feel under any time pressure unless there is a good reason.

- They may want photos of the baby both dressed and naked, alone and in the arms or lying on one or both parents.

- They may want close-ups of the baby's hands and feet and of the baby's hand in the mother's or father's hand.

- They may want to photograph the baby in a Moses basket and on a blanket or shawl.

- They may want family photographs of both parents with the baby and of each parent separately with the baby.

- They may want photographs of their baby with a brother or sister and with other members of the family. These may be very valuable when parents talk about the loss with their children and other people in the future.

- When babies have died on a neonatal unit, parents may want photos of their baby without tubes, wires and machines.

- In a multiple birth, if all the babies have died, or if some but not all of the babies have died, parents may want to have photographs of all their babies together if this is possible (Bryan 2002). This may be the only record of all of the babies together. This may be important as a surviving twin, for example, may find that photographs are a precious, tangible confirmation of his or her twinship. If the parents do not think of it themselves, staff might suggest to them that some other parents have found this helpful.

- Staff may also be able to help them take documentary-style shots of the family interacting with the baby (see Gifts of Remembrance training in Appendix 2 for more details).

Photographs taken as part of the post mortem examination should not be considered as a substitute for the photographs described above. However, some parents may request these photos and find them helpful.

Other keepsakes

Many parents want to gather keepsakes such as their baby's cot card, name band, a lock of hair, prints or plaster casts of feet or hands, stills from scans, a copy of a fetal monitor tracing and/or a baptism or baby blessing card. They may value anything that will help them to remember their baby and staff should offer as much as possible. Some parents may ask for these keepsakes to be saved for them so that they can have them later (see *Storing keepsakes* above).

It is possible to take hand and foot prints without using ink. This method is more expensive but avoids having to remove ink from the baby's skin. The Sands Shop sells inkless *Hand and Footprint Kits* or see other retailers such as *Creative Casting Ltd*. It is important to note that the baby's skin will peel more if it is macerated when hand and footprints are taken, which can make prints rather moist and fuzzy. As this may be disappointing for parents, they should be warned about this possibility.

Some parents may wish to keep the blanket that their baby was wrapped in as they find the smell of their baby on the blanket comforting. Other parents may want to have this blanket buried or cremated with their baby.

Although many parents find it helpful to have keepsakes of their baby, some may decline on personal, cultural or religious grounds. Some parents may find certain specific keepsakes unacceptable. For example, some people from the Indian subcontinent may object to cutting the baby's hair. For some traditional Sikhs, this may be because they never cut hair. In other cultures, the baby's head may usually be shaved to remove the pollution of birth. It is very important to always ask parents before a lock of hair is cut or a foot or handprint is taken.

Memory boxes and booklets

One way of collecting keepsakes is to use memory boxes such as those available from Sands and other organisations. These boxes can be used to store photographs and other keepsakes of the baby. The Sands memory boxes also contain two small bears (one that can be placed in the baby's coffin and one for parents to keep) and a knitted white blanket.

I cherish my daughter's memory box and would like to thank Sands for enabling the hospital to provide it. The hospital staff put the photos in the box along with the blanket that had covered her, her knitted hat and the wires that had monitored her heart – all the things that had been close to her. A hand and footprint and a tiny piece of hair were also included when the midwife gave us our daughter's memory box. Mother

Sands also provides memory booklets. This is a four-page booklet with a place for the baby's name, hand and footprints, a photograph, a lock of hair and space for the parents to record their memories of their baby.

Other family members

Some parents want to be alone at this time. They may need staff to restrict visitors and be firm but tactful on their behalf. Other parents may want their family and friends to visit and comfort them. Visiting hours for other family members should be relaxed so that the family can be together if this is what the parents want. If parents are not in a separate room, they will need somewhere private and quiet where they can be with their family. In some families and cultures it is important for family members and friends to visit parents after a baby's death. In these instances, there may be a large number of visitors.

If parents have chosen to see their baby, they may also want other people such as grandparents and other children to see him or her. It may be helpful for siblings to see their dead brother or sister as what they might imagine is often more frightening than the reality. If the parents agree and other family members want to see the baby, this may also be helpful for the parents in the long-term as they will have shared memories that they may be able to talk about with their family. Parents should be sensitively supported in doing whatever they feel is right for them and should not be put under any pressure to fit in with other people's expectations.

Some parents may want to take photographs of their baby with other family members (see also *Photographs* in this chapter). For more information about support for other family members, see *Other children*, *Grandparents* and *Other family members and friends* in Chapter 3.

Religious ceremonies

Whether they are religious or not, some parents may want to ask the hospital chaplain or another person to give a blessing, hold a naming ceremony or say prayers for their baby. Some may want to ask their own religious adviser or an older relative. Some parents may want to pray, possibly with other family members or members of their faith community.

Parents' time with and access to their baby

 We spent a few hours with her to try and remember everything about her, her curly dark hair, round face, ten fingers and ten toes. Mother

If parents want to spend time alone with their baby, they should be given privacy when they are ready. Parents should know that staff are available if needed. Some parents may want to keep the baby with them for longer periods of time or overnight. They should not be asked to part from their baby before they feel ready to do so. They should then be reassured that their baby will be kept safely for them for a stated period of time and that they can ask to see him or her again if they want. They should be given details about whom to contact and how to ask to see their baby again (see also *Taking the baby's body home* in Chapter 15 and *Transfer to the mortuary* in Chapter 16).

 I combed her soft hair, held her, kissed and stroked her soft sweet cheek, and told her how proud I was of her, that she was mine, and so brave to hang on and fight. I hung onto her as long as I could. I was sure I could feel a pulse as I lay next to her form, holding her tiny palm in mine, willing her back to life. Mother

Parents should be able to see their baby's body whenever they want but they need to know whom to ask. The body should normally be kept on or near the ward for as long as the mother is in hospital. Parents may be able to keep the baby beside them in their room for longer if a cold cot is available or ice-packs are discreetly placed under the bottom sheet of the cot or Moses basket.

 I never thought that the staff would care so beautifully for a baby that had died. Seeing her dressed in proper baby clothes and handled so gently was very comforting. Mother

In order to facilitate easy access for parents to the bodies of their babies following a childbearing loss, Trusts, Health Boards and managers should ensure that a cold cot is available to parents. Some units also have a mortuary fridge near the ward where the mother is receiving care. The staff caring for the mother should have direct access to the fridge. The body must be labelled and the fridge should be monitored and locked. The date and time must be logged whenever a baby's body is placed in or removed from the fridge. This could be beneficial as some parents have had difficulties accessing their baby's body after it has been taken to the mortuary.

If the baby's body must be transferred to the mortuary while the mother is still in hospital, this should be explained to the parents. However, a mother and/or her partner should not have to go to the mortuary to see their baby. Instead the baby should be brought to them in a place that is private and comfortable. This might be in a bereavement room, another room on the ward or a quiet room. The baby should be dressed or wrapped according to the parents' wishes and should be carried in a suitably sized Moses basket or cot. Staff may need to explain to the parents beforehand that their baby will feel cold and they should be told how the body is likely to look and feel. Holding the baby may feel more natural if he or she is wrapped in a shawl. For more about the transfer and storage of babies' bodies see *Transfer to the mortuary* in Chapter 16.

The parents should be reassured that their baby will be kept safely in the hospital for a stated period of time depending on whether the baby is being sent for a post mortem examination or to a funeral director (see Chapter 16 for more information). They should also be gently told that the body is likely to deteriorate as time passes.

Parents may also choose to spend time with their baby away from the hospital by taking their baby home or to a hospice (see *Taking the baby's body home* in Chapter 15).

Postnatal care

Other relevant chapters

The recommendations given in this chapter may be relevant for the care of women who experience any type of childbearing loss at any gestation. This care could take place at home or in any healthcare facility. Healthcare facilities where postnatal care may occur can include hospitals (on labour wards, gynaecological wards, midwifery led units or neonatal units), birth centres, termination clinics or community-based services (GP clinics, surgeries or hospices). Some women may also need critical care at this time and have more complex needs, including women requiring medical care for sepsis, pre-eclampsia or other conditions (RCOG 2010a).

Listening to Parents highlights the disparities in the postnatal care offered to women after their baby's death. This report showed that three-quarters of women had been given a midwife's name and contact details and saw a midwife following the stillbirth or neonatal death of their baby (Redshaw *et al*. 2014). However, a small number of the women surveyed (7 per cent) did not receive the offer of a midwife visit after their baby died neonatally, one-third (33 per cent) were not advised regarding lactation management following the stillbirth of their baby and one-quarter (26 per cent) did not receive information about counselling services (Redshaw *et al*. 2014). Notably, a small number of women did not want to see a midwife postnatally (Redshaw *et al*. 2014).

Almost overwhelmed with support – Bereavement Midwife, Health Visitors etc. All a bit much, wanted to be left alone, just wanted to get physical problems sorted. (Redshaw et al. 2014: 36)

 There wasn't much postnatal care. Midwife visited me twice and it felt like she didn't want to be there. She also offered several times that I can see a different midwife. (Redshaw et al. 2014: 23)

Concerns have also been raised about general postnatal care in the UK. One study found that 45 per cent of women felt their care was rushed or that their check-up was not thorough enough (NCT 2014). Additionally, women from migrant communities have been found to be at an increased risk of receiving substandard postnatal care and/ or experiencing poor perinatal outcomes (Cross-Sudworth et al. 2011). It is worth considering how the general challenges that women face when receiving postnatal care may be exacerbated in instances where women do not receiving sufficient care and information after the death of their baby.

Place of care

In hospital

Listening to Parents highlighted that many women whose baby was stillborn or died in the neonatal period were cared for in private or single rooms (Redshaw et al. 2014). However, more than half of these women could hear the sounds of crying babies, were unable to have their partner stay with them or were located far away from their baby on the neonatal unit (Redshaw et al. 2014).

 I was put into a family room, which was perfect except [for] the fact that all I could hear was crying babies which distressed me even more than I already was. (Redshaw et al. 2014: 22)

If a woman is being cared for in hospital after the birth, she should be offered a designated single room on a side ward unless she prefers to be on a ward with others. The room should have a double bed or an additional single bed so that her partner or another supporter can stay with her through the night if she wishes. The room should be large enough to accommodate extra chairs for any partners or other supporters and a cold cot or crib so that parents can have their baby's body with them if they wish. The mother should have her meals brought to her unless she prefers to eat with others (if there is a communal dining table). Designated members of staff should check on her regularly and ensure that she does not become isolated because she is in a single room. Partners or other supporters should be made to feel welcome and their need for empathy and support should be acknowledged and met. For more information, also see *Parents' time with and access to their baby* and *Place of care* in Chapter 14.

Ideally, each unit should also have a designated sitting room, furnished with a sofa, comfortable chairs, facilities for making tea and coffee and boxes of tissues. This room can be used for parents to spend time together, be with their baby and, if they want, see relatives and friends. It can also be used by staff for discussions with parents.

In the community

Postnatal care may take place at home, in GP clinics or in the hospital when parents start receiving care in the community after the death of their baby (see also Chapter 17). The location could be discussed with parents as they may feel more comfortable in a particular setting.

Medical notes used during postnatal care

If a woman consents, it is important that her medical notes are appropriately marked to alert staff that her baby has died. See the boxed text about Teardrop Stickers in Chapter 14 for more details.

Specially designed bereavement postnatal notes, such as those developed by the Perinatal Institute, may also be helpful to ensure that staff are meeting the specific individualised care requirements of bereaved mothers. These notes are designed to be used after late miscarriage, stillbirth or neonatal death and are available from the Perinatal Institute website (see Appendix 2). These notes also contain a discharge summary letter that can be given to primary care staff including GPs and health visitors.

Physical, emotional and practical care

It is essential that women receive excellent practical and physical care after a loss, as well as emotional support (Mander 2006). Therefore, women should be offered ongoing midwifery care that should be documented in their medical notes (Draper *et al.* 2015). This care can include offering pain relief and advice about lactation, contraception, coping with a sore perineum, infection, lochia, stitches, bathing, constipation and other physical problems. Providing information about infection and bleeding is important for losses at any gestation.

The *MBRRACE-UK* report (Knight *et al.* 2014) also highlights that postnatal care is particularly needed for women who had anaesthesia or pregnancy-related or underlying medical conditions (including mental health problems). This recommendation would include bereaved women who had anaesthesia and/or a medical condition.

Lactation

Some women may find that lactation is a very distressing physical experience after the death of their baby. Engorgement and milk leakage may be a constant painful reminder for a woman of her baby's death. Women may also find lactation, engorgement and leakage particularly challenging around the time of their baby's funeral or wake (McGuinness *et al*. 2014).

The stage of pregnancy when the loss occurred can affect whether women lactate but some women (especially those who have breastfed before) may lactate after an early miscarriage or termination. It may be some time before lactation and pain or discomfort stop completely and women should be given this information.

Woman should also be given empathetic support and practical help regarding their options for lactation and lactation suppression along with information and advice about mastitis and its prevention. Continuing to lactate may be important for some women who may feel that lactation is a tangible link to their baby, be interested in the health benefits of lactation or wish to delay stopping lactation for other reasons (Gillian Weaver 2015, Imperial College Healthcare NHS Trust and UK Association for Milk Banking, personal communication).

Lactation suppression

The most recent Cochrane Review on lactation calls for larger studies of lactation suppression methods as there is limited evidence for many pharmacological interventions, no trials comparing the use of non-pharmacological methods with no treatment and no studies of women's satisfaction with various methods (Oladapo and Fawole 2012).

Women should be given information about their choices for lactation suppression and be informed of the relative advantages and disadvantages of each approach.

Current recommendations are that pharmacological methods of lactation suppression are effective and well-tolerated by many women (RCOG 2010a). However, there are potential side effects for some medications used to suppress lactation such as Cabergoline, which women may wish to consider (NHS Choices [n.d.(b)]). Certain medications may also not be suitable for all women (NHS Choices [n.d.(b)]). Some medications such as bromocriptine should not be used routinely for lactation suppression because of their potentially serious side effects (European Medicines Agency 2014).

Some women may prefer to use non-pharmacological approaches to suppress lactation and all of their options should be discussed with them. Around one-third of women who choose to supress lactation using non-pharmacological methods, such as ice packs, analgesics and support bras, have been found to experience excessive discomfort (RCOG 2010a). To help with discomfort, women may want to:

- Express milk and gradually decrease the frequency of expression.
- Take warm showers.

- Use cloths cooled with cold water.

- Wear a well-fitting bra.

- Avoid touching their breasts (particularly the areola area) to avoid stimulating milk production.

- Use analgesia (for example, paracetamol) if needed (Gillian Weaver 2015, Imperial College Healthcare NHS Trust and UK Association for Milk Banking, personal communication).

Milk donation

Some women may also choose to donate their milk to a breast milk bank. While discussing milk donation may be difficult, staff should sensitively give women information about donating their milk. Some mothers may want to donate their milk to a milk bank and other mothers may not.

The United Kingdom Association for Milk Banking (UKAMB) can provide more support if a there is not a local milk bank. UKAMB offers support for staff and bereaved mothers across the UK who are looking for information about donating milk (see Appendix 2).

Healthcare staff can help a woman to determine if she is eligible to donate her milk to a milk bank and explain how to express and store her milk for donation (see the NICE 2010 guidance on *Donor milk banks* for more information). The woman should also be told about the necessary blood tests, local milk bank dietary and alcohol intake requirements and any emotional and practical support that is available to her when she is donating milk (NICE 2010). Blood tests and health questionnaires can be completed at a place and time that is convenient for the mother after she makes a decision (Gillian Weaver 2015 Imperial College Healthcare NHS Trust and UK Association for Milk Banking, personal communication). If a woman wishes to donate her breast milk but is not able, staff could suggest that she donates her milk for research or has it buried with her baby (Gillian Weaver 2015, Imperial College Healthcare NHS Trust and UK Association for Milk Banking, personal communication).

Stored milk

If a mother has been expressing breast milk for a baby who has died on the neonatal unit, she should be approached sensitively to find out what she would like to be done with any stored milk. This milk could be stored according to the necessary standards at the milk bank while a mother decides whether she would like to donate, take home or discard this milk.

Discussing sex and contraception

There is no ideal time to raise the issue of sexual relationships and contraception when parents are mourning the loss of their baby. Discussion about preventing another pregnancy can seem extremely insensitive and inappropriate and some grieving parents may be very offended and distressed when the subject is raised (Sands Helplines Staff 2006, personal communication).

While there is no specific time frame for resuming sexual relations after the birth of any child, women will need to be given information on preventing infection and how their body will need time to heal (Sands 2014a). Parents should also be told that they may have different sexual needs and desires from their partner and that some women or their partners may have difficulty becoming aroused (Sands 2014a).

 I had absolutely no physical urge, no desire whatsoever, but felt obliged to have sex with my husband, to offer him some form of physical comfort. So I pretended and went along with his needs. Mother

 I was keen for our sex life to become more fun again and for us to really want it instead of just doing it because we thought we should. But my partner found sex a bit of a chore – he was still grieving strongly for our daughter. He struggled to put his pain aside for a while so we could have sex. Mother

 I wanted to feel close to her as I nearly lost her as well as our baby. But I was also scared of getting close to her, I didn't know how she would react. Father

Advice on contraception should be offered tentatively and sensitively, preferably by a member of staff whom the parents already know and trust (See also *Couples* in Chapter 3 and *Pre-conception care* in Chapter 23 for more information). It may be helpful to start the conversation by acknowledging that although this may not seem to be the right time to talk about contraception, it is important that parents give it some thought and to let parents know that their GP, midwife or obstetrician may be able to offer them additional contraceptive or pre-conception advice when they are ready (see *Follow-up appointments* in Chapter 17 and *Pre-conception care* in Chapter 23). It is also important to be aware that, for some women, another pregnancy may not be an option.

Women should be aware that if they have unprotected sex before their next period, they could become pregnant. In some cases there may be compelling medical reasons for waiting to become pregnant again. For example, it may be advisable for parents to wait for all the test results in case there are implications for another pregnancy or to allow the woman's body to heal following the birth. In most cases, however, there is no *medical* reason to wait.

Parents may find it helpful to know that it is not unusual for couples to have different views and feelings about if and when to have another baby. It may be important for parents to allow time to grieve for the baby or babies that have died before becoming pregnant again. Parents should be gently warned that the anniversary of their baby's death or due date is likely to be very difficult and that it may be hard emotionally if a new baby is born around that time. However, it is important to be clear that there are no rules and that all parents should make their own informed decision.

Sands' booklet on *Sexual relationships after the death of a baby* may also provide useful information for parents about sexual relationships and contraception after the death of their baby.

Support and listening

 My story is all I have got. Father

Although many members of staff feel that there is little they can offer, *simply listening is often more helpful than anything else.* It is particularly important that staff are able to listen actively to parents' stories with openness and without taking a defensive position (Kenworthy and Kirkham 2011). Listening can be very difficult, even more so if the parents are angry or blame the staff for their loss (see *Responding to parents' feedback about their care* in Chapter 22).

Giving time to listen to parents after a pregnancy loss or the death of a baby potentially has major benefits for the parents, both in the short and in the longer term (Leoni 1997; Moulder 1998; Swanson 1999; Kenworthy and Kirkham 2011; Crawley *et al*. 2013). Staff should give parents as much time as they are able. Managers should support staff who do this and make arrangements to release staff so that they have time to listen wherever possible. Staff who cared for the mother antenatally and who feel close to the parents may like to offer their sympathy by visiting or sending a card.

Many parents whose baby has died may very much want and need to talk about what has happened but are often given little or no opportunity to do so (Mander 2006). Sometimes parents who want to share their memories of their baby may feel unable to do so (Brierley-Jones *et al*. 2014). This could be because other people may feel uncomfortable and avoid these discussions, not appreciate parents' need to talk or not see parents' grief and loss as being as legitimate as that for other losses (Crawley *et al*. 2013).

It can be potentially helpful if the staff who were involved in the events are available to listen to parents, answer their questions and perhaps contribute their memories of what happened (Kenworthy and Kirkham 2011; Redshaw *et al*. 2014). This process can be important for parents who can receive support and encouragement from staff as they develop their story about their baby's birth and/or death (Kenworthy and Kirkham 2011).

 The midwife who delivered our baby was wonderful. She would pop in when she had a minute and sit with us for a little while, just letting us talk and admiring the baby. You could tell she was upset and she really cared. Mother

Mothers may be more likely to receive this type of support. However, it is important that fathers and partners are also offered this support and care.

 The hospital staff were very good at making sure that Martin was OK. Every time the midwife came round she'd ask him, "How are you?" Our families watched the midwives taking care of him as well as me. And they took a lead from that. Mother

Some parents may welcome the chance to talk about the events surrounding their baby's death to a member of staff who was not involved and who is therefore hearing an account of the loss for the first time. Some parents may also want to speak to a hospital chaplain, their own religious adviser or a counsellor.

Some parents may be anxious about how they are going to feel in the next few weeks and months. It may be helpful to discuss the wide range of normal and sometimes intense feelings that they may experience and the individual and personal nature of grief (see also Chapter 3). Sometimes bereaved parents are told that they are depressed or feel that they are "going mad" when they are grieving. It is important to normalise grief when discussing emotions with bereaved parents. It is also important to give parents details of sources of help and support should they feel they need it at that time or in the future. More information about mental health difficulties that parents may face following the death of a baby (for example, depression, anxiety, PTSD, etc.) is available in Chapter 18.

Before parents leave the hospital

Parents may need a lot of practical information at this time about what they need to do and this information should be communicated sensitively and clearly. It may be necessary to give the same information several times and parents should feel able to ask as many questions as they need. They should be given clear written information and/or information in other formats to back up what they have been told – preferably in their own language.

Before they leave the hospital, and depending on the gestation and the circumstances, staff should offer to discuss and give parents information about:

- The physical and emotional reactions that parents may experience.

- A post mortem or other pathology investigation (see *Post mortem examination* in Chapter 16).

- The need to register the stillbirth or birth and death. The parents should be given clear written information about where and when to register, directions to the Registrar's office, opening hours and telephone numbers (see also *Registration* in Chapter 19).

- Parents' options for burying or cremating the baby's body and whether they want to organise or participate in a funeral. For losses before 24 weeks, sensitive incineration is also an option (except in Scotland) (see *Offering choices to parents* in Chapter 20).

- Any medical certificates and forms that parents are given and may need to register their baby's stillbirth, birth and/or death or arrange a burial or cremation. The purpose of each form should be explained to parents (see also *Certificates and forms issued by healthcare staff* in Chapter 19).

- Leaving the baby (or the remains) at the hospital if parents are doing this while they make decisions about burial, cremation, sensitive incineration or a funeral. Following a discussion, parents should be asked to sign a document that states that the hospital staff can make suitable arrangements if the parents have not told the hospital how they want to dispose of the baby's remains after a stated period of time (for example, six months). Parents who sign such a document should be given a copy to take home. They should also be sent a reminder prior to the date when the hospital will dispose of the baby's remains. Parents must also know whom to contact when they have decided on the arrangements that they want (see also Chapter 20).

- A six-week follow-up appointment with either the mother's GP or a hospital doctor (Draper *et al*. 2015). The mother should be told that the purpose of this appointment is to check on her physical and emotional well-being and give her an opportunity to raise any concerns. Parents' expectations should be managed regarding any results being available by this appointment (see also *Follow-up appointments* in Chapter 17).

- Parents may want to consider whether they want to inform any facilitators of antenatal classes or groups that they were attending of their baby's death. They might also want to decide whether to have the facilitator tell other groups members and what information to share (Thomas 2010). Facilitators of antenatal classes should respect parents' wishes regarding who should be given information and should offer parents their condolences and an opportunity to discuss their baby or feelings (Thomas 2010).

- The support that parents should be offered by the primary health care team. They should also be given information about relevant voluntary and counselling support.

- Sands' booklet on *Saying goodbye to your baby* may be a useful resource for parents before and after they leave the hospital.

In addition, the mother should be given a phone number and/or email address so that she can contact a named designated member of staff who has cared for her. The designated member of staff responsible for the care of the mother should also make sure that:

- The mother's notes contain the address and phone number where the mother can be contacted in the time immediately after leaving hospital. Parents sometimes go away to stay with relatives and it may be necessary to get in touch with them regarding postnatal visits, to let them know when the funeral will be held or regarding post mortem investigations.

- The appropriate primary care staff are informed immediately so that they know what has happened and can offer postnatal care and emotional support. This should also help to ensure that the parents do not receive invitations to baby clinics or for immunisation. If there is time, some women may find it helpful to be visited in hospital by a community midwife before they go home (see also *Home visits* in Chapter 17).

Many parents leave hospital fairly shortly after their baby's death. They are likely to be shocked, distressed and exhausted. They may find it very hard to focus on what needs to be done or to make decisions. If it has not been possible to discuss any of the topics listed above, or the discussion was incomplete, the designated member of staff should inform the community midwife and ask her to fill in any gaps.

The designated member of staff (this may or may not be a bereavement midwife) should also make sure that all outstanding antenatal and scan appointments are cancelled and the antenatal class co-ordinator is informed if necessary.

The woman's lead carer should also cancel the Bounty Pack (although they may need the forms in this pack - see *Entitlement to time off work and benefits* below). Failure to do this may cause bereaved parents extra unnecessary distress. Parents may also be grateful for information about the Baby Mailing Preference Service (MPS) (see Appendix 2). They can register online and prevent or reduce mailings about baby-related samples and advertisements.

> *I spent many months contacting various companies asking them to stop sending information about baby products. I received a lot of free samples and nappies through the post which I found particularly distressing.*
> Mother

Depending on the length of their stay, the parents may also want to discuss other questions and concerns before they leave the hospital. Some example of topics they may wish to discuss are listed below although parents may have other queries:

- *Their chances of having a live, healthy baby in the future.* If there is to be a post mortem examination or other tests, detailed discussion about a possible future pregnancy will probably be more appropriate when the results are available. However, the subject of another baby may be a major source of anxiety and concern for many parents at this time and it is important to listen and respond sensitively if parents raise the subject. Staff should explain honestly that what they can say at this point is limited and should be careful not to speculate or present possibilities to parents as though they are facts. If the cause of death is unknown, it is important to warn parents that sometimes no reason can be found for a baby's death even following a post mortem examination. If appropriate, parents should be offered a referral to a genetic counsellor.

- *The timing of a future pregnancy.* See *Discussing sex and contraception* in this chapter for more information.

- *Time off work and going back to work.* Some women may not benefit from going back to work as soon as possible while others may wish to return more quickly. There is no right or wrong time to return to work but many women need more time to recover than they, their family members, friends or employers may anticipate. It could be suggested to women (including those who have had a miscarriage or an early termination) that they may benefit from taking time off work for emotional as well as physical recovery.

Parents may also want to discourage well-meaning relatives from removing clothing and other items that were prepared for the baby before parents return home. Some bereaved parents find it helpful to deal with baby clothes and equipment in their own time even if they find this distressing. Other parents may specifically request that these items are removed before they go home.

> *We can't come home to a house that pretends he was never there.* Father (Hansen 2003)

Discussing entitlement to time off work and benefits

These paragraphs contain the regulations at the time of going to press (April 2016). As this information is subject to change, see the Sands and Money Advice Service websites for more detail (see Appendix 2). Parents may also find it helpful to look at the Sands' booklets on *Returning to work after the death of your baby* and *Information for employers: helping a bereaved parent return to work.*

Losses before 24 weeks

- *Sick leave.* A woman who experiences a miscarriage or has had a termination before 24 weeks' gestation is not entitled to maternity leave (Money Advice Service 2013). If a woman in this situation does not feel able to return to work immediately, she should be advised to talk to her GP about taking sick leave or her employer about compassionate leave. Sick leave related to a miscarriage may or may not be "protected" in the same way as any sick leave taken during pregnancy. If it is protected, this means that the amount of sick leave that a woman can take is not limited and must be recorded separately from other sick leave (Working Families 2015; see Working Families in Appendix 2). However, some women whose loss occurred before 24 weeks may have to go to back to work out of financial necessity. If the woman has a partner (including a female partner), they may also be entitled to compassionate leave, time off for family and dependents (TOFD) or unpaid leave through their employer.

- *Benefits.* A woman who has a miscarriage or termination before 24 weeks' gestation is not entitled to statutory maternity pay or maternity allowance (Money Advice Service 2013).

Stillbirths (babies born dead after 24 weeks)

- *Maternity and paternity leave*. A woman whose baby is stillborn after 24 weeks' gestation or who gives birth to a live baby who then dies at any gestation is entitled to the full maternity leave if she is eligible. She is also entitled to free prescriptions and dental care until her Maternity Exemption Certificate expires. If the woman has a partner (including a female partner) who is entitled to parental leave, this entitlement is still valid up to 28 days after the baby's birth. Otherwise, partners may be eligible for compassionate leave, TOFD or unpaid leave.

- *Benefits*. A woman whose baby is stillborn is entitled to statutory maternity pay or maternity allowance if she is eligible for these. See Working Families (Appendix 2) for more details about eligibility for statutory maternity pay and maternity allowance. Maternity allowance claim forms are available on the UK Government website at https://www.gov.uk/maternity-allowance/overview. The woman's partner is still entitled to statutory parental pay if they are eligible. Parents of a stillborn baby who are on a low income may also be eligible for Sure Start Maternity Grants and funeral payments (Working Families 2015; see Appendix 2 and also *Parents on a low income* in Chapter 20).

Neonatal deaths

- If a baby is born alive at any gestation and then dies, the parents are entitled to the leave and benefits described under *Stillbirths* above. They are also entitled to child tax credits (this form is usually in the Bounty Pack and this benefit is being gradually replaced with Universal Credit) and child benefit if they are eligible. More information is available on the UK Government website at https://www.gov.uk/child-tax-credit/overview and https://www.gov.uk/child-benefit.

Leaving the hospital

 There are no words to describe the utter devastation of walking empty-armed out of the hospital. Of travelling home with the child seat you bought locked in the boot of the car because you can't bear to look at it. Of shutting the door to your baby's beautifully decorated bedroom and not opening it again for months. Mother

Leaving the insulated environment of the hospital and going home to face the world without the baby can be frightening and painful. Some women want to leave soon after the loss. Others prefer to stay a little longer but some may feel unable to stay. This may be because facilities are inappropriate or they do not feel that they have received sensitive care. For example, women may not have the degree of privacy or contact with others that they would like, they may feel pressured to leave if their bed is needed for other patients or staff may be unable to listen and provide support. Women should not automatically be sent home as soon as possible as women may feel abandoned and unwanted and support may not be available at home (Moulder 2001; Mander 2006).

Early discharge may also mean that the discussions and decisions recommended earlier in this chapter are either rushed or omitted.

Some parents may feel that leaving their baby is unnatural and that this disrupts their sense of motherhood (Lindgren *et al.* 2013). Taking the baby home could be discussed with parents. Otherwise, it may be helpful to discuss the place and time of leaving the hospital with the parents and appoint a person who is known to the parents to hold the baby when the parents leave (Lindgren *et al.* 2013).

All parents should be told about the services and support available to them once they are at home. Some may be reassured if they know that a member of the primary health care team will visit or contact them shortly after their discharge from hospital if this has been scheduled.

Taking the baby's body home

Some parents find it very helpful to have time with their baby and say goodbye away from a clinical setting. This may allow some parents to have privacy and feel more comfortable. If the parents wish, this can also be an opportunity for siblings, relatives and friends to see the baby, create memories and grieve with the parents.

Some parents may also want to take their baby's body home as they may wish to spend a day, and perhaps a night, in the home where he or she would have lived and grown up. Others may want to take the baby's body to a place that has special significance for them. Some areas may also have a local hospice with a cold room where parents can spend time with their baby if they do not wish to take the baby home.

 It was especially helpful to be able to bring Louisa's body home for a few days to the house where she was meant to live and grow up. We let our elder daughter, Natasha, who was then aged three, hold and care for Louisa, as she was bursting to do. She sang to Louisa, carried her into every room to "show her round", brushed her hair and did This Little Piggy with her toes. It was heartrending but beautiful at the same time. Mother

There are no legal reasons to prevent parents from taking their baby's body home unless the death has been referred to the coroner or procurator fiscal. In these cases, a Medical Certificate of Cause of Death (MCCD) cannot be issued (see Chapter 19). Wherever possible, parents should be given the choice to take their baby home or out of the hospital. When parents are not comfortable or there are good clinical reasons to discourage parents from taking their baby's body home, parents should be offered a longer stay in the hospital (Sands 2015k). For mothers with existing mental health problems, advice should be sought from a mental health professional if necessary and extra support should be offered in the community (Sands 2015k).

Sensitive and efficient procedures should be in place that enable staff to provide good support to parents who wish to take their baby's body out of the hospital. If parents plan to take the baby's body home, it is important to take any post mortem examination arrangements into account. A post mortem examination may be carried out first. In these instances, parents should be told about the condition of the body and how to handle it after the post mortem examination (see *Restoring the body* in Chapter 16). Alternatively, it may be possible for parents to take their baby's body home for a short time and then back to the hospital for post mortem examination.

Parents also need to know that it is important to keep the body cool. They may be able to borrow a cold cot from their hospital, a local support group such as Sands or a local hospice. It is important that staff know what local resources are available before offering these options to parents. If parents plan to return the body to the hospital before the funeral, they also need to know when and where they should go. Alternatively, the funeral director (if applicable) can collect the baby's body from the parents' home before the funeral.

Parents can take the baby home by car in a Moses basket secured by a seatbelt or in the parents' arms (Sands 2015k). Depending on the baby's gestation, another suitable container may be used to transport the baby's remains. The type of container offered should be discussed with parents who may wish to use an alternative receptacle of their choice. Staff might suggest using an opaque container for unidentifiable remains. If necessary, parents could arrange to take the baby home in a taxi or minicab if this is agreed with the driver in advance, although using other forms of public transport is not advisable (Sands 2015k). Local funeral directors may also be willing to help transport the baby's body home or to a hospice.

There is no legal reason to inform the police if parents take their baby's body home or out of the hospital. However, for the protection of the parents and to prevent misunderstandings, Trusts and Health Boards should issue a form to accompany the body. The form should confirm that the body has been released to the parents and that they will be taking it back to the hospital or making their own funeral arrangements. It should include the name and contact details of the member of staff who can be contacted if any difficulties arise (for example, in the unlikely event of a traffic accident). For Sands' sample form, see Appendix 1: Form 1. If the parents are collecting the baby's body from the mortuary rather than the ward, the ward should also give them a mortuary release form. The parents are legally responsible for ensuring that the body is lawfully buried or cremated if the baby died after 24 weeks' gestation (Sands 2015k).

CHAPTER 16

Transfer to the mortuary and post mortem investigations

Other relevant chapters

1: Providing holistic care

2: Providing inclusive care

3: Loss and grief

4: Communication

5: Communication across language and other barriers

14: After a loss

15: Postnatal care

17: Follow-up appointments and ongoing care

19: Certificates and registration

20: Funerals and sensitive disposal

In England, Wales and Northern Ireland, the Human Tissue Act 2004 and the Human Tissue Authority (HTA) Codes of practice and Licensing Standards govern how the bodies and remains of babies are handled and stored by institutions, including during and after post mortem examinations. In Scotland, this is regulated through the Human Tissue (Scotland) Act 2006. These pieces of legislation apply to babies who are stillborn or die shortly after birth. Additional guidance has been issued by the HTA (2015) regarding the handling of remains following losses that occur before 24 weeks' gestation. The best practice points highlighted in this chapter relate to the handling of babies' remains and tissues for losses at all gestations.

> *Establishments should have suitable procedures in place for ensuring proper compliance with the HT Act and observing the good practice set out in the HTA's codes of practice, which includes ensuring that the bodies of the deceased and tissue taken from them are treated with respect and the dignity of the person is maintained.* (HTA Code 3 2014: 5)

Transfer to the mortuary

Depending on parents' wishes, the baby should be kept with or near the parents before transfer to the mortuary (see *Parents' time with and access to their baby* in Chapter 14). If the baby is going to have a post mortem examination, it is important to inform parents that keeping the baby's body out of refrigerated storage might affect the information that can be gained from the post mortem examination and discuss how this may affect their time with their baby.

The baby's body is normally transferred to the mortuary for a post mortem examination or when the mother leaves hospital and has not chosen to take the baby home or to a hospice. In some cases, the baby may need to be transferred to the mortuary or funeral director while the mother is still in hospital.

If the baby's body or remains are to be transferred to the mortuary, this should be discussed with parents beforehand and their consent should be sought before any transfer. Parents should be assured that the baby will be treated with dignity and respect at all times. Parents should also be told how the baby will be transferred and cared for in the mortuary. Before any transfer, the baby's body should be labelled with the baby's name and that of the mother and placed in a discreet container of a suitable size such as a cardboard coffin (see *Storage and tracking* below). Babies could also be transferred in a Moses basket or carried to the mortuary by family members or a member of staff (possibly accompanied by one or more family members). If parents want to send items with their baby such as clothing or soft toys, this should be accommodated but they should be advised that these items may become soiled.

Some parents may take comfort from knowing about mortuary procedures and security and that their baby is being cared for by a named member of the mortuary staff (Sands 2015e). They may also have specific questions and concerns. For example, they may want to know whether a light can be left on so that their baby will not be alone in the dark (Sands 2015e). Wherever possible, staff should accommodate parents' preferences about the handling, transportation or storage of their baby's body or remains as this may have an effect on their bereavement experience (Wilson 2015).

During these discussions, parents should be told that they can see their baby again after the transfer to the mortuary (including before and after a post mortem examination if they have chosen to have one). Parents should be given the contact details of a named staff member whom they can contact should they wish to see their baby again.

There must be good communication between the staff caring for the parents and the mortuary staff to facilitate parents' access to their baby after transfer to the mortuary. If parents wish to see their baby again, staff should offer to bring the baby to the parents on the ward. Parents should not be expected to go to the mortuary to see their baby unless they want to accompany their baby or visit the mortuary. The mortuary should have suitable facilities that offer comfort and privacy where a family can see and hold their baby if they do wish to go to the mortuary (Wilson 2015). If family members accompany the baby to the mortuary, they should be told in advance what to expect and what will happen when they arrive. Mortuary staff should also be informed that parents or other family members are coming to the mortuary in advance so that they can prepare the area for their visit.

Transporting babies' bodies and remains outside the hospital

Trust and Health Board contracts and arrangements for transport with ambulance services, funeral directors and other service providers should ensure that the bodies and remains of all babies should be handled and treated respectfully, regardless of gestation or circumstances.

When a baby is transported from home to hospital with the mother, the baby's body or remains should never be placed in a clinical waste bag. This is inappropriate and could also lead to the remains being lost or accidentally disposed of as clinical waste.

Any transfer of the baby outside the hospital should be discussed and agreed with parents beforehand (see also *Location* under *Consent for a post mortem examination* below). Drivers should know what they are carrying and should be given appropriate documentation when transporting babies' bodies between hospitals, to a regional paediatric pathology centre, home or to a cold room at a children's hospice. It is also important that the mode of transport is appropriate in these instances. For example, babies' bodies should not be transported using bicycle or motorcycle couriers.

Storage and tracking

Before storing or transferring a baby, the baby's body or remains should be labelled with the mother's name and NHS number or unique identification number, the baby's date and time of birth and/or death, the baby's name if they have been named, the baby's sex (if known) and the name and details of the person who verified the death (Wilson 2015). If the baby's last name is different from the mother's, a record must be kept and the mortuary staff should be informed. Items such as clothing, shawls or soft toys that parents want to accompany the baby should also be listed.

With the parents' consent, all babies' bodies and remains should be stored regardless of gestational age until parents make a decision about post mortem investigations or their options for disposal (HTA Code 1 2014; HTA Code 5 2014; HTA 2015) (see Chapter 20 for more information). Babies' bodies and remains must be scrupulously labelled, logged and stored individually with any personal or valuable items that have been sent with the baby (HTA Code 3 2014). When a baby's body is incomplete or in pieces, the remains should be kept in a clearly-labelled opaque container.

All mortuaries and storage facilities should have an adequate amount of carefully maintained refrigeration equipment and appropriate security measures and records should be kept of who has access to these areas (HTA Code 3 2014). Babies' bodies and remains should be appropriately covered (HTA Code 3 2014), kept in the best possible condition and protected against accidental damage and avoidable deterioration.

Establishments are responsible for creating and maintaining good records of the babies' bodies or remains that are in their care or that they transfer to other institutions (HTA Code 3 2014). It must be possible at any time to track and locate individual bodies, body parts and tissue while they are in the care of a hospital, ward, mortuary, pathology department or in transit (HTA Code 3 2014). Trusts, Health Boards and managers should ensure that all hospital departments (including accident and emergency, maternity, gynaecology wards, mortuaries and laboratories) have efficient procedures and tracking systems for transferring babies' bodies and fetal remains between them (HTA Code 3 2014). These systems should be understood by all the staff concerned (including labour ward and neonatal unit staff) and an audit trail should be maintained for any transferred remains (HTA Code 3 2014).

Any local policies or guidelines on handling, storing and transporting babies' bodies and fetal remains should be reviewed regularly.

Post mortem examination

There are legal and regulatory requirements governing post mortem examination and the removal, storage and use of any body parts, organs and tissues of babies who are stillborn or who die shortly after birth. These requirements are set out in the Human Tissue Authority's Codes of Practice and reflect the statutory framework of the Human Tissue Act 2004 that applies in England, Wales and Northern Ireland. There is separate legislation in Scotland under the Human Tissue (Scotland) Act 2006. The legislation promotes good practice and ensures that parents' informed consent (called authorisation in Scotland) is sought for a post mortem examination unless a baby's death has been referred to the coroner or procurator fiscal (see *Consent for a post mortem examination* below). These regulations do not extend to post mortem examinations of babies who are born dead before 24 weeks' gestation. However, these good practice points regarding post mortem examinations and consent are relevant to all childbearing losses, regardless of the gestation or type of loss.

The potential benefits of a post mortem examination

Many parents want to know as much as possible about why their pregnancy ended or why their baby died. Many also hope that a post mortem examination can tell them whether there are any implications for future pregnancies or siblings (Mancini *et al.* 2014; Sands 2015f). All parents should be offered a full post mortem examination even if the cause of death is thought to be obvious as more information about the baby's death may be gained (Mancini *et al.* 2014; Draper *et al.* 2015). The InSight Study found that:

> *Although parents may find it difficult to agree to the post mortem they often find it helpful, sometimes because it provides evidence that the baby's death was not due to their own actions, sometimes because the post mortem can provide hope for future pregnancies. Participants felt that parents were more likely to regret not having a post mortem than they were to regret having one. Some participants suggested that*

the post mortem was important in helping the parents to find closure.
(Siassakos *et al.* 2015, unpublished results)

A post mortem examination can often provide helpful information (Sands 2014d) such as:

- It may confirm the cause of the baby's death.

- It can confirm or change an existing clinical diagnosis.

- It may identify conditions that might not have been diagnosed otherwise.

- It can exclude some common causes of death or possible factors such as fetal anomaly, infection or growth restriction.

- It can help assess the chances of problems recurring in a future pregnancy.

- For some families, it can help them resolve specific questions and may help them to come to terms with what happened and facilitate emotional closure (Heazell *et al.* 2012).

- In the case of a genetic condition, a post mortem examination may also indicate the need for other members of the family to be offered investigation.

If it was not possible to determine the baby's sex at birth, parents may also want a post mortem examination because they want to find out the baby's gender. Knowing the baby's sex may help some parents to name or mourn their baby. Other parents will not need or want to know the gender of their baby.

Parents of a surviving baby from a multiple pregnancy may also want to know whether the baby who died was genetically identical to the surviving baby. Not all genetic laboratories offer this service unless there is also a specific medical reason for doing so (RCOG, RCP 2001: 25–6). However, parents may want to consider having the test performed privately (see the Multiple Births Foundation website for more information – Appendix 2).

Some parents may also find comfort in the knowledge that a post mortem examination of their baby might be used in research to benefit other babies and their families, which could contribute towards the prevention of other deaths (Rankin *et al.* 2002; Heazell *et al.* 2012).

Why parents may not want a post mortem examination of their baby

Some parents are very distressed by the idea of their baby undergoing a post mortem examination and find it difficult to contemplate, even if they think it might provide useful information. Some parents may feel that their baby has suffered enough and that they should be left in peace. Not wanting the baby to be "cut open" or harmed in any way are reasons that have been cited by some parents for not wanting a post mortem examination (Arthurs *et al.* 2015; Siassakos *et al.* 2015, unpublished results). It may be helpful to discuss alternative options to a full post mortem examination with these parents (see *Parents who do not consent to a post mortem examination* below).

Parents may also feel that a post mortem examination is not necessary (Redshaw *et al*. 2014). In some instances, this may be because health professionals have suggested to parents that further investigations to understand the case of death is unnecessary (Siassakos *et al*. 2015, unpublished results). However, this stance assumes that there are not multiple contributing factors that led to the baby's death (Siassakos *et al*. 2015, unpublished results). Staff's beliefs about or personal experiences of post mortem examination may also affect the information they give to parents about post mortem investigations (Downe *et al*. 2012). The quality of the information given to parents by healthcare professionals has been identified as a barrier to some parents consenting to a post mortem examination (Heazell *et al*. 2012). Professional training for staff who discuss post mortem examinations with parents may help to remove this barrier to post mortem examination consent (Heazell *et al*. 2012).

For some parents, it is important to hold the funeral as soon as possible after the death (sometimes within 24 hours) for personal, cultural or religious reasons. These parents may refuse a post mortem examination because it might delay the funeral. However, some pathology departments will carry out an urgent post mortem examination. It is important to be aware that access to an urgent post mortem examination may be restricted depending on whether it is a weekday and the availability of staff.

The time it takes to receive results after a post mortem examination may also be a significant barrier to some parents giving consent (Heazell *et al*. 2012). Explaining the reason for the timings of the post mortem procedures and giving parents a realistic idea of when the results might be available is very important (Arthurs *et al*. 2015; Siassakos *et al*. 2015, unpublished results) (see also *Explaining post mortem examinations and discussing options with parents* below).

Time with their baby

Some parents may fear that agreeing to a post mortem examination will shorten the time they can have with their baby as they know the benefits of conducting the post mortem examination as soon as possible after the baby's death. Some parents may be more likely to consent when they know they will have another opportunity to be with their baby after the post mortem examination (see also *Restoring the body* later).

In order to make an informed choice, parents should be told that an early post mortem examination may provide better information. However, parents should also be told that other factors may also affect the information that can be provided by a post mortem examination. For example, parents may also want to consider how results may be affected by where the baby's body is kept prior to the post mortem examination (e.g. in a fridge or beside the parents), the gestation of the baby and, importantly, how long before the birth the baby died (where applicable). If staff are not sure how to advise parents, they should discuss the situation and available options with the pathologist. For example, it may be possible to take a small skin biopsy for genetic study or to slightly delay the full post mortem examination. In addition, placental examination should be discussed with all parents and placentas should be sent for investigation wherever possible (see *Placental examination* below).

The need to transfer the baby to another hospital or facility for a post mortem examination may also be an important barrier for some parents who want to spend more time with their baby (Heazell *et al*. 2012). It is important that staff know local arrangements for transferring the baby to a specialist pathology centre. If transfers take place on specific days of the week, this may affect the amount of time parents can spend with their baby before a post mortem examination. For example, if the transfer cannot be arranged for several days, the parents may be able to spend more time with the baby before the transfer or they may decide against or delay a post mortem examination if the baby would need to be transferred within a day or two of the baby's death (see also *Location* below).

Religious and cultural concerns

Some parents may refuse a post mortem examination for religious or cultural reasons. For example, a post mortem examination may be unacceptable to many observant Jews and Muslims because it is important to bury the body complete and whole. There may also be religious reasons for wanting the funeral to take place as soon as possible, sometimes within 24 hours.

It is important to offer a post mortem examination to all parents regardless of their religious or cultural background. Some religiously observant parents may consent to a post mortem examination despite religious or other restrictions and feel strongly that they want to understand as much as they can about why their baby died. In such cases, particular importance may be put on confidentiality and meticulous repair of the body in order to avoid possible conflict with other family members. However, if it is traditional for family members or religious representatives to wash the body before burial, parents need to know that the signs of the post mortem examination will be visible (see also *Explaining post mortem examinations and discussing options with parents* below).

Consent for a post mortem examination

The *Listening to Parents* report highlighted that 5 per cent of parents whose baby was stillborn or died shortly after birth were not offered a post mortem examination (not including instances where a coroner's post mortem examination was required) (Redshaw *et al*. 2014). It has also been found that some healthcare staff do not discuss post mortem examinations with parents as they underestimate its value, do not want to cause further distress or are concerned about issues regarding organ retention (Downe *et al*. 2012; Heazell *et al*. 2012; Siassakos *et al*. 2015, unpublished results) (see also *The potential benefits of a post mortem examination* above). A recent Cochrane review has also highlighted the need for more research into strategies for overcoming barriers to post mortem examination consent and interventions that would better support parents when they are deciding about a post mortem examination for their baby (Horey *et al.* 2013). Staff should also be aware that it is also the parents' right to be offered a post mortem examination of their baby.

Assumptions should never be made about whether or not parents will want a post mortem examination.

All parents should be offered the opportunity to discuss and make an informed choice about having a post mortem examination (full or limited) of their baby (Sands 2013a). In the case of a neonatal death or stillbirth, it is a legal requirement that consent is obtained from the parents before a post mortem examination takes place. Regardless of the gestational age of the baby, consent or authorisation should always be sought for any post mortem examinations, tests or investigations.

The only exception to this is if an investigation is required by a coroner or procurator fiscal. Consent or authorisation is not required for investigations carried out under the instructions of a coroner or procurator fiscal, nor for the retention of tissue, organs or fluids if they are required for the coroner's or procurator fiscal's purposes (HTA Code 1 2014) (Human Tissue (Scotland) Act 2006) (see also *Deaths reported to the coroner or procurator fiscal* below). However, consent is required in England, Wales and Northern Ireland to retain samples (including block and slides) or specimens for any purposes beyond those of the coroner (HTA Code 1 2014). In Scotland, once the procurator fiscal no longer requires the retained samples and tissues, these automatically become part of the baby's medical record and can be used without authorisation for the following purposes (Human Tissue Act (Scotland) 2006: Section 39):

(i) providing information about or confirming the cause of death;

(ii) investigating the effect and efficacy of any medical or surgical intervention carried out on the person;

(iii) obtaining information which may be relevant to the health of any other person (including a future person);

(iv) audit.

Authorisation is required, however, if these samples or specimens are to be used for research, training or education (Human Tissue Act (Scotland) 2006).

For a post mortem examination that is not ordered by the coroner or procurator fiscal, specific consent or authorisation must be obtained from the parents for any procedures and a detailed consent form should be completed (see *Consent forms* below). Consent must be sought for each of the following activities related to the examination (HTA Code 1 2014; HTA Code 3 2014) (Human Tissue (Scotland) Act 2006):

- *A post mortem examination* (including the removal, storage or use of any material from the deceased baby).

- *Retention of any tissue or organ*, including keeping blocks, slides and frozen samples of tissue as part of the baby's medical record for possible future examination (HTA Code 3 2014). Parents should be given the details of anything that is kept as part of the medical record. In **Scotland**, blocks and slides removed during a post mortem examination may be used for diagnostic or audit purposes without authorisation (Human Tissue (Scotland) Act 2006).

- *Genetic testing or the retention of DNA samples.* It is an offence to hold bodily material with the intention to analyse DNA and use the results of analysis without consent, except in some circumstances (HTA Code 1 2014) (see the HTA Codes of Practice for further details).

- *The use of tissue, fluids or organs for research, audit, quality control or educational purposes.*

- *The making and use of identifiable images of the baby* (even though these do not fall under the Human Tissue Act 2004 or Human Tissue (Scotland) Act 2006).

Consent for one procedure does not imply consent for any others.

Placental examination

Consent for histological examination of the placenta is not covered by the Human Tissue Act 2004 or Human Tissue (Scotland) Act 2006 as this is considered to be examination of tissue from the living for diagnostic purposes. That is in this case, placental tissue is considered to be from a living person (the mother) rather than from a deceased person (the baby). While consent for examination is not legally required, it is good practice to seek consent from parents for examination of the placenta, umbilical cord, membranes or amniotic fluid (HTA Code 1 2014). Additionally, whether parents have consented to a post mortem examination or not, placental examinations should be discussed with all parents. Wherever possible, all placentas from babies who have died should be sent for examination by a specialist pathologist.

If there is to be a post mortem examination, the placenta should always be sent fresh (rather than in formalin) with the baby's body, unless otherwise agreed with the pathologist. If parents do not want the placenta to be examined for any reason, the placenta is usually treated as a surgical specimen in the same way as following a live birth. Some parents may want to bury the placenta for personal, cultural or religious reasons. The parents do not need permission to do this, nor is there a need to inform any other authority.

Consent forms

In line with the principle of informed consent, most consent forms are very detailed and parents are asked to make explicit choices and decisions when considering a post mortem examination of their baby. This may be distressing for some parents and the consent seeker should acknowledge that this process may be difficult.

Completing post mortem consent or authorisation forms with parents should be a process where the person seeking consent gives the parents information and answers parents' questions (Sands 2013a). The form is only a record of parents' decisions and should not be given to parents without a discussion about the purpose of a post mortem examination and their options (Sands 2013a). Sufficient time should be allocated for a trained member of staff to discuss the form with parents and this should be done at an appropriate time for parents and in a private place (see also *Who seeks consent?* and *Discussing a post mortem examination with the parents* below). Also, parents should not be given the form to complete on their own unless they make this request (Sands 2013a).

The HTA has model consent forms for post mortem examination of an adult on its website and states that:

The forms are not prescriptive due to local variations in practice and may be adapted as necessary, providing they comply with the HT Act and the codes of practice. Consent forms are part of the consent process and should be supplemented with further discussion and more detailed explanation where necessary. (HTA Code 3 2014: 91)

The HTA was consulted on the Sands post mortem consent form that was designed to support consent takers, ensure clarity for pathologists and be sensitive to the needs of bereaved parents. All forms can be adapted based on the local needs of hospitals and Trusts. These forms have also been endorsed by the relevant professional organisations. However, the forms are currently only available for use in England. In Wales, Northern Ireland and Scotland, the standard consent or authorisation form must be used. However, the other content in the Sands Post Mortem Consent Package (such as the consent takers' guidance and information for parents) are relevant across the UK. In Northern Ireland, separate forms are available for miscarriages before 12 weeks' gestation, intrauterine deaths after 12 weeks' gestation and for neonatal deaths (HTA Code 3).

If they have not already done so, hospitals, Trusts and Health Boards should consider using the Sands post mortem consent form to update their current forms and make them more suitable for parents whose baby dies during pregnancy or shortly after birth. This is important as the length and complexity of some consent forms has been cited as a barrier to the consent process for some parents and staff (Downe *et al.* 2012).

While written consent or authorisation should generally be sought for a post mortem examination or a specific procedure, parents can give consent by phone, email or fax (Sands 2013a). For example, parents may need to give consent in another way if they are not able to be present to give consent or if further consent is sought after the post mortem examination has started (for example, to retain an organ).

In any case, parents' decisions about post mortem examinations should be documented as this information may be useful when reviewing babies' deaths (Draper *et al.* 2015).

Who seeks consent?

Consent should be sought by a member of staff who has received training in seeking post mortem consent and the process and who has a good understanding of the procedures for which they are seeking consent (Sands 2013a; HTA Code 1 2014). Seeking consent for a post mortem examination may differ from consent for other types of procedures as staff are often not performing or involved with the investigations themselves (Sand 2015f). Instead, they are frequently seeking consent on behalf of the pathologist who must rely on the accuracy and clarity of the completed form (Sands 2013a).

The member of staff who discusses consent with parents should:

- Preferably be someone who is experienced in the consent process and whom the parents know and trust. Responsibility for seeking consent should never be delegated to an inexperienced or untrained staff member (HTA Code 3 2014).

- Have had recent training and updates that cover information about working with bereaved parents and the purposes and procedures of a post mortem examination (HTA Code 1 2014; HTA Code 3 2014). They should also know that it is an offence under the Human Tissue Act (2004: s5(2)) to knowingly provide inaccurate information to the pathologist about the extent of the parents' consent.

- Have witnessed a post mortem examination (HTA Code 1 2014; HTA Code 3 2014).

- Understand what a post mortem examination involves and its potential benefits and that no definite cause may be found for the baby's death, particularly for earlier gestation losses.

- Have read the notes and avoid asking for information that is already documented unless clarifying the parents' wishes.

- Be familiar with the consent form and able to take parents through it confidently.

- Be aware of local post mortem practices and procedures for their hospital.

- Have read any local policies on consent for their hospital, any written information that is given to parents, the Human Tissue Authority's relevant Codes of Practice (1, 3 and 5), the Sands *Guide for consent takers* and the Sands booklet on *Deciding about a post mortem examination: Information for parents*.

The member of staff who seeks consent should also understand the purpose of the different procedures and be able to answer parents' questions about:

- Different types of post mortem examination.

- External examination of the body.

- Examination of the internal organs.

- Photographs and x-rays.

- Tissue sampling.

- The retention of tissue samples for review of the diagnosis.

- Why organs might be retained.

- Restoring the body.

- The options for the parents regarding tissue blocks and slides.

- How and where the post mortem report will be discussed with the parents.

- Any reasons for potential delays in the return of the baby's body or results.

- Who parents should speak to if they have any concerns.

- What the local processes are regarding transporting the baby's body and visiting the mortuary.

- Local policies and procedures for urgent post mortem examinations.

It is important that the member of staff seeking consent knows how to clearly and accurately complete the consent form to avoid delays that may arise if the pathologist is unclear about the information provided (Sands 2015f). All staff who discuss consent for post mortem examinations with families should be in contact with the pathologist and/or mortuary involved in the post mortem examinations. They should regularly exchange information in order to ensure best practice as well as optimal care and support for parents.

Consent seeker training

Training for post mortem consent seekers does not currently adhere to an agreed standard and provision for this training is variable (Sands 2013b). All post mortem consent seeker training should cover information about:

- Legal requirements.

- How to seek consent for a hospital post mortem examination, including completion of the consent form.

- What happens at a post mortem examination, including the examination of internal organs and the retention of organs and tissue for later examination.

- What happens after the post mortem examination, including the disposal, return or retention of any tissue samples.

- Dealing with disagreements between the parents about whether or not to consent to a post mortem examination.

- The written information to be provided to the parents.

- Information about local post mortem examination arrangements, including that the parents may change their minds and the timeframe in which they have to do this.

- Dealing with this situation where parents want less information but where they need sufficient information to ensure their consent is valid.

- Communication skills (Sands 2013b).

Training and support for consent seekers is important as it helps "to ensure the essential processes are effectively undertaken, and that empathic attitudes are developed" (Downe *et al.* 2012: 35). More information about consent taker training is available from the HTA website (See Appendix 2).

Discussing a post mortem examination with the parents

All parents should be offered the opportunity to discuss a post mortem examination of their baby (Draper *et al*. 2015).

Seeking consent is a process that should involve careful listening and discussion. It should be unhurried (a minimum of one hour should be allocated for this process) and should help parents to reach decisions that are right for them. The HTA states that:

> *Consent is valid only if proper communication has taken place. Particular consideration should be given to the needs of individuals and families whose first language is not English. Any difficulties in communicating with the person interviewed (e.g. because of language, literacy or hearing difficulties), and an explanation of how these difficulties were overcome (e.g. through an independent translator), should be recorded.* (HTA Code 1 2014: 67)

All discussions should take place in a quiet, private place where parents and staff will not be disturbed (Sands 2013a).

The first mention of a post mortem examination

The first step is to establish the parents' willingness to discuss the possibility of a post mortem examination. Some parents may ask about a post mortem examination and welcome the discussion. For other parents, there may not be a good time to discuss the topic and staff may need to gently mention a post mortem examination and give more details when parents are ready. Parents who do not wish to discuss a post mortem examination should be told that staff will check with them again later (Sands 2013a). If parents do not want to be asked again later or refuse a second time, this should be respected and recorded in the parent's medical notes (Sands 2013a). They should not be asked more than twice to avoid parents feeling pressured (Sands 2013a).

Mentioning the possibility of a post mortem examination as soon as possible and in advance of seeking consent may be beneficial (Sands 2013a). For some parents, this discussion may be appropriate antenatally when parents have decided to have a termination for fetal anomaly or an intrauterine death has been diagnosed (Sands 2013a). Thinking about a post mortem examination before a termination for fetal anomaly may be important as this may affect the choice of method of termination (Sands 2013a). A post mortem examination could also be mentioned when staff are discussing moving to palliative care on the neonatal unit (Sands 2013a). However, consent should not usually be sought until after the baby's death and at a time that is suitable for the parents.

Explaining post mortem examinations and discussing options with parents

The member of staff seeking consent should familiarise themselves with the mother's and/or baby's medical notes and the baby's name (if one has been given) before meeting the parents. This is particularly important if they have not been caring for the parents prior to seeking consent (Sands 2013a).

The consent seeker should start by expressing their sympathy to parents (Sands 2013a). It should be made clear to parents that no investigations or tests will be done without their consent and that their views and wishes will be respected. It is also important that the consent process is presented to parents as an ongoing process, during which the parents will have time to consider their options, request more information or ask questions (Sands 2014d). At the beginning of the consent process, parents should also be told that they will be able to request more information or change their minds after signing the form and be told how long they would have to withdraw consent before any examinations take place (Sands 2013a; HTA Code 3 2014). The minimum time that parents should have to withdraw consent is 12 hours but the HTA recommends 24 hours (HTA Code 3 2014). Parents should be given written information with the name and phone number of the person to contact if they change their minds.

All information provided to parents should be impartial and explained using clear, simple, carefully chosen language (Downe *et al.* 2012; Heazell *et al.* 2012; Sands 2013a). Information may need to be repeated more than once as it may be difficult for grieving parents to absorb information (see also Chapter 4). Parents may need to know why a post mortem examination would be valuable (see *The potential benefits of a post mortem examination* above) and also that it may not provide conclusive answers in all cases (Rankin *et al.* 2002). Staff should also be aware that parents may want different amounts of details about the post mortem procedure. Parents who want more information should sensitively be given full and honest details about the procedure (HTA Code 3). If parents want less information this should be respected but they will need to be given sufficient information to ensure that their consent is valid (HTA Code 3 2014). A professional interpreter should be involved if the parents speak little or no English (see also Chapter 5).

In addition to verbal information and discussions, the parents should be offered written information in advance of the meeting, although staff should not assume that parents have read or absorbed this material (Sands 2013a). This information should be available in all the main languages spoken locally and in different formats. The Sands booklet on *Deciding about a post mortem examination: Information for parents* may also be a helpful resource for parents.

Some of the topics covered during the discussion should include:

- **The possible findings of an investigation and what could be gained by having the information.** Parents should also be told that an investigation may provide valuable information about what did *not* cause the death or loss (even if the cause of death is not determined).

- **Where, when and by whom the examination would be performed.** Parents need to know where their baby's body will be examined, how long this would take, details of transport arrangements if required and when they can see the baby's body again if they wish (see also *Location* below).

- **The types of post mortem examinations available and the potential benefits and limitations of each option.** Parents can decide to have:

  - **A full post mortem examination.** This is a thorough post mortem examination and may involve investigations of the outside of the body, internal organs, tissues samples and the placenta. Genetic tests may also be carried out. This may provide the most information.

  - **A limited post mortem examination.** Parents may decide that they only want a specific part of the body to be examined or they may not want particular parts to be examined.

  - **An external post mortem examination.** This involves an examination of the outside of the baby's body, x-rays and medical photographs. It may also involve examination of tissue from the placenta or a small skin sample.

  - **Minimally invasive autopsy (MIA).** This option is not yet widely available. However, research has found that this type of post mortem examination provides the same major findings as a full post mortem examination in 90 per cent of cases (Thayyil *et al.* 2013). This type of examination involves the use of imaging technology such as magnetic resonance imaging (MRI) and computed tomography (CT) scans (Arthurs *et al.* 2015). It may also include placental examination and tissue biopsies being taken from small incisions using an endoscope or image guidance (Arthurs *et al*. 2015).

- **What investigations are proposed or available and how long each would take.**
Parents may need to know if some investigations will take longer. The reasons for the extra time needed and the potential benefits of these examinations should be explained (Sands 2013a). For example, the examination of the brain takes longer than the rest of the post mortem examination because the brain has to be specially prepared. In most cases, this should not delay the funeral by more than a few days (if at all) before the brain can be returned but parents should be told if this may happen.

- **That tissue samples are likely to be taken.**

- **What would happen to the baby's tissue samples after the examination.**
Parents' wishes should be sought regarding what will happen to tissue samples in the form of blocks, slides or frozen samples in **England, Wales** and **Northern Ireland** (HTA Code 3 2014; HTA Code 5 2014). Parents can choose whether to have blocks, slides and frozen samples retained as part of the mother or baby's medical record for possible future examination, disposed of or returned to them (HTA Code 3 2014; HTA Code 5 2014). No tissue samples can be kept unless the parent's consent has been given. In **Scotland**, authorisation is not required and tissue samples automatically become part of the medical record. See *Retention and disposal of blocks, slides and frozen tissue samples* below for more information.

- **Retention of organs.** If examinations are being proposed that may require organs to be retained after the body is returned, parents' consent will need to be obtained (HTA Code 3 2014) (Human Tissue Act (Scotland) 2006). Parents may also decide that they want these examinations to be completed before the baby's body is returned so that no organs are retained. Before they consent to the longer preparation of an organ for examination, it is important that parents understand that they may need either to delay the funeral (possibly for several weeks) until the examination has been completed or decide to bury or cremate the baby's body without the organ. Some parents may decide against having specific investigations because of the extra time required.

- **What would happen to retained organs after the examination.** If organs are to be retained for further investigation, parents' wishes should be sought to determine what should happen to any organ(s) once the examination has been completed (HTA Code 3 2014; HTA Code 5 2014) (Human Tissue Act (Scotland) 2006). Parents can choose for organs to be disposed of by the hospital, returned to the parents or funeral director for separate burial or cremation or returned to the baby's body before burial or cremation. Organs can also be kept for use for research or education and training, provided that the parents have given their express consent.

- **Options for donating any tissue samples or retained organs for training or research.** Parents' consent must be sought for any tissue samples or retained organs to be used to train health professionals or for ethically approved medical research (HTA Code 3 2014; HTA Code 5 2014) (Human Tissue Act (Scotland) 2006). Research is important to help understand what causes babies' deaths and to help in the prevention of babies' deaths. Materials such as tissue samples, x-rays and medical photographs may also be important training materials for future doctors and pathologists (including specialist pathologists) (Sands 2014d). Where applicable, parents should be given the option of consenting to tissue samples or organs being used for training or research. A secondary reason for having a post mortem examination of their baby for many parents is to contribute to research that will help prevent other parents from having the same experience (Heazell *et al*. 2012). All identifying details will be removed from samples and organs and these should be disposed of respectfully when they are no longer required (Sands 2014d). Parents should be informed of these arrangements and that any research that the samples will be used for must be ethically approved (Sands 2014d). They must also be told that they can change their mind at any time in the future and be given the contact details of the histopathology department that they would need to contact to withdraw their consent (Sands 2014d).

- **Placental investigation.** Consent is not required under the Human Tissue Act for placental investigations although consent should be sought from parents as a matter of good practice (HTA Code 1 2014). Useful information about the cause of the baby's death or contributing factors can be obtained from examining the placenta and histopathological placental investigations (Heazell and Martindale 2009; Ptacek *et al*. 2014). It is important that healthcare staff do not underestimate the value of placental investigation and the placenta should always be sent for investigation unless parents object (Ptacek *et al*. 2014; Draper *et al*. 2015).

- **That photographs and x-rays are usually taken as part of the investigation.** Parents should be told that any photographs or x-rays would be stored in the medical record. Unless they are anonymised, photographs and x-rays will not be used for teaching purposes without the parents' consent.

- **That in most cases they would be able to see or hold the baby's body after the post mortem examination if they want.** Parents should be able to see and hold their baby after the post mortem examination if they wish. However, if the baby's body is very small, macerated or oedematous, they should be told how the baby's appearance might change during the post mortem examination or that it may not be possible to restore the baby's body afterwards. These parents may want to consider saying goodbye to the baby before the post mortem examination. If the parents want to see the body again, the mortuary staff must be informed and parents should be given information about where and when they can see their baby.

- **How the baby's body would look after the post mortem examination,** including where the suture lines would be (see *Restoring the body* below). Parents who choose to see their baby after the post mortem examination should not see incisions or other marks that they were not warned about. Parents should be asked if they want to provide clothes for their baby to be dressed in after the post mortem examination. Hospitals should also have clothes and coverings available (including very small ones) for parents to choose from. A list of any items or clothing that are sent to the post mortem examination with the baby should be sent to the mortuary.

- **The potential implications of the results.** Parents should be told that the examination may contradict some information they have already been given. This may include the cause of death, information about any conditions present or, on rare occasions, the sex of the baby.

- **When the results would be available and how and when they would be given to the parents.** The timeframe given to parents should be realistic to avoid causing unnecessary distress (see also *Follow-up appointments at the hospital* in Chapter

17). To some extent, this will be dependent on local procedures and the diagnostic tests that have been proposed or performed as a result of the initial post mortem examination findings (Henley and Schott 2014). For example, some results, such as specialist neuropathology tests, may not be available until up to 12 weeks after the post mortem examination. For more information, see the Sands document on *What happens at a hospital post mortem on a baby – procedures and likely timings* (see Appendix 2). Providing the mortuary with the date of the scheduled follow-up appointment when sending other post mortem documents may also help the mortuary to plan to have the results ready in time.

- **How the post mortem examination might affect the timing of the funeral.**

Parents should have time to consider their decisions carefully, ask questions and decide what is right for them before they are asked to sign a consent form (McHaffie *et al.* 2001a; HTA Code 1 2014). Whenever possible and appropriate, the parents should be asked *together* for their consent. Some parents may not agree with each other about having a post mortem examination of their baby. These parents may need sensitive support and more time to reach a decision, even if only one parent's consent is legally required for the procedure (HTA Code 1 2014).

If the parents are uncertain, anxious or want to know more, it may be helpful to offer them the option of talking to the pathologist or mortuary team who will undertake the procedure if they are not involved in seeking consent.

Parents who do not consent to a post mortem examination

Parents' decisions regarding a post mortem examination of their baby should be respected and accepted. They should not be pressured to consent to any post mortem investigations. However, it may be appropriate to explore possible alternatives to a full post mortem examination with these parents. For example, some parents may consent to:

- External examination only.
- Partial examination confined to a specific region of the body.
- Blood or urine tests.
- Skin biopsy, needle biopsy and aspiration of body fluids.
- Post mortem imaging.
- Placental examination.

Where it is available, minimally invasive autopsy or less invasive techniques may be acceptable to many parents who decline a traditional post mortem examination (Cannie *et al.* 2012; Kang *et al.* 2014). It is important that the staff member seeking consent is aware of the available options before suggesting them to the parents and is aware of the potential benefits and availability of each option. They should speak to their referring pathology service if they are uncertain about any of these potential options.

Location

All post mortem examinations on fetuses and babies should be carried out by specialists in perinatal pathology in regional centres (RCOG, RCP 2001).

During the consent process, parents must be informed if the post mortem examination is to be carried out at another hospital and the reasons for this transfer. They should also be told where their baby's body is being sent, when and how it will be transported and when it will be returned so that parents can see their baby or arrange a funeral after a post mortem examination if they wish (Sands 2014d). Some parents may appreciate being told about who will be transporting the baby and caring for them in the mortuary (Sands 2014d).

The timing of the transfer should allow parents as much time as possible with their baby. Staff should be aware of local transport arrangements where applicable and be able to tell parents about how these might affect their time with their baby (see also *Time with their baby* above). The body should also be returned as soon as possible after the post mortem examination.

All transport arrangements and handling of the baby must be respectful and the baby's body must be clearly labelled and tracked (see also *Transporting babies' bodies and remains outside the hospital* and *Storage and tracking* above).

Restoring the body

Mortuary staff should always assume that the parents will want to see the baby's body again regardless of gestation. Each baby's body should be restored and carefully dressed. Pathology staff should use any list of items sent with the baby to dress and wrap the baby's body after the post mortem examination.

Parents of very premature babies should be informed during the consent process if it is likely to be difficult to repair the baby's skin. Anatomical pathology technologists (APTs) should be able to at least repair the baby so that the parents are able to see the baby even if holding the baby is not advised. This may not be possible if formalin is used and this should be discussed with the parents during the consent process.

 I was dreading visiting her in the mortuary but I wanted to see her after the post mortem. I was so relieved to find that she was dressed in the same clothes and hat that she had been in when we'd last seen her. It so comforting to know that people had taken such good care of her. Mother

Unless parents have given explicit permission for certain organs to be retained, they should all be put back and the body should be complete for the funeral. Whenever possible, the brain should be replaced in the skull rather than the abdomen. However, the decision about where organs will be replaced will be based on the individual baby and depend on the condition of the skin on specific parts of the body. Every effort should be made to avoid seepage of body fluids. The APT should communicate or send instructions for staff so that they can advise parents wishing to hold the baby regarding how best to avoid seepage.

Retention and disposal of blocks, slides and frozen tissue samples

In **England, Wales** and **Northern Ireland**, blocks, slides and frozen samples of tissue may be retained with consent as part of the medical record for use for purposes defined in the Human Tissue Act 2004. They may also be returned to parents with (but not in) the body. In **Scotland**, the blocks, slides and frozen samples are automatically kept as part of the medical record under the Human Tissue Act (Scotland) 2006.

If parents choose to have blocks and slides returned to them, they may choose to bury these with their baby, although they cannot generally be cremated (see also Chapter 20). If frozen tissue or blood samples are returned to parents, these will be processed into cassettes (small plastic cases) so they can be safely transported and stored.

Some units retain blocks, slides and frozen samples indefinitely when these become part of the medical record. Parents should be consulted about options for disposal when units intend to dispose of these samples.

Deaths reported to the coroner or procurator fiscal

The doctor must report the death of a baby to the coroner or the procurator fiscal (in Scotland) if the cause of a neonatal death is uncertain, it is possible that a "stillborn" baby was born alive or the baby was not receiving care from a doctor while they were alive. In Northern Ireland, most stillbirths are also now referred to the coroner (see *The coroner and stillbirths in Northern Ireland* below). When a baby's death is reported to the coroner or procurator fiscal, the parents must always be informed and the reasons for reporting the death should be explained. Staff should acknowledge that this may be difficult for parents and they should be offered support.

Some parents may request that the coroner or procurator fiscal holds an inquest into their baby's stillbirth or death. This is often in cases where parents do not feel that an adequate review of their baby's death has taken place or in instances where the hospital has not addressed their concerns about the events leading to their baby's death (Sands 2016d) (see also *Recording, reporting and reviewing the baby's cause of death* below and *Being open and honest with parents* in Chapter 22). Stillbirths are not currently covered by coronial law in England and Wales or under the jurisdiction of procurator fiscals in Scotland, although some coroners in England have agreed to investigate the circumstances of a stillbirth (Sands 2016d). The jurisdiction of coroners and procurator fiscals should be extended to include stillbirths (Sands 2016d). However, stillbirths should not be automatically reported to a coroner or procurator fiscal as this may not be appropriate in all instances (Sands 2016d). Additionally, some parents may be distressed or not find it beneficial to have a coroner's or procurator fiscal's inquest, which can be a lengthy and complex process that involves the police and legal proceedings (Sands 2016d).

The coroner or procurator fiscal may or may not decide that a post mortem examination should be carried out to try to establish the cause of death. A coroner or procurator fiscal-ordered post mortem examination is usually carried out as soon as possible but may occasionally delay the baby's burial, cremation or funeral and this should be discussed with parents (see also Chapter 20). The coroner or procurator fiscal must also ensure that options for disposing of any retained tissue samples and any retained organs are discussed with, and consented to or authorised, by parents (see also *Explaining post mortem examinations and discussing options with parents* and *Retention and disposal of blocks, slides and frozen tissue samples* above). The coroner's or procurator fiscal's office should inform parents and their GP about the date and location of the post mortem examination.

Parents' consent is not required to perform a post mortem examination in these instances. If parents want to object to a coroner or procurator fiscal-ordered post mortem examination for any reason, they should be advised to contact the coroner's or procurator fiscal's office immediately to discuss their objections and the situation. In some areas, the coroner or procurator fiscal or one of their officers can be contacted 24 hours a day. A coroner or procurator fiscal has the legal right to go ahead with a post mortem examination. However, they may be able to arrange for the post mortem examination to be performed as quickly as possible if time is a concern for parents. If a post mortem examination is ordered after parents object, they can apply to the High Court to try to prevent this post mortem examination. Staff should acknowledge that it may be very distressing for parents when a post mortem examination is carried out despite their objections and support should be offered.

In these circumstances, the baby's body will be restored to the same standard as following a hospital post mortem examination (see *Restoring the body* above). When the coroner or procurator fiscal authorises the release of the baby's body, it will then be handed to the parents, funeral director or hospital for burial or cremation (see Chapter 20). The family may also wish to see the baby or create other memories when the baby's body is released following the post mortem examination (see *Creating memories* in Chapter 14 and *Taking the baby's body home* in Chapter 15).

If the coroner or procurator fiscal is not satisfied with the results of the post mortem examination, they may hold an inquest. In some cases, the baby's body may not be released until after the inquest. In Scotland, the procurator fiscal may also order a Fatal Accident Inquiry in specific circumstances such as when a death occurs after an accident at work, in police custody or in prison. When this happens, the baby's death or stillbirth cannot be registered until after the inquest. For registration procedures following a coroner's or procurator fiscal's post mortem examination, see *Obtaining certificates and registration in coroner's or procurator fiscal cases* in Chapter 19.

Medical staff should tell parents about how to obtain the post mortem examination results in these instances and offer to discuss the results of the post mortem examination with parents (see *Results* below):

- **England and Wales**. Parents can request a copy of the pathologist's report from the coroner and may be charged a small fee. Some coroners may also prefer to send this report directly to a hospital doctor who is caring for the parents.

- **Scotland**. Parents can request that the procurator fiscal sends a copy of the pathologist's report to them or their general practitioner.

- **Northern Ireland**. The coroner will discuss the preliminary results of the post mortem examination with parents and the full report will be sent to the mother's or baby's doctor when they are available. Parents can also request the pathologist's report directly from the coroner.

If an inquest is held, the results may not be available until after it is concluded.

The coroner and stillbirths in Northern Ireland

The majority of stillbirths are referred to the coroner in Northern Ireland following the court of appeal ruling that extended the definition of a deceased person to include *a foetus in utero then capable of being born alive* (McBride and McArdle 2014). These referrals to the coroner often result from uncertainty about the cause of stillbirth. Staff should explain to parents why the stillbirth is being referred to the coroner and what will happen (McBride and McArdle 2014). Staff should also allow plenty of time to answer any questions that parents might have (McBride and McArdle 2014). When referring the death to the coroner, staff should request that police officers visit parents wearing plain clothes as this may be less distressing for parents. All police officers should have training in communicating sensitively with parents.

Usually, the coroner will be satisfied for the doctor to issue a stillbirth certificate if the parents have given consent for a hospital post mortem examination unless they have concerns that the stillbirth occurred under suspicious circumstances or as a result of medical negligence. If the coroner orders a post mortem examination, the doctor must provide a clinical summary to the pathologist and the post mortem examination may be delayed if this is not provided (DHSSPSNI 2008). If the pathologist discovers any evidence that the stillbirth was "unnatural" (for example, if there is evidence of trauma or medical negligence), the hospital post mortem examination can be converted to a coronial post mortem. The coroner may also order further coronial investigation if they feel it is needed after the post mortem results are reported (see also *Obtaining certificates and registration in coroner's or procurator fiscal cases* in Chapter 19).

After the post mortem examination

Releasing the baby's body or remains to the parents

Trusts and Health Boards should have procedures and paperwork in place (including a mortuary release form) to give parents when they wish to take their baby's body home or to arrange for burial or cremation after a post mortem examination. No documentation is legally necessary for parents to take the baby's body from the hospital or mortuary but they should be given a form confirming that this has been done so that there is a record of the baby's body being released in case problems arise. See Appendix 1: Form 1 for a sample form and *Taking the baby's body home* in Chapter 15 for more information.

 I was dealt with in such a professional and sensitive way at the mortuary at my local hospital. The attendant asked me to sign some forms and handed me a white box that he had made containing Noah. He explained what I could do with Noah's remains ... I have spoken to several other parents whose babies were born dead before 24 weeks, and they were not given this choice. Not everyone will want it, but some do, and they should always be told. Mother

If parents are coming to the mortuary to pick up their baby, it is best if an appointment is arranged so that staff are available to offer parents information and support. Staff should give parents information about handling and storing the baby before burial or cremation (see *Restoring the body* above). Parents should also be given written contact details for a named staff member who can advise them if they need further information or help. If the body or remains have been placed in formalin or another fixative, parents should be given advice about avoiding accidental exposure to the fixative and what to do if this occurs.

Results

After the post mortem examination, the parents will have a follow-up appointment to discuss the results. If there is a delay to the post mortem examination results, it is important that this information is shared with the healthcare team supporting parents and that this information is conveyed to parents as soon as possible. It can be very distressing for parents who expect to receive results and do not receive them when expected or feel they need to chase results. Therefore, good communication across teams and with parents is paramount (Siassakos *et al.* 2015, unpublished results).

Policies and practices should be in place to ensure that there is good communication between pathology staff and healthcare teams. This coordination between services will help to ensure that staff are aware of the time scale for receiving results when booking follow-up appointments with parents and help them to keep parents informed of any delays. A named contact should be designated within each pathology and midwifery team to facilitate the return of post mortem examination results and ensure that a specific person on the healthcare team is responsible for following up on results. See *Follow-up appointments* and *Follow-up appointments at the hospital* in Chapter 17 for more information about who should attend appointments to discuss results with parents, preparing for the meeting and the consultation itself.

Recording, reporting and reviewing the baby's cause of death

Mothers and Babies: Reducing Risk through Audits and Confidential Enquiries across the UK (MBRRACE-UK) are responsible for the surveillance of maternal and perinatal deaths in the UK. As part of their remit:

> *MBRRACE-UK aims to better understand the causes, risks and inequalities which impact on the health and survival rates of babies, so that organisations can measure whether they are providing the right care.* (Manktelow et al. 2015: x)

In order to meet this aim, they are reliant on complete and accurate information about babies' deaths (including maternal data) being supplied in a timely manner by healthcare staff on MBRRACE-UK's online reporting system (Manktelow *et al.* 2015). MBRRACE-UK request that Trusts and Health Boards supply information about all late miscarriages at 22 and 23 weeks' gestation, stillbirths and neonatal deaths (Manktelow *et al.* 2015). Doing this will help Trusts and Health Boards comply with recommendations from the Morecambe Bay Investigation to systematically record and track perinatal deaths and target their own needs for improvement while contributing to a better overall understanding of the causes of these deaths (Manktelow *et al.* 2015).

Good communication between healthcare organisations is required to gather complete information in instances where the care of the mother and/or baby was transferred to another unit or hospital (Manktelow *et al.* 2015). It is also important that the cause of death classification options available to healthcare staff are clear, consistent, comprehensive and that these are applied consistently by healthcare staff across the UK (Manktelow *et al.* 2015; Ptacek *et al.* 2014). It should be possible for multidisciplinary discussions to take place to review these deaths and determine the most accurate classification for each baby's death (Draper *et al.* 2015; Sands 2016e).

A named member of staff on each unit should be the designated Lead Reporter who is responsible for liaising with MBRRACE-UK and feeding back information to colleagues (Manktelow *et al.* 2015). Community midwifery staff and independent healthcare practitioners, such as independent midwives, should also ensure that they are involved with MBRRACE-UK and that they are reviewing deaths with colleagues including their Local Supervising Authority Midwifery Officer (LSAMO).

The relevant member of staff or healthcare professional should ensure that all perinatal deaths are reported to MBBRACE-UK after the information about the baby's death is as complete as possible (Manktelow *et al.* 2015). For example, reporting should take place after the results of any tests or post mortem examinations have been completed, particularly as information found on MCCDs may not be accurate (Cockerill *et al.* 2012) (see also Chapter 19). More information about reporting babies' deaths is available from the MBRRACE-UK website (see Appendix 2).

Good reporting will then facilitate a robust review of the causes of deaths to help hospitals and healthcare staff better understand the causes of babies' deaths (Draper *et al.* 2015). There is currently variation in the quality and existence of reviews into babies' deaths across the UK. Therefore, it is important that reviews are standardised by using a nationally-accepted, robust system for review (Draper *et al.* 2015; Sands 2016e). This system should be a web-based tool that includes a rating system for quality of care (Sands 2016e). The quality of these reviews should also be checked using internal and external monitoring systems (Sands 2016e).

Reviews should include parent's perspectives wherever possible, which will help to better understand the events leading to the death and identify ways to improve care provision (Draper *et al.* 2015; Sands 2016e). Parents should be offered opportunities to provide information from the beginning of the review process (Sands 2016e). A summary of the reviews' findings should also be shared with parents in a sensitive and timely manner (Draper *et al.* 2015; Sands 2016e) (see also *Being open and honest with parents* in Chapter 22).

The outcomes of reviews should also be used to implement and monitor action plans for improving care (Sands 2016e). The information contained in these reports should be shared with Trusts, Health Boards and service commissioners twice a year to promote organisational learning (Sands 2016e). Additionally, this information should be shared at the national level to promote learning across all healthcare services (Sands 2016e).

See also the *Sands Principles of Review*, developed in conjunction with the Department of Health, that is available on the Sands website (see Appendix 2). Sands and the Department of Health are working to develop a standardised audit tool for perinatal mortality review (see the Sands website details in Appendix 2 for more information).

CHAPTER 17

Follow-up appointments and ongoing care

Other relevant chapters

1: Providing holistic care

2: Providing inclusive care

3: Loss and grief

4: Communication

5: Communication across language and other barriers

6: Antenatal screening and diagnostic tests

7: Continuing the pregnancy

8: Termination of pregnancy for fetal anomaly or maternal medical conditions

10: Early miscarriage before 14 weeks' gestation

11: Late miscarriage between 14 and 24 weeks' gestation and stillbirth

14: After a loss

15: Postnatal care

16: Transfer to the mortuary and post mortem investigations

18: Mental health

19: Certificates and registration

20: Funerals and sensitive disposal

21: Memorials

22: Receiving and responding to feedback: parent experiences

23: Another pregnancy?

Trusts, Health Boards, local authorities and managers should develop and implement a policy to ensure that both immediate and long-term follow-up care are available to all parents who experience a pregnancy loss or death of a baby.

The criteria for providing ongoing care should be based on the needs of the parents and not on the type or gestation of the loss. Support should be available for, and offered to, parents who have experienced a stillbirth, neonatal death, miscarriage at any gestation or termination of pregnancy. Support should continue to be available to all women in all subsequent pregnancies or after the birth of another baby. This requires co-ordination and good communication between hospital and community services (see also Chapter 23).

The importance of care and support for parents in the community

The care received by parents following the death of their baby is very important. It has been identified that:

> Bereaved parents are between two and four times more likely to die or become widowed in the first 10 years after the experience of stillbirth or the death of their child than non-bereaved parents. (Harper et al. 2011: 308)

More research is needed to determine the reasons why bereaved parents might have an increased chance of dying but some suggested causes include an increased risk of suicide or alcohol misuse (Harper *et al.* 2011). Parents with health problems may also be more likely to have babies who are stillborn or die in the neonatal period (Harper *et al*. 2011). The provision of comprehensive ongoing support and care for bereaved parents may help to decrease parents' risk of mortality after the death of their baby.

Hospital staff and primary care staff, such as GPs, community midwives and health visitors, are all important sources of ongoing care and support for many bereaved parents.

 I had thought that terms like "your arms aching to hold him" belonged in trashy romance novels. But they are true. Your arms do ache. Your chest does feel as if a huge stone has settled on it. Your heart does break into a million pieces. It's the loneliest feeling in the world. Mother

 I remember the morning after Emma died so clearly. I awoke and after barely a moment realised that she was gone. I sobbed and sobbed. Father

 Coming home from hospital was the hardest thing and instead of time healing I believe it is getting harder for me. My husband is back to work and I feel devastated and lost without our little boy. I now have to face returning to work and going back to my old life instead of the happy times we had planned. Mother

In the first few days at home, some parents may be in shock. At this time, they may also be busy with visits from family members and friends as well as organising and preparing for a funeral. However, many parents are left to cope on their own or feel alone once other people return to their normal routines. In the days and weeks that follow, some parents may also experience their loss and grief more intensely.

Nothing is ever the same after losing a baby. But people want you to get back to how you were. They expect you to do it fairly quickly. Mother

Some parents may appear to be well supported by their family and friends. However, these parents may not be getting the help that they need (Cacciatore 2010). Some may distance themselves from family members or try to hide their grief. Some parents may also find that friends and relatives avoid them or are unable to listen. This may be because they do not know what to say, they are experiencing their own grief for the baby or they may be experiencing renewed grief for past losses (Sands 2014b) (see also Chapter 3). This can add to the isolation many parents may feel following a pregnancy loss or the death of their baby. Women who have had early miscarriages or terminations may never have told anyone that they were pregnant due to the timing of their loss. Other women who have had a termination for fetal anomaly may not have told friends and family members who they feel might disapprove of their decision.

 Both my husband and I found out who our friends were. Many have become closer whilst others have disappeared from our lives completely. Some people would cross to the other side of the street to avoid us whilst others would come up and hug you, then walk away. Mother

It is at this time that parents may have the greatest need for ongoing care and support from primary care staff (Sands Helpline Staff 2006, personal communication). Parents may only feel able to freely talk with skilled staff. Some parents may also value opportunities to talk with staff about their baby in the months and years after the baby's death or a pregnancy loss when other people may feel they should be "over it". Parents may also feel uncomfortable mentioning the baby in case it causes upset.

Therefore, it is important that parents receive information about the support available from their primary care team and that the primary care team have the training required to offer good bereavement care (Nagraj and Barclay 2011). It is also crucial that GPs and other primary care staff take the initiative to offer support to parents, rather than wait for parents to ask.

Communication and co-ordination

 The day my baby died I came home and got a call from the Health Visitor the next day. She clearly didn't know the situation and just thought baby and mother were home and she wanted to visit. She was very apologetic but it was something I didn't want to speak to a stranger about. Parent (Redshaw et al. 2014: 43)

In the *Listening to Parents* report, some parents highlighted that information about their baby's death had not been handed over from hospital to community health care teams (Redshaw *et al.* 2014). In most cases, primary care staff should be promptly informed that a woman has experienced a pregnancy loss or the death of her baby. The appropriate member of staff can then contact her and ensure that she is not sent reminders for antenatal appointments and immunisation clinics.

Hospital staff should explain the benefits and importance of receiving support from their primary care team to bereaved parents. Many women will give consent to the hospital contacting their GP or primary care team. Other women may not want their GP or primary care team to be informed and it is always important to check. If a woman declines to have her primary care team informed, this decision must be respected (see *Communication between staff and confidentiality* in Chapter 4). The woman should also be told where she can receive additional care if required. Additionally, she should be given a letter summarising her history and treatment to give to her GP or another doctor if she needs further medical care. Staff can also offer to help women register with a GP or change their GP if necessary.

With the woman's consent:

- A designated member of staff at the hospital should phone her GP and community midwife when the woman is discharged. This is important as letters may take several days to arrive.

- The hospital or clinic should also immediately send a summary of the woman's obstetric history and care to her GP when she is discharged. Depending on the gestation at which the loss occurred, the summary should also be sent to the community midwife and the health visitor.

- The woman should be given a summary of her care that she can give to her GP at their first appointment (see also *Communication between units and healthcare teams* in Chapter 4.).

- The GP and community midwifery team (where applicable) should also be informed where the mother will be staying after she is discharged from hospital. This is particularly important if the mother if going to stay with relatives or on the neonatal unit so that the primary care team know where and how to contact her or arrange for her care.

> *Because I wasn't at home but on the ward with Joseph who was very ill, I wasn't having midwifery care after the caesarean. My health visitor arranged for a midwife to come and check my scar, which was a good thing as I was on bedside vigil and wasn't taking care of myself.* Mother

Communication across teams in the community

If different members of the primary care team are involved with the woman and her partner (if she has one), it is important that they communicate with each other. This helps to ensure that someone continues to visit for as long as the parents want and that the parents do not receive conflicting information.

It can be helpful if the GP, community midwife or health visitor marks bereaved parents' electronic and hard copy medical records with an alert or sticker to notify other healthcare professionals to their bereavement. See the boxed text about Teardrop Stickers in Chapter 14 for more details.

Follow-up appointments

This section provides information that may be relevant for all types of follow-up appointments with bereaved parents.

General information for arranging follow-up appointments

All parents should be offered follow-up appointments for postnatal care and to discuss any results from tests or post mortem investigations. It is important that parents do not fall through the gaps. Staff may need to take extra care to ensure that appointments are arranged for parents who:

- Do not live near the neonatal unit where their baby died.

- Have one or more surviving babies from a multiple pregnancy on a neonatal unit.

- Are staying with relatives after leaving the hospital where they received care (McHaffie *et al*. 2001b).

It is important to make sure that the parents know the purpose of each follow-up appointment (Siassakos *et al*. 2015, unpublished results). This will ensure that parents know what to expect at the appointment as they may experience distress if their expectations are not met (Siassakos *et al*. 2015, unpublished results). For example, parents may arrive at an appointment expecting to hear post mortem examination results but learn that the appointment is for a physical check-up, which may cause frustration, disappointment or distress. Letters that are sent to confirm the appointment with parents should clearly state the purpose of the appointment (Siassakos *et al*. 2015, unpublished results).

It is also important to ensure confidentiality in situations where other family members may not know about the loss or about post mortem investigations. Staff who telephone should check they are speaking directly to the woman. The envelope of any letters that are sent should be marked "Private and confidential".

Some women may want to bring a partner, relative and/or friend to appointments. Where relevant, both parents should be encouraged to attend appointments together. When the appointment is booked, parents should also be encouraged to write down any questions and worries and to bring the list with them to the appointment. Additionally, they should be told whom to contact if they need to talk to someone urgently in the time before the appointment and be given contact details.

All staff who visit or contact parents after a pregnancy loss or the death of a baby should have had training in bereavement care and should feel confident and competent in supporting distressed parents (see *Staff training* in Chapter 24).

If staff are not fluent in a parent's language, they should work with a professional interpreter during appointments (with parents' consent). Staff should also ask the interpreter to help them make contact with parents by phone to arrange and explain the purpose of appointments. The interpreter should be well informed beforehand about the situation and the reason for the visit (see also *Working well with an interpreter* in Chapter 5).

With her consent, the mother's medical notes should be marked so that all staff (including receptionists) are aware of her loss. This should help to avoid distressing comments or the woman needing to explain her situation. See the boxed text about Teardrop Stickers in Chapter 14 for more details.

It is important that any partners also receive the offer of follow-up care after their baby has died. *Listening to Parents* found that most women received follow-up support from a health professional after the death of their baby (72 per cent whose babies were stillborn and 78 per cent whose babies died after birth) (Redshaw *et al.* 2014). However, their partners were much less likely to receive support from a healthcare professional (47 per cent whose babies were stillborn and 56 per cent whose babies died after birth) (Redshaw *et al.* 2014). Both women and their partners should be offered support following the death of their baby as both parents may experience intense grief and/or mental health problems (Cacciatore 2013; Koopmans *et al.* 2013; Flenady *et al.* 2014 (see also *Fathers and same-sex partners* in Chapter 3).

> *I think as a man you expect, and people expect you, to be strong for your partner … but I don't remember being strong. I remember crying a lot when I was alone and when I went back to work.* Father

Ongoing follow-up appointments

In addition to the initial follow-up appointment, an offer of ongoing care (beyond the initial follow-up appointment) should be made to all bereaved parents. This offer should also be repeated some weeks later if parents initially decline the offer. Parents may find that they need support later and/or be surprised by a lack of support offered by friends, family or other services.

Place of care for follow-up appointments

Follow-up appointments may take place at home, in the GP's surgery or at the hospital. Some parents may find it too distressing to go back to the place where their baby died

(Siassakos *et al.* 2015, unpublished results). If this is the case, arrangements should be made for follow-up appointments to take place in another suitable setting or outside normal clinic hours.

Bereaved parents should not have to sit with other mothers with healthy babies or attend an appointment in an antenatal or postnatal clinic if they do not wish to do so.

Discussions at follow-up appointments

Parents often have very high expectations of follow-up appointments. They may be hoping for clear answers about why their baby died that will help them make sense of what has happened. If it is not possible to provide these answers, healthcare professionals should acknowledge that this may be difficult for parents and recognise any emotions that parents may feel.

> *One of the hardest things is not knowing why. I am a logical person and I know I could accept it if I could understand it. It has taken me almost a year to accept that we will not find an answer.* Mother

While parents should be told the purpose of an appointment or visit, it is always important to avoid imposing a set agenda and to respond to the woman's and (where applicable) her partner's needs. Some examples of things parents may want from follow-up appointments may include:

- To ask questions about what has happened and to check their understanding of the information they were given at the hospital.

- To discuss the events surrounding the pregnancy loss or baby's death so that they can clarify and confirm what happened.

- To discuss how they are feeling. It is important to ask parents how they feel and to offer them an opportunity to talk. Grief should not be treated as a mental health concern but parents should also be assessed for mental health problems that may be compounding their grief (see Chapters 3 and 18).

- Help in preparing questions for their consultant or GP.

- Suggestions about dealing with the reactions and questions of other family members (for example, other children, their partner, grandparents, a pregnant relative, etc.), friends and neighbours.

- Information and advice about registration and certification (see *Registration* in Chapter 19).

- Help with decisions about and arranging a funeral for their baby (see *Offering choices to parents* in Chapter 20).

- Advice about sex and contraception (see *Discussing sex and contraception* in Chapter 15 and *Pre-conception care* in Chapter 23).

- To discuss the timing of another pregnancy, their chances of having a live healthy baby and how they can reduce or manage any risks. They may also want to talk about any related implications for any existing children (see Chapters 15 and 23).

- To discuss concerns about coping with anxiety in another pregnancy or the possibility of never having a child.

- Information about local or national support organisations (see *Voluntary support* later).

- Advice about parental leave and claiming benefit payments (see *Entitlement to time off work and benefits* in Chapter 15).

- Advice about coping with or returning to work, including what to say to colleagues and how to deal with their reactions. Parents may find it helpful to read Sands' booklets entitled *Returning to Work after the death of your baby* and *Information for employers – Helping a bereaved parent return to work*.

- Advice about bereavement counselling that is available to parents and other family members.

- Referral for further investigations including genetic counselling. If they do not want genetic counselling immediately, they should be told how to access these services at a later date.

> *What I really needed was someone to talk to. It is incredible how common this problem is. I do feel there is very little support available for people, both women and their partners.* Parent (Redshaw *et al*. 2014: 43)

Written information for parents attending follow-up appointments

Staff should offer parents written information and/or information in other formats about appropriate sources of continuing support, both professional and voluntary. The Sands Bereavement Support Pack contains a number of support booklets that may be helpful for parents. These support packs can be ordered free of charge from the Sands Shop (see Appendix 2). All staff should also have access to an up-to-date list of local and national resources that are available to bereaved parents. One member of their team should be responsible for updating this list at least every six months.

At the end of the appointment, parents should be told whom to contact if they have further questions, problems or concerns. They should be given a named contact and a telephone number and/or email address for that person. In some cases, it may be appropriate to offer another appointment. Also, a written summary of the discussion should be sent to the woman, her GP and to the referring hospital if necessary.

After our genetic counselling appointment, the consultant wrote to us to confirm what he'd told us. He wrote that it was nice to meet our daughter Rosie (whom we had had to take to the appointment), that he was pleased that we had a pleasant time in Donegal for Daisy's due date, and that he considered us to be a low-risk in terms of future babies being affected by Down's Syndrome. The personal touches in the letter had a tremendous impact: it was very comforting for us that a specialist saw us as a family and not as an abstract de-personalised "case". Father

Information regarding follow-up appointments with specific staff

The information provided under *Follow-up appointments* above is general information that applies to all follow-up appointments with parents. The sections below cover specific considerations for follow-up appointments with different healthcare professionals and in different settings.

Follow-up appointments with primary care staff

Primary care staff such as community midwives, GPs and health visitors have an important role in providing follow-up care to bereaved parents. Healthcare visits with such primary care staff may take place in the clinic or at home (see also *Place of care for follow-up appointments* above and *Home visits* below).

Follow-up appointments with community midwives

All women who have given birth should receive postnatal care and the offer of emotional support from a community midwife. This includes women who have had a late miscarriage or termination. Some women may prefer to see a midwife who they met during their pregnancy or a specialist bereavement community midwife. Some parents may find it helpful to know that community midwives who cared for them in pregnancy are also experiencing sadness and grief after their baby's death (Downe *et al.* 2012).

Community midwives may also visit with women in the hospital or on the neonatal unit if needed to offer postnatal care and support.

In addition to providing postnatal care and listening, community midwives may be able to offer support and answer questions based on the mother's and her partner's (if she has one) needs and concerns. This could include offering advice and information about registering the baby's death, entitlement to benefits, funeral arrangements, preparing for consultant or GP appointments, sexual intercourse, contraception or the timing of another pregnancy (see *Discussions at follow-up appointments* above).

Community midwives may also be providing care and support for women and their families in subsequent pregnancies (see also Chapter 23).

Follow-up appointments with the GP

Unless a woman does not consent, the hospital should inform her GP when she experiences a pregnancy loss or her baby dies. It is important that GPs are trained to provide bereavement care and make contact with parents (Nagraj and Barclay 2011).

Many parents welcome a phone call or visit from their GP after their baby's stillbirth or death, an early or late miscarriage or a termination for fetal anomaly. Having their GP acknowledge the loss, express sympathy, ask how they are feeling and offer support can be very important for parents (Moulder 1998; Statham *et al.* 2001). The GP should always initiate contact with the woman and perhaps offer a home visit, particularly if there are specific concerns for the woman's physical or emotional well-being.

Primary care staff may not have met the parents as a result of the changing structure of general practice. However, staff should still make contact with bereaved parents who they have not met previously (Nagraj and Barclay 2011). Even with the changing structure of general practice, the GP may be the one health professional who is in touch with bereaved parents over many years and who can inform newly arrived primary care staff about the parents' situation. GPs are also well-placed to provide ongoing care (Nagraj and Barclay 2011) as they may be able to monitor parents' physical and emotional well-being for a longer period and offer care as appropriate. This can be important as some parents may not experience or seek help for mental health problems until a long time after the death of their baby. Additionally, a GP may be better placed to notice depression in parents than other healthcare professionals (Siassakos *et al.* 2015, unpublished results). The GP may also be providing care and support to other members of the family including siblings or grandparents. The ongoing care that GPs can offer could also include:

- Physical care (see Chapter 15 for more information about postnatal care).

- Ongoing emotional support.

- Information on maternity leave and benefits following pregnancy loss (see *Entitlement to time off work and benefits* in Chapter 15).

- Contraceptive advice.

- Discussing relationship and sexual concerns with parents (for example, loss of libido, sexual anxiety, emotional responses to sex, etc.) (Sands 2014a).

- Discussing and clarifying the results of investigations if parents have questions after appointments with hospital staff.

- Referral to other specialist services such as genetic counselling.

- Referral to appropriate support organisations and/or counselling services.

- Pre-conceptual advice.

- Support in subsequent pregnancies.

It is important that bereaved parents are aware that this care and support is available.

As soon as we could we started trying for a baby. I have felt extremely excluded from everyday life and do not feel that I should "bother" my GP as I have not been "trying for a baby for long enough". Parent (Redshaw *et al.* 2014: 48)

Follow-up appointments with health visitors

Some women and their partners (where relevant) may also appreciate the offer of a visit from the health visitor, especially if they have met before or if there are other children in the family. At an initial visit, the health visitor can ask whether future visits would be helpful. They can then negotiate the frequency and length of any follow-up visits and phone calls with the parents (Schott and Henley 2014).

 The health visitor wrote and said if we wanted to talk she would be happy to listen. She said a lot of people don't have anyone to talk to and that was what she wanted to offer us. She came a couple of times, once when we were both here, and once when I was on my own. Mother

The role of the health visitor in supporting bereaved parents can be very important (Schott and Henley 2014). Schott and Henley (2014) highlight how health visitors are able to:

- Offer emotional support that may involve listening to parents' stories or having parents share their memories and keepsakes of their baby on more than one occasion.

- Advise parents regarding ongoing physical concerns.

- Signpost parents to organisations and services that can offer additional support.

- Be aware of significant dates and anniversaries such as the dates when the baby was due or of their birth and death. Health Visitors can offer additional support by offering to contact or visit parents at that time.

- Offer additional care and support when parents are considering another pregnancy as well as during and after any subsequent pregnancies.

Health visitors are also able to check on the well-being of the whole family including any partners or other children and provide ongoing support over a longer period of time. *You Are My Sunshine* (2011) by Shirley Gittoes and Rosemary Elliot describes the long-term support that one health visitor was able to provide for a bereaved mother after the stillbirth of her daughter.

Home visits

First contact

The initial home visit after a woman leaves the hospital should be made by the woman's GP or community midwife. She may appreciate seeing a GP or midwife who she has seen and built a relationship with during her pregnancy. If the woman does not want a visit at this point, a date for a postnatal visit should be discussed and determined. Women may also receive later home visits from a health visitor.

It can be very difficult to make a first visit to a bereaved woman or family. Staff are likely to feel more confident and better able to help if they have been informed about key details of the loss (see *Communication and co-ordination* above) and feel well prepared and supported.

Staff should telephone the woman to offer a visit, rather than visit unannounced (see *Arranging follow-up appointments* above). Some women may want to be visited but may fear the reactions of family members or neighbours if a uniformed member of staff arrives at their home. In this case, staff should suggest not wearing a uniform or arrange to meet the woman elsewhere.

The purpose of a home visit

 The local professionals saw us through some hard times. The care that my health visitor gave helped us both through the emotional turmoil of memories of Heulwen's stillbirth that came back to us when Joe was so ill after he was born. Mother

The purpose of a home visit is often a physical and emotional well-being check-up for the mother. Women may want help with physical symptoms such as bleeding, lactation, stitches and pain (see more about postnatal care in Chapter 15). They may also want to know about postnatal exercises.

As mentioned under *Follow-up appointments* above, the woman may wish to discuss a range of topics and it is best to respond to her needs and those of her partner if she has one.

Follow-up appointments at the hospital

A follow-up appointment should be made with the consultant obstetrician and/or neonatologist who cared for the mother and/or baby. This appointment is usually arranged for a time when all the results from any investigations including post mortem examinations will be available. It may be preferable for parents if staff arrange for any blood test results to be ready before this appointment so that parents do not need to return to the hospital on several occasions (Siassakos *et al.* 2015, unpublished results).

Parents may also want other members of staff (for example, a midwife, neonatal nurse, genetic counsellor and/or pathologist) to be invited to this appointment (see *Who should attend the appointment* below).

Many parents are anxious to have an early appointment with the consultant and to receive post mortem investigation or test results as soon as possible. They should be told in advance how long it is likely to be before these results are available and staff should be as realistic as possible when discussing this timeframe to avoid distress if the results take more time (see also Chapter 16). A follow-up appointment may also be more useful or productive if it is delayed for a few weeks while waiting for the results. Parents may find it more difficult to think clearly or to take in and remember medical information and its implications in the first few weeks after their baby's death.

However, some parents have also found that delayed follow-up appointments were unnecessary as their questions had been answered by their GP or community midwife before they attended the hospital appointment (Siassakos *et al.* 2015, unpublished results). This has particularly been the case for some parents who have not chosen to have a post mortem examination for their baby (Siassakos *et al.* 2015, unpublished results).

Additionally, delays to follow-up appointments where parents are expecting to receive results from post mortem examinations may be very difficult for parents (Siassakos *et al.* 2015, unpublished results). Parents should not have to follow-up on when these appointments will take place and a designated member of staff should be responsible for keeping parents updated regarding when the results are likely to be available (Siassakos *et al.* 2015, unpublished results). If the post mortem examination results are delayed, the parents should be contacted before they see the consultant. The reasons for the delay should be explained and a new appointment time should be offered.

 At first I was told it was four weeks, then it was six weeks, and then time went on and on, I just didn't hear nothing, and in the end I spoke to my doctor, and said I still hadn't had no results, he said he hadn't heard nothing, and he was gonna chase it up. Parent
(Siassakos *et al.* 2015, unpublished results)

 I did ring up and had to chase up, because I'd hadn't heard anything at all, this was about, maybe nine or ten weeks, and I didn't hear, it would've been nice to hear, to speak to someone. Parent
(Siassakos *et al.* 2015, unpublished results)

Parents should have the name and contact details of a member of staff (possibly a midwife or neonatal nurse) who they can contact if they have any questions or concerns during the time when they are waiting for a follow-up appointment.

Preparation for the appointment

Before the appointment, the doctor and all the members of staff seeing the parents should read the notes in order to familiarise themselves with the mother's and baby's history. They should also know the baby's name if one was given so that they can refer to the baby by name. They should be prepared and able to provide detailed information and to answer a wide range of questions as honestly as possible. All staff (including receptionists) should be alerted of the reason for the appointment and, with the parent's consent, the medical notes should have been marked with a Sands teardrop or other sticker (see *Informing other carers* in Chapter 14).

 When I went back to the hospital for my follow-up appointment the doctor said cheerfully, "Who's watching your baby?". Mother

Who should attend the appointment

When both an obstetrician and a paediatrician have been involved in a baby's care, they should ask the parents whether they would prefer for one or both of them to attend the appointment. Continuity may be important to parents and they may want to have had some contact with the consultant before the meeting (Siassakos *et al.* 2015, unpublished results).

If the baby had a complex anomaly that may have a genetic component, it may be helpful for parents to see the local clinical genetics team at the same meeting so that they get comprehensive information and advice. It may also be helpful for a member of the pathology team who carried out any post mortem examinations to be present as they may be able to better answer parents' questions about the post mortem investigation report. These options should be offered to parents when they book the follow-up appointment.

It can be very helpful for a midwife who is experienced in bereavement support or another midwife who the woman knows and trusts to be present at the follow-up appointment. During the consultation she can assess how the woman or couple are feeling and whether they have further needs that should be addressed. She can also be the contact for parents if they need further care or support including in a future pregnancy.

If the baby was on a neonatal unit, the neonatal nurse who provided the most care for their baby might also attend. This could be particularly important for parents who may have built relationships with staff on the neonatal unit (see also *Keeping in touch and ongoing support for parents* in Chapter 13).

Some parents may want staff who were involved in their or their baby's care to attend the meeting. However, other parents may find it distressing if health professionals with whom they have had contact are present at the appointment. It is important to let parents know who will be attending the meeting in advance as many parents want to know this information (Siassakos *et al.* 2015, unpublished results).

Parents may also wish to invite other family members or friends to this appointment for additional support.

The consultation

These discussions with parents should include providing parents with honest information about the results of any investigations and their implications (Draper *et al.* 2015) as well as any other concerns raised by parents (see *Discussions at follow-up appointments* above). Staff should be prepared to allow as much time as possible. All of the parents in the InSight study found that they had plenty of time during their hospital follow-up appointment to discuss their experiences, test results and planning for the future (Siassakos *et al.* 2015, unpublished results). The pathology results could also raise many issues and the parents may have a lot of questions. Extra time may be needed to deal with these concerns.

In some hospitals, the parents are given, or at least offered, a copy of the full pathologist's report. Elsewhere, they are given a summary. The full report should be sent to their GP. Parents should be told whom to contact if they have any further questions and be given a name and their contact details. It is very important that any medical terminology used in the results is interpreted to the parents and unfamiliar medical concepts and events explained (Rankin *et al.* 2002).

At follow-up appointments, most parents are looking for a full, compassionate and clear account of why their baby died that makes sense to them. It is important that parents are not given conflicting information. If a decision was made to withdraw or withhold life-sustaining treatment for a baby, parents may want reassurance that the decision was correct (Goggin 2012). This may also be the case for parents who decided to have a termination for fetal anomaly. Parents may be anxious that the post mortem examination will not confirm the diagnosis on which they based their decision. Parents often find it helpful to have the results of post mortem examinations and may even be reassured if the results do not show a reason for their baby's death (Siassakos *et al.* 2015, unpublished results). However, not having an explanation about why their baby died may also be difficult for some parents and staff should also acknowledge this difficulty.

 We waited 12 weeks for the appointment that would tell us what had gone so incredibly wrong and at times I was so scared they would tell me I had done something wrong, but they found no reason at all and again I found myself asking WHY? I think I will always question why? Mother

Although most parents want to know as much as possible about why their baby died, some find the catalogue of findings that may be listed in a post mortem investigation report extremely distressing. Staff should gently ask parents if they have had enough information at this stage and whether they would like to continue or put the written report away to discuss later or at another appointment (McHaffie *et al.* 2001b). If parents would like to continue to discuss the report at a later date, staff should offer to arrange another appointment before parents leave.

Parents may be particularly concerned about the implications of what has happened and risks for a future pregnancy or existing children (McHaffie *et al.* 2001b; Siassakos *et al.* 2015, unpublished results). Staff should offer to describe the kind of care and support that would likely be given without raising expectations beyond what is deliverable. If there are indications that further investigations or treatment would be necessary in a future pregnancy or for existing children, staff should offer to tell parents how this care would be organised.

This is also a good time to ensure that women have had appropriate postnatal care and to discuss their health and that of their partner when they have one. Parents may also want to ask questions about their recent pregnancy and birth of their baby.

Many parents also appreciate sharing memories of their baby and discussing the events in their baby's life with the staff who were most involved. Parents are often grateful when staff show that they understand the impact that the baby's life and death has had on them (McHaffie *et al.* 2001b).

A clear summary of this appointment should be sent to women and their GP afterwards (Draper *et al.* 2015).

Longer-term support

 Day and night I have an ache of yearning for him. Even simple tasks seem a big effort as if I am moving through treacle. Mother

 The pain is still deep inside, surfacing occasionally, but you get through somehow. You have to. I still cry, with some days being better than others. Seeing all the other mothers passing with toddlers her age and imagining what she would look like, it always brings a tear or two so I have to turn away. Mother

Many parents will grieve for their baby over the following months and years. Many will value continuing professional support but the kind of support that they need and the timing may vary. It is important that parents know that they can ask for support long after their loss. They should also know whom to contact.

Long-term support should also be offered to partners who may feel out of place and marginalised when most support and care is directed toward the mother (see also *Fathers and same-sex partners* in Chapter 3).

Support at home? Almost none at all. The only person who got any support at all was my wife Heather. The midwife visited but at no point asked me how I was. Father

Sometimes support that is given only to the mother may help to strengthen a partnership but this can also be divisive. Some couples may find it helpful to see a member of staff together, perhaps in the evening or at weekends. Some partners may also appreciate an offer to see a member of staff alone so that they can discuss their feelings and concerns more openly. Support groups such as Sands, the Miscarriage Association and ARC have leaflets for fathers and male volunteers whom fathers can contact.

If there were problems and conflicts in relationships within the family before the baby died, these may become worse. Sometimes professional help with family relationships can seem an unwelcome intrusion but some families may find this support helpful to relieve tensions and pressures. For example, with parents' permission, a GP or health visitor may be able to talk to other children in the family. Other family members may also benefit from talking to their own GP or to a counsellor.

As time passes, parents may have more questions about why the pregnancy ended or why their baby died. It can be particularly difficult if an explanation was not found for their baby's death. Some parents may need help in accepting that no cause will be found and they may need reassurance or support to help them believe that they did not somehow cause their baby's death.

There is currently no consensus regarding the "normal" length of grief or when grief is considered to be complicated (Shear 2015). However, parents who continue to find it very difficult to cope with daily life several months after the loss might benefit from specialist help and should be offered a referral (see Chapter 18).

Voluntary support

 We are members of a club that we never wanted to join. Father

 If you are lucky you find support from other parents. Sands helps keep you sane, to realise that you are not alone. To find out that you aren't going mad when you scream yourself hoarse in the car because you can't keep it in any more. It offers that safe place where you can talk about your child when your family and friends would rather you moved on, like they do in TV soap land. Where you can remember your baby, give thanks for them, find out that other parents hate Christmas just as you do for the presents that are missing, can't function in the weeks after their child's birthday even though no one else mentions it. The discovery that you are not a freak and not going mad is a huge relief. Mother

Many parents find it helpful to talk to other people who have been through similar experiences. They may prefer to access this support one-to-one or in a group. However, it is better to refer parents to specialist voluntary groups that have specially trained supporters, rather than to individual local bereaved parents. Staff should offer parents information about national and local organisations that offer support and how to contact them. They should have an up-to-date list prepared with this information and a member of staff should have the responsibility of ensuring that it is updated every six months. Some information about voluntary organisations that offer support and information for bereaved parents can be found in Appendix 2. It may sometimes be helpful for staff to offer to help parents make the first contact with a group.

> *No-one can explain the emotions of losing a child, the only people who understand are those who have had a similar experience. Your life is over. The nursery is empty. Your heart is broken and your inside feels empty. You go to the hospital to have a baby, your whole life is geared up for this little person and you come home with nothing but a few memories.*
> Mother

It is important that voluntary support groups are seen as *complementing* professional support rather than replacing it and that staff do not automatically withdraw their support if parents develop local contacts. Staff should also consider the possible limitations of local support groups. For example, parents in minority communities or whose first language is not English, fathers, parents on a low income and single mothers may be less likely to contact support groups. In such cases, healthcare professionals may be able to help build bridges between parents and these groups or help to set up new groups where these parents may feel more comfortable.

Mental health

This chapter on mental health highlights some of the mental health concerns that staff should be aware of when working with bereaved parents. This includes staff such as health visitors, GPs, midwives, obstetricians, neonatal nurses and any other practitioners who work with women and their families during pregnancy, childbirth, the postnatal period and the first few years of a child's life.

It is important to recognise that some bereaved parents or family members will not experience mental health problems following a perinatal loss. However, some bereaved parents and other family members (for example, grandparents and siblings) may benefit from the offer of support and treatment for mental health difficulties following a pregnancy loss or the death of a baby at any gestation. Parents should be asked questions to identify potential mental health problems (NICE 2014a). Mental health assessment and treatment should also be offered to women, their partners (NICE 2014a), other children and family members (where relevant) after any type of perinatal loss (see also *Fathers and same-sex partners* and *Grief experiences of other family members and friends* in Chapter 3).

Mental health support and information about self-care should also be available for staff working with bereaved parents as providing care and support following a pregnancy loss or the death of a baby can also be stressful and distressing for staff (see Chapter 24).

Grief, prolonged grief and depression

While grief can affect a person's emotional and mental well-being, it is crucial to acknowledge that grief is not a mental health problem but a typical response to bereavement. The experience, expression and intensity of grief following a pregnancy loss or the death of a baby are also very personal and unique to each individual (Worden 2003) (see also *Parents' experiences and expressions of grief* in Chapter 3). Parents may experience a wide range of feelings that may include (not exclusively) sadness, anger, helplessness, guilt and/or shame. In the period immediately following a perinatal loss, some women may also experience a sense of the baby's presence where they hear the baby cry or feel the baby kicking inside them. The wide range of experiences and the individual nature of grieving makes it difficult to define what is meant by grief (Worden 2003).

Prolonged grief

There is also no universally accepted length of "normal" grief, although the duration is often far longer than most people expect following perinatal loss (Wallerstedt *et al*. 2003; Shear 2015). Some parents may find that other people's expectations may cause them to feel that they have been grieving for "too long" (see also *How staff can offer emotional support to parents* in Chapter 3). For many parents, grief decreases over time and their feelings are no longer overwhelming after a time. However, it is also common for many parents to continue to grieve for their baby for months or years and to experience resurgences of intense grief on anniversaries and other important occasions (Worden 1991). Parents may also have a continuing bond with their baby that some parents may find beneficial as long as it does not prevent them from living their lives (Klass 1996) (see also *Resolution or continuing bonds?* in Chapter 3).

All of these factors can make it difficult to determine what is meant by prolonged grief disorder (PGD) (also referred to as complicated or "pathological" grief) (Worden 2003). In contrast to "normal" grief, prolonged grief is generally characterised by prolonged yearning for the deceased (that occurs for more than six months) as well as an inability to carry out usual social and occupational functions and at least five of the following symptoms:

- Feeling emotionally numb, stunned or that life is meaningless.
- Experiencing mistrust.
- Bitterness over the loss.
- Difficulty accepting the loss.
- Identity confusion.
- Avoidance of the reality of the loss.
- Difficulty moving on with life (Prigerson *et al*. 2009: 1).

Prolonged grief disorder was not included as a diagnostic category in the latest version of the Diagnostic and Statistical Manual of Mental Disorders (DSM-5) but is being considered for inclusion in the next version of the International Classification of Diseases (ICD-11) (Bryant 2014). Bereaved parents who are unable to carry out their usual daily functions after six months should be offered a referral for specialist help. However, it is also important to recognise that grief may last for one or two years for some parents (American Psychiatric Association 2013). It may also be necessary to consider the relationship between potential symptoms of what is thought to be prolonged grief disorder and PTSD (Maercker and Lalor 2012) (see also *Post-traumatic stress and post-traumatic stress disorder* below).

Depression

Clinical depression is diagnosed when a person experiences a persistent low mood or sadness and takes little, or reduced, interest in or enjoyment from activities that they enjoyed previously (NHS Choices 2014a; WHO 2016). Depression may also be characterised by a wide range of other symptoms such as tearfulness, feelings of guilt, decreased self-esteem and self-confidence, feelings of worthlessness, disturbed sleep, reduced concentration and decision-making abilities, changes in appetite, loss of libido or difficulties at home or at work (NHS Choices 2014a; WHO 2016).

When working with bereaved parents, it is important to recognise that many of these symptoms of depression overlap with feelings and experiences that parents may have following the death of their baby (American Psychiatric Association 2013) (see also Chapter 3). While many of these feelings are typical for bereaved parents, the DSM-5 no longer excludes bereaved individuals from being diagnosed with a major depressive disorder (also referred to as clinical depression) within two months of their bereavement (American Psychiatric Association 2013). It is important for staff to be aware of this change as it is likely that the DSM-5 will affect diagnostic categories in the next version of the ICD (ICD-11) that is used in the UK (NHS Choices 2013).

There may be some benefits to bereaved parents as a result of this change in diagnostic guidance. For example, an earlier diagnosis of clinical depression may be beneficial for some bereaved parents who are experiencing depression alongside their grief as this change may help them to access support and treatment sooner (American Psychiatric Association 2013). Earlier diagnosis and treatment may also help to prevent some parents from developing more severe mental or physical health problems (American Psychiatric Association 2013). If parents or staff have concerns about parents' mental health following a perinatal loss, it is important that staff offer support, an assessment for mental health difficulties and appropriate treatment options when necessary. Staff should also offer women information about the "baby blues" and postnatal depression as experiencing the death of a baby does not prevent women from potentially experiencing these difficulties.

However, it is important that staff avoid pathologising grief when supporting parents and that parents are not expected to fit into a prescribed pattern of grieving (Thieleman and Cacciatore 2013; Bandini 2015). In order to avoid such pathologisation of a potentially "normal" grief response, staff should be aware that bereaved parents may experience grief that is more intense and lasts longer than other types of bereavement, which means that a diagnosis of clinical depression may need to be more carefully considered in these circumstances (Thieleman and Cacciatore 2013). When working with bereaved parents, staff should offer emotional support to parents as this may be beneficial for parents' well-being and help with depressive symptoms and other long-term effects of loss (Cacciatore 2010; Stroebe *et al.* 2010) (see *Support and listening* in Chapter 15). However, staff should also be aware that some parents may need to experience grief in their own time and way and that parents may still experience emotional benefits from receiving support even if their grief or yearning for their baby is not diminished (Stroebe *et al.* 2005; Cacciatore 2010).

Recognising symptoms and offering assessment and treatment for mental health problems

It is important that assessments and treatment for mental health problems are offered to bereaved parents and family members who are experiencing or are at risk of developing these conditions. Early detection of risk factors for, and the existence of, mental health problems and offering support and treatment to parents may help to prevent these conditions from developing or worsening (Hogg 2012) (see also *The importance of recognising and support for mental health problems* below).

Staff awareness of mental health problems and treatments

When staff are not aware of the signs and symptoms of mental health conditions or they do not have sufficient time to spend with parents during follow-up appointments, it is possible that mental health difficulties in bereaved parents and other family members may remain undiagnosed and untreated (Khan 2015). Therefore, it is crucial that staff who care for bereaved parents and families (including midwives, health visitors, GPs, counsellors and hospital chaplains) are trained to recognise signs of mental health difficulties, offer assessments for these conditions and discuss all of the available treatment options that are offered locally and in other areas (Khan 2015). This includes staff who are offering immediate and/or long-term care and support for parents after a perinatal loss. Provisions for long-term care (including assessments and treatments) may be particularly important as some parents may not experience or disclose mental health problems until months or years after their experience of loss or during a subsequent pregnancy (see also *Longer-term support* in Chapter 17). Staff must also have sufficient time during appointments with parents and family members to offer information and assessments.

Trusts, Health Boards, service commissioners and managers should ensure that perinatal mental health training is required for all relevant staff and that this training includes information about bereavement following a pregnancy loss or the death of a baby. Trusts, Health Boards, service commissioners and managers should also ensure that policies and practices are in place to offer bereaved parents ongoing follow-up care, further assessment and treatment for mental health problems. Policies and practices should also be in place to ensure that sufficient time is available in follow-up appointments with bereaved parents to enquire about their emotional well-being and offer assessments for mental health conditions where necessary (see also *Follow-up appointments* in Chapter 17).

Staff should also be aware that some parents or their families may feel stigmatised if they are labelled as having a mental health condition, particularly if they fear that other children may be removed from their care as a result (Khan 2015). Experiences of, or fears about, stigma or losing their children may cause some parents to hide or downplay any symptoms they are experiencing as they may want to avoid being labelled as having a mental illness or being a mental health service user (Foulkes 2011; Maternity Action, Women's Health and Equality Consortium 2014). Staff should be sensitive and compassionate when raising mental health concerns with parents and it is important that parents feel that staff are able to listen without judgement (CQC 2015). Staff should also acknowledge and listen to parents concerns about stigma, reassure them that their confidentiality will be maintained and offer them information about the potential benefits of being assessed and receiving treatment and support for mental health concerns.

Policies and practices should also be in place to ensure that there is good communication between staff and healthcare teams regarding parents who may be at risk of developing or who have been diagnosed as having mental health problems after a perinatal loss (see *Predisposing and protective factors for mental health problems* below and *Communication and co-ordination* in Chapter 17). When there is a lack of continuity of carer for parents, insufficient communication between staff or when medical notes are incomplete, this may mean that staff are unaware that parents have or are at risk of developing mental health problems, which may mean that parents are not offered assessments or treatments for these conditions (Oates and Cantwell 2011; Boots Family Trust 2013; Cantwell *et al.* 2015; Khan 2015).

Staff should also be aware of some of the mental health disorders that may be experienced by bereaved parents. The experience of bereavement may result in the onset of mental health problems for some parents or it may cause a recurrence or exacerbation of prior mental health conditions. Some parents may also be experiencing symptoms of more than one mental health problem and parents should be offered assessments for different conditions to ensure that they are then offered appropriate treatment and support. Some parents may also have difficulties with the misuse of substances, such as drugs and alcohol, and staff should offer parents non-judgemental support and information about the help available to them.

Some of the more common mental health problems that may affect bereaved parents include prolonged grief, clinical depression, anxiety disorders and post-traumatic stress (PTS) or PTSD. The information provided here about these conditions is not intended to provide a comprehensive list of symptoms or mental health problems that may be experienced by bereaved parents. As mentioned above, mental health training should be required for staff to help them recognise and offer assessment and treatment to parents who may be experiencing a range of symptoms and/or mental health problems after a perinatal loss.

Prolonged grief and clinical depression

Bereaved parents may have a higher risk of experiencing prolonged grief and/or clinical depression (Bennett *et al*. 2008; Hogue *et al*. 2015) (see *Grief, prolonged grief and depression* above for a more detailed discussion of these conditions). These conditions are distinct mental health problems that parents should be offered assessments and treatment for and these diagnostic categories should not be used to redefine any co-existing mental health difficulties that may be experienced by parents. As mentioned above, it is important for staff to understand the differences between grief, prolonged grief and depression in order to avoid pathologising or imposing time limits on parents' "normal" experiences of grief.

Anxiety disorders

Parents who experience a perinatal loss at any gestation may have an increased risk of experiencing an anxiety disorder (Brier 2004; Kreicbergs *et al*. 2004). Anxiety disorders (where people feel persistent worry or fear) cover a range of mental health problems including:

- Generalised anxiety disorder where people feel anxious about a variety of situations or events.

- Panic disorder where panic attacks characterised by overwhelming fear, anxiety and apprehension may be experienced alongside physical symptoms such as palpitations, nausea, trembling and sweating.

- Phobias where a person feels extreme or "irrational" fear in relation to an object, place, situation, animal or feeling (for example, social anxiety where social situations are a source of persistent and overwhelming fear).

- PTSD (see below) (NHS Choices 2014c, 2014d, 2014e).

These feelings or experiences of anxiety may also be accompanied by other symptoms such as an inability to relax, irritability, feelings of dread or worry, insomnia, sweating, muscle aches and pain, amongst a number of other possible symptoms (NHS Choices 2014f).

It is important to recognise that some fear and anxiety may be typical responses to situations or circumstances (NHS Choices 2014c) and some parents may appreciate an offer to discuss their fear or concerns. However, staff should offer parents a referral for specialist help if parents' feelings of fear or anxiety are persistent, affecting their daily lives and/or are causing them concern or distress (NHS Choices 2014c).

Post-traumatic stress and post-traumatic stress disorder

Approximately one-third of women are expected to experience PTS following a stillbirth (Gravensteen *et al*. 2013). However, bereaved parents may experience symptoms of PTS after a loss at any stage in pregnancy, including early miscarriage (Engelhard *et al*. 2001; Brier 2004). PTS occurs when an individual experiences involuntary repetition of stress-related thoughts, emotions or behaviours following a traumatic event (Daugirdaitė *et al.* 2015).

Bereaved parents may also be at risk of developing PTSD (Daugirdaitė *et al.* 2015). PTSD is found when an individual vividly re-experiences aspects of a traumatic event through symptoms that may include flashbacks, nightmares and/or intrusive images or other sensory impressions (Daugirdaitė *et al.* 2015; NICE 2005). Other common symptoms that may be experienced by people with PTSD are avoidance of reminders of the trauma, hypervigilance, heightened startle responses, irritability, difficulty with concentration, insomnia and emotional numbing (NICE 2005). PTSD often develops immediately after the traumatic event but may also develop months or years afterwards for some people (NICE 2005).

PTS is more commonly found in parents following a perinatal loss than PTSD although it is possible for PTS to develop into PTSD (Daugirdaitė *et al.* 2015). PTS and PTSD are also more common in women than men following a perinatal loss (Daugirdaitė *et al.* 2015). However, it is still important to offer fathers assessment for PTSD symptoms as they too may be at risk of developing this condition (Christiansen *et al.* 2014). Despite this possibility, staff should also be aware that many parents will experience a great deal of distress as a result of their experience of loss but that not all parents will experience trauma.

Without treatment, PTSD may last for prolonged periods of time and some bereaved parents have been found to experience PTSD symptoms for up to 18 years after the death of their baby (Christiansen *et al.* 2013). Some women may also experience PTSD in a subsequent pregnancy (Turton *et al.* 2001) (see *Mental health risks during and after a subsequent pregnancy* below).

It is important to offer bereaved parents assessments and any necessary treatment for PTS and PTSD as symptoms of PTSD can have significant effects on the daily lives of parents with PTSD and their family (NICE 2005; NHS Choices 2015b).

Offering support and treatment

When parents have been diagnosed as having a mental health condition, they should be offered a referral for further support and treatment as soon as possible. This care should be readily available and treatment should be offered within two weeks for individuals experiencing psychosis and six weeks for those who have other mental health problems (CQC 2015; NHS England *et al.* 2015). Despite these recommended waiting standards, however, it is important that staff are aware that some parents may need more timely or immediate access to care if they are experiencing psychosis or suicidal thoughts (NHS England *et al.* 2015).

It is also important that all mental health care offered to parents and families is high quality, compassionate and accessible (CQC 2015). Mental health professionals (including counsellors, psychologists, mental health support workers and psychiatrists) should be available locally to offer support and intervention (where necessary) to bereaved parents and families. These professionals should receive training in bereavement following a perinatal loss and understand the unique experiences and challenges that bereaved parents and families may be facing.

Trusts, Health Boards, service commissioners and managers should ensure that specialist perinatal mental health services are available in all areas of the UK and that these services are available for bereaved parents and their families. Efforts should be made to implement these services in the large number of areas where specialist perinatal mental health services do not currently exist and to decrease long waiting lists in other areas (Bauer *et al*. 2014).

NICE's clinical guidance on *Antenatal and postnatal mental health* (NICE 2014a) and *Post-traumatic stress disorder: management* (NICE 2005) offers more details of the treatments and interventions that should be offered for different mental health problems. It is also important that more research is undertaken examining the efficacy and benefits of different types of support, treatments and interventions for bereaved parents and other family members following perinatal loss.

Offering support and treatment in subsequent pregnancies

It is important that mental health support continues to be available to women and their partners (where relevant) during and after pregnancies following perinatal losses, as this may benefit both parents and children (Robertson Blackmore *et al*. 2011; Gaudet *et al*. 2010) (see *The importance of recognising mental health problems and offering support* above). Some parents may benefit from being able to talk openly about their feelings, concerns and any grief they are experiencing as a result of their previous experiences of loss (Gaudet *et al*. 2010) (see Chapter 23 for more information about supporting parents experiencing a subsequent pregnancy before, during and after birth).

The importance of recognising mental health problems and offering support

It is crucial that staff are able to recognise symptoms of mental health problems and offer bereaved parents or other family members information, assessments and treatment for these conditions, as they may have implications for both parents and their families.

For example, Harper *et al*. (2011) found that bereaved parents are two to four times more likely to die or be widowed within ten years of their baby's death. The causes of these deaths are uncertain but it is possible that some of these deaths are attributed to suicide or substance misuse (Harper *et al*. 2011) (see also *The importance of care and support for parents in the community* in Chapter 17). The MBRRACE-UK confidential enquiry into maternal deaths also found that some of the women who died by suicide between 2011 and 2013 had experienced a miscarriage, stillbirth or neonatal death (Cantwell *et al*. 2015). One of the recommendations of this report was that women who experienced a perinatal loss should be offered additional monitoring and support as they were more at risk of developing a mental health problem (Cantwell *et al*. 2015).

In addition, mental health problems may not only affect the person experiencing one of these conditions but they may also have implications for the well-being of other members of that individual's family. In the case of bereaved parents, these effects may extend to older children or future children who are born after the baby has died. For example, the older children of bereaved parents may be affected by the perinatal loss and some grieving parents may be unable to offer support or meet the emotional needs of these children and help them adjust to the death of their sibling (Fauth *et al.* 2009; Cacciatore 2010). This is important as the support that a bereaved child receives may help to prevent potential short and long-term effects on their well-being (Akerman and Statham 2014). See *Other children* in Chapter 3 for more information about support for children.

Furthermore, parental mental health problems may also affect attachment, cognitive, behavioural and emotional outcomes for infants and children (Beck 1995; Atkinson *et al.* 2000; Grace *et al.* 2003; Goodman *et al.* 2011; Sutter-Dallay *et al.* 2011; Milgrom *et al.* 2016). As has been seen in studies of the impact of maternal mental health problems on paternal mental health, it is possible that one parent's mental health difficulties may also affect the other parent and have an even greater impact on the well-being of their surviving children (Goodman 2004; Ramchandani *et al.* 2005; Stevenson-Hinde *et al.* 2007, 2013; Paulson and Bazemore 2010).

Maternal mental health problems during subsequent pregnancies after a perinatal loss may have additional effects on children who are born following a perinatal loss. For example, maternal anxiety during pregnancy may increase the risks of premature birth, low birth weight babies and infants and children experiencing behavioural and/or developmental difficulties (Mulder *et al.* 2002; Dunkel Schetter and Tanner 2012; Ding *et al.* 2014; Graignic-Philippe *et al.* 2014).

Predisposing and protective factors for mental health problems

The presence of protective and/or predisposing factors for mental health problems do not necessarily determine whether parents or other family members will or will not develop these conditions after a perinatal loss. Rather, predisposing factors are elements that may indicate that a parent has an increased risk of developing a mental health problem while the presence of protective factors may decrease this risk (Carr 2006). Staff should be aware of ways in which they might offer parents support that may be beneficial for their well-being while also being aware of general and individual risk factors that may increase parents' risk of developing a mental health problem following a perinatal loss.

Protective factors

Factors that may help to protect bereaved parents from developing mental health problems include the perceived support that they receive from healthcare professionals, partners and family members during and following their loss and their ability to create and share memories of their baby (Cacciatore *et al.* 2009; Cacciatore 2010; Crawley *et al.* 2013; Gravensteen *et al.* 2013; Brierley-Jones *et al.* 2014; Redshaw *et al.* 2014) (see also Chapter 14 and *Support and listening* in Chapter 15). Attendance at support groups may also help to prevent PTSD symptoms for some parents as they may feel more able to talk and share memories of their baby in these settings (Cacciatore 2007).

Parents may also be less likely to experience depression if they are able to see, hold and/or spend as much time as they wish with their baby (Surkan *et al.* 2008). While some parents may experience psychological benefits from seeing and holding their baby, it is important to recognise that this may not be the case for all parents and parents should not be pressured to see or hold their baby (Turton *et al.* 2009b) (see *Seeing and holding the baby* in Chapter 14). Parents may also benefit from follow-up support if they decide to see and hold their baby (Ryninks *et al.* 2014).

Predisposing factors

There are a number of predisposing factors that may increase a parent's risks of developing a mental health problem following their experience of loss. Some parents may have a higher risk of developing mental health problems after a perinatal loss if they experience a perceived lack of support from healthcare professionals and/or feel unable to talk about or share memories of their baby (Crawley *et al.* 2013; Brierley-Jones *et al.* 2014; Redshaw *et al.* 2014).

Some risk factors may also be specific to parents in certain circumstances. For example, women who are single, divorced or widowed may be more likely to experience depression following a stillbirth (Cacciatore *et al.* 2009). Additionally, parents who do not experience a subsequent pregnancy following a perinatal loss may also be more likely to develop depression later on (Surkan *et al.* 2008).

With regard to PTSD, women may have a higher risk of developing this condition if they have less perceived social support, are younger, have a lower income, have a lower education level, have experienced a previous trauma or mental health problem and/or have had fewer previous pregnancies (Daugirdaitė *et al.* 2015; Horsch *et al.* 2015). There may also be an increased risk of parents developing PTSD if they had a traumatic experience of childbirth where a woman and/or her partner felt out of control (vulnerable and powerless), alone, abandoned, a loss of dignity, uncared for by those around them, disconnected from and ignored by health care providers due to a lack of communication, that care was unsafe so feared for their own safety and that of their baby, invisible, degraded, and/or that care was inhumane (Beck *et al.* 2013). This highlights the importance of good communication with parents, including in emergency situations (see *Good communication with parents* in Chapter 4).

Some parents may have an increased risk of experiencing mental health problems after a perinatal loss if they have a previous history of mental illness (Hogg 2012). It is important that parents with a history of psychiatric illness are identified by healthcare staff and offered additional information, assessments and support following their experience of loss. This may be particularly important for parents with a history of severe mental illness, such as severe depression or a bipolar disorder, who may re-experience these conditions after a loss.

Some women with a previous history of mental illness (particularly a bipolar disorder or schizoaffective disorder) may also have an increased risk of experiencing postpartum psychosis, although it can occur in women with no previous history of experiencing these illnesses (APP 2014). Postpartum psychosis is a serious condition and the symptoms can worsen rapidly; therefore, it is important that treatment and support are available promptly (APP 2014). The causes of postpartum psychosis are currently unknown but they may be related to genetic and biological factors that occur around pregnancy and birth (APP 2014). Postpartum psychosis affects approximately 0.1 per cent to 0.2 per cent of all childbearing women, not only women who experience a perinatal loss (Sit *et al.* 2006). While postpartum psychosis is rare, it is possible that some women who experience a perinatal loss may be affected by this condition and staff should be aware of the associated symptoms and risk factors.

Domestic violence may be another predisposing factor for mental health problems (Howard *et al.* 2013) and women who experience domestic abuse may also be more at risk of experiencing a perinatal loss (NHS Choices 2015c). Consequently, it is important that staff are trained to recognise signs of violence and abuse, facilitate a disclosure of these experiences and offer intervention and support (Knight 2015).

Mental health risks during and after a subsequent pregnancy

Women who have experienced a previous perinatal loss are more likely to experience grief, distress and symptoms of anxiety and depression in a subsequent pregnancy (Hutti 2005; Gaudet *et al.* 2010). Experiences of anxiety and depression may predict difficulties with prenatal attachment to the baby and/or persist after the subsequent birth of a baby who is healthy (Gaudet *et al.* 2010; Robertson Blackmore *et al.* 2011).

Some women who have experienced a previous perinatal loss may also be more likely to experience PTSD in a subsequent pregnancy (Turton *et al.* 2001). Additionally, parents who are experiencing PTS or PTSD following a perinatal loss may find that their symptoms are exacerbated during a subsequent pregnancy, particularly if these conditions have been undiagnosed, misdiagnosed or untreated.

Staff should be aware of these potential mental health problems that may be experienced by parents in a subsequent pregnancy and offer assessments for these difficulties and specialist support where needed (Debackere *et al.* 2008) (see also *Feelings, emotional well-being and mental health* in Chapter 23).

CHAPTER 19

Certificates and registration

Other relevant chapters

1: Providing holistic care

2: Providing inclusive care

3: Loss and grief

4: Communication

5: Communication across language and other barriers

14: After a loss

15: Postnatal care

16: Transfer to the mortuary and post mortem investigations

20: Funerals and sensitive disposal

This chapter provides information for staff about the certification and registration process following a loss at any gestation. Some of the certificates and forms mentioned are statutory documents while others are intended to support the needs of bereaved parents. Additional information about registering a stillbirth, birth or death can be found on the relevant government websites or from the Bereavement Advice Centre (see Appendix 2). The *Certificates and registration* section of the Sands support booklet entitled *Saying goodbye to your baby* may also be a helpful resource for parents. Information in this Chapter was correct at time of going to press (April 2016), but professionals should check whether changes to legislation or regulations have altered these processes.

Certificates and forms issued by healthcare staff

The forms and certificates that staff give to parents who experience a childbearing loss depend on the gestation and type of loss. Depending on how the loss is legally defined (see the *Legal definitions* box below), some forms and certificates are required by law. Other documents should be offered to parents by hospitals and medical practitioners as part of good practice.

Many parents greatly value copies of certificates and forms that are issued for their baby. Parents may feel that these documents provide a tangible record of their baby's existence when they may otherwise have few or no keepsakes. The following best practice points should be considered when providing parents with forms and certificates:

- Staff should explain the purpose of each document to parents.

- Any copies should be good quality.

- All locally-produced documents should be worded sensitively and sympathetically. It is always possible to use plain, non-bureaucratic language without compromising meaning or clarity (see also *Written information and information in other formats* in Chapter 4).

- Locally-produced forms and certificates should also be available in the main local languages for parents who do not read English. If translated documents are not yet available or if parents still need help, an interpreter should explain to the parents what the form or certificate says and its purpose.

Legal definitions

Stillbirth

A stillborn child is defined in law as "a child which has issued forth from its mother after the twenty-fourth week of pregnancy and which did not at any time after being completely expelled from its mother breathe or show any other signs of life" (Births and Deaths Registration Act 1953 s 41, Amended by Stillbirth Definition Act 1992).

Relevant laws:
- England and Wales: Section 41 of the Births and Deaths Registration Act 1953 as amended by the Stillbirth Definition Act 1992.

- Scotland: Section 56(1) of the Registration of Births, Deaths and Marriages (Scotland) Act 1965 as amended by the Stillbirth Definition Act 1992.

- Northern Ireland: Births and Deaths Registration Order 1976 as amended by the Stillbirth Definition Northern Ireland Order 1992.

Neonatal death
"Death before the age of 28 completed days" (CEMACH 2006).

The status of the fetus
Under Article 2 of the Human Rights Convention, which was incorporated into English law by the Human Rights Act (1998) and into Scottish Law by the Scotland Act 1998, a fetus has no legal status. Therefore, in the UK, the interests of the fetus cannot outweigh those of the mother.

Certification and forms for a baby born dead before 24 weeks' gestation

When a baby is born dead before 24 weeks' gestation (the current legal age of viability), the law does not require or permit the birth to be certified or registered. It can be very distressing for some parents who do not receive a certificate or cannot register their baby who was born dead before 24 weeks' gestation (Sands 2015a). However, other parents would find it very distressing if they were required to register their baby's birth (Sands 2015a).

For parents whose baby is born dead before 24 weeks' gestation, there may be few opportunities to create memories of their baby and they may value any tangible keepsakes that are available (Sands 2015a). Parents should be offered an unofficial "certificate of birth" from the hospital, which could be based on one of the templates available from Sands' website (see Appendix 1: Form 2). Sands offers five templates as it is important that healthcare staff select and use the form template that is most appropriate for each family.

In most cases, the baby's remains will be disposed of by the hospital but all available options should be discussed with parents (see Chapter 20). Before fetal remains or those of a baby born dead before 24 weeks can be buried, cremated or sensitively incinerated (sensitive incineration is no longer an option in Scotland), the following must take place:

- A doctor, registered midwife or nurse who was present at the birth, and/or has examined the baby, issues a form or letter confirming that the baby was born dead at less than 24 weeks' gestation. Parents should be given this document as they may need it if they wish to arrange for a private cremation or burial, even though there are no legal regulations for burying and cremating fetal remains (ICCM 2014; HTA 2015).

- Healthcare professionals in **England, Wales** and **Northern Ireland** should not complete statutory cremation forms for a loss that occurs before 24 completed weeks' gestation where there have been no "signs of life" (DHSSPSNI 2008; Ministry of Justice 2012a). For a sample form see Appendix 1: Form 3. Following a discussion with parents, this form could be adapted and the word "baby" could be inserted in place of "fetal remains" (which occurs twice in the form) in order to avoid causing unnecessary distress. This should be discussed with parents beforehand and their wishes should be accommodated.

- In **Scotland**, the new legislation proposed under the Burial and Cremation (Scotland) Bill aims to include a requirement for statutory forms for burial and cremation for losses before 24 weeks' gestation (Marsh 2015). However, the process is currently similar to that detailed above for England, Wales and Northern Ireland and no statutory forms are required.

- Depending on the arrangements to be made, parents or healthcare staff may also need to complete documentation required by the cemetery or crematorium (see *Paperwork required for cremation* in Chapter 20 and sample forms 3 and 4 in Appendix 1).

If a miscarriage occurs at home or outside a medical setting without the presence of a health professional, some parents may have difficulty obtaining a letter or form confirming that their baby was born dead before 24 completed weeks' gestation (Miscarriage Association *et al*. 2015). This can be problematic if parents wish to bury or cremate their baby as the cemetery or crematorium will require confirmation that the miscarriage occurred before 24 weeks' gestation (Miscarriage Association *et al*. 2015). In these instances, the Miscarriage Association, Sands and the Institute of Cemetery and Crematorium Management (ICCM) (Miscarriage Association *et al*. 2015) recommend that parents take the baby to the hospital or GP and request a letter or form stating that healthcare staff's professional opinion is that the loss occurred prior to 24 weeks' gestation. This can be a very distressing situation for parents and staff should accommodate this request. If there are questions around the gestation, staff should consult with a colleague.

Certification following a termination before 24 weeks' gestation

Once the termination has taken place, the doctor responsible for initiating it fills out an abortion notification form, which is sent in confidence to the Chief Medical Officer for England, Wales or Scotland as appropriate.

For a certificate that may be offered to the parents, see *Certification and forms for a baby born dead before 24 weeks' gestation* above.

Certification for a baby who was born at or after 24 weeks but had died before 24 weeks

If it is known or can be proven that a baby died in utero before 24 weeks based on the fetal stage of development, the baby should *not* be certified or registered as stillborn even if he or she was expelled from the mother after 24 weeks' gestation (RCOG 2010a). Legal advisers from the Department of Health and the Office for National Statistics confirmed that these babies should not be certified or registered (RCOG 2010a; Fairbairn 2014) (see the Legal definitions box under *Certificates and forms issued by healthcare staff* above). Additionally, it has been accepted throughout the UK that this is how registration law should be interpreted and implemented in these cases (RCOG 2010a; Fairbairn 2014).

This situation might arise if, for example, there is a delay between a diagnosed intrauterine death and delivery. See *Certification and forms for a baby born dead before 24 weeks' gestation* for more details about certificates that can be given to parents in these circumstances. If the baby's gestation is not known, they will be examined to determine the stage of development and whether the baby is considered to have been stillborn or born dead before 24 weeks' gestation (RCOG 2010a). It should be acknowledged that this may be very distressing for parents and all information should be explained sensitively to parents.

Certification for a fetus papyraceous

If a fetus papyraceous is identified at the birth of one or more other babies, this must be documented in the mother's notes and the parents should be informed. A fetus papyraceous should not be certified as a stillbirth (RCM 2008). Some parents may, however, appreciate the offer of a certificate from the hospital confirming the existence of this baby (see *Certification and forms for a baby born dead before 24 weeks' gestation* above).

Certification and forms following a stillbirth

When a baby is stillborn, the procedure for issuing a certificate of stillbirth and cremation form depends on the country where the baby is born. The stillbirth certificate must be taken to the register office within a specified time period which varies by country (see *Registering a stillbirth* below).

England and Wales

In England and Wales, the doctor or the registered midwife who attended the delivery or examined the baby's body after the birth gives the parents a Medical Certificate certifying the stillbirth.

Scotland

In Scotland, the doctor or the registered midwife who attended the delivery or examined the baby's body after the birth gives the parents a Medical Certificate certifying the stillbirth.

Northern Ireland

If a cause of death is known for a stillborn baby in Northern Ireland, a doctor or registered midwife can issue a Medical Certificate for the Cause of Death for the stillbirth although it is also recommended that they consult with the coroner in these cases. Examples of known causes of death would include antenatal diagnoses of the baby having a major congenital anomaly or a maternal medical condition.

The majority of stillbirths are referred to the coroner in Northern Ireland following a court of appeal ruling that has extended the definition of a deceased person to include *a foetus in utero then capable of being born alive* (McBride and McArdle 2014). These referrals for the baby often result from uncertainty about the cause of stillbirth. Usually, the coroner will be satisfied for the doctor to issue a stillbirth certificate if the parents have given consent for a hospital post mortem examination unless they have concerns that the stillbirth occurred under suspicious circumstances or as a result of medical negligence (see the section on *Obtaining certificates and registration in coroner's or procurator fiscal cases* below). It should be acknowledged that this may be difficult for parents and they should be offered support.

If parents wish to cremate their baby, a cremation form will also need to be completed for a stillborn baby by a medical practitioner who attended the baby, even in coroner's cases (DHSSPSNI 2008). This is usually done by the medical practitioner who completed the stillbirth Medical Certificate (DHSSPSNI 2008). A confirmatory medical form should then be completed by a medical practitioner who has been practicing for no less than five years, is independent of the practitioner who signed the initial cremation form, who ideally, was not involved in the baby's care and who was not related to the baby (DHSSPSNI 2008). No fee should be charged for signing a cremation form for a stillborn baby.

Certification following a termination after 24 weeks' gestation

Once the termination has taken place, the doctor responsible for initiating the termination fills out an abortion notification form that is sent in confidence to the Chief Medical Officer for England, Wales or Scotland as appropriate.

If the baby is born dead after the termination, the doctor or registered midwife who attended the delivery or who examined the baby's body after the birth gives the parents a medical certificate certifying the stillbirth (see *Certification and forms following a stillbirth* above). This certificate must be taken to the registrar of births and deaths for the stillbirth to be registered (see *Certification and forms following a stillbirth* above and *Registering a stillbirth* below for more information).

Certification and forms following a neonatal death

If a baby is born alive at any gestation and dies within 28 days of birth, a birth and death certificate must be issued for the baby. The doctor who provided medical care for the baby or mother before death should issue a Medical Certificate for the Cause of Death (MCCD) which certifies the death. This certificate must always be issued, even if the baby lived for only a few minutes. These certificates must be taken to the registrar of births and deaths (see *Registering a neonatal death* and *Registering the baby's birth and death at the same time* below). It should be acknowledged that this may be difficult for parents and they should be offered support.

If no doctor saw the baby while the baby was still alive or the baby's death was unexpected, the death cannot be medically certified until it has been reported to the coroner or procurator fiscal. The doctor responsible for the care of the mother and baby should contact the coroner or procurator fiscal to discuss the circumstances of the death. The parents must be informed that their baby's death has been referred to the coroner or procurator fiscal and the procedure and the reasons should be sensitively explained to them (see also *Obtaining certificates and registration in coroner's or procurator fiscal cases* below).

If the baby is to be cremated, a registered doctor (usually the doctor who verified the death and signed the medical certificate) must complete and sign a cremation form unless the baby's death has been referred to the coroner or procurator fiscal.

In **England** and **Wales**, if there is no post mortem examination or the medical referee has specific concerns about the form, a second doctor who has been registered for at least five years must sign a confirmatory medical certificate (Ministry of Justice 2012a). Doctors may waive the fees for signing confirmatory cremation certificates for babies.

In **Scotland**, the process for reviewing Medical Certificates for the Cause of Death means that cremation forms are no longer required (Health Improvement Scotland 2015b).

In **Northern Ireland**, one doctor will need to complete a cremation form and another will need to complete a confirmatory medical form even if the baby's death has been reported to the coroner (see *Northern Ireland* in *Certification and forms for a stillbirth* above).

Certification following a termination if the baby is born alive and then dies

If a baby is born alive following a termination of pregnancy at any gestation and subsequently dies, both the birth and the death of the baby must be registered with the registrar of births and deaths (RCOG 2010b).

The doctor who provided care for the baby while the baby was still alive will issue a birth certificate for the baby and a medical certificate certifying the baby's death (see *Certification and forms following a neonatal death* above).

If no doctor was present while the baby was still alive, the death cannot be medically certified until it has been reported to the coroner or procurator fiscal (see *Obtaining certificates and registration in coroner's or procurator fiscal cases* below). The parents should be told that the death cannot be registered until any investigations have been completed. It should be acknowledged that this may be difficult for parents and they should be offered support.

Forms for parents who take their baby's body or remains home

If parents wish to take their baby's body or remains out of the hospital or home, before a post mortem examination or funeral or for a private burial, the hospital should give the parents a form. Parents do not legally require a certificate or letter if they want to take the baby's body or remains home for burial on private land (or any other reason) (see *Burial on private land* and *Releasing the body or remains to the parents* in Chapter 20).

However, parents should be given a form or letter acknowledging the gestation of the loss and that the responsibility is with the parents to dispose of the remains appropriately. This form may be useful if the parents run into difficulties. The form should confirm that the body or remains have been released to the parents and that they will be taking it back to the hospital or making their own funeral arrangements. This document should include a contact telephone number in case of difficulties. A copy of this document should be kept in the medical records.

For Sands' sample form see Appendix 1: Form 1. If the parents are collecting the baby's body from the mortuary rather than the ward, the ward should also give them a mortuary release form.

See also *Taking the baby's body home* in Chapter 15 for more details.

Medical Reviewers and Examiners

Recommendations have been made to have Medical Examiners verify the MCCD for all deaths including stillbirth and neonatal deaths (Home Secretary and Secretary of State for Health 2007; Kirkup 2015; RCPath 2015a). The role of the Medical Examiner was set out in the Coroners and Justice Act (2009). The recommendation for this role resulted from the need to better scrutinise patients' deaths to improve the accuracy of MCCDs, improve the understanding and public health information about causes of death and ensure that the process of death certification is robust (Health Improvement Scotland 2015b; RCPath 2015b). Issues with inaccuracy of MCCDs following stillbirths have been highlighted as a concern and the data provided is not reliable enough to be used for research into stillbirth (Cockerill *et al.* 2012). Training has also been suggested to help improve MCCDs issued for stillborn babies (Cockerill *et al.* 2012).

Pilots of the review process have found that review of MCCDs may make death certification a more rigorous process and does not cause significant delays to providing a MCCD (Sheffield LMC 2012). However, concerns were raised in the pilots about issues that may arise if the Medical Examiner is unavailable and the process is delayed when an urgent burial or cremation is required (Sheffield LMC 2012) (see *Urgent burials and cremation* below).

In **England and Wales**, the implementation of the Medical Examiner role is currently pending (RCPath 2015b).

In **Scotland**, some MCCDs are now being checked by Medical Reviewers who are experienced doctors that are responsible for ensuring that the required numbers of MCCDs are reviewed each year and for educating doctors who are certifying death (Health Improvement Scotland 2015a). The implementation of this review process means that separate cremation forms are no longer required to cremate the baby but that all deaths must be registered before burial or cremation can take place (Health Improvement Scotland 2015b). The certificates for stillborn babies or deaths that are referred to the procurator fiscal are not subject to this review process (Health Improvement Scotland 2015a).

The MCCDs that are to be reviewed in **Scotland** will be randomly selected. The review of the MCCD may cause slight delays to registration and the funeral but should only take one working day for a Level 1 review and three working days for a Level 2 review (Health Improvement Scotland 2015b). A Level 1 review will involve having the death certificate reviewed by the Medical Reviewer who will also speak to the doctor who completed the MCCD (Health Improvement Scotland 2015b). The Medical Reviewer will also check the relevant medical records for a Level 2 review (Health Improvement Scotland 2015b). Parents will not be charged for this review.

Registration

Registration is required by law for all stillbirths, live births and deaths in **England, Wales**, **Scotland** and **Northern Ireland**. If a baby is born dead before 24 weeks' gestation, the law does not require registration. Information about all stillbirths, live births and deaths must be given in person at a register office. It cannot be given by letter or telephone.

How healthcare staff can help parents with registration

Many parents find the process of registering the stillbirth or death of their baby very distressing. However, many parents are also pleased that there is tangible legal evidence of their baby's existence. Most registrars do what they can to support parents and avoid causing unnecessary additional distress.

Healthcare staff can help parents by offering to explain what the registration process involves and alerting them to decisions they may want to make before they go to the register office. For example, parents may wish to name the baby as the name cannot be changed after registration. Also, the parents may want to consider having both parents' names on the certificate if they are not married (see below for more details about the regulations for each type of loss.) Staff who discuss registration with parents should have easy access to well-written local reference guides on registration, certification, burial and cremation.

There should be separate leaflets for parents about registering a stillbirth and registering a neonatal death. These leaflets should be available in different formats and in all the main languages spoken locally. These leaflets should include what parents need to know about registering their baby's stillbirth, birth or death (including when the parents are or are not married, fertility treatments that have been used, the father is unknown or untraceable or neither parent is able to attend the register office in person) and key local information about:

- When they must legally register their baby's stillbirth, birth and/or death.
- The register office for births and deaths, including addresses, directions, telephone numbers, opening hours and details of the documents they require from parents.
- Whether or not parents need to make an appointment to see the registrar. It is generally a good idea to advise the parents to telephone the registrar's office to say that they will be coming to register a stillbirth or neonatal death. They can then usually be seen quickly and will not have to wait with other parents registering new births. If parents prefer, a member of staff could make this phone call.
- The coroner/procurator fiscal.
- Funeral directors, crematoria and cemeteries.

The leaflets for parents and the guide for staff should be checked and updated at least every six months by a designated member of staff.

Before the parents leave the hospital, a member of staff should make sure that: (see also Before parents leave the hospital in Chapter 15)

- **They have discussed the information about registering the baby's stillbirth, birth or death with parents and that parents understand what is required of them.** These discussions are important and staff should not solely rely on parents reading leaflets.

- **Parents are given written information leaflets about registration and organising a funeral** (see also *Written information* in Chapter 20).

- **They have given parents the medical certificate and any other information that the registrar will need** (see sections below for specific details). With the parents' permission, it may be helpful for the registrar if "Death of a baby" is written in the corner of the envelope containing the medical certificate.

- **Parents who need an interpreter know whether the register offices can provide an interpreting service and how to book it.** If no interpreter is provided, parents should be advised to take a relative or friend along to help them understand and answer the registrar's questions.

If there are likely to be any problems with registration, the parents or, if they prefer, the member of staff who is caring for them should telephone the registrar for advice. For example, delays may result if the mother is ill or there are complications with entering the father's or another parent's name in the register. In particularly difficult situations, the parents may also appreciate an offer from a member of staff to go with them to the register office.

Urgent burials and cremation

Some parents may require that their baby's burial takes place within 24 hours or as soon as possible after the death. For example, an urgent burial may be required as a result of long-distance travel arrangements for family members attending the funeral or for religious reasons. When an urgent burial is needed for religious reasons, a community or religious leader may be able to help with the necessary arrangements. The local registrar may also provide an out of hours service where burial or cremation is required urgently. However, staff should verify whether this service is available locally.

England, Wales and Northern Ireland

Although registration must normally take place before a body can be buried, the local registrar should make arrangements to provide the necessary documents before registration in **England, Wales** and **Northern Ireland** so that urgent burials can take place wherever possible. This may be needed if the death or stillbirth occurs on or just before a weekend or public holiday. Families may need help from healthcare staff with getting the documentation completed as quickly as possible and with contacting the registrar out of hours.

It is important that staff are aware of local arrangements for out of hours services and know about how to deal with these circumstances in areas where urgent burials are not frequently requested. Staff should look on their local council's website and contact their local registrar if they have any questions about local procedures. There is currently no provision for out of hours registration service provided in **Northern Ireland**.

If an urgent burial is required, the registrar will normally issue a certificate of burial to allow the burial to go ahead. This is unlikely to be possible if the death needs to be reported to a coroner or procurator fiscal. Parents should be able to contact the coroner's or procurator fiscal's office to explain the circumstances although arrangements for an urgent burial may not be possible.

Formal registration of the death after the burial can take place up to five days after a neonatal death (which can be extended to 14 days) and up to 42 days after a stillbirth. In **Northern Ireland**, the person responsible for the burial ground must give notice to the registrar that burial has taken place within seven days if they have not received documentation from the registrar or coroner to authorise the burial.

Cremation

In **England** and **Wales**, the regulations have been amended to enable a certificate for cremation to be issued before registration following a neonatal death - in the same way as for burials. However, it is still not possible to issue a certificate for cremation before the registration of a stillborn baby. In **Northern Ireland**, it is not currently possible to organise an urgent cremation in the same way.

Scotland

In **Scotland**, all deaths must now be registered before burial or cremation can take place. If a death is selected for review during registration, the initial funeral arrangements can still be made, although the funeral cannot take place until after the review is complete (NAFD 2015). If families require an urgent funeral under special circumstances for religious, cultural, compassionate or practical reasons (for example, when travel arrangements have been made), they can apply for advance registration (NAFD 2015). The Medical Reviewer will review the request and the MCCD and they can usually confirm whether advance registration will be possible within two hours (NAFD 2015). The registrar can then tell the family whether or not their request can be granted (NAFD 2015).

Where to register a birth, death or stillbirth

Information for the registration of a birth, death or stillbirth can be given in any registration district within the same country.

In **England**, the process will take a few days longer if the death is registered in another registration district than where the death occurred (Bereavement Advice Centre 2013). This is because the information must be forwarded by post to the register office in the district where the death did occur (Bereavement Advice Centre 2013). This office will then post the appropriate certificate(s) (of birth, death or stillbirth) to the parents. In the case of a stillbirth or a neonatal death, this may mean a slight delay to the funeral because burial or cremation cannot normally take place until after the registrar in the district where the event occurred has issued the necessary paperwork.

Registering a stillbirth

In **England** and **Wales**, a stillbirth should be registered within 42 days although the register office can explain when exceptions might be made to extend this time period.

In **Scotland**, a stillbirth must be registered within 21 days.

In **Northern Ireland**, a stillbirth must be registered within one year.

Who can register a stillbirth?

Either parent can register their baby's stillbirth if they are married. This includes when the baby was conceived following fertility treatment and applies to a second female parent who was in a civil partnership with the mother when treatment occurred.

When the parents are not married, they should follow the procedures below:

- The mother can register the stillbirth when the parents are not married or if the father cannot be traced or is unknown.
- Both parents should attend the register office together to include both of their names on the register.
- Alternatively, the parents can follow these procedures to have both names registered:
    - The father can register the stillbirth if he has a signed declaration from the mother (information about how to do this can be obtained from the register office).
    - If the mother attends the register office alone and both parents want the father's name in the register, the mother must have a signed declaration from the father (information about how to do this can be obtained from the register office).
    - The mother can register the stillbirth and include the father's name if a court declares his paternity of the baby.

If neither parent can attend to register the baby's stillbirth, this can be done by anyone who was present at the stillbirth, anyone with responsibility for the baby or the occupier of the premises where the stillbirth occurred. In **Scotland** and **Northern Ireland**, the stillbirth could also be registered by a relative of the baby under these circumstances.

What documentation and information must the parents take?

In **England** and **Wales**, parents will need to take the medical certificate issued by the doctor or midwife who certified the stillbirth.

In **Scotland**, parents will need to take the medical certificate certifying the stillbirth and the parents' marriage certificate if applicable.

In **Northern Ireland,** parents will need to take the medical certificate of the stillbirth signed by a registered medical practitioner or midwife and have the following details:

- The baby's full name and sex.

- The date, time, district and place of the stillbirth.

- The full names, addresses and occupations of the parents.

For more information about medical certificates, see *Certification and forms following a stillbirth* above.

In addition to the documents above, parents will also need to take the appropriate signed declaration of parentage if they are not married and not attending the register office together (see *Who can register a stillbirth* above).

Parents may also want to have their baby's name(s) entered in the register. It is important that they know about registering their baby's name(s) before attending the register office. They may need time to think about the baby's name(s) and this information cannot be entered or changed later.

Staff should also be able to advise parents on any other information that they need to register the stillbirth including:

- The baby's sex (where known).

- The date and time of the stillbirth

- The parents' names, addresses, occupations, date and place of birth and marriage date (if applicable).

- The mother's maiden or previous names (if applicable).

- The details of the mother's previous children (if applicable).

What certificates will parents receive?

Certificates are generally given to parents when they register their baby's stillbirth. It is important to tell parents that the registrar will keep the medical certificate of their baby's stillbirth.

See *Obtaining copies of stillbirth, birth and death certificates* below for more information about how parents can obtain copies of these documents after registration.

England and Wales

The registrar gives the parents a *certificate of registration of stillbirth*. This certificate is issued free of charge and shows that the stillbirth has been registered.

The parents can also purchase a *stillbirth certificate* if they want for a small fee. This is a certified copy of the complete entry in the stillbirth register. It is helpful if healthcare staff tell parents that they will be able to purchase this certificate before they attend the register office.

The registrar will also give the parents a *certificate for burial or cremation*. This will be required before parents can bury or cremate their baby. Where applicable, parents should give this document to their funeral director or the hospital if they are arranging the funeral.

Scotland

The registrar will give parents a *certificate of registration of stillbirth*. This will be required before parents can bury or cremate their baby. Where applicable, parents should give this document to their funeral director or the hospital if they are arranging the funeral.

If parents are registering the stillbirth, they can also request an *extract of the stillbirth entry* in the register. This is a certified copy of the full entry in the stillbirth register. It is helpful if healthcare staff tell parents that they can request this form before they attend the register office.

Northern ireland

The registrar will offer parents a *certificate of stillbirth* when they register the stillbirth. This is an exact copy of the entry in the stillbirth register and is free of charge.

The registrar will also give the parents a *form to permit the disposal of the body*. Where applicable, parents should give this document to their funeral director or the hospital if they are arranging the funeral.

Registering a neonatal death

All deaths, including neonatal deaths, must normally be registered within five days (eight days in **Scotland**). If it is necessary to go beyond the time limit, the registrar should be contacted as soon as possible for advice.

When a baby is alive when they are born and then dies, the baby's birth and death must both be registered (see *Premature labour* in Chapter 11). If the birth has not yet been registered, this can either be done at the same time as the death or later if necessary. No medical certificate is needed to register the birth.

See *Obtaining certificates and registration in coroner's or procurator fiscal's cases* below for more information about registration if the baby's death has been reported to the coroner or procurator fiscal.

Who can register a neonatal death?

Either or both parents can register the baby's death, whether they are married or not. Alternatively, another relative, someone else who was present at the death, a funeral director or a hospital administrator can register the death if the parents cannot do it themselves.

What documentation must the parents take?

Parents must take the medical certificate issued by the doctor who saw the baby before death. It may also be helpful if parents take the baby's birth certificate and NHS medical card if they have these documents.

Parents may also need to bring identification or supporting documents that show their name and address (for example, a utility bill).

What information will the registrar need?

Staff should advise parents regarding the information that they will need to have available when they register their baby's death:

- The date and place of the baby's death (and the time in **Scotland**) (on the medical certificate).
- The baby's full name (see below).
- The date and place of the baby's birth (on the birth certificate).
- The baby's age at death (on the medical certificate).
- The cause of death (on the medical certificate).
- The parents' full names, addresses and current or previous occupations.
- The name and address of the mother's or baby's GP (where available).

Parents will need to have their baby's name(s) entered in the register. It is important that they know about registering their baby's name(s) before attending the register office. They may need time to think about the baby's name(s) and this information cannot be entered or changed later.

What certificates will parents receive?

The registrar will offer the parents a *death certificate* (a certified copy of the baby's entry in the death register). There is a small fee that parents will need to pay for this certificate, although parents in **Scotland** will be given a free abbreviated extract of this certificate. See *Obtaining copies of stillbirth, birth and death certificates* below for more information about how parents can obtain additional copies of these documents after registration.

The registrar will give the parents a certificate that allows for burial or cremation to take place. Where applicable, parents should give this document to their funeral director or the hospital if they are arranging the funeral. If parents are arranging their own funeral without a funeral director, they can give the certificate directly to the appropriate cemetery or crematorium office.

The registrar will also give the parents a certificate that they will need for any social security benefits that may be payable. Parents will also need the baby's birth certificate to claim Child Tax Credit and/ or other benefits to which they are entitled (see *Discussing entitlement to time off work and benefits* in Chapter 15).

Registering the baby's birth and death at the same time

By law, all live births must be registered within 42 days (21 days in **Scotland**). If the parents have not already registered their baby's birth, they can do this when they register the death. No medical certificate or other documentation is needed to register a birth.

For details of the requirements for registering the baby's death, see *Registering a neonatal death* above.

Who can register a baby's birth?

Either parent can register the baby's birth if the parents are married or were married when the baby was conceived. This is also the case for female parents in a civil partnership. For men in a civil partnership, they will need a court order before they can be registered as their baby's parents.

When parents are not married, the mother can register the birth without the father's details. If the parents wish to have the father listed on the birth certificate, they can register the birth together or have the other parent sign a declaration of parentage if only one parent attends the register office. Alternatively, the father's details can be added to the birth certificate with a court order that grants the father parental responsibility.

Female partners who are not in a civil partnership can have both mothers registered on the birth certificate if they have a parental agreement or received treatment together at a licensed UK clinic. They will, however, need to register the birth together, obtain a court order and complete a *statutory declaration of acknowledgment of parentage form*.

If the parents are unable to register the birth, this can be done by another person who is responsible for the baby, someone who was present at the birth or a hospital administrator where the baby was born. In **Scotland** and **Northern Ireland**, a relative can also register the birth.

What documentation must the parents take to register the birth?

Parents will need to bring a piece of identification or supporting document that shows their name and address. Depending on who is registering the birth and the names that are to be included on the birth certificate, a declaration of parentage may also be required (see *Who can register a birth?* above).

In **Scotland**, parents are also advised to bring the card issued by the hospital and the parents' marriage certificate if applicable. However, the birth can still be registered without these documents.

What information will the registrar need to register the birth?

Parents will need all of the information listed in *What information will the registrar need?* under *Registering a neonatal death* above (with the exception of the details about the baby's death).

Parents will also need information about the baby's sex, the parents' place and date of birth and the date of the parents' marriage or civil partnership (if applicable).

Parents will need to have their baby's name(s) entered in the register. It is important that they know about registering their baby's name(s) before attending the register office. They may need time to think about the baby's name(s) and this information cannot be entered or changed later in most cases.

What certificates will parents receive?

An abbreviated version of the baby's *birth certificate* will be issued to parents free-of-charge by the registrar. This certificate is required for parents to claim Child Benefit and any other benefits to which they are entitled (see *Discussing entitlement to time off work and benefits* in Chapter 15).

Parents can order copies of their baby's birth certificate (including copies of the full certificate) at a later date. There is a small fee. See *Obtaining copies of stillbirth, birth and death certificates* below for more details.

Obtaining certificates and registration in coroner's or procurator fiscal cases

If there is any uncertainty surrounding the cause of a neonatal death, there is reason to believe that a "stillborn" baby was born alive or a doctor was not providing care for a baby when they were alive, the doctor must report the case to a coroner or, in Scotland, a procurator fiscal. The parents should always be informed when a death is reported to a coroner or procurator fiscal and the reasons should be explained to them (See also *Deaths reported to the coroner or procurator fiscal* in Chapter 16).

This referral does not necessarily delay registration or the funeral. In most cases, the coroner or procurator fiscal will not wish to examine the case further and will instruct the doctor to issue the medical certificate to parents so that registration and the funeral can go ahead.

In some cases, the coroner or procurator fiscal may order a post mortem examination. The doctor should explain the reasons for this post mortem examination to the parents, give them the telephone number and address of the coroner's or procurator fiscal's office and encourage them to contact the office. They should also give parents information about how this will affect the way their baby's stillbirth or death will be registered and the timing of the funeral. It should also be acknowledged that this may be difficult for parents and support should be offered.

Parents should be informed if the coroner or procurator fiscal orders further investigations or an inquest after a post mortem examination. They should also be contacted by the coroner when their baby's stillbirth or death is registered by the coroner.

England and Wales

In England and Wales, the coroner will usually register the cause of death with the registrar and release the baby's body for the funeral after the post mortem examination. The coroner will also issue a cremation form if the baby is to be cremated.

If the coroner decides to hold an inquest, they will inform the registrar of the cause of death to be included in the register after the inquest is completed.

Parents can obtain a copy of their baby's death certificate from the local registrar after the death has been registered by the coroner. If parents wish to obtain copies of their baby's death certificate, they can also order this through the General Register Office.

Scotland

The procurator fiscal is responsible for establishing the cause of death in all sudden, unexpected, unexplained or suspicious deaths. After initial investigations, a cause of death may be identified and the procurator fiscal may have a doctor issue a certificate of death and give this to the parents (Crown Office and Procurator Fiscal Service [n.d.]).

If deemed necessary, the procurator fiscal will order a post mortem examination and the parents will be provided with a cause of death certificate that will be issued by the pathologist; this certificate may not reflect the final record of the cause of death (Crown Office and Procurator Fiscal Service [n.d.]). Depending on local arrangements, the death certificate may then be delivered to parents by the police or a funeral director or parents may have to collect the certificate from the mortuary (Crown Office and Procurator Fiscal Service [n.d.]). The mortuary staff, funeral director or police officer who have contact with the family at this stage should explain how to register the death now that they have received the death certificate (see *Registration* above). If a police officer is delivering this certificate to the family, they should wear plain clothes.

Once the cause of death has been established and the parents have received the death certificate, the procurator fiscal normally releases the body to allow for burial or cremation to proceed. However, there may be a delay in releasing the body if further investigations are required (Crown Office and Procurator Fiscal Service [n.d.]).

Northern Ireland

When the results of the post mortem examination are available, the coroner will contact the family to obtain their views on further investigation and inquest. When it has been deemed that further investigation or an inquest is not necessary, the coroner will notify the register of deaths that the stillbirth or neonatal death can be registered with the cause of death on the post mortem report. If an inquest is required, the coroner will contact the register to have the cause of death registered for the stillbirth or death after the hearing.

The coroner will often release the baby's body for burial or cremation after the post mortem examination has been performed (this usually takes place within a few days). In the case of a stillborn baby, the coroner does not need to issue a burial or cremation order for the baby's body to be released for the funeral and the baby can be buried or cremated without further delay. For a baby who died in the neonatal period, the coroner will authorise a cremation or burial order. This usually happens on the day that the post mortem examination is completed and the preliminary results are available. However, doctors will still need to complete cremation forms for stillborn babies and babies who died in the neonatal period before a cremation can proceed (see *Northern Ireland* in *Certification and forms following a stillbirth* above).

Parents can obtain copies of their baby's stillbirth or death certificates through the General Register Office Northern Ireland (GRONI). See *Obtaining copies of stillbirth and death certificates* for more details.

Obtaining copies of stillbirth, birth and death certificates

If the parents did not get a full certificate when they registered their baby's stillbirth, birth or death, if they want more copies of these certificates, or wish to order copies if their baby died many years ago and they did not receive these certificates (Sands 2014e), parents can order these copies from:

- The General Register Office in **England** and **Wales**.
- National Records for Scotland in **Scotland**.
- The General Register Office Northern Ireland (GRONI) in **Northern Ireland**.

See Appendix 2 for details of these organisations.

Parents will be charged a small fee for any certificates that they order.

In **Scotland** and **Northern Ireland**, one of the baby's parents must complete an application form to obtain a *stillbirth certificate* although some exceptions will be made.

In **Northern Ireland**, another relative can only apply for a *stillbirth certificate* if the parents are deceased or unable to apply and they supply a reason for their application.

In **Scotland**, the siblings of the stillborn baby can apply for a stillbirth certificate only if their parents are deceased or on their parents' behalf (with their parents' consent). These certificates are available for stillbirths from 1939 and afterwards. If no name was added previously, the parents (but not siblings) can also request that the baby's name is added to the stillbirth certificate in these instances.

CHAPTER 20

Funerals and sensitive disposal

Other relevant chapters

1: Providing holistic care

2: Providing inclusive care

3: Loss and grief

4: Communication

5: Communication across language
   and other barriers

14: After a loss

15: Postnatal care

16: Transfer to the mortuary and post
    mortem investigations

19: Certificates and registration

21: Memorials

This chapter discusses burial, cremation and sensitive incineration of babies' bodies and fetal remains. It covers what staff and parents need to know about funerals or disposal and the choices that parents should be offered. This includes information about hospital policies and contracts with funeral service providers, private arrangements, legal considerations and other regulations relating to burial, cremation and disposal.

 In the natural, logical order of things, parents are not expected to outlive their children. I should not be burying my son, I should not be burying him. Father

Offering choices to parents

There is growing awareness of the importance of what happens to fetal remains and the bodies of babies who are stillborn or die shortly after birth. Parents' needs and wishes may not be related to the gestational age of their baby or of the nature of their loss.

Legal requirements and guidance

All stillborn babies and babies who die after birth must be buried or cremated by law. This also applies in cases of termination after 24 weeks' gestation. Parents have a legal responsibility to bury or cremate their baby's body although they can consent to have a Trust or Health Board carry this out on their behalf. Parents whose babies are stillborn or die in the neonatal period should be informed about their choices for their baby's burial or cremation.

There is no legal requirement to bury or cremate fetal remains although the legal options for disposal are burial, cremation or incineration in England, Wales and Northern Ireland (HTA Code 5 2014). In Scotland, incineration is not permitted and fetal remains must either be cremated or buried (Scottish Government 2015a). The use of maceration or sluicing for disposing of fetal remains is not permitted.

There is also no legal requirement under the Human Tissue Act 2004 or the Human Tissue (Scotland) Act 2006 to seek parents' consent for the disposal of fetal remains. However, guidance documents issued by the HTA and the Scottish Government highlight the importance of offering women (and their partners if appropriate) information and choices about their available options (HTA 2015; Scottish Government 2015a). Additionally, the Burial and Cremation (Scotland) Bill proposes that new legislation in Scotland should specify who has the right to give instructions for the disposal of the fetal remains (Marsh 2015). The HTA states that:

> The Human Tissue Act 2004 (HT Act) makes no distinction between the disposal of pregnancy remains and the disposal of other tissue from a living person; pregnancy remains are regarded as the tissue of the woman. Although under the HT Act, consent is not required for the disposal of pregnancy remains, the particularly sensitive nature of this tissue means that the wishes of the woman, and her understanding of the disposal options open to her, are of paramount importance and should be respected and acted upon. (HTA 2015: 2)

Women who experience a miscarriage or termination for any reason before 24 weeks' gestation should be given the opportunity to discuss and make choices about their available options for the disposal of fetal remains (RCN 2015; Scottish Government 2015a). Some women may decline information about these options or involvement in decision-making processes regarding the disposal of fetal remains and this should be respected (RCN 2015; Scottish Government 2015a).

Staff in **Scotland** should also be aware that new legislation will be issued as a result of the Burial and Cremation (Scotland) Bill, which had not been passed at the time that this guidance went to press.

See the relevant sections below for more information about *Burial*, *Cremation* and *Sensitive incineration*.

Some parents may also wish to arrange a funeral or other ceremony for their baby although they are not required to have a funeral. Staff should offer to discuss the various funeral options available with all parents. See the section on *Funerals* below for more information.

Written information

All parents should be offered written information that is relevant to the stage at which the pregnancy ended or the baby died, outlining (as appropriate):

- What choices they have if they want the hospital to make the arrangements.

- What choices they have and what they need to do if they want to make their own arrangements or use the services of a funeral director.

- What costs are involved (if any) and what to do if they might be eligible for a Funeral Payment through the government (see *Parents on a low income* later).

When this information is given to parents, staff should make it clear that they are willing and available to talk about any aspect of the arrangements and/or to discuss the range of possibilities.

If possible, written information should also be available in other formats and in the other main languages spoken locally. The content should also take account of any predominant cultural and religious concerns that may be relevant locally.

Discussions with parents

Staff should offer all parents the opportunity to discuss their options for a funeral, burial and/or cremation. For losses before 24 weeks' gestation, this will also include giving parents information about sensitive incineration in England, Wales and Northern Ireland and collective cremation or burial in Scotland.

Some parents may not want to discuss these options and may choose to leave all arrangements to the hospital. This decision should be respected. However, some parents may change their minds later or may want to know what arrangements were made at a later date. In these instances, parents should be told whom to contact and the timescale in which they are able to change their mind.

 The nurse insisted that I choose between burial and cremation and that we must attend the funeral, but I didn't want to be involved in any of that. It seemed weird and unnatural to me to be having a funeral for a pregnancy that ended at 12 weeks. Mother

Other parents will want to discuss the arrangements and their options. These discussions should not be rushed as parents may need time to decide what they want. Some parents may find it difficult to make decisions, especially if they are experiencing shock or grief. Other parents may wish to discuss their options with family, friends or a spiritual advisor. Parents may also want different things and they may need time to reach a decision together (Sands 2014f). Many parents may know nothing or very little about the practical arrangements that have to be made or the choices that are available to them. For some parents, this may be the first time they have had to make decisions about or attend a funeral (Sands 2014f). Parents may also find it difficult to think about what they could do and some may welcome tentative suggestions (Siassakos *et al.* 2015, unpublished results). It is important that staff offer to discuss funeral options with parents and not assume that chaplains or other staff have spoken to parents about these decisions (Siassakos *et al.* 2015, unpublished results).

> *Of all the plans and decisions we had started to make, we never dreamed that deciding about our baby's funeral would be one of them.* Father

Where the option is offered, parents will need to decide whether they want the hospital to make some or all of the arrangements (see also *Funerals arranged by the hospital* below). If parents decide to organise the funeral themselves or use the services of a funeral director, they may still need information from staff about their options or support while making decisions (see also *Arranging a private funeral or ceremony* below).

Staff should also mention any additional options that are available to parents. These options might include an entry in the hospital remembrance book or an individual or shared memorial service (see Chapter 21). Parents should be given the name and contact details of a member of staff whom parents can contact for more information.

Staff who talk with parents should have a thorough understanding of the available local options for babies of different gestations and should know what is possible at local cemeteries and crematoria. Many burial and cremation authorities will arrange for hospital staff to visit and will explain all options available for the burial, cremation and commemoration of babies. Staff should also be able to tell parents who have decided to have a post mortem examination for their baby or whose baby's death has been referred to the coroner or procurator fiscal about how this may affect any arrangements. See Chapter 16 and *Obtaining certificates and registration in coroner's or procurator fiscal cases* in Chapter 19 for more information.

Staff should also be aware of, and open to, different personal, religious and cultural needs (see below). It may be helpful if staff have reflected on their own feelings about the options available and how these may affect their discussions with parents. It is important that staff do not question parents' choices unless there are legal reasons why their wishes cannot be carried out.

Staff may sometimes find checklists or funeral consent forms helpful in ensuring that essential questions are asked and procedures are followed. These should be used for guidance only. Any checklists that staff use when they are eliciting the views and preferences of parents should make it clear that the overriding principle is parental choice. See also *Documentation of parents' choices* below and *Parental choice and checklists* in Chapter 14.

It is important to create an atmosphere where parents are able to honestly express what they want and do not want, ask questions and raise any concerns. Staff should listen carefully and try to support parents to make choices that reflect their own wishes and values. Staff should also acknowledge that these decisions may be difficult and offer parents as much time as they need to make choices.

If parents have not made a decision before they leave the hospital, they should be given the details of whom to contact when they have reached a decision (Sands 2014f). If parents are not taking their baby's body home, they should also be given details of where their baby's body or pregnancy remains will be stored and the length of time that they will be stored (RCN 2015). If parents want the information, they should also be told what arrangements will be made if they do not make a decision within the time stated (RCN 2015). Where hospitals are unable to store remains beyond a specific timeframe, parents should be contacted or sent a reminder before any arrangements are carried out by the hospital. The HTA (2015) recommends that the parents are allowed a defined timeframe in which to advise hospitals of their decision regarding their baby's body or pregnancy remains and suggest that this timeframe does not exceed 12 weeks.

Additional considerations that may affect parents' choices

Costs

It is important that the person who is supporting the parents knows the kinds of costs that may be involved and what is possible locally in terms of making private burial, cremation or funeral arrangements. This person should also advise parents regarding whether they might be eligible for financial support (see *Parents on a low income* below).

To decrease costs for parents, hospital medical staff should waive fees for signing cremation forms for stillborn babies and babies who die shortly after birth.

Some funeral directors might either charge a nominal fee or make no charge for their standard private funeral for a baby. However, parents may have to pay for any additional features. Many cemeteries and crematoria do not charge for funerals for babies.

Depending on their wishes, parents may need to consider other fees such as:

- The fees linked to having a funeral service if they choose to have one. This may include fees for a religious service, humanist celebrant, flowers or a coffin if the parents want these options.

- Crematorium fees that parents may need to pay if their baby is cremated (these may not always be charged).

- The costs of a plaque or any other form of memorial at a crematorium if their baby is cremated.

- In England, Wales and Northern Ireland, the Medical Referee at the crematorium must sign a form to authorise the cremation of a stillborn baby or a baby who died shortly after birth. There may be a fee for this. However, in the case of the individual or shared cremation of fetal remains or babies born dead before 24 weeks, guidance from the Ministry of Justice (2012c) states that a Medical Referee should not complete a form to authorise cremation. Therefore, no fee is payable under these circumstances.

- The cost of buying a private burial plot in a municipal cemetery. This may be expensive, although sometimes, it is possible to buy a smaller child's plot that is less costly. Alternatively, it may be possible to buy a place in a shared grave, although many cemeteries do not charge for a place in a shared grave.

- If the family already owns the exclusive right to a grave in a cemetery (i.e. a family plot), the baby can normally be buried there provided that the family member that owns the exclusive right for burial gives written permission. There will be a charge for digging or reopening the grave.

- Additional fees for burial in a churchyard if space and local regulations permit. This option is less expensive although there will still be fees for services such as digging the grave.

- The purchase of a headstone if parents wish to buy one for their baby's grave and this is permitted. For advice on gravestones and memorials, parents can contact cemetery staff, a local funeral director or a monumental mason. To find a local monumental mason, parents can contact the National Association of Memorial Masons (see Appendix 2). Parents should be advised to seek a number of quotations for the provision of a memorial and seek assurance that it will be installed in accordance with British Standard 8415. A local Sands group or another bereavement support group may also be able to give advice.

Parents on a low income

Parents of babies who are stillborn at or after 24 weeks or who are born alive and then die at any gestation may be eligible for a Funeral Payment. To be eligible, one or both parents must be receiving at least one benefit or tax credit.

This payment will cover:

- Burial fees and exclusive rights to burial on a plot.
- Cremation fees.
- Travel expenses to arrange and attend the funeral.
- Up to £700 for funeral expenses.

A Funeral Expenses Payment must be claimed within three months of the funeral. However, these payments are currently under review by the Department of Work and Pensions.

In **England, Wales and Scotland**, parents can download and print a claim form from the government website and take this to their local Job Centre Plus or return it by post. They can also phone the Bereavement Services Helpline to file a claim (see Appendix 2). Parents must attach receipts or invoices for all expenses along with payment details. These expenses can be paid directly to a funeral director or to the parents if they have already paid any relevant bills.

More information and claims forms are available in the Funeral Payments section of the UK Government website (see Appendix 2). Parents can also call the Pension Service or visit their local Job Centre Plus to access claim forms and information. If parents need help with the application form, they should make an appointment at the Job Centre Plus.

In **Northern Ireland**, parents can access more information or download and print a claim form from the Funeral Payments section of the NI Direct website (see Appendix 2). They can also obtain claim forms and file claims at their local Social Security or Jobs and Benefits office.

For information about other benefits for which parents may be eligible, see *Entitlement to time off work and benefits* in Chapter 15.

Multiple births

If parents have twins or more babies who were multiples and have died, they may wish to consider whether or not they want their babies to share a funeral, burial, cremation and/or coffin (Sands 2014f). In these circumstances, parents are legally able to bury or cremate more than one baby in the same coffin (ICCM 2014), although some parents may decide to have separate coffins for each baby.

If one or more surviving babies is still on the neonatal unit after their sibling dies, parents may also wish to delay the funeral (Sands 2014f). Parents should be given time to consider the options and arrangements that are right for them and their family (Sands 2014f).

Personal, cultural and religious considerations

Different people, cultural groups and religious groups have various ways of managing death and funerals. Assumptions should not be made about what any individual will want on the basis of their heritage or religion. There may be differences in practice between different denominations and traditions of the same religion. Individual parents' decisions and wishes may also be different even if they belong to the same religious or ethnic group.

The following is a list of potential examples of cultural or religious practices that healthcare professionals may encounter. This is not an exhaustive list as it is not possible to list all of the personal, cultural and religious factors that may influence parents' choices about their baby's body or funeral arrangements.

- For some families, the extended family may be heavily involved in making funeral arrangements.

- Some women may expect or prefer their husbands to be excluded from decisions about funeral arrangements. In some instances, older female relatives may be a more significant source of support for a bereaved mother. Conversely, men may be more involved in some formal and public religious events such as funerals and women may sometimes be excluded.

- Some parents may want members of their own religion to prepare the baby's body for the funeral.

- Although attending a funeral is right for many parents, this is not always an option. For example, some religions or denominations do not traditionally hold funerals or other ceremonies for a stillborn baby or a baby born dead before 24 weeks. Others may not allow women to go to the graveside.

- For many parents, the decision about burial or cremation is a personal one. For some parents, their choices may also be affected by religious requirements. For example, burial traditionally takes place within 24 hours of death for some observant Jews and Muslims. Some observant Jews and Muslims may also want to bury all fetal remains if the loss occurs at an early gestation. Although Sikh and Hindu adults are normally cremated, it is traditional in these communities for babies to be buried as soon as possible after the death.

Staff should discuss all available options with all parents regardless of their religious or cultural background. Parents may also wish to speak to a spiritual or religious leader from their own faith if they are uncertain about specific religious or cultural requirements for their baby's funeral. Wherever possible, the personal, cultural or religious needs of parents should be met in these circumstances (HTA 2015). It is important that individualised care is provided for all parents and that assumptions are not made based on their cultural or religious background.

Urgent burials or cremation

For some parents, personal circumstances or religious considerations may mean that they need to organise an urgent burial or cremation for their baby. This may not always be possible, particularly when the baby's stillbirth or death has been referred to the coroner or procurator fiscal. However, staff should do what they can to support parents who wish to organise an urgent burial or cremation for their baby. See *Urgent burials and cremation* in Chapter 19 for more information.

Documentation of parents' choices

Any decisions that parents make regarding their options for their baby's burial or cremation, the disposal of fetal remains or a hospital arranged funeral should be documented in the woman's or baby's medical records (HTA 2015). It should also be documented if a woman chooses not to receive information or be involved in these decisions (HTA 2015).

A written record of any decisions made should be given to the parents. This may be helpful if parents wish to double check any arrangements that they have made or agreed to in discussions with staff. It is good practice to have a separate funeral consent form that is signed by the parents and that details the options discussed with parents and the choices parents have made (Scottish Government 2015a). See Appendix 1: Form 5 for a sample funeral consent form that could be adapted for local needs. This form can also be downloaded from the Sands website.

Releasing the body or remains to the parents

There is no legal reason why parents should not be able to take their baby's body or remains from the hospital or mortuary and make their own arrangements. They may also wish to take their baby home before a hospital arranged funeral or take the baby to the funeral, cemetery or crematorium themselves. Staff should support parents who want to do this and there should be sensitive and efficient procedures in place. Parents may wish to carry their baby in their arms or a Moses basket and should be offered a suitable container for fetal remains. Parents of a stillborn baby or of a baby who died shortly after birth should also be given information about the regulations relating to funerals, burial and cremation (see *Legal requirements and guidance* above).

If parents are picking up their baby's body following a post mortem examination, the mortuary staff should ensure that fetal remains and babies' bodies are well presented and the appropriate paperwork is ready. See *Releasing the baby's body or remains to the parents* in Chapter 16 for more information.

No documentation is legally required but a form should be issued by staff to accompany the body to protect the parents and avoid misunderstandings. For a sample form, see Appendix 1: Form 1. The hospital or mortuary should also keep a record that the body has been released to the parents.

 We left the hospital ... bringing Matthew and his tiny coffin with us. Matthew was buried the next afternoon and it was such a sad day. For me the worst part was walking away from the graveyard knowing that I would never get to see my baby again. Mother

For more information, see *Taking the baby's body home* in Chapter 15.

What options are available to parents?

Staff should be aware of, and have access to, information about local burial and cremation options. Parents should be given the details of all available options for burial and cremation that can be arranged by the hospital or privately before they make a decision. If the loss occurred prior to 24 weeks' gestation, they should also be told about their options for sensitive incineration in England, Wales and Northern Ireland or "collective cremation" in Scotland.

If parents decline to be involved in these decisions or discuss any information related to these options, this should be respected (RCN 2015). However, parents should be told that this information is available should they wish to access this information later (RCN 2015). When parents have not made a decision before leaving the hospital or clinic, they should be told how long the baby or remains will be stored for and what arrangements will be made if they do not make a decision in this timeframe (RCN 2015) (see also *Discussions with parents* above).

This guidance does not cover arranging for burial or cremation outside of the country where the baby died. Staff should offer to help parents contact the registrar for advice in these circumstances.

Burial

Burial can be arranged by the hospital in some areas or parents may choose to make private burial arrangements. Parents may wish to wash or dress their baby or ask a funeral director, hospital staff or member of their religious community to do this before the burial. Parents who wish to bury their baby may also wish to include special items such as a cuddly toy, blanket, religious item, letter or poem for burial with their baby.

Burial arranged by the hospital

Some hospitals offer parents a choice as to whether their baby is buried in a shared or an individual grave. Other hospitals only offer parents the options of having their baby buried in a shared grave and others may be unable to offer parents the offer of burial in areas where graves are very expensive (Sands 2014f). However, many cemeteries do not charge a fee for the burial of a baby and staff should check local arrangements.

In a shared burial, each baby or fetus should be in an individual sealed container or coffin that is contained within a larger sealed container (HTA 2015; RCN 2015; Scottish Government 2015a). The written information that is available to parents should include the details of these arrangements and the cemetery where the baby will be buried. Staff should also be aware of the details of the hospital's contract with the local cemetery if applicable (see *Contract with a cemetery* below).

If their baby will be buried in a shared grave, parents should be given the full details of this arrangement in advance. They should be told how many babies will be in the grave and be given an estimate of how long it is likely to be before the grave is closed and the ground properly reinstated (see *Contract with a cemetery* below). Parents should also be told that once a baby of any gestation has been buried in a *shared grave* it may not be possible to exhume the body later and bury it elsewhere (see *Exhumation* later). Some parents find it comforting to know that their baby will be buried with other babies. Other parents find the idea upsetting and might prefer to make their own arrangements.

 At first the idea of a shared grave seemed very strange. But when we thought about it, we were comforted by the thought that our baby would not be alone. Father

Parents also need to know in advance about any local regulations affecting shared and individual graves. This will prevent parents from discovering that they cannot commemorate their baby in the way that they planned when it is too late for them to consider alternatives. These regulations are decided locally. Some examples of local policies and options that may affect parents' decisions include:

- Some cemeteries do not permit headstones of any kind on a communal grave as space would not be available to accommodate memorials for all babies buried within the grave. If no headstone is permitted, there is sometimes a communal memorial nearby and it may be possible to have the baby's name and dates of birth and death engraved on this.

- Other cemeteries have regulations about the type and size of headstone that is permitted.

- Rules in some cemeteries do not allow any flowers on a shared grave.

- Some cemetery policies do not permit having personal items such as pictures or a teddy bear on any grave.

- Some cemeteries have a specific area set aside where flowers and personal items can be placed.

- Some cemeteries have a book of remembrance in which the baby's name can be entered.

When a baby is stillborn or dies in the neonatal period, parents should also be told to give the certificate issued by the registrar that allows for the baby's burial to the relevant hospital administrator. This is not required for a loss that occurs before 24 weeks' gestation. See also *Registration* in Chapter 19 for more details.

Records should be kept by the hospital and cemetery of the date and location of all individual and shared burials arranged by the hospital.

Privately arranged burial

Some parents may decide to pay for a private, single plot in a cemetery although this may be expensive (see *Costs* above). Parents may wish to purchase a smaller plot in the children's section of the cemetery or purchase a full-size plot where they could also be buried in the future. If parents purchase a full-size plot, they should check local policies and regulations concerning the reuse of used or partially used plots. Staff may also wish to suggest that parents consider having both of their names registered when they purchase the plot so that they both have the right of burial there in the future. The deed for the exclusive right of burial will be issued to parents after the plot is purchased. Many cemeteries have regulations about the kinds of memorials allowed on single graves and parents should be told about these before purchasing a plot.

Some parents may want to have their baby buried in a nearby or familiar cemetery. Others parents may want their baby to be buried in a cemetery or an area of a cemetery that is specifically reserved for members of their faith. The availability of these options will depend on space and local regulations.

When a baby is stillborn or dies in the neonatal period, parents will need the certificate issued by the registrar that allows for the baby's burial to arrange the burial themselves or to give to a funeral director (see *Registration* in Chapter 19 for more details). This is not required for a loss that occurs before 24 weeks' gestation. However, some cemeteries may require proof that the baby was not born after 24 weeks' gestation and staff should provide parents with a form or letter confirming that this is the case (see

Certification and forms for a baby born dead before 24 weeks' gestation in Chapter 19). Local authority cemeteries will also require parents or the person responsible for the burial to complete an additional burial application. The information provided on this form is used to register full details in the cemetery registers and records. These registers and records can be inspected in the future free of charge.

Cemeteries and burial grounds will retain a register of the date and location of burials.

Burial on private land

Some parents may want to bury their baby in their own garden or in some other place that holds special meaning for them. Alternatively, there are an increasing number of woodland and natural or green burial sites where parents can bury their baby in England, Wales and Scotland. There is currently no provision for this service in Northern Ireland. For more information and details of local sites and information about burial on private land, contact the Natural Death Centre (see Appendix 2).

Staff may be able to help parents consider their options. They could also offer to put parents in touch with other professionals (such as a funeral director, the local council's Environmental Health Department or the local authority cemetery office) and the Natural Death Centre for more information. Some local authorities provide a natural burial area within their cemeteries and this can be checked locally.

There is no legal prohibition affecting the burial of a body on private land. However, parents may need to think carefully about burying their baby on private land as they might move house or the land could possibly be used for new purposes. They may want to consider exhumation requirements if they may later wish to move their baby's body in these instances (see below). Parents should also consider how this will affect the value of their property and potential resale.

Parents who wish to bury their baby on private land in **England and Wales** will also need to check that:

- The owner of the freehold of the land gives permission, if the parent(s) is not the freeholder.

- The freeholder has checked that there are no deed or registration restrictions prohibiting burial. If the property is mortgaged it may be prudent to inform the mortgage company before the burial takes place as it may affect the resale of the property. It may also be prudent to consult the appropriate authority if the property is in a conservation area.

- The burial meets Environment Agency regulations regarding the depth of burial, preparation of the grave and the distance of burial from specific water and drainage sources. See the Environment Agency's (n.d.) document *Funeral practices, spreading ashes and caring for the environment: meeting the needs of families and the environment* for more details.

- The owner of the land or their agent must also keep a register of the details of the burial (Jarvis and Natural Death Centre 2010).

In **Scotland,** parents will need to check local laws and regulations about burial on private land along with those pertaining to public health and planning (South Ayrshire Council [n.d.]). They should also check with the Scottish Environment Protection Agency (SEPA) regarding the proximity of the burial to water supplies and obtain permission from their mortgage provider if applicable (South Ayrshire Council [n.d.]). There is no legal requirement to register home burials on private land (South Ayrshire Council [n.d.]). However, details of the burial should be noted and kept with the deeds of the property (South Ayrshire Council [n.d.]). Legislation is also being considered in Scotland that will offer more clear guidance for burial on private land (Marsh 2015). The Burial and Cremation (Scotland) Bill proposes that an application for approval of a burial on private land is made to the local authority and that the burial will be registered with the local authority.

Exhumation

Occasionally, a family might want to exhume the baby's body after burial. For example, some families may later decide that they want to have the baby buried in the same grave as another family member or wish to move the grave to another location. It is important that accurate records are kept so that the location of the grave and the exact position of the coffin in the grave can be identified. It is also important that parents are aware that this process may be difficult and costly.

Depending on the condition of the body at burial and the length of time that has elapsed, it may not be possible to find identifiable remains. If this is likely, parents should be told before they start the process of gaining permission to exhume the baby's body.

It is an offence to exhume the body of a baby born at or after 24 weeks' gestation or who died after birth without the necessary permissions. This will vary based on local regulations, which parents should check with their local authority. No permission is required to exhume a baby born dead before 24 weeks' gestation from private land.

In **England** and **Wales,** parents will require an exhumation licence from the Ministry of Justice. The parents will also need permission from the grave owner, burial authority and/or land owner (for private burial).

In **England**, parents will also need a Faculty (a type of authorisation) from the local Church of England Diocese if the grave is situated on consecrated ground in churchyards and cemeteries.

In **Scotland,** parents will require a solicitor to gain permission from the cemetery administrator to check whether exhumation is feasible and obtain a warrant from the local Sheriff Court. The Burial and Cremation (Scotland) Bill also proposes that new legislation includes a recommendation to facilitate the application process for exhumation (Marsh 2015).

In **Northern Ireland,** parents will need to obtain permission from the local authority, the appropriate Public Health Agency and the consent of the Department of the Environment for Northern Ireland. If the burial is on consecrated ground, they need the consent of the church authority. In all cases, the Police Service of Northern Ireland (PSNI) must be informed when the body is exhumed.

The exhumation of a baby who died before 24 weeks' gestation does not require a licence unless the burial was on consecrated ground; in which case, parents will need to obtain the permission of the church.

It is also highly unlikely that permission will be granted to exhume a baby or fetal remains that have been buried in a shared grave. If the remains of other babies will need to be removed or disturbed, permission will need to be sought from the parents of all other babies in the grave. This may be difficult to obtain, particularly if all parents must first be traced to request consent. A licence will also be needed to exhume the graves of any babies who were stillborn or died after birth and were placed in the grave after the baby who is to be exhumed. This may be more complicated if baby's coffins are stacked on top of each other rather than side by side.

The exhumation procedure must be carried out in such a way that complies with the conditions set out in the licence, warrant or permission granted by the church. Respect for the deceased must be maintained and public health must also be protected during the exhumation. Details of the regulations and requirements are available from the relevant local authority.

Cremation

Cremation can often be arranged by the hospital or parents may choose to make private cremation arrangements. Hospitals may offer parents the choice of shared or individual cremation. Others may only offer one of these options. The recovery of ashes and alternative options should be discussed with all parents and they should be given the choice of receiving ashes when their baby is cremated (see *Ashes* below).

Parents may wish to wash or dress their baby or ask a funeral director, hospital staff or member of their religious community to do this before the cremation. They should also be told about any crematorium policies or regulations about materials that can or cannot be cremated with their baby. This is because some parents like to purchase their own coffin or include toys or other items in the coffin with the baby.

Many crematoria have a designated area for memorials to babies that have died. The crematorium's regulations regarding placing items or memorials near the place where their baby's ashes may be buried or scattered should also be explained to parents (Sands 2014f). In some places, parents can have their baby's name inscribed on a plaque or memorial stone.

All crematoria have books of remembrance in which the baby's name can be entered.

Shared cremation

A shared cremation is when a hospital arranges for the bodies or remains of several babies to be cremated at the same time. This may be referred to as "collective cremation" in Scotland. Collective cremation is the minimum standard allowed for the disposal of any fetal remains in Scotland. For a shared cremation, each baby or fetus should be in an individual sealed container or coffin that is contained within a larger sealed container (HTA 2015; RCN 2015; Scottish Government 2015a).

Crematoria cremate the shared cremation on a tray in order to protect the ashes. Parents should be told that no individually identifiable ashes will be available following a shared cremation. Staff should also be aware of local arrangements regarding where ashes from shared cremations are scattered. Many crematoria have a dedicated area for scattering babies' ashes where it might be possible to arrange for a small memorial. Parents should be given the choice of having information about where their baby's ashes will be buried or scattered by the crematorium and any options for having a memorial.

Parents should also be told about alternative options for arranging an individual cremation or burial, particularly as some parents may wish to have individually identifiable ashes (see more about *Ashes* below).

Individual cremation

An individual cremation is when a baby is placed in the cremator one at a time. The baby is placed on a tray that protects and maximises the recovery of ashes. Some hospitals might arrange individual cremations or parents may choose to make their own arrangements with a crematorium. Cremation outside of a crematorium is not legal in the UK.

Parents should be given information about the likelihood of recovering ashes after cremation before they make a decision about cremating their baby (see *Ashes* below).

Ashes

The Infant Cremation Commission's (2014) report called for ashes to be statutorily defined as:

> *All that is left in the cremator at the end of the cremation process and following the removal of any metal.* (Infant Cremation Commission 2014: 5, Section 2.3)

This definition should be applied for ashes irrespective of their composition (Scottish Government 2015a). While this definition has not yet been made statutory, any ashes left in the cremator should routinely be offered to parents following the individual cremation of their baby (Sands 2015b). A definition of ashes is expected to be included in new legislation in **Scotland** that is to be implemented following the proposals of the Burial and Cremation (Scotland) Bill (Marsh 2015). A definition may also be included in legislation in **England** and **Wales** following a review of the Cremation (England and Wales) Regulations 2008.

Many bereaved parents view what is left in the cremator as their baby's ashes regardless of what they contain. Some parents may be distressed if they do not receive ashes after their baby's cremation or later learn that ashes were produced following their baby's cremation that were stored, scattered or buried (see *When ashes have been stored or scattered without parents' knowledge* below).

In very few cases, there may not be any ashes left in the cremator following the individual cremation of a baby. This is more likely if the baby was born before 17 weeks' gestation (Sands 2014f). Whether or not a crematorium can produce ashes during the cremation of babies also depends on the technique used and the ability to reduce turbulence during the cremation cycle.

Parents should be told about the likelihood of receiving ashes based on their baby's gestation, condition and the practices of the crematorium where the hospital has a contract (see also *Contract with a crematorium* below). Parents should also be told to ask the crematorium about their policy regarding the recovery of ashes if they are making private arrangements (ICCM and Sands 2014).

If parents cannot be offered ashes, they should be provided with information about other options such as using an alternative crematorium or burial. This will give parents the choice of making other arrangements even if they must pay for these options.

Offering parents choices when ashes are recovered

All of the choices that parents make regarding their baby's ashes should be documented and a copy should be given to parents by hospital staff, a funeral director or the crematorium depending on who is discussing these choices with parents (see also *Documentation of parents' choices* above).

Following a shared cremation where there are no identifiable individual ashes, parents should be given the choice to know where any ashes are buried or scattered. A record of the date and location when this occurred should be kept by the crematorium and the hospital. This information should remain available to parents should they wish to know the location of their baby's ashes in the future.

When individual ashes are available following a baby's cremation, parents should be offered the choice of receiving these ashes. They should also be given the following options regarding what will happen with the ashes:

- Scattering or burial of the ashes by the crematorium with or without the parents in attendance.

- Collection of the ashes by the parents or their appointed representative (this may be a funeral director or a hospital administrator).

- Storage of the ashes at the crematorium. If the crematorium is only able to store the ashes for a limited time period, the parents should be given this information in writing and told what will happen if they do not make arrangements to have the ashes collected within the allotted time (Scottish Government 2015b).

Some parents may need more time to decide whether they wish to have their baby's ashes or if they wish for the crematorium to scatter or bury their baby's ashes. Parents should be told how long they have to make a decision and whether the crematorium will scatter or bury the ashes if they do not make a decision in the allotted time. The crematorium should contact or send a reminder to parents before they scatter or bury the ashes. Some crematoria will continue to store ashes if a parent asks for more time to make a decision. A funeral director may also be able to store the ashes for a longer period of time than the crematorium while the parents make a decision. When the crematorium scatters or buries the ashes, the location and date should be recorded and this information should be offered to parents and remain available should they want to know more in the future.

If parents wish to receive ashes and the hospital is arranging the cremation, they should also inform parents about when and where they can collect their baby's ashes. For a privately arranged cremation, the funeral director or crematorium should tell parents when their baby's ashes can be collected.

Parents should also be told about the usual methods of disposal for metal recovered from an individual cremation and be told about their options for disposal of this metal (ICCM and Sands 2014). Parents' consent should be obtained before disposal (ICCM and Sands 2014).

If parents wish to receive their baby's ashes, they may also like to consider what they would like to do with them. Parents should be reassured that they can take time to make these decisions.

Some parents may choose to scatter or bury the ashes at the crematorium or another place of their choice. If parents choose to scatter the ashes on water, the Environment Agency (n.d.) states that they must check that they are not scattering ashes:

- Within one kilometre upstream of any water supply (they can call the local Environment Agency office to check).
- Near buildings, bathers, anglers or marinas.
- In windy weather to avoid the risk of ashes affecting other people or businesses.

They should also scatter the ashes as close to the water's surface as possible and check whether they will affect anyone else who is downstream (Environment Agency [n.d.]). No other items or tributes should be placed in or near the water because of the potential risk to wildlife and pollution concerns (Environment Agency [n.d.]). Burial of ashes is not believed to pose a risk to the environment (Environment Agency [n.d.]).

Other parents may want to keep their babies' ashes. Some may choose to place their baby's ashes in an urn, have jewellery made with the ashes or consider other options.

When ashes have been stored or scattered without parents' knowledge

When ashes have been stored or scattered by crematoria or funeral directors without parents' knowledge, parents should be contacted and, depending on the circumstances, be offered the options of being told where their baby's ashes have been scattered, collecting the ashes or having the ashes sent to them (Sands 2015b). This correspondence should contain:

- An acknowledgement that receiving the letter may be distressing for parents.

- Information about the support offered by Sands.

- A note stating that the information about the location of their baby's ashes will be available should they wish to receive it in the future (Sands 2015b).

Contacting parents will offer them transparent information about their baby's ashes and the choice to know the location of or receive these ashes (Sands 2015b). If the hospital was the applicant for the cremation, the crematorium or funeral director may need to contact the hospital to obtain contact details for parents.

Paperwork required for cremation

Paperwork for cremation of stillborn babies or babies who die shortly after birth

The forms required to bury or cremate a stillborn baby or a baby who died shortly after birth are different in each UK country (see the details for each country below). Parents should give the relevant documentation to the hospital if they are arranging the cremation, the funeral director or directly to the crematorium if they are making their own arrangements. If a baby's death has been referred to the coroner or procurator fiscal, the procedures will be different than those listed below and they will issue the forms required for the baby to be cremated. Parents will still need to complete any application forms required by the crematorium and, in Northern Ireland, cremation forms will still need to be completed by medical practitioners (see *Obtaining certificates and registration in coroner's or procurator fiscal cases* in Chapter 19 for more information).

More details about the specific forms that are required from healthcare staff and registrars to cremate babies born dead before 24 weeks' gestation, stillborn babies or babies who die shortly after birth are available in Chapter 19.

England and Wales

If parents wish to cremate their baby who died shortly after birth, they will need a cremation form to be signed by a registered doctor and a certificate from the registrar authorising the cremation. They will also need to complete an *Application for cremation of a deceased person* or ask a member of the hospital bereavement staff to complete this form. If they have specific concerns, the medical referee at the crematorium may also require that a second medical practitioner completes and signs a cremation form. The medical referee will issue a form to authorise the cremation unless they are not satisfied with the cause of death listed on the forms and the coroner does not request an inquest or post mortem examination. In these instances, the medical referee would refuse the cremation application and order a post mortem examination to be performed (Ministry of Justice 2012c). It should be acknowledged that this may be distressing for parents and they should be offered support.

Parents who wish to cremate their stillborn baby will need the certificate authorising cremation that is issued by the registrar after they register the stillbirth. They will also need to complete an *Application for cremation of stillborn baby* following a stillbirth or ask a member of the hospital bereavement staff to complete this form for them (Ministry of Justice 2012b). If the medical referee who is employed by the local council to check cremation certificates is satisfied with the cremation application and certificate of stillbirth, they will then complete an *Authorisation of cremation of remains of stillborn child by medical referee* form (Ministry of Justice 2012b).

Scotland

If parents wish to cremate their baby in Scotland, a separate cremation form is no longer required from healthcare staff under the Certification of Death (Scotland) Act 2011. However, parents or a member of the hospital staff will need to complete an *Application for cremation* that details whether or not the parents have given consent for the cremation before the baby can be cremated.

There is no longer a legal requirement for medical referees to be employed by crematoria to check cremation forms in Scotland (NAFD 2015). Crematoria managers will now be responsible for ensuring that a neonatal death or stillbirth has been registered and that a Certificate of Stillbirth has been issued for stillborn babies as these are not being checked by Medical Reviewers (NAFD 2015). They will also check the *Application for cremation* to ensure that there are no hazards linked with cremating a stillborn baby or baby who died shortly after birth (NAFD 2015).

Northern Ireland

To cremate their baby, parents will need a form from the registrar after registering the stillbirth or neonatal death that allows for the cremation to take place.

A cremation form and a confirmatory medical certificate form must be completed and signed by different medical practitioners before a baby who dies shortly after birth or a stillborn baby can be cremated in Northern Ireland (DHSSPSNI 2008) (see *Northern Ireland* under *Certification and forms following a stillbirth* in Chapter 19 for more details). These forms must still be completed even when the stillbirth or neonatal death has been referred to the coroner (DHSSPSNI 2008). A medical referee must then complete an additional form for the Cremation Authority to authorise the cremation (DHSSPSNI 2008).

Paperwork for the cremation of fetal remains or babies born dead before 24 weeks' gestation

For fetal remains and babies who are born dead before 24 weeks' gestation, there are no statutory cremation forms required. However, crematoria may still cremate fetal remains and babies born dead before 24 weeks' gestation. The crematorium will need confirmation of the gestation of the loss, which is usually in the form of a medical form or letter (see *Certification and forms for a baby born dead before 24 weeks' gestation* in Chapter 19 for more information).

Parents or healthcare professionals may also need to complete additional forms required by the crematorium before the cremation can take place. Some crematoria do not have standard forms covering the cremation of fetal remains and babies born dead before 24 weeks' gestation. It may be helpful to suggest that they use the following forms found in Appendix 1 of these guidelines or in the Appendices of the ICCM document called *Policy and Guidance for Baby and Infant Funerals* (see Appendix 1):

- Appendix 1: Form 3. *Medical form for burial or cremation confirming that fetal remains are less than 24 weeks' gestation.*

- Appendix 1: Form 4. *Application form for the individual burial/ cremation of fetal remains.*

- ICCM document: Appendix B. *Application for Shared/Communal Burial/Cremation of Fetal Remains at Crematorium.*

Notifying the registrar after a burial or cremation following stillbirth or neonatal death

In **England and Wales**, the registrar must be notified within 96 hours of the burial or cremation of a baby who dies in the neonatal period. The person who notifies the registrar must return the counterfoil, called Part C, which is attached to the certificate issued by the registrar or coroner to authorise the burial or cremation. The person who is responsible for completing Part C of this certificate is usually a cemetery or crematorium officer or the parents if they are making their own arrangements for burial on private land.

If the registrar is not notified within 14 days of the burial or cremation, they must make enquiries. If the registrar finds that the body has not been disposed of in an appropriate manner, he or she must inform the relevant authorities. If it appears that no suitable arrangements for disposal have been or are being made, the local council has a duty to dispose of a body under Section 46 of the Public Health (Control of Disease) Act 1984. If the registrar believes that the body has been buried or cremated and they have not received notice within 96 hours of the event, they must report this matter to the General Register Office.

There is no need to inform the registrar following the cremation or burial of a baby who is stillborn.

In **Northern Ireland**, there is no legislative equivalent to Section 46 of the Public Health (Control of Disease) Act 1984. If a burial takes place in Northern Ireland, the person who is responsible for the burial ground must give notice of the burial to the registrar within seven days if they do not receive the registrar's or coroner's certificate authorising the disposal of the body.

In **Scotland**, the registrar no longer needs to be notified after a burial or cremation takes place as all stillbirths and deaths must now be registered beforehand.

Sensitive incineration

In England, Wales and Northern Ireland, sensitive incineration can be used in specific circumstances to dispose of fetal remains from miscarriage or termination before 24 weeks' gestation. These remains are incinerated separately from clinical waste. The HTA (2015) states that:

> *Incineration should only occur where the woman makes this choice, or does not want to be involved in the decision, or does not express an*

opinion within the stated timescale … and the hospital considers this the most appropriate method of disposal. (HTA 2015: 2–3, paragraph 5)

Sensitive incineration cannot be used to dispose of fetal remains in Scotland where "collective cremation" or "collective burial" are the minimum standards that are permitted for disposal (Scottish Government 2015a).

The option of sensitive incineration should be available to all woman who experience a miscarriage or termination of pregnancy in England, Wales or Northern Ireland (HTA 2015; RCN 2015; Sands 2015c). The difference between sensitive incineration and cremation and the local processes for incineration should be sensitively explained to women when staff are discussing the available options so that they are able to make a fully informed decision (RCN 2015). Any written information given to parents about the disposal options that are available or will be used by the hospital should clearly state if sensitive incineration will be used if parents do not wish to be involved in the decision-making process. Sensitive incineration should not be referred to as cremation by staff.

Sensitive incineration may be the preferred option for some women and their decision should be respected (HTA 2015; RCN 2015). If the woman has not made a decision in the time given, the hospital has the right to dispose of the remains. The means of disposal that will be used by the hospital in these circumstances should be explained to the woman before she leaves the hospital or clinic, unless she declines this information. The woman should also be contacted or sent a reminder by the hospital or clinic before any arrangements are made for disposal.

The disposal process for sensitive incineration should involve having any fetal remains or tissue packaged in suitable containers, stored and incinerated separately from clinical waste (HTA 2015; RCN 2015). The date of collection and the location of incineration should be recorded in the woman's medical notes should she wish to access this information later (RCN 2015).

Funerals or ceremonies

Some parents may wish to organise a funeral or ceremony for their baby, regardless of the gestation or nature of their loss. Other parents will decide not to have a service for their baby. This is not a requirement. The cost of a funeral may also affect some parents' choices about their baby's funeral (see *Costs* above). Some parents may need reassurance that the amount of money they spend on their baby's funeral is not a measure of their love for their baby or their grief. Parents should also be advised of financial support that may be available to help with funeral costs (See *Parents on a low income* above for more details).

Some parents may find having a funeral or ceremony for their baby distressing but may also welcome the opportunity to acknowledge and celebrate their baby's life (Sands 2014f). Funerals and other rituals or blessings have been found to be therapeutic, supportive and comforting for some parents of stillborn babies (Capitulo *et al*. 2014). Having a funeral or ceremony might also provide parents with an opportunity to create and share memories of their baby with any family and friends that they may choose to invite. Additionally, a funeral or ceremony may give family and friends a formal opportunity to express their sympathy and support.

A funeral or ceremony can take many forms. Some funerals or ceremonies may be religious services while others will be non-religious or have a mixture of religious and non-religious content. Parents may wish to hire a funeral director or arrange a funeral or ceremony themselves. Some parents may wish for their baby's funeral to be arranged by the hospital where this option is available. Other parents may want their baby's body or remains to be buried, cremated or sensitively incinerated by the hospital. Some parents may wish to take their baby's body home before the funeral or take their baby to the funeral themselves (see *Releasing the body or remains to the parents* above and *Taking the baby's body home* in Chapter 15).

> *I brushed his hair and put him in the new cardigan I had bought him. I got to do all the things I'd looked forward to doing, it was my chance to show him all the love I had.* Mother

The timing of the funeral may be affected by:

- Any post mortem examinations that are being carried out (see also Chapter 16).
- The baby's death having been referred to the coroner or procurator fiscal (see also Chapter 19).
- The mother's health if she is very ill after the birth.
- The health of any surviving siblings from multiple births (see *Multiple births* above).
- Religious or cultural factors (see *Personal, cultural and religious considerations* above).
- Personal circumstances (for example, family travel arrangements).

It is important that parents are informed about the available funeral options if they wish to have this information and are supported to make decisions that are right for them. Parents may find the Sands booklet *Deciding about a funeral for your baby* helpful when they are making decisions or arrangements regarding a funeral or ceremony for their baby. This is available from the online Sands Shop (see Appendix 2).

Parents may invite staff to their baby's funeral and some staff may choose to attend services that are arranged by the hospital.

Funerals arranged by the hospital

> *We went to the funeral. We felt we just had to be there even though it was incredibly painful. It was a simple one, arranged by the hospital. I am so grateful they did that for us. I couldn't have possibly done it myself.* Mother

Many parents want the hospital to arrange a funeral for their baby. The funeral options available are dependent on the hospital. When a hospital arranged funeral is offered and parents want this information, they should be told whether the funeral that will be arranged will be an individual or shared funeral and whether it is religious or non-denominational. They should also be told whether they have options to have the baby or remains buried, cremated or sensitively incinerated and whether individual or shared burial or cremation will be offered (see more about *Burial*, *Cremation* and *Sensitive incineration* options above).

Any options that are available for a hospital arranged funeral should be discussed with parents so that they can make the choice that is right for them. They should also be told about their options for arranging a funeral privately. Parents who have not made a decision about a funeral before they leave the hospital should be given the details of whom to contact when they have made a decision and how long they have to make a decision before arrangements are made by the hospital.

Before the woman leaves hospital, a note must be made of the address and telephone number where she can be contacted. Unless the parents have asked not to be informed, the member of staff arranging the funeral should try to check by phone that they have received the information about the funeral. They should also contact parents who have not made a decision about a funeral to remind them of the timeframe when a decision must be made before the hospital makes any arrangements.

Parents attending a hospital arranged funeral

Parents should be asked if they would like to attend or be informed of the date and time of the funeral (whether they attend or not). Some parents may not want to attend but may want to know the date and time or send flowers. If the hospital has a set time for shared funerals, the parents should be informed of the date, time and of the type of ceremony that will be performed. If the hospital offers an individual funeral, the date and time should be agreed with the parents before booking and then confirmed in writing. Parents who want to attend or are considering attending the funeral should also be given written directions and the number of someone to phone if they have any queries.

Some parents do not want to be informed of the date of the funeral. Their decision must be recorded to ensure that they are not sent this information. The date and location of the funeral should also be recorded in the woman's or baby's medical notes so that they can access this information if they choose to do so at a later date.

If the parents do not attend the funeral and want the information, the funeral director or the hospital should inform them in writing where the grave is located or where any ashes have been buried or scattered. Both the funeral director and the hospital should keep a record of these details should parents who do not want this information change their mind at a later date.

 When the midwife mentioned a funeral, I told her that she could do as she wished, I wouldn't be going! But I totally changed my mind about 24 hours later. It's just that we hadn't got our heads around what had happened and all the things we were expected to make decisions about. Mother

Parents' options for hospital arranged funerals

In addition to the relevant available options for burial, cremation or sensitive incineration, parents should be told whether or not they are able to make any choices about the funeral. For example, they may want to select the content of the service, a coffin, flowers, readings or music (see also *Arranging a private funeral or ceremony* below for other ideas). The options available if the hospital arranges the funeral will depend to some extent on whether the ceremony will be a shared or individual funeral.

Parents should also be told about any costs that may be associated with these options. For example, there will be costs to parents if they want to buy flowers, purchase a different type of coffin, arrange for a car to take members of the family to the funeral or erect a plaque or memorial. Parents may wish to wash or dress their baby or ask a funeral director, hospital staff or member of their religious community to do this before the funeral.

Parents may also wish to speak with a hospital chaplain beforehand, particularly if the chaplain will be conducting the funeral service. Depending on the parents' wishes, the chaplain may also be able to help parents contact a religious adviser of their own faith, a Humanist adviser or a funeral celebrant who can conduct the service. Parents may need to pay a fee for this person to lead the ceremony.

 We had the twins cremated which was arranged by the hospital chaplain. Letting them go was the hardest and most painful thing I have ever had to do in my life. I wish now that I had touched the coffin, but at the time I couldn't think straight … I had ordered two white roses which were tied together with white ribbon and I placed these on the coffin. Ed held the coffin and carried it in. He said he wanted to do it as it was his only chance of giving them a cuddle. Mother

Arranging a private funeral or ceremony

 We decided to arrange our baby's funeral ourselves. It was the hardest thing we've ever done and I can't imagine how we managed it but I'm glad we did. I so wanted our baby to know how much we loved her, how special she was and how much we wanted her to be safe from harm. I just kept telling her that in my head. Mother

Parents may need information and support from staff to help them think about whether they want to arrange a private funeral or ceremony. They may also need information about the choices and decisions they can make when planning the funeral and their options for burial, cremation and taking the baby's body home or to the funeral.

A private funeral does not need to be expensive or difficult to arrange. Parents on a low income may be eligible for financial help to make these arrangements (see *Parents on a low income* above).

Parents may choose to hire a funeral director to help them make these arrangements or they may organise the funeral, burial or cremation themselves (see *Burial* and *Cremation* above for more information about the potential options that are available to parents and the required paperwork). Organisations such as the ICCM are also able to provide information to parents who wish to arrange a funeral without the services of a funeral director (see Appendix 2). Parents may also ask relatives or close friends to help them organise the funeral.

If the parents decide to use a funeral director:

- The hospital should give parents a list of local funeral directors who should be registered with the National Society of Allied and Independent Funeral Directors (SAIF) or the National Association of Funeral Directors (NAFD). Parents should be told that this is a suggested list but that they are free to go to any funeral director and that that may wish to discuss costs and services with several funeral directors. Parents can have these consultations with funeral directors without making any commitment. Some parents may prefer to use the firm with which the hospital has a contract if this firm has experience of organising funerals for babies.

- Some parents may want to contact their local Sands or other bereavement support group (see Appendix 2) to find out more about local options and get personal recommendations for local funeral directors.

- Some parents may prefer the chaplain, a member of the hospital or community staff or another member of their family to liaise with the funeral director for them. Parents should still be given every opportunity to make decisions themselves and to be involved in planning. Any decisions should always be checked with them.

Parents may also wish to contact a religious leader, Humanist celebrant or funeral celebrant for advice or to perform the ceremony. The funeral director or hospital chaplain should be able to arrange a contact for them or parents can search the internet for local religious leaders or celebrants. Parents may also choose to have a family member or friend lead the funeral service.

Planning a funeral or ceremony

The ceremony may be held in place of worship such as a church, synagogue, mosque or temple. However, some parents may prefer to organise a ceremony at home or another meaningful place for them (Daly 2005).

Parents' choices for a funeral or ceremony may be affected by what is possible under the regulations of the local cemetery, crematorium or religious institution. The person supporting the parents to make funeral arrangements might gently suggest some or all of the following options:

- Parents choose special readings, prayers, music, flowers, candles or prayers for the service.

- Parents, siblings and other family members may wish to contribute to the ceremony in some way. For example, they may wish to offer a reading, song or address at the service.

- Parents might like to have the baby at home before the funeral. They might want to take the coffin to the service with them.

- Parents may want to wash and dress the baby themselves or ask a funeral director or member of their religious community to prepare the baby. They may want the baby to be dressed in a particular outfit or wrapping.

- Parents may wish to arrange for a car or taxi to take them to and from the ceremony.

- Parents may want to carry the coffin to the place where the service, burial or cremation is taking place.

- Parents, siblings or other family members may want to place special items in the coffin (for example, a family photograph, letter, poem, drawing, painting, soft toy, flower, religious item, something they had bought for the baby, etc.). They should be told about any environmental restrictions on items that can be cremated in advance. The funeral director will remove anything that cannot be cremated before the coffin is closed and return it to the parents.

- Parents may want the coffin to be kept open until immediately before or throughout the service.

- Parents may want the baby to be placed in a Moses basket during the ceremony.

- Parents may want to have photographs or a video taken during the service.

- Parents may want to have a printed order of service.

- There could be a memorial book or card for people attending the funeral to sign.

- Parents may want to request that donations are made to a charity rather than having flowers sent.

- Parents may want to arrange a reception or gathering after the service for the people who attend.

 We decided to write a short piece ourselves about our daughter's little life. So many people hadn't had the chance to meet her, but we wanted to tell them about her; that she had big feet. Mother

More details about options that parents might want to consider are found in Sands' booklet entitled *Deciding about a funeral for your baby*, which is available from the online Sands Shop.

Policies and practice

Trusts and Health Boards have a responsibility to ensure that parents are offered choices about burial, cremation, sensitive incineration and funerals for their baby or pregnancy remains. It may be very distressing for parents who are not fully informed about their available options and discover afterwards that arrangements were made that they do not consider to be satisfactory. As has been seen in instances where ashes were retained, scattered or buried without parents' knowledge, it is possible that parents may file complaints or share their stories publically if their needs have not been met (Angiolini 2014; Infant Cremation Commission 2014; Jenkins 2015). Supporting parents' choices and providing sensitive and supportive hospital arranged options for parents is potentially beneficial to parents and may help avoid complaints and publicity that can take up staff time and involve additional expense.

Trust and Health Board policies on funerals and disposal should cover perinatal losses of all types and gestations. The basis for all these policies must be that parents are offered choices about hospital and private arrangements and that babies' bodies and fetal remains are handled with respect. These policies should be carefully worked out in close consultation with representatives from all relevant departments, bereaved parents and representatives from relevant support organisations (see Appendix 2). In **England**, **Wales** and **Northern Ireland**, these policies should also be updated in relation to the Human Tissue Authority's Guidance on the disposal of pregnancy remains following pregnancy loss or termination (HTA 2015). In **Scotland**, guidance has been issued by the Scottish Government regarding the disposal of pregnancy remains that incorporates the Infant Cremation Commission Report recommendations (Scottish Government 2015a). All policies should be reviewed and updated regularly.

In addition to arranging and paying for burial, cremation, sensitive incineration and/or a funeral or other ceremony for stillborn babies and fetal remains, Trusts, Health Boards and managers should also consider offering these options for babies who die shortly after birth. This may be important as women living in poverty have a much higher risk (57 per cent) of experiencing their baby being stillborn or dying in the neonatal period (Manktelow *et al.* 2015).

All policies should be communicated to all relevant staff who should have a good understanding of these policies and easy access to a well-written, regularly updated reference guide.

Negotiating contracts with local service suppliers

Trusts and Health Boards should appoint a multidisciplinary group of staff that negotiates and monitors contracts with local funeral directors, a local cemetery and/or a local crematorium. *One or more members of the staff who regularly provide care for bereaved parents should be part of the negotiating team.*

Trusts and Health Boards should make arrangements for funerals, burials, cremations and sensitive incineration for losses that occur outside the hospital and negotiate contracts accordingly. Alternatively, they may arrange to share in a local hospital's arrangements.

The ICCM have issued a document called *Policy and Guidance for Baby and Infant Funerals*, which is a useful resource for Trusts and Health Boards who are considering contracts with service suppliers and contains a sample agreement for hospitals and cemeteries/crematoria in Appendix A (see Appendix 2).

Contracts with funeral directors

Wherever possible, contracts should be sought with funeral directors who have experience arranging funerals for babies and a reputation for working collaboratively with parents. Many funeral directors have good knowledge of local communities and their needs, and can be an important resource for Trusts, Health Boards and managers. It is important to make sure that the contracted funeral director understands the possible range of personal, religious and cultural needs of different families and can accommodate them. Hospitals may need to arrange additional contracts with specialist funeral directors who have experience in organising funerals for members of particular religious or ethnic groups and who have contacts with the appropriate cemeteries.

Contracts with funeral directors should state clearly the hospital's requirements for funerals for all fetal remains and babies. Contracts should not be awarded on the grounds of price alone. Any funeral service provided should be suitable for parents to attend whether or not they choose to be present at the funeral. A member of staff should attend contract funerals regularly to monitor the standard of provision and ensure that it is acceptable.

The costs of collecting bodies and fetal remains from the hospital mortuary should be included in the agreed fee. The contract should also state that parents should be able to discuss the funeral with the funeral director beforehand and that parents can attend the funeral and/or choose to pay for additional options that are not included in the contract (see *Parents' options for hospital arranged funerals* above).

The funeral director should also provide facilities for parents who want to see their baby before the funeral.

Contract with a cemetery

Wherever possible, a contract should be negotiated with a cemetery so that parents can be offered the choice between burial and cremation. Some hospitals may not be able to provide burial in areas where the cost of graves is prohibitive or as a result of budget constraints. However, many cemeteries do not charge for the burial of babies.

Even if hospitals cannot offer burial as an option for all parents, arrangements should be in place for those whose religion requires burial. The member of staff responsible for arranging funeral contracts should establish links with the relevant local religious groups and specialist funeral directors who can offer help and advice to parents who require a religious burial.

Burials should be in an acceptable area of a cemetery. Many cemeteries have a designated area for babies or children. Some Trusts, Health Boards and local authorities buy a special plot for the burial of babies of all gestations and ages.

Hospitals should know whether the cemetery permits shared graves as some cemeteries only allow the burial of babies in separate graves. Shared graves should normally be located in a special children's area of the cemetery with a general memorial stone.

The contract should describe the services that are to be provided for hospital-arranged funerals and burials and include details of the following:

- The documentation that will be needed.

- The area designated for the burial of babies and fetal remains.

- Whether the cemetery will provide individual and/or shared grave options.

- How many coffins or containers of fetal remains may be placed in a single grave. All fetal remains should be placed in individual containers (HTA 2015).

- How containers of fetal remains should be labelled in order to maintain the confidentiality of the mother where necessary. Where confidentiality is required, a case number should be used instead of a name so that only the healthcare staff can trace the remains to the mother (ICCM 2014).

- The gestation after which a baby should be buried in a separate coffin.

- How coffins should be labelled.

- How the coffins or containers will be arranged within a shared grave. If coffins or containers are stacked on top of each other rather than beside one another, this may make it more difficult or impossible to exhume a specific coffin at a later date (see *Exhumation* above).

- How the exact location of each coffin or container in a shared grave will be recorded.

- That graves will be backfilled immediately after burial and not be left open (ICCM and Sands 2014; Sands 2015d). If this is not possible, the contract should state the maximum amount of time that a grave can be left open and that *lockable* grave covers will be used to ensure that the graves are not disturbed until the grave is filled and the ground re-constituted (ICCM and Sands 2014; Sands 2015d).

- Who will lead any funeral ceremonies and how often funeral ceremonies will take place.

- The responsibilities of the cemetery for keeping records of burials indefinitely and of the Trust or Health Board for keeping records of when and where burials take places so that remains can be traced for a minimum of 50 years (ICCM 2014). In the case of shared burials, a record should be kept of all the babies that a grave contains.

- Details about what memorials or objects parents are or are not able to place on graves and information about the book of remembrance where the names of individual babies can be entered if parents wish.

If the local cemetery does not accept fetal material for burial, the Trust or Health Board should consider finding another cemetery where this can be done. It may be helpful to contact the ICCM for advice (see Appendix 2).

Contract with a crematorium

A contract should be negotiated with a crematorium that gives parents the choice of receiving ashes after the cremation of their baby wherever possible (see the sections on *Cremation* and *Ashes* above). It is important to check the crematorium's policy and practices regarding maximising the recovery of ashes as many crematoria are able to produce ashes following a baby's cremation even for earlier gestations (ICCM and Sands 2014). The ICCM are able to provide information about crematoria that offer these services and specialised training for crematorium technicians (see Appendix 2).

The contract should describe the services to be provided for hospital-arranged funerals and cremations and include information about:

- The documentation that will be needed (see *Paperwork required for cremation* above for a list of the forms required for the cremation of babies and fetal remains).

- The types of coffins or containers that can be used for cremating babies and fetal remains and any restrictions regarding materials that can be cremated to ensure compliance with crematorium regulations. This information will help hospitals and clinics purchase appropriate coffins and containers and may also be useful when discussing the types of coffins that parents may wish to buy or items that they wish to have cremated with their baby.

- How containers of fetal remains will be labelled in order to maintain the confidentiality of the woman where required. A case number should be used so that only the health care staff can trace the remains to the woman (ICCM 2014).

- How many containers of fetal remains may be placed in a single coffin.

- The gestation after which a baby should always be cremated in a separate coffin.

- How individual coffins should be labelled.

- When and how often cremations will take place.

- Who will lead any funeral ceremonies and when these services will take place.

- The likelihood of recovering ashes, techniques and practices that will be employed to maximise their recovery. Information about where ashes will be buried or scattered in the case of shared cremations or when parents wish for this to be done by the crematorium.

- The responsibilities of the crematorium and of the Trust or Health Board for keeping records of when and where the cremation of individual babies and fetal remains take place and where any ashes are buried or scattered for a minimum of 50 years (ICCM 2014).

- Details about parents' options for erecting a plaque or memorial for their baby and the book of remembrance where the names of individual babies can be entered if the parents wish.

Some crematoria will not accept fetal material for cremation or will not carry out shared cremations. Some will not cremate tissue that results from a molar, anembryonic or ectopic pregnancy on the grounds that it contains tissue from a living person (the mother). In these situations, Trusts and Health Boards should seek out the services of a crematorium that will undertake shared cremation of fetal remains and will cremate tissue from early pregnancy losses. The ICCM can be contacted for advice (see Appendix 2).

Contract for sensitive incineration

Hospitals, clinics, Trusts and Health Boards in **England**, **Wales** and **Northern Ireland**

 must negotiate with clinical waste service suppliers to ensure that the appropriate procedures are in place to make certain the sensitive incineration of fetal remains. The contract with the service provider should state:

- That fetal or pregnancy remains should be incinerated separately from other clinical waste (HTA 2015).

- Details of how remains will be packaged and stored separately from other clinical waste (HTA 2015).

- What containers can be placed in incinerators.

- Any details about local arrangements for chaplains or spiritual leaders to be involved in the process and how to ensure that women's choices are respected when they do not want the pregnancy remains to be acknowledged in this manner (HTA 2015).

- How the date of collection and location of incineration will be recorded (HTA 2015).

- How frequently and when sensitive incineration services will be provided.

- How the sensitive incineration process will be monitored to ensure that fetal and pregnancy remains are being incinerated separately.

CHAPTER 21

Memorials

Other relevant chapters

1: Providing holistic care

2: Providing inclusive care

3: Loss and grief

4: Communication

5: Communication across language
and other barriers

20: Funerals and sensitive disposal

Many parents want to create a lasting memorial to their baby. Sometimes parents choose to do this shortly after their baby's death while others may decide to make a memorial later – sometimes many years after the baby died. Parents may welcome reassurance from staff that it is never too late to commemorate and show their love and grief for their baby.

Some parents may choose to have a headstone or a plaque in a cemetery or the grounds of a crematorium (see *What options are available to parents?* in Chapter 20). However, there are many other public and private ways in which parents can create memorials to their babies. Some parents may welcome memorial suggestions from healthcare staff or want to contact their local Sands, Miscarriage Association, ARC, TAMBA or other bereavement support group (see Appendix 2) to find out what other parents have done.

Sands' *Long ago bereaved* booklet also offers suggestions of ways that parents may like to create a memorial for their baby and could be a helpful resource for parents whose baby died years previously.

Books of remembrance

Many cemeteries and all crematoria have books of remembrance in which parents can have their baby's name entered. This can be done when the baby is buried or cremated or at a later date. The funeral director or local crematorium or cemetery manager can tell parents how to arrange this entry. Many crematoria can also provide a personalised miniature book of remembrance or remembrance card for parents that only shows the entry for their baby.

Many hospitals also have books of remembrance that are kept in the hospital chapel, multi-faith room, maternity unit and/or neonatal unit (see *Keeping in touch and ongoing support for parents* in Chapter 13). Staff should offer all parents the opportunity to enter their baby's name and an inscription after a perinatal loss.

Some maternity and neonatal units have memorial books in which parents and other family members are invited to insert photographs, poems and personal messages about the baby who died. It is important to ensure that hospital books of remembrance, memorial books, sympathy cards and other materials are not religious in content. This will help to ensure that these items are as inclusive as possible.

Memorial services

Some parents may wish to organise a memorial ceremony for their baby even if they have already arranged or attended a funeral service. This ceremony might be held shortly after the baby's death or later when parents feel ready. Many parents find a ceremony to be helpful and comforting, even many years after their loss.

Parents may find it helpful to contact the hospital chaplain, a religious adviser, Humanist celebrant or funeral celebrant to discuss the form and location of the service and how it can best meet their needs. Staff can offer to put parents in touch with local contacts if needed. See *Planning a funeral or ceremony* in Chapter 20 for more ideas and information.

Some hospital chaplains hold regular shared, non-denominational memorial services in the hospital chapel, multi-faith room or local church. These services should be sensitive to the needs of parents who have lost a baby at any gestation and for any reason. The ceremony should also reflect that parents may be from different religious backgrounds or have no religious faith or affiliation. Written information about these services should be given to all parents and include an open invitation.

Some hospitals, churches and crematoria hold an annual act of remembrance or memorial service to which all bereaved parents are invited. Some units send out personal invitations to all parents who have lost a baby since the last memorial service and/or advertise the service in the local media. Some Sands, Miscarriage Association and ARC groups around the country also organise services for all bereaved parents and families. This includes Sands' annual memorial service at the Sands Garden in the National Memorial Arboretum in Staffordshire and the annual Sands Lights of Love services that are held across the UK (see the Sands website for more details). These services should also be open and suited to the needs of bereaved parents from different backgrounds and who have experienced any type of loss.

Other memorials

 Daisy was due on 18th April. We spent the day with our family on the beach where we had had our wedding photos taken, remembering her. We scattered her ashes and then we released a bunch of helium balloons tied to pictures that the kids had drawn. We said goodbye. And now we have some happy memories of her, alongside the pain. Father

There are many options available to parents who wish to commemorate their baby. Parents may want to create a memorial or remember their baby in some of the following ways (see also *Creating memories* in Chapter 14):

- Framing and hanging a photograph, drawing or painting of the baby. Drawings and paintings may be made using photographs of the baby.

- Making a book or memory box about the pregnancy, birth and/or the baby's life and death. Some examples of items that may be included are: the confirmation of the pregnancy, any test results, hospital appointment cards, photographs taken during the pregnancy or of the baby, a scan photo, drawings by siblings, the baby's cot card and name band if the baby died after birth, hand or footprints, cards and letters received, a photo of the cemetery, crematorium or the baby's grave, a toy, clothes or other keepsakes.

- Pressing flowers from their baby's funeral to keep or to display in a frame.

- Making an embroidery or piece of patchwork.

- Making, buying, or commissioning a special picture, sculpture, engraving or piece of jewellery. For example, this may be of the baby, a special place associated with the pregnancy or baby or a symbol of the baby. It might also incorporate a lock of the baby's hair, the baby's ashes or hand and footprints.

- Lighting a candle on anniversaries or other special days. Parents may have a special candle holder for this purpose.

- Putting flowers on the baby's grave or in the crematorium grounds on anniversaries and other important dates where this is permitted (see *What options are available to parents?* in Chapter 20).

- Buying a special vase and having flowers on anniversaries or at other times.

- Visiting a special place or sending flowers or a gift to a hospital or nursing home on anniversaries.

- Planting a tree or shrub in a special place, where the baby is buried or where the ashes have been scattered (if this is permitted).

- Writing a poem or letter to the baby or choosing a piece of writing or a poem to be framed.

- Writing an account of their experience of loss. Charities that support bereaved parents, such as Sands, the Miscarriage Association and ARC sometimes publish parents' stories in their newsletters or other publications.

- Putting up a bench with a memorial plaque in a well-loved place, in the cemetery where the baby is buried or in the crematorium grounds.

- Raising money or making a donation to a charity in memory of their baby.

- Naming their baby if the baby has not already been named. Parents may choose a name that is suitable for a boy or a girl if they do not know their baby's sex.

- Adding the baby to a family tree.

- Requesting a stillbirth, birth or death certificate for their baby if they did not receive one when their baby died (see *Obtaining copies of stillbirth, birth and death certificates* in Chapter 19). Parents who experienced a loss before 24 weeks' gestation (or 28 weeks' gestation before 1992) may wish to download and complete their own certificate (see *Certification and forms for a baby born dead before 24 weeks' gestation* in Chapter 19).

CHAPTER 22

Receiving and responding to feedback: parent experiences

Other relevant chapters

1: Providing holistic care

2: Providing inclusive care

3: Loss and grief

4: Communication

5: Communication across
   language and other barriers

14: After a loss

15: Postnatal care

17: Follow-up appointments
    and ongoing care

Why it is important for parents to provide feedback

The *Listening to Parents* report highlighted that many parents received good quality care around the time of their baby's death (Redshaw *et al*. 2014). However, other parents did not receive care that met their needs or they felt that their care could have been better managed (Redshaw *et al*. 2014).

These findings emphasise the need for good feedback mechanisms to be in place to provide parents with opportunities to let healthcare staff know about their experiences of care. When parents have had a good experience of care at what is often a very difficult time, it can be important for the staff who cared for them to know that the care they provided was beneficial. Conversely, it is important for staff and healthcare services to receive feedback when parents have not received optimal care as this allows for reflection and learning and promotes the improvement of services (NMC 2015).

By actively gathering feedback from parents, this will help services to work together with bereaved parents and families to improve their experiences of care and the care of other parents and families in the future (NHS Institute for Innovation and Improvement 2013).

The Health and Social Care Act 2012 also provides the legal framework that stipulates the need for patient involvement and input into healthcare services.

It may also be important for some parents to express their gratitude to staff who provided care that helped them to have the best experience possible under very difficult circumstances.

Other parents may need the opportunity to express their feelings about their care, including any anger or concerns regarding the care that they or their baby received. It may be very important for some parents to have their feelings about their care or any concerns about their care recognised and acknowledged by staff (see also *Responding to parents' feedback about their care* below).

How to obtain feedback from parents

It may be challenging for staff and healthcare services to obtain feedback about care from bereaved parents. However, it is crucial that Trusts, Health Boards and managers ensure that appropriate feedback mechanisms are in place to obtain this feedback.

It can be difficult to determine what may be "appropriate" feedback mechanisms for requesting and obtaining feedback from parents after a pregnancy loss or the death of their baby. It is also important to recognise that there may not be a single mechanism of feedback that will meet the needs of all parents (Henley and Turner 2013). The most important thing about any feedback mechanism is that it does not add to parents' distress and that the wording and approach of any technique are sensitive (Henley and Turner 2013).

It is clear that some feedback mechanisms are not appropriate for asking bereaved parents about their experiences of care. For example, Sands surveyed bereaved parents in 2013 to ask whether they thought the Friends and Family Test (FFT) used by NHS England was suitable for asking parents about their experiences of care when their baby died (Henley and Turner 2013). The FFT is a feedback tool that asks patients whether they would recommend the services they received to friends or family if they needed similar care or treatment (Henley and Turner 2013; NHS England 2015c). The FFT is usually given to patients following discharge from hospital or at the end of an appointment (NHS England 2015c). Most parents surveyed felt that the content and timing of the FFT was inappropriate when asking bereaved parents for feedback (Henley and Turner 2013).

However, most parents surveyed felt that it was a good idea to ask bereaved parents for feedback and obtain feedback from parents who wish to provide it (Henley and Turner 2013). Some of the recommendations that parents made for requesting this feedback include:

- Asking parents a question about how they experienced care.

- Requesting feedback at a time when parents may feel more able to reflect on the care that they received when responding to questions. Some parents suggested that feedback was requested several months after their experience of loss while other parents felt that it would be more appropriate to ask years later. Services may need to be flexible in their timing when requesting feedback about care from parents.

- Using a questionnaire that is open enough to capture the variety of experiences that bereaved parents may have had.

- Offering parents an opportunity to discuss their care face-to-face with a healthcare professional rather than completing a questionnaire. In a face-to-face interview, it is recommended that this member of staff has undertaken bereavement care training, has time to listen and is able to listen supportively even if parents are very critical of their care (see *Responding to parents' feedback about their care* below). While some parents may prefer to discuss their care face-to-face (and this should be accommodated), a Cochrane review has found that there is not sufficient evidence to suggest that these psychological debriefing sessions are beneficial or harmful (Bastos *et al*. 2015). However, it is important to recognise that this review is focusing on the use of debriefing interventions to prevent PTSD after a traumatic birth and that these findings may not be relevant for all bereaved parents (see Chapter 18).

- Discussing feedback at an existing appointment such as a postnatal care appointment or when the post mortem examination results are discussed (if relevant). However, it was highlighted that time may already be very pressured during these appointments. Additionally, some parents may not be ready to discuss their care at these appointments.

- Giving or sending parents a feedback questionnaire when they leave the hospital or a few months later. However, it should be made clear that there is no time limit for parents completing and returning the questionnaire. It may also be helpful if an addressed, stamped envelope was provided with this questionnaire.
(Henley and Turner 2013)

It is clear that there is no single way of requesting feedback that would be acceptable or preferred by all parents. A flexible approach to this process and requesting input from bereaved parents is important. It may also be helpful to consider how obtaining feedback could be incorporated into the roles of bereavement midwives and nurses or by forming local bereavement groups (see *Bereavement midwives and nurses* in Chapter 25).

Trusts, Health Boards and managers should ensure that local feedback mechanisms are developed in collaboration with staff and bereaved parents who have received care from their services. This will help to ensure that specific feedback on local services is available and that the feedback mechanism is relevant for the needs of parents from different local communities.

Maternity Services Liaison Committees (MSLCs) may also be a useful forum for receiving feedback from bereaved parents. Information about local MSLCs and how to become involved should be widely publicised so that parents are aware of these services. Additionally, Trusts, Health Boards and managers should ensure that invitations are extended to local support groups and organisations who may be able to send a representative to participate in the MSLC.

Another important way of obtaining feedback from parents is during reviews of babies' deaths. It is important that parents' perspectives regarding their care should be incorporated into these reviews wherever possible (Draper *et al.* 2015). Staff should ask parents for their views of their care and include these views when reviewing a baby's death (Draper *et al.* 2015) (see also *Being open and honest with parents* below and *Recording, reporting and reviewing the baby's cause of death* in Chapter 16).

Large-scale surveys of bereaved parents, such as *Listening to Parents*, also provide very useful information about parents' experiences of care and ways of improving care. However, it is important that the emphasis on improving care also occurs at the local level and that all parents are offered opportunities to provide feedback about their experiences of care.

Being open and honest with parents

When something has gone wrong during treatment or care, healthcare staff have a duty to inform patients of what has happened and the potential implications (GMC 2013a; GMC and NMC 2015; NMC 2015).

When a baby dies, staff should review the baby's death in a multidisciplinary meeting and parents' feedback about their care should be requested and included in these reviews (Draper *et al.* 2015; PASC 2015). After the review, staff should offer parents an opportunity to discuss the findings of the review and a summary of the findings (Draper *et al.* 2015). The aim of discussing the clinical and any pathological findings of the review with parents is to ensure that parents gain the best understanding possible of the events leading to the death and any implications for future pregnancies (Draper *et al.* 2015).

When a baby has died after something has gone wrong during care, it is important that staff acknowledge this and tell parents what happened to the best of their ability. Not only is it important that parents are offered this information but staff also have a professional duty to inform parents of what has happened as soon as possible (GMC 2013a; GMC and NMC 2015; NMC 2015). These discussions should take place in a private place and information should be given sensitively and so that parents can understand (GMC and NMC 2015) (see *Good communication with parents* in Chapter 4).

When staff offer this information to parents, they should apologise to parents and fully inform them about what has happened and the potential implications (GMC 2013a; GMC and NMC 2015). Staff who apologise to parents are not accepting legal liability for what has happened (GMC and NMC 2015). They should also not be expected to accept personal responsibility for what has happened if it is not their fault (GMC and NMC 2015). However, their apology should be genuine and personalised to reflect the situation (GMC and NMC 2015). Any uncertainty should be acknowledged (GMC and NMC 2015).

Staff should also be aware that parents may become angry or distressed when they hear this information. They should be prepared to supportively listen to parents without becoming defensive or angry (see *Responding to parents' feedback about their care* below). Parents should also be given the contact details for a named contact who they can speak with if they have any additional questions or concerns (GMC and NMC 2015).

If parents decline this offer of information, staff should ask them if there is a reason (GMC and NMC 2015). If parents still do not want this information, staff should respect this decision and let them know that they can request this information in the future and tell them how to do so (GMC and NMC 2015).

Staff should also document these discussions and parents' decisions about receiving information in the medical notes (GMC and NMC 2015).

Being open and honest with colleagues

All staff also have a duty to honestly report any incidents to their colleagues, managers, regulators and any other relevant organisations. They also have a duty to be involved in any relevant reviews and audits, regardless of whether a complaint has been made (GMC and NMC 2015; PASC 2015). If a healthcare team is involved in an incident, one member of that team should be allocated to report the incident (GMC and NMC 2015). Any feedback given to colleagues involved in an incident should also be honest, accurate and constructive (NMC 2015).

These principles should always be followed by staff when reporting, discussing or reviewing any incidents that may have been related to a baby's death (see also *Recording, reporting and reviewing the baby's cause of death* in Chapter 16). It is important that staff reflect upon and learn from these experiences and incidents to improve future care and prevent deaths.

Trusts, Health Boards and managers should make certain that policies and reporting systems are in place to ensure that staff report any incidents that may have been related to a baby's death (GMC and NMC 2015). They should also ensure that a culture of learning is created around reporting errors and incidents rather than a culture of blame (GMC and NMC 2015; PASC 2015). Reporting an error or incident may be very stressful and distressing for staff and they should be encouraged and supported during this process (see *Support for staff* in Chapter 24).

Responding to parents' feedback about their care

When parents provide positive feedback about their care, this should be acknowledged and shared with any relevant staff.

Other parents may feel angry after their baby dies and this anger may be directed towards the health professionals who were involved in their care (see *Parents' experiences and expressions of grief* in Chapter 3). Some parents find it helpful to be able to express their anger and pain to someone who simply listens. Some parents may be angry if they did not receive an empathetic response to their loss. For example, some parents may want to hear staff say "I am so sorry your baby died" (Enkin *et al*. 2000: 479). Some parents may wish to speak with a member of staff who they feel is responsible for their baby's death or their poor experience of care and express their feelings. If the needs of parents are not met during their discussions with staff, parents may continue to be angry, consider filing a complaint, consider litigation or express their feelings to staff if they encounter them in public.

It may difficult for staff to listen to parents who are angry or who blame the hospital or a particular member of staff for what happened without feeling threatened, becoming defensive or arguing with parents' perspectives. However, it is important for staff to be able to supportively listen to parents in these circumstances and remain calm (see *Listening and support* in Chapter 4). It may also be appropriate for staff to offer their condolences or apologise for what has happened (without accepting personal responsibility if they are not personally at fault) (GMC and NMC 2015) (see *Being open and honest with parents* above).

Some women may also wish to access their medical notes to better understand what happened when their baby died. Women have the legal right to access their notes under the Data Protection Act 1998 and staff should provide women with information about how to access their notes and any fees that they may need to pay. They should also offer women an appointment to discuss their notes and explain any medical terminology that women do not understand (The Patients Association 2009).

When parents provide feedback about their care or file a complaint, it is important that this is responded to fully, promptly and honestly (GMC 2013a; PASC 2015). Parents should be offered an appointment to discuss what has happened with a senior member of staff. In most cases, parents' concerns or complaints can be resolved informally (NHS Choices 2014b). However, parents should be given clear information about how to file a formal complaint as some parents may not feel that their concerns have been addressed informally. Trusts, Health Boards and managers should ensure that information is readily available for parents and that mechanisms for providing feedback and filing complaints are accessible for parents in different formats and languages (see Chapter 5). It is important that additional harm and distress is not caused to parents and families as a result of the complaints process (PASC 2015). When parents provide feedback or file a complaint against a member of staff or a healthcare service, it is also crucial that this does not affect the care that they receive (GMC 2013a; NMC 2015).

Any feedback or complaints should be viewed by staff and healthcare services as opportunities to reflect on current policies and practices. It should be an opportunity make changes to improve services and care where necessary without the need to find blame (NMC 2015; PASC 2015). When investigating complaints from parents, all relevant staff should be involved and offer honest information about what has happened (GMC 2013a) (see *Being open and honest with colleagues* above). This information should also be included as part of the review following a baby's death (see *Recording, reporting and reviewing the baby's cause of death* in Chapter 16).

Trusts, Health Boards and managers should ensure that policies and procedures are in place to investigate issues of patient safety and parents' feedback and complaints in an efficient and effective manner (PASC 2015). Investigations should be conducted in a way that is supportive to staff and encourages them to be open and honest (PASC 2015) (see *Being open and honest with colleagues* above).

Parents' feedback should be taken seriously. Changes in policies and procedures should be made if parents have raised concerns relating to clinical safety or organisational failure. However, Trusts, Health Boards and managers should carefully consider any other major changes in practice and consult other bereaved parents and relevant organisations before instituting these changes. All parents are different and some parents may be satisfied with care and procedures that other parents find distressing. In some instances, it may be best to consider policies and procedures that emphasise the need to provide parents with individualised care that is tailored to their needs.

There should also be transparency regarding any outcomes of investigations and reviews and these should be published and disseminated (PASC 2015). Parents should be offered an opportunity to discuss the outcome of any investigation of a complaint or feedback with a senior member of staff and policies should be in place to ensure that this happens standardly and as quickly as possible.

It is also important that staff receive support from colleagues and managers during and after any feedback or complaints are received. Listening to parents in these circumstances or receiving complaints can be very stressful or distressing for staff (see *Support for staff* in Chapter 24). This may particularly be the case if staff feel they are to blame, fear complaints or litigation or feel that the baby's death is a professional failure (Kenworthy and Kirkham 2011).

CHAPTER 23

Another pregnancy?

Other relevant chapters

1: Providing holistic care

2: Providing inclusive care

3: Loss and grief

4: Communication

5: Communication across language and other barriers

15: Postnatal care

17: Follow-up appointments and ongoing care

18: Mental health

Both primary and maternity care staff may provide care for parents relating to subsequent pregnancies in both community and hospital settings. It is important that all healthcare staff who may come into contact with bereaved parents before, during and after a pregnancy following a childbearing loss are aware of the potential difficulties and challenges that these parents might face.

Parents considering subsequent pregnancies

Listening to Parents found that of the bereaved mothers surveyed, 39 per cent were pregnant when they completed the questionnaire, 44 per cent were planning to become pregnant in the future, 12 per cent were unsure about becoming pregnant again and 5 per cent had decided against another pregnancy (Redshaw *et al.* 2014).

Some parents may want to become pregnant again as soon as possible after their baby dies. Other parents may need more time before they are emotionally or physically ready or may find it difficult to decide whether to have another baby. Parents may long to be pregnant again but also fear the pain and grief of another loss. They may also have lost confidence in their ability to have a healthy baby.

I wanted to try again from day one. I just wanted to be pregnant again. It was all I could think about. Mother

 At first, I couldn't think of having another baby. It wasn't till I was back at work and had done a lot of grieving that I started to feel emotionally ready. We didn't really try for a baby, getting pregnant wasn't my main focus. We just thought if it happens, it happens. Mother

Some parents may disagree with each other about when and if they will try to become pregnant again (Sand 2014g) (see also *Couples* in Chapter 3). These parents may need time to discuss their individual needs and concerns with each other or someone else who is able to offer them support (Sands 2014g). A parent's sex does not determine whether they will be ready sooner or later (Swanson 2003; Turton *et al.* 2006).

For some parents, another pregnancy is not possible. Some may have medical problems that make it impossible or dangerous for a woman to become pregnant again. Other women may have reached menopause. If the baby who died had a medical or genetic condition that may affect subsequent babies, the risk of another loss may feel too difficult for some parents to consider. Some parents do not want to face the stresses and worries of another pregnancy that could end in loss, even when there is no specific risk or difficulty (Kohner and Henley 2001).

Parents who had treatment for fertility problems in order to conceive the baby who died may also face grief related to infertility. Some may decide that they cannot face the stresses and uncertainty of another round of fertility treatment. Others may not be able to be able to afford any more fertility treatment.

 It was torture to have to face IVF again. Kindly meant advice to "try again" rang very hollow. We were lucky enough to conceive again eventually and to have a healthy second daughter. Later we had a miscarriage. We live with a continuing sense of loss. The pain of infertility endures until you feel that your family is complete. Mother

Some parents may find it difficult to have sexual intercourse. For some parents, having sex may trigger distressing memories, feelings of grief or fears about becoming pregnant again (Sands 2014a). Parents' sex drive may also be affected by depression, anxiety, flashbacks or intrusive thoughts after a traumatic birth or low self-esteem after their baby's death (Sands 2014a; Cacciatore *et al.* 2008). Some men may have concerns about hurting their partner (Sands 2014a).

 We had stopped having sex when I found out I was pregnant, so I just kept thinking, the last time I did this we made our daughter. Mother

When we did make love I was scared of hurting her. Father

Despite these potential challenges, people sometimes assume that a couple will go on to have more children after a loss, which may lead to inadvertently intrusive questions such as, "When are you going to try again?" (Moulder 2001: 54). Some parents may feel under pressure to have another baby as soon as possible to relieve the anxiety of other people who love them and want them to be happy again.

 When we told people I was pregnant again, you could almost hear the collective sigh of relief from people who thought that everything would be alright now and that we would forget our daughter. Mother

Well-meaning friends and family members may also offer false reassurance such as "Everything will be okay next time". This may make it difficult for parents to discuss their fears and difficulties with close friends and family. Healthcare staff may be the only people with whom parents feel that they can talk openly.

Parents who are thinking about becoming or are pregnant again may want to contact a support organisation such as Sands, the Miscarriage Association or ARC (see Appendix 2). These organisations may also have local support groups specifically for parents in this situation. Parents may also find it helpful to look at Sands' *Another Pregnancy?* or *Sexual relationships after the death of a baby* booklets that are available from the Sands website or online shop. Parents may need this care and support in any subsequent pregnancy after a childbearing loss, not only the first pregnancy.

Pre-conception care

The timing of subsequent pregnancies, the risks involved, concerns about their ability to conceive, sexual difficulties and the chances of having a live, healthy baby may be some of the concerns for parents who are thinking about becoming pregnant again (see also *Discussing sex and contraception* in Chapter 15 and *Follow-up appointments* in Chapter 17). Parents may need support and an opportunity to discuss their concerns and any questions with healthcare staff before trying to conceive. Healthcare staff may also be able to help by offering parents time (separately or together) to discuss their feelings and by supporting them to make decisions regarding another pregnancy.

Staff can reassure parents that there is no one right time to try for another baby. Staff can also support parents to make an informed choice about timing that is right for them by outlining the possible advantages and disadvantages of delaying or going ahead (Franche 2001; Hutti 2005; Gold *et al*. 2010) (see also *Discussing sex and contraception* in Chapter 15). It should be gently suggested to parents that they may want to consider the timing of the next baby's birth in relation to significant dates. For example, it may be difficult for parents if the next baby's birthday is close to the anniversary of their baby's death. Parents may also need time to grieve for their baby before having another child.

 The doctors asked us to wait six months before trying for another baby as they wanted to complete some more tests. In fact it was good to wait – it gave us time to come to terms with what had happened and to grieve for our daughter. Mother

It is important that staff sensitively provide full information, recommendations and advice to bereaved parents who may be at a higher risk of blaming themselves if they experience another loss (Gold *et al*. 2010). Parents should be offered information about how the mother may need time to heal physically after the previous birth and about any illness that the woman experienced in her previous pregnancy (Sands 2014g).

For some parents, it is also important to find out as much as they can about why their baby died and future risks before embarking on another pregnancy, particularly if the baby had a genetic condition (Siassakos *et al*. 2015, unpublished results). It could be suggested that parents may wish to wait to receive the results of any post mortem investigations or tests before trying to conceive. Some parents may find another pregnancy particularly difficult if no reason was found for the loss. In these instances, there may be nothing that the parents can do to try to ensure that it does not happen again. However, the post mortem results may also provide parents with hope for future pregnancies (Siassakos *et al*. 2015, unpublished results).

Once results are received, staff may be able to better discuss any potential risks for another baby and/or measures that could be taken to prevent another loss (Sands 2014g). Even when parents decide not to have a post mortem examination, staff should offer parents an opportunity to discuss the risks for another pregnancy based on what is known about why the previous loss occurred and the mother's obstetric history. Some parents may overestimate the risk that the problem will recur. At the same time, it is important for staff to be realistic when attempting to reassure parents and parents may value an acknowledgement of their risk of experiencing similar problems in a subsequent pregnancy (Redshaw *et al*. 2014).

Staff can also support parents before conception by:

- *Encouraging both parents to look after themselves* physically and emotionally. They can support parents to find practical ways of trying to reduce their anxiety. For example, staff could encourage parents to learn and practice relaxation techniques.

- *Offering pre-conceptual advice* such as stopping smoking, taking folic acid, eating well, managing their weight and reducing alcohol intake as appropriate. Such measures may also help parents feel that they are taking some control and doing something positive.

- *Offering to organise referrals* to appropriate medical or genetic specialists and/or a counsellor.

- *Acknowledging that a future pregnancy may be stressful* and outlining any additional antenatal support that would be offered and any support that is available from other organisations (see Appendix 2). It is also important to acknowledge parents' fears and concerns.

Staff should highlight that parents may not become pregnant immediately once they start trying but that this is a possibility. Parents should be told that they may wish to speak with their GP or obstetrician if they are still not pregnant six months after they start trying for another baby (Sands 2014g).

Antenatal care during subsequent pregnancies

Antenatal care in subsequent pregnancies may involve offering parents extra antenatal appointments, screening options, scan appointments and/or opportunities to discuss an antenatal care plan and birth plan (see also Chapter 6 for information about screening and diagnostic tests and *Care during labour and birth* below). Parents may also need longer antenatal appointments in subsequent pregnancies so that they can get the information they need and discuss any concerns (Hutti 2005). Staff should allocate extra time for these appointments. Parents should also be able to bring another support person such as a family member or friend to attend some or all of these appointments with them.

It is crucial that there is good communication between staff providing antenatal care for parents in a subsequent pregnancy so that parents do not have to retell their story if they do not wish to do so (see *Place of care and continuity of carer* below).

Many healthcare staff feel that more frequent contact with bereaved parents is a positive way of providing support (Siassakos *et al.* 2015, unpublished results). Parents may welcome this offer of extra care and want all available screening and diagnostic tests. For some parents, this may reassure them of the healthy progression of the pregnancy although this may be a short-lived reassurance for some parents (Mills *et al.* 2014). Many parents, however, may not need or want extra care but they should have the contact details for a named contact in case they have any concerns. Other parents may find additional appointments, screening and tests stressful and decline some or all of this care. Staff should explain the reason why parents have been offered additional antenatal tests or checks based on the cause of the previous baby's death (for example, growth restriction) and ask parents if there are ways for staff to decrease their stress and/or offer extra support. However, parents' decisions about care should be respected.

Parents should also be offered regular contact with staff, emotional support and screening for mental health difficulties (Mills *et al.* 2014). *Listening to Parents* found that:

> *While women appreciated the easier and more frequent access to antenatal care with a subsequent or further pregnancy, they also recognised the importance of this for their own mental health and wellbeing as well as for more medical reasons.* (Redshaw *et al.* 2014: 48)

Feelings, emotional well-being and mental health

 When I got pregnant after 8 months, I wanted to be delighted but I didn't dare let myself in case all our hopes were dashed again. Mother

 She was pregnant ... again. What should have been fantastic news filled me with sheer terror. I did not know if I could go through this again. Father

It is never possible to predict how individual parents will feel during subsequent pregnancies. For some parents, the main feelings during another pregnancy may be grief, anxiety and distress (Rillstone and Hutchinson 2001; Wallerstedt *et al.* 2003; Mills *et al.* 2014). They may experience these feelings in the first pregnancy after a loss but also later pregnancies following the birth of a healthy baby.

Many parents describe the experience of another pregnancy as being like an emotional rollercoaster that they cannot get off. Some describe the exhaustion of trying to keep their hopes and fears in check. One of the most important things that staff can offer parents is sensitive support to help them deal with the range of feelings and worries that they have (Mills *et al.* 2014). Parents may appreciate the offer of one-to-one sessions at times when their anxiety levels are particularly high. Some parents may also be grateful for the offer of an early ultrasound scan or additional scans and checks for reassurance that all is well.

 It's an excruciating time not knowing if your next baby will live or die. You know you have been chosen once and there is no reason why fate will not strike again. It is about understanding, empathy, and a kind heart and smile but very few words - just a giant pair of ears will do! Mother

Certain stages, events or dates during the pregnancy may be particularly difficult for parents, depending on what happened during the previous pregnancy. For example, parents may be very anxious and distressed in the period leading up to the gestational week or date when the previous baby died or an anomaly was diagnosed. Some parents may feel less frightened after this point if all is well (Debackere *et al.* 2008). Other parents may remain fearful until after the new baby is born.

Some parents may worry that they will be unable to love the new baby or that they will be disloyal to the baby or babies who died by loving the new baby. Some parents may feel that a single baby is insufficient if they had one or more babies who died during or following a multiple pregnancy. It may be helpful for staff to offer parents an opportunity to discuss the mixture of emotions they may feel or expect to feel when their baby is born.

I didn't want to love the baby I was carrying. I was so afraid that she would die as well and I knew I wouldn't be able to cope with the pain. Mother

Parents may also worry about the effects of the fear and anxiety they are feeling on the well-being of this baby. It is important that staff acknowledge the validity of parents' concerns and take them seriously.

 I was terrified that I wouldn't want him when he was born and I felt so guilty. I couldn't tell anyone. They all thought I was looking forward to having a beautiful new baby but all I could think about was our son who died two days after being born. Mother

Bereaved parents may also have a higher risk of experiencing mental health difficulties such as anxiety, depression and/or PTSD during pregnancies after a perinatal loss (Turton *et al*. 2001; Debackere *et al*. 2008). Mental health screening should be available for parents and some parents may need to be offered specialist mental health support (Debackere *et al*. 2008) (see also Chapter 18). More information about treatments and interventions that may be beneficial or are recommended during pregnancy are found in NICE's (2014a) *Antenatal and postnatal mental health* guideline. These interventions and treatments for mental health problems should be available for all bereaved parents.

In addition to the mother, it is important to also ensure that fathers and partners are offered support. Fathers and partners may want to be more actively involved during this pregnancy as they may wish to support the mother and may also want reassurance for themselves (Mills *et al*. 2014). Where appropriate, and with the mothers' consent, staff can include fathers and partners during appointments and discussions by encouraging them to voice any questions and concerns that they have about the baby and mother (Armstrong 2001). Some fathers and partners may be reluctant to voice their fears in the mother's presence as they are concerned about distressing her. Staff should offer fathers and partners an opportunity to speak with staff on their own.

Discussing previous losses with parents

Some parents may try to protect themselves from feeling overwhelmed by fear and anxiety by distancing themselves from what is happening, either throughout the pregnancy or until the point at which they feel their baby is safe (Rillstone and Hutchinson 2001; Debackere *et al*. 2008; Mills *et al*. 2014). Some parents may prefer to avoid discussing their emotions or previous loss with staff and try to focus on the practical tasks at hand. However, some women may find this distancing more difficult after the baby starts to move (Mills *et al*. 2014).

Other parents are grateful for opportunities to talk to staff about how they are feeling and their baby or babies who died (Mills *et al*. 2014). Parents should be encouraged to discuss their feelings about their previous loss(es) with staff and be offered counselling or information about other support available (Debackere *et al*. 2008) (see Appendix 2).

During these discussions, staff should use the previous baby's name where one has been given (Mills *et al.* 2014).

 I had counselling during my pregnancy. It was a safe place to voice my fears. I could talk freely about my stillborn daughter and not just about my bump. Mother

Parents may fear that the problem that led to the loss of their baby will recur in this pregnancy. It may be helpful to offer to go over the obstetric history, medical notes and/ or genetic test results with parents. Staff should ensure that parents understand what happened previously and how previous difficulties may relate to the outcome of this pregnancy. These details may have been discussed with the parents after the baby's death but they may not have been able to fully take in or remember information given at the time.

Some parents' fears may be medically unfounded and they should be given the correct information sensitively while having their anxiety acknowledged. Some parents may be anxious because their baby has a higher risk of being affected by medical or genetic factors. Staff should be realistic but offer hope to these parents when providing support throughout the pregnancy. It is important not to offer false reassurance as this may increase parents' sense of isolation and prevent them from talking openly about their fears. However, a gentle reminder that parents may have a healthy baby could potentially be helpful for some parents as this may help them to maintain hope (Mills *et al.* 2014). Staff may also need to be aware that statistical probabilities may not provide comfort for parents (Rillstone and Hutchinson 2001; Wallerstedt *et al.* 2003).

 I was monitored regularly but nothing anyone said could reassure me. I didn't believe that she would be born alive until I was in the operating theatre awaiting my caesarean section. Mother

A woman who feels that she was to blame for her baby's death or who feels that she missed warning signs before the baby's death may find any subsequent pregnancies particularly difficult (Franche and Mikail 1999; Franche 2001; Debackere *et al.* 2008; Mills *et al.* 2014). These women may carefully monitor their pregnancy and this may provide them with some comfort and/or increase their anxiety and need to have contact with staff (Mills *et al.* 2014). It may be helpful to find out why the woman believes that she is to blame and support her to reflect on the validity of her feelings. If there was no confirmed cause for the baby's death, it may be helpful to acknowledge the potential difficulty of coming to terms with this lack of information.

Telling other people about the pregnancy

Pregnancies following a childbearing loss may also be very stressful for other family members, including other children and grandparents. Some parents may welcome discussions with staff about how to cope with the reactions of other family members.

 My community midwife was wonderful and did the early booking at my home. We live in a close community and if I had been seen going to the hospital it would have been common knowledge that I was pregnant. Mother

Some parents may tell very few people about the pregnancy or limit the amount of information they share with others. Some prefer not to tell anyone until after they have had test results or after the gestation at which the previous baby died and this may mean that they have little support in early pregnancy (Mills *et al.* 2014). After telling family members and friends, parents may not feel able to be open about their fears or speak about the baby who died. They may also feel isolated if family or friends assume that parents will move on from their grief because they are pregnant again (Mills *et al.* 2014).

Some parents are also unsure about how to answer well-meaning questions from strangers. For example, they may be asked whether this is their first baby. Parents may find it helpful to have discussions with staff about what to say in different situations, how to cope with hurtful comments and how they might tell family members and friends what support they need (Rillstone and Hutchinson 2001; Hutti 2005).

Place of care and continuity of carer

Parents should feel well supported in any pregnancy following a childbearing loss. Parents who have a good relationship with staff in a particular hospital or midwifery team may want to return there for their antenatal care. This may be because some parents want to receive care from a member of staff whom they had built a relationship with previously or because their trust had been reinforced by their positive experience of care under difficult circumstances (Redshaw *et al.* 2014). Despite this, it is sometimes necessary to rebuild parents' trust (Redshaw *et al.* 2014). Rebuilding trust may be particularly needed if parents are unhappy about aspects of the care they or their baby received.

 I cannot say enough, how wonderful the midwife was when our son was stillborn. She subsequently delivered Charlie and her presence at his birth was a reassurance and felt "right". She probably has no idea how important she is to us and how glad I am that she was there at the birth of both my sons. Mother

Some parents may prefer to be cared for in a different hospital or by different members of staff, even if their previous care was good (Wallerstedt *et al.* 2003). This may be because they find it too distressing or may fear that traumatic memories will be triggered if they return to the place where their baby died or see staff who had cared for them at that time (Mills *et al.* 2014). Healthcare staff should refer parents to another unit or another consultant if this is requested.

 I was given a new community midwife. The community midwife I had had when I was pregnant with Heulwen who was stillborn was really considerate. She understood that I felt uneasy seeing her even though she hadn't done anything wrong. When I did run into her she always chatted to me and was so caring. Mother

 I got a consultant in a different hospital, a fantastic antenatal midwife and a great anaesthetist and doctors all of whom buoyed me up all the way through and during delivery of a baby boy by caesarean. The staff thought I would need special care afterwards so they arranged for me to go to a cottage hospital near home. Mother

Special consultant-led clinics are available for women with high-risk pregnancies in some areas. These clinics can offer women additional monitoring and care during subsequent pregnancies. However, attending a high-risk antenatal clinic can also have disadvantages for some parents. Although parents may have things in common with other parents, hearing their stories can raise new fears and worries. Staff need to be aware that this may happen and ensure that all parents are encouraged and have time to talk about their concerns.

 At my booking appointment the midwife said, "Absolutely any time if you're concerned about something you just pick up the phone; we'll never think you're a nuisance. Even if it's every single day, just phone. We don't want to think of you sat at home worrying". I haven't phoned but just knowing that I can has taken that worry away. Mother

For some women having the same staff providing their care throughout the pregnancy, birth and postnatal period may be an important part of feeling supported. At the first antenatal visit, each woman should be allocated a named midwife and consultant obstetrician. These practitioners should provide most of the woman's care throughout her pregnancy, birth and the postnatal period. They should also carefully read the woman's notes thoroughly before the first appointment and ask parents if it is okay to refer to the baby who died by name if one has been given (Mills *et al.* 2014; Redshaw *et al.* 2014). Depending on parents' wishes, it may be appropriate for both the named midwife and consultant to attend some appointments.

Offering parents continuity of carers and the option of having their notes clearly marked may also help to ensure that parents do not need to explain their situation repeatedly (Redshaw *et al.* 2014). For example, staff might label parents' notes with the Sands Teardrop Sticker (with their consent) (see Chapter 14). Some parents have also explicitly stated that they want carers to be aware of their previous experiences and that good communication between staff (including across teams and departments) is essential in subsequent pregnancies (Redshaw *et al.* 2014) (see also *Informing other carers* in Chapter 14). All staff who care for bereaved parents in subsequent pregnancies should be well-informed about parents' history so that they can respond sensitively to any anxieties or concerns that parents may express.

I am pregnant again now and it would be useful to see her [bereavement midwife] again now, but I don't think I am allowed or encouraged to do so. Also we thought there would be a "flag" for our next pregnancy to help staff know what had happened, but there is not, so we find ourselves explaining each time we see someone new. Parent
(Redshaw *et al.* 2014: 47)

I would also like to see her [bereavement midwife] now I am pregnant again. Also I would like a "label" on my notes indicating a previous neonatal death to staff, especially sonographers so that they ... understand what we have already gone through. Parent
(Redshaw *et al.* 2014: 47)

Parents may also become strongly attached to the staff who care for them and the understanding and support that staff can offer to parents can be extremely important (Rillstone and Hutchinson 2001). Managers and colleagues should recognise that staff may value being able to support these parents, but that this work may also be emotionally difficult and that these staff may need additional support (see also Chapter 24). Support should be available for all staff who are caring for bereaved parents in subsequent pregnancies.

Antenatal classes

They were all so positive and happy and I felt I had to act the same way. It was exhausting because inside I was grieving for my daughter and worrying that this baby could die too. Mother

Many bereaved parents feel unable to attend standard antenatal classes during pregnancies after a childbearing loss (Mills *et al.* 2014). This may be because parents do not feel they can share their experiences for fear of their own emotional response or the potential effects on other parents (Mills *et al.* 2014).

Wherever possible, these parents should be offered individual preparation sessions for labour, birth and caring for a baby by a member of the team caring for them. If group sessions are offered for parents during subsequent pregnancies, class sizes should be limited whenever possible and classes should be spread over a few weeks to give parents time to talk or express their feelings (including anger) (Thomas 2010; O'Leary *et al.* 2012). This time will also give the facilitator an opportunity to focus on the individual concerns of all attendees (Thomas 2010; O'Leary *et al.* 2012).

Specialist antenatal classes for parents during subsequent pregnancies should be flexible in content and timing to ensure that they are sensitive to parents' individual needs and experiences (O'Leary *et al.* 2012). Parents may or may not want to discuss their previous experiences during antenatal classes (O'Leary *et al.* 2012). Additionally, some visual aids, videos, visualisations or relaxation techniques that are used in other antenatal classes may not be appropriate or may cause distress for some parents (O'Leary *et al.* 2012).

Facilitators should also be aware that some parents may not have previously attended antenatal classes (particularly if their loss occurred at an earlier gestation) and information about pregnancy, labour and birth should still be discussed (O'Leary *et al.* 2012). Some parents may want to have information about caring for the baby during these classes. Other parents may not want this information until after the baby is born (O'Leary *et al.* 2012).

Some parents may want to attend standard antenatal classes and may welcome help from staff when deciding what they want to say to the class facilitator and to the group (if they decide to say anything). If parents choose to disclose their previous experience, antenatal class facilitators should have access to more information about supporting parents who have experienced a perinatal loss. It may also be helpful for the facilitator to be aware that supporting bereaved parents in these classes may be emotionally challenging (Thomas 2010).

In any antenatal class, some parents may be angry about their previous experience and direct this anger at the facilitator (Thomas 2010). Offering support for parents during these sessions may also trigger the facilitator's own experiences of grief (Thomas 2010). It is important that facilitators are able to access support for themselves after running these sessions.

Support groups and clinics

Some hospitals run a drop-in clinic where pregnant women who have previously experienced recurrent early miscarriages, late miscarriage, stillbirth or neonatal death can meet and support each other in a relaxed and informal setting. Some women may choose to bring a partner, relative or friend to these clinics.

Sometimes these clinics are led by a bereavement support midwife with support from other midwives and gynaecology nurses. It is helpful if they are run at the same time as a consultant-led antenatal clinic so that women can seek a consultant's opinion if they are anxious. Such clinics give women access to regular and ongoing emotional support throughout their pregnancy and are generally highly appreciated (Bereavement support midwife 2006, personal communication).

 I was fortunate in that the midwife who ran the baby loss support group I attended was with me throughout the pregnancy, time in hospital and was there waiting in the delivery suite when I came out of theatre with my second son. She and another Mum who had lost a child were the only people who understood my fear of another loss. Others just got angry.
Mother

For some parents, support from a local parents' group can also be very helpful during subsequent pregnancies. This may help parents to meet and build a relationship with other parents who have experienced situations similar to their own (Hutti 2005) (see also *Voluntary support* in Chapter 17).

Care during labour and birth

 My biggest fear was going into the hospital. Though the staff were wonderful, would they understand when I needed the "medical jargon" explained to me? My community midwife was with us when Charlie was born. She explained the scores and that they meant he was fine. She stayed with us that day and helped me with breastfeeding and the initial emotional rollercoaster that I went through once Charlie had arrived safely.
Mother

During antenatal care, parents should be offered an opportunity to visit the labour ward and meet some of the staff. Parents should also be asked if they would like to make a birth plan and staff should offer to discuss their available options for the labour, birth and meeting their baby. Some parents may feel that this gives them a sense of control during the pregnancy and some may start planning in early pregnancy (Mills *et al.* 2014). There may be certain things that parents want to avoid or do differently during this labour and birth. Parents should be reminded that it may be beneficial to think about the "birth plan" as a list of preferences and that flexibility may be needed if the birth does not go exactly as they planned (Sands 2014g).

If a baby died during a previous labour or at birth, parents may find this time particularly distressing. Parents should be offered an opportunity to discuss how their baby will be born and the timing of the birth with their obstetrician and/or midwife before the due date. Some women may be fearful or mistrust their bodies and their ability to have a healthy baby and may request a very premature delivery if they believe this is safer for their baby (Mills *et al.* 2014). Staff need to sensitively and gently offer information about the potential risks of a very premature birth for the baby in these situations.

Women who had a traumatic birth previously may also benefit from a discussion about how they may or may not experience flashbacks, anxiety and/or panic attacks in labour. They should be assured that continuous support will be available from staff during the labour and birth. All staff should be aware of how to care for women who experience flashbacks or panic attacks during labour and birth.

Parents' plans or preferences must be shared with all staff supporting parents during labour and birth and these staff should read this information carefully and meet parents' requests wherever possible. Additionally, the woman's notes should be clearly marked with a Sands teardrop sticker or another sticker (with the woman's consent). Some maternity units also use a special sticker on the notice board when a bereaved mother is in labour (see *Continuity of carers, bereavement midwives and communication between staff* in Chapter 12). These stickers and good communication between staff will help to ensure that all staff are alerted to a woman's previous experience and that she receives sensitive support and care.

 In my birth plan we asked that, when my baby was delivered, he was put straight onto me, without being cleaned or weighed. I desperately needed to see him and hold him before anyone else. After a few minutes they weighed him, but I am forever grateful that I had those first precious moments with him. Mother

Women may need additional support and encouragement during labour and the birth in a subsequent pregnancy. Women should be offered continuous support from their midwives throughout the labour unless they request privacy. If parents do want privacy, they should be aware that support is always available and know how to access staff members. It is also important that support is offered to any partners or birth supporters who are with the woman.

Staff should be prepared for parents' possible emotional reactions during labour and at the birth. Some parents may not believe that everything will be okay until after the baby is born. Some parents may also need constant reassurance and reminders during labour that this is a different birth and a different baby (Wallerstedt *et al.* 2003).

 I felt disconnected during the labour and just couldn't believe that everything would be OK. Mother

Parents may also need support when they meet their baby. Some parents may be reminded of the baby who died or experience grief for that baby (Sands 2014g). Other parents may have a positive experience of welcoming their baby (Sands 2014g). Staff should be aware of the range of potential experiences that parents may have and be available to offer support if needed.

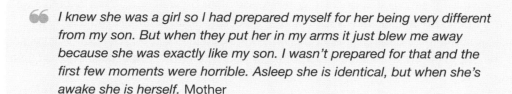

I knew she was a girl so I had prepared myself for her being very different from my son. But when they put her in my arms it just blew me away because she was exactly like my son. I wasn't prepared for that and the first few moments were horrible. Asleep she is identical, but when she's awake she is herself. Mother

I had been worried that I might confuse him with my first baby and feel very sad when he was born. But I didn't. He was a different baby. Mother

Another baby and ongoing support

Our first son, Jordan, made his entrance into the world. After four years of not being able to deal with how I was feeling, all of a sudden I was presented with a whole new set of emotions. Father

Some parents may be surprised and confused if they experience renewed grief for the baby or babies who have died, have mixed feelings or find life difficult when a healthy baby is born. For some parents, these feelings may be more complicated if the baby resembles or is the same sex as the baby who died. Some parents may not feel they are able to love this baby immediately and it may take a while before they start to experience these feelings (Hutti 2005). Some parents may feel guilty if they love their new baby. A lack of sleep and the demands of a new baby may also compound the feelings that parents are experiencing (including how they feel about their new baby) (Sands 2014g). Some parents may feel that babies born in a subsequent pregnancy have more problems or that the quality of their interactions with the baby may be affected and this may last into childhood (Turton *et al*. 2009a). Other parents may welcome these demands as they are happy to have a healthy baby (Sands 2014g).

I kept thinking of our perfect baby and imagining how easy it would have been to look after him. But then I realised that if he had lived, he would have been just as demanding as our daughter. It wasn't fair to assume he would have been easier to look after. Mother

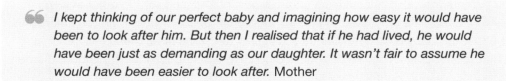

At postnatal group meetings, when others were moaning about sleepless nights, I just smiled because it was so amazing and wonderful to have a live baby, even if it was hard work. Mother

Staff should offer sensitive support to parents after their baby is born. They should also normalise parents' feelings and acknowledge that such feelings are shared by many parents and that they usually pass. If these feelings continue for long periods of time after the baby is born, staff should also offer parents a referral for specialist support (see Chapter 18).

 The staff were fantastic. One member of staff had also lost a child, a boy, and was great with me. They encouraged me to stay in the hospital as long as possible. They asked if I was supported enough emotionally at home and were just fantastic. I will always remember them all with absolute fondness and heartfelt thanks. Mother

 My partner was disconnected during my pregnancy, but now our son is born, his dad looks at him every day and cries. He's a lot more emotional now than I am. This baby has really brought his grief out. Mother

Some parents may also become overprotective towards this baby and/or any other children that they have. Staff should try to reassure parents that this is understandable and common. However, parents should be offered a referral for specialist help if they feel that their anxiety is affecting their ability to cope or their relationships with the baby or other people.

Primary care staff (such as GPs or health visitors) or local support groups may be able to offer parents long-term support and an opportunity to discuss their feelings (see also Chapter 17). Staff should be aware that some parents try to hide their feelings from relatives and friends and may become isolated. This may be important as some parents may find it difficult to watch other children grow and pass milestones that the baby who died did not experience. Parents may also find it difficult to answer questions about how many children they have and be grateful for opportunities to discuss how they might respond to such questions (Sands 2014g).

Some parents may also benefit from staff suggestions for supporting other siblings. For example, parents may need to also support older children who might be anxious to ensure that the baby is all right (Sands 2014g). At the same time, these children might also be experiencing a mixture of common positive and negative feelings about the new baby (Sands 2014g). Parents may also need to consider how to discuss the baby who died with subsequent siblings (Sands 2014g).

Among those parents who go on to have another pregnancy, a few may experience the death of another baby. This can be deeply shocking and distressing for the parents and staff who are caring for them. These parents may need additional immediate and long-term support from staff. See Chapters 14, 15 and 17 for more information about the support that parents should be offered.

CHAPTER 24

Staff support and training

Trusts, Health Boards and managers should ensure that there is good provision for staff support and training. It is also important that staff recognise that they have a professional responsibility to access support and training when they feel they need it. This chapter provides a general overview of support and training for staff who work with parents whose baby has died.

Specific training and support needs have also been identified in particular chapters that relate to:

- Communication (Chapter 4).

- Working with interpreters and communicating with parents whose first language is not English or who have a sensory impairment (Chapter 5).

- Discussing screening and diagnostic tests and results with parents (Chapter 6).

- Supporting parents experiencing a termination for fetal anomaly or a maternal medical condition (Chapter 8).

- Supporting parents during labour and birth when their baby has died (Chapter 12).

- Caring for parents and babies on the neonatal unit (Chapter 13).

- Post mortem examinations (Chapter 16).

The importance of support and training for staff

When a baby dies, it is important that parents receive good quality care from staff as parents' experiences of care can have lasting effects (Downe *et al.* 2013). Ensuring that staff who care for bereaved parents have good support and training is important as this can improve the quality of the care that parents receive.

Research has shown that both parents and staff have identified that it is crucial for staff to receive bereavement care training (Downe *et al.* 2013; NHS Improving Quality 2014; Redshaw *et al.* 2014; Sands 2015h, 2015i; Siassakos *et al.* 2015, unpublished results). Bereavement care training can help staff to develop skills in communicating more sensitively and empathetically with parents and increase their awareness of the potential needs of bereaved parents (Downe *et al*. 2013; NHS Improving Quality 2014; Redshaw *et al*. 2014; Sands 2015h, 2015i; Siassakos *et al*. 2015, unpublished results). Training can also help staff to feel more confident in the care that they provide and help to reduce staff stress (Kenworthy and Kirkham 2011).

There can also be significant emotional effects on staff who support parents during pregnancy loss or when their baby dies. Support is essential for staff well-being. The stress and distress of individual staff can also affect the quality of care that parents receive as well as their colleagues and the entire organisation (Kirkham and Stapleton 2004; Mander 2009; Kirkham 2011; Wallbank and Robertson 2013). Worden (2003) and Kenworthy and Kirkham (2011) also highlight that support and training are essential to ensure staff well-being and avoid staff burn out. Stress is most likely to occur in situations where the pressure and demands on maternity care staff are high, staff have little control over their workload or working practices and there is limited support or help available from colleagues and managers (Kirkham and Stapleton 2004; West 2015).

In contrast, care can be positively affected when staff experience good morale and feel motivated (Finlayson 2002). Receiving emotional and practical support from colleagues and managers can help staff to provide ongoing support for bereaved parents and deal with their own experiences of grief and distress (Kenworthy and Kirkham 2011). It can also be important for some staff to be able to express their grief with their colleagues and managers (Mander 2009).

When considering support for staff, it is important to consider the many reasons why it can be stressful and demanding to care for and support parents during a pregnancy loss or when a baby dies. Some of the reasons why providing this care can be stressful include:

- The way in which individual parents experience loss and grief is intensely personal and unpredictable. Therefore, staff have to work with a great deal of uncertainty.

- Many staff are aware that what they say and do at this time is vitally important and that parents may remember it for years to come (Downe *et al*. 2013). This awareness may cause staff to be very anxious about inadvertently saying the wrong thing and causing additional distress.

- Staff have a role in alleviating pain and distress and can find it particularly hard to deal with parents' grief that cannot be alleviated (Siassakos *et al*. 2015, unpublished results). Some staff may also find it difficult to take a less active role, listen and give parents time. Staff need patience, self-awareness and self-control in order to offer parents genuine choices and support their decision-making process.

- Staff have to deal with their own emotional reactions, often without acknowledgement or support. Some staff may be reminded of their own experiences of loss and may find it very hard to manage (Kenworthy and Kirkham 2011; Siassakos *et al*. 2015, unpublished results). They are also likely to feel distressed when a baby dies, especially if they have developed a close relationship with the parents. This relationship with parents, however, may also be beneficial for staff as they deal with their own feelings (Kenworthy and Kirkham 2011).

- Staff may also feel that the death of a baby represents a professional failure (Mander 2006; Kenworthy and Kirkham 2011). Some may blame themselves and fear complaints and litigation (Kenworthy and Kirkham 2011; Kirkham 2013). It can be distressing for staff if a mistake has been made even if it would not have affected the outcome (Siassakos *et al.* 2015, unpublished results).

- Parents may express anger and hostility towards staff if they feel that mistakes have been made. This is stressful in itself and may be even more stressful if the parents' accusations have some justification. Staff who are doing their best in difficult circumstances are likely to feel demoralised by parents' complaints (Jennings 2002). Speculation around the preventability of the death can also cause blame, guilt, anger and stress for staff (Worden 2003).

- Staff with little experience in caring for parents who are experiencing pregnancy loss may be anxious about their ability to cope. In a crisis, they may react with shock, panic and fear and may not know what to do. Less experienced staff may need more support to help them cope with caring for parents (Siassakos *et al.* 2015, unpublished results).

- The policies, guidelines and procedures in a unit may not accommodate the wishes and needs of individual parents and staff may feel frustrated and guilty that they cannot meet parents' needs (Anderson 2004; Edwards 2004b; Kirkham and Stapleton 2004; Levy 2004; Edwards *et al.* 2011; Kirkham 2011).

- Caring for parents experiencing childbearing losses may sometimes raise ethical issues for some staff members. For example, some staff may have a conscientious objection to the termination of pregnancy for a fetal anomaly or find it difficult to continue to provide active care for a baby when they do not feel that this is in their best interests.

- Staff often work under great pressure and in stressful circumstances with staff shortages affecting working environments (Sandall *et al.* 2011; Kirkham 2013). The numbers of staff on units is also unlikely to change with current financial constraints on the healthcare system (Sandall *et al.* 2011). This means that the time that staff can give to parents is often limited by other demands (Siassakos *et al.* 2015, unpublished results). As a result, staff may feel frustrated and anxious if they do not have enough time to give the best possible care (Ashcroft *et al.* 2003). This may particularly be the case if staff worry that the pressures under which they work may lead to adverse events, near-misses and poor outcomes for parents (Ashcroft *et al.* 2003).

Offering high-quality supportive bereavement care for parents can be difficult and this is why it is crucial that all staff have training and support for providing this care.

Support for staff

Trusts, Health boards and managers should ensure that adequate support and supervision are in place for all staff who offer care for parents experiencing a pregnancy loss or the death of their baby. The culture of healthcare services and teams should also be supportive and encouraging of staff who seek help and support.

Practitioners who work independently, such as independent midwives, interpreters and doulas, should also ensure that they have adequate support in place for themselves. Some of the information below may not be relevant to these practitioners. However, some of this information may be helpful for those who are considering the support that they may need.

Basic support requirements for all staff

The quality of care that parents receive depends entirely on the staff who care for them. To provide parents with high quality, individualised care, staff must be well-supported and receive regular supervision. This applies to all members of staff – at all levels and in all disciplines. It also applies to all primary care staff who may have long-term relationships with the family and who may be working in greater isolation. This support for staff should be built into the systems in which they work.

The type and amount of support that staff need can vary depending on the individual and the situation. It is important to have different support options available for members of staff to use as they need.

All staff should have access to:

- *Practical support and breaks while providing care for bereaved parents* (Kenworthy and Kirkham 2011).

- *Organisational support around patient allocation.* No member of staff should be expected to provide all care for bereaved parents. There may be implications for the well-being of a staff member who has to deal with several losses within a short space of time (Kenworthy and Kirkham 2011). They may also distance themselves from parents and be unable to provide empathic care (Kenworthy and Kirkham 2011). It is important that this is recognised by managers so they can ensure that workload allocation is appropriate in order to help mitigate the potential impact on individuals who are providing this care and avoid de-skilling other members of the team (see *The role of managers and bereavement midwives and nurses* below).

- *Systems that ensure that staff have a break between caring for parents who are experiencing a loss and caring for other parents* (Kenworthy and Kirkham 2011). Staff should also not be expected to provide bereavement care and care for parents expecting live babies at the same time (Kenworthy and Kirkham 2011).

- *An open and supportive atmosphere in which the stress and difficulty of caring for parents and families who are experiencing a childbearing loss are acknowledged.* All staff (regardless of their level of experience) should have team debriefing opportunities where they are able to discuss any issues or concerns that arise and talk about how they feel (Kenworthy and Kirkham 2011). There may be pressures on the time available for staff to engage in these activities but it is important that time is allocated for these discussions.

- *Opportunities to discuss, in confidence, their own feelings, difficulties or concerns about a particular case with a professional who has appropriate counselling skills.* There should be no stigma attached to accessing this support and staff should be able to access it in confidence.

- *Opportunities to reflect on and discuss particular cases or areas of their practice.* Staff should have access to a bereavement support worker or other experienced practitioner so that they can improve their skills and confidence (Jennings 2002).

- *Support and encouragement when they are open and honest about things that have gone wrong or practice that may have been inappropriate* (GMC and NMC 2015). When support is in place for staff to meet and openly review a baby's death without a fear of blame, this can help all staff to learn from what happened and aim to improve future care (Webster 2005; Sands 2016e). This support will also help to ensure that robust information about the death can be collected and reviewed (Manktelow *et al*. 2015) (see also *Recording, reporting and reviewing the baby's cause of death* in Chapter 16).

- *Support from colleagues who are available to scrutinise the documentation that must be completed following a baby's death to ensure that it has been fully and accurately completed* (Kenworthy and Kirkham 2011). This can help staff who are experiencing emotional distress and are also concerned about making errors while completing the documentation required after a baby's death (Kenworthy and Kirkham 2011). This is important as any errors in these records may affect whether disciplinary action is taken against staff following a review of the death (Kenworthy and Kirkham 2011).

- *Bereavement midwives and support from managers* (see *The role of managers and bereavement midwives and nurses* below).

Fear of getting it wrong should not be a reason for staff to avoid giving bereavement care or being over-cautious about what they say and do. There are bound to be occasions when a member of staff "gets it wrong" for a particular woman or couple even if they are very sensitive and thoughtful. When this happens, the member of staff should be actively supported and given time for reflection.

Support networks can be of great benefit to staff during times of stress and professional grief (Kenworthy and Kirkham 2011). Some individuals might like to set up personal support networks with two or three people. These might be trusted colleagues or friends who would be prepared to give each other informal, confidential support when wanted, either on the phone or face-to-face. For more about setting up personal support networks, see Schott and Priest 2002: 248–50.

Staff should also be aware of the support available to them through the Sands helpline and the Bereavement Care Network (See Appendix 2).

Staff training

Many health care staff are expected to cope with very distressing events and highly emotional situations without appropriate education and training (Burden & Stuart 2005; Deery 2004). Undergraduate, postgraduate and in-service training and updating in bereavement care should be provided for all staff (Downe *et al*. 2013; NHS Improving Quality 2014; Redshaw *et al*. 2014; Siassakos *et al*. 2015, unpublished results).

Provisions should also be made to ensure that staff can be released for this training (NICE 2015).

All staff involved in giving care during pregnancy loss and the death of a baby need to:

- Learn about and develop some understanding of the experience of loss and grief in general and the uniqueness of childbearing loss in particular (see Chapter 3).

- Learn about the possible needs of bereaved parents and how to provide individualised and inclusive care that meets the particular needs of women and families (see Chapters 1 and 2).

- Understand what is meant by parent-led care, informed choice and the implications of providing this type of care. Develop the skills and knowledge to enable bereaved parents to make informed choices about their bereavement care, including the memories they create with their baby (see Chapter 14), post mortem examinations (see Chapter 16) and what happens to their baby's body (see Chapter 20).

- Develop and use appropriate communication skills and techniques to deliver difficult and bad news and communicate sensitively and effectively with bereaved parents (see Chapter 4). This includes skills for communicating across language barriers and using interpreters (see Chapter 5).

- Recognise the impact of pregnancy loss and the death of a baby on health professionals and be able to access available support.

- Recognise the importance of on-going support for bereaved parents and the potential impact of their loss on all subsequent pregnancies.

- Know about local procedures and arrangements and the choices open to parents, and local and national sources of information and support for parents.

- Explore their own anxieties and concerns about providing care to bereaved parents (Mitchell 2005).

Sands recognises the importance of training that provides both information and skills to help healthcare professionals feel competent and confident in providing care for bereaved parents. Therefore, Sands has developed bereavement care workshops for midwifery, student midwifery, multidisciplinary groups and other professionals that enables the attendees to develop the knowledge, insight and skills to provide high quality, sensitive care to parents who experience the death of a baby, before, during or shortly after birth (see Appendix 2). These skills-based workshops focus on translating communication skills and best practice into providing better bereavement care. During these workshops, facilitators use a wide variety of teaching methods to increase healthcare professionals' confidence in working with bereaved parents and parents facing loss.

Multidisciplinary training that includes both hospital and community staff also provides an opportunity for participants to review and contribute to policy and practice, share information and solve problems with their colleagues.

All Trust and Health Board policies for the management of pregnancy loss and the death of a baby should recognise the need for staff training and updating. Training and updating in bereavement care should also be specified in staff contracts.

The role of managers and bereavement midwives and nurses

The NHS Constitution states that:

> *All staff should have rewarding and worthwhile jobs, with the freedom and confidence to act in the interest of patients. To do this, they need to be trusted, actively listened to and provided with meaningful feedback. They must be treated with respect at work, have the tools, training and support to deliver compassionate care, and opportunities to develop and progress. Care professionals should be supported to maximise the time they spend directly contributing to the care of patients.* (NHS 2013: 12)

Managers and senior staff have a particular duty to provide encouragement, support and training for staff for whom they are responsible, to watch for signs of strain or difficulty in individuals and within teams and to facilitate discussion between colleagues and teams. To meet the needs of staff and those of bereaved parents, managers should ensure that:

- *The unit has a shared philosophy of care and shared standards and aims.*

- *All staff working with bereaved parents feel that they are working as part of a team.* If there are problems or communication difficulties within a team, managers need to address these, and if necessary, organise intra-team and inter-professional team-building workshops using an experienced and skilled facilitator (Statham *et al*. 2001).

- *No individual member of staff bears sole responsibility for the care of all parents experiencing a loss and allocation of bereavement care is fairly distributed amongst staff.* It is essential that managers and colleagues are alert to this possibility and take steps to ensure that the care of parents who are experiencing a loss is allocated fairly and that no single member of staff carries an undue responsibility.

- *Bereavement midwives, nurses or coordinators are employed on every maternity and neonatal unit.* A bereavement midwife's role should include ensuring that all staff are supported and trained in providing bereavement care (Sands 2015i). The bereavement midwife, nurses and coordinators should also ensure that all members of the healthcare team are competent and confident in providing bereavement care and that specific members of staff are not providing all of this care in isolation (Sands 2015i) (see also *Continuity of carers, bereavement midwives and communication between staff* in Chapter 12 and *Bereavement midwives and nurses* in Chapter 25).

- *Staff feel valued for their work and receive positive feedback when they provide good care to parents.* Ensuring that staff feel valued can be an important factor for promoting staff morale (Finlayson 2002).

- *Staff morale is promoted by ensuring that staff workloads are designed to reduce stress and that staff have control and autonomy to provide effective care to parents (within safe boundaries)* (West 2015). These measures go beyond promoting staff well-being programmes and resilience, which deal with the symptoms of staff stress rather than the causes (West 2015). This also involves reviewing staffing levels, changes in the demand for maternity care services and staff absenteeism while ensuring that mechanisms are in place to ensure that adequate numbers of staff are available (NICE 2015).

- *Staff are shown compassion and listened to when they express their concerns or feelings* (West 2015).

- *Support and multidisciplinary training are provided for all staff, teams and departments.* This support and training should be integrated into day-to-day practice. Training should also be extended to community and non-clinical staff.

- *The procedures and guidelines that staff are expected to follow are appropriate for the care of families who are experiencing a childbearing loss* (Sands 2015i). Knowing that they are providing a good service to bereaved parents can enable staff to better cope with their own feelings when dealing with loss (Enkin *et al.* 2000). All staff should have opportunities to influence policy, protocols and procedures on the basis of their experience (NICE 2015).

- *All staff know how to access staff counselling services.*

- *That appropriate clinical supervision or access to a trusted mentor is in place for all staff and that they are aware of how to access this support and of its supportive function* (NICE 2015). Clinical supervision is particularly important for staff working with loss and bereavement as it provides opportunities for support, reflection on practice, personal and professional development and giving positive feedback.

Managers and bereavement midwives should also make sure that they themselves get support so that they can support their staff.

CHAPTER 25

Guidance for trusts, health boards, service commissioners and managers

This chapter is intended as guidance for all entities and individuals who are responsible for commissioning and organising services that provide care and support for bereaved parents who experience a pregnancy loss or the death of a baby. This includes the entities and individuals who are responsible for the policies, organisational systems and resources that enable frontline healthcare staff to work effectively. It also includes services provided by both the NHS and independent healthcare services. This chapter should be read in conjunction with Chapter 24 on *Staff support and training*.

This chapter highlights the relevant guidance and information for Trusts, Health Boards, service commissioners and managers. Additional information is available in the chapters highlighted.

There are a number of recommendations in the guidance that are related to policies and practices that will help services to meet the needs of bereaved parents. Many of these recommendations are cost neutral and require few resources to implement. However, some recommendations may have cost implications. Many recommendations reflect the need to ensure that staffing levels are adequate [see also NICE (2015)] and that care is organised in a way to enable staff to provide good bereavement care. A strategic approach is required to address how the recommendations could be achieved through short and long-term planning and implementation.

These recommendations should be regarded as important goals to improving the care received by parents following a pregnancy loss or the death of their baby. Providing good bereavement care for parents is crucial as this can affect their experiences of care and have long-term implications for their well-being (Schott and Henley 2009; Crawley *et al*. 2013; Downe *et al*. 2013; Redshaw *et al*. 2014; Ryninks *et al*. 2014).

The Sands Audit Tool for Maternity Services is an excellent resource for service commissioners, managers and staff members to use when assessing the care that they provide and identifying any improvements that should be made to this care (see the Sands website in Appendix 2 for more details). This tool can be used by any member of staff working in a healthcare setting.

It is crucial to ensure that care for parents experiencing a perinatal loss is effective and can be transferred smoothly between hospitals, community services and independent services when necessary. Therefore, it is important that hospitals, Trusts, Health Boards, service commissioners, managers and healthcare staff work together to develop policies, plan services and set standards.

Planning and providing services (See Chapter 1)

1. When designing and implementing policies and reviewing current practice, it is crucial that service users are key contributors to these processes. Trusts, Health Boards, service commissioners and managers should consult bereaved parents in their local area as well as organisations such as Sands, ARC, the Miscarriage Association, Bliss, Child Bereavement UK, Cruse Bereavement Care, the Multiple Births Foundation, TAMBA and the Ectopic Pregnancy Trust (see Appendix 2). Parents from different backgrounds, such as parents from minority backgrounds, should also be actively involved in these consultations and it is important to recognise that these parents may not be involved with local support organisations.

2. There is a responsibility to ensure that all parents are able to receive good care, regardless of their location in the UK (see Chapter 1).

Inclusive care (see Chapters 2 and 3)

3. Services should be accessible to parents from different backgrounds and systems and standard practices should not discriminate against parents. Services should be flexible so that they can be adapted wherever possible to meet the needs of all parents.

4. There is a need to be aware of the costs that parents may incur if they or their baby need specialist care and, wherever possible, funding should be available to assist parents on low incomes. It is also important that staff are aware of the benefits and resources that may be available for these parents (see also *Discussing entitlement to time off work and benefits* in Chapter 15).

5. Specialist midwives and nurses (for example, those that focus on bereavement, mental health, teenage pregnancy, substance misuse, etc.) should be identified and trained. These specialist staff should develop knowledge and skills for supporting vulnerable parents with specific needs. See *Bereavement midwives and nurses* below for more information about their role.

6. All staff should have training in supporting parents in same-sex relationships and sensitive documentation (for example, official forms and documents) should be available to support the needs of all parents (Cacciatore and Ratho 2011).

7. All staff should have training and awareness of all family types and be aware of the potential needs and experiences of bereaved parents who have used assisted reproductive technology to conceive their baby (Cacciatore and Ratho 2011).

8. Chaplaincies should have contacts with religious and spiritual advisers of all local faiths and spiritual organisations. Chaplains who work in health care settings should receive specialist training in communicating and supporting individuals and families during very distressing times (NHS England 2015a). They should also be responsible for checking and maintaining multi-faith rooms to ensure that they meet the needs of people from different spiritual backgrounds (NHS England 2015a) (see Chapter 1).

Loss and grief (see Chapter 3)

9. All staff should have adequate support and training to support bereaved parents (see also Chapter 24).

Bereavement midwives and nurses

10. Bereavement midwives and nurses should be available in all units and in community midwifery teams. These staff have specialist training and knowledge in bereavement care and should have an overview of all of the care that should be offered to bereaved parents (Sands 2015i). They are a resource for staff, bereaved parents and families and are also familiar with the relevant protocols and policies around the bereavement care that should be provided (Sands 2015i). Ideally, two or more specialist bereavement nurses or midwives will be designated so that they can offer each other support in this demanding role.

11. It is important that the roles of bereavement midwives and nurses are properly recognised, that a job description is available for these staff and that sufficient hours are allocated for them to complete the tasks associated with this role (Sands 2015i). This includes ensuring that these staff have an official job title and that their pay grade is adjusted accordingly (Sands 2015i).

12. It is important that bereavement midwives and nurses are not expected to provide care for all bereaved parents as this can be very demanding, these staff may not always be available and this can de-skill other staff (Sands 2015i). These specialist staff should be responsible for:

    - Ensuring that all protocols are regularly reviewed and are up-to date.

- Ensuring the relevant paperwork and equipment (such as cameras and equipment to take hand and footprints) are always available and ensuring that staff are familiar with how to complete paperwork and use equipment.

- Supporting staff who come into contact with bereaved parents at any stage of their care in hospital. This helps to ensure that parents receive sensitive and confident care when the bereavement midwife is not present and empowers other members of staff.

- Organising and evaluating multidisciplinary training sessions to include midwives, obstetricians, trainee medical staff, sonographers, gynaecology and neonatal nurses, receptionists and all other staff that see bereaved parents.

- Helping to ensure high standards of bereavement care in every relevant department.

- Liaising with other staff such as chaplains, neonatal staff, fetal medicine specialists, pathologists and mortuary staff.

- Promoting good communication between all relevant hospital departments and primary care staff.

- Building working relationships with external bodies such as the registrar of births and deaths, the coroner, local GP practices, funeral directors, crematorium and cemetery managers and local support groups such as Sands.

- Ensuring that parents are offered support literature such as the Sands booklets for parents.

- Monitoring contracts with funeral directors, the cemetery and the crematorium and the services they provide where hospitals offer to arrange and pay for funerals.
  This material has been copied from Sands' position statement on Bereavement midwives (Sands 2015i).

Communication (see Chapters 4 and 5)

13. Good communication is a crucial part of providing bereavement care (Redshaw *et al.* 2014; Siassakos *et al.* 2015, unpublished results). It is therefore crucial that all staff who work with bereaved parents receive training in the relevant communication skills (Redshaw *et al.* 2014; Siassakos *et al.* 2015, unpublished results) (see *Staff training* in Chapter 24). Sands Bereavement Care Training enables the attendees to develop the knowledge, insight and skills to provide high quality, sensitive care to parents who experience the death of a baby, before, during or shortly after birth (see Appendix 2). These skills-based workshops focus on translating communication skills and best practice into providing better bereavement care.

14. Policies should be in place to ensure that parents are told as soon as it is suspected that something is wrong, even if it is not yet confirmed or certain.

15. Good communication between staff and healthcare teams is also essential to providing good bereavement care. Policies should be in place to ensure that there are efficient processes for keeping all staff informed (with a woman's consent) about a pregnancy loss, a diagnosis of a fetal anomaly or the death of a baby and any treatment or care that has been received or decided upon. These policies should be developed and agreed to by primary and secondary care staff.

16. Many Trusts, Health Boards and clinics produce their own leaflets and other materials that provide information for parents. Some also use material produced by support organisations. All material should be developed in consultation with parents, sensitively worded and checked on a regular basis (at least every six months) to ensure that the information is consistent, up-to-date, relevant and easy to read. Information should be available in the main languages spoken locally and in formats suitable for parents with a sensory impairment.

17. Under the Equality Act 2010, adjustments should be made to all services to ensure that the needs of bereaved parents with disabilities such as sensory impairments or bereaved parents who need language support can access and receive good quality care that is tailored to their individual needs (Government Equalities Office 2010).

18. Interpreters should be available to support parents for whom English is not their first language so that they receive the same quality of care as other parents (NHS England 2015b). This is an essential part of providing safe and effective care and the best and most comprehensive service possible should be offered (NHS England 2015b). More guidance is available in *Providing interpreters for parents* in Chapter 5.

19. Support and training should be available for interpreters who work with bereaved parents (Sheldon 2005).

20. All staff should have adequate training in supporting parents with sensory impairments and other disabilities (Government Equalities Office 2010).

Antenatal screening and testing (see Chapter 6)

21. Policies and practices regarding antenatal screening and testing should emphasise the importance of informed choice. Policies should be in place to ensure that flexible appointment times are available when discussing antenatal screening and diagnostic testing with parents so that healthcare staff have time to give women sufficient information and women have time to ask questions (Tsouroufli 2011; Ahmed *et al*. 2013). It should also be ensured that staff receive adequate training to provide information that is consistent, reliable, up-to-date and clear. Parents should be given information verbally and in written or other formats and they should be informed of results as soon as possible.

22. A policy should be in place that ensures prompt and accurate communication between the different specialties involved in screening and diagnostic testing (for

example, teams working in midwifery, obstetrics, haematology, gynaecology and genetic counselling). Good coordination and regular communication between specialties are essential to ensure that policies and procedures are coherent, that parents are offered the best possible care and that the information given to parents by staff in different specialities is consistent.

23. A policy should be in place that ensures prompt and accurate communication between secondary and primary care staff about women whose baby is suspected to have, or has, been diagnosed with a fetal anomaly (with a woman's consent). Primary care staff should have information about test results and know what support and information they are expected to offer to parents in this situation.

Continuing a pregnancy (see Chapter 7)

24. Policies should be in place to ensure that continuity of carer, flexible access to services and support with travel costs to appointments (where applicable) can be offered for parents who continue a pregnancy after a fetal anomaly has been diagnosed.

25. Antenatal palliative care planning should also be available and offered to parents where relevant.

26. When a baby may or is expected to die around the time of birth, arrangements should also be in place for staff to refer parents to a local hospice where possible.

Termination of pregnancy for fetal anomaly, maternal medical conditions or other reasons (see Chapters 8 and 9)

27. Wherever possible, managers should support staff with a conscientious objection to opt out of providing care before and after a termination of pregnancy procedure to ensure that women and parents receive the best care possible (RCN 2013).

28. Policies should be in place to ensure that women are able to access the termination procedure of their choice. Regardless of gestation, terminations can be performed medically (using medicines to induce the expulsion of the pregnancy) or surgically (the physical removal of the pregnancy from the uterus using surgical tools such as vacuum aspiration or forceps).

29. Policies should be in place to ensure that women who are undergoing a medical termination of pregnancy for fetal anomaly or maternal medical condition are able to access care in their place of choice (on a gynaecological ward, a labour ward or at home). The location of the procedure may be important for some women and

they may be distressed if they are admitted to the "wrong ward" (Fisher and Lafarge 2015).

30. Where needed, financial support should be in place for women who need to travel to access specialist services such as feticide.

31. Policies should be in place to ensure that there is good communication between NHS services and any independent clinics or services where women are referred for terminations.

32. Training should be available for staff so that they are aware of the potential needs of women who have a termination of pregnancy for fetal anomaly or a maternal medical condition to ensure that these women are offered appropriate care following the termination procedure and that staff (including those in the private sector) are aware of their potential needs (RCOG 2010b; Fisher and Lafarge 2015). For example, some women may find it distressing if they are offered contraception following a termination procedure for fetal anomaly or a maternal medical condition (Fisher and Lafarge 2015).

33. To minimise delays in referral for termination, Trusts and Health Boards should consider setting up contracts with service providers that enable women to access termination services directly without referrals. Access routes should be widely publicised and any referrals should be made without delay.

34. A centralised booking system should be commissioned to cover all local service providers that carry out terminations after 20 weeks' gestation. This would decrease delays in referrals for women who are nearing the end of the second trimester of pregnancy.

35. Trusts and Health Boards should ensure that there is provision within the NHS for women with complex health problems seeking termination. These women cannot usually be cared for by independent service providers because they require specialist medical care as well as a termination. This may be particularly difficult for women seeking later terminations, which are more often provided by the independent sector.

Early miscarriage before 14 weeks' gestation (see Chapter 10)

36. All Trusts and Health Boards should provide an EPAU that can be accessed directly by primary care physicians, midwives and accident and emergency units (RCOG 2010c). EPAUs should be available on a daily basis and women should be able to access care within 24 hours of referral (RCOG 2010c). Where it is not possible for an EPAU to be open every day because of resource constraints, it should be open five days a week as a minimum (RCOG 2010c). In these cases, women should be able to access an emergency gynaecological unit at any time, although it is

important to note that these units do not always provide specialist support for women who are experiencing a miscarriage (NHS Improving Quality 2014).

37. All EPAUs should have access to transvaginal ultrasound and staff who are trained to use this equipment (RCOG 2010c).

38. When a woman visits or calls any medical service (including their GP or midwife) because of pain or bleeding in early pregnancy, she should be offered a referral for an assessment to confirm whether she is miscarrying as soon as possible. Ideally, this referral should be made to an EPAU. Women should also be able to self-refer to an EPAU if they have previously experienced recurrent miscarriages, ectopic pregnancy or molar pregnancy (NICE 2012). Information about EPAU referral criteria should be disseminated to all the relevant primary care staff.

39. Policies should ensure that time is allocated for staff to talk to parents and listen to their feelings and concerns during miscarriage. This is important as staff caring for parents during miscarriage do not always feel that they have time to offer adequate emotional support (Murphy and Merrell 2009; NHS Improving Quality 2014).

40. Policies should be in place so that women are offered information about and are able to decide on their place of care and whether their miscarriage care will be expectant, medical or surgical (where medically appropriate).

41. Policies should be in place to ensure that women experiencing an early pregnancy loss are able to access continuity of carer wherever possible.

42. Care pathways should be in place for women who experience miscarriage that include the offer of a follow-up appointment with either their GP or with a member of their consultant team if appropriate. Some parents may want to have a follow-up appointment in person while others may only wish to receive a telephone call (Jansson and Adolfsson 2010).

Late miscarriage between 14 and 24 weeks' gestation and stillbirth (see Chapter 11)

43. Policies, practices and procedures should be in place to make sure that the emotional and practical care needs of parents are met around the time when their baby has died (Redshaw *et al*. 2014) (see *Support and care for parents who experience a late miscarriage or stillbirth* in Chapter 11 for further details).

44. Policies and systems should be in place to offer parents care from a known carer and/or the same team of staff during late miscarriage and stillbirth.

45. Care pathways should be developed detailing the stillbirth or late miscarriage care that parents should receive. These care pathways should act as reminders for staff of the care options that should be offered to parents. However, care pathways

should not be used as checklists that must be completed (see *Parental choice and checklists* in Chapter 14).

46. During and after labour, it is important that parents are offered a private room away from the sounds of other women in labour and crying babies (Redshaw *et al.* 2014). Policies should be in place and facilities made available to provide such rooms for women and that ensure that any partners and supporters are able to stay with the woman overnight (Redshaw *et al.* 2014). See *Place of care* in Chapter 14 for more details of how these facilities should be arranged and maintained.

47. Local policies should be in place so that women who are experiencing late miscarriage and stillbirth should be offered a special bereavement room on the labour ward and provisions should also be in place for women who wish for their baby to be born at home (see Chapter 12). Most commonly, the cut-off point for access to the labour ward is 20 weeks' gestation although a small number of units do not allow women onto the labour ward before 24 weeks' gestation (Sands 2010; NHS Improving Quality 2014). These restrictions on place of care are important as many parents feel that their baby is not acknowledged as a baby if they are not admitted to the labour ward (Sands 2010).

Labour and birth when a baby has died (see Chapter 12)

48. Policies should be in place to ensure that women are able to make fully informed choices about their care during labour and birth after their baby has died. These policies should also ensure that women whose babies have died are offered the same quality and content of care as other women (Draper *et al.* 2015).

Care in neonatal units (see Chapter 13)

49. Policies should be in place to ensure that parents and family members are able to spend as much time as they want with their baby. Visiting should only be restricted when absolutely necessary (for example, if there is a risk of infection).

50. Policies should be in place so that parents are offered the opportunity to participate in all important decisions about the care of their baby, including critical care decisions when their baby is in a very critical condition (Bliss 2010).

51. Guidelines should be available for staff such as those published by the RCPCH (Larcher *et al.* 2015) to help them determine when life-sustaining treatment should be withheld or withdrawn. However, policies should acknowledge that making these decisions may be more difficult than simply following clinical guidance (Smith 2005).

52. Palliative and end of life care pathways should be developed and provisions should be in place to allow staff to provide good quality palliative and end of life care. The guidance document entitled *Practical guidance for the management of palliative care on neonatal units* (Mancini *et al.* 2014) offers additional practical guidance on preparing families and providing palliative care for babies.

53. All staff should receive training in providing palliative and end of life care and be aware of its importance and the potential benefits.

54. Policies should be in place to ensure that staff are aware of, and offer parents, referral to local hospices that offer support to parents before and after their baby's death.

55. Policies should be in place so that parents are offered the option of taking the baby home or to a hospice for extubation wherever possible (ACT 2009; McNamara 2013; Mancini *et al.* 2014). This includes ensuring that there is good communication and policies have been agreed between the transport team, the neonatal unit team and any community-based care providers (for example, a GP, nurse or hospice staff) (Mayer 2014).

56. Policies should be in place so that there is good inter-disciplinary communication between all staff involved in decision-making about a baby's care (Bloomer *et al.* 2015).

57. Private, comfortable rooms should be available on the unit for discussions with parents and single family rooms should be available where parents and families can spend time with the baby.

58. Policies should be in place to ensure that parents are made aware of the financial support available to them through benefits, the health service or local charities.

59. Policies should be in place so that women who are hospitalised can be brought to their baby on the neonatal unit in a wheelchair or hospital bed if possible. If the baby is transferred to a regional unit where specialist care can be provided and it is not possible to move the mother with the baby, policies should be in place so that midwifery staff at the referring hospital can contact the regional unit regularly to check the baby's progress and pass this information to the mother.

After a loss (see Chapter 14)

60. A dedicated, sound-proofed bereavement room or suite should be available where parents can spend time with their baby. This should include space and facilities for partners and other supporters. See item number 43 and 46 above and *Place of care* in Chapter 14 for more information.

61. A cold cot should be available to parents and units should consider having a mortuary fridge near the ward where the mother is receiving care. The baby's body

must be labelled and the fridge should be monitored and locked. These measures will help to facilitate parents' access to their babies.

62. Policies should be in place so that all parents have the choice of seeing and holding their baby and creating memories. These policies should include provisions for careful notes being kept about what has been offered to parents and what has or has not been done.

63. When hard copy keepsakes are part of the medical notes and can no longer be stored by a hospital, the parents should be contacted and given the choice of whether to have these items sent to them (Sands 2015j). When storing any keepsake, parents must also be informed that this may happen. See *Storing keepsakes* in Chapter 14 for more information.

64. Visitors should not be restricted from visiting parents unless parents request privacy.

65. Policies should be in place and forms should be available to facilitate the process when parents want to take their baby home or to a hospice. Forms should be given to parents confirming that their baby's body has been released to them. These policies should also ensure that parents are offered these options (see also Chapter 15 and Sample Form 1 in Appendix 1).

Postnatal care (see Chapter 15)

66. Policies should be in place to ensure that all women are offered and receive adequate postnatal care after the death of their baby (Draper *et al*. 2015).

67. If a woman consents, it is important that her medical notes are appropriately marked to alert staff that her baby has died. See the boxed text about Teardrop Stickers in Chapter 14 for more details.

68. Specially designed Bereavement Postnatal Notes, such as those developed by the Perinatal Institute, could also be used to ensure that staff are meeting the specific individualised care requirements of bereaved mothers. These notes are designed to be used after late miscarriage, stillbirth or neonatal death and are available from the Perinatal Institute website (see Appendix 2). These notes also contain a discharge summary letter that can be given to primary care staff including GPs and health visitors.

Transfer to the mortuary and post mortem examinations (see Chapter 16)

69. Contracts and arrangements for transport with ambulance services, funeral directors and other service providers should be negotiated to ensure that the bodies and remains of all babies are handled and treated respectfully, regardless of gestation or circumstances. Clinical waste bags should never be used and all drivers should be made aware of what they are transporting.

70. It should be ensured that all hospital departments (including accident and emergency units, maternity units, gynaecology wards, mortuaries and laboratories) have efficient procedures and tracking systems for transferring babies' bodies and fetal remains between them (HTA Code 3 2014). These systems should be understood by all the staff concerned (including labour ward and neonatal unit staff) and an audit trail should be maintained for any transferred remains (HTA Code 3 2014).

71. Sensitive post mortem examination consent forms should be available for use when discussing post mortem examinations with parents. If they have not already done so, hospitals, Trusts and Health Boards should consider using one of the HTA's model forms to update their current forms and make them more suitable for parents whose baby dies during pregnancy or shortly after birth. This is important as the length and complexity of some consent forms has been cited as a barrier to the consent process for some parents and staff (Downe *et al.* 2012).

72. Policies and provisions should be in place to ensure that consent is always sought by a member of staff who has received training in taking post mortem examination consent and has a good understanding of the procedures for which they are taking consent (Sands 2013a; HTA Code 1 2014).

73. Policies should be in place to ensure that all parents are offered the opportunity to discuss a post mortem examination of their baby and that this is documented (Draper *et al.* 2015). This should include offering parents information about different types of post mortem and placental examinations that are available.

74. All post mortem examinations on fetuses and babies should be carried out by specialists in perinatal pathology in regional centres (RCOG and RCP 2001). Policies should be in place to ensure that parents are informed during the consent process about any transfer that may be required and how and when this will take place.

75. Policies should be in place to ensure that parents are accurately informed of how long the results of a post mortem examination will take and to ensure that they are informed immediately of any delays that arise.

76. Procedures and paperwork should be in place (including a mortuary release form) to give parents when they wish to take their baby's body home or to arrange for

burial or cremation after a post mortem examination. No documentation is legally necessary for parents to take the baby's body from the hospital or mortuary but they should be given a form confirming that this has been done in case problems arise.

77. A policy to ensure that there is a robust system of reporting and reviewing each baby's death should be in place on every unit and time should be allocated for multidisciplinary reviews and reporting at the local and national levels (Ptacek *et al.* 2014; Draper *et al.* 2015; Manktelow *et al.* 2015) (see also *Recording, reporting and reviewing the baby's cause of death* in Chapter 16). A named member of staff on each unit should be the designated Lead Reporter who is responsible for liaising with MBRRACE-UK and feeding back information to colleagues (Manktelow *et al.* 2015). Parents' perspectives regarding their care should be incorporated into these reviews wherever possible (Draper *et al.* 2015).

Follow-up appointments and ongoing care (see Chapter 17)

78. Policies should be developed and implemented to ensure that both immediate and long-term follow-up care are available to all parents who experience a pregnancy loss or the death of a baby.

Mental health (see Chapter 18)

79. Mental health assessment and treatment should be offered to women as well as their partners (NICE 2014a), other children and family members (where applicable) after any type of perinatal loss.

80. Perinatal mental health training should be required for all relevant staff that includes information about bereavement following a pregnancy loss or the death of a baby.

81. Policies and practices should be in place to offer bereaved parents ongoing follow-up care, further assessment and treatment for mental health problems.

82. Policies and practices should be in place to ensure that sufficient time is available in follow-up appointments with bereaved parents to enquire about their emotional well-being and offer assessments for mental health conditions where necessary.

83. Policies and practices should be in place to ensure that there is good communication between staff and healthcare teams regarding parents who may be at risk of developing or who have been diagnosed as having mental health problems after a perinatal loss.

84. Specialist perinatal mental health services should be available in all areas of the UK and these services should be available for bereaved parents and their families. Efforts should be made to implement these services in the large number of areas where specialist perinatal mental health services do not currently exist and to decrease long waiting lists in other areas (Bauer *et al.* 2014).

Certificates and registration (see Chapter 19)

85. Parents who experience a loss before 24 weeks' gestation should be offered an unofficial "certificate of birth". This form could be based on one of the templates available from Sands' website (see Appendix 1: Form 2 as an example) and should reflect the needs of individual families.

86. Policies should be in place to ensure that healthcare staff can help parents by offering to explain what the registration process involves when necessary and alerting them to decisions they may want to make before they go to the register office.

Funerals and sensitive disposal (see Chapter 20)

87. Trusts and Health Boards have a responsibility to ensure that parents are offered choices about burial, cremation, sensitive incineration and funerals for their baby or pregnancy remains. It may be very distressing for parents who are not fully informed about their available options and discover afterwards that arrangements were made that they do not consider to be satisfactory. See *Policies and practices* in Chapter 20 for full information.

88. Trust and Health Board policies regarding funerals and disposal should cover perinatal losses of all types and gestations. The basis for all these policies must be that parents are offered choices about hospital and private arrangements and that babies' bodies and fetal remains are handled with respect. The policies should be carefully developed in consultation with representatives from all relevant departments, bereaved parents and representatives from relevant support organisations (see Appendix 2). In England, Wales and Northern Ireland, these policies should also be updated in relation to the Human Tissue Authority's Guidance on the disposal of pregnancy remains following pregnancy loss or termination (HTA 2015). In Scotland, guidance has been issued by the Scottish Government regarding the disposal of pregnancy remains that incorporates the Infant Cremation Commission Report recommendations (Scottish Government 2015a). All policies should be reviewed and updated regularly.

89. In addition to arranging and paying for burial, cremation, sensitive incineration and/ or a funeral or other ceremony for stillborn babies and fetal remains, Trusts, Health Boards and managers should also consider offering these options for babies who die shortly after birth. This may be important as women living in poverty have a

much higher risk (57 per cent) of experiencing their baby being stillborn or dying in the neonatal period (Manktelow *et al.* 2015).

90. Trusts and Health Boards should appoint a multidisciplinary group of staff that negotiates and monitors contracts with local funeral directors, a local cemetery and/or a local crematorium. One or more members of the staff who regularly provide care for bereaved parents should be part of the negotiating team. See *Negotiating contracts with local service suppliers* in Chapter 16 for more details of what these contracts should include.

91. Trusts and Health Boards should make arrangements for funerals, burials, cremations and sensitive incineration for losses that occur outside the hospital and negotiate contracts accordingly. Alternatively, they may arrange to share in a local hospital's arrangements.

92. The ICCM document called *Policy and Guidance for Baby and Infant Funerals* should be used by Trusts and Health Boards who are considering contracts with service suppliers and it contains a sample agreement for hospitals and cemeteries/crematoria in Appendix A (see Appendix 2).

Memorials (see Chapter 21)

93. It is important to ensure that hospital memorial services, books of remembrance, memorial books, sympathy cards and other materials are not religious in content. This will help to ensure that these items are as inclusive as possible.

Receiving and responding to feedback: parent experiences (see Chapter 22)

94. Appropriate feedback mechanisms should be in place to obtain feedback from parents about their care. Local feedback mechanisms should be developed in collaboration with staff and bereaved parents who have received care from their services. This will help to ensure that specific feedback on local services is available and that the feedback mechanism is relevant for the needs of parents from different local communities.

95. Information about local MSLCs and how to become involved should be widely publicised so that parents are aware of these services. Additionally, Trusts, Health Boards and managers should ensure that invitations are extended to relevant local support groups and organisations who may be able to send a representative to sit on the MSLC.

96. Policies and reporting systems should be in place to ensure that staff report any incidents that may have been related to a baby's death (GMC and NMC 2015).

Trusts, Health Boards and managers should also ensure that a culture of learning is created around reporting errors and incidents rather than a culture of blame (GMC and NMC 2015; PASC 2015).

97. Information should be readily available for parents about feedback. Complaint procedures and mechanisms for providing feedback and filing complaints should be accessible for parents in different formats and languages (see also Chapter 5). It is important that additional harm and distress is not caused to parents and families as a result of the complaints process (PASC 2015).

98. Policies and procedures should be in place to investigate issues of patient safety and parents' feedback and complaints in an efficient and effective manner (PASC 2015). Investigations should be conducted in a way that is supportive to staff and encourages them to be open and honest (PASC 2015).

99. Parents' feedback should be taken seriously. Changes in policies and procedures should be made if parents have raised concerns relating to clinical safety or organisational failure. However, Trusts, Health Boards and managers should carefully consider any other major changes in practice and consult other bereaved parents and relevant organisations before instituting these changes. All parents are different and some parents may be satisfied with care and procedures that other parents find distressing. In some instances, it may be best to consider policies and procedures that emphasise the need to provide parents with individualised care that is tailored to their needs.

100. There should be transparency regarding any outcomes of investigations and reviews and these should be published and disseminated (PASC 2015). Parents should be offered an opportunity to discuss the outcome of any investigation of a complaint or feedback with a senior member of staff and policies should be in place to ensure that this happens standardly and as quickly as possible.

101. It is also important that staff receive support from colleagues and managers during and after any feedback or complaints are received. Listening to parents in these circumstances or receiving complaints can be very stressful or distressing for staff (see *Support for staff* in Chapter 24).

Support in subsequent pregnancies (see Chapter 23)

102. Policies should be in place so that parents can be offered continuity of carers during pregnancies, labour and birth that they experience following a loss (Redshaw *et al.* 2014). The option of having their notes clearly marked may also help to ensure that parents do not need to explain their situation repeatedly (Redshaw *et al.* 2014). For example, staff might label parents' notes with the Sands Teardrop Sticker (see Chapter 14). Policies should be in place so that there is flexibility regarding the place of care or specific carers who provide parents with care wherever possible.

103. Ensuring that there is good communication between staff (including across teams and departments) is essential in subsequent pregnancies (Redshaw *et al.* 2014). See also *Informing other carers* in Chapter 14. All staff who care for bereaved parents in subsequent pregnancies should be well-informed about parents' history so that they can respond sensitively to any anxieties or concerns that parents may express.

Staff support and training (see Chapter 24)

104. Trusts, Health Boards and managers should ensure that adequate support and supervision are in place for all staff who offer care for parents experiencing a pregnancy loss or the death of their baby. The culture of healthcare services and teams should also be supportive and encouraging of staff who seek help and support.

All Trust and Health Board policies for the management of pregnancy loss and the death of a baby should recognise the need for staff training, updating and support. Training and updating in bereavement care should also be specified in staff contracts.

Appendix 1:
Sample forms and certificates

These sample forms and certificates are provided free of copyright for individual Trusts, Health Boards, hospitals and healthcare staff to adapt and reproduce as needed. It is very important that all forms and certificates that staff might give to parents are attractively laid out and produced. They are available to download from the Sands website (see Appendix 2).

Forms 3 and 4 have been adapted with the kind permission of Eltham Crematorium Joint Committee and the Institute of Cemetery and Crematorium Management.

1: Form to give to parents who take the baby's body out of the hospital

There is no legal reason why parents should not take the fetal remains or body of their baby out of the hospital. However, for the protection of the parents and to avoid misunderstandings, staff should give them a copy of Form 1. For more information, see *Taking the baby's body home* in Chapter 15

2: Certificate to be offered to parents of a baby who was born dead before 24 weeks' gestation

For more information, see *Certification and forms for a baby born dead before 24 weeks' gestation* in Chapter 19. One sample form is included here and five forms are available from the Sands website with spaces to include:

- Only the mother's name.
- Only the father's name.
- The names of a mother and a father.
- The names of two mothers.
- The names of two fathers.

The appropriate form from the Sands website should be used or modified for each family.

3: Medical form for burial or cremation confirming that fetal remains are less than 24 weeks' gestation

For more information, see *Certification and forms for a baby born dead before 24 weeks' gestation* in Chapter 19 and *Paperwork for the cremation of fetal remains or babies born dead before 24 weeks' gestation* in Chapter 20.

4: Application form for the individual burial or cremation of fetal remains

For more information, see *Certification and forms for a baby born dead before 24 weeks' gestation* in Chapter 19 and *Paperwork for the cremation of fetal remains or babies born dead before 24 weeks' gestation* in Chapter 20.

For the application forms needed for a shared burial or cremation of fetal remains, please see the ICCM's sample form in Appendix B of their *Policy and Guidance for Baby and Infant Funerals* document that is available at http://www.iccm-uk.com/iccm/library/Fetal%20Remains%20Policy%20Updated%20Sept2015%20.pdf

5: Funeral consent form

This consent form can help staff to ensure that parents are asked essential questions about their baby's funeral but should not be used as a checklist where all items must be completed (see *Parental choice and checklists* in Chapter 14). This form should be used for guidance only. This form can be signed by the parents and they should be provided with a copy so that they have a record of their choices.

FORM 1

Form to give to parents who take the baby's body out of the hospital

Name of hospital/trust/health board
Form for parents who take their baby's body home
TO WHOM IT MAY CONCERN

This is to confirm that (name(s) of parent(s)

_____

of (address) _____

_____

Have taken their baby's body from (name and address of hospital)

_____

Date _____

I / We, the parent(s), hereby take full responsibility for our baby whilst they are in our care. We will (tick as appropriate):

☐ return our baby to the hospital on (date) _____

☐ make our own funeral arrangements.

Parent(s) Name(s) (please print):

_____   _____

Signature _____ Signature _____

Position (please print) _____

In case of need or concern please contact:

Staff member's name _____ Job Title _____

Department direct line _____ Signature _____

24-hour phone contact for support _____

FORM 2

Certificate to be offered to parents of a baby who was born dead before 24 weeks' gestation

Certificate of Birth
before the 24ᵗʰ week of pregnancy

Mother

_____

Father

_____

Home Address

_____

Name of baby

_____

Date of birth

_____

Time of birth

_____

Gestational age at birth

_____

Born at

_____

The baby showed no signs of life

Issued by

_____

(signature)

_____

Name

_____

Registered qualifications

_____

Date

_____

FORM 3

Medical form for burial or cremation confirming that fetal remains are less than 24 weeks' gestation

MEDICAL FORM FOR CREMATION OR BURIAL CONFIRMING THAT FETAL REMAINS ARE LESS THAN 24 WEEKS' GESTATION

I hereby certify that I have examined _____
[insert name if given], the fetus of:

[Parent(s)' names] _____

Delivered on *[date]* _____ 20 _____
was of a gestation up to and no more than 24 weeks and showed no signs of life.
I know of no reason why any further enquiry or examination should be made.

Name _____

Signature _____

Registered qualifications _____

Address _____

Telephone number _____

Date _____

The above signatory must be a registered doctor, nurse or midwife who delivered or examined the fetus.

FORM 4

Application form for the individual burial or cremation of fetal remains

APPLICATION FORM FOR THE INDIVIDUAL BURIAL OR CREMATION OF FETAL REMAINS

Name of baby, if given _____

Date and time of burial /cremation _____

Place of burial/ cremation _____

Family to attend _____

Service details _____

Funeral director *(if applicable)* _____

Address _____

I *[name of applicant]* _____

Telephone _____

Address _____

_____

am the parent or am acting with the knowledge and consent of the parent(s) *[delete as applicable]* to apply for the cremation or burial of the remains of the baby described in the attached *Medical form for burial or cremation confirming that fetal remains are less than 24 weeks' gestation.*

I would like to receive details about the Book of Remembrance [please tick the box] ☐

Signature of Applicant _____

Date _____

FORM 5

Funeral consent form

FUNERAL CONSENT FORM FOR PARENTS

This is to confirm that (name(s) of parent(s))

_____

Have decided to have a funeral arranged for their baby _____

☐ By *[Name of hospital/trust/health board]*   ☐ By private arrangement

☐ Have not yet decided on a funeral for their baby but will contact the member of staff
named below by [date] _____ to inform them of their decision.

[Amend the list below based on the locally available options for the baby's gestation]
Where **[Name of hospital/ trust/ health board]** is to make the funeral arrangements, all available
options have been fully explained and the parents have decided on:

☐ Individual burial   ☐ Shared burial
☐ Individual cremation   ☐ Shared cremation
☐ Sensitive incineration

☐ Staff have explained whether and when ashes will be available following a cremation

☐ An individual funeral   ☐ A shared funeral   ☐ Not to have a funeral

☐ Parents have been informed that an **[individual/ shared]** funeral will be provided by the
hospital that is **[non-denominational/name of religion]**

☐ Parents have been offered information about additional options available to them (for
example, they have been offered details about their options for a coffin, music, flowers,
readings, etc.) and any related expenses have been explained. Include details below.

_____

_____

_____

☐ Parents will attend the funeral   ☐ Parents will not attend the funeral and
☐ Parents may attend the funeral   ☐ have been informed of the details
                                                ☐ have declined information about
                                                   the funeral

☐ Parents are aware that the funeral will be held on [date] _____ at [time] _____ at
[location] _____

☐ The baby will be transported to the funeral by:

☐ The hospital   ☐ A funeral director: ☐ The parents
                         _____

Parent(s) Name(s) (please print):

_____

Signature _____   Signature _____

Date _____

Appendix 2: Useful organisations and resources

Action on Pre-Eclampsia (APEC)
Helps and supports women and their families who are affected by or worried about pre-eclampsia and aims to raise public and professional awareness of pre-eclampsia.
http://action-on-pre-eclampsia.org.uk/

Antenatal Results and Choices (ARC)
Offers non-directive individualised information and support for parents making decisions around antenatal testing, including when a baby has a significant anomaly.
http://www.arc-uk.org/

Baby Mailing Preference Service (MPS) online
Free site where parents can register online to stop or help reduce baby-related mailings.
http://www.mpsonline.org.uk/bmpsr/

Bereavement Advice Centre
Offers information and advice for people with practical concerns after the death of someone close to them.
https://www.bereavementadvice.org/

Bereavement Care Network
Online network for bereavement care professionals who offer or are interested in care for parents when a baby dies.
http://bereavement-network.rcm.org.uk/

Bliss
Offers support for families of premature or sick babies, including bereaved families.
http://www.bliss.org.uk/

Financial advice for families is available at:
http://www.bliss.org.uk/financial-advice-for-families
In addition, Bliss provides the Bliss Baby Charter and Audit Tool to help professionals assess and improve the family-centred care provided for premature and sick babies.
http://www.bliss.org.uk/baby-charter-audit-tool

British Pregnancy Advisory Service (BPAS)
Offers advice and treatment for termination of pregnancy in the UK.
https://www.bpas.org/

Child Benefit Office

Parents can contact the Child Benefit Office at HM Revenues and Customs for information about eligibility, claiming and stopping Child Benefit.
https://www.gov.uk/government/organisations/hm-revenue-customs/contact/child-benefit

Child Bereavement UK (CBUK)

Provides support for families when a baby or child has died or is dying and offers support for children faced with bereavement. Offers training for professionals.
http://www.childbereavementuk.org/

The Compassionate Friends

An organisation of bereaved parents, siblings and grandparents that offer support to others after the death of a child or children.
http://www.tcf.org.uk/

Contact a Family

Provides support, information and advice for families with disabled children.
http://www.cafamily.org.uk/

Cruse Bereavement Care

Offers support to bereaved people and training for professionals.
http://www.cruse.org.uk/

Each Baby Counts

The Royal College of Obstetricians and Gynaecologists' programme to reduce the number of babies who die or are severely disabled as a result of incidents occurring during term labour in the UK.
https://www.rcog.org.uk/eachbabycounts

Ectopic Pregnancy Trust

Provides support and information for people who have had or been affected by an ectopic pregnancy, including health professionals.
http://www.ectopic.org.uk/

Federation of British Cremation Authorities (FBCA)

Professional organisation of burial and cremation authorities in the UK.
http://www.fbca.org.uk/

Funeral Payments – NI Direct

Financial help that is available for individuals on low-incomes in Northern Ireland who need help to pay for a funeral that they are arranging.
http://www.nidirect.gov.uk/funeral-payments

Funeral Payments – UK Government

Financial help that is available for individuals on low-incomes in England, Wales and Scotland who need help to pay for a funeral that they are arranging.
https://www.gov.uk/funeral-payments

Gifts of Remembrance

Provides photography training for hospital staff and volunteers who support parents after a stillbirth or neonatal death.
http://giftsofremembrance.co.uk/

Human Fertilisation and Embryology Authority (HFEA)

Independent regulator overseeing the use of gametes and embryos in fertility treatment and research that provides information for parents about the fertility process and fertility clinic.
http://www.hfea.gov.uk/

Human Tissue Authority (HTA)

Regulator for human tissue and organs and organisations that remove, store and use tissue.
https://www.hta.gov.uk

Also provides learning outcomes for perinatal post mortem consent taker training:
https://www.hta.gov.uk/policies/learning-outcomes-perinatal-post-mortem-consent-taker-training#legal

Infertility Network UK

Provides support for people dealing with infertility and/or who are facing involuntary childlessness.
http://www.infertilitynetworkuk.com

Institute of Cemetery and Crematorium Management (ICCM)

Professional organisation of burial and cremation authorities in the UK that promotes the improvement of cemeteries, crematoria and public services.
http://www.iccm-uk.com

Also offers fully accredited training for cemetery and crematorium staff.
http://www.iccm-uk.com/iccm/index.php?pagename=training

International Stillbirth Alliance (ISA)

International alliance of organisations and individuals working to prevent stillbirth and improve bereavement care worldwide.
http://www.stillbirthalliance.org

Jobcentre Plus – Bereavement Services Helpline

Provides information about benefits claims.
https://www.gov.uk/contact-jobcentre-plus

Telephone: 0345 608 8601
Information is also available from the Pension Service helpline on (0345) 6060265 (option 2).

Lullaby Trust
Offers support and advice for parents whose baby dies suddenly and advice on safer sleep.
https://www.lullabytrust.org.uk/

Marie Stopes International
Independent provider of sexual and reproductive health services in the UK.
https://www.mariestopes.org.uk/

Mothers and Babies: Reducing Risk through Audits and Confidential Enquiries across the UK (MBRRACE-UK)
Provides surveillance of maternal, perinatal and infant deaths in the UK.
https://www.npeu.ox.ac.uk/mbrrace-uk

Also provides an online reporting system for healthcare units to report maternal, perinatal and infant deaths.
https://www.mbrrace.ox.ac.uk

Miscarriage Association
Offers support and information for individuals affected by pregnancy loss and health care professionals.
http://www.miscarriageassociation.org.uk/

Money Advice Service
Provides free and impartial money advice, including information for bereaved parents about benefits and entitlements after the death of their baby.
https://www.moneyadviceservice.org.uk

Multiple Births Foundation (MBF)
Provides support and information for multiple birth families (including bereavement support) and information for professionals.
http://www.multiplebirths.org.uk

National Association of Funeral Directors
Provide support and guidance for funeral firms and bereaved families using their services.
http://www.nafd.org.uk/

National Association of Memorial Masons (NAMM)
Sets standards for memorial stones and provides information for individuals who are choosing a memorial.
http://www.namm.org.uk

National Perinatal Epidemiology Unit (NPEU)
Multidisciplinary research unit at the University of Oxford who provide evidence to improve care for women and their families in the perinatal period and promote the effective use of resources by perinatal health services.
https://www.npeu.ox.ac.uk/

The Natural Death Centre

Offers support, advice and guidance for families and other individuals who are arranging a funeral, including information about environmentally-friendly funerals and woodland burial sites.

http://www.naturaldeath.org.uk/

Neonatal Data Analysis Unit and North West London CLAHRC Map

A map that has information about all neonatal units of different levels, children's hospitals and hospices in the UK.

https://www.google.com/maps/d/viewer?mid=zvO6tbj1tNpI.k6W-xh0w52nM

NHS Antenatal and newborn screening timeline

Visual reference developed to show the optimal timings of antenatal and newborn screening tests offered through the NHS.

http://cpd.screening.nhs.uk/timeline

Now I lay me down to sleep

An American website that puts bereaved parents in touch with professional photographers who will take photographs of their babies at no cost. Site shows examples of photographs of babies of all gestations. Photographers in the UK can also be found through the *Find a Photographer* page.

https://www.nowilaymedowntosleep.org/

Perinatal Institute for maternal and child health

National non-profit organisation that aims to enhance the safety and quality of maternity care and provides resources for healthcare professionals.

http://www.perinatal.org.uk/

Rainbow Trust Children's Charity

Offers support to families in England with life-limiting and life-threatening conditions.

https://rainbowtrust.org.uk/

Registry Offices for England and Wales, Scotland, and Northern Ireland

- England and Wales: General Register Office
  http://www.gro.gov.uk/gro/content/

- Scotland: National Records for Scotland
  http://www.nrscotland.gov.uk/registration

- Northern Ireland: General Register Office Northern Ireland (GRONI)
  http://www.nidirect.gov.uk/gro

Relate

Offers relationship support to help people strengthen their relationships.

http://www.relate.org.uk/

Remember My Baby Remembrance Photography

UK-based charity who have professional photographers who voluntarily provide their photography services to parents whose baby dies before, during or shortly after birth.

http://www.remembermybaby.org.uk/

Sands, the stillbirth and neonatal death charity

Provides support and information for anyone affected by the death of a baby, before or after birth. National helpline, local parent-led support, literature and online support. Works to improve care when a baby dies and promotes research to reduce the loss of babies' lives. More information about Sands' work and resources is available at the end of these guidelines.

https://www.uk-sands.org/

Samaritans

Offers confidential support that is available 24 hours a day to people who need to talk. Telephone: 116 123 (UK) or 116 123 (ROI) for free.

http://www.samaritans.org/

Sibs

Offers support to individuals who are growing up with or have grown up with a disabled sibling.

https://www.sibs.org.uk/

Sure Start Maternity Grant

One-off payment that some bereaved parents may be eligible to claim to help with the costs of having a child.

https://www.gov.uk/sure-start-maternity-grant/overview

Tamba Bereavement Support Group

Offers support for families who have lost one or more children from a multiple birth during pregnancy, birth or at any time afterwards.

http://www.tamba.org.uk/bereavement

(Part of the Twins and Multiple Births Association (Tamba) https://www.tamba.org.uk/)

Tax Credits Office

Provides information and claim forms for parents looking to claim Child Tax Credit.

https://www.gov.uk/government/organisations/hm-revenue-customs/contact/tax-credits-enquiries

Telephone: 0345 300 3900

For information about the online tool that can be used for claims, parents can visit:

https://www.gov.uk/child-tax-credit/how-to-claim

Together for Short Lives

Offers support for families with children who have life-threatening or life-limiting conditions and professionals and services (including children's hospices).

http://www.togetherforshortlives.org.uk/

United Kingdom Association for Milk Banking (UKAMB)

Supports human milk banking and aims to provide safe and screened donor breastmilk for premature and sick babies.

http://www.ukamb.org/

UK Government, population screening programmes

List of NHS screening programmes.
https://www.gov.uk/topic/population-screening-programmes

UK National Screening Committee (UK NSC)

Advises the UK government and the NHS about screening and supports the implementation of screening programmes.
https://www.gov.uk/government/groups/uk-national-screening-committee-uk-nsc

Winston's Wish

Offer support to bereaved children, their families and professionals.
http://www.winstonswish.org.uk

Working Families

Helps working parents, carers and their employers balance home and work responsibilities. They also provide information about parents' rights at work and to benefits after they experience miscarriage, stillbirth and neonatal death.
http://www.workingfamilies.org.uk/articles/
miscarriage-stillbirth-and-neonatal-death-your-rights-at-work/

References

Aagaard H, Hall EOC (2008) Mothers' experiences of having a preterm infant in the neonatal care unit: a meta-synthesis. *Journal of Paediatric Nursing* 23: e26–e36.

Abramsky L, Fletcher O (2002) Interpreting information: what is said, what is heard – a questionnaire study of health professionals and members of the public. *Prenatal Diagnosis* 22: 1188–1194.

Abramsky L, Hall S, Levitan J, Marteau TM (2001) What parents are told after prenatal diagnosis of a sex chromosome abnormality: interview and questionnaire study. *British Medical Journal* 322: 463–466.

ACT (2009) *A Neonatal Pathway for Babies with Palliative Care Needs*. Bristol: ACT: Valuing Short Lives.

AFFIRM (2014) Welcome to AFFIRM. AFFIRM website. Edinburgh: University of Edinburgh. Available at http://www.crh.ed.ac.uk/affirm/ (accessed 2 January 2016).

Ahmed S, Bryant LD, Cole P (2013) Midwives' perceptions of their role as facilitators of informed choice in antenatal screening. *Midwifery* 29: 745–750.

Ahmed S, Green J, Hewison J (2002) What are Pakistani women's experiences of beta-thalassaemia carrier screening? *Public Health* 116: 297–299.

Ahmed S, Green J, Hewison J (2005) Antenatal thalassaemia carrier testing: women's perceptions of "information" and "consent". *Journal of Medical Screening* 12: 69–77.

Ahmed S, Green J, Hewison J (2006) Attitudes toward prenatal diagnosis and termination of pregnancy for thalassaemia in pregnant Pakistani women in the north of England. *Prenatal Diagnosis* 26: 248–257.

Akerman R, Statham J (2014) Bereavement in childhood: the impact on psychological and educational outcomes and the effectiveness of support services. Working Paper No. 25. London: Childhood Wellbeing Research Centre (CWRC). Available at http://www.cwrc.ac.uk/news/documents/Revised_Childhood_Bereavement_review_2014a.pdf (accessed 2 January 2016).

Aladangady N, de Rooy L (2012) Withholding or withdrawal of life sustaining treatment for newborn infants. *Early Human Development* 88: 65–69.

American Psychiatric Association (2013) Highlights of Changes from DSM-IV-TR to DSM-5. Arlington: American Psychiatric Publishing. Available at http://www.dsm5. org/documents/changes%20from%20dsm-iv-tr%20to%20dsm-5.pdf (accessed 28 December 2015).

Anderson T (2004) The misleading myth of choice: the continuing oppression of women in childbirth. In: Kirkham M (Ed.) *Informed Choice in Maternity Care* (pp. 257–264). Basingstoke: Palgrave Macmillan.

Alfirevic Z, Milan SJ, Livio S (2013) Caesarean section versus vaginal delivery for preterm birth in singletons. *Cochrane Database of Systematic Reviews* 9: CD000078.

Angiolini E (2014). Mortonhall Investigation: Report. Edinburgh: City of Edinburgh Council. Available at http://www.edinburgh.gov.uk/info/20242/mortonhall_ investigation/957/mortonhall_investigation_-_report (accessed 31 July 2015).

APP (2014) *Planning Pregnancy: A Guide for Women at High Risk of Postpartum Psychosis*. Birmingham: Action on Postpartum Psychosis (APP).

ARC [n.d.] *Supporting You Throughout Your Pregnancy: A Handbook for Parents after a Prenatal Diagnosis.* London: Antenatal Results and Choices (ARC).

ARC (2005) *Supporting Parents' Decisions: a Handbook for Professionals.* London: Antenatal Results and Choices (ARC).

ARC (2012) *A Handbook to be Given to Parents When an Anomaly is Diagnosed in Their Unborn Baby*. London: Antenatal Results and Choices (ARC).

Armstrong D (2001) Exploring fathers' experiences of pregnancy after a prior perinatal loss. *American Journal of Maternal Child Nursing* 26: 147–153.

Arockiasamy V, Holsti L, Albersheim S (2008) Fathers' experiences in the neonatal intensive care unit: a search for control. *Pediatrics* 121: e215–222.

Arthurs OJ, Bevan C, Sebire NJ (2015) Less invasive investigation of perinatal death: emphasis is shifting to a service driven by parental acceptability and involvement. *BMJ* 351: h3598.

Ashcroft B, Elstein M, Boreham N, Holm S (2003) Prospective semistructured observational study to identify risk attributable to staff deployment, training, and updating opportunities for midwives. *British Medical Journal* 327: 584–588.

Atkinson L, Paglia A, Coolbear J, Niccols A, Parker KCH, Gugerd S (2000) Attachment security: a meta-analysis of maternal mental health correlates. *Clinical Psychology Review* 20: 1019–1040.

Avelin P, Rådestad I, Säflund K, Wredling R, Erlandsson K (2013) Parental grief and relationships after the loss of a stillborn baby. *Midwifery* 29: 668–673.

Bagchi D, Friedman T (1999) Psychological aspects of spontaneous and recurrent abortion. *Current Obstetrics and Gynaecology* 9: 19–22.

Bandini J (2015) The medicalization of bereavement: (ab)normal grief in the DSM-5. *Death Studies* 39: 347–352.

BAPM (2010a) Palliative Care (Supportive and End of Life Care): A Framework for Clinical Practice in Perinatal Medicine: Report of the Working Group August 2010. London: British Association of Perinatal Medicine (BAPM). Available at http://www.bapm.org/publications/documents/guidelines/Palliative_care_final_version_%20Aug10.pdf (accessed 9 June 2015).

BAPM (2010b) Service Standards for Hospitals Providing Neonatal Care (3rd edition). London: British Association of Perinatal Medicine (BAPM). Available at http://www.bapm.org/publications/documents/guidelines/BAPM_Standards_Final_Aug2010.pdf (accessed 9 June 2015).

Barr P (2004) Guilt- and shame-proneness and the grief of perinatal bereavement. *Psychology and psychotherapy* 77: 493–510.

Barr P, Cacciatore J (2007) Problematic emotions and maternal grief. *OMEGA--Journal of Death and Dying* 56: 331–348.

Bastos MH, Furuta M, Small R, McKenzie-McHarg K, Bick D (2015) Debriefing interventions for the prevention of psychological trauma in women following childbirth. *Cochrane Database of Systematic Reviews* 4: CD007194.

Bauer A, Parsonage M, Knapp M, Iemmi V, Adelaja B (2014) *The Costs of Perinatal Mental Health Problems.* London: Centre for Mental Health. Available at http://www.centreformentalhealth.org.uk/costs-of-perinatal-mh-problems (accessed 6 November 2015).

Bazian (2012). Twins "more likely to die before first birthday". NHS Choices website. Available at http://www.nhs.uk/news/2012/06june/Pages/twins-five-times-more-likely-to-die-in-first-year.aspx (accessed 23 November 2015).

Beck CT (1995) The effects of postpartum depression on maternal-infant interaction: a meta-analysis. *Nursing Research* 44: 298–304.

Beck CT, Watson Driscoll J, Watson S (2013) *Traumatic Childbirth*. Abingdon: Routledge.

Bennett J, Dutcher J, Snyders M (2011) Embrace: addressing anticipatory grief and bereavement in the perinatal population: a palliative care case study. *Journal of Perinatal and Neonatal Nursing* 25: 72–76.

Bennett SM, Litz BT, Lee BS, Maguen S (2005) The scope and impact of perinatal loss: current status and future directions *Professional Psychology: Research and Practice* 36(2): 180–187.

Bennett SM, Litz BT, Maguen S, Ehrenreich JT (2008) An exploratory study of the psychological impact and clinical care of perinatal loss. *Journal of Loss and Trauma* 13: 485–510.

Bereavement Advice Centre (2013) When and where to register a death. Bereavement Advice Centre website. Available at http://www.bereavementadvice. org/registering-a-death-and-tell-us-once/when-and-where-to-register.php (accessed 10 July 2015).

Bergh C, Möller A, Nilsson L, Wikland M (1999) Obstetric outcome and psychological follow-up of pregnancies after embryo reduction *Human Reproduction* 14(8): 2170–2175.

Bijma HH, van der Heide A, Wildschut HIJ (2008) Decision-making after ultrasound diagnosis of fetal abnormality. *Reproductive Health Matters* 16 (Suppl. 31): 82–89.

Birth Control Trust (1997) *Abortion Provision in Britain – How Services Are Provided and How They Could Be Approved*. London: Birth Control Trust.

Bliss (2010) *Making Critical Care Decisions for Your Baby*. London: Bliss.

Bliss (2011) Bliss Baby Charter Standards. London: Bliss. Available at http://www.bliss. org.uk/baby-charter-audit-tool (access 5 June 2014).

Bliss (2014) It's Not a Game: The Very Real Costs of Having a Premature or Sick Baby. London: Bliss. Available at http://www.bliss.org.uk/campaigns-and-policy-reports (accessed 09 June 2015).

Blood C, Cacciatore J (2014) Parental grief and memento mori photography: narrative, meaning, culture, and context. *Death Studies* 38: 224–233.

Bloomer MJ, O'Connor M, Copnell B, Endacott R (2015) Nursing care for the families of the dying child/infant in paediatricand neonatal ICU: nurses' emotional talk and sources of discomfort: a mixed methods study. *Australian Critical Care* 28: 87–92.

BMA (2014) *The Law and Ethics of Abortion: BMA Views*. London: British Medical Association.

Boots Family Trust (2013) Perinatal Mental Health Experiences of Women and Health Professionals. Boots Family Trust Alliance. Available at http://www.bftalliance.co.uk/ wp-content/uploads/2014/02/boots-perinatal-mental-health-09-10-13-web.pdf (accessed 15 November 2015).

Bottomley C, Van Belle V, Mukri F, Kirk E, Van Huffel S, Timmerman D, Bourne T (2009) The optimal timing of an ultrasound scan to assess the location and viability of an early pregnancy. *Human Reproduction* 24: 1811–1817.

Breeze AC, Lees CC, Kumar A, Missfelder-Lobos HH, Murdoch EM (2007) Palliative care for prenatally diagnosed lethal fetal abnormality. *Archives of Disease in Childhood: Fetal and Neonatal Edition* 92: F56–F58.

Breeze ACG, Lees CC (2013) Antenatal diagnosis and management of life-limiting conditions. *Seminars in Fetal and Neonatal Medicine* 18: 68–75.

Brier N (2004) Anxiety after miscarriage: a review of the empirical literature and implications for clinical practice. *Birth* 31: 138–142.

Brierley-Jones L, Crawley R, Lomax S, Ayers S (2014) Stillbirth and stigma: the spoiling and repair of multiple social identities. *Omega* 70: 143–168.

Brinchmann BS, Førde R, Nortvedt P (2002) What matters to the parents? A qualitative study of parents' experiences with life-and-death decisions concerning their premature infants *Nursing Ethics* 9: 388–404.

Brunkhorst J, Weiner J, Lantos J (2014) Infants of borderline viability: the ethics of delivery room care. *Seminars in Fetal and Neonatal Medicine* 19: 290–295.

Bryan E (2002) Loss in higher multiple pregnancy and multifetal reduction. *Twin Research* 5: 169–174.

Bryant RA (2014) Prolonged grief: where to after Diagnostic and Statistical Manual of Mental Disorders, 5th Edition? *Current Opinion in Psychiatry* 27: 21–26.

Bulman KH, McCourt C (2002) Somali refugee women's experiences of maternity care in West London: a case study *Critical Public Health* 12: 365–380.

Burden B, Stuart PC (2005) Bereavement, grief and the midwife. In Wickham S (Ed.) *Midwifery Best Practice*, Vol. 3. Oxford: Books for Midwives.

Butt MMZ (2012) Islamic law and the limitations of medical intervention. *Early Human Development* 88: 83–85.

Cacciatore J (2007) Effects of support groups on post traumatic stress responses in women experiencing stillbirth. *Omega* 55: 71–90.

Cacciatore J (2010) The unique experiences of women and their families after the death of a baby. *Social Work in Health Care* 49: 134–148.

Cacciatore J (2013) Psychological effects of stillbirth. *Seminars in Fetal and Neonatal Medicine* 18: 76–82.

Cacciatore J, Ratho Z (2011) An exploration of lesbian maternal bereavement. *Social Work* 56: 169–177.

Cacciatore J, DeFrain J, Jones KLC, Jones H (2008) Stillbirth and the couple: a gender-based exploration. *Journal of Family Social Work* 11: 351–372.

Cacciatore J, Erlandsson K, Rådestad I (2013) Fatherhood and suffering: a qualitative exploration of Swedish men's experiences of care after the death of a baby. *International Journal of Nursing Studies* 50: 664–670.

Cacciatore J, Schnebly S, Froen JF (2009) The effects of social support on maternal anxiety and depression after stillbirth. *Health and Social Care in the Community* 17: 167–176.

Callander G, Brown GP, Tata P, Regan L (2007) Counterfactual thinking and psychological distress following recurrent miscarriage. *Journal of Reproductive and Infant Psychology* 25: 51–65.

Calman K, Royston G (1997) Personal paper: risk language and dialects. *British Medical Journal* 315: 939–942.

Campbell-Yeo M, Johnston C, Benoit B, Latimer M, Vincer M, Walker CD, Streiner D, Inglis D, Caddell K (2013) Trial of repeated analgesia with Kangaroo Mother Care (TRAKC Trial). *BMC Pediatrics* 13:182.

Canadian Paediatric Society (2001) Guidelines for health care professionals supporting families experiencing a perinatal loss (Canadian Paediatric Society: Fetus and Newborn Committee). *Paediatric Child Health* 6: 469–476.

Cannie M, Votino C, Moerman PH, Vanheste R, Segers V, Van Berkel K, Hanssens M, Kang X, Cos T, Kir M, Balepa L, Divano L, Foulon W, De Mey J, Jani J (2012) Acceptance, reliability and confidence of diagnosis of fetal and neonatal virtuopsy compared with conventional autopsy: a prospective study. *Ultrasound in Obstetrics and Gynecology* 39: 659–665.

Cantwell R, Knight M, Oates M and Shakespeare J (2015) Lessons on maternal mental health. In Knight M, Tuffnell D, Kenyon S, Shakespeare J, Gray R, Kurinczuk JJ (Eds) on behalf of MBRRACE-UK. *Saving Lives, Improving Mothers' Care – Surveillance of Maternal Deaths in the UK 2011–13 and Lessons Learned to Inform Maternity Care from the UK and Ireland Confidential Enquiries into Maternal Deaths and Morbidity 2009–13* (pp. 22–41). Oxford: National Perinatal Epidemiology Unit, University of Oxford.

Capitulo KL, Huang Z, Lu X (2014) Should parents and families of stillborn babies be encouraged to see, hold, and have funerals for the babies? *MCN, The American Journal of Maternal/Child Nursing* 39: 146–147.

Carr A (2006) *The Handbook of Child and Adolescent Clinical Psychology: A Contextual Approach*, 2nd Edition. Hove: Routledge.

Cavinder C (2014) The relationship between providing neonatal palliative care and nurses' moral distress: an integrative review. *Advances in Neonatal Care* 14: 322–328.

CBUK (2011) How Children and Young People Grieve. Information Sheet. Saunderton: Child Bereavement UK. Available at http://www.childbereavementuk.org/files/5414/0868/5878/How_Children_and_Young_People_Grieve.pdf (accessed 23 November 2015).

CEMACH (2006) Perinatal Mortality Surveillance, 2004: England, Wales and Northern Ireland. London: Confidential Enquiry into Maternal and Child Health. Available at http://cemach.org.uk/publications/PMR2004_March2006.pdf (accessed on 19 June 2006).

Chapple A, Ziebland S (2010) Viewing the body after bereavement due to a traumatic death: qualitative study in the UK. *BMJ* 340: c2032.

Charchuk M, Simpson C (2005) Hope, disclosure, and control in the neonatal intensive care unit. *Health Communication* 17: 191–203.

Chiswick M (2001) Parents and end of life decisions in neonatal practice. *Archives of Disease in Childhood: Fetal and Neonatal Edition* 85: 1–3.

Chiswick M (2008) Infants of borderline viability: ethical and clinical considerations. *Seminars in Fetal and Neonatal Medicine* 13: 8–15.

Chitty LS, Barnes CA, Berry C (1996) Continuing with pregnancy after a diagnosis of lethal abnormality: experience of five couples and recommendations for management. *British Medical Journal* 313: 478–480.

Christiansen DM, Olff M, Elklit A (2014) Parents bereaved by infant death: sex differences and moderation in PTSD, attachment, coping and social support. *General Hospital Psychiatry* 36: 655–661.

Christiansen DM, Elklit A, Olff M (2013) Parents bereaved by infant death: PTSD symptoms up to 18 years after the loss. *General Hospital Psychiatry* 35: 605–611.

Clare A (2000) *On Men – Masculinity in Crisis.* London: Chatto and Windus.

Clement S, Candy B, Heath V, To M, Nicoliades KH (2003) Transvaginal ultrasound in pregnancy: its acceptability to women and maternal psychological morbidity. *Ultrasound Obstetrics and Gynecology* 22: 508–514.

Cockerill R, Whitworth MK, Heazell AEP (2012) Do medical certificates of stillbirth provide accurate and useful information regarding the cause of death? *Paediatric and Perinatal Epidemiology* 26: 117–123.

Conde-Agudelo A, Díaz-Rossello JL (2014) Kangaroo mother care to reduce morbidity and mortality in low birthweight infants (Review). *Cochrane Database of Systematic Reviews* 4: CD002771.

Coogler C (2012) Your body's talking: moulding your body language into a confident you. Nursing Times, 26 May. Available at http://www.nursingtimes.net/clinical-subjects/leadership/your-bodys-talking-moulding-your-body-language-into-a-confident-you/5045146.fullarticle (accessed 24 November 2015).

Cortezzo DE, Sanders MR, Brownell E, Moss K (2013) Neonatologists' perspectives of palliative and end-of-life care in neonatal intensive care units. *Journal of Perinatology* 33: 731–735.

Coulter A, Entwistle V, Gilbert D (1999) Sharing decisions with patients: is the information good enough? *British Medical Journal* 318: 318–322.

Cowles KV (1996) Cultural perspectives on grief: an expanded concept analysis. *Journal of Advanced Nursing* 23: 287–294.

CQC (2014) The importance of choice and control. Care Quality Commission website. Available at http://www.cqc.org.uk/content/importance-choice-and-control (accessed 24 November 2015).

CQC (2015) *Right Here Right Now: People's Experiences of Help, Care and Support During a Mental Health Crisis: Summary*. Gallowgate: Care Quality Commission.

Craig F, Mancini A (2013) Can we truly offer a choice of place of death in neonatal palliative care? *Seminars in Fetal and Neonatal Medicine* 18: 93–98.

Crawley R, Lomax S, Ayers S (2013) Recovering from stillbirth: the effects of making and sharing memories on maternal mental health. *Journal of Reproductive and Infant Psychology* 31: 195–207.

Cross-Sudworth F, Ecclestone L, Williamson A, Gardosi J (2011). Confidential case review of the care of migrant mothers in pregnancies resulting in stillbirth or neonatal death [Abstract]. *Archives of Disease in Childhood: Fetal and Neonatal Edition* 96 (Suppl. 1): 1359–2998.

Crown Office and Procurator Fiscal Service [n.d.] Information for bereaved relatives: the role of the procurator fiscal in the investigation of deaths. Available at http://www.copfs.gov.uk/images/Documents/Deaths/The%20role%20of%20the%20Procurator%20Fiscal%20in%20the%20investigation%20of%20deaths%20-%20Information%20for%20bereaved%20relatives%20-%20June%202015.pdf (accessed 16 July 2015).

da Costa DE, Ghazal H, Al Khusaiby S (2002) Do Not Resuscitate orders and ethical decisions in a neonatal intensive care unit in a Muslim community. *Archives of Disease in Childhood: Fetal and Neonatal Edition* 86: 115–119.

Daly N (2005) *Sasha's Legacy: A Guide to Funerals for Babies.* Aotearoa, New Zealand: Steele Roberts.

Das A (2012) Withdrawal of life-sustaining treatment for newborn infants from a Hindu perspective. *Early Human Development* 88: 87–88.

Davies MM, Bath PA (2001) The maternity information concerns of Somali women in the United Kingdom. *Journal of Advanced Nursing* 36: 237–245.

Davies R (2004) New understandings of parental grief: literature review. *Journal of Advanced Nursing* 46: 506–513.

Daugirdaitė V, van den Akker O, Purewal S (2015) Posttraumatic stress and posttraumatic stress disorder after termination of pregnancy and reproductive loss: a systematic review. *Journal of Pregnancy* 2015: 646345.

Debackere KJ, Hill PD, Kavanaugh KL (2008) The parental experience of pregnancy after perinatal loss. *JOGNN* 37: 525–537.

Deery R (2004) An action-research study exploring midwives' support needs and the effect of group clinical supervision *Midwifery* 21: 161–176.

Denton J, Bryan E (2002) Multiple birth children and their families following ART. In Vayena E, Rowe PJ, Griffin PD (Eds). *Current Practices and Controversies in Assisted Reproduction. Report of a Who Meeting On Medical, Ethical and Social Aspects of Assisted Reproduction* (pp. 243–251). Geneva: World Health Organization.

Department of Health (2015) Abortion Statistics, England and Wales: 2014. Summary Information from the Abortion Notification Forms Returned to the Chief Medical Officers of England and Wales. London: UK Government, Department of Health. Available at https://www.gov.uk/government/uploads/system/uploads/attachment_data/file/433437/2014_Commentary__5_.pdf (accessed 20 August 2015).

de Rooey L, Aladangady N, Aidoo E (2012) Palliative care for the newborn in the United Kingdom. *Early Human Development* 88: 73–77.

DHSSPSNI (2008) Guidance on Death, Stillbirth and Cremation Certification. Department of Health, Social Services and Public Safety. Available at http://www.dhsspsni.gov.uk/guidance-death-stillbirth-and-cremation-certification-pt-b.pdf (accessed 8 July 2015).

DHSSPSNI (2013) The Limited Circumstances for a Lawful Termination of Pregnancy in Northern Ireland: A Guidance Document for Health and Social Care Professionals On Law and Clinical Practice. London: Department of Health, Social Services and Public Safety. Available at http://www.dhsspsni.gov.uk/guidance-limited-circumstances-termination-pregnancy-april-2013.pdf (accessed 21 August 2015).

Di Clemente M (2004) *Living with Leo.* London: Bosun Publications/SANDS.

Ding X-X, Wu Y-L, Xu S-J, Zhu R-P, Jia X-M, Zhang S-F, Huang K, Zhu P, Hao J-H, Tao F-B (2014) Maternal anxiety during pregnancy and adverse birth outcomes: a systematic review and meta-analysis of prospective cohort studies. *Journal of Affective Disorders* 159: 103–110.

DoH (2003) Confidentiality: NHS Code of Practice (Gateway 2003). London: Department of Health. Available at http://www.dh.gov.uk/assetRoot/04/06/92/54/04069254.pdf (accessed on 8 July 2006).

Dodd JM, Crowther CA (2012) Reduction of the number of fetuses for women with a multiple pregnancy. *Cochrane Database of Systematic Reviews* 10: CD003932.

Don A (2005) *Fathers Feel Too: a Book for Men on Coping with the Death of a Baby.* London: Bosun Publications/SANDS.

Downe S, Kingdon C, Finlayson K, Thomson G, Fleming A, Eichmann H, Edge E, Byrom S (2009) *Hard to reach? Access to Maternity Services for "Vulnerable" Women in the North West.* Preston: NHS, University of Central Lancashire.

Downe S, Kingdon C, Kennedy R, Norwell H, McLaughlin M-J, Heazell AEP (2012) Post-mortem examination after stillbirth: views of UK-based practitioners. *European Journal of Obstetrics & Gynecology and Reproductive Biology* 162: 33–37.

Downe S, Schmidt E, Kingdon C and Heazell AEP (2013) Bereaved parents' experience of stillbirth in UK hospitals: a qualitative interview study. *BMJ Open* 3: e002237.

Draper ES, Kurinczuk JJ, Kenyon S (2015) *MBRRACE-UK Perinatal Confidential Enquiry:* Term, Singleton, Normally Formed, Antepartum Stillbirth. Leicester: The Infant Mortality and Morbidity Studies. Available at https://www.npeu.ox.ac.uk/downloads/files/mbrrace-uk/reports/MBRRACE-UK%20Perinatal%20Report%20 2015.pdf (accessed 1 December 2015).

Duncan D (1995) Fathers have feelings too. *Modern Midwife* 5: 30–31.

Dunkel Schetter C, Tanner L (2012) Anxiety, depression and stress in pregnancy: implications for mothers, children, research, and practice. *Current Opinion in Psychiatry* 25: 141–148.

Dyson L, While A (1998) The "long shadow" of bereavement. *British Journal of Community Nursing* 3: 432–439.

Dyson S (2005) *Ethnicity and Screening for Sickle Cell/Thalassaemia: Lessons for Practice from the Voices of Experience.* London: Elsevier Churchill Livingstone.

Eden LM, Clark Callister C (2010) Parent involvement in end-of-life care and decision making in the newborn intensive care unit: an integrative review. *Journal of Perinatal Education* 19: 29–39.

Edwards A (2004a) Flexible rather than standardized approaches to communicating risks in health care. *Quality and Safety in Health Care* 13: 169–170.

Edwards A, Elwyn G, Mulley A (2002) Explaining risks: turning numerical data into meaningful pictures. *British Medical Journal* 324: 827–830.

Edwards NP (2004b) Why can't women just say no? In Kirkam M (Ed.) *Informed Choice in Maternity Care* (pp. 1–29). Basingstoke: Palgrave MacMillan.

Edwards N, Murphy-Lawless J, Kirkham M, Davies S (2011) Attacks on midwives, attacks on women's choices. *AIMS Journal* 23: 3–7.

Engelhard IM, Van den Hout MA, Arntz A (2001) Posttraumatic stress disorder after pregnancy loss. *General Hospital Psychiatry* 23: 62–66.

Enkin M, Keirse MJ, Neilson J, Crowther C, Hodnett E, Hofmeyr J (2000) *A Guide to Effective Care in Pregnancy and Childbirth.* Oxford: Oxford University Press.

Environment Agency [No date] *Funeral Practices, Spreading Ashes and Caring for the Environment: Meeting the Needs of Families and the Environment.* Bristol: Environment Agency.

EPICure (2012a) EPICure2 – outcome at 2–3 years. EPICure website. Available at http://www.epicure.ac.uk/epicure-2/epicure2-outcome-at-2-3-years/ (accessed 14 January 2016).

EPICure (2012b) Survival: Survival after birth before 27 weeks of gestation. EPICure website. Available at http://www.epicure.ac.uk/overview/survival/ (accessed 20 October 2015).

European Medicines Agency (2014) Bromocriptine-Containing Medicines Indicated in the Prevention or Suppression of Physiological Lactation Post-Partum: Restrictions in Use of Bromocriptine for Stopping Breast Milk Production. London: European Medicines Agency website. Available at http://www.ema.europa.eu/ema/index.jsp?curl=pages/medicines/human/referrals/Bromocriptine-containing_medicinal_medicines_indicated_in_the_prevention_or_suppression_of_physiological_lactation_post-partum/human_referral_prac_000031.jsp&mid=WC0b01ac05805c516f (accessed 24 July 2015).

EPT (2016) Treating an ectopic pregnancy. The Ectopic Pregnancy Trust (EPT) website. Available at http://www.ectopic.org.uk/patients/treatment/ (accessed 14 January 2016).

Evans R (2012) Emotional care for women who experience. *Nursing Standard* 26: 35–41.

Fairbairn C (2014) Registration of Stillbirth. Standard Note: SN/HA/5595. London: Library, House of Commons, Home Affairs Section, 30 April. Available at http://researchbriefings.files.parliament.uk/documents/SN05595/SN05595.pdf (accessed 5 August 2015).

Fauth B, Thompson M, Penny A (2009) Associations Between Childhood Bereavement and Children's Background, Experiences and Outcomes. Secondary Analysis of the 2004 Mental Health of Children and Young People in Great Britain Data. London: National Children's Bureau (NCB). Available at http://ncb.org.uk/media/60128/fullreportassociationswithchildhoodbereavement.pdf (accessed 2 January 2016).

Finlayson B (2002) *Counting the Smiles: Morale and Motivation in the NHS.* London: King's Fund.

Fisher J, Lafarge C (2015) Women's experience of care when undergoing termination of pregnancy for fetal anomaly in England. *Journal of Reproductive and Infant Psychology* 33: 69–87.

Fisher J, Lohr PA, Lafarge C, Robson SC (2015) Termination for fetal anomaly: are women in England given a choice of method? *Journal of Obstetrics and Gynaecology* 35: 168–172.

Flenady V, Boyle F, Koopmans L, Wilson T, Stones W, Cacciatore J (2014) Meeting the needs of parents after a stillbirth or neonatal death. *BJOG* 121 (Suppl. 4): 137–140.

Foulkes M (2011) Enablers and barriers to seeking help for a postpartum mood disorder. *JOGNN* 40: 450–457.

Fowlie PW, McHaffie HE (2004) Supporting parents in the neonatal unit. *British Medical Journal* 329: 1336–1338.

Franche R-L (2001) Psychologic and obstetric predictors of couples' grief during pregnancy after miscarriage or perinatal death. *Obstetrics and Gynecology* 97: 597–602.

Franche R-L, Mikail SF (1999) The impact of perinatal loss on adjustment to subsequent pregnancy. *Social Science and Medicine* 48: 1613–1623.

Fraser E (2010) *TAMBA Bereavement Support Group Booklet for Parents Who Have Lost One Or More Babies from a Multiple Birth.* Guildford: TAMBA BSG.

FSRH (2009) UK medical eligibility criteria for contraceptive use. Faculty of Sexual and Reproductive Healthcare, Royal College of Obstetricians and Gynaecologists. Available at http://www.fsrh.org/pdfs/UKMEC2009.pdf (accessed 20 August 2015).

Garcia J, Bricker L, Henderson J, Martin MA, Mugford M, Nielson J, Roberts R (2002) Women's views of pregnancy ultrasound: a systematic review. *Birth* 29: 225–250.

Garros D, Rosychuk RJ, Cox PN (2003) Circumstances surrounding end of life in a paediatric intensive care unit. *Paediatrics* 112: 371–379.

Gaudet C, Séjourné N, Camborieux L, Rogers R, Chabrol H (2010) Pregnancy after perinatal loss: association of grief, anxiety and attachment. *Journal of Reproductive and Infant Psychology* 28: 240–251.

Geerinck-Vercammen CR (1999) With positive feeling: the grief process after stillbirth in relation to the role of the professional caregivers. *European Journal of Obstetrics and Gynecology* 87: 119–121.

Gittoes S, Elliot R (2011) *You Are My Sunshine*. Central Milton Keynes: AuthorHouse™ UK Ltd.

GMC (2008) *Consent: Patients and Doctors Making Decisions Together.* London: General Medical Council. Available at http://www.gmc-uk.org/static/documents/content/Consent_-_English_1015.pdf (accessed 24 November 2015).

GMC (2009) *Confidentiality*. London: General Medical Council. Available at http://www.gmc-uk.org/static/documents/content/Confidentiality_-_English_1015.pdf (accessed 21 November 2015).

GMC (2013a) *Good Medical Practice*. London: General Medical Council. Available at http://www.gmc-uk.org/static/documents/content/Good_medical_practice_-_English_1015.pdf (accessed 2 December 2015).

GMC (2013b) *Personal Beliefs and Medical Practice*. London: General Medical Council. Available at http://www.gmc-uk.org/static/documents/content/Personal_beliefs_and_medical_practice.pdf (accessed 21 August 2015).

GMC, NMC (2015) *Openness and Honesty When Things Go Wrong: The Professional Duty of Candour.* London: General Medical Council and Nursing and Midwifery Council. Available at http://www.nmc.org.uk/globalassets/sitedocuments/nmc-publications/openness-and-honesty-when-things-go-wrong--the-professional-duty-of-candour.pdf (accessed 28 October 2015)

Goggin M (2012) Parents perceptions of withdrawal of life support treatment to newborn infants. *Early Human Development* 88: 79–82.

Goh AYT, Lum LCS, Chan PWK, Bakar F, Chong BO (1999) Withdrawal and limitation of life support in paediatric intensive care. *Archives of Disease in Childhood* 80: 424–428.

Gold KJ, Leon I, Chames MC (2010) National survey of obstetrician attitudes about timing the subsequent pregnancy after perinatal death. *American Journal of Obstetrics and Gynecology* 202: 357.e1–6.

Goodman JH (2004) Paternal postpartum depression, its relationship to maternal postpartum depression, and implications for family health. *Journal of Advanced Nursing* 45: 26–35.

Goodman SH, Rouse MH, Connell AM, Robbins Broth M, Hall CM, Heyward D (2011) Maternal depression and child psychopathology: a meta-analytic review. *Clinical Child and Family Psychology Review* 14: 1–27.

Government Equalities Office (2010) Equality Act 2010: What Do I Need to Know? Disability Quick Start Guide. London: Government Equalities Office. Available at https://www.gov.uk/government/uploads/system/uploads/attachment_data/file/85011/disability.pdf (accessed 30 November 2015).

Grace SL, Evindar A, Stewart DE (2003) The effect of postpartum depression on child cognitive development and behavior: a review and critical analysis of the literature. *Archives of Women's Mental Health* 6: 263–274.

Graignic-Philippe R, Dayan J, Chokron S, Jacquet A-Y, Tordjman S (2014) Effects of prenatal stress on fetal and child development: a critical literature review. *Neuroscience and Biobehavioral Reviews* 43: 137–162.

Gravensteen IK, Helgadóttir LB, Jacobsen E-M, Rådestad I, Sandset PM, Ekeberg Ø (2013) Women's experiences in relation to stillbirth and risk factors for long-term post-traumatic stress symptoms: a retrospective study. *BMJ Open* 3: e003323.

Guirdham M (1990) *Interpersonal Skills at Work*. London: Prentice Hall.

Haines HM, Rubertsson C, Pallant JF, Hildingsson I (2012) The influence of women's fear, attitudes and beliefs of childbirth on mode and experience of birth. *BMC Pregnancy and Childbirth* 12: 55.

Hall C (2014) Bereavement theory: recent developments in our understanding of grief and bereavement. *Bereavement Care* 33: 7–12.

Hansen D (2003) I Hate This (a play without a baby) www.davidhansen.org. First performed at Cleveland Public Theatre, Cleveland, Ohio, February 2003.

Harper M, O'Connor RC, O'Carroll RE (2011) Increased mortality in parents bereaved in the first year of their child's life. *BMJ Supportive and Palliative Care* 1:306–309.

Harris R, Ayers S (2012) What makes labour and birth traumatic? A survey of intrapartum "hotspots". *Psychology and Health* 27: 1166–1177.

The Health Foundation (2014) Person-Centred Care Made Simple: What Everyone Should Know About Person-Centred Care. London: The Health Foundation. Available at http://www.health.org.uk/sites/default/files/PersonCentredCareMadeSimple.pdf (accessed 9 November 2015).

Health Improvement Scotland (2015a) Death Certification Briefing Note: Ready for Review. Number 4, May 2015. Edinburgh: Health Improvement Scotland. Available at http://www.healthcareimprovementscotland.org/our_work/governance_and_assurance/death_certification.aspx (accessed 16 July 2015).

Health Improvement Scotland (2015b) Death Certification: Questions and Answers. Edinburgh: Health Improvement Scotland website, available at http://www.healthcareimprovementscotland.org/our_work/governance_and_assurance/death_certification/questions_and_answers.aspx (accessed 16 July 2015).

Health Scotland (2008) *Now We're Talking: Interpreting Guidelines for Staff of NHS Scotland*. Edinburgh: Health Scotland. Available at http://www.healthscotland.com/uploads/documents/7833-Nowwe'retalkinginterpretingguidelines.pdf (accessed 30 November 2015).

Heazell AEP, Martindale EA (2009) Can post-mortem examination of the placenta help determine the cause of stillbirth? *Journal of Obstetrics and Gynaecology* 29: 225–228.

Heazell A, McLaughlin M-J, Schmidt E, Cox P, Flenady V, Khong T, Downe S (2012) A difficult conversation? The views and experiences of parents and professionals on the consent process for perinatal postmortem after stillbirth. *BJOG: An International Journal of Obstetrics and Gynaecology* 119: 987–997.

Henley A, Schott J (1999) *Culture, Religion and Patient Care in a Multiethnic Society*. London: ACE Books.

Henley A, Schott J (2014) What Happens at a Hospital Post Mortem on a Baby – Procedures and Likely Timings. London: Improving Bereavement Care Team, Sands. Available at https://www.uk-sands.org/sites/default/files/What%20happens%20at%20a%20post%20mortem%20-%20procedures%20and%20timings.pdf (accessed 18 January 2016).

Henley A, Turner V (2013) *Acceptability of the Friends and Family Test (FFT) with Parents Whose Baby Has Died: A Survey of Parents' Views by Sands, the Stillbirth and Neonatal Death Charity* [unpublished report]. London: Sands Improving Bereavement Care Team.

HESonline (2012) NHS Maternity Statistics 2011–12: Summary Report. Hospital Episode Statistics (HES) and the Health and Social Care Information Centre. Available at http://www.hscic.gov.uk/catalogue/PUB09202/nhs-mate-eng-2011-2012-rep.pdf (accessed 28 September 2015).

Hogg S (2012) Prevention in Mind: All Babies Count: Spotlight on Perinatal Mental Health. London: The NSPCC. Available at https://nspcc-web-stage.amaze.com/globalassets/documents/research-reports/all-babies-count-spotlight-perinatal-mental-health.pdf (accessed 6 November 2015).

Hogue CJR, Parker CB, Willinger M, Temple JR, Bann CM, Silver RM, Dudley DJ, Moore JL, Coustan DR, Stoll BJ, Reddy UM, Varner MW, Saade GR, Conway D, Goldenberg RL (2015) The association of stillbirth with depressive symptoms 6–36 months post-delivery. *Paediatric and Perinatal Epidemiology* 29: 131–143.

Home Secretary, Secretary of State for Health (2007) *Learning from Tragedy, Keeping Patients Safe: Overview of The Government's Action Programme in Response to the Recommendations of the Shipman Inquiry. London:* The Stationary Office. Available at https://www.gov.uk/government/uploads/system/uploads/attachment_data/file/228886/7014.pdf (accessed 10 July 2015).

Horey D, Flenady V, Heazell AEP, Khong TY (2013) Interventions for supporting parents' decisions about autopsy after stillbirth (Review). *The Cochrane Library* 2: CD009932.

Horsch A, Jacobs I, McKenzie-McHarg K (2015) Cognitive predictors of PTSD and its relationship with perinatal grief following stillbirth: a longitudinal study. *Journal of Traumatic Stress* 28: 1–8.

Howard LM, Oram S, Galley H, Trevillion K, Feder G (2013) Domestic violence and perinatal mental disorders: a systematic review and meta-analysis. *PLoS Medicine* 10: e1001452.

HSG (1991) *Disposal of Fetal Tissue: Executive Summary*. Health Service Guidelines (91)19. London: Department of Health.

HTA (2015) Guidance on the Disposal of Pregnancy Remains Following Pregnancy Loss or Termination. London: Human Tissue Authority. Available at https://www.hta.gov.uk/sites/default/files/Guidance_on_the_disposal_of_pregnancy_remains.pdf (accessed 8 July 2015).

HTA Code 1 (2014) Code of practice 1: consent. London: Human Tissue Authority. Available at https://www.hta.gov.uk/sites/default/files/Code_of_practice_1_-_Consent.pdf (accessed 7 July 2015).

HTA Code 3 (2014) Code of practice 3: post-mortem examination. Version 14.0. London: Human Tissue Authority. Available at https://www.hta.gov.uk/sites/default/files/Code_of_practice_3_-_Post-mortem_examination.pdf (accessed 13 July 2015).

HTA Code 5 (2014) Code of practice 5: disposal of human tissue. Version 14.0. London: Human Tissue Authority. Available at https://www.hta.gov.uk/sites/default/files/Code_of_practice_5_-_Disposal_of_human_tissue.pdf (accessed 7 July 2015).

Hugill K, Letherby G, Reid T, Lavender T (2013) Experiences of fathers shortly after the birth of their preterm infants. *Journal of Obstetric, Gynecologic and Neonatal Nursing* 42: 655–663.

Hunter A (2015) "One chance to get it right": providing bereavement care after stillbirth or the death of a baby. *AIMS Journal* 27: 9–10.

Hutti MH (2005) Social and professional support needs of families after perinatal loss. *Journal of Obstetric, Gynecologic, and Neonatal Nursing* 34: 630–638.

Hutti MH, Armstrong DS, Myers JA and Hall LA (2015) Grief intensity, psychological well-being, and the intimate partner relationship in the subsequent pregnancy after a perinatal loss. *Journal of Obstetric, Gynecologic, and Neonatal Nursing* 34: 42-50.

ICCM (2014) The Sensitive Disposal of Fetal Remains: Policy and Guidance for Burial and Cremation Authorities and Companies. London: Institute of Cemetery and Crematorium Management. Available at http://www.iccm-uk.com/iccm/library/FetalRemainsPolicyNOV2014ReviewFINAL.pdf (accessed 8 July 2015).

ICCM, Sands (2014) Policy and Guidance for Baby and Infant Funerals. London: Institute of Cemetery and Crematorium Management. Available at http://www. iccm-uk.com/iccm/library/BabyandInfantFuneralsNovember%202014.pdf (accessed 23 July 2015).

Infant Cremation Commission (2014) Report of the Infant Cremation Commission. Edinburgh: The Scottish Government. Available at http://www.gov.scot/ Resource/0045/00453055.pdf (accessed 23 July 2015).

Inwald D, Jakobovits I, Petros A (2000) Brain stem death: managing care when accepted medical guidelines and religious beliefs are in conflict: consideration and compromise are possible. *British Medical Journal* 320: 1266–1267.

Jansson C, Adolfsson A (2010) A Swedish study of midwives' and nurses' experiences when women are diagnosed with a missed miscarriage during a routine ultrasound scan. *Sexual and Reproductive Healthcare* 1: 67–72.

Jarvis M, Natural Death Centre (2010) Private land burial. The Natural Death Centre website. Available at http://www.naturaldeath.org.uk/index.php?page=home-burial (accessed 23 July 2015).

Jenkins D (2015) Report into Infant Cremations at the Emstrey Crematorium Shrewsbury. Shrewsbury: Shropshire Council. Available at http://www.shropshire. gov.uk/media/1540025/Independent-inquiry-report.pdf (accessed 31 July 2015).

Jennings P (2002) Should paediatric units have bereavement support posts? *Archives of Disease in Childhood* 87: 40–42.

Jones L, Othman M, Dowswell T, Alfirevic Z, Gates S, Newburn M, Jordan S, Lavender T, Neilson JP (2012) Pain management for women in labour: an overview of systematic reviews. *Cochrane Database of Systematic Reviews* 3: CD009234.

Kaempf JW, Tomlinson MW, Campbell B, Ferguson L, Stewart VT (2009) Counseling pregnant women who may deliver extremely premature infants: medical care guidelines, family choices, and neonatal outcomes. *Pediatrics* 123: 1509–1515.

Kai J, Beavan J, Faull C, Dodson L, Gill P, Beighton A (2007) Professional uncertainty and disempowerment responding to ethnic diversity in health care: a qualitative study. *PLoS Medicine* 4: e323.

Kain VJ (2013) An exploration of the grief experiences of neonatal nurses: a focus group study. *Journal of Neonatal Nursing* 19: 80–88.

Kang X, Cos T, Guizani M, Cannie MM, Segers V, Jani JC (2014) Parental acceptance of minimally invasive fetal and neonatal autopsy compared with conventional autopsy. *Prenatal Diagnosis* 34: 1106–1110.

Kenworthy D, Kirkham M (2011). *Midwives Coping with Loss and Grief: Stillbirth, Professional and Personal Losses*. London: Radcliffe Publishing Ltd.

Kersting A, Dorsch M, Kreulich C, Reutmann M, Ohrmann P, Baez E, Arolt V (2005) Trauma and grief 2–7 years after termination of pregnancy because of fetal anomalies – a pilot study. *Journal of Psychosomatic Obstetrics and Gynecology* 26: 9–14.

Khan L (2015) Falling Through the Gaps: Perinatal Mental Health and General Practice. London: Centre for Mental Health. Available at http://www.rcgp.org.uk/clinical-and-research/our-programmes/~/~/media/Files/CIRC/Perinatal-Mental-Health/RCGP-Exec-Summary-Falling-through-the-gaps-PMH-and-general-practice-Mar-2015.ashx (accessed 6 November 2015).

Kilby MD, Pretlove SJ, Bedford Russell AR (2011) Multidisciplinary palliative care in unborn and newborn babies: coordinated clinical care and psychological, spiritual, and social support must be provided throughout the process. *BMJ* 342: d1808.

Kirkham M (2011) A duty of obedience or a duty of care? *AIMS Journal* 23: 13–14.

Kirkham M (2013) Modern birth: processes and fears. *Midwifery Matters* 136: 3–6.

Kirkham M, Stapleton H (2004) The culture of maternity services in Wales and England as a barrier to informed choice. In Kirkham M (Ed.) *Informed Choice in Maternity Care* (pp. 117–145). Basingstoke: Palgrave Macmillan.

Kirkup B (2015) The Report of the Morecambe Bay Investigation. London: Morecambe Bay Investigation, Department of Health. Available at https://www.gov.uk/government/uploads/system/uploads/attachment_data/file/408480/47487_MBI_Accessible_v0.1.pdf (accessed 10 July 2015).

Kirschner AK, Atteneder M, Schmidhuber A, Knetsch S, Farnleitner AH, Sommer R (2012) Holy springs and holy water: Underestimated sources of illness? *Journal of Water and Health* 10: 349-357.

Klass D (1996) The deceased child and the psychic and social worlds of bereaved parents during the resolution of grief. In Klass D, Silverman P, Nickman S (Eds) *Continuing Bonds: New Understandings of Grief (Death Education, Aging and Health Care)* (pp. 199–216). London: Routledge.

Knight M (2015) Learning from homicides and women who experienced domestic abuse. In Knight M, Tuffnell D, Kenyon S, Shakespeare J, Gray R, Kurinczuk JJ (Eds) on behalf of MBRRACE-UK. *Saving Lives, Improving Mothers' Care – Surveillance of maternal deaths in the UK 2011–13 and Lessons Learned to Inform Maternity Care from the UK and Ireland Confidential Enquiries into Maternal Deaths and Morbidity 2009–13* (pp. 62–70). Oxford: National Perinatal Epidemiology Unit, University of Oxford.

Knight M, Kenyon S, Brocklehurst P, Neilson J, Shakespeare J, Kurinczuk JJ (Eds) (2014) Saving Lives, Improving Mothers' Care: Lessons Learned to Inform Future Maternity Care from the UK and Ireland Confidential Enquiries into Maternal Deaths and Morbidity 2009–2012. Oxford: National Perinatal Epidemiology Unit, Nuffield Department of Population Health, University of Oxford. Available at https://

www.npeu.ox.ac.uk/downloads/files/mbrrace-uk/reports/Saving%20Lives%20 Improving%20Mothers%20Care%20report%202014%20Full.pdf (accessed 15 May 2015)

Knight M, Tuffnell D, Kenyon S, Shakespeare J, Gray R, Kurinczuk JJ (Eds) (2015), on behalf of MBRRACE-UK. *Saving Lives, Improving Mothers' Care - Surveillance of maternal deaths in the UK 2011-13 and lessons learned to inform maternity care from the UK and Ireland Confidential Enquiries into Maternal Deaths and Morbidity 2009-13.* Oxford: National Perinatal Epidemiology Unit, University of Oxford.

Kobler K, Limbo R, Oakdale C (2012) Childbirth education for parents receiving perinatal palliative care. *International Journal of Childbirth Education* 27: 26–32.

Kohner N, Henley A (2001) *When a Baby Dies* (revised edition). Abingdon: Routledge.

Kollantai JA, Fleischer LM (undated) Multiple Birth Loss and the Hospital Caregiver. Anchorage: Center for Loss In Multiple Birth (CLIMB). Available at http://www.climb-support.org/pdf/mblnicu.pdf (accessed on 6 June 2006).

Koopmans L, Wilson T, Cacciatore J, Flenady V (2013) Support for mothers, fathers and families after perinatal death (review). *Cochrane Database of Systematic Reviews* 6: CD000452.

Korenromp MJ, Christiaens GC, Van den Bout J, Mulder EJH, Hunfeld JAM, Bilardo CM, Offermans JPM, Visser GHA (2005) Long-term psychological consequences of pregnancy termination for fetal abnormality: a cross-sectional study. *Prenatal Diagnosis* 25: 253–260.

Kreicbergs U, Valdimarsdóttir U, Onelöv E, Henter J-I, Steineck G (2004) Anxiety and depression in parents 4–9 years after the loss of a child owing to a malignancy: a population-based follow-up. *Psychological Medicine* 8: 1431–1441.

Kübler-Ross E, Kessler D (2005) *On Grief and Grieving: Finding the Meaning of Grief Through the Five Stages of Loss.* London: Simon & Schuster.

Lally JE, Thomson RG, MacPhail S, Exley C (2014) Pain relief in labour: a qualitative study to determine how to support women to make decisions about pain relief in labour. *BMC Pregnancy and Childbirth* 14: 6.

Lalor J, Begley CM, Galavan E (2009) Recasting hope: a process of adaptation following fetal anomaly diagnosis. *Social Science and Medicine* 68: 462–472.

Lalor JG, Devane D, Begley CM (2007) Unexpected diagnosis of fetal abnormality: women's encounters with caregivers. *Birth* 34: 80–88.

Larcher V (2013) Ethical considerations in neonatal end-of-life care. *Seminars in Fetal and Neonatal Medicine* 18: 105–110.

Larcher V, Craig F, Bhogal K, Wilkinson D, Brierley J (2015) Making decisions to limit treatment in life-limiting and life-threatening conditions in children: a framework for practice. *Archives of Disease in Childhood* 100 (Suppl. 2): S1–26.

Leon IG (1992) Perinatal loss: a critique of current hospital practices. *Clinical Pediatrics* 31: 366–374.

Leonard L (2002) Prenatal behavior of multiples: implications for families and nurses. *Journal of Obstetric, Gynecologic, and Neonatal Nursing* 31: 248–255.

Leoni LC (1997) The nurse's role: care of patients after pregnancy loss. In: Woods JR, Woods JLE (Eds) *Loss During Pregnancy or in the Newborn Period* (pp. 361–386). Pitman: Jannetti Publications.

Levy V (2004) How midwives used protective steering to facilitate informed choice in pregnancy. In: Kirkham M (Ed.) *Informed Choice in Maternity Care* (pp. 57–70). Basingstoke: Palgrave Macmillan.

Lewis H (2012) *Body Language*, 3rd revised edition. London: SAGE Publications Ltd.

Lindgren H, Malm MC, Rådestad I (2013) You don't leave your baby--mother's experiences after a stillbirth. *Omega* 68: 337–346.

Lindholm M, Hargraves JL, Ferguson WJ, Reed G (2012) Professional language interpretation and inpatient length of stay and readmission rates. *Journal of General Internal Medicine* 27: 1294–1299.

Lindquist A, Kurinczuk JJ, Redshaw M, Knight M (2015) Experiences, utilisation and outcomes of maternity care in England among women from different socio-economic groups: findings from the 2010 National Maternity Survey. *BJOG* 122: 1610–1617.

Littlewood J (1992) *Aspects of Grief.* London: Tavistock.

Lovett KF (2001) PTSD and stillbirth. *British Journal of Psychiatry* 179: 367.

Lundqvist A, Nilstun T and Dykes A-K (2002) Both empowered and powerless: mothers' experiences of professional care when their newborn dies *Birth* 29: 192–199.

Lyus R, Creed K, Fisher J, McKeon L (2014) Termination of pregnancy for fetal abnormality. *British Journal of Midwifery* 22: 332–337.

Maercker A, Lalor J (2012) Diagnostic and clinical considerations in prolonged grief disorder. *Dialogues in Clinical Neuroscience* 14: 167–176.

Maifeld M, Hahn S, Titler MG, Mullen M (2003) Decision making regarding multifetal reduction *Journal of Obstetric, Gynecologic, and Neonatal Nursing* 32: 357–369.

Mancini A, Uthaya S, Beardsley C, Wood D, Modi N (2014) Practical Guidance for the Management of Palliative Care on Neonatal Units, 1st edition. London:

Chelsea and Westminster Hospital NHS Foundation Trust. Available at http://www.
togetherforshortlives.org.uk/assets/0000/6890/NICU-Palliative-Care-Feb-2014.pdf
(accessed 9 June 2015).

Mander R (2006) *Loss and Bereavement in Childbearing*, 2nd edition. Abingdon:
Routledge.

Mander R (2009) Good grief: staff responses to childbearing loss. *Nurse Education
Today* 29: 117–123.

Manktelow BN, Seaton SE, Field DJ, Draper ES (2013) Population-based estimates of
in-unit survival for very preterm infants. *Pediatrics* 131: e425–e432.

Manktelow BN, Smith LK, Evans TA, Hyman-Taylor P, Kurinczuk JJ, Field DJ, Smith
PW, Draper ES (2015) Perinatal Mortality Surveillance Report: UK Perinatal
Deaths for births from January to December 2013 on behalf of the MBRRACE-UK
collaboration. Leicester: University of Leicester. Available at https://www.npeu.
ox.ac.uk/downloads/files/mbrrace-uk/reports/MBRRACE-UK%20Perinatal%20
Surveillance%20Report%202013.pdf (accessed 17 August 2015).

Marsh R (2015) Financial Scrutiny Unit Briefing: Burial and Cremation (Scotland) Bill.
Edinburgh: Scottish Parliament Information Centre (SPICe). Available at http://www.
scottish.parliament.uk/ResearchBriefingsAndFactsheets/S4/SB_15-70_Burial_and_
Cremation_Scotland_Bill.pdf (accessed 16 January 2016).

Marteau T, Dormandy E (2001) Facilitating informed choice in prenatal testing: how well
are we doing? *American Journal of Medical Genetics* 106: 185–190.

Marteau TM, Saidi G, Goodburn S, Lawton J, Michie S and Bobrow M (2000) Numbers
or words? A randomized controlled trial of presenting screen negative results to
pregnant women. *Prenatal Diagnosis* 20: 714–718.

Maternity Action, Refugee Council (2013) When Maternity Doesn't Matter:
Dispersing Pregnant Women Seeking Asylum. London: Maternity Action, Refugee
Council. Available at https://www.refugeecouncil.org.uk/assets/0002/6402/When_
Maternity_Doesn_t_Matter_-_Ref_Council__Maternity_Action_report_Feb2013.pdf
(accessed 9 November 2011).

Maternity Action, Women's Health and Equality Consortium (2014) Women's
Voices on Health: Addressing Barriers to Accessing Primary Care. London:
Maternity Action, Women's Health and Equality Consortium. Available at http://www.
maternityaction.org.uk/wp/wp-content/uploads/2014/05/Access-to-Primary-Care-
report-FINAL.pdf (accessed 10 November 2015).

Mayer A-PT (2014) Redirection in treatment goals: withdrawal of mechanical ventilation
outside of the intensive care unit. *Archives of Disease in Childhood* 99: 795–797.

MBF (1997a) *Bereavement: Guidelines for Professionals.* London: Multiple Births
Foundation.

MBF (1997b) *Selective Feticide: A Leaflet for Parents.* London: Multiple Births Foundation.

MBF (2000) *When a Twin or Triplet Dies: A Booklet for Bereaved Parents and Twins.* London: Multiple Births Foundation.

McBride M, McArdle C (2014) Guidance on Death, Stillbirth and Cremation Certification Following the Court of Appeal Decision on the Death of a Fetus In Utero. Letter, 1 December. Belfast: Department of Health, Social Services and Public Safety (DHSSPS). Available at http://www.dhsspsni.gov.uk/hss-md-38-2014.pdf (accessed 8 July 2015).

McCourt C, Pearce A (2000) Does continuity of carer matter to women from minority ethnic groups? *Midwifery* 16: 145–154.

McGuinness D, Coughlan B, Butler M (2014) An exploration of the experiences of mothers as they suppress lactation following late miscarriage, stillbirth or neonatal death. *Evidence Based Midwifery* 12: 65–70.

McHaffie H (2000) Supporting families when treatment is withdrawn from neonates: parental views on the role of the chaplain. *Scottish Journal of Healthcare Chaplaincy* 3: 2–7.

McHaffie H (2001) *Crucial Decisions at the Beginning of Life: Parents' Experiences of Treatment Withdrawal from Infants.* Abingdon: Radcliffe Medical Press.

McHaffie HE, Fowlie PW (1996) *Life, Death and Decisions: Doctors and Nurses Reflect on Neonatal Practice.* Cheshire: Hochland and Hochland.

McHaffie HE, Fowlie PW, Hume R, Laing IA, Lloyd DJ, Lyon AJ (2001a) Consent to autopsy for neonates. *Archives of Diseases in Childhood* 85: 4–7.

McHaffie HE, Laing IA, Lloyd DJ (2001b) Follow up care of bereaved parents after treatment withdrawal from newborns. *Archives of Disease in Childhood: Fetal and Neonatal Edition* 84: 125–128.

McHaffie HE, Lyon AJ, Fowlie PW (2001c) Lingering death after treatment withdrawal in the neonatal intensive care unit. *Archives of Disease in Childhood: Fetal and Neonatal Edition* 85: 8–12.

McNamara K (2013) Framework for Children's Palliative Care. Bristol: Together for Short Lives. Available at http://www.togetherforshortlives.org.uk/assets/0000/5003/Standards_framework_update_2013.pdf (accessed 24 June 2015).

Mendel TR (2014) The use of neonatal palliative care: reducing moral distress in NICU nurses. *Journal of Neonatal Nursing* 20: 290–293.

Meyer EC, Ritholz MD, Burns JP, Truog RD (2006) Improving the quality of end-of-life care in the pediatric intensive care unit. *Pediatrics* 117: 649–657.

Milgrom J, Ericksen J, Sved-Williams A (2016) Impact of parental psychiatric illness on infant development. In Sutter-Dallay AL, Glangeaud-Freudenthal NM-C, Guedeney A, Riecher-Rössler A (Eds) *Joint Care of Parents and Infants in Perinatal Psychiatry* (pp. 47–78). London: Springer International Publishing.

Mills TA, Ricklesford C, Cooke A, Heazell AEP, Whitworth M, Lavender T (2014) Parents' experiences and expectations of care in pregnancy after stillbirth or neonatal death: a metasynthesis. *BJOG* 121: 943–950.

Mitchell L (2004) Women's experiences of unexpected ultrasound findings. *Journal of Midwifery and Women's Health* 49: 228–234.

Mitchell M (2005) Preparing student midwives to care for bereaved parents. *Nurse Education in Practice* 5: 78–83.

Ministry of Justice (2012a) The Cremation (England and Wales) Regulations 2008 Guidance to Medical Practitioners Completing Forms Cremation 4 and 5. London: Ministry of Justice. Available at https://www.gov.uk/government/uploads/system/uploads/attachment_data/file/325750/cremation-doctors-guidance.pdf (accessed 8 July 2015).

Ministry of Justice (2012b) The Cremation (England and Wales) Regulations 2008: Guidance to Funeral Directors. London: Ministry of Justice. Available at https://www.gov.uk/government/uploads/system/uploads/attachment_data/file/325616/cremation-funeral-directors-guidance.pdf (accessed 10 July 2015).

Ministry of Justice (2012c) The Cremation (England and Wales) Regulations 2008: Guidance to Crematorium Medical Referees. London: Ministry of Justice. Available at https://www.gov.uk/government/uploads/system/uploads/attachment_data/file/325789/guidance-medical-referees.pdf (accessed 30 July 2015).

Miscarriage Association (2011) Late Miscarriage: Second Trimester Loss. Wakefield: The Miscarriage Association. Available at http://www.miscarriageassociation.org.uk/wp/wp-content/leaflets/Late-Miscarriage.pdf (accessed 20 October 2015).

Miscarriage Association (2012) Time for a change. Miscarriage Association website. Available at http://www.miscarriageassociation.org.uk/2012/11/time-for-a-change/ (accessed 9 October 2015).

Miscarriage Association (2013) Molar Pregnancy (Hydatidiform Mole). Wakefield: The Miscarriage Association. Available at http://www.miscarriageassociation.org.uk/wp/wp-content/leaflets/Molar-Pregnancy.pdf (accessed 4 October 2015).

Miscarriage Association (2014) Ectopic Pregnancy. Wakefield: The Miscarriage Association. Available at http://www.miscarriageassociation.org.uk/wp/wp-content/leaflets/Ectopic-pregnancy.pdf (accessed 9 October 2015).

Miscarriage Association (2015a) Feelings after pregnancy loss. Miscarriage Association website. Available at http://www.miscarriageassociation.org.uk/support/feelings-after-pregnancy-loss/ (accessed 24 September 2015).

Miscarriage Association (2015b) Management of Miscarriage: Your Options. Wakefield: The Miscarriage Association. Available at http://www.miscarriageassociation.org.uk/wp/wp-content/leaflets/Management-of-miscarriage.pdf (accessed 28 September 2015).

Miscarriage Association, Sands, ICCM (2015) Guidance for miscarriages that occur at home. Available at http://www.uk-sands.org/sites/default/files/Guidance%20for%20miscarriages%20that%20occur%20at%20home.pdf (accessed 8 July 2015).

Money Advice Service (2013) *Late Miscarriage, Stillbirth, Neonatal Death: A Guide to the Financial Help Available*. London: Money Advice Service.

Moulder C (1998) *Understanding Pregnancy Loss: Perspectives and Issues in Care.* London: Macmillan.

Moulder C (2001) *Miscarriage: The Guidelines for Good Practice.* Wakefield: The Miscarriage Association.

Mulder EJH, Robles de Medina PG, Huizink AC, Van den Bergh BRH, Buitelaar JK, Visser GHA (2002) Prenatal maternal stress: effects on pregnancy and the (unborn) child. *Early Human Development* 70: 3–14.

Murphy FA (1998) The experience of early miscarriage from a male perspective. *Journal of Clinical Nursing* 7: 325–332.

Murphy F, Merrell J (2009) Negotiating the transition: caring for women through the experience of early miscarriage. *Journal of Clinical Nursing* 18: 1583–1591.

Murphy S (2012) Reclaiming a moral identity: stillbirth, stigma and "moral mothers". *Midwifery* 28: 476–480.

Murray Parkes C (1985) Bereavement. *British Journal of Psychiatry* 146: 11–17.

Myers AJ, Lohr PA, Pfeffer N (2015) Disposal of fetal tissue following elective abortion: what women think. *Journal of Family Planning and Reproductive Health Care* 41: 84–89.

NAFD (2015) Death Certification in Scotland: Guidance for the Funeral Industry. Solihull: National Association of Funeral Directors (NAFD). Available at http://www.iccm-uk.com/iccm/library/Scottish%20Death%20Certification%20A5%20Booklet.pdf (accessed 30 July 2015).

Nagraj S, Barclay S (2011) Bereavement care in primary care: a systematic literature review and narrative synthesis. *British Journal of General Practice* 61: e42–e48.

National Collaboration for Integrated Care and Support (2013) *Integrated Care and Support:*

Our Shared Commitment. London: Department of Health, Health and Social Care Integration. Available at https://www.gov.uk/government/uploads/system/uploads/attachment_data/file/198748/DEFINITIVE_FINAL_VERSION_Integrated_Care_and_Support_-_Our_Shared_Commitment_2013-05-13.pdf (accessed 9 November 2015).

NCT (2014) NCT and Netmums research finds the six week postnatal check-up unsatisfactory. NCT, Press Releases, October 6. Available at http://www.nct.org.uk/press-release/nct-netmums-research-finds-six-week-postnatal-check-unsatisfactory (accessed 3 June 2015).

NDSSPE (2004) Antenatal Screening: Working Standards. National Down's Syndrome Screening Programme for England. Available at http://www.screening.nhs.uk/downs/working_standards.pdf (accessed on 10 December 2006).

Neonatal Expert Advisory Group (2013) *Neonatal Care in Scotland: A Quality Framework*. Edinburgh: The Scottish Government.

Ngo TD, Park MH, Shakur H, Free C (2011) Comparative effectiveness, safety and acceptability of medical abortion at home and in a clinic: A systematic review. *Bulletin of the World Health Organization* 89: 360-70.

NHS (2013) The NHS Constitution: The NHS Belongs to Us All. London: Department of Health. Available at http://www.nhs.uk/choiceintheNHS/Rightsandpledges/NHSConstitution/Documents/2013/the-nhs-constitution-for-england-2013.pdf (accessed 16 November 2015).

NHS Choices [n.d.(a)] Abortion. NHS Choices website. Available at http://www.nhs.uk/conditions/Abortion/Pages/Introduction.aspx (accessed 20 August 2015).

NHS Choices [n.d.(b)] Cabergoline (Cabergoline 500microgram tablets). NHS Choices website. Available at http://www.nhs.uk/medicine-guides/pages/MedicineOverview.aspx?condition=Breast%20milk%20production&medicine=cabergoline (accessed 24 July 2015).

NHS Choices (2013) News analysis: controversial mental health guide DSM-5. NHS Choices website. Available at http://www.nhs.uk/news/2013/08August/Pages/controversy-mental-health-diagnosis-and-treatment-dsm5.aspx (accessed 28 December 2015).

NHS Choices (2014a) Clinical depression – Symptoms. NHS Choices website. Available at http://www.nhs.uk/Conditions/Depression/Pages/Symptoms.aspx (accessed 29 December 2015).

NHS Choices (2014b) Making a complaint. NHS Choices website. Available at http://www.nhs.uk/choiceintheNHS/Rightsandpledges/complaints/Pages/NHScomplaints.aspx (accessed 3 December 2015).

NHS Choices (2014c) Generalised anxiety disorder in adults. NHS Choices website. Available at http://www.nhs.uk/conditions/Anxiety/Pages/Introduction.aspx (accessed 3 January 2016).

NHS Choices (2014d) Panic disorder. NHS Choices website. Available at http://www.nhs.uk/Conditions/Panic-disorder/Pages/Introduction.aspx (accessed 3 January 2016).

NHS Choices (2014e) Social anxiety disorder (social phobia). NHS Choices website. Available at http://www.nhs.uk/conditions/social-anxiety/Pages/Social-anxiety.aspx (accessed 3 January 2016).

NHS Choices (2014f) Generalised anxiety disorder in adults – Symptoms. NHS Choices website. Available at http://www.nhs.uk/Conditions/Anxiety/Pages/Symptoms.aspx (accessed 3 January 2016).

NHS Choices (2015a) What is the Mental Capacity Act? NHS Choices website. Available at http://www.nhs.uk/conditions/social-care-and-support-guide/pages/mental-capacity.aspx (accessed 24 November 2015).

NHS Choices (2015b) Symptoms of post-traumatic stress disorder (PTSD). NHS Choices website. Available at http://www.nhs.uk/Conditions/Post-traumatic-stress-disorder/Pages/Symptoms.aspx (accessed 3 January 2016).

NHS Choices (2015c) Domestic abuse. NHS Choices website. Available at http://www.nhs.uk/conditions/pregnancy-and-baby/pages/domestic-abuse-pregnant.aspx#close (accessed 3 January 2016).

NHS Commissioning (2015) Briefing on Improving the Quality of Interpreting and Translation Services in Primary Care (Community Languages* and British Sign Language), February 2015. London: NHS Commissioning, NHS England. Available at https://www.england.nhs.uk/commissioning/wp-content/uploads/sites/12/2015/03/quality-standards-is-pc-briefing.pdf (accessed 30 November 2015).

NHS Education for Scotland (2009) Spiritual Care Matters: An Introductory Resource for all NHS Scotland Staff. Edinburgh: NHS Education for Scotland. Available at http://www.nes.scot.nhs.uk/media/3723/spiritualcaremattersfinal.pdf (accessed 9 November 2015).

NHS England [n.d.] Implementing our mission – high quality care for all: What do we mean by high quality care? NHS England website. Available at https://www.england.nhs.uk/about/our-vision-and-purpose/imp-our-mission/high-quality-care/ (accessed 9 November 2015).

NHS England (2015a) NHS Chaplaincy Guidelines 2015: Promoting Excellence in Pastoral, Spiritual and Religious Care. Leeds: Commissioning Strategy: Equality and Health Inequalities. Available at https://www.england.nhs.uk/wp-content/uploads/2015/03/nhs-chaplaincy-guidelines-2015.pdf (accessed 9 November 2015).

NHS England (2015b) Principles for high quality interpreting and translation services [Version 1.19]: Policy Statement [Draft]. NHS Commissioning, NHS England. Available at https://www.england.nhs.uk/commissioning/wp-content/uploads/sites/12/2015/03/it_principles.pdf (accessed 30 November 2015).

NHS England (2015c) FAQs for the Friends and Family Test – updated 01/10/2015, Publications Gateway Ref No. 01789. NHS England website. Available at https://www.england.nhs.uk/wp-content/uploads/2015/10/fft-imp-guid-faqs-oct15.pdf (accessed 2 December 2015).

NHS England, Medical Directorate, Mental Health Team (2015) Guidance to Support the Introduction of Access and Waiting Time Standards for Mental Health Services in 2015/16. London: Mental Health Team, Medical Directorate. Available at https://www.england.nhs.uk/wp-content/uploads/2015/02/mh-access-wait-time-guid.pdf (accessed 31 December 2015).

NHS Improving Quality (2014) A Review of Support Available for Loss in Early and Late Pregnancy. Leeds: NHS Improving Quality. Available at http://www.nhsiq.nhs.uk/resource-search/publications/pregnancy-loss.aspx (accessed 8 October 2015)

NHS Institute for Innovation and Improvement (2013) NHS Patient Feedback Challenge. NHS Institute for Innovation and Improvement website. Available at http://www.institute.nhs.uk/innovation/spread_and_adoption/nhs_patient_feedback_challenge.html (accessed 2 December 2015).

NHS National Services Scotland (2015) Termination of Pregnancy Statistics: Year ending 31 December 2014. Edinburgh: NHS National Services Scotland: Information Services Division. Available at http://www.isdscotland.org/Health-Topics/Sexual-Health/Publications/2015-05-26/2015-05-26-Terminations-2014-Report.pdf (accessed 20 August 2015).

NHS Screening Programmes (2015) Fetal Anomaly Screening Programme Standards 2015–16. London: NHS Screening Programmes. Available at https://www.gov.uk/government/uploads/system/uploads/attachment_data/file/421650/FASP_Standards_April_2015_final_2_.pdf (accessed 27 August 2015).

NHS Sickle Cell and Thalassaemia Screening Programme (2012) *NHS Screening Programmes: Sickle Cell and Thalassaemia: Information for Healthcare Professionals*. London: NHS Sickle Cell and Thalassaemia Programme Centre.

NICE (2005) Post-traumatic stress disorder: management, NICE clinical guideline 26. Available at http://www.nice.org.uk/guidance/cg26/resources/posttraumatic-stress-disorder-management-975329451205 (accessed 3 January 2016).

NICE (2008a) Antenatal care for uncomplicated pregnancies, NICE clinical guideline 62. Available at https://www.nice.org.uk/guidance/cg62/resources/guidance-antenatal-care-pdf (accessed 10 November 2015).

NICE (2008b) Inducing labour, NICE clinical guideline 70. Available at http://www. nice.org.uk/guidance/cg70/resources/inducing-labour-975621704389 (accessed 3 November 2015).

NICE (2010) Donor milk banks: the operation of donor milk bank services, NICE clinical guideline 93. Available at https://www.nice.org.uk/guidance/cg93/resources/ guidance-donor-milk-banks-the-operation-of-donor-milk-bank-services-pdf (accessed 3 June 2015).

NICE (2012) Ectopic pregnancy and miscarriage: diagnosis and initial management in early pregnancy of ectopic pregnancy and miscarriage, NICE clinical guideline 154. Available at http://www.nice.org.uk/guidance/cg154 (accessed 28 September 2015).

NICE (2013) Caesarean section, Quality standard. Available at http://www.nice.org. uk/guidance/qs32/resources/caesarean-section-2098602884293 (accessed 2 November 2015).

NICE (2014a) Antenatal and postnatal mental health: clinical management and service guidance, NICE clinical guideline 192. Available at http://www.nice.org.uk/guidance/ cg192 (accessed 18 December 2014).

NICE (2014b) Intrapartum care for healthy women and babies, NICE clinical guideline 190. Available at https://www.nice.org.uk/guidance/cg190/resources/intrapartum-care-for-healthy-women-and-babies-35109866447557 (accessed 2 November 2015).

NICE (2015) Safe midwifery staffing for maternity settings, NICE guideline 4. Available at http://www.nice.org.uk/guidance/ng4 (accessed 16 November 2015).

NMC (2007) *The Care of Babies Born Alive at the Threshold of Viability: NMC Circular 03.* London: The Nursing and Midwifery Council.

NMC (2015) The Code: Professional Standards of Practice and Behaviour for Nurses and Midwives. London: Nursing and Midwifery Council. Available at http://www.nmc. org.uk/globalassets/sitedocuments/nmc-publications/revised-new-nmc-code.pdf (accessed 21 August 2015)

NNAP (2014) NNAP – dataset and audit questions. National Neonatal Audit Programme (NNAP), Royal College of Paediatrics and Child Health (RCPCH). Available at http:// www.rcpch.ac.uk/improving-child-health/quality-improvement-and-clinical-audit/ national-neonatal-audit-programme-nn-2#Questions for the 2014 audit (accessed 11 June 2015).

Nuffield (2006) Critical Care Decisions in Fetal and Neonatal Medicine: Ethical Issues. London: Nuffield Council on Bioethics. Available at http://www.nuffieldbioethics. org/fileLibrary/pdf/CCD_web_version_8_November.pdf (accessed on 19 November 2006).

Oates M, Cantwell R (2011) Chapter 11: Deaths from psychiatric causes. In Lewis G (Ed.) *Saving Mothers' Lives: Reviewing Maternal Deaths to Make Motherhood*

Safer: 2006–2008. Published in *BJOG: An International Journal of Obstetrics and Gynaecology* 118: 130–142.

Ogden J, Maker C (2004) Expectant or surgical management of miscarriage: a qualitative study. *British Journal of Obstetrics and Gynaecology* 111: 463–467.

Oladapo OT, Fawole B (2012) Treatments for suppression of lactation (Review). *Cochrane Database of Systematic Reviews* 9: CD005937.

O'Leary J, Warland J, Parker L (2012) Childbirth preparation for families pregnant after loss. *International Journal of Childbirth Education* 27: 44–50.

Örtenstrand A (2014) The role of single-patient neonatal intensive care unit rooms for preterm infants. *Acta Pædiatrica* 103: 462–463.

Parliamentary and Health Service Ombudsmen (2014) *Complaints About Acute Trusts* 2013-14 and Q1, Q2 2014-15. London: Parliamentary and Health Service Ombudsman. Available at http://www.ombudsman.org.uk/__data/assets/pdf_file/0004/28876/Complaints_about_acute_trusts_2013-14_and_Q1,-Q2_2014-15.pdf (accessed 24 November 2015).

Parry G, Van Cleemput P, Peters J, Walters S, Thomas K, Cooper C (2007) Health status of Gypsies and Travellers in England. *Journal of Epidemiology and Community Health* 61: 198–204.

PASC (2015) *Investigating Clinical Incidents in the NHS: Sixth Report of Session 2014–15: Report, Together with Formal Minutes Relating to the Report*. House of Commons, The Public Administration Select Committee (PASC). London: The Stationery Office Limited.

Patients Association (2009) How to Obtain Access to Your Medical Records: A Patient's Guide. Harrow: The Patients Association. Available at http://www.patients-association.org.uk/wp-content/uploads/2014/07/How-to-obtain-access-to-your-medical-records.pdf (accessed 2 December 2015).

Paulson JF, Bazemore SD (2010) Prenatal and postpartum depression in fathers and its association with maternal depression: a meta-analysis. *JAMA* 303: 1961–1969.

Pector EA, Smith-Levitin M (2002) Mourning and psychological issues in multiple birth loss. *Seminars in Neonatology* 7: 247–256.

Peel E (2010) Pregnancy loss in lesbian and bisexual women: an online survey of experiences. *Human Reproduction* 25: 721–727.

Permalloo N (2006) Antenatal screening: choices for ethnic minority women. *British Journal of Midwifery* 14: 199–203.

Pitkin Derose K, Escarce JJ, Lurie N. (2007). Immigrants and health care: sources of vulnerability. *Health Affairs* 26: 1258–1268.

Platts J, Mitchell EA, Stacey T, Martin BL, Roberts D, McCowan L, Heazell AEP (2014) The Midland and North of England Stillbirth Study (MiNESS). *BMC Pregnancy and Childbirth* 14: 171.

Pointon T (1996) Telephone interpreting service is available (Letter). *British Medical Journal* 312: 53.

POPPY Steering Group (2009) *Family-Centred Care in Neonatal Units. A Summary of Research Results and Recommendations from the POPPY Project*. London: NCT.

Pradhan F (2011) Change management and neonatal palliative care. *Infant* 7: 184–186.

Prigerson HG, Horowitz MJ, Jacobs SC, Parkes CM, Aslan M, Goodkin K, Raphael B, Marwit SJ, Wortman C, Neimeyer RA, Bonanno G, Block SD, Kissane D, Boelen P, Maercker A, Litz BT, Johnson JG, First MB, Maciejewski PK (2009) Prolonged grief disorder: psychometric validation of criteria proposed for *DSM-V* and *ICD-11*. *PLoS Medicine* 6: e1000121.

Ptacek I, Sebire NJ, Man JA, Brownbill P, Heazell AEP (2014) Systematic review of placental pathology reported in association with stillbirth. *Placenta* 35: 552–562.

Puddifoot J, Johnson M (1999) Active grief, despair and difficulty coping: some measured characteristics of male response following their partner's miscarriage. *Journal of Reproductive and Infant Psychology* 17: 89–93.

Purcell C, Cameron S, Caird L, Flett G, Laird G, Melville C, McDaid LM (2014) Access to and experience of later abortion: accounts from women in Scotland. *Perspectives on Sexual and Reproductive Health* 46: 101–108.

Rådestad I (2001) Stillbirth: care and long-term psychological effects *British Journal of Midwifery* 9: 474–480.

Rådestad I, Surkan PJ, Steineck G, Cnattingius S, Onelöv E, Dickman PW (2009) Long-term outcomes for mothers who have or have not held their stillborn baby. *Midwifery* 25: 422–429.

Ramchandani P, Stein A, Evans J, O'Connor TG (2005) Paternal depression in the postnatal period and child development: a prospective population study. *The Lancet* 365: 2201–2205.

Rance S, McCourt C, Rayment J, Mackintosh N, Carter W, Watson K, Sandall J (2014) Women's safety alerts in maternity care: is speaking up enough? *BMJ Quality and Safety* 23: 26–34.

Rankin J, Wright C, Lind T (2002) Cross sectional survey of parents' experience and views of the post-mortem examination. *British Medical Journal* 324: 816–818.

RCM (2008) Registration of stillbirths and certification for pregnancy loss before 24 weeks' gestation. Guidance paper from the RCM. Published in Midwives magazine

(2005). Available at https://www.rcm.org.uk/news-views-and-analysis/analysis/ registration-of-stillbirths-and-certification-for-pregnancy-loss (accessed 10 July 2015).

RCM (2014) High Quality Midwifery Care. London: Royal College of Midwives. Available at https://www.rcm.org.uk/sites/default/files/High%20Quality%20Midwifery%20 Care%20Final.pdf (accessed 18 January 2016).

RCN (2013) Termination of Pregnancy: An RCN Nursing Framework. London: Royal College of Nursing. Available at https://www.rcn.org.uk/__data/assets/pdf_ file/0004/529654/Termination_of_pregnancy_WEB.pdf (accessed 20 August 2015).

RCN (2015) Managing the Disposal of Pregnancy Remains: RCN Guidance for Nursing and Midwifery Practice. London: Royal College of Nursing. Available at https://www. rcn.org.uk/__data/assets/pdf_file/0008/645884/RCNguide_disposal_pregnancy_ remains_WEB.pdf (accessed 30 November 2015).

RCOG (2010a) Late Intrauterine Fetal Death and Stillbirth: Green–top Guideline No. 55. London: Royal College of Obstetricians and Gynaecologists. Available at https:// www.rcog.org.uk/globalassets/documents/guidelines/gtg_55.pdf (accessed 15 May 2015).

RCOG (2010b) Termination of Pregnancy for Fetal Abnormality in England, Scotland and Wales. London: Royal College of Obstetricians and Gynaecologists. Available at https://www.rcog.org.uk/globalassets/documents/guidelines/ terminationpregnancyreport18may2010.pdf (accessed 16 July 2015).

RCOG (2010c) The Management of Tubal Pregnancy: Green-top Guideline No. 21. London: Royal College of Obstetricians and Gynaecologists. Available at https:// www.rcog.org.uk/globalassets/documents/guidelines/gtg21_230611.pdf (accessed 29 September 2015).

RCOG (2010d) The Management of Gestational Trophoblastic Disease: Green-top Guideline No. 38. London: Royal College of Obstetricians and Gynaecologists. Available at https://www.rcog.org.uk/globalassets/documents/guidelines/ gt38managementgestational0210.pdf (accessed 4 October 2015).

RCOG (2011a) The Care of Women Requesting Induced Abortion: Evidence-based Clinical Guideline Number 7. London: RCOG Press, Royal College of Obstetricians and Gynaecologists. Available at https://www.rcog.org.uk/globalassets/documents/ guidelines/abortion-guideline_web_1.pdf (accessed 20 August 2015).

RCOG (2011b) The Investigation and Treatment of Couples with Recurrent First- trimester and Second-trimester Miscarriage: Green–top Guideline No. 17. London: Royal College of Obstetricians and Gynaecologists. Available at https://www.rcog. org.uk/globalassets/documents/guidelines/gtg_17.pdf (accessed 12 October 2015).

RCOG (2011c) Reduced Fetal Movements: Green–top Guideline No. 57. London: Royal College of Obstetricians and Gynaecologists. Available at https://www.rcog.org.uk/globalassets/documents/guidelines/gtg_57.pdf (accessed 20 October 2015).

RCOG (2012) Information for You: When Your Baby Dies Before Birth. London: Royal College of Obstetricians and Gynaecologists. Available at https://www.rcog.org.uk/globalassets/documents/patients/patient-information-leaflets/pregnancy/pi-when-your-baby-dies-before-birth.pdf (accessed 30 October 2015).

RCOG (2015a) Ultrasound from Conception to 10+0 Weeks of Gestation: Scientific Impact Paper No. 49. London: Royal College of Obstetricians and Gynaecologists. Available at https://www.rcog.org.uk/globalassets/documents/guidelines/scientific-impact-papers/sip-49.pdf (accessed 27 August 2015)

RCOG (2015b) Each Baby Counts. Royal College of Obstetricians and Gynaecologists website. Available at https://www.rcog.org.uk/eachbabycounts (accessed 28 October 2015).

RCOG (2015c) Obtaining Valid Consent: Clinical Governance Advice No. 6. London: Royal College of Obstetricians and Gynaecologists. Available at https://www.rcog.org.uk/globalassets/documents/guidelines/clinical-governance-advice/cga6.pdf (accessed 30 October 2015).

RCOG, RCP (2001) *Fetal and Perinatal Pathology: A Report of a Joint Working Party.* London: Royal College of Obstetricians and Gynaecologists/Royal College of Pathologists.

RCPath (2015a) The Royal College of Pathologists statement - Morecambe Bay Investigation Report. Press Statement, 3 March. London: Royal College of Pathologists. Available at http://www.rcpath.org/Resources/PDF/RCPath%20statement%20-%20Morecambe%20Bay%20Investigation%203%20March%202015.pdf (accessed 8 July 2015).

RCPath (2015b) Medical Examiners Committee. London: Royal College of Pathologists website, Committees. Available at http://www.rcpath.org/committees/committees/medical-examiners-committee/medical-examiners-committee (accessed 8 July 2015).

Redshaw M, Rowe R, Henderson J (2014). Listening to Parents After Stillbirth or the Death of Their Baby After Birth. Oxford: National Perinatal Epidemiology Unit, University of Oxford. Available at https://www.npeu.ox.ac.uk/downloads/files/listeningtoparents/report/Listening%20to%20Parents%20Report%20-%20March%202014%20-%20FINAL%20-%20PROTECTED.pdf (accessed 6 May 2015).

Richards J, Graham R, Embleton ND, Campbell C, Rankin J (2015) Mothers' perspectives on the perinatal loss of a co-twin: a qualitative study. *BMC Pregnancy and Childbirth* 15: 143.

Rijken M, Veen S, Walther FJ (2007) Ethics of maintaining extremely preterm infants. *Paediatrics and Child Health* 17: 58–63.

Rillstone P, Hutchinson SA (2001) Managing the reemergence of anguish: pregnancy after a loss due to anomalies. *Journal of Obstetric, Gynecologic, and Neonatal Nursing* 30: 291–298.

Roberts C, Moss B, Wass V, Sarangi S, Jones R (2005) Misunderstandings: a qualitative study of primary care consultations in multilingual settings, and educational implications. *Medical Education* 39: 465–475.

Robertson Blackmore E, Côté -Arsenault D, Tang W, Glover V, Evans J, Golding J, O'Connor TG (2011) Previous prenatal loss as a predictor of perinatal depression and anxiety. *The British Journal of Psychiatry* 198: 373–378.

Robinson J (2002) Stillbirth: is seeing the baby harmful? *British Journal of Midwifery* 10: 640.

Rocca CH, Kimport K, Roberts SCM, Gould H, Neuhaus J, Foster DG (2015) Decision rightness and emotional responses to abortion in the United States: a longitudinal study. *PLoS ONE* 10: e0128832.

Rowlands IJ, Lee C (2010) "The silence was deafening": social and health service support after miscarriage. *Journal of Reproductive and Infant Psychology* 28: 274–286.

Roy R, Aladangady N, Costeloe NK, Larcher V (2004) Decision making and modes of death in a tertiary neonatal unit. *Archives of Disease in Childhood: Fetal and Neonatal Edition* 89: 527–530.

Ryder IH (1999) Prenatal screening for down syndrome: a dilemma for the unsupported midwife. *Midwifery* 15: 16–23.

Ryninks K, Roberts-Collins C, McKenzie-McHarg K, Horsch A (2014) Mothers' experiences of their contact with their stillborn infant: An interpretative phenomenological analysis. *BMC Pregnancy and Childbirth* 14: 203.

Säflund K, Sjögren B, Wredling R (2004) The role of caregivers after a stillbirth: Views and experiences of parents. *Birth* 31: 132–137.

Samsel C, Lechner BE (2015) End-of-life care in a regional level IV neonatal intensive care unit after implementation of a palliative care initiative. *Journal of Perinatology* 35: 223–228.

Samuelsson M, Rådestad I, Segesten K (2001) Waste of life: fathers' experiences of losing a child before birth *Birth* 28: 124–130.

Sandall J, Homer C, Sadler E, Rudisill C, Bourgeault I, Bewley S, Nelson P, Cowie L, Cooper C, Curry N (2011) *Staffing in Maternity Units: Getting the Right People in the Right Place at the Right Time.* London: The King's Fund.

Sands (2010) *Bereavement Care Report 2010: Survey of UK Maternity Units and the Care They Provide to Parents Whose Baby Dies Before, During or Shortly After Birth.* London: Sands.

Sands (2013a) *Guide for Consent Takers: Seeking Consent/ Authorisation for the Post Mortem Examination of a Baby.* London: Sands.

Sands (2013b) Learning outcomes for consent taker training: seeking consent/ authorisation for a hospital post mortem examination of a baby. London: Sands. Available at https://www.hta.gov.uk/sites/default/files/Sands_Post_Mortem_ Learning_Outcomes.pdf (accessed 13 August 2015).

Sands (2013c) *When a Baby Dies Before Labour Begins.* London: Sands.

Sands (2014a). *Sexual Relationships After the Death of a Baby.* London: Sands.

Sands (2014b) *For Family and Friends.* London: Sands.

Sands (2014c) *Mainly for Fathers.* London: Sands.

Sands (2014d) *Deciding About a Post Mortem Examination: Information for Parents.* London: Sands.

Sands (2014e) *Long Ago Bereaved.* London: Sands.

Sands (2014f) *Deciding About a Funeral for Your Baby.* London: Sands.

Sands (2014g) *Another Pregnancy? After a Late Miscarriage, Stillbirth or Neonatal Death.* London: Sands.

Sands (2014h) *Saying Goodbye to Your Baby: For Parents Who Have Had a Late Miscarriage, Stillbirth or Neonatal Death.* London: Sands.

Sands (2014i) *Supporting Children When a Baby Has Died.* London: Sands.

Sands (2015a) Certificates and registration for babies born dead before 24 completed weeks of pregnancy: Sands position statement. Improving Bereavement Care Team, Sands. Available at http://www.uk-sands.org/sites/default/files/Position%20 statement%20Certificates%20and%20Registration.pdf (accessed 8 July 2015).

Sands (2015b) Cremation and ashes: Sands position statement. Improving Bereavement Care Team, Sands. Available at https://www.uk-sands.org/sites/default/files/ Position%20statement%20Cremation%20and%20ashes.pdf (accessed 18 January 2016).

Sands (2015c) Disposal of fetal remains: Sands position statement. Improving Bereavement Care Team, Sands. Available at http://www.uk-sands.org/sites/default/files/Position%20statement%20Disposal%20of%20Fetal%20Remains%202015.pdf (accessed 30 July 2015).

Sands (2015d) Shared graves and lockable grave covers: Sands position statement. Improving Bereavement Care Team, Sands. Available at https://www.uk-sands.org/sites/default/files/Position%20statement%20Shared%20graves%20and%20lockable%20grave%20covers.pdf (access 18 January 2016).

Sands (2015e) Transferring babies to the mortuary or another hospital for a post mortem examination: Sands position statement. Improving Bereavement Care Team, Sands. Available at https://www.uk-sands.org/sites/default/files/Position%20statement%20The%20mortuary%20and%20transfer%20fr%20PM%20exmaination_0.pdf (accessed 18 January 2016).

Sands (2015f) Post mortem examination after a pregnancy loss or death of a baby before, during or shortly after birth: Sands position statement. Improving Bereavement Care Team, Sands. Available at https://www.uk-sands.org/sites/default/files/Position%20statement%20The%20mortuary%20and%20transfer%20fr%20PM%20exmaination_0.pdf (accessed 18 January 2016).

Sands (2015g) Seeing and holding the baby after a pregnancy loss or the death of a baby before, during or shortly after birth: Sands position statement. Improving Bereavement Care Team, Sands. Available at https://www.uk-sands.org/sites/default/files/Position%20statement%20Seeing%20and%20holding%20a%20baby%20after%20death_0.pdf (accessed 18 January 2016).

Sands (2015h) 5 ways to improve care: improving bereavement care. Sands. Available at https://www.uk-sands.org/professionals/principles-of-care/5-ways-to-improve-care (accessed 19 October 2015)

Sands (2015i) Bereavement midwives: Sands position statement. Sands. Available at https://www.uk-sands.org/sites/default/files/Position%20statement%20Bereavement%20midwives_0.pdf (accessed 19 October 2015).

Sands (2015j) Storing keepsakes in hospitals: Sands position statement. Improving Bereavement Care Team, Sands. Available at https://www.uk-sands.org/sites/default/files/Position%20statement%20Storing%20keepsakes%20in%20hospitals_1.pdf (accessed 18 January 2016).

Sands (2015k). Taking the baby home: Sands position statement. Improving Bereavement Care Team, Sands. Available at https://www.uk-sands.org/sites/default/files/Position%20statement%20Taking%20the%20baby%20home_2.pdf (accessed 18 January 2016).

Sands (2016a) Your health. Sands website. Available at https://www.uk-sands.org/why-babies-die/advice-for-a-safer-pregnancy/your-health (accessed 2 January 2016).

Sands (2016b) Your baby's health. Sands website. Available at https://www.uk-sands. org/why-babies-die/advice-for-a-safer-pregnancy/your-babys-health (accessed 2 January 2016).

Sands (2016c) Advice for a safer pregnancy. Sands website. Available at https://www. uk-sands.org/why-babies-die/advice-for-a-safer-pregnancy (accessed 2 January 2016).

Sands (2016d) Coroners' inquests into stillbirths. Sands position statement. Research and Prevention Team, Sands. Available at https://www.uk-sands.org/sites/default/ files/Position%20statement%20inquests%20into%20stillbirths-updated%20 Jan%202016.pdf (accessed 24 February 2016).

Sands (2016e) Improving the review of deaths. Sands website. Available at https://www. uk-sands.org/why-babies-die/preventing-more-deaths/improving-the-review-of-deaths (accessed 9 February 2016).

Sawyer A, Rabe H, Abbott J, Gyte G, Duley L, Ayers S (2013) Parents' experiences and satisfaction with care during the birth of their very preterm baby: a qualitative study. *BJOG* 120: 637–643.

Schaap A, Wolf H, Bruinse H, Barkhof-van de Lande S, Treffers P (1997) Long-term impact of prenatal bereavement: comparison of grief reactions after intrauterine versus neonatal death. *European Journal of Obstetrics and Gynaecology* 75: 161–167.

Schott J, Henley A (1996) *Culture, Religion and Childbearing in a Multiracial Society.* Oxford: Butterworth Heinemann.

Schott J, Henley A (1999) *Culture, Religion and Patient Care in a Multi-Ethnic Society: A Handbook for Professionals.* London: Age Concern.

Schott J, Henley A (2009) After a stillbirth – offering choices, creating memories. *British Journal of Midwifery* 17: 798–801.

Schott J, Henley A (2014) Working with Bereaved Families After a Late Miscarriage, Stillbirth or Neonatal Death. Good Practice Points for Health Visitors: Working with Minority Groups. London: Institute of Health Visiting. Available at http://www.ihv.org. uk/uploads/07%20MG_Breavement.pdf (accessed 3 July 2015).

Schott J, Priest J (2002) Leading Antenatal Classes: A Practical Guide. Oxford: Butterworth Heinemann.

Scott-Joynt M (2012) Withdrawal of life-sustaining treatment for newborn infants from a Christian perspective. *Early Human Development* 88: 89–90.

Scottish Government (2015a) Revised guidance on the disposal of pregnancy loss up to and including 23 weeks and 6 days' gestation. Edinburgh: The Scottish

Government, Directorate of Chief Medical Officer, Directorate of Chief Nursing Office, Patients, Public and Health Professions, 17 April.

Scottish Government (2015b) Consultation on a proposed Bill relating to burial and cremation and other related matters in Scotland. Edinburgh: The Scottish Government, Health Protection Team. Available at https://consult.scotland.gov.uk/burial-cremation/consultation-on-a-proposed-bill-relating-to-burial (accessed 24 July 2015).

Scrutton S (1995) *Bereavement and Grief: Supporting Older People Through Loss.* London: Age Concern.

Shackman J (1984) *The Right to be Understood: A Handbook on Working with, Employing and Training Community Interpreters.* Chippenham: Jane Shackman.

Shahheidari M, Homer C (2012) Impact of the design of neonatal intensive care units on neonates, staff, and families: a systematic literature review. *Journal of Perinatal and Neonatal Nursing* 26: 260–266.

Shear MK (2015) Complicated grief. *New England Journal of Medicine* 372:153–160.

Sheffield LMC (2012) Medical Examiner (ME) pilot: response to comments from Sheffield GPs/practices. Sheffield Local Medical Committee. Available at http://www.sheffield-lmc.org.uk/Reports/Medical%20Examiner%20Pilot%20Feedback%20Report%20Mar12.pdf (accessed 3 August 2015).

Sheldon H (2005) *Language Support in Neonatal Care Research Project: Stage 4: Interpreters' Views* (unpublished interim project report).

Siassakos D, Jackson S, Storey C, Chebsey C, Ellis A (2015) *InSight Investigation after Stillbirth to Inform and Guide Healthcare Training: Understanding and Improving Care for Parents after a Baby Has Died. Multicentre Case Study Analysis of Parent Interviews, Staff Focus Groups and Service Provision Data* (unpublished results). Perinatal and Reproductive Loss research hub (PEARL).

Sit D, Rothschild AJ, Wisner KL (2006) A review of postpartum psychosis. *Journal of Women's Health (Larchmont)* 15: 352–368.

Skirton H, Barr O (2010) Antenatal screening and informed choice: a cross-sectional survey of parents and professionals. *Midwifery* 26: 596–602.

Smith H (2014) Giving hope to families in palliative care and implications for practice. *Nursing Children and Young People* 26: 21–25.

Smith L (2005) The ethics of neonatal care for the extremely preterm infant. *Journal of Neonatal Nursing* 11: 33–37.

Smith L, Frost J, Levitas R, Bradley H and Garcia J (2006) Women's experiences of three early miscarriage management options: a qualitative study. *British Journal of General Practice* 56: 198–205.

Soffritti S, Monari C, Sandri F (2014) Changing the focus of care: from curative to palliative care. *Journal of Pediatric and Neonatal Individualized Medicine* 3: e030261.

Soni R, Vasudevan C, English S (2011) A national survey of neonatal palliative care in the UK. *Infant* 7: 162–163.

South Ayrshire Council [n.d.] Home burials. Ayr: South Ayrshire Council website. Available at http://www.south-ayrshire.gov.uk/registrationandbereavement/cemeteries/homeburials.aspx (accessed 23 July 2015).

Sovio U, White IR, Dacey A, Pasupathy D, Smith GCS (2015) Screening for fetal growth restriction with universal third trimester ultrasonography in nulliparous women in the Pregnancy Outcome Prediction (POP) study: a prospective cohort study. *Lancet* 386: 2089–2097.

Statham H (2002) Prenatal diagnosis of fetal abnormality: the decision to terminate the pregnancy and the psychological consequences. Fetal and Maternal Medicine Review 13: 213–247.

Statham H, Solomou W, Green JM (2001) *When a Baby has an Abnormality: A Study of Parents' Experience.* Cambridge: Centre for Family Research, University of Cambridge.

Statham H, Solomou W, Green J (2003) Communication of pre-natal screening and diagnosis results to primary-care health professionals. *Public Health* 117: 348–357.

Stevenson-Hinde J, Chicot R, Shouldice A, Hinde CA (2013) Maternal anxiety, maternal sensitivity, and attachment. *Attachment and Human Development* 15: 618–636.

Stevenson-Hinde J, Curley JP, Chicot R, Jóhannsson C (2007) Anxiety within families: Interrelations, consistency, and change. *Family Process* 46: 543–556.

Stroebe M, Schut H (1999) The dual process model of coping with bereavement: rationale and description. *Death Studies* 23: 197–224.

Stroebe W, Abakoumkin G, Stroebe M (2010) Beyond depression: yearning for the loss of a loved one. *Omega* 61: 85–101.

Stroebe W, Zech E, Stroebe MS, Abakoumkin G (2005) Does social support help in bereavement? *Journal of Social and Clinical Psychology* 24: 1030–1050.

Stroebe M, Schut H, Finkenauer C (2013) Parents coping with the death of their child: from individual to interpersonal to interactive perspectives. *Family Science* 4: 28–36.

Surkan PJ, Rådestad I, Cnattingius S, Steineck G, Dickman PW (2008) Events after stillbirth in relation to maternal depressive symptoms: a brief report. *Birth* 35: 153–157.

Sutter-Dallay AL, Murray L, Dequae-Merchadou L, Glatigny-Dallay E, Bourgeois ML, Verdoux H (2011) A prospective longitudinal study of the impact of early postnatal vs. chronic maternal depressive symptoms on child development. *European Psychiatry* 26: 484–489.

Swanson KM (1999) Effects of caring, measurement, and time on miscarriage impact and women's well-being. *Nursing Research* 48: 288–298.

Swanson KM (2003) Miscarriage effects on couples' interpersonal and sexual relationships during the first year after loss: women's perceptions. *Psychosomatic Medicine* 65: 902–910.

Swanson PB, Kane RT, Pearsall-Jones JG, Swanson CF, Croft ML (2009) How couples cope with the death of a twin or higher order multiple. *Twin Research and Human Genetics* 12: 392–402.

Swanson PB, Pearsall-Jones JG, Hay DA (2002) How mothers cope with the death of a twin or higher multiple. *Twin Research* 5: 156–164.

TAMBA (2014) In hospital. TAMBA website, Parenting. Available at https://www.tamba. org.uk/Parenting/First-Year/In-Hospital (accessed 9 June 2015).

Tay JI, Moore J, Walker J (2000) Regular review: ectopic pregnancy. *British Medical Journal* 320: 916–919.

Thayyil S, Sebire NJ, Chitty LS, Wade A, Chong WK, Olsen O, Gunny RS, Offiah AC, Owens CM, Saunders DE, Scott RJ, Jones R, Norman W, Addison S, Bainbridge A, Cady EB, De Vita E, Robertson NJ, Taylor AM (2013) Post-mortem MRI versus conventional autopsy in foetuses and children: a prospective validation study. *Lancet* 382: 223–233.

Thieleman K, Cacciatore J (2013) When a child dies: a critical analysis of grief-related controversies in DSM-5. *Research on Social Work Practice* 24: 114–122.

Thomas K (2010) Supporting parents when a baby dies. *NCT News Digest* 52: 6–7.

Tosello B, Dany L, Bétrémieux P, Le Coz P, Auquier P, Gire C, Einaud M-A (2015) Barriers in referring neonatal patients to perinatal palliative care: a French multicenter survey. *PLoS One* 10: e0126861.

The Traveller Movement (2014) Child Poverty in the Gypsy and Traveller Communities. London: The Traveller Movement. Available at http://www.travellermovement.org. uk/wp-content/uploads/2015/09/Child-Poverty-GRT-January-2014.pdf (accessed 9 November 2015).

Trulsson O, Rådestad I (2004) The silent child – mothers' experiences before, during, and after stillbirth. *Birth* 31: 189–195.

Tsouroufli M (2011) Routinisation and constraints on informed choice in a one-stop clinic offering first trimester chromosomal antenatal screening for Down's syndrome. *Midwifery* 27: 431–436.

Turton P, Badenhorst W, Hughes P, Ward J, Riches S, White S (2006) Psychological impact of stillbirth on fathers in the subsequent pregnancy and puerperium. *British Journal of Psychiatry* 188: 165–172.

Turton P, Badenhorst W, Pawlby S, White S, Hughes P (2009a) Psychological vulnerability in children next-born after stillbirth: a case-control follow-up study. *Journal of Child Psychology and Psychiatry, and Allied Disciplines* 50: 1451–1458.

Turton P, Evans C, Hughes P (2009b) Long-term psychosocial sequelae of stillbirth: phase II of a nested case-control cohort study. *Archives of Womens Mental Health* 12: 35–41.

Turton P, Hughes P, Evans CD, Fainman D (2001) Incidence, correlates and predictors of post-traumatic stress disorder in the pregnancy after stillbirth. *British Journal of Psychiatry* 178: 556–560.

Twamley K, Craig F, Kelly P, Hollowell DR, Mendoza P, Bluebond-Langner M (2014) Underlying barriers to referral to paediatric palliative care services: Knowledge and attitudes of health care professionals in a paediatric tertiary care centre in the United Kingdom. *Journal of Child Health Care* 18: 19–30.

UK NSC (2005) Understanding and communicating risk. In: *Screening Choices: A Resource for Health Professionals Offering Antenatal and Newborn Care*. UK National Screening Committee. Available at http://www.screening.nhs.uk/cpd/webfolder/units/understanding-risk.pdf (accessed on 5 April 2006).

UK NSC (2014) *Screening Update: May 2014*. London: NHS Screening Programmes, Public Health England.

van der Kooy B (2015) What happens next? *AIMS Journal* 27: 6.

Walker J (2002) *The Ectopic Pregnancy: Diagnostic Guidelines.* London: Ectopic Pregnancy Trust.

Wallbank S, Robertson N (2013) Predictors of staff distress in response to professionally experienced miscarriage, stillbirth and neonatal loss: a questionnaire survey. *International Journal of Nursing Studies* 50: 1090–1097.

Wallerstedt C, Higgins P (1996) Facilitating perinatal grieving between the mother and the father. *Journal of Obstetric, Gynecologic, and Neonatal Nursing* 25: 389–394.

Wallerstedt C, Lilley M, Baldwin K (2003) Interconceptional counseling after perinatal and infant loss. *Journal of Obstetric, Gynecologic, and Neonatal Nursing* 32: 533–542.

Walsh A (2000) Can a life ever not be worth living? *British Journal of Midwifery* 8: 537–538.

Walter T (1999) *On Bereavement: the Culture of Grief.* Maidenhead: Open University Press.

Walther FJ (2005) Withholding treatment, withdrawing treatment, and palliative care in the neonatal intensive care unit. *Early Human Development* 81: 965–972.

Webster CS (2005) The iatrogenic-harm cost equation and new technology. *Anaesthesia* 60: 843–846.

Weitzman G (2012) Withdrawal of life sustaining treatment for newborn infants from a Jewish perspective. *Early Human Development* 88: 91–93.

West M (2015) Are we supporting or sacrificing NHS staff? The King's Fund. Available from The King's Fund blog at http://www.kingsfund.org.uk/blog/2015/10/are-we-supporting-or-sacrificing-nhs-staff (accessed 16 November 2015).

WHO (2016) ICD-10 Version: 2016. Geneva: World Health Organization. Available at http://apps.who.int/classifications/icd10/browse/2016/en#/F30-F39 (accessed 29 December 2015).

Wilkinson AR, Ahluwalia J, Cole A, Crawford D, Fyle J, Gordon A, Moorcraft J, Pollard T, Roberts T (2009) Management of babies born extremely preterm at less than 26 weeks of gestation: a framework for clinical practice at the time of birth. *Archives of Disease in Childhood Fetal and Neonatal Edition* 94: 2–5.

Wilkinson D, de Crespigny L, Xafis V (2014) Ethical language and decision-making for prenatally diagnosed lethal malformations. *Seminars in Fetal and Neonatal Medicine* 19: 306–311.

Williams C, Alderson P, Farsides B (2002) Is nondirectiveness possible within the context of antenatal screening and testing? *Social Science and Medicine* 54: 339–347.

Wilson AL, Fenton LJ, Stevens DC, Soule DJ (1982) The death of a newborn twin: an analysis of parental bereavement. *Paediatrics* 70: 587–591.

Wilson J (2015) Care After Death: Guidance for Staff Responsible for Care After Death. London: Hospice UK. Available at http://www.hospiceuk.org/what-we-offer/publications?cat=72e54312-4ccd-608d-ad24-ff0000fd3330 (accessed 7 July 2015).

Wilson R (2001) Parents' support for their other children after a miscarriage or perinatal death. *Early Human Development* 61: 55–65.

Wisborg K, Ingerslev HJ, Henriksen TB (2010) IVF and stillbirth: a prospective follow-up study. *Human Reproduction* 25: 1312–1316.

Wocial LD (2000) Life support decisions involving imperiled infants. *Journal of Perinatal and Neonatal Nursing* 14(2): 73–86

Woodroffe I (2013) Supporting bereaved families through neonatal death and beyond. *Seminars in Fetal and Neonatal Medicine* 18: 99–104.

Woods JR (1997) Pregnancy-loss counselling: the challenge to the obstetrician. In: Woods JR, Esposito Woods JL (Eds) *Loss During Pregnancy or in the Newborn Period* (pp. 71–124). Pitman: Jannetti Publications.

Wool C (2013) State of the science on perinatal palliative care. *JOGNN* 42: 372–382.

Worden WJ (1991) Grief Counselling and Grief Therapy: *A Handbook for the Mental Health Practitioner*. London: Routledge

Worden WJ (1996) *Children and Grief – When a Parent Dies*. New York: Guilford Press.

Worden WJ (2003) *Grief Counselling and Grief Therapy: A Handbook for the Mental Health Practitioner* (4th edition). London: Tavistock Publishing.

Working Families (2015) Miscarriage, stillbirth and neonatal death – your rights at work and to benefits. Available at http://www.workingfamilies.org.uk/articles/miscarriage-stillbirth-and-neonatal-death-your-rights-at-work/ (accessed 3 June 2015).

Wortman CB, Silver RC (1989) The myths of coping with loss. *Journal of Consulting and Clinical Psychiatry* 57: 349–357.

Wright JCE, Barlow AD (2015) The current status of neonatal organ donation in the UK. *Archives of Disease in Childhood: Fetal and Neonatal Edition* 100: F6–F7.

Younge N, Smith PB, Goldberg RN, Brandon DH, Simmons C, Cotton CM, Bidegain M (2015) Impact of a palliative care program on end-of-life care in a neonatal intensive care unit. *Journal of Perinatology* 35: 218–222.

Zeanah CH, Dailey JV, Rosenblatt M, Saller DN (1993) Do women grieve after terminating pregnancies because of fetal anomalies? A controlled investigation. *Obstetrics and Gynecology* 82: 270–275.

About us

Sands, the stillbirth and neonatal death charity

Sands was founded in 1978 by a small group of bereaved parents.

Since that time, we have supported many thousands of families whose babies have died, offering emotional support and information. Today, Sands operates throughout the UK and focuses on three key areas:

1) We support anyone affected by the death of a baby

We offer a wide range of bereavement support services. We run a national telephone and email helpline for anyone affected by the death of a baby including parents, families, carers and healthcare professionals. We host an online forum and message boards enabling bereaved families to connect with others. We provide a wide range of specialist support booklets, leaflets and other resources such as memory boxes, all of which are available on our website. We also have a network of support groups across the UK that are run by trained befrienders who provide face to face and group support locally to parents and families.

2) We work in partnership with professionals to try to ensure that bereaved parents and families receive the best possible care

We produce a wide range of online and printed resources to support professionals in delivering sensitive, empathic bereavement care, focused upon the needs of parents.

We deliver high quality training in bereavement care to professionals across the country, offering accredited, evidence based workshops. These services provide professionals with the latest information and support in working with bereaved parents, ensuring that parents receive the best quality care when a baby dies and professionals receive the support they need.

3) We promote and fund research to reduce the loss of babies' lives

We believe many babies' deaths could be prevented with better care and information. We raise vital funds for research and work with clinicians and experts to understand why babies die and how to save lives. We also provide policy expertise at government level and campaign to make addressing the tragedy of too many baby deaths a policy priority nationally and locally.

Sands

www.uk-sands.org

Charity registration number 299679.
Company limited by Guarantee Number 2212082.
Scottish Charity Registration Number SC042789.

About the authors

Amanda Hunter is a researcher, freelance writer, birth worker and previous member of Sands' Improving Bereavement Care team. Her training is in medical anthropology, psychology and birth education and she has a particular interest in issues related to perinatal mental health, bereavement, informed choice and healthcare policy and practice.

Judith Schott has been a freelance writer and trainer on health issues for many years. Judith ran workshops throughout the UK for health professionals at all levels, on a range of topics including cultural and religious aspects of health care and loss and grief.

Alix Henley is a freelance writer, researcher and consultant. She has a particular interest in communication between health professionals and service users, and in equal opportunity issues.

Judith and Alix were the principal authors of the 3rd edition of the Guidelines and were for many years members of the Sands Improving Bereavement Care team, developing many of the Sands support booklets and position statements.

Nancy Kohner was an advisor to Sands for many years and worked closely with bereaved parents and the professionals who cared for them. She also advised government and professional organisations on a wide range of issues related to perinatal loss. She was the author of the first two editions of the *Guidelines* and wrote and collaborated on a large number of other publications. Nancy died in 2006.

Index

471

232, 242, 294, 326, 346, 347, 353, 356

chaplaincies, 17, 18

clinical supervision, 385, 386, 390

ceremonies. *See* religious ceremonies

certificates, 217, 243, 303–322, 340, 409

    abortion notification form, 306

    baby born dead before 24' weeks gestation, 304, 305

    baby born at or after 24 weeks but had died before 24 weeks, 306

    burial, 284

    coroner or procurator fiscal cases, 319

    coroner cases (England and Wales), 320

    coroner cases (Northern Ireland), 320, 321

    England and Wales, 305, 307, 308, 310, 315, 320, 321

    issued by healthcare staff, 303, 304

    fetus papyraceous, 306

    following a neonatal death, 308

    following a stillbirth, 307

    following a termination if the baby is born alive and then dies, 309

    legal definitions, 304

    medical reviewers and examiners, 310

    Northern Ireland, 305, 307, 309, 310, 316, 320, 321

    obtaining copies, 321, 322

    obtaining copies (England and Wales), 321

    obtaining copies (Northern Ireland), 321

    obtaining copies (Scotland), 321

    procurator fiscal cases (Scotland), 320

    Scotland, 305, 307, 308, 310, 316, 321

    taking the baby's body or remains out of the hospital, 309

    termination after 24 weeks' gestation, 308

    termination before 24 weeks' gestation, 306

    what the parents receive, 315, 317

    what the parents receive (England and Wales), 315

    what the parents receive (Northern Ireland), 316

    what the parents receive (Scotland), 316, 317

Child Bereavement UK (CBUK), 37, 101, 171, 189, 200, 417

childbearing loss

    terminology explanation, 5

clothing, 172, 205, 207, 209, 224, 228, 245, 250, 251, 264, 266, 357

Cochrane Reviews, 160, 238, 255, 361

cold cot, 223, 233, 236, 248

collective cremation, 325, 331, 336, 343

communication, 2, 3, 11, 12, 14, 22, 39, 47–63, 65–77, 80, 88, 95, 96, 99, 103, 119, 134, 135, 155, 156, 166, 181, 196, 199, 214–217, 260, 275–277, 295, 362, 371, 377, 380, 388–390

    across language barriers, 14, 66–69, 188

    after a loss, 214–217

    at the end of each discussion, 52

    between departments, 135, 156

    between hospital and primary care teams, 2, 12, 14, 52, 62, 63, 91, 95, 135, 156, 189, 201, 270, 275–277, 295, 377, 385, 389, 390

    between staff, 12, 14, 52, 57, 61–63, 80, 99, 100, 135, 156, 174, 180–182, 198, 276, 295, 371, 377, 380, 389, 390

    between units and healthcare teams, 62, 135, 276

    Braille, 59, 75

    CDs, 59

    challenges, 65, 66

    choosing words, 50, 51, 74, 139, 143

    confidentiality, 16, 50, 62, 67, 71, 72, 81, 94, 112, 124, 126, 130, 255, 277, 295, 351, 352

    decisions about care, 39, 57–59, 162

    discharge, 246, 247, 276

    DVDs, 59

    giving information, 49, 55–59, 70, 92, 102–104, 133, 134, 140, 155, 170, 182–184, 194, 195, 214, 225, 226

    informed choice, 2, 14, 40, 41, 49, 50, 56–59, 70, 80–82, 89–92, 96, 102, 111, 116, 126–128, 140, 155, 169–172, 182, 183, 191, 194, 195, 214, 220, 221, 225, 254–256, 369, 388

    keeping records, 61, 351, 352

X

This publication has been endorsed by the following organisations: